The Virtue of Agency

The Virtue of Agency

Sôphrosunê and Self-Constitution in Classical Greece

CHRISTOPHER MOORE

OXFORD
UNIVERSITY PRESS

Oxford University Press is a department of the University of Oxford. It furthers
the University's objective of excellence in research, scholarship, and education
by publishing worldwide. Oxford is a registered trade mark of Oxford University
Press in the UK and certain other countries.

Published in the United States of America by Oxford University Press
198 Madison Avenue, New York, NY 10016, United States of America.

© Christopher Moore 2023

All rights reserved. No part of this publication may be reproduced, stored in
a retrieval system, or transmitted, in any form or by any means, without the
prior permission in writing of Oxford University Press, or as expressly permitted
by law, by license, or under terms agreed with the appropriate reproduction
rights organization. Inquiries concerning reproduction outside the scope of the
above should be sent to the Rights Department, Oxford University Press, at the
address above.

You must not circulate this work in any other form
and you must impose this same condition on any acquirer.

Library of Congress Cataloging-in-Publication Data
Names: Moore, Christopher, author.
Title: The virtue of agency : Sôphrosunê and Self-Constitution in
Classical Greece / Christopher Moore.
Description: New York, NY, United States of America : Oxford University Press, [2023] |
Includes bibliographical references and index.
Identifiers: LCCN 2023004777 (print) | LCCN 2023004778 (ebook) |
ISBN 9780197663509 (hardback) | ISBN 9780197663523 (epub)
Subjects: LCSH: Temperance (Virtue) | Moderation.
Classification: LCC BV4647.T4 M667 2023 (print) | LCC BV4647.T4 (ebook) |
DDC 179/.9—dc23/eng/20230425
LC record available at https://lccn.loc.gov/2023004777
LC ebook record available at https://lccn.loc.gov/2023004778

DOI: 10.1093/oso/9780197663509.001.0001

Printed by Integrated Books International, United States of America

for my mother,

σωφρονεστάτη

> Nor do not saw the air
> too much with your hand, thus, but use all gently;
> for in the very torrent, tempest, and, as I may say,
> the whirlwind of passion, you must acquire and beget
> a temperance that may give it smoothness.
>
> —*Hamlet*

> I have no impulse to join those the Buddha describes, those who strain always after fulfillment and in fulfillment strive to feel desire. It has seemed to me that my commitments are often more important than my impulses or my pleasures, and that even when my pleasures or desires are the principal issue, there are choices to be made between better and worse, bad and better, good and good.
>
> —Wallace Stegner, *The Spectator Bird*

> Your constitution is what gives you the kind of volitional unity you need to be the author of your actions. And it is the person who acts in accordance with the best constitution, the most unified constitution, who is most truly the author of her actions. For Kant as for Plato, integrity is the metaphysical essence of morality.
>
> —Christine Korsgaard, *The Constitution of Agency*

Contents

Acknowledgments	ix
Selected Abbreviations and Editions	xi
1. Debating a Virtue	1
2. The Early History of *Sôphrosunê*	27
3. Heraclitus, Self-Knowledge, and the Greatest Virtue	54
4. Tragic *Sôphrosunê* in Two Plays of Euripides	75
5. The Late Fifth Century	100
6. The Figure of Socrates	133
7. Xenophon on *Sôphrosunê* and *Enkrateia*	157
8. Plato 1—*Sôphrosunê* and the Capacity for Action	185
9. Plato 2—Two Formulations of Agency	212
10. Plato 3—*Sôphrosunê* with Wisdom in Two Late Dialogues	236
11. Aristotle and the Later Fourth Century	257
12. Pythagorean *Sôphrosunê*	281
13. *Sôphrosunê* for Later Greek Women	307
Epilogue: Translating an Ancient Virtue for Modern Times	335
Epigraphical Appendix	341
Bibliography	347
Index Locorum	373
Index	383

Acknowledgments

I began thinking seriously about *sôphrosunê* in infinite discussions with Chris Raymond, my "other self" in ancient philosophy, as we tried to make sense of Plato's *Charmides* and its central topic of discussion. We made good progress there, but not enough; hence this book. He read a number of the present chapters, as did Mirjam Kotwick, Alex Lee, Pamela Mensch, Sarah Nooter, and David Williams, to each of whom I am deeply grateful. Audiences in several venues—Boulder, Verona, Siracusa, and the Sophists-and-Public-Intellectuals-Network Zoom group—helped with parts of various chapters. All the chapters were read by two highly engaged referees for Oxford University Press, who succeeded in getting me to rewrite the entire book, twice. The National Humanities Center supported my writing of the last several chapters and the beginning of the book's revision. Lucy Randall has been an ideal editor: responsive, professional, and encouraging. And, well, I have learned a lot about *sôphrosunê* from members of my family, often as models of the virtue, sometimes as acolytes to its embodiment; in every case, as objects of love.

Selected Abbreviations and Editions

A.	Aeschylus: Page, D., ed., *Aeschyli Septem Quae Supersunt Tragoedias* (Oxford: Oxford University Press, 1972).
fr.	fragment (in **TrGF**)
Pers.	*Persians*
Ag.	*Agamemnon*
Eum.	*Eumenides*
Choe.	*Choephoroi (Libation Bearers)*
Sept.	*Seven against Thebes*
Supp.	*Suppliant Maidens*
[PB]	*Prometheus Bound*
Aesch.	Aeschines
Anon. Iambl.	*Anonymus Iamblichi* (in Iamblichus)
Antiph.	Antiphon: Pendrick, G., *Antiphon the Sophist: The Fragments*. Cambridge Classical Texts and Commentaries (Cambridge: Cambridge University Press, 2002).
Antisth.	Antisthenes: Prince, S., *Antisthenes of Athens: Texts, Translations, and Commentary* (Ann Arbor: University of Michigan Press, 2016).
Ar.	Aristophanes: Wilson, N. G., ed., *Aristophanis Fabulae*. 2 vols. (Oxford: Oxford University Press, 2007).
Ach.	*Acharnians*
Nub.	*Clouds*
Ran.	*Frogs*
Th.	*Women at the Thesmophoria*
Pl.	*Plutus (Wealth)*
Arist.	Aristotle
EE	*Eudemian Ethics*: Susemihl, F., ed. *Eudemi Rhodii Ethica* (Leipzig: Teubner, 1884).
NE	*Nicomachean Ethics*: Bywater, I., ed., *Aristotelis Ethica Nicomachea* (Oxford: Oxford University Press, 1894).
Metaph.	*Metaphysics*: Jaeger, W., ed., *Aristotelis Metaphysica* (Oxford: Oxford University Press, 1957).
MM	*Magna Moralia*: Susemihl, F., ed., *Aristotelis quae feruntur Magna moralia* (Leipzig: Teubner, 1883).
[Probl.]	*Problemata*: Bekker, I., ed., *Aristotelis Opera*, vol. 2 (Berlin: Reimer, 1831).
Pol.	*Politics*: Ross, W. D., ed., *Aristotelis Politica* (Oxford: Clarendon Press, 1957).
Rhet.	*Rhetoric*: Ross, W. D., ed., *Aristotelis Ars Rhetorica* (Oxford: Oxford University Press, 1959).
Top.	*Topics*: Ross, W. D., ed., *Aristotelis topica et sophistici elenchi* (Oxford: Clarendon Press, 1958).

Aristox.	Aristoxenus
Pyth. pr.	*Pythagorean Precepts*: Huffman, C., ed., *Aristoxenus of Tarentum: The Pythagorean Precepts* (Cambridge: Cambridge University Press, 2019).
VA	*Life of Archytas*: Huffman, C., ed., *Archytas of Tarentum: Pythagorean, Philosopher, and Mathematician King* (Cambridge: Cambridge University Press, 2005).
Bacchyl.	Bacchylides: Snell, B. and H. Maehler, eds., *Bacchylides. Carmina cum fragmentis*, 10th ed. (Leipzig: Teubner, 1970).
BNJ	Worthington, I., ed., *Brill's New Jacoby*. 2nd ed. (Leiden: Brill, 2018–).
CEG	Hansen, P. A., ed., *Carmina epigraphica Graeca*, 2 vols. (Berlin: De Gruyter, 1983–89).
Democr.	Democritus (in **LM**)
Diss. Log.	*Dissoi Logoi* (in **LM**)
DK	Diels, H., and W. Kranz, eds., *Die Fragmente der Vorsokratiker*, 6th ed. (Berlin: Weidmann, 1951).
DL	Diogenes Laertius: Dorandi, T., ed., *Diogenes Laertius: Lives of Eminent Philosophers* (Cambridge: Cambridge University Press, 2013).
DPhA	Goulet, R. ed., *Dictionnaire des Philosophes Antiques* (Paris: CNRS Éditions, 1989–2003).
Eur.	Euripides: Diggle, J., ed., *Euripides Fabulae*, 3 vols. (Oxford: Oxford University Press, 1981–94).
Bacch.	*Bacchae*
Cycl.	*Cyclops*
Hipp.	*Hippolytus*
IA	*Iphigenia at Aulis*
Med.	*Medea*
Or.	*Orestes*
fr.	fragments (in *TrGF*)
Hdt.	Herodotus: Wilson, N. G., ed., *Herodoti Historiae*, 2 vols. (Oxford: Oxford University Press, 2015).
Hes.	Hesiod: Most, G. W., ed., *Hesiod*, rev. ed., 2 vols. Loeb Classical Library (Cambridge, MA: Harvard University Press, 2018).
WD	*Works and Days*
Th.	*Theogony*
Hom.	Homer
Il.	*Iliad*: West, M. L., ed., *Homeri Ilias*, 2 vols. (Leipzig: Teubner, 1998–2000).
Od.	*Odyssey*: West, M. L., ed., *Homerus: Odyssea* (Berlin: De Gruyter, 2017).
Iambl.	Iamblichus of Chalcis
Protr.	*Protreptic*: Pistelli, E., ed., *Iamblichi Protrepticus* (Stuttgart: Teubner, 1967).
VP	*On the Pythagorean Way of Life*: Nauck, A., ed., *Iamblichi De vita Pythagorica* (St. Petersburg: Eggers, 1884).
Ibyc.	Ibycus (in **PMG**)
Isoc.	Isocrates: Mandilaras, B. G., ed., *Isocrates: Opera Omnia*, 3 vols. (Munich: Teubner/Saur, 2003).
LM	Laks, A., and G. Most, eds., *Early Greek Philosophy*, 9 vols., Loeb Classical Library (Cambridge, MA: Harvard University Press, 2017).

LSJ	Liddell, H. G., R. Scott, and H. S. Jones, *A Greek-English Lexicon*, 9th ed. (Oxford: Clarendon Press, 1925–40).
Lys.	Lysias: Carey, C., ed., *Lysiae Orationes cum Fragmentis* (Oxford: Oxford University Press, 2007).
OCD	Hornblower, S., A. Spawforth, and E. Eidinow, eds., *Oxford Classical Dictionary*, 4th ed. (Oxford: Oxford University Press, 2012).
PCG	Kassel, R., and C. Austin, eds., *Poetai Comici Graeci*, 8 vols. (Berlin: De Gruyter, 1983–95).
Pind.	Pindar: Race, W. H., ed., *Pindar*, rev. ed., 2 vols., Loeb Classical Library (Cambridge, MA: Harvard University Press, 2012).
Isthm.	*Isthmian Odes*
Nem.	*Nemean Odes*
Ol.	*Olympian Odes*
Pyth.	*Pythian Odes*
fr.	fragment
Paeans	Rutherford, I., *Pindar's Paeans* (Oxford: Oxford University Press, 2001).
Pl.	Plato: Burnet, J., ed., *Platonis Opera* (Oxford: Oxford University Press, 1900–1907).
Alc.	*Alcibiades*
Chrm.	*Charmides*
Crat.	*Cratylus*
Euthd.	*Euthydemus*
Grg.	*Gorgias*
La.	*Laches*
Phd.	*Phaedo*
Phdr.	*Phaedrus*
Phlb.	*Philebus*
Pol.	*Statesman, Politicus*
Prot.	*Protagoras*
Rep.	*Republic*: Slings, S. R., ed., *Platonis Rempublicam* (Oxford: Oxford University Press, 2003).
Symp.	*Symposium*
Tim.	*Timaeus*
Plut.	Plutarch: Nachstädt, W., W. Sieveking, and J. B. Titchener, eds., *Plutarchi Moralia*, 7 vols. (Leipzig: Teubner, 1966–71).
PMG	Davies, M., and D. L. Page, eds., *Poetarum Melicorum Graecorum Fragmenta*, vol. 1 (Oxford: Clarendon Press, 1991).
Σ	Scholiast
SEP	Zalta, E., *Stanford Encyclopedia of Philosophy*, Metaphysics Research Laboratory, Department of Philosophy, Stanford University, 2022. Online.
Soph.	Sophocles: Lloyd-Jones, H., and N. G. Wilson, eds., *Sophoclis Fabulae* (Oxford: Oxford University Press, 1990).
Aj.	*Ajax*
Ant.	*Antigone*
El.	*Electra*

xiv SELECTED ABBREVIATIONS AND EDITIONS

OC	*Oedipus at Colonus*
OT	*Oedipus Tyrannos*
Ph.	*Philoctetes*
fr.	fragment (in **TrGF**)
SSR	Giannantoni, G., ed., *Socratis et Socraticorum Reliquiae* (Naples: Bibliopolis, 1991).
Stob.	Stobaeus: Wachsmuth, C., and O. Hense, eds., *Joannis Stobaei Anthologium*, 5 vols. (Berlin: Weidmann, 1884–1912).
Thg.	Theognis: West, M. L., ed., *Iambi et Elegi Graeci*, 2 vols. (Oxford: Oxford University Press, 1989–92).
Thuc.	Thucydides: Jones, H. S., and J. E. Powell, eds., *Thucydidis Historiae*, 2 vols. (Oxford: Oxford University Press, 1942).
TrGF	Snell, B., R. Kannicht, and S. Radt, eds., *Tragicorum Graecorum Fragmenta*, 6 vols. (Göttingen: Vandenhoeck and Ruprecht, 1971–2004).
Xen.	Xenophon: Marchant, E. C., ed., *Xenophontis Opera Omnia*, 2nd ed., 5 vols. (Oxford: Clarendon Press, 1921).
Anab.	*Anabasis*
Ap.	*Apology of Socrates*
Cyn.	*Cynegeticus (On Hunting with Dogs)*
Cyr.	*Cyropedia*
Hell.	*Hellenika (History of Greece)*
Hipparch.	*Hipparchus (On the Cavalry Commander)*
Lac. Pol.	*Constitution of the Spartans*
Mem.	*Memorabilia (Memoirs of Socrates)*
Oec.	*Oeconomicus (On Estate Management)*
Symp.	*Symposium (Banquet)*

Other abbreviations are generally from *OCD*.

Translations are my own unless otherwise credited.

Note on Reference to "Presocratic" Fragments

The text of ancient writings by and about the early Greek writers eventually called "philosophers" comes from LM, unless noted, and is cited by both DK and LM number, if available. In DK, "A" precedes testimonia, "B" precedes fragments. In LM, "P" precedes information about the philosopher, "D" precedes fragments or doctrinal statements, and "R" precedes later reception of the philosophers' thought (according to the editors' judgment).

1
Debating a Virtue

Sôphrosunê, a Virtue of Agency

This book tells a story about the Greek virtue *sôphrosunê* (σωφροσύνη) during the classical era.[1] It is a story of a virtue coming to increased attention and esteem, the queries and debates that followed, and the theories put forward to resolve those puzzles and disagreements.

By the fifth century *sôphrosunê* was becoming canonical—one among three or four other virtue-terms which, together, name the competences of the wholly good person. By the fourth century, this canon generally included, besides *sôphrosunê*, wisdom (σοφία), courage (ἀνδρεία), justice (δικαιοσύνη), and sometimes piety (εὐσέβεια). All are familiar, but *sôphrosunê* least so. Accordingly, the descriptive purpose of this book is to show how writers in the classical period used the term, and especially what they said about it, how they esteemed it, what they contended over, and how the philosophically minded of them sought to clarify or articulate or redefine the term in response to those contentions. Without surveying usages exhaustively or taxonomizing every variety, the goal is to reconstruct how these authors understood *sôphrosunê* as a fundamental human excellence.

Hardly separable from the descriptive purpose of this book is its interpretative purpose. It seeks to answer questions that may not have been asked in such explicit terms by the Greeks themselves: Why was *sôphrosunê* so esteemed? Why did it merit such disagreement? Why did fourth-century writers include it in their quadripartite or other-sized canons of virtues? Why was it sometimes even treated as the condition for the other virtues? In brief: What fundamental aspect of human excellence did the term *sôphrosunê* actually point to?

---

[1] I pronounce σωφροσύνη, which I transliterate as *sôphrosunê* (though other authors write *sophrosyne*), *soe-froe-SUE-nay*, as though the Greek accent over the υ serves as a stress marker; some others pronounce it *suh-FRAH-zoo-nay*, preferring the English pattern of stressing the antepenult and giving the omicron a broader sound. I always transliterate the term (for discussion of English translations of the term, see the epilogue) and usually use the abstract nominal form as a stand-in for the other main parts of speech (unless the form is important or English grammar prefers another part of speech): *sôphronein* (verb); *sôphrôn* (adjective); *sôphronôs* (adverb). Other forms include *sôphronizein* (verb: "to cause to be *sôphrôn*"), *sôphronismos* (noun: "result of *sôphronizein*"), and *sôphronikos* (adjective: "*sôphrôn*-like").

Despite the range of contexts in which Greek authors used the term *sôphrosunê*, their divergent sensibilities and judgments about it, and their distinctive elaborations on the virtue's nature, we come to see that they shared a basic assumption. *Sôphrosunê* is the capacity to act well in the face of a distinctive human challenge: the conflicting heterogeneity of our ends. Given our range of interests, relationships, and needs, we may simultaneously feel several opposed inclinations to act, and often the one we feel most strongly is not the one we should act on now. *Sôphrosunê* allows us to choose our action on grounds independent of the phenomenological quality of our inclinations—their strength or noisiness or urgency—when that quality does not actually convey practical wisdom. This capacity for a more deliberative and hopefully more successful action may be formulated in various ways, depending on one's preferred moral-psychological formulations—as the capacity to act only on certain desires, to pursue only certain goals, to acknowledge only certain norms, to accept only certain reasons. However we put it, we need *sôphrosunê* because we sometimes feel like doing things that, outside the cramped experience of that feeling, differ from what we can realize we should do.

The other virtues can be seen as solutions to human challenges: justice to our living among others who have rights and interests; courage to the fact that defending our rights and interests causes risk of harm to ourselves; piety to the invisible and aloof gods who may nevertheless demand our fealty; wisdom to the obscurity of practical problems and the uncertainty of future outcomes. These are not exclusive, sharply delineated, or equal-sized domains; their scope and reach depend on the conception of the situation. For instance, wisdom might assess who has which rights and interests and the best way to respect them; it may take courage to respect those rights that seem contrary to tradition. Because of these overlapping domains, *sôphrosunê* can sometimes seem a particular capacity—the capacity to deal with desiderative plurality—but also the general term for every other virtue. Analyzing courage as the competition between the desire for safety and the desire for honor turns it into a class of *sôphrosunê*; so, too, justice as wanting to respect others but also to keep one's money, or piety as the wish to benefit the gods but also to keep to human affairs. Hence *sôphrosunê*'s distinctive association with those conflicted desires less readily found in martial, political, or religious contexts, such as those for bodily pleasure or self-aggrandizement. Still, the solution *sôphrosunê* provides has a general character.

The problem with having multiple simultaneous desires or goals or action-guiding principles is plain: they cannot all be satisfied, they may not be equally good, and one's appraisal of them at one moment may not match one's appraisal at other moments. Though one may experience a given desire as supremely urgent, it may not warrant so much attention. What feels like an emergency may be no such thing. Indeed, satisfying a dominating desire may prevent satisfying desires that, with a few moments' distance, would reveal themselves to be more valuable from the long-term perspective or otherwise more deserving of satisfaction. Further, if one acts only as the seemingly strongest desire demands, and the relative strength of desires fluctuates for physiological or psychological reasons, one may keep switching actions, and many of the most important actions need prolonged and stable engagement. And sometimes there is not even a single strongest desire, so something else is needed to decide what to do. These three problems—false alarms, mercuriality, and indeterminacy—represent the sorts of problems that *sôphrosunê* addresses.

Sôphrosunê is a power of practical discrimination, but it is also one of self-constitution. You observe that you have many inclinations to do one thing or another, but you commit yourself to acting only on those that advance what you, as an ongoing and farsighted being, really want to be doing. Not every inclination does so equally. You deem some of those inclinations as less representative of yourself, as alien or adventitious or merely bodily or from a less authoritative part of the soul. Others you deem more representative and identify with them, so to speak, saying, "This is what *I* want," and, in committing yourself to them, incorporating them, you become them and they become you. *Sôphrosunê* is thus the virtue that makes each of us count as a "self," something or someone that has practical integrity through time. The alternative is being a mere site of desire-satisfaction and desire-frustration. A self originates actions for which it takes full responsibility. Adult human individuals do not merely embody movements or behaviors, as do animals and babies, and they do not merely carry out actions for somebody else, as do tools, robots, and, in a qualified way, slaves. They are agents. As agents, they act rather than simply move; it is they, rather than physiological energies or social pressures, who do the acting.

The achievement of the agency that comes from self-constitution is the goal of nearly every regimen of maturation, what parents hope for their children and good societies hope for their citizens. A person may not in every instance strive to act independently of her potent feelings. But we do expect people to attain some degree of agency, some authority over the desires that prompt them to action. Only in this way does a person's actions belong to *that person*, and not just to the impulses and habits imputed by nature, society, or happenstance.

Yet is *sôphrosunê* just an executive virtue of prudence and rationality, of an enlightened self-interest, concerned with being an even-keeled captain of one's actions, whatever they are? Is it not also an ethical virtue, concerned with doing the right thing toward others? The answer depends on the desires that we should act on, the goals to which we should strive, the norms that should guide us. It depends on the correspondence between what *I* really want or value, what I identify with as most properly my desire or goal or self-defining ruling, and the norms we might take as objective: what the gods deserve, what justice demands, what the laws of reason require. That correspondence is controversial. One might suppose that they do correspond: we are supremely vulnerable to the gods, and so we do ideally desire to furnish them with what they deserve; personal well-being depends on civic comity, and so we do ideally desire to meet the demands of justice; hard practical or theoretical problems do not get solved through sloppy thinking, and so we do ideally desire to think carefully and well. Or the ethical life is for some other reason supremely valuable and desirable, or even already valued and desired. But one might equally doubt that the norms of pious, just, and reasonable action are really one's own self-constituting norms, and deny that they reflect one's deepest, most stable, and most internally consistent desires. They might seem merely distant and alien authorities. By desiring to propitiate some mysterious gods, or following the decrees of a hyperventilating democratic assembly, or obeying a logician's parameters for valid inference, am I not in fact abdicating from or alienating my agency, submitting myself to someone else's will, being mastered rather than mastering myself? This doubter might go on to expand his criticism. Might not any standard deployed to judge between my desires involve something external to those desires and thus external to myself? Isn't agency simply the capacity to satisfy the desires that I happen to have? Isn't *sôphrosunê*, in seeking to separate myself from my desires, precisely the virtue that undermines agency?

The drama to be found in our story of *sôphrosunê* in classical Greece comes from the discovery of these questions and the refinements and response they prompted. The apologists for the virtue must show how ignoring or neutralizing some of one's desires, and adopting what may appear an external regime of value, can constitute oneself as a self, an agent, an effective and responsible actor. The critics of the virtue must show how a life meritorious even in one's own terms can unfold without any selection between and consequent commitment to the ends or guidelines or desires that motivate or guide one's actions.

The story is not so simple as pro and con, however; there are alternative formulations, inchoate presentiments, idiosyncratic takes, and rabbit holes of one depth or another. But its significance should be clear. Greek discourse about *sôphrosunê* is to be seen as discourse about the ideal of agency: How do we become people who act for ourselves?

A Laudatory Attribution Becomes Contentious

The term *sôphrosunê* appears in the Homeric epics, where it denotes the admirable capacity not to blurt or act out in situations where doing so, no matter how natural or satisfying, would be contrary to one's broader goals or commitments. This rational self-discipline becomes thematic a century later, in the sympotic poetry of Theognis, as an admirable trait of reliable individuals and loyal citizens. By the early fifth century, it appears among the cardinal virtues of Pindar and Aeschylus, as it does on celebratory tombstones and in the philosophical aperçus of Heraclitus, now glossing the virtue in terms of Delphic self-knowledge. By the later fifth century, the term appears across the literary genres—historiography, tragedy, comedy, and oratory—reflecting its essential position in Greek evaluative and ethical vocabulary.

As the social importance of *sôphrosunê* grows, so too does its correct application or retraction. Ascription, or withholding of ascription, becomes eminently valuable. This raises the possibility of disagreement—about the virtue's scope, criteria, acquisition, operation, and real significance. The historical record reveals this disagreement. Three-quarters through the fifth century, extant literature first depicts and dramatizes debates about *sôphrosunê*. It does so vigorously and expansively. As the characters of this literature valorize themselves as *sôphrôn* and contend with that valorization, its authors prove the centrality of the virtue for thinking about the life successfully carried out—as a leader, a parent, a citizen, and generally as a grown-up person. In their querying of the virtue's nature, they raise and refine deep questions about human maturity, in particular about our being actors rather than patients in our own lives. We see that these debates concern our capacity to act on our own behalf, our constituting ourselves as agents.

Three debates from the decade around 425 BCE—the period of Socrates' maturity, the height of the sophistic period, the beginning of the Peloponnesian War—capture three dimensions of disagreement about *sôphrosunê*, and thereby three dimensions on which the term serves as commendation. An exchange early in Herodotus' *Histories* (finished in the 420s BCE) concerns the evaluation of competent action, formulated in the language of *sôphrosunê*. The text asks, Against what background of goals and interests do we judge a person a successful agent, someone who does what *he* really wants, rather than simply a tool to satisfy the whims of madness? A series of conversations in Euripides' *Medea* (431 BCE) concerns the type of considerations and kind of reasoning necessary for being deemed *sôphrôn*. What makes certain motivations count as proper to oneself, and thus acting from them *sôphrôn*, and what makes others count as extraneous, as the grounds only of foolish action? Finally, the famous contest between Better and Worse Argument in Aristophanes' *Clouds* (first production 423 BCE) concerns the viability and value of an education to *sôphrosunê*. What could bring the virtue about, and would having it do more good than harm?

These are not the only debates about *sôphrosunê* from the period; in Chapters 4–6 we return to more in Euripides and look closely at implied or actual debates attributable to Critias, Democritus, Antiphon, Thucydides, and Socrates, other major intellectuals of the period. The present selection of discussions of *sôphrosunê* only hints at the rich and profound inquiry into the virtue to be found in the decades that follow. In the second half of this chapter, I lay out why I think a study of this classical Greek inquiry into *sôphrosunê* matters, how earlier studies went about that inquiry, and how this one will go.

Herodotus' *Histories*

In Book 3 of his *Histories*, Herodotus tells the story of Cambyses' insanity. This story culminates in a debate about the proper attribution of *sôphrosunê*. Cambyses, the king of Persia, wants to disprove the Persian view that he is crazy and out of his mind (παραφρονέειν καὶ οὐκ εἶναι νοήμονα).[2] He proposes a test that, should he pass, will show the Persians have mistaken his state of mind, but should he fail, will show that he in fact, as he puts it, lacks *sôphrosunê* (ἢν δὲ ἁμάρτω, φάναι Πέρσας τε λέγειν ἀληθέα καὶ ἐμὲ μὴ σωφρονέειν).[3] This test of his *sôphrosunê* is a test of ability to do precisely what he intends do. He will try to shoot an arrow at a small target far away. As it turns out, his target is the chest of a boy, the son of his most trusted messenger, Prexaspes, the man indeed to whom he addresses this proposal. He hits his target exactly. Full of pride at his accomplishment, he laughs, "Now it's clear—I'm not crazy; it's the Persians who are out of their minds!" (οὐ μαίνομαι . . . παραφρονέουσι).[4] Prexaspes is not convinced: he sees that Cambyses has indeed lost his mind (οὐ φρενήρεα).[5] Herodotus notes that it is only much later, when Cambyses comes to recognize the circumstances of his own immediate death, that he regains his *sôphrosunê* (ἐσωφρόνησε).[6]

Cambyses believes that he has shown himself *sôphrôn* through his competence to execute his plans, in this case through perfect perceptual and body control. He has understood "out of one's mind" to mean a failure of agency, a disconnect between intention and accomplishment. He has a reason to do something, namely to prove his prowess, and he does it, unimpeded by cognitive or physical distraction or obstacle. The Persians think he cannot; he shows them that he can. For him, *sôphrosunê* is the virtue of agency. So, too, for Prexaspes and Herodotus; and this is precisely why they deny that he is *sôphrôn*: he is not acting on his own authority; he is not in control.

So there is disagreement about the ascription of *sôphrosunê* and the ascription of agency. How Herodotus denies ascriptions of *sôphrosunê* elsewhere clarifies

[2] Hdt. 3.34.3.
[3] Hdt. 3.35.2.
[4] Hdt. 3.35.4.
[5] Hdt. 3.35.4.
[6] Hdt. 3.64.5.

this disagreement.⁷ A *sôphrôn* people would not have set sail for Troy simply because Helen was abducted—that was a disproportionate and even mistaken response, presumably their jealousy or contentiousness taking charge.⁸ One should not attack enemies without due diligence (ἀβούλως) and without being very *sôphrôn* about what one is doing (ἐπὶ τὸ σωφρονέστερον αὐτὴν λάμβανε), for example by delaying until one has adequate forces; again, being hot to fight can undermine one's overall campaign.⁹ Though other Greeks may know more, the Spartans have more *sôphrôn* conversations, evidently preferring to listen and respond carefully over putting themselves forward as experts.¹⁰ Xerxes presents *sôphrosunê* as precisely this sensitivity to others' insights and not just to one's own immediate inclinations:

Ἀρτάβανε, ἐγὼ τὸ παραυτίκα μὲν οὐκ ἐσωφρόνεον¹¹ εἴπας ἐς σὲ μάταια ἔπεα χρηστῆς εἵνεκα συμβουλίης· μετὰ μέντοι οὐ πολλὸν χρόνον μετέγνων, ἔγνων δὲ ταῦτά μοι ποιητέα ἐόντα τὰ σὺ ὑπεθήκαο. (Hdt. 7.15.1–2)

Artabanus, there was a moment when I was lacking *sôphrosunê*, uttering nonsense to you for your useful advice; after not much time, however, I changed my mind, recognizing that I should do the things that you advised.

In each of these cases, being *sôphrôn* amounts to being responsive to something other than one's pressing inclinations—to go after Helen, to attack, to mansplain—in order to satisfy one's longer-term, more fundamental, or more considered goals and interests. This framework holds for whatever these goals and interests are, whether self-regarding or other-regarding, and in whatever way they are judged superior to those sought by one's present inclinations. The basic assumption is that people have a sometimes inconsistent complex of ends, that certain of those ends have an evaluative priority, and yet that sometimes quite other ends have an attentional or visceral priority. Accordingly, people sometimes want to act on a desire that, with more or deeper reflection, they would take to be less worth acting on—for example, the desire for glory or revenge or self-confidence. By satisfying such a desire, they would prevent themselves from satisfying others they might more closely identify with—for example, the desire for safety or victory or other form of long-term success. In every case, *sôphrosunê* marks the capacity to distinguish one's feeling about what to do now from one's

---

⁷ For more general remarks, see Rademaker (2005, 194–201).
⁸ Hdt. 1.4.2. This is the Persian view; they consider the abduction of women unjust but the avenging of abductions senseless (ἀνοήτων).
⁹ Hdt. 3.71.3.
¹⁰ Hdt. 4.77.
¹¹ This is in all manuscripts except A, which has ἐφρόνεον.

judgment about what one should in general be doing, and to act in accordance with the latter rather than the former in cases where they diverge.

All this clarifies the competing judgments about Cambyses' *sôphrosunê*. There is a disagreement about what Cambyses' goals, interests, or desires really are, and thus whether his arrow strike has satisfied them. Cambyses constructs his goals narrowly: to execute his immediate intentions, to express his anger at being dishonored, to show his total authority over life and death. Prexaspes and Herodotus construe his goals differently, imagining that should Cambyses be in a position to reflect on his overarching commitments he would see that they include much else (a position he enters only once he must confront the nearness of his death). Those commitments might include treating his close associates with respect, cultivating appreciation for his leadership, avoiding needless death, and exercising his persuasive powers. He lacks *sôphrosunê* because he does not act on their basis; he is insane because he is currently incapable even of considering doing so. So each party agrees that *sôphrosunê* is the virtue of agency; they disagree, so to speak, about the conditions for ascribing agency. For Cambyses, it is narrow: a single desire and its direct satisfaction; for others, it is wide: a complex of desires, some adventitious and others intrinsic, their satisfaction either immediate or deferred.

Euripides' *Medea*

The *Medea* of 431 BCE depicts Medea's anger (ὀργή) in light of her insight (σοφία) and dramatizes competing assessments of the quality of her reasoning. It prompts the play's audience to reflect: What makes acting on a certain motivation consistent with *sôphrosunê*? What makes for *sôphrôn* decision-making? This is a version of the question Herodotus asked about Cambyses, but Euripides does it with fine-grained attention to the various possible motivations for Medea's actions—as it turns out, again, the killing of someone's children.

Talk of *sôphrosunê* begins in an exchange between Medea and Creon. Creon is the father of the woman for whom Jason left Medea. Creon hopes to exile Medea, since he fears her vindictiveness and worries that he himself may come in for retribution. Medea, refusing exile, reassures him that she directs no animosity toward him, despite his family connection. Creon did no injustice (ἠδίκηκας) in following his heart (θυμὸς ἦγεν) when he gave his daughter to Jason; in her eyes, she says, he was *sôphrôn* in doing so.[12] Medea must be saying that Creon acted wholeheartedly, so to speak, from his fatherly sentiment, his deep interest in marrying off his daughter well, and broke no overriding obligations in the

---

[12] Eur. *Med.* 309–11.

process.¹³ He did not act out of anger or pride or some other momentary emotion reprehensibly inconsistent with a humane consideration for others.¹⁴

Medea's praise of Creon's *sôphrosunê*, whether noble or strategic, puts in sharper focus a later sequence of problematic *sôphrosunê* self-attributions. The sequence begins with Jason's major self-defense speech, justifying his marriage to Creon's daughter. He claims that he was, first, wise, then *sôphrôn*, and, finally, a great friend to Medea and the children.¹⁵ He gives negative and positive reasons for the triple virtuosity of the marital realignment.¹⁶ Negatively, he claims not to have been motivated by sex or ambition; he did not seek conjugal novelty or more children.¹⁷ Positively, "the main thing" (τὸ μὲν μέγιστον) he says he wanted was for his family to "live well" (οἰκοῖμεν καλῶς), with sufficient prosperity and society for his children. In sum, he says, he wanted to flourish (εὐδαιμονοίην), and for this he deliberated (βεβούλευμαι) well.¹⁸ Medea he chastises for not seeing this, obsessed as she is with the marriage bed, which for her trumps everything else desirable and worthwhile (τὰ λῷστα καὶ κάλλιστα).¹⁹

Jason has called himself *sôphrôn* on the grounds that his primary desideratum was his own maximal well-being, which includes his flourishing and helping his offspring live well, and he has deliberated on the way to accomplish both. Like Creon, he has acted in ways fundamental for a father, and he has done so thoughtfully and reflectively. He does not deny the existence of libidinal or honor-bound feelings, but presents them as not "the main thing"—they were not decisive for

---

¹³ LSJ s.v. θυμός II.1.
¹⁴ Later in the play, θυμός, "heart," has a more equivocal sense: Medea says, "despite knowing what bad things I will suffer, my heart gets the better of my deliberation" (θυμὸς δὲ κρείσσων τῶν ἐμῶν βουλευμάτων, 1079). She means that her sentiments—to avenge herself against Jason—go so deep in her that she cannot reason herself out from them. For further discussion, see Kovacs (1986, 351n12). In the seventh *Homeric Hymn* (To Dionysus), the pilot of a pirate ship has a *sôphrôn* heart (θυμός, 49): unlike his crewmates, he is calm when the god appears in the form of a lion.
¹⁵ Eur. *Med.* 550–51.
¹⁶ I take the reasons to pertain equally to *sophia*, *sôphrosunê*, and *philia* rather than some reasons pertaining exclusively to wisdom, some to *sôphrosunê*, and some to *philia*. For a contrasting view, see Mastronarde (2002 ad 548): his "demonstration is mostly about his prudence" (*sophos*); friendship is his "planning for the future"; *sôphrosunê* "lies only in his claim not to have acted from desire for a new, young sexual partner." But this is inconsistent with the Creon exchange discussed above (which Mastronarde does not discuss) and with what follows; line 884 in particular, discussed below, seems to confirm it, as even Mastronarde seems to recognize (p. 313).
¹⁷ Eur. *Med.* 555–58: σὸν μὲν ἐχθαίρων λέχος | καινῆς δὲ νύμφης ἱμέρωι πεπληγμένος | οὐδ' εἰς ἅμιλλαν πολύτεκνον σπουδὴν ἔχων· | ἅλις γὰρ οἱ γεγῶτες οὐδὲ μέμφομαι.
¹⁸ Editors have taken issue with the first-person singular form, εὐδαιμονοίην, doubting that he could really be saying that *he* wanted to flourish rather than that he wanted himself *and* Medea to flourish. Whereas some editors have suggested emending the text, Mastronarde (2002) and Page (1938 ad 565) treat the verb form as evidence for Jason's "very self-centred" nature. But Jason is explaining *his* decision-making; his flourishing is, as it were, the ultimate reason for action; his flourishing depends (as he implies) on the overall flourishing of his family, where the well-being of his children contribute most to this.
¹⁹ Eur. *Med.* 559–72. When she reacts to his self-praise as *sôphrôn*, etc., Jason chastises her, "Hold your peace" (ἀλλ' ἔχ' ἥσυχος, 550), which, as we will see, basically means "Be *sôphrôn*."

his action.[20] So *sôphrosunê* means the capacity to let what is really important to you (if and once you have figured it out) govern your actions. According to Jason, Medea fails to let what is more important win out. Whether Jason is right about her, and about himself, are open questions.

Jason's vaunting of his *sôphrosunê* echoes through the play. About three hundred lines later, Medea pretends, for a spell, to reconcile with him. She says she now realizes how *sôphrôn* Jason in fact is.[21] This realization came to her, she says, as she deliberated with herself, resolved her misapprehensions, and succeeded at appreciating his reasons.[22] She appears to be presenting herself as *sôphrôn* in the very recognition of another's *sôphrosunê*—she can now see where authoritative judgment resides. Jason accepts Medea's improved self-understanding: your anger was reasonable, he says, but now your heart has come to see what is better, more desirable (ἐς τὸ λῷον); through time, you have recognized "the superior plan" (τὴν νικῶσαν ... βουλήν). This discovery, Jason says, is exactly the task of the *sôphrôn* woman.[23] Jason treats *sôphrosunê* as the capacity to forgo acting on the basis of one's reactive attitudes and to treat what is actually best as the proper motivation for action.

Of course, what Jason deems "best" rather than a merely reactive attitude— what is a core commitment rather than a superficial resentment—is tendentious. Later in the play he says again that a properly *sôphrôn* woman should find the loss of a marriage a mere triviality (σμικρόν) rather than a matter affecting her identity generally, and that Medea finds everything bad (σοὶ δὲ πάντ' ἐστὶν κακά), implying that she does not know how to order her desires (e.g., to maintain her marriage versus to help her children flourish).[24] Jason's analysis at least clarifies the stakes: *sôphrosunê* is the virtue whereby one can flourish by being motivated by some interests or desires rather than others; it is a virtue of distinguishing between various reasons for action. How we characterize the more proper interests will be an ongoing source of disagreement. Whatever they are, however, the

---

[20] When the Chorus of women later sings in the second stasimon, requesting that "*sôphrosunê* favor me, fairest gift of the gods" (στέργοι δέ με σωφροσύνα, δώρημα κάλλιστα θεῶν, 636), they request only as much love (ἔρως) as would be sufficient for happiness but would not make them contentious or mad (627–44). Page (1938 ad 635) compares this passage to A. *Ag*. 927–28, τὸ μὴ κακῶς φρονεῖν | θεοῦ μέγιστον δῶρον (not to think badly is god's greatest gift).

[21] Eur. *Med*. 884–85: νῦν οὖν ἐπαινῶ σωφρονεῖν τέ μοι δοκεῖς | κῆδος τόδ' ἡμῖν προσλαβών, ἐγὼ δ' ἄφρων.

[22] The speech runs 869–905.

[23] Eur. *Med*. 908–13. This usage does not mean sexual propriety but, as Mastronarde (2002 ad 913) puts it (though over-specifically), "meekly following the lead of a supervising male."

[24] Eur. *Med*. 1367–69. Mastronarde (2002 ad 1369) glosses *sôphrôn* as having "good sense and self-control." The present interpretation of σοὶ δὲ πάντ' ἐστὶν κακά, "everything is bad to you, i.e., in your eyes," which is influenced by the preceding statements and the overall interpretation of the virtue, and follows Kovacs, is not shared by all translators. (Page [1938 ad 1369] thinks that such a reading "has no proper relevance here," though it evidently does.) Mastronarde (2002 ad 1369) gives "you have all wicked qualities," taking ἐστιν as ἔνεστιν, but this does not seem responsive to what Medea just said, and Page despairs over finding a parallel for "such extraordinary phraseology."

Medea capitalizes on the sense that *sôphrosunê* is the virtue needful for being the self-possessed creator of one's life: identifying one's major ends, and pursuing them, whatever the domestic habits or conventional pieties that may interfere.

Aristophanes' *Clouds*

More extensive than either of the previous disagreements about *sôphrosunê* is the one found in Aristophanes' *Clouds*. This occurs in the "Debate" (Ἀγών) in the play's second half, where two instructors compete for the tuition of Pheidippides, a potential student at Socrates' Thinkery.[25] The Chorus tells one instructor, "Better Argument," to describe how he used to teach, and the other, "Worse Argument," to describe his new way of doing so.[26] The two instructors end up describing two perspectives on *sôphrosunê*: as a route to effective agency and as the very inhibition of agency.

Most readers of the debate have taken it to concern justice and modes of education, but *sôphrosunê* is evidently its real focus.[27] Better opens by saying that in the old days, "I flourished, saying what's just [τὰ δίκαια λέγων], and *sôphrosunê* was the norm ['νενόμιστο]."[28] As it turns out, he never comes to focus on justice. Instead he enumerates those *sôphrosunê*-related norms and presents them as having contributed to Athenian military success at Marathon. Such norms could govern a boy's upbringing now, he suggests, in which case that boy would become *sôphrôn* and have physical vigor.[29] The Chorus caps his speech by emphasizing the relevant virtue and its outcome: "How sweet is the *sôphrôn* flower in your

---

[25] The contestants of the *agôn* begin arguing at Ar. *Nub.* 889–948; their display competition for Pheidippides' benefit is 961–1114. The version of the *Clouds* we possess is evidently Aristophanes' revision of the 423 script; it is uncertain how much of this *agôn* is a result of Aristophanes' revision. Hypothesis A7 states that Aristophanes revised a bit of everything and created anew "where Better Argument chatters to [πρὸς ... λαλεῖ] Worse Argument," referring to the present section. Sommerstein (1982, 4n9) and Henderson (2007, 296) claim this means only 889–948; MacDowell (1995, 144, with 138–47) would assign all of 889–1114 to the revision. See Dover (1968, lxxxiii–lxxxiv, xc–xcvii) for careful discussion, though he gives no final judgment. I note that Better Argument describes Worse Argument's talking with the verb we find in the Hypothesis (λαλούντων, 1053). Were the entire *agôn* new, in its focus on *sôphrosunê* it could be seen as solving a problem with the previous version, perhaps comparable to the situation of Euripides' two *Hippolytus* plays (see Chapter 4). Were the *agôn* not entirely new, it would mean that the problem of *sôphrosunê* concerned Aristophanes even by 423.

[26] Ar. *Nub.* 935–36.

[27] *Sôphrosunê* in the *agôn* is not mentioned by Starkie (1911, xviii–xx) or by Dover (1968, lviii–lxiv) in their introductory discussions of it. MacDowell (1995, 138–43) finds the speech mainly about sophistry, and finds the banter about *sôphrosunê*, which he glosses as "abstention from sexual misconduct," basically irrelevant to the rest of the play; similarly Claughton and Affleck (2012, 72). More sensitive to *sôphrosunê*'s structuring role in the debate are North (1947, 10–11; 1966, 97–99); Fisher (1984, 192–202); Freydberg (2008, 41–44).

[28] Ar. *Nub.* 962.

[29] Ar. *Nub.* 986, 1006, 1002, 1012.

words; people were really happy [εὐδαίμονές] then."[30] When Worse takes his turn, he appears to start equally generally: he says that he pioneered arguing against "norms and matters of justice" (τοῖσιν νόμοις καὶ ταῖς δίκαις).[31] And yet he too addresses specifically the norms of *sôphrosunê* brought up by his opponent; then he repeatedly addresses *sôphrosunê* explicitly.[32] It is not surprising that both instructors begin their speeches mentioning "matters of justice," since Strepsiades wants his son to learn how to speak justly and unjustly.[33] But it is just as clear that the debate proceeds in terms of *sôphrosunê*.[34]

Better Argument describes the code of conduct that prevailed when *sôphrosunê* was the norm.[35] Young men practiced silence; they walked through the streets in good order (εὐτάκτως); they wore austere clothing; they sang only traditional tunes; they did not goof around; there was no musical innovation; and sexual modesty in personal bearing was practiced.[36] In other words, the youth did not act however they wished; they followed established and authoritative norms. Some of these norms concerned body control, others desire control, but most concerned a person's bearing and types of activity. For those of Pheidippides' age, there was avoidance of the agora, bathhouses, and dancing girls' houses, and the young men were encouraged to reject what was considered shameful and to respect their elders.[37] Social and sexual impulses are addressed, but Better emphasizes the broader picture: recognition of judgments that transcend one's personal preference. Should Pheidippides follow these rules, Better says, he would be exercising at the gymnasium or a park, not anemically theorizing in the agora or disputing in the courts.[38] This preferred regime would build bodily strength, endurance, and control and would limit the scenarios in which sexual feelings could be aroused or exacerbated. It encourages the adoption of preexisting norms and respect for those promulgating and enforcing them, the recognition and rejection of what is considered disgraceful and shameful. The practice of silence provided a training in self-control, discouraged idleness, and warded

---

[30] Ar. *Nub.* 1026–27.
[31] Ar. *Nub.* 1040.
[32] Ar. *Nub.* 1067, 1071, 1078.
[33] E.g., Ar. *Nub.* 99, 115–16. There is a similar movement from talk of justice to talk of *sôphrosunê* in Plato's *Gorgias*; see Chapter 8.
[34] In the "Great Speech" attributed to Protagoras in Plato's *Protagoras*, set in the same era, Socrates dings Protagoras for speaking imprecisely about the relationship between justice and *sôphrosunê*. See Chapter 10.
[35] There is considerable debate whether Better Argument represents Aristophanes' view or quite the opposite. For example, Green (1868, 10 and Habib (2014, 39–40) think that it does represent his view; against this see, e.g., Fisher (1984, 197–201); MacDowell (1995, 147).
[36] Ar. *Nub.* 963, 964, 965, 966–68, 969–72, 973–83.
[37] Ar. *Nub.* 991, 992 (τοῖς αἰσχροῖς αἰσχύνεσθαι), 993–94, 994–95 (ἄλλο τε μηδὲν | αἰσχρὸν ποιεῖν ὅ τι [οὐ Henderson] τῆς Αἰδοῦς μέλλεις τἄγαλμ' ἀναπλήσειν), 998–99, 996–97.
[38] Exercise: Ar. *Nub.* 1002, 1005–14; talking: 1003-4 (οὐ στωμύλλων κατὰ τὴν ἀγορὰν τριβολεκτράπελ', οἷάπερ οἱ νῦν | οὐδ' ἑλκόμενος περὶ πραγματίου γλισχραντιλογεξεπιτρίτου), 1015–23.

off the dangers associated with unnecessary talk. It was feared that such talk might undermine the norms.³⁹

Worse starts his rebuttal of Better's austere regimen with a telling counterexample. Better advocates cold baths, but Heracles is associated with warm baths, and "who was more manly [ἀνδρειότερος] than he?"⁴⁰ Heracles' excellence of soul (ἄριστον ψυχήν) and toil-confronting nature (πλείστους πόνους πονῆσαι) precisely represent the activity of spirit that Better's education in *sôphrosunê* is meant to promote.⁴¹ Worse then splits his argument into two parts: one dealing with *sôphrosunê* in general, the other focused on speech. He doubts that any good has ever come from *sôphrosunê*. Better rejoins that it served Peleus well,⁴² but Worse quips that it yielded only an unhappy marriage.⁴³ Worse then asserts that *sôphrosunê* interferes with such pleasures as consorting with boys and women, playing cottabus, and indulging one's desires for rich foods, drink, and hearty laughter. These are the key sources for a worthwhile (ἄξιον) life, at least when imagined by those for whom partying exemplifies human enjoyment.⁴⁴ Then, Worse says, if you lack the argumentative capacity that Better's *sôphrosunê*-building curriculum prevents you from developing, you cannot get yourself out of the troubles that the "necessities of nature" (ἡ τῆς φύσεως ἀνάγκη) get you into, such as the lust that can lead to adultery. Instead of training yourself in *sôphrosunê* as a prevention against falling into trouble, you should train in argumentative power and pull yourself out of trouble, benefiting first from having the pleasures that get you into trouble. Rather than going against your inclination, you should prevent others from punishing you for it: "indulge your nature [χρῶ τῇ φύσει], gambol, laugh, and take nothing to be shameful."⁴⁵

---

³⁹ Ar. *Nub*. 1020–21: καί σ' ἀναπείσει τὸ μὲν αἰσχρὸν ἅπαν | καλὸν ἡγεῖσθαι, τὸ καλὸν δ' αἰσχρόν.
⁴⁰ Ar. *Nub*. 1050. For warm baths, Ibyc. fr. 300; Hdt. 7.176.3.
⁴¹ Ar. *Nub*. 1048–49.
⁴² Peleus is explicitly called *sôphrôn* in Pind. *Isthm*. 8.26 (with 27–53; note the related *eusebestaton* at 40) and *sôphronestatos* at Pl. *Rep*. 3.391c. The specific relevance of the virtue in the Thetis case is uncertain. It might be because Peleus' *sôphrosunê* made him an appealing candidate husband in the eyes of Zeus and Poseidon, who were arranging the marriage of Thetis, or it was his *sôphrosunê*—as steadfastness—that allowed him to capture Thetis despite her attempt to escape his grasp through Protean changes. For the story, see Apollod. *Bibl*. 3.13; Σ Pind. *Nem*. 4.54 and 4.59; Σ Ar. *Nub*. 1063; Σ Apol. Rhod. 1.224.
⁴³ Ar. *Nub*. 1068–69. Worse Argument says Thetis left him because he was neither *hubristês* nor a pleasure to spend all night with in bed. (Sommerstein [1982 ad 1068] says that this explanation is "the speaker's ad hoc invention.") *Hubristês*, a common opposite of *sôphrôn*, seems here to mean "unbridled" (as of animals or natural forces) and thus "tending to act on one's lusts" (*hubrizein* with sexual connotation: Ar. *Th*. 63; Xen. *Mem*. 2.1.30). Soph. fr. 155 has Thetis leaving Peleus because he spoke to her harshly; *Il*. 18.429ff. and Pind. *Nem*. 4.62ff. present her as not wishing to marry him.
⁴⁴ Ar. *Nub*. 1072–74. As we will see in Chapter 5, Critias had a notably scornful attitude toward cottabus, since it encouraged overdrinking at symposia; he himself recommends moderate drinking as an expression of *sôphrosunê*: Critias B6; Xen. *Hell*. 2.3.56. Cottabus is often focalized in this period: see Eur. fr. 562 (*Oeneus*); fr. 631 (*Pleisthenes*); Soph. fr. 537; Cratin. fr. 299; Ar. *Ach*. 525.
⁴⁵ Ar. *Nub*. 1078. For "indulge your nature," see LSJ s.v. χράομαι 2 ("ὀργῇ or θυμῷ χρῆσθαι *to indulge one's anger, give vent to it*, Hdt."). Sommerstein (1982 ad 1075) offers that *phusis* may also be euphemistic for "genitals."

Worse has a distinctive view of human nature: we are the totality of our desires, especially our natural desires, and our reason should help us satisfy them. Recognizing and acting on them just is self-realization. From this perspective, *sôphrosunê* as desire-suppression is self-inhibition, and so cannot be "the finest of god's gifts." This was not Better's perspective. As we see from children's uncontrolled behavior and the way people respond to it, everyone thinks that maturation requires selecting for certain motivations rather than others, in particular ones that are tried and true. The exemplars of human efficacy and durability—in this case, the Athenians of the Marathon generation—achieved those capacities by such selection. They achieved much thanks to their sacrifice of the immediate pleasures, and in particular by ignoring the metadesire for unimpeded freedom; had they failed in those great achievements, they could not—even with the best rhetorical education—have talked themselves out of the consequences: the Persians would not have been convinced. *Sôphrosunê* involves sacrificing immediate liberty, a trivial thing, for the sake of future power.

Thinking about the goods possibly achieved by *sôphrosunê* leads us to think about the prerequisites for mature human action; debates about those goods amount to debates about those prerequisites. What does it take to constitute oneself as an effective actor? Does it take suppression of certain desires, development of certain skills, and an eventual focus on long-term goods, including the preservation of one's city? Or should one keep the desires but work to eliminate whatever obstacles or costs to their satisfaction one may confront? We have already seen versions of these questions prompted by the *sôphrosunê* debates in Herodotus and Euripides, though the emphasis in Aristophanes is on desire-management rather than on ideals of agency or the relative significance of one's concerns. In subsequent chapters, we will examine attempts to answer them.

The Purposes of This Book

This book has two primary but closely related aims. The first is to understand the way classical Greek authors thought about *sôphrosunê*, one of the most prized and eventually canonical virtues of the age, though also one of the least appreciated by modern readers. We see that these authors shared a basic concept of *sôphrosunê*, as shown by their use of the term and the tenor of debates about it. Where authors differ is to be explained by their analytic choices, for example whether to speak of *sôphrosunê* in terms of desires or not and, if so, which kinds of desires to emphasize. The second aim is to give content to this basic concept, which I argue concerns rational agency and self-constitution. Both aims are philosophical, the first principally descriptive and the second interpretative: I am trying to set out what these authors were in fact saying and then what they could have meant by saying it. The book also has subordinate aims, chief among them to dispel various contemporary misapprehensions of *sôphrosunê*. Some of these current attitudes toward the virtue will be familiar to or even shared by readers: that it has disparate "intellectual" and "moral" connotations or even denotations; that despite its polysemy it might fairly be translated "moderation" or "temperance"; that it mainly concerns control of certain bodily desires; and that it has no English or contemporary equivalent. Of course something might be said in favor of each of these, but I do not think they are altogether accurate and I do not think they capture the significance and appeal of the virtue. My hope is to inspire greater interest in *sôphrosunê*, the classical discussions of which, across the literary genres in which they appear, reveal Greek thinking about selfhood in ways both distinctive and unfamiliar.

The approach of this book is in the first instance lexicographic; it studies people's mentioning or discussing *sôphrosunê*.[46] It is also selective, since it studies only the most provocative uses of and statements about *sôphrosunê*. In these parameters it diverges from the key earlier study of *sôphrosunê*, in fact one of only two ever published: Helen North's *Sophrosune: Self-Knowledge and Self-Restraint in Greek Literature*, from 1966.[47] North's study revises her dissertation and a series of articles from 1947.[48] It aims at comprehensive coverage from the archaic period until Augustine, mentioning all prominent uses of the term. Indeed, it even exceeds this; on the assumption that "the feeling is older than the word," North infers some authors' views about *sôphrosunê* even where they do not use the word itself.[49] Fair enough, to the extent that the book concerns a complex of ideas about knowing and restraining oneself. But in doing so North is assuming that *sôphrosunê* labeled that preexisting complex of ideas, and she is not ultimately focused on the way Greeks used the term.[50] Those uses reveal a complex set of dynamics, connected with but not always determined by those ideas. Where her book does stick to uses of the term itself, it emphasizes the variety in

---

[46] Havelock (1969) exemplifies this approach, for justice (δικαιοσύνη), though in much smaller compass.
[47] The early bibliography on *sôphrosunê* is sparse. The Göttingen dissertation of Ernst Weitlich (1922), *Quae fuerit vocis sōphrosyne vis ac natura apud antiquiores scriptores graecos usque ad Platonem*, does not circulate and has been seen by few. Einarson (1927) is a valuable source but only twenty-five pages long. Kollmann (1941) and De Vries (1943) are even briefer. The greatest density of contemporary writing on *sôphrosunê* is found in scholarship on Plato's *Charmides*, though these works tend not to give especially synoptic or substantive analyses of the virtue: Tuckey (1951, 5–9), Hazebroucq (1997, 138–48), Tuozzo (2011, 90–98), Moore and Raymond (2019, xxviii–xxxvii).
[48] North (1947: "A Period of Opposition to *Sôphrosynê* in Greek Thought"; 1948a: "The Concept of *Sophrosyne* in Greek Literary Criticism"; 1948b: "Pindar *Isthmian* 8.24–28"; 1977: "The Mare, the Vixen, and the Bee: Sophrosyne as the Virtue of Women in Antiquity"). Her 1979 *From Myth to Icon: Reflections of Greek Ethical Doctrine in Literature and Art* has been little noticed; it develops issues from the 1966 book, and it mostly forgoes the lexical approach.
[49] North (1966, 7; see also ix).
[50] Similar criticisms made by Adkins (1968, 712); Else (1969, 362–63).

their connotations. Such variety does constitute one of the fascinating aspects of the term, for instance that it can refer as much to clear thinking as to chastity. But North is often satisfied to believe that *sôphrosunê* simply came to mean many different things rather than to hypothesize a single human competence named by *sôphrosunê* that has a range of aspects and manifestations accounting for the range of usages of the term. This latter option is perhaps to be preferred, given that the Greeks were in fact using a single word.[51] For instance, North, among other authors, considers *sôphrosunê* to fall into two major categories—intellectual and moral—as is reflected in the subtitle of her book. And yet if, as I propose, *sôphrosunê* denotes the faculty of acting only on authoritative desires, then the same faculty could be characterized as intellectual or moral. It will depend on the author's purposes, whether emphasizing the recognition of the authoritative desires or the self-mastery allowing one to act only on that recognition. So while the variety of usage explored in North's study provides an excellent foundation for thinking about the sweep of this virtue-term's appearance in Greek literature, it leaves unresolved what holds those usages together and what questions about the human condition talk of *sôphrosunê* was answering.

Exploration of variety is the dominant mode of the second book written on the subject, four decades later: Adriaan Rademaker's (2005) *Sophrosyne and the Rhetoric of Self-Restraint: Polysemy and Persuasive Use of an Ancient Greek Value Term*. Rademaker explicitly rejects the urge to find unity across uses of the term. He asserts that *sôphrosunê* is more a cluster term for human dispositions ideologically parsed than the name of a single disposition: "What we have here is a number of quite distinct uses of the word that are connected by . . . family resemblance. . . . These uses are 'nodes' . . . of a network of related, if clearly distinct, uses."[52] He then works to associate agent types, such as men, women, children, and slaves, with prototypical uses of the term, such as desire-control, chastity, orderliness, and obedience. But Rademaker does not show that unity is not findable or, more important, that Greek speakers would not have assumed that *sôphrosunê* is a coherently integrated concept. Had he looked, maybe he would have found, in place of networks of discrete meanings, "overlapping circles" where the word had "a single set of meanings all related to a central concept."[53] He disregards the existence of fifth- and fourth-century debate and analysis of the term, especially that found in Xenophon, Isocrates, and Aristotle, which show that the Greeks assumed unity.[54] Thus we again have a book that provides provocative readings of individual remarks about *sôphrosunê* in all its classical variety but that does

---

[51] Cf. Adkins (1968, 713).
[52] Rademaker (2005, 5).
[53] Harris (2011, 117).
[54] Cf. Johnson (2006).

not investigate how Greek thinkers sought to make sense of the variety, and what that sense-making process shows about their thinking about themselves.

The books of Helen North and Adriaan Rademaker take *sôphrosunê* seriously, even if Rademaker seems to do so mainly as a case study in political rhetoric and of what he sees as Plato's habit of logical equivocation. So much cannot be said for two major statements on the ethical-philosophical phenomenon to which I argue a study of *sôphrosunê* must be connected: the development of ideas about selfhood and self-constitution. These are the books that appeared in the turbulent wake of Bruno Snell's *The Discovery of the Mind*, which historicized the conceptions classical Greeks had about agency, their capacity for responsible action.[55] A. W. H. Adkins' (1960) *Merit and Responsibility*, reprised ten years later in *Moral Values and Political Behaviour in Ancient Greece* (1972), explains how the Greeks came to associate virtue (ἀρετή) with morality, by which he means with other-regarding actions. Adkins argues that, in archaic times, *aretê*, the term of highest personal approbation, referred only to excellence in competition, especially defense of one's home and city: "Life is a matter of skill and courage; hence skill and courage are most highly commended."[56] What he calls the "quiet/cooperative virtues," including being prudent (πινυτός), wise (πεπνυμένος), *sôphrôn*, and just, were simply not so highly commended, and thus not yet *aretai*. It was only in city life of the classical period that cooperation became evidently valuable for "smooth, successful, and efficient civic organization" and that these "quiet" competences became commended as *aretai*, true personal excellences.[57] Justice is Adkins' main case in his sociological account of a change in the Greek canon of *aretai*. *Sôphrosunê* is not much mentioned, mainly because it is seen as simply one more of these cooperative virtues.

But Adkins' quietness about *sôphrosunê* may also result from how uneasily it fits into his taxonomy of competitive and cooperative virtues. After all, *sôphrosunê* is not obviously cooperative, altruistic, or other-directed. Even Adkins says that, from Homer's time, being *sôphrôn* means being "prudent in one's own interests," which emphasizes not cooperation but success in achieving one's personal, even competitive, ends. This reference to efficacy, which Adkins calls "non-moral," is found throughout the uses of *sôphrosunê*, which is "moralized" only in extreme cases, such as those of Hippolytus and Bellerophon.[58] Nevertheless, Adkins asserts that *sôphrosunê* was "so much attached to the practice of ... [and had] too

---

[55] English edition: Snell (1953); German: *Die Entdeckung des Geistes* (1946).
[56] Adkins (1960, 36–37, 50).
[57] Adkins (1960, 349).
[58] These are not especially convincing cases themselves, since *sôphrosunê* in these people is far from cooperative; it may be religious and purificatory rather than ostensibly "competitive," but, as we will see in the case of Hippolytus (Chapter 4), it is a matter of distinct personal pride, with perhaps some covert competitiveness, connected to scrupulosity.

much flavor of the quiet virtues" that it need not be assessed separately from them. "Nor would one expect the ordinary man to value *sôphrosunê* very highly; the normal usage of *aretê* does not readily bring *sôphrosunê* to mind."[59] This last point does not seem borne out by the fifth-century evidence. At any rate, *sôphrosunê* transcends Adkins' simple distinction in types of personal excellence, and so it does not get a proper analysis. The other major book of post-Snellian reflection on human agency, Bernard Williams' (1993) *Shame and Necessity*, is in part a corrective to Adkins' factitious division of non-moral and moral reasons for action. But Adkins had already set the terms: *sôphrosunê* is not mentioned in Williams' book.

One book in this vein that does discuss *sôphrosunê* effectively, though from a different scholarly vantage, is Michel Foucault's (1984) *The Use of Pleasure*.[60] In fact, its thirty pages on *sôphrosunê* (63–93) may be the most capacious and engaging from the period. Foucault develops a sensitive distinction between *sôphrosunê* and *enkrateia*, in his focus on evolving conceptions of self-mastery, and the connection between *sôphrosunê* and freedom and agency: "[T]o be free in relation to pleasures was to be free of their authority; it was not to be their slave."[61] His discussions will be amplified in what follows; he wrote them mostly with an eye to the attitudes Greeks took toward their pleasures.

The question remains: Why has there been relatively little scholarly attention to *sôphrosunê*? We might consider four explanations. The first is the absence of a recognizably great work on *sôphrosunê* in classical Greek philosophy. Plato's *Republic* takes up the question of justice and comes to focus on knowledge of what is good.[62] Aristotle's *Nicomachean Ethics* focuses on virtue in general, but again gives pride of place to justice and (practical) wisdom (φρόνησις). Both are evidently distant offspring of Hesiod's *Theogony* and *Works and Days*, poems that emphasize justice and omit any reference to *sôphrosunê*. Plato's *Charmides*, which is in fact about *sôphrosunê*, received little scholarly attention until about five decades ago, but even now it tends to be thought a short and aporetic Socratic fantasia, significant mainly as an example of *elenchus* and the epistemologization of virtue. Scholarship coalesces around central problems, and *sôphrosunê* has not come to be seen as one of the central problems.

A second explanation is the apparent beige-ness of *sôphrosunê*. It has frequently been translated as "moderation." Far from suggesting an exciting or aspirational state, it seems rather a default condition, the ground from which exciting states, like courage and wisdom, are launched.[63] Similarly, though when

---

[59] Adkins (1960, 246–48).
[60] This is *The History of Sexuality*, volume 2; the English translation was published in 1985.
[61] Esp. 63–65 (*enkrateia* comparison), 79 (quotation).
[62] For this formulation, see Broadie (2021).
[63] Geach (1977, 131), in a well-known book on virtue, famously denied that "temperance" (*sôphrosunê*) is an "exciting topic," calling it instead "a humdrum, common-sense matter." He argued that "unlike prudence and justice, temperance is not an attribute of God," only of those

translated as "temperance" *sôphrosunê* now sounds like something of an achievement, the achievement itself sounds like only a fine-tuning, a getting one's desires within acceptable boundaries. It lacks the sense of boldness and adventure attributable to cases of pure piety, pure courage, or pure justice or reason. This sense of a muted status quo state may be encouraged by etymological reflection, in that *sôphrosunê* seems to mean "security/preservation of one's judgment." As long as nothing aggressive derails one's judgment, all is fine.[64]

A third and related explanation for *sôphrosunê*'s minimal role in our ethical perspective is its moral marginality or preliminarity. Whereas other virtues seem directed at the social sphere or at action, *sôphrosunê*—pace Adkins—may seem directed mainly inward and to be something that serves as a precondition of action. One can imagine a contest of justice or a crisis of courage, but it is harder to imagine a contest or crisis of *sôphrosunê*.

Finally, there is the view that *sôphrosunê* has no true English-language (or modern?) correlate, either because it is distinctly Greek or because it is not a unified concept. This was famously stated by Edith Hamilton in her preface to the translation of the *Charmides* in the Bollingen edition of Plato, the dominant English-language translation before the 1997 Hackett edition and the one still regularly carried in American chain bookstores: "This quality . . . which to the Greeks was an ideal second to none in importance, is not among our ideals. We have lost the conception of it. . . . [We can] describe it in some fashion, but we cannot give it a name."[65] This remains the dominant position.[66] This

---

beings (animals and humans) that have distracting bodily needs. What causes temperance's boringness is the fact that "men need temperance because they need to observe a mean of virtue if they are to pursue and attain any great or worthy end": it is a mere precondition for the more exciting virtues. But see Frey (2022) for an attempted recuperation along Aristotelian-Thomistic lines.

[64] Bourgault (2013, 122–25, 130–32) gives a related though more pluralistic and polemical explanation: *sôphrosunê* is thought to be at once too close to chastity, conservativism, "woman's virtue," and, remarkably, in its form as "moderation" and anti-pleonexia, hostile to the capitalism that keeps everybody going.

[65] Hamilton and Cairns (1961, 99). She continues, however, quite reasonably: "It meant accepting the bound which excellence lays down for human nature, restraining impulses to unrestricted freedom, to all excess, obeying the inner laws of harmony and proportion."

[66] De Vries (1943, 84, 99): these are divergent aspects, even if "ils ne sont pas [always] séparés dans la conscience grecque primitive." Tuckey (1951, 8–9): this word "cannot be translated by any one word in English. It means wisdom, discretion, self-respect, moderation, chastity, temperance." Santas (1973, 109–10): there is "no apparent unifying thread" between various uses of the term; "we must take this diversity at its face value and not search in vain for unity or a continuous line of development." Adkins (1976, 302n5): "*Sophrosune* spans 'moderation,' 'self-control,' and 'prudence.' No English word adequately renders it." Schofield (2013, 11): "it is virtually impossible to find any single satisfactory equivalent for *sôphrosunê*, in whatever context—Stoic or non-Stoic—we find it." Herman (2006, 102–3) makes a blanket claim against confidence in our translation of Greek virtue terms but for historiographical reasons: they do not "help social historians to achieve a better understanding of their evaluative meaning."

nonunifiability thesis gets another imprimatur from North and Rademaker, as discussed above.

Among the subordinate tasks of this book is to undermine or at least qualify these four reasons for analytical diffidence about *sôphrosunê*. To start, then, it is true that the two great works of classical Greek ethics do not give *sôphrosunê* top billing; despite this, the virtue had a central role in two centuries of ethical thought. Euripides' plays, especially *Medea*, *Hippolytus*, and *Bacchae*, but also the fragmentary *Oedipus* and *Hypsipyle*, treated the virtue as thematic, and it was not incidental in other tragedies. The sophists debated it, and Thucydides presented it as a major matter of geopolitical dispute. Plato's texts make it central, notably in the *Charmides* and *Republic*, but also in the *Protagoras*, *Gorgias*, *Statesman*, and *Laws*. Much of Xenophon's *Memorabilia* presents an account of Socrates' *sôphrosunê*, both his embodiment of and thoughts about it. Early fourth-century Pythagorean communities organized themselves around the norm of *sôphrosunê*. Several leading fourth-century Academics wrote books titled *On Sôphrosunê*, though these are now lost. Taken together, it looks like much of Classical Greek literature has taken *sôphrosunê* as a fundamental preoccupation.

For the connoisseur of the inner life, *sôphrosunê* provides as much excitement as an item of moral psychology can offer. There are inner battles, pressured assimilations, and seductive harmonizations, with Heracles, Cyrus, and Socrates as heroes, Phaedra, Pentheus, and Critias as victims. There are the partisans of *sôphrosunê* against self-control, wisdom, and justice, and the advocates of those other capacities against *sôphrosunê*. There are also the great diplomats, who subsume those virtues to *sôphrosunê* as the basic capacity to act for good reasons.

Finally, despite the great range of contexts in which the term *sôphrosunê* gets used, there is a core meaning of *sôphrosunê* that is identifiable and that is more or less mappable to English-language terms (though the issue of translation I leave to the epilogue). The ancient Greeks who thought about *sôphrosunê* saw it as contributing to the generating of action-guiding beliefs, on the one hand, and the controlling of desires, on the other. The latter seems the domain of a nonintellectual virtue, the former of an intellectual virtue. But it is easy to see these as simply two aspects of a single process, whereby certain judgments are motivationally authorized. Within the shouting match of wants and opinions, *sôphrosunê* picks out those that should direct our actions and inferences. It does this picking-out by, so to speak, judging candidate desires and beliefs against norms, authoritative standards for decision-making. So it is the same capacity that enables one not to treat one's desire to eat *right now* as a reason for acting, given its inconsistency with the norm to finish one's project first, and discourages one from believing that the pleasurable route is superior to the toilsome, given its inconsistency with the norm to consider all the consequences of a trade-off.

To be sure, there are context-dependent and stereotyped uses of *sôphrosunê* in Greek literature. *Sôphrosunê* may refer to female domesticity, which is related to the good order of the household, feminine silence about political matters, and sexual chastity. But these are local applications of general principles more broadly applicable than female domesticity: careful arrangement of one's resources, tactful and circumspect speech, and wariness about physical attraction. There is bodily comportment, related to the integration of youth into society, female reticence to attract attention, and the ideal of natural or authentic self-presentation. There is the context of the feast or festival, whereby alcoholic temperance, avoidance of overeating, and keeping one's hands to oneself are salient. In the professional realm, *sôphrosunê* refers to a clear-eyed self-assessment of one's competence; this generalizes to the self-knowledge appropriate in any of these contexts. Then there is the civic analogue, where *sôphrosunê* means an isolationist foreign policy, keeping free of obligations to potentially irascible allies, and, relatedly, a resistance to direct democracy, in which momentary majority preference can alter policy and constitution without due deliberation. *Sôphrosunê* is a single virtue that has application in each of these domains: there is a reason beyond historical linguistic connection that these various behaviors and attitudes all manifest *sôphrosunê*. In each, one's actions flow from stable commitments to norms or principles that obtain beyond the immediate circumstance. This involves an appreciation that there are grounds for action that are deep, objective, better justified, or simply those that one continues to identify with by contrast with grounds for action that are shallow, adventitious, irrational, or simply alien to one's self-conception, and that having *sôphrosunê* means acting on those in the first group.

The Structure of This Book

We have already seen some of the most telling debates about *sôphrosunê* in the later fifth century. They were motivated by a shared high estimation of the virtue but disagreement about its conditions of use. They brought out that estimation and those conditions: *sôphrosunê* is a virtue of acting rather than merely behaving, with due appreciation of all the relevant considerations, even if one's field of attention is captivated by only a few of them. To the extent that this means acting in one's long-term or more significant personal or social interests, it involves the construction or maintenance of something deserving to be called a "self."

Chapter 2 reveals that the late fifth-century conception of *sôphrosunê*, as just articulated, is not novel; it is anticipated by the earliest uses of the term, in archaic and early classical poetry, and is to be expected by the dynamics of the word's formation. The chapter thus begins with an etymological study of *sôphrosunê*, comparing it to other *-phrosunê* nouns (or *-phrôn* adjectives), a favored type of word in early Greek. This analysis suggests that the word had something to do with having a *phrên*, a seat of judgment, that was insulated from distortion. The several instances of the term in Homer support this impression: *sôphrosunê* is the capacity to forbear from doing what one most immediately would like, by attending to one's standing commitments to do otherwise. But this is a rare word in Homer, so we get corroboration from Theognis and Pindar. In the latter poet, as well as in Aeschylus and contemporaneous sepulchral epigraphy, we begin to see the inclusion of *sôphrosunê* in stereotyped lists of human traits of excellence—proto-canons. These lists witness *sôphrosunê*'s increased centrality to reflection on the thoughtfully active and so flourishing life.

Chapter 3 presents the pinnacle of this canonization and the advent of philosophical reflection on *sôphrosunê*: Heraclitus' vaunt of *sôphrosunê* as the "greatest virtue" and his pairing of it with self-knowledge as core human desiderata. We find these remarks about *sôphrosunê* in two fragments, B112 and B116, brief sentences whose authenticity has until recently been mostly denied. For that reason, they have appeared infrequently in studies of *sôphrosunê*; the chapter begins with a defense of their authenticity. Further evidence of their authenticity comes from their susceptibility to meaningful interpretation in light of Heraclitus' view of self-knowledge. I argue that Heraclitus treats *sôphrosunê* as a virtue of epistemic agency, as what lets us count as knowers and live in a way responsive to the reality of the world. Whether or not this puts too fine a point on his exiguous writings, Heraclitus' perspective on *sôphrosunê* and its centrality for human excellence sets up terms of the debates about the virtue in the decades to come.

With Chapter 4 we return to Euripides, who two years after the *Medea* wrote the *Hippolytus*, a play that truly makes *sôphrosunê* thematic. Its main characters treat *sôphrosunê* as the greatest virtue, and each believes he or she embodies it, but their conceptions of the virtue as it applies to themselves differ, with tragic consequences. Those conceptions fail in part because they exaggerate one or another familiar aspect of *sôphrosunê*, for example reverence of a single god or the absence of libidinal feelings or the manifestation of chastity. The characters' downfalls appear to come from their not appreciating what *sôphrosunê* overall might demand and thus what human maturity properly entails, including a more inclusive piety, a less austere attitude toward one's feelings, and a reasonableness that takes into account the range of phenomena outside human power. But Euripides does not give a simple formula for *sôphrosunê*, since he recognizes many hard problems: how simultaneous respect for gods with different expectations—that is, competing absolute norms—is possible; what attitude to take toward seemingly unmanageable erotic longings; where someone might justifiably break a social norm for the sake of personal integrity. *Sôphrosunê* remains a vital concern of Euripides a quarter-century later, in his *Bacchae*, whose dramatic backbone is provided by disagreement about the virtue. Can *sôphrosunê* be manifest through *mania*? Pentheus thinks not, and his supercilious confidence is akin to Hippolytus'. Euripides thus presents to his audience another character callow about the details of human maturity and the complexities of ethical agency.

Chapter 5 continues with late fifth-century debates and discussion about *sôphrosunê*, specifically those in prose. Four figures get special notice: Critias, Antiphon, Thucydides, and Democritus. Critias, on evidence from the first half of Plato's *Charmides*, defined *sôphrosunê* as "doing one's own things." This solves some problems with defining a virtue and emphasizes the theme of self-constitution we will have already seen in preceding chapters. Critias' analysis proves especially useful for seeing its application equally to individuals and to cities. Antiphon, in several preserved excerpts of his own words, gives an alternative account of *sôphrosunê*, in which the suppression of felt bad desires is key. Notable here is that he disclaims the necessity that reason or insight must do the suppressing. He is evidently contributing to an ongoing discussion about the relationship between *sôphrosunê* and the intellectual virtues. Some later authors will decompose his view of the virtue into a matched set, *sôphrosunê* and self-control (ἐγκράτεια). Thucydides' *History of the Peloponnesian War* develops a tack indicated in the *Charmides*, that cities may be judged *sôphrôn* and not just because they contain *sôphrôn* citizens. *Sôphrôn* cities are those that, on first analysis, abstain from foreign affairs. Several major paired speeches debate the nature, value, and presence of *sôphrosunê* in cities; one speech in particular, by Archidamus, king of Sparta, gives the most extensive argument about *sôphrosunê* yet seen in this book. This chapter ends with a reflection on Democritus. The half-dozen precepts about *sôphrosunê* ascribed to him resonate with his moral-psychological theory. In that theory he presents a rational agent's duty as acting only on the noblest of his desires.

A figure so far not mentioned except in the Critias discussion, but whose relevance to *sôphrosunê* studies is surely among the highest of the period, is Socrates. Unfortunately for our purposes he wrote nothing, and thus nothing about *sôphrosunê*; what thoughts he may have had about it are only to be inferred from those writing about him. Later chapters deal expressly with Xenophon and Plato, our fullest witnesses to Socrates despite neither of them writing factual reports about their teacher. In Chapter 6 we deal with a variety of other sources that speak to a Socratic perspective on *sôphrosunê*. We begin with the Old Comedy evidence, which links him to the *sôphrosunê-agôn* described above and characterizes him as dubiously *sôphrôn*. Then we turn to the small evidence from Antisthenes, the oldest of the Socratics, and to the sayings on *sôphrosunê* attributed to Socrates by Stobaeus, who may even be drawing from lost works of Antisthenes. Finally we look at the *Alcibiades* found in the Platonic corpus, which has Socrates identify *sôphrosunê* with self-knowledge, a plausibly Socratic equation.

Chapter 7 continues the Socratic focus, with an account of Xenophon's extended analysis of *sôphrosunê*. A key finding is the distinction he draws between *sôphrosunê* and self-control (ἐγκράτεια). This is the first episode in fourth-century reflections on their differences; he, Plato, and Aristotle each divvy up aspects of the rich phenomenon of *sôphrosunê* between those two concepts. (Plato gives almost nothing to *enkrateia*; Aristotle gives little to *sôphrosunê*.) But we also see Xenophon attributing views of *sôphrosunê* to Socrates that practically identify it with wisdom and with the following of authoritative norms, and defending him against the claims that he failed to teach *sôphrosunê* to Critias and Alcibiades before teaching them political efficacy.

The next three chapters provide a complex of treatments of Plato's dialogues, for which *sôphrosunê* is a recurring and vibrant concept of discussion. Chapter 8 starts with the *Phaedo* and then the *Protagoras*, where, after Protagoras places *sôphrosunê* and justice at the heart of civic success, Socrates tries to argue for the coincidence of *sôphrosunê* with wisdom and with justice. This tentative unification of the virtues is seen again in the *Gorgias*. There, Socrates' argument with Callicles becomes most heated once they disagree on the value of *sôphrosunê* for life and talk of justice falls away (as it did in the *Clouds*' contest between Better and Worse). Socrates cannot defend *sôphrosunê* as a reduction of desire, since for Callicles the excellent human life amounts to the full manifestation and realization of desire. So Socrates must defend *sôphrosunê* as a virtue of agency, of human power and responsibility; he therefore argues that it amounts to a well-functioning soul that includes, as subordinate aspects of *sôphrosunê*, at least courage, one of the instrumental virtues of agency (with wisdom) Callicles has already accepted.

Chapter 9 turns to the *Republic* and *Charmides*. Both defend a view of *sôphrosunê* as agency, the competence to originate actions, but from different perspectives, the former affective and the latter epistemic—the one focusing on desire, the other on self-knowledge. We see that these come to about the same thing. The *Republic*'s account of *sôphrosunê* is notoriously entwined with its account of justice, and the absence of talk about desire-control in the *Charmides* is surprising but explicable; like the dialogues discussed in Chapter 8, neither dialogue here gives a complete account of the virtue.

Among Plato's last dialogues, the *Statesman* and *Laws* both give signal importance to *sôphrosunê*, especially in the context of constitutional reflection. As we see in Chapter 10, the big question that arises in both concerns the relationship between *sôphrosunê* and wisdom. Both identify two sorts of states associated with the virtue, one a set of desiderative dispositions and the other a virtue proper, where those dispositions are guided by rational insight. Neither dialogue really determines what the status of these two states are and what role wisdom plays in them, but both raise issues that consolidate matters of debate we will have seen throughout this book and partially explain Aristotle's particular take.

In Chapter 11, we get to Aristotle and the only robust theory of *sôphrosunê* from the classical period, *Nicomachean Ethics* 3.10–12. It is a remarkable theory: it limits the virtue's pertinence to some of the pleasures of touch, specifically those associated with nutrition and reproduction. Desire-control in general gets shunted off to self-control, judgment about authoritative norms to practical judgment or wisdom. Aristotle's theory is a solution to a taxonomic problem, not, despite appearances, an attempt to understand how people have used the term and what role it plays in their reflections on human nature. For Aristotle, *sôphrosunê* retains a basal role in maturity—it is a core precondition for rational agency—but it loses its position as a primary concept for that maturity. In this chapter we also address various Peripatetic and contemporary Academic accounts of *sôphrosunê*, noting their difference from Aristotle's.

A leading student of Aristotle's, Aristoxenus of Tarentum, grew up in Pythagorean communities of the early fourth century. Among other works on Pythagoreanism, he wrote a *Life of Archytas* and *Pythagorean Precepts*. The first contains a debate about the value or disvalue of *sôphrosunê*; the second depicts a community's constitution as largely structured by the pursuit of *sôphrosunê*. Chapter 12 discusses both texts, which are relatively unfamiliar but provide essential testimony to the importance of *sôphrosunê* in early fourth-century ethical and political thought largely outside the Socratic and Athenian traditions. The Archytas debate appears as a parallel to the Socrates-Callicles debate (studied four chapters earlier), with arguments in favor of and against unimpeded desire-satisfaction. In the *Pythagorean Precepts*, desire is considered naturally wayward; *sôphrosunê* amounts to subservience to authoritative norms, through belief in the gods and a conservative obedience to rules promulgated by civic elders. As *sôphrosunê* was advocated by Cleon in Thucydides, as discussed in Chapter 5, here too the appetitive stability characteristic of *sôphrosunê* is seen as more important than the fruits of prudential or ethical innovation.

Only in the final chapter does the book leave the classical period, when in Chapter 13 we address head-on the problem of gendered virtue. Aristotle thought that virtue was gendered, but Xenophon and Plato were less sure. None, however, pursued the issue at length. So we focus on two Roman-era texts that were clearly influenced by all three classical writers. One is *On Women's Sôphrosunê*, attributed to Phintys, which opens with a theory about gendered virtue and proceeds to vaunt a conservative *sôphrosunê* to women. Our question for that text is whether she enjoins submissiveness, the abandonment of agency, or, by contrast, an active self-possession governed by norms of women's thoughtful acceptance, the constitution of agency. The other text is Iamblichus' letter to a woman named Arete on the subject of *sôphrosunê*. Unlike Phintys, Iamblichus does not assume that this virtue is gendered, and he leaves no doubt whether *sôphrosunê* is the virtue of agency; it is. These authors highlight the challenges that remain to understand agency.

An epilogue discusses English equivalences of *sôphrosunê*.

An appendix reproduces and translates epigraphical texts referring to *sôphrosunê* during the classical period, material not readily available to those studying our topic.

2
The Early History of *Sôphrosunê*

Etymological Considerations

Etymologies of complex terms have limited probative value. But they may get us into the semantic territory and, if produced in the period of interest, represent cases of direct reflection on our terms of interest. We know two putative etymologies of *sôphrosunê* from the Classical period, from Plato and Aristotle.[1] The seriousness of Plato's is questionable, though its context is telling.[2] It occurs in the *Cratylus*, where Socrates answers his interlocutor Hermogenes' request that he explain the aptness of the various terms for the virtues, "such as thought, reason, justice, and all those sorts of things."[3] Socrates complies, beginning by stating that all register an assumption of motion; this he instances with "thought" (φρόνησις, also "[practical] wisdom"), "judgment" (γνώμη), and "intelligence" (νόησις), sometimes giving multiple possible etymologies.[4] Having just discussed *phronêsis*—analyzed as either "intelligence of motion and flowing" (φορᾶς... καὶ ῥοῦ νόησις) or "benefit of motion" (ὄνησιν... φορᾶς)—he goes on to etymologize *sôphrosunê*: it is the "preservation (σωτηρία) of thought (φρόνησις)."[5] He then goes on to longer and more ornate explanations of "knowledge" (ἐπιστήμη), "comprehension" (σύνεσις), "wisdom" (σοφία), "good" (ἀγαθόν), and, with by far the longest and strangest discussion, "justice" (δικαιοσύνη and, mostly, τὸ δίκαιον).[6] For *sôphrosunê*, *sôteria* ("preservation") is chosen as a plausibly related noun with the right initial letters; it pertains to the motion signified by *phronêsis*. *Sôphrosunê* is notable for the company it keeps: it is preceded by three terms of normative intellect, and followed by three more (justice and courage come later).[7] But it is clear that Socrates does not mean to belabor the etymology; he

---

[1] The Platonic *Definitions* gives six glosses or definitions, but no etymologies; see Chapter 11.
[2] Sedley (2003, 108–9); Ademollo (2011, 217–18); Ewegen (2014, 134–40).
[3] Pl. *Crat.* 411a2-4: τὰ καλὰ ὀνόματα... τὰ περὶ τὴν ἀρετήν, οἷον "φρόνησίς" τε καὶ "σύνεσις" καὶ "δικαιοσύνη" καὶ τἆλλα τὰ τοιαῦτα πάντα. In his assent to Hermogenes' request, Socrates repeats the first two, then instead of justice mentions "judgment" (γνώμην) and "knowledge" (ἐπιστήμην) (a7–8).
[4] Pl. *Crat.* 411d4–e4.
[5] Pl. *Crat.* 411e4–412a1.
[6] These are at 412a1–4, a5–b1, b2–8, c1–5, 412c6–413d2 (to give a sense of their length).
[7] Courage is at 413e1–414a6. On Socrates' order of discussion, see Sedley (2003, 113, 120); Ademollo (2011, 185).

mentions it only as an easy add-on to *phronêsis*. This whole section strikes one as a tour de force of etymological fancy.

Aristotle gives his own etymology of *sôphrosunê* again in relation to *phronêsis*, this time in a parenthetical digression in Book 6 of his *Nicomachean Ethics*. He has been distinguishing between *phronêsis* and knowledge (ἐπιστήμη). *Phronêsis* is a truth-sensible and rational state concerned with good and bad human action.[8] As a kind of illuminating or justifying example, Aristotle has just noted that we consider Pericles and such men "thoughtful/sensible people" (φρόνιμοι), given that they are able to descry what is good for themselves and for men in general.[9] Then he turns to a further observation:

> ἔνθεν καὶ τὴν σωφροσύνην τούτῳ προσαγορεύομεν τῷ ὀνόματι, ὡς σῴζουσαν τὴν φρόνησιν. σῴζει δὲ τὴν τοιαύτην ὑπόληψιν. οὐ γὰρ ἅπασαν ὑπόληψιν διαφθείρει οὐδὲ διαστρέφει τὸ ἡδὺ καὶ λυπηρόν, οἷον ὅτι τὸ τρίγωνον δύο ὀρθὰς ἔχει ἢ οὐκ ἔχει, ἀλλὰ τὰς περὶ τὸ πρακτόν. αἱ μὲν γὰρ ἀρχαὶ τῶν πρακτῶν τὸ οὗ ἕνεκα τὰ πρακτά: τῷ δὲ διεφθαρμένῳ δι' ἡδονὴν ἢ λύπην εὐθὺς οὐ φαίνεται ἀρχή, οὐδὲ δεῖν τούτου ἕνεκεν οὐδὲ διὰ τοῦθ' αἱρεῖσθαι πάντα καὶ πράττειν: ἔστι γὰρ ἡ κακία φθαρτικὴ ἀρχῆς. (Arist. *NE* 6.5 1140b11–20)

> Thence, too, we call *sôphrosunê* by this name, as "preserving (σῴζουσαν) *phronêsis*." And it does save such belief [as concerns our good]. For pleasure and pain do not ruin or deflect every belief, for instance that a triangle amounts or does not amount to two right angles, but only those concerning action. The principles of action are that [end] which one's actions are for the sake of; but to the one having been ruined by pleasure or pain [that end] simply does not appear a principle, nor that he ought to choose and do everything towards it and for its sake; for badness is destructive of the principle.

Aristotle's account differs from the *Cratylus* account, with which it is in basic agreement concerning word parts and concerning ethical significance, in using the verb rather than the abstract noun; in giving an explanation based in his erudite moral psychology; and in being earnest. The view, compressed as it is, is that *sôphrosunê* involves control of pleasure and pain; when uncontrolled, those feelings can obscure the goals of action; yet those goals are the object of *phronêsis*' concern, and so *sôphrosunê* prevents an obstacle—excessive pleasure and pain— to the correct working of *phronêsis*.

---

[8] Arist. *EN* 6.5 1140b5: ἕξιν ἀληθῆ μετὰ λόγου πρακτικὴν περὶ τὰ ἀνθρώπῳ ἀγαθὰ καὶ κακά.
[9] Arist. *EN* 6.5 1140b9: ὅτι τὰ αὑτοῖς ἀγαθὰ καὶ τὰ τοῖς ἀνθρώποις δύνανται θεωρεῖν. Aristotle says that we attribute this capacity to those we consider experts in household and city management.

In both cases, these etymologies express the centrality of *sôphrosunê* to the highest concerns about human activity, and both reflect ideas about *sôphrosunê*'s fundamental connection to practical judgment that we will see throughout this book. Nevertheless, as instances of linguistic history they may possess little validity. Benedict Einarson, in one of the earliest extended studies of "the meaning of *sôphrosunê*," suggests that these authors give a mistaken priority to the noun *sôphrosunê* over the more fundamental and earlier adjective *sôphrôn*. The adjective applies to people, yet the putatively active "preserving *phronêsis*," which follows from attributing powers to a virtue, is absurd when so applied to a person. It is better to see the *sô-* first element as coming from σῶς, "safe, sound," and the *-phrôn* second element as from φρήν, "seat of intellect and desires." This would give the meaning "unharmed, intact in mind," where this could have an intellectual connotation of "sensible" and an appetitive connotation of "self-contained."[10] Most modern studies share this basic etymology.[11]

Such atomic etymology might not, however, give the whole picture. The *-phro(sunê)* second element was highly productive by the time of Homer and Hesiod. Table 2.1 includes all such terms recorded in the Liddle-Scott-Jones Greek lexicon, with an approximate translation of the word or prefix associated with the first element, a selection of the definitions of the word provided by that lexicon, and some earliest locations of the term.

Focusing just on what may be the oldest such formations—those with an abstract *-phrosunê* form by the archaic period—we see that the *-phro-* element suggests "thoughtfulness," where the attitudinal or affective aspect is as prominent as the reasoning aspect, in the way our English idioms "to be considerate" or "to be feeling" suggest. The sympathy of sensibility and judgment indicated by *philophrosunê* and *homophrosunê* are good representatives of this quality. Odysseus counsels Achilles to give up his anger toward Agamemnon and cites Peleus' advice to his son: your strength comes from Athena and Hera, but it comes from "you to restrain (ἴσχειν) your great-hearted anger (θυμόν) in your breast, for *philophrosunê* is better" (Hom. *Il.* 9.255–56). This is friendliness, interpreting others' attitudes toward oneself optimistically and forbearing from quarrelsome action. In the *Odyssey*, Odysseus expresses his hope for Nausicaa: may the gods grant you a husband, a house, and "great (ἐσθλήν) *homophrosunê*," for nothing is stronger or better than when a man and woman run a household with such like-mindedness (ὁμοφρονέοντε νοήμασιν) (Hom. *Od.* 6.181–84). The spouses

---

[10] Einarson (1927, 1–3).
[11] North (1966, 3n10; 1979, 89–90); Chantraine (1968, 1047); Frisk (1954, 844); Beekes (2010, 1441). But now Bigio (2021), in by far the closest etymological analysis, argues for a verbal formation, "saving the mind." A provocative use of the verb *sôzô* as "maintaining coherence" is in Aeschylus, referring to a rhythm (σῳζόμενον ῥυθμόν, *Ch.* 798).

Table 2.1 *-phro(sunê)* Terms in the Archaic and Early Classical Periods

-φροσύνη nominal form dating to epic period			
ἀγανοφροσύνη	ἀγανός (mild)	gentleness, mildness	*Il.* 24.772, *Od.* 11.202
ἀεσιφροσύνη	ἀασθείς (damaged)	folly	*Od.* 15.470; Hes. *Th.* 502
ἀφροσύνη	ἀ- (lacking)	folly, thoughtlessness	*Il.* 7.110, *Od.* 24.457
δολοφροσύνη	δόλος (trick)	craft, subtlety	*Il.* 19.97, 19.112
ἐπιφροσύνη	ἐπι- (upon)	thoughtfulness, wisdom	*Od.* 5.437, 19.22; Hes. *Th.* 658
εὐφροσύνη	ἐυ- (well-)	mirth, merriment	*Od.* 20.8, 10.465, 9.6
ὁμοφροσύνη	ὁμο- (together)	unity of mind and feeling	*Od.* 6.181, 15.198
φιλοφροσύνη	φίλος (dear, friend)	friendliness, kindliness	*Il.* 9.256
χαλιφροσύνη	[uncertain]	thoughtlessness	*Od.* 16.310 (cf. 23.13)

-φρων adjectival form dating to epic period			
ἀλλόφρων	ἄλλος (another)	thinking of other things, heedless	*Il.* 23.698, *Od.* 10.374
ἀταλάφρων	ἀταλός (tender, of youth)	tender-minded (of a child)	*Il.* 6.400
δαΐφρων	δαΐς (war, battle)	warlike, fiery	*Il.* 2.23
δαΐφρων	δάω (learn)	wise, prudent	*Il.* 11.482, *Od.* 1.48
δεινόφρων—see λυκόφρων			
ἐχέφρων	ἔχω (to have)	sensible, prudent	*Il.* 9.341, *Od.* 13.332
κερδαλεόφρων	κερδαλέος (cunning, profitable)	greedy of gain	*Il.* 1.149, 4.339
κλεψίφρων	κλέψ (thief)	dissembling	*h.Merc.* 413
κρατερόφρων	κρατερός (strong, mighty)	stout-hearted, dauntless	*Il.* 14.324, *Od.* 4.333, Hes. *WD* 147
λυκόφρων	λυκός (wolf)	wolf-minded	Λυκοφρων as proper name

Table 2.1 Continued

μελίφρων	μέλι (honey)	sweet to the mind, delicious	Il. 2.34, Od. 7.182
μετάφρενον, τό	μετά (after)	behind the midriff, one's back	Il. 5.40, Od. 8.528
ὀλοόφρων	ὀλοός (destructive)	baleful, crafty	Il. 2.723; Od. 11.322
περίφρων	περι- (around)	very thoughtful	Il. 5.412; Od. 16.435
πολύφρων	πολυ- (much)	ingenious, inventive	Il. 21.367; Od. 14.424
πρόφρων	προ- (before)	willingly, gladly	Il. 1.543, 1.77; Od. 2.387
πυκινόφρων	πυκνός (compact)	shrewd	Hes. fr. 143; h.Merc. 538
ταλασίφρων	*τλάω (suffering)	patient, stout-hearted	Il. 4.421, Od. 11.466
ταλάφρων	" "	" "	Il. 13.300
χαρμόφρων	χάρμα (joy)	of joyous heart	h.Merc. 127

-φρων dating to early Classical period

αὐτόφρων	αὐτός (same)	of shared mind	Ion BNJ 392 F10
βαρύφρων	βάρυς (heavy)	gloomy, savage	lyr. adesp. 140.8; Lyc. 464
γυναικόφρων	γυνή (woman)	of woman's mind	Eur. fr. 362.34
δύσφρων	δύσ- (ill-)	sorrowful, ill-disposed, senseless	A. Ag. 547, Supp. 511, Th. 875
σιδηρόφρων	σίδηρος (iron)	iron-hearted	A. Sept. 52
ὑψηλόφρων	ὑψηλός (lofty)	haughty	Eur. IA 919
ὠμόφρων	ὠμός (raw, savage)	savage-minded	A. Choe. 421

must share their valuation of the many elements in running a house: they share judgments about what ought to be done.

Even a cursory glance at the other terms shows that the *-phro-* element stands in for something like "good judgment," a sensitivity to relevant considerations, and not an austere "reasoning" separated from "mood" or "feeling." The disposition of *euphrosunê* shows this particularly well: it does not mean "excellence in ratiocination" or "goodness in means-end reasoning" but "merriment"; it takes place characteristically at a festival and marks one's deeming everything to be going well. So here it refers to the bias or tilt of one's judgment. The "mildness" named by *aganophrosunê* follows the same pattern: judging things, or being disposed to judge things, as not panic-inducing or confrontation-causing. The *-phro-* element seems built from the root *phrên* as a seat of normative judgment, that place whence comes one's evaluative response to the world.[12] Different first elements determine the implied part of the world or the distinctive character of that response.

We cannot read off from those first elements alone, however, the meaning of the word: the *eu-* of *euphrosunê* is a good example. In what way is the judgment "good" or "going well"? It is not the *eu-* itself that makes the term mean "merriment" in convivial contexts. The precise meaning of the compound depends on the imputation of the earliest (and then continued) users, which is to be found only in instances of its use.[13] From this perspective, *sôphrosunê*'s first element, *sô-*, surely has something to do with one's judgment being "sound or safe." These are judgments that may involve or amount to dispositions, moods, or evaluations relevant to one's actions. But which judgments, and "sound" relative to what, or "safe" from what, or "preserving" what and how, will be inferable only from instances of the term's use.[14]

So we will turn to some of those instances, where we will find important patterns of use. Authors from Homer, by the seventh century, to Theognis, in the sixth century, to Pindar, by the early fifth century, and Aeschylus toward the middle of the fifth century, use the term *sôphrosunê* to mean, roughly, prudence or discipline: not being impetuous, being motivated to action by perhaps something other than one's immediate impulses, and reasoning about those of one's interests or commitments or identity that transcend the present moment. We might connect this to the term's elements by thinking of the *phrên* as the source of considered judgments about the best way to live, more or less long term, and the safety or soundness as against whatever undermines the authority of those considered judgments, especially instantaneous reactions to novelties in our milieu.

---

[12] On *phrên*, and its ambiguous status as body part and abstract seat of judgment, see Onians (1951, 23–38); Ireland and Steel (1975); Snell (1977); Claus (1981, 16); Sullivan (1988); Padel (1992, 20–23; cf. 73, 113).

[13] This was a major contention of Moore (2020b), discussing *phil-* prefixed terms.

[14] Murray (1911, 26): "the meaning of *sôphrosynê* can only be seen by observation of its usage."

Homer

The noun *sôphrosunê* and adjective *sôphrôn* appear together four times in Homeric poetry (each time using the older σαοφρ- in place of σωφρ-). On each occasion, the term indicates a person's capacity to act on the basis of a broader set of considerations than their immediate impulses.[15] The term arises once in the *Iliad*, when Apollo says to Poseidon that he, Apollo, would not be *sôphrôn* were he to contend with Poseidon over mere mortals.

ἐννοσίγαι' οὐκ ἄν με σαόφρονα μυθήσαιο
ἔμμεναι, εἰ δὴ σοί γε βροτῶν ἕνεκα πτολεμίξω
δειλῶν, οἳ φύλλοισιν ἐοικότες ...
                               ... ἀλλὰ τάχιστα
παυώμεσθα μάχης·   (Hom. *Il*. 21.462–66)

[APOLLO]: Earth-shaker, you'd deny that I am *sôphrôn*
were I to fight *you* for the sake of worthless
mortals, who are like leaves ...
                         ... but let's stop
fighting right now.

Saying this, Apollo then turns away, feeling a respectful diffidence or sense of shame (αἴδετο) about fighting with his uncle. He incurs a cost in doing so: his sister Artemis lambastes him for cowardice, for not competing and thereby allowing Poseidon to brag of a victory that he did not really earn; she believes that Apollo *did* have sufficient reason to contend over mere humans.[16]

Apollo presents what he takes to be, or wants Poseidon to believe to be, Poseidon's perspective: leaving human disputes alone is an exercise of *sôphrosunê*. One should not get wrapped up in such disputes, since they matter much less than other concerns, for instance familial comity. Apollo's putative *sôphrosunê* gets recapitulated as his turning away from and feeling shame toward his uncle, manifesting his respect and acknowledgment—for his greatness, his family connections, and the long-term nature of their relationship.[17] Artemis does not buy Apollo's claim to exercise *sôphrosunê*. It sounds to her like a veiled claim to weakness: Apollo chooses peace not because he sees something

---

[15] Compare North (1966, 2–8): "Sophrosyne at this stage in its history is devoid of moral and religious implications; in three of the four passages it clearly denotes 'prudence' or 'shrewdness' in one's own interests" (at 3); briefer comments at Kollmann (1941, 12–14); De Vries (1943, 84).

[16] Turning away: 468–69; lambasting: 470–77.

[17] In scholarship, Apollo is often taken as archetypally connected with *sôphrosunê*, e.g., Otto (1954, 66–67); Richardson (1993, 93). But the evidence is often insufficient; see Moore (2015c, 22–23).

of greater value in doing so but because he fears he lacks the strength to win, and maybe pacifism is the wrong approach. In response, Apollo asserts his strength and promises to show it off another time, evidently when its exercise would conduce to a proper goal. The exchange between Apollo and Artemis presages fifth-century debates about *sôphrosunê*: does it involve acting only in the ways that really count, thereby concentrating one's overall power, or is it mere hesitation and self-limitation in the name of caution and suspicions of impotence? It is always open to query the benefit of standing down in some present conflict for the putative benefit of standing up for something else in the future; *sôphrosunê* is the ability to decide that it is better to wait, not the proof that it is in fact better.

Sôphrosunê or *sôphrôn* show up three times in our text of the *Odyssey*, now only in the human realm, yet with the same basic meaning. When Telemachus visits great Menelaus, seeking news of his father, he does not speak. Helen and Menelaus have just noticed the similarities between the young man now and the baby they remember him to have been. Telemachus' host, Peisistratus, explains his silence:

κείνου μέν τοι ὅδ᾽ υἱὸς ἐτήτυμον, ὡς ἀγορεύεις·
ἀλλὰ σαόφρων ἐστί, νεμεσσᾶται δ᾽ ἐνὶ θυμῷ
ὧδ᾽ ἐλθὼν τὸ πρῶτον ἐπεσβολίας ἀναφαίνειν
ἄντα σέθεν, τοῦ νῶϊ θεοῦ ὣς τερπόμεθ᾽ αὐδῇ. (Hom. *Od*. 4.157–60)

Of that one he is indeed the son, it's true, as you say—
but he is *sôphrôn*, and resents in his heart the idea,
coming here for the first time, that he might blare out hasty speech
before you, in whose voice we delight as in a god's.[18]

Telemachus' imputed *sôphrosunê* in his respect for an elder, a withholding of speech despite his urgent desire to request information about his father and satisfy his longing to know of Odysseus, is glossed as felt judgment about the impropriety or wrongness of some action, namely speaking out of turn.[19] It is

---

[18] The last three lines quoted, accepted in West (2017, 68), are said not to have been in the text of Rhianus (b. ca. 275 BCE) and to have been athetized in Aristarchus' (ca. 216–144 BCE). A scholiast claims that the formulation ἀλλὰ σαόφρων is "contrary to custom" (παρὰ τὰ πάτρια) and its assertion is out of character for Peisistratus (οὐχ ἁρμόττοντα τῷ Π. προσώπῳ); Homer would have used αἰδεῖται rather than νεμεσσᾶται; and ἐπεσβολία is ridiculous. Later scholars have thought that these lines may have been interpolated to explain Peisistratus' role as spokesman. See Bolling (1925, 230–31); Heubeck, West, Hainworth (1988, 204); more generally on *aidôs* and *nemesis* in Homer, see Murray (1911, 103–12). But the parallels cited below show that nothing is obviously wrong with these lines.

[19] Cf. Hom. *Od*. 1.119, where Telemachus notices that Athena has been standing at the door and "resents in his heart" (νεμεσσήθη δ᾽ ἐνὶ θυμῷ) that a stranger has been so long unattended; and Hom. *Il*. 17.254, where Menelaus tells the Greeks to "resent in [your] heart" (νεμεσιζέσθω δ᾽ ἐνὶ θυμῷ) Patroclus' being given to Trojan dogs. The adjective ἐπεσβολίας ("uninvited") sometimes means "scurrilous."

a self-restraint animated by an appreciation of larger values, namely social requirements, formulated in affective terms: a feeling of anger at himself should he give in to his eager curiosity, aware as he is of the awe he should entertain toward Menelaus.

The other two occurrences of *sôphrosunê*, as a noun, appear in proximity at the start of Book 23, both in reaction to Odysseus' return. When Eurycleia, Penelope's slave-maid, wakes her mistress up to announce Odysseus' return, Penelope "thoughtfully" (περίφρων) impugns Eurycleia's judgment:

μαῖα φίλη, μάργην σε θεοὶ θέσαν, οἵ τε δύνανται
ἄφρονα ποιῆσαι καὶ ἐπίφρονά περ μάλ' ἐόντα,
καί τε χαλιφρονέοντα σαοφροσύνης ἐπέβησαν·
οἵ σέ περ ἔβλαψαν· πρὶν δὲ φρένας αἰσίμη ἦσθα. (Hom. *Od.* 23.12–15)

Dear mama, gods have made you crazy, they who can
make foolish even the most conscientious person,
and who have put the dimwitted on the path to *sôphrosunê*—
they have harmed you, you who were till now wholly reasonable.

Penelope impugns the reliability of Eurycleia's announcement by saying that she is out of her mind. For otherwise her slave-maid would not be trying to aggravate a grieving woman with such absurdities. Eurycleia's excitement has led her to ignore what is really important, which is preserving her mistress from greater miseries.

The *phro-* root of *sôphrosunê* becomes thematic in this passage; there are six uses of the root across five lines (περίφρων, ἄφρονα, ἐπίφρονά, χαλιφρονέοντα, σαοφροσύνης, φρένας). Each of the positively inflected terms—*epiphrôn, phrên aisimê, periphrôn*—involves considering the whole situation rather than just what one's immediate attention rests upon, and thinking through what is best. We are told about *sôphrosunê* only that it is what a dimwitted (χαλιφρονέοντα) person lacks insofar as she is dimwitted; context suggests that this is perspective or insight into what matters.[20] If its use here is consistent with that of the previous two uses, perhaps it means respect for authority—namely Eurycleia's for Penelope, which respect Penelope accuses Eurycleia of lacking.

An obstacle to interpreting *sôphrosunê* with total precision here is Penelope's having used the term only in a hypothetical: it serves in the counterfactual half of her argument from opposites. Gods can make thoughtful people thoughtless,

---

[20] Russo, Fernández-Galiano, Heubeck (1992, 316) provide "simple" for χαλιφρῶν, but this suggests as its opposite "sophisticated" rather than "thoughtful" or "broad-minded," which is what we need.

which is what Penelope says happened to Eurycleia; they can also make thoughtless people thoughtful.[21] The reverse direction is presumably meant to give persuasive force to the argument: while we can imagine non-divine reasons for mental deterioration, we cannot so readily do so for instantaneous goodness; thus gods really must have a part to play here. The point of emphasizing divine interference is to soften the blame; Penelope is saying that, bad as Eurycleia's actions are, they are not the maid's fault; the gods have, after all, "harmed" (ἔβλαψαν) her. But there is something provocative about *sôphrosunê*'s being a gift of the gods that has a magnitude or quality equal to that of the harm they can do. The harm apparently amounts to a person's being prevented from doing what she has taken such care to maintain herself toward—unkeeling her, in effect unpersoning her. The happy reverse, then, would be giving her a keel, a stability and directedness to reach or maintain her standing commitments. That capacity to take and hold a line is *sôphrosunê*.

Once Penelope finishes her excoriation, Eurycleia responds. She has not been mocking her mistress, she says; she is telling the truth. It turns out, she reveals, that the abused beggar whom Penelope has seen is actually Odysseus.

Τηλέμαχος δ' ἄρα μιν πάλαι ᾔδεεν ἔνδον ἐόντα,
ἀλλὰ σαοφροσύνῃσι νοήματα πατρὸς ἔκευθεν,
ὄφρ' ἀνδρῶν τείσαιτο βίην ὑπερηνορεόντων. (Hom. *Od.* 23.29–31)

Telemachus had long known that he was inside,
but he kept concealing, each time thanks to his *sôphrosunê*, the intentions
   of his father
until he could avenge the violence of the overweening men.

The meaning matches what we saw in Book 4, during Telemachus' visit to Menelaus. In both cases, Telemachus keeps quiet, despite the strength of his emotions, to preserve something greater: in the early book, the respect due to an elder; here, the caution due to a great event. Silence is not, of course, at the heart of *sôphrosunê*; whereas Telemachus is silent through *sôphrosunê*, Eurycleia, implicitly exercising her own *sôphrosunê*, is speaking up—but to the right person, her mistress, at the right time, at the earliest reasonable moment.

The infrequency of the term *sôphrosunê* in the Homeric poems, and the consistency of use across those four occurrences, allows us to draw several important conclusions. Some are negative. The term does not set the theme of either

---

[21] This statement is proverbial, as discussed below in the section on Theognis, and in Eur. *Hipp.* 920: mankind "cannot teach the senseless to be sensible" (φρονεῖν διδάσκειν οἷσιν οὐκ ἔνεστι νοῦς); cf. 921. This is the question of Plato's *Protagoras* and *Meno*, whether a person might become virtuous independent of divine dispensation.

poem and does not represent a principal topic of praise. It hardly occupies the poet's attention at all, except during the few lines cited.[22] Connected ideas do play considerable roles in the poems, such as respect and restraint, but their not being articulated as instances of the virtue *sôphrosunê* itself shows that the term is rather narrowly tailored. Yet despite its limited role, or even because of it, we can also draw positive conclusions. The term *sôphrosunê* is narrowly tailored to refer to the capacity to follow norms that do not have the same felt urgency as the immediate impulses to act otherwise. Obedience to such norms appears salient in self-restraint: Apollo is not to fight his uncle; Telemachus is not to query his host or fight too soon; Eurycleia is not to wake her mistress so early in the morning. The actions dismissed as improper have a range of desiderative causes: loyalty toward some humans; anxiety about a father's whereabouts and the disposition of his household; enthusiasm about a master's homecoming; public celebration of one's relief at a father's homecoming. Each here concerns tender social feelings. *Sôphrosunê* does not militate against those feelings as such, only against treating them as authoritative motives for action when doing so would undermine more important goals. We do not hear of *sôphrosunê* as concerning the appetites of consumption and procreation, but surely nothing stops it from being used in such contexts. *Sôphrosunê* would be describable both as one of the cognitive virtues (continuous with the *Cratylus* analysis seen above), the capacity to commit oneself to important action-guiding norms; and as one of the affective virtues (continuous with Aristotle's analysis), an inner force against nonnormative desires, in the way hard exercise involves affective virtue to push past moments of discomfort and shortness of breath. *Sôphrosunê*'s joint cognitive/epistemic and affective/practical qualities evidence not a Homeric inability to distinguish these two dimensions of human life but instead an ability to recognize a way of being that pertains to both of them, one that makes sense without a reliance on any such conceptual distinction.

We see the range of applications of *sôphrosunê* broaden considerably as we leave Homer, as the sheer increase in available cases allows; they turn out to be relatively consistent with the ones we see here. (There are no uses of *sôphrosunê* in Hesiod, but given that his extant work has fewer than a quarter as many lines as Homer's, this is neither surprising nor suspicious.) To Theognis we turn first.

Theognis

Theognis probably wrote in the late sixth century, though this is uncertain, and the manuscript of 1,400 verses coming down to us under his name preserves

[22] Cf. North (1966, 2).

much that would have been written by others into the next century.²³ For the most part, then, the poem does not serve well to mark changes in the meaning of *sôphrosunê*, though it does give a composite perspective for the time up to the Classical period.²⁴ What we see is a *sôphrosunê* that amounts to being guided by broadly acceptable rules or norms rather than by immediate felt inclination. The poem's use of the term sounds to some ears haughty and aristocratic; at any rate, it strikes the note of principle.²⁵

For what it's worth, one of the poem's leading editors, Martin West, identifies two of the ten passages in the poem that mention *sôphrosunê* as authentically Theognis'.²⁶ We will give closest attention to them. The first provides a political context for *sôphrosunê*:

Κύρνε, κύει πόλις ἥδε, δέδοικα δὲ μὴ τέκῃ ἄνδρα
 εὐθυντῆρα κακῆς ὕβριος ἡμετέρης.
ἀστοὶ μὲν γὰρ ἔθ' οἵδε σαόφρονες, ἡγεμόνες δέ
 τετράφαται πολλὴν εἰς κακότητα πεσεῖν. (Thg. 39–42)

Cyrnus, this city is pregnant, and I fear she might give birth to
 one who chastises our bad hubris.
While these townsmen are still *sôphrôn*, their leaders
 have changed and fallen into great badness.

These four lines give us *sôphrosunê* as opposite to "great badness" (πολλὴν . . . κακότητα) and to "bad hubris" (κακῆς ὕβριος), both in a civic context.²⁷ If hubris means exceeding the social or religious boundaries on the exercise of one's free choice ("Do whatever you want as long as you don't slap someone, for instance, or reveal the gods' secrets"), *sôphrosunê* means staying within those boundaries, irrespective of one's other desires, and, in particular, living in a way consistent with a stable constitution.²⁸ (Theognis could have

---

²³ For dates around 500 BCE, see Fränkel (1975, 401–25); Nagy (1983); Friis Johnson (1991). West (1974, 65–71) argues for the mid-seventh century, near the time of Homer.
²⁴ See generally Kollmann (1941, 17). North (1966, 17–20) seeks to identify an evolution in the term's use.
²⁵ Rademaker (2005, 82): Theognis' poetry is "the expression of an unmistakably 'conservative,' 'elitist' ideology." This view follows, for example, North (1979, 91–93). Donlan (1980, 80–95) argues that Theognis' attitude toward *sôphrosunê* is part of his "internalization" of aristocratic qualities, after the crisis of understanding aristocracy on the basis of external qualities; Nagy (1983, 85) goes further to say that Theognis is non-oligarchic. Porubjak (2019) argues for Theognis' narratorial self-characterization as *sôphrôn*; see Porubjak (2013, 57–60) for more on *sôphrosunê* in Theognis.
²⁶ West (1971).
²⁷ For textual issues ancillary to this discussion, see Rademaker (2005, 82–86).
²⁸ MacDowell (1976); Fisher (1992, 209); Rademaker (2005, 84–85). Demosth. 21.180 (cf. 185) glosses hubris as treating free men as though they were slaves (ὡς δούλοις χρώμενος τοῖς ἐλευθέροις).

ideological reasons to say so—to discourage revolt or reform even when the stability is unjust and intolerable—but then all virtue terms can be deployed for political reasons, without their thereby being mere slogans.) It is hard to say to what extent *sôphrosunê* is being conceived by Theognis as other-regarding or, in a word, "moral." In the Homeric examples, *sôphrosunê* involved a kind of self-restraint that put standing interests over instantaneous ones. Sometimes those standing interests involved respect for others (and thus following social norms), but sometimes they simply involved success in one's long-term plans (and thus following prudential norms); *sôphrosunê* appears indifferent to the object of those standing interests. In Theognis' civic context, the social norms seem emphasized, but probably not absolutely, since self-impeding failures of *sôphrosunê* would be detrimental both to oneself and to one's city, and if one, then the other. (I break a contract to pay; this harms a seller; but it also lessens commercial trust in the city; and this redounds to my own disadvantage.)

If we accept the ten lines that follow as a continuation of the poem (as does another recent editor, Douglas Gerber), we see that bad and hubristic leaders ruin the populace and rule in favor of the unjust for the sake of their own profit and power, destroying the city's considerable preexisting peace (πολλῇ ἐν ἡσυχίῃ).[29] Thus *sôphrôn* rule, which is "peaceful," does not destroy, does not side with injustice, and does not make self-interested exceptions. It respects others and follows the demands of justice, whatever the cost to private preference. It means being guided by a principle other than "what I feel like doing right now." Theognis emphasizes a moral norm, though again we still have no reason to call *sôphrosunê* moral rather than prudential; it is just that in this context, the moral significance has salience.

Other poems from the *Theognidea* reinforce the connection between *sôphrosunê* and justice. The narrator complains that Zeus treats people equally, "whether the mind of men is turned toward *sôphrosunê* or toward hubris, being entreated to do injustice."[30] He goes on to specify: the men turned toward *sôphrosunê* refrain from worthless deeds but become poor, despite "loving what is just" (τὰ δίκαια φιλεῦντες), "bearing in mind what is just" (τὰ δίκαια φρονεῖ νόος) and "having judgment in [their] breast" (γνώμη στήθεσιν).[31] *Sôphrosunê* involves committing oneself to justice—presumably the generic name for the norm of civic comity—in a way that is indifferently cognitive and affective, as the language of "loving," "thinking," and "judging" suggest. Later in the *Theognidea*, the narrator puts the matter succinctly: being *sôphrôn* means not being bad and not doing injustice for the sake of wealth.[32] Satisfying the desire for money can

---

[29] Thg. 43–52; Gerber (1999, 181).
[30] Thg. 379–80: ἤν τ' ἐπὶ σωφροσύνην τρεφθῇ νόος ἤν τε πρὸς ὕβριν | ἀνθρώπων, ἀδίκοις' ἔργμασι πειθομένων.
[31] Thg. 384–85, 387, 395.
[32] Thg. 753–56.

lead someone to disregard other interests that, according to the narrator, are more authoritative.

The other poem mentioning *sôphrosunê* that West attributes to Theognis looks like a meditation on Eurycleia's speech in the *Odyssey*, again with a cascade of *-phro-* roots.[33]

φῦσαι καὶ θρέψαι ῥᾷον βροτὸν ἢ φρένας ἐσθλὰς
  ἐνθέμεν· οὐδείς πω τοῦτό γ' ἐπεφράσατο,
ᾧ τις σώφρον' ἔθηκε τὸν ἄφρονα κἀκ κακοῦ ἐσθλόν.
  εἰ δ' Ἀσκληπιάδαις τοῦτό γ' ἔδωκε θεός,
ἰᾶσθαι κακότητα καὶ ἀτηρὰς φρένας ἀνδρῶν,
  πολλοὺς ἂν μισθοὺς καὶ μεγάλους ἔφερον.
εἰ δ' ἦν ποιητόν τε καὶ ἔνθετον ἀνδρὶ νόημα,
  οὔποτ' ἂν ἐξ ἀγαθοῦ πατρὸς ἔγεντο κακός,
πειθόμενος μύθοισι σαόφροσιν· ἀλλὰ διδάσκων
  οὔποτε ποιήσει τὸν κακὸν ἄνδρ' ἀγαθόν. (Thg. 429–38)

Bringing about and nurturing someone's life is easier than placing in it
  a good *phrên*. No one has yet contrived that
by which one makes a foolish person *sôphrôn* and a fine man from someone bad.
  If the god had given this to the Asclepiads,
to cure badness and benighted *phrên*,
  they would be bringing home a lot of money.
And if intelligence could be made and placed in a man,
  never would a bad man come from a good father,
obedient as he would be to *sôphrôn* words. But by teaching
  you will never make the bad man good.

We wondered earlier why Penelope said that the gods could turn the dimwitted *sôphrôn*, given that she wanted to observe only that it must have been the gods who made the normally thoughtful Eurycleia foolish. Theognis provides us part of an answer: mortals (by contrast with the gods) fail to make the dimwitted *sôphrôn*—a point repeated here a remarkable six times. In this expression of frustration at the incorrigibility of people's idiocy, we can see a simple negative definition of *sôphrosunê*: "not doing stupid stuff." The implication is that *sôphrosunê* amounts to being reasonable, being sensitive to the descriptive and evaluative variety of reasons for action.[34] That simple equation is repeated with the contrast

---

[33] For another poem with much *-phro-* language, see 1323–26.
[34] Rademaker (2005, 78–79) focuses only on the last point, about bad sons of good fathers, when concluding that this poem concerns people with noble birth not living up to the level of their class and those without noble birth not being able to make up for that misfortune.

"*sôphrôn—aphrôn*, thought (γνώμης)—thoughtlessness (ἄνοια)" in a nearby poem.[35] A more complex form of that equation appears in a lament about the unavoidability of change in the world: life is uncertain; the gods act; good and bad switch places; so too poverty and wealth; "the *sôphrôn* person errs; reputation often accompanies the thoughtless; and someone bad obtains honor."[36] Being *sôphrôn* means acting correctly, which means in accordance with some practical norm. Theognis' point here is not that *sôphrosunê* is generally unstable, only that nothing good can be counted on as permanent. This view gets mythological formulation when Rhadamanthys, a great judge, is said to be *sôphrôn*, Sisyphus wise, and both qualities better than being wealthy.[37]

Sôphrosunê, which appears more frequently in the *Theognidea* than in the Homerica, has so far had two emphases. One is commitment to broadly applicable norms for the sake of civic stability and justice; it is an eminently social virtue, conducive of action sensitive to the fact that others wish to act as well. It is construable as both intellectual and affective, taking form as a thoughtfulness and a consideration of one's fellow citizens. The other emphasis is less overtly political: it amounts to being reasonable. This must mean being sensitive to the considerations relevant to good decision-making and not simply doing whatever strikes one's fancy at the moment. It is the skill of suitable judgment. These are differences in emphasis, not in form.

Until now we have not come across uses of *sôphrosunê* connected to drunkenness, a state that eventually takes a prominent position in discussions that involve *sôphrosunê*. Where they appear in the *Theognidea*, *sôphrosunê* is not control over the desire for drink; it is rather a capacity obliterated by drink. The most interesting is a sympotic poem from the *Theognidea* sometimes attributed to the late fifth-century sophist Evenus:[38]

ὃς δ' ἂν ὑπερβάλλῃ πόσιος μέτρον, οὐκέτι κεῖνος
τῆς αὐτοῦ γλώσσης καρτερὸς οὐδὲ νόου,
μυθεῖται δ' ἀπάλαμνα, τὰ νήφοσι γίνεται αἰσχρά,
αἰδεῖται δ' ἔρδων οὐδέν ὅταν μεθύῃ,
τὸ πρὶν ἐὼν σώφρων, τότε νήπιος. (Thg. 479–83)

Whoever drinks beyond measure, that person is no longer
    master of his tongue or his mind;

---

[35] Thg. 453–54.
[36] Thg. 657–66; 665–66: καὶ σώφρων ἥμαρτε, καὶ ἄφρονι πολλάκι δόξα | ἕσπετο, καὶ τιμῆς καὶ κακὸς ὢν ἔλαχεν.
[37] Thg. 699–702. For Rhadamanthys' qualities, see Pind. *Pyth*. 2.73 (on his *phrên*); Ibyc. fr. 28 (on his justice).
[38] The Evenus attribution is accorded plausibility by Gerber (1999, 245n2) but is doubted by Rademaker (2005, 94n40) with Van Groningen (1966, 198).

> he talks aimlessly, about things that are disgraces for the sober;
>   he is ashamed of nothing he does when drunk—
> earlier he was *sôphrôn*, now he is childish.

Drinking makes one no longer a rational agent: a drunk person no longer directs his speech or his thoughts as we expect of mature people, as responsive to various norms of reason, practice, and communication. More generally, the drunk person fails to be governed by the norms that cause the otherwise influential feelings of disgrace or shame, which presumably track social proprieties—as we have seen already in the *Iliad*. Being *sôphrôn* is the state that may obtain when sober, when master of one's articulated thoughts, and when one avoids hubris. In the following poem of the *Theognidea*, we learn again that drinking prevents a person from the serious pursuit of purposes typical of the *sôphrôn* person: "Wine makes the mind light (κοῦφον), of both the foolish and the *sôphrôn* man, when he drinks beyond measure."[39] Again we see *sôphrosunê* presented not as the inhibitor of drinking (though it may be) but as something whose action is defeated by drinking.

A final passage from *Theognidea* has a mythographic puzzle of some relevance. The narrator bemoans the social degradation of his time. Of all the gods, only *Elpis* ("Help," "Expectation") remains. Gone are *Pistis* ("Trustworthiness"), *Sôphrosunê*, and the *Charites* ("Graces").[40] The following lines might tell us what each of the gods originally provided:

> ὅρκοι δ' οὐκέτι πιστοὶ ἐν ἀνθρώποισι δίκαιοι,
>   οὐδὲ θεοὺς οὐδεὶς ἅζεται ἀθανάτους,
> εὐσεβέων δ' ἀνδρῶν γένος ἔφθιτο, οὐδὲ θέμιστας
>   οὐκέτι γινώσκουσ' οὐδὲ μὲν εὐσεβίας. (Thg. 1139–42)

> Oaths of justice are no longer trusted among men,
>   nor does anyone respect the immortal gods,
> the race of reverent men has wasted away, nor do they any longer
>   recognize things of rectitude or reverence.

The eight lines that follow 1142 repeat the importance of reverence to the gods; unjust men with crooked words, who ignore the gods, set their minds instead on others' property and make evil contracts for their shameful ends.[41]

---

[39] Thg. 497–98.

[40] Thg. 1135–38: Ἐλπὶς ἐν ἀνθρώποισι μόνη θεὸς ἐσθλὴ ἔνεστιν, | ἄλλοι δ' Οὔλυμπόν ἐκπρολιπόντες ἔβαν· | ᾤχετο μὲν Πίστις, μεγάλη θεός, ᾤχετο δ' ἀνδρῶν | Σωφροσύνη, Χάριτές τ', ὦ φίλε, γῆν ἔλιπον·

[41] Thg. 1143–50: ἀλλ' ὄφρα τις ζώει καὶ ὁρᾷ φῶς ἠελίοιο, | εὐσεβέων περὶ θεοὺς Ἐλπίδα προσμενέτω· | εὐχέσθω δὲ θεοῖσι, καὶ ἀγλαὰ μηρία καίων | Ἐλπίδι τε πρώτῃ καὶ πυμάτῃ θυέτω. |

The first line quoted above, about the loss of trust (πιστοί) in oaths, evidently pertains to the absence of *Pistis*. The absence of the Graces probably results in an unpleasant atmosphere of disharmony and deception. The absence of *Sôphrosunê*, then, presumably accounts for the lack of reverence (εὐσεβία) continuously adverted to. This makes sense; reverence is the acknowledgment of matters of ultimate value. *Sôphrosunê* would be a "recognition" (γιγνώσουσ') of exemplary models, ones consistent with the divine norms of excellence. Without that divine guidance, people may fail to keep to themselves and use social bonds for good.

The *Theognidea* gives a more central place to *sôphrosunê* than the Homerica, and in its more frequent deployments of the term—drawing both from the Homeric poems themselves and from gnomic wisdom more broadly—we see its broader application: it speaks to civil peace, rational action, self-mastery, sobriety, and piety. This shows the poem's robust appreciation of that reverence for socially sanctioned and prudentially authoritative norms in a range of departments of life. That is, some *sôphrôn* actions might be called "good," others "efficacious," depending on the type of norm one privileges over a particular desire. In any event, it is clear that *sôphrosunê*, which in this sixth-century collection has attributed to it signal importance, means being sensible, capable of recognizing what really must get done.

As an addendum to the *Theognidea*, we must mention a fascinating text from Theognis' likely contemporary, Phocylides, a poet known to us from his gnomic couplets. In one fragment, now found only in Stobaeus, Phocylides draws explicit attention to two aspects of *sôphrosunê* that risk separation: the cognitive and the behavioral. This is the first we see of *sôphrosunê* as manifest in orderly comportment, an aspect frequently noted in the fifth and fourth centuries.

πολλοί τοι δοκέουσι σαόφρονες ἔμμεναι ἄνδρες
σὺν κόσμῳ στείχοντες, ἐλαφρόνοοί περ ἐόντες. (Phoc. fr. 9 West)

Look, many think they are *sôphrôn* men
who walk in an orderly way, but really they are weak-minded.

One visible quality of *sôphrosunê* is bodily self-control; this trope recurs explicitly in Aristophanes, Xenophon, and Plato. Phocylides observes that people—whether onlookers or the putative *sôphrôn* people themselves; the verb *dokein* is ambiguous here—take this visible quality as the external manifestation of *sôphrosunê*'s invisible internal quality: thoughtfulness. He does not describe the

φραζέσθω δ' ἀδίκων ἀνδρῶν σκολιὸν λόγον αἰεί, | οἳ θεῶν ἀθανάτων οὐδὲν ὀπιζόμενοι | αἰὲν ἐπ' ἀλλοτρίοις κτεάνοις' ἐπέχουσι νόημα, | αἰσχρὰ κακοῖς' ἔργοις σύμβολα θηκάμενοι.

assumed or actual causal connection between a sound mind and orderly comportment, though it may be that flexible and acute attention may be directed as much to bodily movements as to mental ideas. What is clear, however, is that Phocylides gives priority to the cognitive side of *sôphrosunê* over its physical side, while treating both as expressions of the virtue.[42] Since the verb translated as "walk" (στείχω) often means "march," he could be speaking of putative military competence: though orderly in the line, they may have little real courage.

Pindar

Our next author is Pindar, who wrote in the early fifth century. Admittedly he uses *sôphrosunê* infrequently: three of the six extant instances of the term appear in highly fragmentary poems, and four of them simply praise morally exemplary individuals.[43] Still, we can tell even from these that each refers to the capacity for principled action. They refer to lawfulness and impartiality, something distinctive of the arbitrator and good ruler, and to the qualification of ambition and courage.[44]

Paean I ends with (.) . . .]φρονος ἄνθεσις εὐνομίας; on the basis of a line from Bacchylides, this has been plausibly reconstructed as σαο]φρονος.[45] This "flower of *sô]phrôn* well-orderedness" represents the value that the poet has just finished vaunting.

πρὶν ὀδυνηρὰ γήραος σ[. . . .μ]ολεῖν,
πρίν τις εὐθυμίᾳ σκιαζέτω
νόημ' ἄκοτον ἐπὶ μέτρα, ἰδών
    δύναμιν οἰκόθετόν.
. . .
Παιὰ]ν δὲ λαῶν γενεὰν δαρὸν ἐρέπτοι
σαό]φρονος ἄνθεσιν εὐνομίας. (Pind. fr. 52a.1–4, 9–10)

---

[42] Donlan (1973) describes this passage as a "criticism of the mere appearance of soundness based on outward appearance" and part of the criticism of "epic-heroic values" (similarly Donlan 1980, 67).

[43] Rumpel (1883, 429) lists only *Pyth.* 3 and *Isthm.* 8 (the *Paian* fragments were first published, initially from *P.Oxy.* 841, in 1908 by Grenfell and Hunt; the *Partheneian* comes from *P.Oxy.* 659, first published in 1904), and translates the adjective "temperans." Slater (1969, 483) includes all but the reconstructed *Paian* VI and translates them as "sagacious."

[44] Compare Kollmann (1941, 17); De Vries (1943, 85); North (1966, 24–26); Donlan (1980, 105–6).

[45] Text from Rutherford (2001, 254) = Race (1997, 242–44). Bowra (1935, 191) supplies σ[χεδὸν μ]ολεῖν for line 1, and with Grenfell and Hunt prints σώ] in place of σαό]. Bacchyl. 13.186 speaks of a festival-guarding *sôphrôn* Well-orderedness (Εὐνομία τε σαόφρων). As with others of the Pindaric references considered below, it is about (the island of) Aeacus, in the context of "guarding cities of pious men in peace" (189), which *eunomia* does with *eukleia*. See further Rademaker (2005, 86–88).

Before the pains of old age ... arrive,
before this, let someone shelter in cheerfulness
a mind without rancor in moderation, having seen
    the ready stores in his house.
...
May Paian keep wreathing the children of men
with the flower of *sô]phrôn* well-orderedness.

Pindar praises the happy and even-keeled man who has saved for future eventualities.⁴⁶ The well-being of this man is represented as the "flower" of a *sôphrôn eunomia*, a well-ordered life and household. He has avoided animosity, seeks moderation, and looks to the long term. What the adjective *sôphrôn* adds to *eunomia* is uncertain; it may simply amplify the praise of norm-following. But it may suggest something more cognitively active, a forethoughtfulness, a self-restraint, a sensitivity about which misfortunes deserve one's reaction. Whatever its tenor, *sôphrosunê* is here signifying a laudatory life of reasonableness, and signifies this with enough gravity as suitably to cap the poem.⁴⁷

Parthenian II contains the adjective *sôphrôn* modifying now "ambition" or "concern" (μέριμνα), perhaps the anxiety to achieve virtue or honor.⁴⁸ This poem includes a richer though somewhat ambiguous context. It is addressed to a Theban, and immediately preceding the relevant lines, in a lacuna, there may have been a reference to the Seven against Thebes.⁴⁹

ἐνῆκεν καὶ ἔπειτ[.........]λος
    τῶνδ᾽ ἀνδρῶν ἕνε[κε]ν μερίμνας σώφρονος
ἐχθρὰν ἔριν οὐ παλίγ-
    γλωσσον, ἀλλὰ δίκας [ὁ]δοὺς
π[ισ]τὰς ἐφίλη[σ.]ν (Pind. fr. 94b.61–64)

and then ... provoked
on account of the men's *sôphrôn* ambition
a hateful strife, not *palinglôsson*—
but he/they cared for faithful paths of justice

---

⁴⁶ Rademaker (2005, 90–91) provides political background that is probably not decisive for interpreting these verses.
⁴⁷ North (1966, 24), by contrast, notes mainly the "aristocratic bias" here, though she also judges this to be the earliest extant connection between Apollo and *sôphrosunê*.
⁴⁸ LSJ s.v.; Slater (1969, s.v.). Cf. Rademaker (2005, 91).
⁴⁹ ῥίζα τέ [... | σε]μνὸν αν[....] Θ[. | ...] ἑπταπύλοισ‹ιν›, 58–60. Preceding these lines is a gap of probably eight lines (Prodi 2014, 101–3). The following text is from Race (1997, 326–38) except reading [σ.] for his [σε], for which he follows Grenfell and Hunt.

Some men, evidently referred to in the lacuna, had some pursuit or ambition that Pindar qualifies as *sôphrôn*. This may suggest that it could have been excessive or outrageous but was either moderated or aimed at something good. Not everyone got the memo of good tidings, unfortunately; a strife, presumably instigated by an interpretation of the ambition as problematic, was instigated. All the same, Pindar says, justice was not eradicated: either the men with *sôphrôn* ambition still cared for justice (reading ἐφίλη[σα]ν), or someone in particular, probably involved in that strife (reading ἐφίλη[σε]ν), did. In the quite plausible first case, *sôphrosunê* may be thought responsible for maintaining their "caring" and "faithful" following of the norms of justice. In the latter, we might at least imagine a resonance between the two evaluative conditions. (The meaning of the term παλίγλωσσον is too uncertain to be interpreted here.)[50] At any rate, by contrast with the *Paean* I usage, where *sôphrôn* seemed simply to reinforce the glory of *eunomia*, here it seems to specify the appropriateness of an otherwise contentious ambition. A parallel formulation is found in *Paean* IX, where Teneros, a prophetic son of Apollo, is said to have ruled Thebes thanks to his "*sôphrôn* courage."[51]

Two other (probable) uses of *sôphrosunê* in Pindar pertain to Aeacus, eventual judge in the underworld with Minos and Rhadamanthys. We have already seen him referred to as *sôphrôn* in the *Theognidea*. In a reconstructed fragment of *Paean* VI, Aeacus seems to be called the most *sôphrôn* (σωφρο]νέστατον) son of Zeus.[52] In *Isthmian* 8, Aeacus is said to have judged disputes among gods (ὃ καί δαιμόνεσσι δίκας ἐπείραινε, 23–24) and implicitly passed down that capacity:

τοῦ μὲν ἀντίθεοι
ἀρίστευον υἱέες υἱ-
έων τ' ἀρηΐφιλοι παῖδες ἀνορέᾳ
χάλκεον στονόεντ' ἀμφέπειν ὅμαδον,
σώφρονές τ' ἐγένοντο πινυτοί τε θυμόν. (Pind. *Isthm.* 8.24–26)

---

[50] In a comic fragment (Com. Adesp. 1098), παλίγλωσσον means δύσφημος, the quality of a bad utterance, something that bodes ill or is slanderous, shameful, or abusive (in Pind. *Nem.* 8.37, modifying κλέος, ill-famed). In Pindar it means "lying" (*N.* 1.58, the gods' messages) or "of backward speech" (? *I.* 6.24, referring to distant and non-Greek cities). As received from the papyrus, this adjective, negated, modifies the strife, but quite bafflingly. Grenfell and Hunt, followed by Race, conjectured a meaning "(un)relenting." Wilamowitz, followed by Bowra (1935, 225), emended to οὐ παλίγλοσσος, so that it would agree with the subject of ἐφίλη[σε]ν: he cared for the faithful paths of justice without deception.

[51] *Paean* IX, fr. 52k.42–46: ἀνορέας ... σαόφρονος. For the idea, see Xen. *Anab.* 2.6.18, treating of Proxenus' hearty ambition as just, by contrast to Meno's.

[52] *Paean* VI, fr. 52f.144–45: the supplement is in Snell and Maehler (1975) but not Race (1997); Bowra (1935, 203) does not print the lines. See also Radt (1958, 185–86).

his god-equaling
sons and children of their sons
were the best in courage, Ares-loving,
went around in the bronze groan-causing battle-din
and were *sôphrôn* and prudent in heart.

This poem, from ca. 478 BCE, has been thought to represent something of an early canon of virtues. As god-equaling, these offspring—Peleus and Telamon as sons, Achilles and Ajax as grandsons—are presumably perfectly good, glossed here as "best in courage" (ἀνόρεος = ἀνδρεῖος), *sôphrôn*, and prudent (πινυτός), as well, perhaps, as capable with justice (δίκη) as their father or grandfather.[53] Perhaps like the sentiment in *Parthenian* II and *Paean* IX, Pindar presents the offspring's *sôphrosunê* and prudence as a balance to the putative boldness in battle.[54]

Finally, Chiron is called *sôphrôn* at *Pythian* 3.63. The point in this poem is only praise, though in the *Iliad* Chiron is spoken of as "most just," and elsewhere in mythology Chiron is contrasted temperamentally with the lascivious other centaurs.[55] Probably, then, Chiron's *sôphrosunê* explains his superiority as a teacher, eventually of Heracles.

One might wonder whether the relative infrequency of *sôphrosunê* in Pindar's epinician poetry depends on its not being a salient trait for athletic champions—even if they need it as much as anyone. In any event, the lesson about the term is clear in outline. Being *sôphrôn* is being prudent, acting with a sensitivity to overall temporal and social considerations, taking into account long-term and other-person effects. It means setting and following good laws for oneself (εὐνομία), following just paths, and judging impartially—and thus in terms of stable canons of evaluation. That the term probably concludes *Paean* I, and characterizes the jurisprudentially and pedagogically leading legendary figures, speaks to its fundamentality.

---

[53] The D scholiast on this passage distinguishes courage, as pertaining to battle, from the two other virtues, as pertaining to soul (ψυχή); similarly, Carey (1981, 193) says that Aeacus' progeny "possess civil as well as military virtues." It seems likely that Pindar knew of a canon of virtues; *Nemean* 3.74 speaks of a chariot team of four virtues (τέσσαρας ἀρετάς) that drive our mortal lives (Pindar had just referred to, without specifying them, the excellences of each of three stages of life, 71–74); *Pythian* 6.47–51 formulates, partly negatively, something like the four Platonic cardinal virtues: ἄδικον ("[not] being unjust" = justice), οὔθ' ὑπέροπλον ("nor being insolent" = *sôphrosunê*?), σοφίαν (wisdom), τίν τ' . . . μάλα ἁδόντι νόῳ, Ποσειδάν, προσέχεται ("to you, Poseidon, with a mind that delights you, he keeps close" = piety?). See further North (1948b; 1966, 27); Sparshott (1970, 41, 43); Aurelio Privitera (1982, 232).

[54] The description of martial valor is epic, however; cp. *CEG* 145, from ca. 600 BCE: χαροπὸς τόνδ' ὄλεσεν Ἄρες | βαρνάμενον παρὰ ναυσὶν ἐπ' Ἀράθθοιο ῥοϝαῖσι | πολλὸν ἀριστεύϝοντα κατὰ στονόϝεσσαν ἀϝυτάν.

[55] Hom. *Il*. 11.831: δικαιότατος; cf. *Il*. 4.219. For fifth-century centaurs, see Osborne (1994).

Aeschylus

Aeschylus wrote in the final decades of Pindar's life. In 472 BCE, in his *Persians*, the Ghost of Darius advises his overly ambitious son to practice *sôphrosunê*, since Zeus "as chastiser sets himself upon those overweening in excessive pride."[56] *Sôphrosunê* involves not thinking too highly of one's capacities or fortunes; a person may be mistaken, or his luck may turn. Fifteen years later, in the *Agamemnon*, Clytemnestra warns that the Chorus, in demanding her exile despite Agamemnon's being the true source of injustice, has yet to learn *sôphrosunê*, and yet will learn it in their forthcoming comeuppance by the gods.[57] Aegisthus makes the same charge against the Chorus, for speaking harshly against a superior.[58] Both uses had been presaged by the famous "learning through suffering" (πάθος μάθει) ode early in the play, where the Chorus says that *sôphronein* and *to phronein* ("reason") come unwillingly through toil and the subsequent memory of pain.[59] *Sôphrosunê* is linked with reason as the capacity to find and concern oneself with what really matters: from Clytemnestra's perspective, not simply getting rid of her but finding the actual source of trouble; from Aegisthus' perspective, not simply speaking one's mind but acknowledging hierarchies of authority. In *Persians*, *sôphrosunê* is a kind of self-knowledge, which includes the appreciation that the world does not always bow to one's ambitions. It may manifest itself in self-restraint, but of a sort that allows long-term success: the avoidance of Zeus' chastisement. In *Agamemnon*, *sôphrosunê* is a kind of openness of mind or clarity of vision, which involves recognizing various pertinent reasons for action, not just one's most present inclination.

All of Aeschylus' adjectival uses of *sôphrôn* work in similar ways, to the extent we can tell.[60] A pair of such uses, in *Seven against Thebes* (467 BCE), which otherwise give little information about the content of *sôphrosunê*, are especially illuminating about the position of the virtue in Greek culture. They reiterate what we already saw in Pindar's *Isthmian* 8 and probably *Parthenian* II above. Amphiaraus, one of the Seven, is presented as an all-around great guy. A scout describes him:

ἕκτον λέγοιμ' ἂν ἄνδρα σωφρονέστατον
ἀλκήν τ' ἄριστον, μάντιν, Ἀμφιάρεω βίαν. (A. *Sept.* 568–69)

The sixth I should speak about is a most *sôphrôn* man,
greatest in prowess, a mantis, powerful Amphiaraus.

---

[56] A. *Pers.* 827–28: κολαστὴς τῶν ὑπερκόμπων ἄγαν | φρονημάτων ἔπεστιν.
[57] A. *Ag.* 1425.
[58] A. *Ag.* 1620.
[59] A. *Ag.* 176–81. See also A. *Eum.* 521, 1000.
[60] A. *Ag.* 351; *Choe.* 140, 786; *Eum.* 44, 136; *Supp.* 710; *Sept.* 186, 568, 610, 645; fr. 137.

Amphiaraus here gets the equivalent of *sôphrosunê*, courage, and perhaps the insight mixed with piety appropriate to the seer. The scout does not list his justice, but that allotment comes out forty lines later, when Eteocles recapitulates the scout's description:

οὕτως δ' ὁ μάντις, υἱὸν Οἰκλέους λέγω,
σώφρων δίκαιος ἀγαθὸς εὐσεβὴς ἀνήρ,
μέγας προφήτης, ἀνοσίοισι συμμιγεὶς
θρασυστόμοισιν ἀνδράσιν βίᾳ φρενῶν. (A. *Sept.* 609–12)

This mantis, I mean the son of Oecles,
a *sôphrôn*, just, *agathos*, pious man,
a great prophet, got mixed up with
impious men, his judgment forced.

The line at 610 lists four virtue terms.[61] Since *agathos* is not a summary term, it may well mean "good in a manly way," thus courageous; and being called a great mantis and prophet, as at 609 and 611, probably indicates insight and prudence in addition to piety.[62] Eteocles has just been giving examples of good people brought low by bad people: a pious man (εὐσεβὴς ἀνήρ), he says, perishes in storms sent to punish evil-doers (those with πανουργία); someone who is just (δίκαιος ὤν) is caught unjustly (ἐκδίκως) among those who forget the gods (θεῶν ἀμνήμοσιν).[63] So the context may seem to privilege piety and justice, but the priority of *sôphrosunê* in the asyndetonic list in line 610 as well as in the multipart description in lines 568–59 may suggest that *sôphrosunê* in a sense includes those two.

Epigraphy

These accumulations of *sôphrosunê* with other virtue-names in Pindar and Aeschylus have an important precedent: funeral epitaphs of the late sixth century.[64] At least a half-dozen epitaphs are known from before 500 BCE that memorialize the dead person's *sôphrosunê*, often as "good (ἀγαθός) and *sôphrôn*," sometimes with the noun "virtue" (ἀρετή).[65] (See Epigraphical Appendix for

---

[61] On Amphiarus and the canon of virtues, see North (1948b, 304; 1966, 41–42; 1979, 39–40, 104–5, 149–51, 175–76).
[62] For this usage of *agathos*, see Hom. *Il.* 1.131, 21.280; Hdt. 5.109; LSJ s.v. I.2.
[63] A. *Sept.* 602–8; cf. 598: δίκαιον ἄνδρα.
[64] For context, see Bowie (2010).
[65] *CEG* 30,b2, 34, 36, 41, 58, 67, 69.

the evidence.) With *agathos* or *aretê* understood as "valiant"/"courage," this pair has often been taken as a polar expression, "bold/valiant in war, restrained/reliable in peace."⁶⁶ But instead of indexing the two virtues to two periods of life, two seasons of the year, we might gloss the pair as "active and thoughtful," the two complementary sides of the powerful life. The person actually got things done, and they were not stupid things. This gloss is suggested by Clement of Alexandria's attribution to Gorgias: "one needs two virtues, daring and wisdom" (διττῶν ἀρετῶν δεῖται, τόλμης καὶ σοφίας).⁶⁷ Fine action requires intensity and norm-guidance.

Some epitaphs from that early period include a longer canon of virtues.⁶⁸ A young horse-racer is lauded as "*sôphrôn*, prize-winning, and smart" (σόφρονα, ἀεθλοφόρον καὶ σοφόν): the second term names his particular form of athletic goodness, probably bold and energetic; the third term praises his mental competence.⁶⁹ Another epitaph, badly worn, has been reconstructed as follows: [σό]φρον, εὐ[χσύν]ετος, χσε[νικό]ς, πι[νυ]τός, τὰ κάλ' [εἰδό]ς, evidently a list of positive traits, plausibly "*sôphrôn*, sharp, hospitable, faithful/prudent, knowing what's best."⁷⁰ And a woman, Alkimachus, is said to be "well-reputed, *sôphrôn*, and prudent (πινυτόν), having every (or the whole of) virtue."⁷¹ These lists of ultimately praiseworthy traits show both *sôphrosunê*'s salience on such occasions and the early formation of canons of virtue. The last example makes the point explicitly.⁷²

---

⁶⁶ E.g., Friedländer (1948, texts 6 and 31; pp. 15, 35).

⁶⁷ Gorgias B8/D32. Clement may be reformulating something from Gorgias' Funeral Oration (B6/D28), which was known into late antiquity: Gorgias praises the virtue of the fallen soldiers, who have "have practiced the two things which most of all must be, thought <and strength>" (καὶ δισσὰ ἀσκήσαντες μάλιστα ὧν δεῖ, γνώμην <καὶ ῥώμην>, τὴν μὲν βουλεύοντες τὴν δ' ἀποτελοῦντες). This line happens to be absent from the earlier of two witnesses to the text, Syrianus' (late fourth–early fifth century CE), but is present in Planudes' (late thirteenth century CE). What has been supplied by Foss and Sauppe and accepted by later editors as ῥώμη could well be τόλμη. More evidence that this view is Gorgias' comes from Plato's *Gorgias*; there, Callicles, putatively a student of Gorgias', advances this very view: "The [best people] are the ones who are thoughtful about the city's affairs—like how it should be managed—but not only thoughtful, but also brave, enough to accomplish what they've considered to do, and not giving up from weakness of spirit" (οἳ ἂν εἰς τὰ τῆς πόλεως πράγματα φρόνιμοι ὦσιν, ὅντινα ἂν τρόπον εὖ οἰκοῖτο, καὶ μὴ μόνον φρόνιμοι, ἀλλὰ καὶ ἀνδρεῖοι, ἱκανοὶ ὄντες ἃ ἂν νοήσωσιν ἐπιτελεῖν, καὶ μὴ ἀποκάμνωσι διὰ μαλακίαν τῆς ψυχῆς, 491b1–4).

⁶⁸ See Dover (1974, 64–66).

⁶⁹ *CEG* 136; the dedicator gives the summary comment that he is an ἄνδρα ἀ[γα]θ[ό]ν, "good man."

⁷⁰ *CEG* 67.

⁷¹ *CEG* 69. It is unclear whether to read πᾶσαν ἠέχον|τ' ἀρετέν as "having every *or* the whole of virtue"; similar phrasing is found in an epitaph from about 460 BCE, IG I³ 850, and Sophocles' *Trachiniae* 645 of 450–425 BCE.

⁷² Friedländer (1948, 8, 15) claims that the Attic epitaph in particular shows "a new ethical note," a "moral turn." See Whitehead (1993, 2009); Veligianni-Terzi (1997) on ethical terms in Greek epigraphy (219–21 on *sôphrosunê*). Oblique evidence for a wider canon of virtues is (Plato's) Meno's inclusion with the standard group of "generosity" (μεγαλοπρέπεια) and "very many" unstated others (*Meno* 74a4–6), two of which he later specifies as "intelligence and memory" (εὐμαθία καὶ μνήμη, 88a7); this view is said to be Gorgias' (71d7). Gorgias' Funeral Oration contains something close to

In the fifth century, our (exiguous) evidence shows an expansion or modification of the canon.[73] Around 430, a copper-smelter is praised for his justice, *sôphrosunê*, and virtue.[74] Around 400, a certain Cleidemus gets a most poetic epitaph:

πότνια [Σ]ωφροσύνη, θύγατερ μεγαλόφρονος Αἰδῶς,
   πλεῖστα σὲ τιμήσας εὐπόλεμόν τε Ἀρετήν
Κλείδημος Μελιτεὺς Κλειδημίδο ἐνθάδε κεῖται (*CEG* 102)

Lady *Sôphrosunê*, daughter of high-minded Respect,
   having greatly honored you and martial Virtue,
Cleidemus Meliteus son of Cleidemidus lies here.

Here *sôphrosunê* gets first billing, and a deification, and another pairing with virtue (ἀρετή); but now *sôphrosunê* is linked to respect or the sense of shame (αἰδός), which is a sensitivity to social norms, and "virtue" is linked to success in battle, which implies energy and courage.[75]

The fourth century frequently reprises laudation for *sôphrosunê* itself and the *sôphrosunê–aretê* pairing.[76] Occasionally we again see the addition of justice or wisdom; we now see the addition of "orderly" (κόσμον), "piety" (εὐσέβεια), and "mentally sharp" (εὐσύνετος); once we see the more practically oriented "*sôphrôn* and useful and industrious, having all virtue."

These epigraphic records speak of *sôphrosunê* as capping a well-grieved life. They tell us about the continuing broad significance attributed to *sôphrosunê* and about the other virtues related to or distinguished from *sôphrosunê*, but they do not tell us what *sôphrosunê* is, or what precisely its relationship is with other virtues. They do not need to, even if they could; their inscribers do not deploy them in critical contexts, where their boundaries could matter. Nevertheless, since *sôphrosunê* is evidently a term of highest accolade, its proper scope of

---

a four-member canon: σεμνοί ... ὅσιοι ... δίκαιοι ... εὐσεβεῖς as well as a number of other tetrads. Chappell (1993, 13) infers a distinctive Thrasymachean tetrad of virtues: strength (ἰσχύς), unrestraint (ἐλευθερία), imperiousness (δεσποτεία), and practical intelligence (εὐβουλία). He similarly infers a Calliclean tetrad, which to courage and wisdom adds force (ἐπικουρία) and the trio luxury (τρυφή)—indiscipline (ἀκολασία)—unrestraint (15).

[73] For the half-century gap in relevant inscriptions, see Lougovaya-Ast (2004).
[74] *CEG* 96.
[75] Further discussion of this epigram in Clairmont (1970, 153–54); González González (2019, 69–70); Hunter (2022, 75–76). The genealogical presentation of the virtues becomes common by early in the fifth century, especially in Pindar: *Ol.* 13.6–8 (*Themis* mother of *Dikê*, *Eunomia*, and *Eirênê*), 9.14–16 (*Themis* mother of *Eunomia*); 7.44 (*Promêtheia* mother of *Aidôs*); *Pyth.* 8.1–4 (*Dikê* mother of *Hesuchia*); see generally Abel (1943).
[76] See generally Vestrheim (2010, 65, 67, 71, 73); Fantuzzi (2010, 302).

application does matter, and so it will become an object of analysis and dispute in the fifth and fourth centuries. The remaining chapters of this book consider that analysis.

Preclassical Sôphrosunê

In this chapter we studied the forerunners of the classical usage of *sôphrosunê*; as we will see in subsequent chapters, we have come across close antecedents for all such later uses. The earliest instances, drawn from the Homeric epics, stand in well for the rest. In the three *Odyssey* instances, they represent discretion or tact, not blurting out whatever one at some moment wishes, given that doing so could undermine one's standing commitments or ultimate goals. In the *Iliad* instance, *sôphrosunê* comes up beyond the conversational sphere and means diffidence or circumspection, standing down from honor-preserving confrontation when the stakes do not warrant it and other relationships or self-identifications tell against it. Seen together, *sôphrosunê* looks like the virtue of identifying with something other than one's hottest inclinations—whether that is the inclination to learn what one wants, or divulge a secret, or celebrate a homecoming, or defend one's favorites. One identifies instead with the nexus of beliefs about what is truly worth doing seen from a perspective wider than any specific moment of decision. This nexus is untheorized in Homer but appears to be the norm of maturity, reliability, and efficacy.

Theognis extends the application of *sôphrosunê* little beyond the Homeric usages, sometimes even meditating on those Homeric lines or the underlying gnomic formulations. The putatively aristocratic context of his poetry means that his uses tend toward the political, preferring adherence to stabilizing, "conservative," civic norms; his poetry's sympotic context increases the reference to alcohol and sexual lust as the surest obstacles to *sôphrosunê*. But this does not mean that, for Theognis, *sôphrosunê* is control over bodily desires or, for that matter, democratic aspirations, just as reverence is not specifically control over urges to profane or disregard the gods. Rather, in Theognis, *sôphrosunê* is the capacity to follow principles with authoritative provenance, whether they be principles of rational self-government or those set out by a city's constitution.

Our knowledge of Pindar's understanding of *sôphrosunê* has a narrow evidence base, though that evidence base provides some key lessons. By the time of Pindar's writing, *sôphrosunê* is included in what looks like a canon of virtues; it represents forethoughtfulness and keeps ambition limited to that which is just. As in the *Theognidea*, we see here no fundamental change from the Homeric conception of *sôphrosunê* as the capacity for judgment concerning short- and long-term, or narrowly and widely relevant interests.

Aeschylus shows again *sôphrosunê*'s increasing appearance in a canon of virtues; its special ambit seems self-knowledge and practical knowledge of the world of action. That canonicity is evidenced especially in the epigraphic tradition. *Sôphrosunê* comes to represent, in a popular and legible way, one of the signal attainments of human excellence.

3
Heraclitus, Self-Knowledge, and the Greatest Virtue

The Two *Sôphrosunê* Fragments

The first known philosophical reflection on *sôphrosunê* occurs during the young adulthood of Pindar and Aeschylus, in the years around 500 BCE.[1] This is found in the fragments of Heraclitus, a thinker widely apprised of philosophical innovations across the Mediterranean and an innovative epistemologist in his own right.[2] Stobaeus attributes to him two fragments that include the verb *sôphronein*:

B112/D114a + b: σωφρονεῖν ἀρετὴ μεγίστη καὶ σοφίη ἀληθέα λέγειν καὶ ποιεῖν κατὰ φύσιν ἐπαΐοντας. (Stob. 3.1.178)[3]

Sôphronein is the greatest virtue and wisdom, to speak and act true things, perceiving in accordance with nature.

B116/D30: ἀνθρώποισι πᾶσι μέτεστι γινώσκειν ἑωυτοὺς καὶ σωφρονεῖν. (Stob. 3.5.6)

It belongs to all people to know themselves and *sôphronein*.

The first of these fragments, B112, identifies *sôphrosunê* as the superlative virtue (ἀρετή) and evidently links it with wisdom (σοφίη) and a natural and conscientious correctness of thought and action. The statement's directness, and other fragments' gnomic tendencies, suggest that Heraclitus means here to provoke: *sôphrosunê* does not normally get discussed as the greatest virtue—or even as *aretê* at all, given the polar expression *sôphrosunê–aretê* seen in the previous

---

[1] Thibodeau (2019, 146–52) shows that all we know about Heraclitus' dating is that his acme was 510–490 BCE.

[2] Among the extensive bibliography on Heraclitus' epistemological thought, see, simply in the past fifteen years, Huffman (2008); A. G. Long (2008); A. A. Long (2009); Hülsz Piccone (2013); Dilcher (2013); Johnstone (2014); Lesher (2016); Moore (2020, ch. 2).

[3] Text here and below from Hense, with punctuation removed; at Stob. 3.1.178, Hense punctuates with a terminal dot after μεγίστη.

chapter. But we have also seen the increasing importance of *sôphrosunê* in the Greek mentality of the decades around Heraclitus' life, and so he makes a plausible claim, one he goes on to explain and justify. The second fragment, B116, links the verb *sôphronein* again with self-knowledge and picks both out as salient capacities due to all people. We might assume that Heraclitus again means to provoke, giving a surprising if short list of capacities to be widely shared.

Both fragments are frustratingly lapidary, but they reflect a fundamentality that Heraclitus ascribes to *sôphrosunê*. Their importance, and their inauguration of a long tradition of treating *sôphrosunê* in theoretical discussion, motivates the careful if speculative analysis that follows. We want primarily to figure out what Heraclitus was saying when he said that *sôphronein* is the greatest virtue (etc.) and due to all people, and why he said that. But we want secondarily to show that Heraclitus did say what Stobaeus ascribes to him.

Both of Heraclitus' fragments on *sôphrosunê* have had their authenticity so severely questioned over the past two centuries that they have contributed little to reconstructing Heraclitus' philosophy or the history of ethical terminology.[4] B116, on *sôphrosunê* and self-knowledge, has frequently been thought a lax paraphrase of another fragment: "though the *logos* is shared, many live as if they had private insight."[5] In one of the most recent critical editions of Heraclitus' texts, by Miroslav Marcovich, B116 receives no commentary at all, so certain is the editor of its distance from Heraclitus' real views.[6] The reasoning is usually that its putatively simple syntax lacks a Heraclitean fingerprint, or that the connection of the virtue and self-directed epistemic state can only be a Socratic idea that has then been retrojected on an earlier thinker.[7] Fair enough; to modern eyes nothing looks excitingly self-contradictory in these few words. Yet perhaps there is paradox enough to be worthy of Heraclitus; one must first look. B112, on *sôphrosunê*

---

[4] Neither fragment is mentioned, for example, in Kirk, Raven, and Schofield (1983, 211); the authors do state that "Heraclitus' ethical advice [which is similar to others'] ... stresses the importance of moderation," but they do not identify their evidence; apparently it is B43/D112, "insolence (ὕβρις) is more to be extinguished than a conflagration," and B114/D105, "those who speak with sense (ξὺν νόῳ) must rely on what is common to all, as a city must rely on its law, and with much greater reliance. For all the laws of men are nourished by one law, the divine law; for it has as much power as it wishes and is sufficient for all and is still left over" (their translations). B116 does not appear in Barnes (1982); Rademaker (2005, 332) makes mention only of B116, not of B112, and in less than a sentence.

[5] B2/D2: τοῦ λόγου δ' ἐόντος ξυνοῦ ζώουσιν οἱ πολλοὶ ὡς ἰδίαν ἔχοντες φρόνησιν.

[6] Marcovich (1967, 88–97). The term σωφρονεῖν does not appear in his "Index Verborum Heracliti."

[7] E.g., Kirk (1962, 56: "weak paraphrase"; 390: "even more suspect" [than B112]). More baselessly, Vitek (2012, 189): "B116 seems to be a combination of reflections on the first part of B114, B133[R111], and B101[D36]. The thusly created statement is linear, excessively appellative, and moralistic (amounting to a flattened version of the Delphic 'Know thyself'). Moreover, it contains a completely redundant exhortation to 'thinking' (σωφρονεῖν), which Heraclitus would hardly consider necessary." Fronterotta (2013, 285) is also doubtful. For further scholarship, see Moore (2018a, 2–4).

as the greatest *aretê*, has suffered not so much athetization as neglect due to interpretative despair.[8] The syntactic questions following the sentence's third or fifth words (σωφρονεῖν ἀρετὴ μεγίστη καὶ σοφίη...) seem almost hopeless: how does "wisdom" relate to the rest of the sentence; what does "to speak and act true things" refer to; could "to act true things" mean anything at all; what does "in accordance with nature" qualify; where does the participle go? Nobody wants to base a thesis about Heraclitus on word salad. The most recent editors of this text, André Laks and Glenn W. Most, have tried to avoid some of these problems by formalizing what scholars of Heraclitus had sometimes already done: presented "*Sôphronein megistê aretê*" as its own (complete) fragment, the *kai* as a linkage term supplied by Stobaeus (but mistakenly assimilated to the fragment itself) from it to another (independent) fragment, and then "*Sophiê* . . ." as its own fragment.[9] In doing so, though they preserve the claim to *sôphrosunê*'s preeminence, they exclude the greater part of the fragment from informing us about the meaning of this claim. We have yet to see whether some sense, even if eccentric or outlandish, might be made from the full passage, and whether we have better cause to imagine Heraclitus' saying *that* then to have made two rather simpler points.[10]

Even setting aside these burdensome textual problems, which we will address further below, these two fragments do not readily reveal their meanings. Not that we should expect them to, given Heraclitus' intended enigmaticity and the novelty of his thought.[11] There may well be a limit to the sense we can make of them; these fragments are just too short, and we have lost too much of the dialectical context both within and beyond Heraclitus' oeuvre. In one respect, that limit does not much matter for the purpose of this chapter; their existential

---

[8] Kirk (1962) has an ambiguous attitude toward this fragment: "these words can safely be rejected as a banal paraphrase in the language of late fifth-century ethical investigations" (390); yet they are also "a rather clever fusion of Heraclitean phrases which give a possible, but thoroughly banal, resultant sense" (390) and "may include some original phraseology" (229); but "in any case it adds nothing to what Heraclitus tells us elsewhere" (391). (For all that, he goes some way to interpreting the latter part of the fragment: 158, 391). Vitek (2012, 177) includes it among the moral maxims attributed to Heraclitus he judges too banal, too low-register, and too early relative to late fifth-century ethical theorizing actually to be his, though like Kirk he hedges: "B112 consists of some Heraclitean terms and phrases from different sayings, but on the whole it is only a trivial piece of 'wisdom' at a questionable intellectual level, which looks quite out of place within the Heraclitean corpus." I suspect both were influenced by the long scholarly consensus against the fragment, which includes Schleiermacher, Lassalle, Mullach, Bernays, Heidel, Beeretz, Marcovich, Roussos, and Pradeau.

[9] They do not give their grounds for this decision, or parallels for such *kai* confusion; maybe they follow Lebedev (2014, 411) (see n44 below). There is a kind of precedent: following Heidel (1913, 713–14), Kirk (1962, 391) speaks of the "unacceptable first three words," and Barnes (1982, 133) translates B112 as "It is wisdom to speak the truth and to act knowingly in accordance with nature," simply dropping the first four words without explanation (he also says that "the sentence is a paraphrase, not a quotation; but it summarizes Heraclitus' doctrine well enough"—without evidence, though presumably following Marcovich).

[10] Rosella Schluderer (2017) is an impressive attempt to do so.

[11] Bollack and Wismann (1972, 15–28, 387–99); Kahn (1979); Mackenzie (1988); Gallop (1989); Mouraviev (2002, III.3.A.135–210); *SEP* s.v. "Heraclitus," §5; Habash (2019).

significance, so to speak, is plain, as is the conceptual environment they enliven. In another respect, however, we can still make considerable sense of them, even if controversially and indeterminately.[12] Enough, that is to say, to see that Heraclitus understands *sôphrosunê* as the crucial virtue of maturity, of the constitution of oneself into a responsible reasoner and actor, what we might now call an epistemic, rational—or, in more Heraclitean terms, a logical—agent.

B116: Knowing Oneself and *Sôphronein*

We begin with the shorter of the two fragments, B116, "It belongs to all people to know themselves and *sôphronein*." This fragment has been frequently ignored as inauthentic, especially in the nineteenth and earlier twentieth centuries. However, more recent scholarship has shown that such judgments of inauthenticity are either untenable or dubiously subjective, and students of Heraclitus from the past several decades more regularly accept it.[13] Productive interpretative time was lost, however, and so analysis of the fragment remains inchoate. We will see this from two important discussions of Heraclitus' work. Both have seen in the fragment something of great significance, even as, without taking cognizance of the history of *sôphrosunê*, their interpretations prove insufficient.

The earlier of the two studies, Jean Bollack and Heinz Wismann's *Héraclite ou La Séparation*, gives a rightly provocative but in the end incomplete reading.[14] The authors focus on the "knowing oneself" half of the fragment: whereas the Delphic injunction, they claim, tells people to know and keep to their social position, Heraclitus treats the maxim as a call to self-liberation and the discovery of one's identity.[15] Wrestling one's thought from social convictions, from *la mesure*, is to *bien-penser*, "think well," which is their translation of *sôphronein*, a gloss and explanation they justify quasi-etymologically: *sôphronein* is to "*sauve[r] (sôzei) sa pensée*." Thus Bollack and Wismann read B116 as a call to intellectual maveric, shifting the guide rails of reasoning from the group to one's individuality. Heraclitus may well encourage such self-definition, and obviously esteems a thoughtfulness free of cliché and herd notions. But while *sôphronein* can mean "thinking well/effectively," "saving one's thought" (with its Aristotelian ring) is a mysterious locution, and there is little evidence that the exercise of *sôphrosunê* means independence from social conviction or convention or an impulse to spontaneous individuality. The assertion of Heraclitus' radical use of "know

---

[12] For these fragments' programmatic importance, see Bolton (1989, 54–56); Long (2009, esp. 93–95); Curd (2009, 3); Bachmann (2019).
[13] See Moore (2018a, 4–6) for bibliography.
[14] Bollack and Wismann (1972, 321–22).
[15] Bolton (1989, 54) also believes that Heraclitus departed from the Delphic message.

yourself" feels right, but no philological argument substantiates it; indeed, the authors could not have found evidence for their claim about the Delphic injunction, since evidence for its meaning simply does not exist.[16]

Seven years later, and from a different scholarly tradition, Charles Kahn's *The Thought and Art of Heraclitus* gives another charitable interpretation of Heraclitus, but again without adequate philological substantiation.[17] Heraclitus is again treated as innovative, in both his deeming self-knowledge accessible in principle to everyone and his treating it as a route to comprehension of the common *logos*.[18] But though Kahn says that this democratic self-knowledge "presents an apparent contradiction ... with the Delphic motto," in fact nothing about its inscription on the Temple of Apollo implies any such restriction. More important, *sôphronein* does effectively no work in Kahn's analysis of the fragment, though it might seem to deserve an equal part of Kahn's attention. He says that "the connection between self-knowledge and *sôphronein* is taken for granted in the archaic conception of wisdom": at Delphi both the "nothing in excess" (μηδὲν ἄγαν) and the "know yourself" (γνῶθι σαυτόν) "might reasonably be paraphrased as *sôphronein*, 'be of sound mind.'" This claim lacks contemporaneous evidence; and even were it true, it would not explain Heraclitus' use of both *sôphronein* and "know themselves" in this fragment as anything other than sonorous redundancy.[19] In later pages Kahn even speaks of "the Delphic assimilation [of *sôphronein*] to self-knowledge" without explanation.[20]

Bollack and Wismann want *sôphrosunê* to represent an independent mode of thinking that leads to or preserves an individuality-finding self-knowledge. Kahn wants it simply to *mean* self-knowledge, where that is the avenue for cognition of the *logos*. These authors have not marshaled the evidence for their views. But it is hard to disagree with their near equation of *sôphrosunê* and knowing oneself. We probably are indeed to understand *sôphrosunê* as some instantiation of self-knowledge. What neither Bollack and Wismann nor Kahn provides, however, is

---

[16] Moore (2015c, 22–31).
[17] Kahn (1979, 116–17).
[18] Lebedev (2014, 410–11) favors this anti-aristocratic line and believes, on the anachronistic evidence of *Charmides* 164e (dubiously treating Critias' dubious interpretation of the Delphic injunction as Plato's belief), that curbing one's passions is the Delphic exhortation. One might appeal to B20, 29, 110, 117 for this idea.
[19] Kahn's (1979, 309n85) putative evidence comes from Pl. *Chrm.* 164e7; North (1966, "10ff."); and Wilamowitz-Moellendorff (1913, 173). The *Charmides* reference is Critias' equation of the Delphic *Gnôthi sauton* with *Sôphronei*; but this is in a deliberately obtuse speech, one intended as sensational; besides its radicality, its dramatic date is 429, many decades after someone inscribed the motto at Delphi, with a purpose certainly unknown to Critias himself. Further, Critias treats the *mêden agan* as of quite a different nature, not at all as synonymous (165a1–10). North gives no archaic evidence for the equivalence of self-knowledge and either *sôphrosunê* or non-excess; the evidence provided of gnomic maxims by the Seven Sages, which does not support this equivalence, dates at any rate from the late fourth century at the earliest. Wilamowitz's position is even less supported, again mainly inferring from a supposed Apolline religion of self-restraint.
[20] Kahn (1979, 120).

an account of *sôphrosunê* that could show the virtue to be so understood; nor do they provide an account of self-knowledge that could show it to be such a virtue. Admittedly, justifying the identity of *sôphrosunê* and self-knowledge is not an easy thing to do. It becomes a major preoccupation of fifth- and fourth-century thinkers. We will meet such attempts in the subsequent chapters of this book. Heraclitus cannot be known to have inspired those later attempts (the extent of his uptake in subsequent generations is questionable), but he witnesses the plausibility of so attempting.

Heraclitus has written, "It belongs to all people to know themselves and *sôphronein*" (ἀνθρώποισι πᾶσι μέτεστι γινώσκειν ἑωυτοὺς καὶ σωφρονεῖν). To say that successful attainment of this pair of states "belongs to all people" is perhaps his first big point. *Meteinai* means "to have a share in," not necessarily "to possess"; it implies an availability and a propriety.[21] Citing this availability is presumably exhortative: people should strive harder to get what they have not yet gotten, since it is possible to get it; and yet it is likely they have not gotten it, since otherwise citing its possibility would be pointless.[22] We may surmise the reason people do not pursue self-knowledge or *sôphrosunê*: they assume they already know themselves (fourth-century authors frequently point this out) and thus do not actually study themselves;[23] and they think they are *sôphrôn*, insofar as they do not feel deranged at present, even as they might not so readily deem themselves especially courageous or intellectually insightful. So self-knowledge and *sôphrosunê* may seem to be default conditions: both easy to have and not a big deal. Heraclitus' pointed observation that they are universally accessible and proper suggests that they may not actually have yet been accessed or pursued—perhaps for the very reason that they seem easy to have—and that they are a big deal.

Let us hypothesize that the nature of self-knowledge illuminates the nature of *sôphrosunê*, either by being the same or by assuming the same view of selfhood. So getting clear about self-knowledge is the crucial thing to do. Initial interpretative help comes from the shorter and more frequently cited fragment, B101: "I sought out myself (ἐδιζησάμην ἐμεωυτόν)." Its main verb, "to seek out," is found again at B22/D39, in a more instructive fragment: "Those searching for gold dig up much earth and find little (χρυσὸν οἱ διζήμενοι γῆν πολλὴν

---

[21] Hdt. 1.171 (the Carians have a shrine access to which they give to Mysians and Lydians, as to brothers, on grounds of their ethnic connection); see also LSJ s.v. II and Dilcher (1995, 21). Arist. *Pol.* 1292a1–3, using the same verb, speaks of forms of democracy where all have "a share" in governing; he does not mean that all govern simultaneously.

[22] Compare B113: "thinking is common to all" (ξυνόν ἐστι πᾶσι τὸ φρονέειν), which presumably also enjoins actually *thinking*, given that it is possible.

[23] Hussey (1999, 103–4) observes that Heraclitus thinks we have a choice to become better, but also that the conflict between self-knowledge and self-delusion in us is "presumably ... isomorphic to" cosmic conflict. Fourth-century agreement: see, e.g., [Pl.] *Alc.* 129a5; Xen. *Cyr.* 7.2.21, *Mem.* 4.2.24; see earlier Ion of Chios fr. 55.

ὀρύσσουσι καὶ εὑρίκσουσιν ὀλίγον)." That verb of search, δίζημαι, probably means seeking one thing out from among many ultimately irrelevant items, wheat among chaff.[24] Seeking oneself out thus probably implies undergoing a challenge, sorting through flak, seeking an unusual object: oneself. The fascination with fragment B101 comes from the fact that we do not generally think that we need to *seek* ourselves, since we think we are *obviously right here*. Yet it is hardly remarkable, in Heraclitus' thinking, that just as nearly everyone fails to recognize his experiences for what they are (see below on B17/D3), nearly everyone would also start by failing to have already found himself. Indeed, it may not be obvious what counts as "oneself," whether there is something to which this reflexive pronoun refers or whether we are to posit something that could be so referred to.

The specific language of *ginoskein heauton*, given Heraclitus' other uses of those terms, provides a clue. He uses the cognitive verb *ginôskein* throughout his extant fragments.[25] While translated "know" above, the English verbs "recognize" and "acknowledge" get closer and are more consistent with pre-Heraclitean uses of the word.[26] "To recognize," like "to acknowledge," means to identify something correctly in a way that bears normative force. I might learn the content of my city's law, and thus be able to describe its contours, but when I acknowledge that something is the law for me, I correctly identify a social norm *as* law and thus as binding on my actions. When I recognize my friend, I identify this person *as* my friend and thus as a person to whom certain duties are due and certain feelings are apt. The contrast is with other veridical attitudes, such as "noting" or "being familiar with" or "having information about." Heraclitus' verb

---

[24] This has been controversial, of course; see Moore (2020b, 48n36 for B22; 56 for B101). Generally see LSJ s.v. δίζημαι A; Guthrie (1962, 416–19); Robinson (1987, 147). Marcovich (1967, 53–58) and Tonelli (2005, 199) understand δίζημαι as querying (oneself), as of the Oracle; this view seems to imply that Heraclitus also riddles *himself*. DL 9.5 says that Heraclitus inquired of himself alone, not others, and was thus his own teacher (followed by Fronterotta 2013, 283). Kirk, Raven, and Schofield (1983, 204, 211) treat "searching out oneself" as discovery of one's physical nature, the way in which the soul ranges outside oneself and is connected structurally and materially with the world: the soul is a portion of the vast cosmic fire, and the possessor of soul partakes in some part of the fire's directive power. Kahn (1979, 116) takes the view that Heraclitus is looking for his "true self" (similarly Boudouris 1989, 60–61, who calls it "hidden"); yet one wonders what in Heraclitus' language denotes this "true self." Pritzl (1985, 308) treats the reflexive as identifying a repository of (personal) experience on which one draws on the path to knowledge. Long (2001, 27) says that "the cosmic order that [Heraclitus] discovered—a universe governed by divine *logos*—offered itself as a startlingly new paradigm for what to make of oneself: a *microcosm* of psychological balance, self-measurement, internal control, and beauty." Lebedev (2014, 409–10) has it that the world and oneself are the same; to look for one is to look for the other; there's no difference between subject and object. Similarly Fränkel (1975, 379). Suzuki (1989) thinks Heraclitus advocates an investigation into soul.

[25] He uses the verb only in the progressive; he also uses a related noun in B56 (discussed below) and B78.

[26] Lesher (1981, 8–11, 14; 1994, 7–8). See also Lesher (1983, 159–63): "γνῶναι and γιγνώσκειν . . . [mean] knowing not just who or what something is, but what this means, what its signficance is, what the larger situation is, or what the facts really are." Cf. Snell (1953, 13).

ginôskein, we will see, involves a fitting appreciation of something *as* a particular sort of thing and thus of its practical weight.

Heraclitus' most revealing use of *ginôskein* is in his three-clause excoriation of the delusive life. "Most people do not understand (φρονέουσι) such things as they encounter (ἐγκυρέουσιν), nor having learned (μαθόντες) do they recognize (γινώσκουσιν) [sc. what they have learned?], but they seem to themselves (ἑωυτοῖσι δὲ δοκέουσι) [sc. to do so?]" (B17). The translation and interpretation are difficult on their own, aside from this statement's being something of a riddle, the solution to which requires close attention to the difference between these easily conflated cognitive terms.[27]

The common failure denounced here is the conceit that one automatically understands what one has experienced. Most people think they know exactly what they have been through, as though Aeschylus' *pathei mathos* were universally true. Heraclitus responds that enlightenment does not occur simply through the passage of time; his fragment make three observations about the failure to achieve such enlightenment. First, "encountering" something does not suffice for "understanding," since it is too particular and private (cf. B2). This recalls Heraclitus' programmatic opening fragment (B1/D1), where he says that many people seem unfamiliar (ἀπείροισιν) with the *logoi* he goes through, even though they have experienced (πειρώμενοι) them in word and deed. Second, "learning" does not suffice for "recognizing," since it does not render the skill or lesson a person has learned practically salient. This recalls Heraclitus' opposition between "much learning" (πολυμαθίη) and "understanding" (νόον) in B40 and B129. Third, not only does brute intake differ from proper uptake, but people ignore this difference and believe that they have understanding and recognition when they do not.[28] There is a stark contrast between "but they seem to themselves" (ἑωυτοῖσι δοκέουσι) here and "knowing themselves" (γινώσκειν ἑωυτούς) of B116. The possibility of mistaken self-assessment suggests that understanding and recognizing involve acknowledging the way something really is, and having the way it really is matter, rather than going with first impressions, whatever they may be, and letting those impressions reinforce one's current expectations. One can presume to understand how something really is but fail to have verified that presumption. Both acknowledgment and understanding are kinds of "seeing as," a unifying of some experience under the concept of something already (or soon to be even more) meaningful.

Ginôskein cognates arise in a number of additional fragments, each confirming a translation as "recognition" or "acknowledgment" construed as above.[29] They

---

[27] Other Heraclitean riddles: B56/D22, B57/D25a.

[28] On the verb *dokeô*, see B27/D120: "What awaits men at death they do not expect or even consider (δοκέουσιν)."

[29] Most straightforward is: "dogs bark at those they do not know (γινώσκωσι)" (B97/D9), where recognition would change their entire orientation, from alert warnings to companionable

show that Heraclitus' remarks about "recognition," among the most interesting of his fragments, treat humans as regularly failing to appreciate the significance of their perceptions or experiences. What is to be recognized is often *right there*: that day and night are one, for example, and what is otherwise "obvious." Failing to recognize is failing to make the correct sense of what you see; since you see it anyway, it is easy to settle for your current appraisal. We may have hints already relevant to our reconstruction of Heraclitus' use of *sôphrosunê*.

Now to Heraclitus' second clue about the nature of "knowing oneself," the reflexive pronoun. Heraclitus does not specify any particular thing about oneself that one seeks to recognize, for instance, one's beliefs, the structure of one's soul, the limitations on one's period of existence, or one's capacity for knowledge or action. It may be that the imputed object of recognition is simply understood, as though everyone knows what the sage *gnôthi sauton* commends one know. But this is doubtful, both in the general case, since there evidently was no agreed understanding about the force of the maxim, and in Heraclitus' case, since we do not expect him simply to accept such conventional assumptions. This might not leave much for us to say about *ginoskein heauton*. That is, unless Heraclitus means to use the reflexive pronoun in a robust way, as, so to speak, fully reflexive—where the "oneself" is coextensive with the subject of the verb.

The reflexive pronoun appears in about a half-dozen fragments. Besides B101 and B116, one other appears in the accusative, as the direct object in an insecure

tail-wagging. More interesting is: "The teacher (διδάσκολος) of most people is Hesiod: they know (ἐπίστανται) him to know (εἰδέναι) most, he who did not recognize (ἐγίνωσκεν) day and night: for they are one" (B57). (Similarly, B106/D25b has Heraclitus judging Hesiod as "ignorant [ἀγνοοῦντι] of the single nature of each day.") Again we have a riddle. Hesiod did not acknowledge the unity of day and night, giving them distinct identities in *Theogony* (128, 724), misled as he was by the superficial experience of differences in light intensity or by mythological tradition. Heraclitus signals the importance of "recognition" by setting it near three other cognition terms. The unity of the day is significant in two ways: abstractly, as a representative of singularity out of polarity, and concretely, as actually the way humans mark the passage of time (Kahn 1979, 108–10). Hesiod was dazzled by the apparent differences, thought he accounted for those differences in a clever way, and in the process ignored the deep connections. In another fragment, Heraclitus generalizes Hesiod's error: "Beliefs [are what] the most reputed one recognizes, maintains (δοκέοντα ὁ δοκιμώτατος γινώσκει, φυλάσσει)" (B28a/D19; text and translation are uncertain). Those treated as intellectual authorities mistake their reputation as an imprimatur for their perspective. Thus they take as true and important, and retain as warranted and reliable, what they have actually failed to recognize in a clearer light (though compare the reading in Sider 2013, 327). Of course, that clear light need not be so much brighter than it already is: "Men are deceived in the recognition of what is *obvious* (ἐξηπάτηνται οἱ ἄνθρωποι πρὸς τὴν γνῶσιν τῶν φανερῶν), just as Homer was, who was wisest of all the Greeks" (B56). How can we fail to recognize the obvious unless we have focused on something other than what is in front of us? Mystery initiates "pray to images as if they were talking with houses, not recognizing (γινώσκων) what gods or even heroes are like" (B5/D15; see also Adomenas 1999, 101–6). Heraclitus abstracts from these observations about famous men and commoners to state a basic thesis of his intellectual project: "of all those whose accounts I have heard, none has gone so far as this: to recognize (γινώσκειν) that [the] wise is set apart from [them] all" (B108/D43). The understanding for which people ought to seek, and which will be decisive, is distinct from the particulars that people usually look for to direct their lives (cf. B86/D38, B97/D9).

attribution to Heraclitus: "belonging to the soul is a *logos* increasing itself" (ψυχῆς ἐστι λόγος ἑαυτὸν αὔξων).[30] Whatever this means—is it the idea of self-consciousness?—we need not assume that the *logos* increases only a part of itself.[31] Indeed, the appeal of the fragment comes from its suggestiveness about the special nature of soul and *logos*, such that their maturation depends somehow on themselves.

A dative reflexive pronoun is perhaps Heraclitus' most famous reflexive; it comes in his summary view of the world as compounding opposition and unity: "They do not understand how a thing, in differing from itself, self-agrees (διαφερόμενον ἑωυτῷ ὁμολογέει): a back-turning harmony, just as in the bow and the lyre."[32] Whether the reflexive pronoun wholly coincides with the object, and what it would mean for this to be possible (or impossible), is a deep question about Heraclitus' perspective, and it is surely Heraclitus' purpose for us to meditate on the issue. To the extent something agrees with itself (ἑωυτῷ ὁμολογέει), the subject and object are identical. To the extent something differs from itself (διαφερόμενον ἑωυτῷ), they are not. But this paradoxical situation exploits the grammar and the reader's expectation that reflexive pronouns can (even if they do not need to) refer to the whole of the verb's subject.[33]

The other reflexive pronouns are in the genitive: Pythagoras made up his "own" wisdom (ἐποιήσατο ἑαυτοῦ σοφίην, B129/D26); Heraclitus' Ephesians deserve to be hanged for driving out the very best of "themselves" (ἑωυτῶν, B121/D14). In both fragments, the reflexive is surprising.

Against this background, Heraclitus appears sensitive to the substantive and the rhetorical effect of reflexive pronouns, especially the possibility that they may be coreferential with the subject. This does not determine for us the use he makes of them in B101 (ἐδιζησάμην ἐμεωυτόν) and B116 (γινώσκειν ἑωυτούς), but it makes plausible that he would have his readers contemplate the possibility of coreferentiality. If the objects of *dizesthai* and *ginôskein*—that is, what Heraclitus wanted to look for and what he thinks everyone should know—were the same as the subject, we might make a sequence of inferences about its nature. Some of these inferences depend on the kind of thing that engages in *dizesthai*

---

[30] B115/D99 = Stob. 3.1.180a. Attributed in Stobaeus' manuscripts to Socrates, Hermann Diels attributed it to Heraclitus because of its similarity to B45/D98 (λόγος τῆς ψυχῆς) and its relationship to sayings in the Hippocratic corpus. Though one might also find the line unduly paradoxical and abstract for the Socrates familiar to us, it has an approximate parallel in Pl. *Phdr.* 276e6–277a4.

[31] For some phenomenological suggestions, see Robb (1986, 338–39); Long (2009, 102); Jeremiah (2012, 83–86).

[32] B51: οὐ ξυνιᾶσιν ὅκως διαφερόμενον ἑωυτῷ ὁμολογέει· παλίντροπος ἁρμονίη ὅκωσπερ τόξου καὶ λύρης. For relevant discussion, see Vlastos (1955, 348–51); Jeremiah (2012, 86–87).

[33] Another dative reflexive pronoun arises in B17, where people "seem to [or consider] themselves (ἑωυτοῖσι δὲ δοκέουσι)" to understand what they have experienced; but this means only that others may not agree that they do.

and *ginôskein*, others on the kind of thing that is the object of those "epistemic" actions:

1. The self can seek and recognize.
2. The self can be found and recognized.
3. The self might not be found or recognized; it might be mislocated or misrecognized.
4. The self might be ignorant or deluded.[34]
5. Presumably the self can get better at seeking and recognizing; it can improve epistemically.
6. Recognizing itself as something improvable epistemically gives the occasion to improve itself epistemically, since it has been exhorted to seek and recognize (well).

This list of corollaries might be expanded or rephrased, but it already allows that Heraclitus hints at an ideal of epistemic agency. This is a competence to assess one's own claims to knowledge (or recognition, or understanding), such that one may be responsible for one's epistemic states. This matters for actions the deliberation on which depends on knowledge. In other words, consistent with the rest of Heraclitus' statements about human belief and action, Heraclitus counsels taking a second look at what one thinks is true and what one takes as good. First impressions and long-running habits have little claim to authority.

This view of self-knowledge as epistemic agency—the active, effortful seeking out of what is best to think and do—recalls the discussion of *sôphrosunê* in the previous chapter. We saw uses in Aeschylus that hewed close to self-knowledge and to a sound understanding of the world in which one acts. For Pindar, *sôphrosunê* involved recognition of one's long-term benefit, a setting aside of impulse in favor of constituting oneself as a person who might someday wish to retire. It qualified one's ambitions such that they remained consistent with justice, that overriding norm of social life. In the *Theognidea*, *sôphrosunê* was a reverence for the highest order of norms, whether divine or civic, as well as the capacity to act and speak as one would really intend, the opposite of having an unhinged or idiotic mind. And in Homer it was the capacity to appreciate what reasons for action should actually motivate one's action.

Given this background, and its proximity to *ginôskein heautôn*, what could *sôphronein* in Heraclitus mean? We have just treated self-knowledge as conceivably the recognition of oneself as an epistemic agent, someone responsive to the reasons for treating a belief as knowledge or mere opinion, by contrast with someone who takes merely holding a belief as sufficient to act on its basis.

---

[34] Cf. B43/D112, B85/D116, B20/D118, B29/D13, B110/D117, B117/D104.

To exercise *sôphrosunê*, which might be the practical/action-oriented correlate of knowing oneself, could be to take the mere presence of a desire as insufficient for treating it as a motivation; only certain desires, not all of them urgent and felt, deserve to be action-guiding. To save rather than spend, to swallow one's pride rather than react, to keep one's promises rather than take advantage of one's business partners, to say what is true rather than whatever crosses one's mind—these are the choices being *sôphrôn* allows one to make. But it is not just that *sôphrosunê* allows one to choose between two equally valid ways of life; in choosing a life that satisfies only the right desires, one's life becomes unified and thereby one's own, and one's actions integrated and thereby one's own. Simply going along with the most vehement or spontaneous of desires hardly counts as a life at all.

From this perspective, *sôphronein* could be imagined the affective correlate of the epistemic *ginôskein heautôn*, where both amount to founding one's commitment to some action-guiding element—a desire or a belief—on good reasons. Heraclitus does not use the language of "desire" in these fragments, so we may say nothing more detailed here. In any event, these good reasons are to be found beyond the way the world presents itself immediately to one's subjectivity. In Heraclitus' language, those reasons are to be referred to the *logos*, some universal intelligible structure or account of the cosmos. How one is to perceive or conceive of this structure, it is hard to say; presumably it does not matter to his ideas about *sôphrosunê*. What seems clear is that *sôphrosunê* can be treated, with self-knowledge, as *the* virtue everyone can and should have because it is the virtue concerned with acting on the basis of what really matters, of what really is the case. The ethical consequences follow directly. The leading desideratum for a life ought not to be glory, as it was for the Homeric heroes, or a self-satisfied complacency, as Heraclitus implies it is for his contemporaries. It ought instead to be the discovery of the way the world fundamentally is and having that true nature inform how one acts. The leading desideratum for a life is truth, and *sôphrosunê* is the virtue that conforms one's actions to it.

B112: *Sôphronein* as the Greatest Virtue

If this interpretation of B116 is to get any local textual vindication, it must come through an interpretation of the other Heraclitean fragment about *sôphrosunê*, B112 (σωφρονεῖν ἀρετὴ μεγίστη καὶ σοφίη ἀληθέα λέγειν καὶ ποιεῖν κατὰ φύσιν ἐπαΐοντας). What appears as a single continuous fragment in Stobaeus has been taken to speak about *sôphrosunê* in three ways:

1. Only the first three words are relevant: it is the greatest virtue.
2. As in B116, Heraclitus implies a linkage (of uncertain meaning) between two claims, one about *sôphrosunê* and the other about wisdom.

3a. *Sôphrosunê* is both the greatest virtue and the greatest wisdom; he goes on to say more about wisdom (the following words as pendant on *sophia*).
3b. *Sôphronein* is both the greatest virtue and the greatest wisdom; he goes on to say more about *sôphrosunê* (*sôphronein* being the focalized concept).

Recent scholarship has provided the range of interpretations but not a good criterion for deciding between them.[35]

The recent critical edition mentioned above, that of Miroslav Marcovich from the 1960s, follows earlier scholarship in denying authenticity to this fragment, claiming it to be "no more than a late (probably Stoic) imitation," though Marcovich cites no evidence for this view.[36] Nevertheless, in his discussion of the fragment, Marcovich chunks it into semantic units and comments on the latter half:[37]

σ ω φ ρ ο ν ε ῖ ν ἀρετὴ μεγίστη,
καὶ σοφίη ἀληθέα λέγειν
καὶ ποιεῖν κατὰ φύσιν
ἐπαΐοντας.

Marcovich appears to believe there are several linked ideas: *sôphronein* is the greatest virtue; *sophia* is speaking the truth; there is acting in accordance with nature; and there is *epaiein* one or more aspects of the above. Marcovich glosses none of this.

Bollack and Wismann, again with Kahn the most engaged earlier commentators, punctuate differently and provide an intriguing translation:

σωφρονεῖν· ἀρετὴ μεγίστη καὶ σοφίη, ἀληθέα λέγειν καὶ ποιεῖν κατὰ φύσιν ἐπαΐοντας.

Bien-penser, c'est le plus grand exploit et l'art est là, dire des choses varies et faire que, suivant la nature, l'on écoute.

Well-thinking: it's the greatest feat and aptitude that's here, speaking of true things and doing that which, following nature, one hears.

They take the whole sentence to gloss *sôphronein*: the *megistê* clause, which defines *sôphronein*, is in turn glossed in a chiasmus: *alêthea legein* corresponds to *sophiê*, "aptitude," and *poiein* ... (that which) *epaiontas* corresponds to *aretê*.

---

[35] One exception: Rosella Schluderer (2017) provides a convincing case for following 3b.
[36] Marcovich (1967, 96). Doubt is sown over the whole interpretative history when we reflect on Diels' (1903) emendation of σωφρονεῖν to (τὸ) φρονεῖν in both B112 and B116.
[37] Marcovich (1967, 90). He does not say why he kerns σωφρονεῖν; I assume he thinks only this word is authentic, but as noted above (n6), the verb does not appear in his index.

So the greatest virtue is doing only what one hears, as instructed by nature; the greatest wisdom is speaking truthfully. Both superlatives, Bollack and Wismann cleverly observe, are paradoxical: *aretê*, traditionally associated with the exploits of warriors, is here sublimated to having good listening skills; *sophia*, traditionally associated, via *sôphrosunê*, with tactful or selective speech—they cite Telemachus' *sôphrôn* silence about his father's return to Ithaca—is replaced with transparent and forthright speech. They believe that Heraclitus proposes a new meaning of *sôphrosunê*, which according to them had generally been considered "good sense" or "sane thinking," but what that new meaning is supposed to be, they do not make especially clear. They do not cross-reference their discussion of B116.

Kahn runs into similar problems in what he judges Heraclitus' "most interesting utterance as a moral philosopher" on "the paramount virtue of his age."[38] In Kahn's official text of this fragment he punctuates with Bollack and Wismann, though dropping the initial terminal dot, and his translation follows it; but in a footnote he gives an alternative punctuation and translation:

σωφρονεῖν ἀρετὴ μεγίστη καὶ σοφίη, ἀληθέα λέγειν καὶ ποιεῖν κατὰ φύσιν ἐπαΐοντας.

Thinking well is the greatest excellence and wisdom: to act and speak what is true, perceiving things according to their nature.

σωφρονεῖν ἀρετὴ μεγίστη, καὶ σοφίη ἀληθέα λέγειν καὶ ποιεῖν κατὰ φύσιν ἐπαΐοντας.

Sound thinking is the greatest excellence, and wisdom is to speak things true and act according to nature by listening <to the *logos*>.

These two translations differ significantly, and ultimately Kahn thinks we are meant to toggle between them.[39] The first defines *sôphronein* as the greatest in two value categories (virtue and wisdom) and then explains: it amounts to the position of truthful speaking and truthful action, accompanied or allowed by what is in effect a truthful, reality-sensitive, apprehension of the world.[40] The puzzling assertions add up: *sôphronein* is both a virtue-type excellence and an epistemic state; it principally involves the avoidance of lies or nonsense or misapprehensions;

---

[38] Kahn (1979, 43 fr. XXXII). Kahn does not justify his view about *sôphrosunê*'s paramounticity. Fränkel (1975, 391) avoids difficulties and says that this fragment amounts to Heraclitus' "demand[ing] of men that they should be wide awake [and] rational."

[39] The first translation is presaged by Kirk (1962, 391), who, however, ignores the first four Greek words: "it is wisdom to say-and-act the truth, perceiving things according to their real constitution."

[40] This punctuation is now seen in, e.g., *SEP* s.v. "Heraclitus"; Rosella Schluderer (2017); Habash (2019).

it involves (the unfamiliar state of) true action; and, in an echo of B1, it requires a perceptual sensitivity.[41] The second translation, by contrast, simplifies: *sôphronein* is only a great virtue; a parallel item, wisdom, amounts to speaking truly and acting—not specifically truly but—according to nature, where the object of the listening is now to be supplied: the *logos*. These differences are dictated, first, by the shift of a comma, and second, by the disjoining of ἀληθέα from ποιεῖν, on the grounds that "doing the true" has no obvious sense. In accordance with the duck-rabbit switching of the opening of B1 (the temporal adverb in τοῦ δὲ λόγου τοῦδ ἐόντος <u>ἀεὶ</u> ἀξύνετοι can go with what proceeds or what follows), Kahn suggests that when we read the Greek of B112, we toggle between two distinct renderings, able to settle on neither of them but provoked usefully by both of them. This does not tell us much about *sôphrosunê*.[42]

I turn lastly to the most recent edition and translation of Heraclitus, found in the third volume of André Laks and Glenn W. Most's *Early Greek Philosophy*. The editors publish the fragment in two parts, D114a and b:

σωφρονεῖν ἀρετὴ μεγίστη.

To be moderate: the greatest virtue.

σοφίη ἀληθέα λέγειν καὶ ποιεῖν κατὰ φύσιν ἐπαΐοντας.

Wisdom: to speak the truth and to act in conformity with the nature [scil. of each thing], understanding it.

They comment, "These two quotations are linked in Stobaeus by an 'and' that seems to derive from Stobaeus, not Heraclitus. The grammar and meaning of the second sentence are uncertain."[43] On this editorial view, Heraclitus' only observation about *sôphronein* is its superlativity as a virtue; any connection to *sophia* is of Stobaeus' making.[44]

---

[41] Rosella Schluderer (2017, 8–9) remarks that B112 "appear[s] as B1's positive counterpart."

[42] Kahn (1979) does not note the difference between his renderings of *sôphronein* across these two translations, "thinking well" and "sound thinking" (43), nor between those in his analysis, "soundness of mind," "good sense," and "good judgment," even though they are sensible choices. He does assert that *sôphronein* is cognate with *phronein* and thus names a kind of successful thinking (41, 119), which is true enough, as we have seen in the Aeschylean evidence. But Kahn also believes, drawing on B116, that *sôphronein* is (somehow) "modeled on Delphic self-knowledge," and accordingly he explicates the first five Greek words as follows: "valor and discretion . . . in their highest form are united in thinking well, in salvaging one's thought in the self-knowledge that is also a recognition of what is common to all." (I am not sure what "salvaging" means here.) He later explicates the remaining: *sôphrosunê* involves "communicating the *logos* in 'words and deeds,' sharing with others one's perception of how things hang together in unity and are also distinguished in their own nature." This is appealing but difficult.

[43] LM 3.197.

[44] This editorial decision may follow Lebedev (2014, 411 fr. 100 Leb.). Lebedev's reasoning appears to be that we have two *gnômai* with parallel structures, one headed by *sôphronein*, the other by *sophiê*,

Their translation here charmingly captures a certain paradox: the extraordinary status of something that sounds quite ordinary, "moderation." Perhaps this is what justifies their confidence that Heraclitus would have written something so short. But it is hard to know what justifies this translation, given what we have seen in the previous chapter: the Homeric usages of *sôphrosunê* do not encourage it, and even for Pindar, where it might work, the translation seems much too general. Further, at B116 (D30), Laks and Most render the verb "thinking with moderation," which is related but not the same. So they have made a bold conjecture, but it is not one that gives us much with which to work productively.

Let us now revisit the fragment as it usually has been reported, without punctuation:

σωφρονεῖν ἀρετὴ μεγίστη καὶ σοφίη ἀληθέα λέγειν καὶ ποιεῖν κατὰ φύσιν ἐπαΐοντας

We can make a sequence of observations as we read from left to right. Only this will give the fine-grained attention to this earliest significant philosophical reflection on *sôphrosunê*:

1. σωφρονεῖν: Heraclitus uses the verbal form rather than the nominal *sôphrosunê*.

The verbal form also occurs in B112, and together they serve as the earliest extant uses of the verb. Aeschylus, along with classical-era authors, shows the commonality of the verbal form. We might suppose that commonality to depend to some extent on the verb *phronein*. It makes it easy to think of *sôphronein* as an activity, not just a state or deprivation.

2. σωφρονεῖν ἀρετή: the disposition is an *aretê*: an excellence or virtue.

This is Heraclitus' only extant use of *aretê*. From contemporary Pindaric uses, we can be confident it means "human excellence."[45] Some interpreters have assumed, like Bollack and Wismann, that *aretê* stands in for a specific human excellence, namely courage, nobility, or some other "warrior" or "manly" quality;

and also that leaving the fragment whole and punctuating after *sophiê*, with *sôphronein* the primary subject, is "tortured." Lebedev translates (in his English version of the fragments), "Self-restraint is the greatest of all virtues" and "Wisdom is to tell the truth and to act according to nature, with understanding." But Lebedev does not explain the "tortured"-ness or show that it cannot be vindicated, and does not show parallels for the putative phenomenon in Stobaeus.

[45] Slater (1969, s.v. ἀρέτη).

this would make the paradox strong. But the epigraphical evidence shows that *aretê* has an increasingly general aspect by this time.⁴⁶ It would be better to assume that, in some contexts, the salient human excellence is taken to be, say, martial skill, but that Heraclitus means to shift the frame, to a less context-dependent claim.

3. σωφρονεῖν ἀρετὴ <u>μεγίστη</u>: it is the greatest of *aretai*.

The contextless, universal claim is that the supreme virtue is (always) *sôphronein*. This would be so even for warriors, who must also manifest courage or boldness. Heraclitus may not be undercutting the value of the warrior or manly qualities; we could imagine that he asserts that a precondition of any true success by them is *sôphrosunê*. It could be that this precondition is frequently overlooked, as B116 seemed to be assuming, and Heraclitus in articulating the supremacy of *sôphrosunê* here at B112 means to draw attention to it. We have seen the plausibility of this view, even if it has never been so directly stated: in Pindar, the term *sôphrosunê* articulates the excellence of judges, the character of the life well lived, and what keeps ambition within the bounds of social agreement. (In other lyric, it represents the overall good domestic life.) In Theognis, it grounds right action and means thoughtfulness. Without a specific derogation of another virtue—justice, piety, perceptual acuity—we cannot say that Heraclitus means to replace anything with *sôphrosunê*; it is not clear, anyway, how such an argument preferring one virtue to another at the same level would work. It seems more likely that Heraclitus, sensitive to the centrality of *sôphrosunê* found in Greek culture of his age, as the capacity for reasonable and deliberate action responsive to a commonly accessible normative schema, puts words to this centrality.

4. σωφρονεῖν ἀρετὴ μεγίστη <u>καὶ σοφίη</u>: it is virtue and wisdom.

As we read from left to right, we may take *sophia* as another predicate of *sôphronein*, with "greatest" either to be distributed or not. Elsewhere in his extant fragments Heraclitus twice speaks of *sophia*. Once, he speaks of Pythagoras' "own wisdom (σοφίη)," which Heraclitus calls an "encyclopedism" (πολυμαθίη) and "deceptive dealing" (κακοτεχνίη) (B129). Here *sophia* marks a distinctive attainment in learning and competence in action. Heraclitus' charge is that Pythagoras' *sophia* is really his idiosyncratic formulations about the way the world is, with untoward consequences from his application or teaching of it. Pythagoras has an ill-gotten authority from his putative *sophia*.⁴⁷ Xenophanes,

---

⁴⁶ See Chapter 2.
⁴⁷ On this passage, see Huffman (2008); Moore (2020b, 40, 46n29, 60).

in the same period, vaunts his own *sophia* as helpful advice-giving or norm-establishing for his city.[48] In Heraclitus' other use of the *sophia* word-group, he writes that "the wisest (σοφώτατος) of men appears as a monkey with respect to a god, in wisdom (σοφίᾳ) and beauty and everything else" (B83/D77). *Sophia* represents excellence in mental capacity as beauty represents excellence in looks.

Heraclitus uses the adjective *sophos* rather more frequently than the noun—we have already seen one instance—and does so with thematic importance. Of greatest connection is his claim that a dry soul is "wisest and best" (σωφοτάτη καὶ ἀρίστη, B118/D103). Presumably the soul's excellence is largely found in its superlative wisdom, though we cannot be sure of a perfect equivalence. The dry soul is the one not bogged down, moistened by drink or any other obstacle to clear thought (B117). Indeed, the dry soul may well be the physiological correlate of or metaphor for the *sôphrôn* soul, which is thereby in the best and wisest condition.[49]

Then there are four fragments about *to sophon*—the object of wisdom, the state of being wise—and unity: that it is one, and called Zeus, and amounts to knowing the "judgment" (γνώμη) that steers all through all, and is separated from all, and leads a person, when listening to the *logos*, to say that all things are one. The unity of *to sophon* is continually repeated. The contrast evidently is with the plurality of things one might know but that do not rise to the level of *to sophon*, wisdom. Presumably a person (or soul) is *sophos*, and has *sophia*, to the extent he (or it) has access to *to sophon*, the unified way things really are, and can focus on that as providing the norms of thought and action.

So for *sôphronein* to be wisdom, or the greatest wisdom, would be for it to be what it takes to assimilate oneself to that overall *to sophon*. Perhaps this equivalence of wisdom, as comprehension of the objective and integrated cosmic order, and *sôphrosune* as the precondition for any virtuous action, is Heraclitus' big point. Xenophanes speaks of *aretê* as something parallel to the "excellent deeds" (ἐσθλά) that one might recall from memory after having drunk—in contrast to telling mythological stories.[50] These *esthla* seem to be, taking a page from Bollack and Wismann, "exploits," superb things done; *aretê* presumably is the underlying capacity to get them done. Heraclitus could be saying that *sôphronein* is an *aretê* but not one of brawn or tactical cleverness—it is the *aretê* of being governed by the way things really are and not as one adventitiously thinks of them.

5. σωφρονεῖν ἀρετὴ μεγίστη καὶ σοφίη <u>ἀληθέα λέγειν</u>: adding "true speech"

---

[48] Xenoph. B2/D61.12, 14.
[49] Cf. Johnstone (2020, 40). See Claus (1981, 122–38), Kirk, Raven, and Schofield (1983, 204–8) (cursorily), and Betegh (2007) for useful reflections on the physiological correlate of these psychological and moral states, though none mentions B112 or B116 in the context.
[50] Xenoph. B1/D59.20.

Whereas before we may have been inclined to see *sophia* as a predicate of *sôphronein*, now we must wonder. The *kai* could link two predicates on *sôphronein*, but it could instead link two independent clauses. In the first case, *alêthea legein* would be apposite to *sôphronein*: "*sôphronein* is the greatest virtue and wisdom—[the reason being that *sôphronein* involves] speaking true things." In the second case, it would be apposite only to *sophia*: "*sôphronein* is the greatest virtue and wisdom, [which latter is itself] speaking true things." Admittedly, even here, where *sophia* is the focus, the content of the latter part of the phrase may eventually redound to *sôphronein*, if *sôphronein* is the greatest wisdom.

In any event, speaking true things matters to the content of *sophia* and to *sôphronein*, whether directly or indirectly. Correct acknowledgment and non-(self)-deception is a recurring theme in the fragments of Heraclitus. He presents himself as reporting the way the world is, as a model for listening to the *logos*, which is somehow the objective articulacy of the world—*logos* is a term that combines the ideas of speaking and what's true, and then helping others to come to hear it. It is *to sophon*, wise, to say that all things are one. *Sôphrosunê* and *sophia*, to the extent they are like self-knowledge, involve acknowledging what one really desires and what one really has reasons to believe—they involve telling oneself how things really are with oneself.

6. σωφρονεῖν ἀρετὴ μεγίστη καὶ σοφίη ἀληθέα λέγειν <u>καὶ ποιεῖν κατὰ φύσιν</u>:
adding a verb of action and a qualifier, "in accordance with nature"

Another syntactic ambiguity arises: just as we wondered whether *sôphronein* takes one or two predicates, here we wonder whether the object *alêthea* takes one or two verbal subjects. Does *poiein* ("acting," "doing," "making") take *alêthea* as a sort of internal accusative object ("doing true things"); or does it take only the following, as accusatives of manner ("acting in accordance with nature"); or does it do both, with the latter explanatory of the former ("doing true things, that is, in accordance with nature")?

The third choice seems best. The perceived oddity of "doing true things" might be lessened by thinking of *poiein* as "making," even "creating," which then tightens the parallel with "speaking." A case of "speaking" is true when its articulations track the structure of the world; thus "creating," as a more general category of articulation than speaking, could also be true in tracking the structure of the world. The prepositional phrase *kata phusin* will thus explain how one may both speak and make true things—namely, by doing so in accordance with nature, which is how things really are. Accordingly, *sôphrosunê* would involve speaking and creating in a way that reflects the actual state of nature, which is to say, truly. Thus it is the background for any virtue, whether intellectual or practical, elocutionary or artistic, peacetime or martial: acting in accordance with the highest norms, not whatever desires or inclinations one might have.

7. σωφρονεῖν ἀρετὴ μεγίστη καὶ σοφίη ἀληθέα λέγειν καὶ ποιεῖν κατὰ φύσιν ἐπαΐοντας: adding a final participle of cognition

There is a final word, *epaiontas* ("giving ear to," "perceiving," "understanding"). It is a masculine plural accusative participle, with accordingly no obvious (plural) subject. Could the implied subject be "those who understand," such that *sôphronein* (etc.) is speaking and making true things, in accordance with nature, so to speak "among those who realize [what that nature is]"?[51] However it is to be construed, this participle appears to be introducing a component of self-knowledge: one is *sôphrôn* when one acts correctly *knowingly*, not merely adventitiously.[52]

In brief, and in rapprochement with B112, then, *sôphrosunê* is the condition for any virtuous action; it is the wisdom that recognizes the essentiality of following the integrated and unified nature of things; and it is akin to self-knowledge in the recognition that good action and thought requires this ability to know, not merely to react to whatever mental states happen to populate oneself at any moment.

A Virtue of Normative Self-Constitution

Heraclitus distinguishes himself from earlier authors by talking about *sôphrosunê*, not just using the term, and also by making explicit its superlative status in human affairs. In B112, calling it the greatest *aretê*, he links it with wisdom, speaking and acting the truth in accordance with nature, and perceiving all of this. In B116, he lists it with self-knowledge as the perquisites—and implicitly the aspirations—of all humans. Nothing about these fragments tells against their authenticity, and they complement his other fragments about wisdom and self-scrutiny. By themselves somewhat inscrutable, once we gave the fragments' instances of *sôphronein* content from the term's application in Homer, Theognis, and Pindar, we saw Heraclitus to be vaunting *sôphrosunê* as the virtue of epistemic agency. In the case of B112, knowing oneself seems realized upon recognizing oneself as a knower, one potentially sensitive to norms of reasoning and truth and not merely reactive or in thrall to feeling and presupposition. *Sôphrosunê*

---

[51] This syntactical reading is supported by Rossella Schluderer (2017, 8–9), though the final participle plays little role in her ultimate interpretation of the fragment.
[52] Cf. Pl. *Chrm.* 164a–d.

seemed best understood as the affective or ethical correlate of this capacity to be guided by epistemic norms: the capacity to be guided by principles of reality, which include principles of value. Appreciation of these principles amounts to wisdom and takes the *logos* as its proper object. This is basically the story told in B116: *sôphrosunê* amounts to wisdom, articulated as perceiving how the world really is (κατὰ φύσιν ἐπαΐοντας), and thereby speaking and acting in line with its actual norms, "what's true" (ἀληθέα). The person with *sôphrosunê* represents the exception to Heraclitus' dour judgment of people castigated in B1, who fail to appreciate how things are despite being told, fail to act as though experienced and thus be norm-guided by speech and acts that accord with nature, and fail to treat the objective world, rather than their private and idiosyncratic dreams, as the proper authority for them.

Heraclitus might be said to advance a view of *sôphrosunê* as a virtue of self-constitution, even of agency: the competence to make of oneself what a human being can fully be, which includes being responsible for one's actions and beliefs. Still, this is conjectural and indeterminate, since Heraclitus does not give explicit expansion, justification, or defense against alternative views. In the next several chapters we will see debates about and investigations into the nature and importance of *sôphrosunê*. Only as we enter the fourth century will we see what we might term systematic "theorizing" about *sôphrosunê*. But depending on one's taste for fragmentary philosophy, perhaps we have already seen the kernel of such theory. Given Heraclitus' adversarial stance in many of his fragments, we may even suppose we have already seen one side of an already running debate about its nature.

4
Tragic *Sôphrosunê* in Two Plays of Euripides

Vaunting *Sôphrosunê* without Fully Understanding It

The *Medea* asks: Who is *sôphrôn*? Could it be Medea, vociferously indignant though righteously so, who, after much deliberation, plans to kill her offspring and does so successfully? Could it be Jason, who glibly abandons his wife to marry into Creon's powerful family, through which he can establish his children in a prosperous life? Is it Creon himself, who allows his daughter to marry Jason? It depends on the meaning of the laudation and even more on the motivations of the person. As we saw in the first chapter, one dramatic conflict in the play depends on the discernment and especially the obscuration of those *sôphrosunê*-related motivations. But we would exaggerate if we were to say that the play was *about sôphrosunê*—that is, that the characters took the virtue as their directing life-ideal but that they disagreed about their or others' attainment of it.

Yet for two other of Euripides' plays, the nature and exemplification of *sôphrosunê* do serve as leading themes. These are plays wherein characters take *sôphrosunê* to be the "greatest virtue," but they do not agree what that virtue commands, either for themselves or for others. Heraclitus' vaunting of *sôphrosunê*, studied in the previous chapter, makes this a conceivable position, and also points to the problems that arise in so taking it. In taking *sôphrosunê* to be best, one may derogate other virtues as worse; in taking oneself to be *sôphrôn*, one may forgive or even justify one's weaknesses as its corollaries. These are plays whose drama depends, wonderfully enough, on conflicting moral ideals: what the good life, under *sôphrosunê*'s aegis, should look like. Together, these plays provide the most vibrant and incisive inquiry into the substance of *sôphrosunê* from the period. None promulgates a theory of *sôphrosunê*, but they do illuminate the main considerations for any such theory and they put special pressure on less promising perspectives on the virtue.

The first of these post-*Medea* plays is *Hippolytus*, from 428, though evidently rewritten from an earlier play of unknown date; the second, *Bacchae*, comes more than two decades later, at the end of Euripides' life. So a concern for *sôphrosunê* spans Euripides' mature career; evidence from the fragments of his lost plays suggests that he wrote even more on the theme.¹ From these two plays we cannot infer an evolution in Euripides' thinking about *sôphrosunê*, or even an evolution in the background debate about the virtue. What we can know are the contours of Euripides' inquiry into its central role in human flourishing and the appeal these issues had to his audience. Of special concern are two issues: the connection between *sôphrosunê* and the proper reverence of the divine, and the assimilation of *sôphrosunê* to chastity or the experience of love. These might be formulated, if blandly and selectively, as *sôphrosunê*'s expression as purity and as reasonableness. In either case, the debates about the duties of *sôphrosunê* concern how we might fit ourselves into a normative order not of our own making and what attitude we might take toward those of our desires with which we do not wholly identify. Both are problems of self-constitution, the one outward-looking (what standing principles guide my maturation) and the other inward-looking (how do my feelings relate to my decisions).

The *Hippolytus*' title character characterizes himself as superlatively *sôphrôn*; for him the virtue amounts to a free-and-easy chastity—he apparently feels no erotic attachments—and the veneration of a favored god, in his case Artemis. His stepmother, Phaedra, also takes herself as *sôphrôn*, but for her this is the competence to overcome violent sexual desire, even at the cost of self-destruction. Phaedra's nurse-attendant advances a third vision of *sôphrosunê*, as the capacity to think through tough circumstances and find the best life-saving compromise. All three glosses on the *sôphrosunê* ideal—the absence of inner struggle, the mastery of inner turmoil, and reasoning about what to do—reflect fifth-century ways of thinking about *sôphrosunê*, as we saw in the first chapter. Euripides does not integrate them, and he does not obviously reject any of them, but the play's tragic conclusion suggests that one perhaps should try.

In the *Bacchae*, Pentheus scorns the Bacchic religious frenzy that has overcome his Theban kingdom, seeing it as a failure of women's *sôphrosunê*: they are obscuring their sexual indiscretion behind a real or fabricated madness. For Pentheus, *sôphrosunê* is especially sexual restraint and a calm, collected comportment. Dionysus, by contrast, sees *sôphrosunê* as the proper acknowledgment of the gods, whatever the behavioral adjuncts to that acknowledgment may be. Unlike in the *Hippolytus*, here Euripides seems to side with one character, Dionysus; Pentheus has a profound comeuppance. But this does not make it simpler to understand *sôphrosunê*: the issue of sexual continence is sidelined, and in its place a new paradox is raised, the possible coincidence of *mania* and *sôphrosunê*, elsewhere evident opposites.²

---

[1] At least *Hypsipyle* frr. 757.829–30, 868–80, 946–49 (= fr. 759); *Oedipus* frr. 543, 545, 545a, 547–48, 552. For *sôphrosunê* in Euripides generally, see North (1966, 68–84); Rademaker (2005, 143–90).

[2] This paradoxical coincidence is raised again in Plato's *Phaedrus*; see Scott (2011).

Hippolytus

Euripides' *Hippolytus* dramatizes the deaths of Phaedra and her stepson Hippolytus as both direct their lives toward *sôphrosunê*. Hippolytus celebrates his own lack of sexual passion, but the goddess Aphrodite, piqued by his dismissal of her charms, avenges herself by inciting Phaedra's sexual passion for him. Phaedra prevents herself from throwing herself upon him, and protects her reputation for perfect sexual restraint, only by suicide and a fatal false accusation against him. The play's fascination comes from its ambiguous portrayal of these two characters: we wonder whether they have done the best they can, entangled as they are in divine jealousies, or whether they misunderstood the crucial norms of human life. The secondary characters with whom they must speak, since the primary characters are prevented by their respective *sôphrosunê* from speaking with one another, are drawn with similar ambiguity: do they have more sensible attitudes toward *sôphrosunê* and life in general, or does their facile confidence belie a superficial appreciation of human ideals or cowardice about their demands?[3]

The flip side of the play's being about *sôphrosunê* is that it is about love. It raises two linked questions: How necessary is love for one's well-being and, to the extent love is out of one's control, how tolerable is it? Hippolytus thinks love is not necessary; Phaedra finds it uncontrollable and thereby intolerable. Phaedra's attendant suggests some ways for Phaedra to tolerate it; Hippolytus' father suggests some ways that Hippolytus misconstrues well-being.

Euripides' lesson, as I read the play, is that whatever *sôphrosunê* is, it must take into account all three (or more) pictures of *sôphrosunê* mentioned above: a holiness and purity that involves the absence of harmful desires, a competence to act on some rather than others of one's complex milieu of desires, and a reflective attitude toward one's situation and long-term goals that allows for creative compromise and doing the best one can. The disaster that strikes each character is related to the intensity of their commitment to *sôphrosunê*. So attractive has the virtue become to them that they require it to take two inconsistent forms. For *sôphrosunê* to be something they can strive to attain, the virtue must be cast narrowly; for it to be something they can justify striving to attain, it must be cast broadly. So it must be, on the one hand, simply keeping the erotic life at bay, or not acting on what erotic impulses one has, or acting on those impulses in as safe

---

[3] Knox (1952, 3–4) argues for the equal importance of all four characters. The present approach to the play has most resonance with the studies by Zeitlin (1985); Goldhill (1986, 118–37, esp. 134: "the correct attitude of mind and observance of bounds and limits in terms of the vocabulary of *sôphronein* and *phronein* is an extremely important part of the discourse of sexuality and the self in this drama"); Gill (1990); Cairns (1993, 317–40); During (2021).

a way as possible; but it must also be, on the other hand, that which provides a total framework for a life well lived.[4]

Hippolytus' Problem

The play starts with a plot overview, from the perspective of a certain interested and powerful party. This is Aphrodite, who says that she esteems those who revere (τοὺς μὲν σέβοντες) her but trips up those who are conceited toward her (σφάλλω δ' ὅσοι φρονοῦσιν εἰς ἡμᾶς μέγα).[5] Hippolytus is included among the latter: he disdains her as "worst of the divinities" (κακίστην δαιμόνων) and avoids sex and marriage.[6] So he does not revere her, and he believes he need not live that aspect of life over which she rules. He spends his time instead in revering Artemis, his companion in the hunt.[7] Aphrodite says she will punish Hippolytus for this; it will be in an ironic way. She will not force him to feel *erôs*; he will instead be mortally cursed by his father for his suspicion that his son felt *erôs* toward his stepmother. The curse will arise from Phaedra's feeling a terrible love (ἔρωτι δεινῷ) that, given her own *sôphrosunê*, as we learn, motivates her suicide and a false explanation for that suicide.[8]

Aphrodite finds Hippolytus irreverent and self-aggrandizing, worthy of death.[9] Her view is that reverence demands attention to all the gods and their domains of life, in her case including love; her view is that one cannot pick and choose among the gods one wishes to favor. Rectitude—and more specifically *sôphrosunê*, though she does not mention the term—is not achieved by the wholesale avoidance of certain attachments. To be sure, the authority of Aphrodite could be put into question.[10] But nothing else in the play suggests that Euripides dismisses Aphrodite's or the gods' claims in general. In the world of

---

[4] There is good reason to believe that the present was the second *Hippolytus* written by Euripides, where the first represented Phaedra as rather less restrained. For the significance Euripides' rewrite has to a study of *sôphrosunê*, see Barrett (1964, 10–45); Zeitlin (1985, 52–56); Carson (2006, 309–12).

[5] Eur. *Hipp*. 5–6. On the language of "undermining" or "tripping up" (σφάλλειν) throughout the play, see Knox (1952, 25–27).

[6] Eur. *Hipp*. 13.

[7] Eur. *Hipp*. 15–19. Artemis as representative of *sôphrosunê*: North (1979, 66–67). On Hippolytus' failed desire to match her divinity: Segal (1979).

[8] Eur. *Hipp*. 28; 38–50.

[9] Linforth (1914): Hippolytus has committed a sin against human nature; the goddesses represent those laws. Rishel (2020, 206–7): Hippolytus as charioteer fits an ancient trope connected to moderation; he restrains his horses too much, to his detriment.

[10] Euripides' epistemic attitude toward the gods is felt as especially pressing in this play. Aren't the deaths of two people a baldly excessive response to a self-sufficiency expressed by a young aficionado of the sporting life? If so, Euripides could be thought to be speaking to the unreasonableness of the *erôs* for which Aphrodite stands. From this Aphrodite-skeptical perspective, Hippolytus is not immoral, just imprudent—it's dangerous, not impious, to try to keep *erôs*-free. For discussion, see, e.g., Norwood (1954, 91–109).

the play, the gods should all be reverenced; humans should not think they know better; and humans should (allow themselves to) feel *erôs*.

The view of Aphrodite, expressed in the first divinity scene, is mirrored by that of Hippolytus' servant in the first human scene. The servant chastises Hippolytus for his favoritism; he thinks it inappropriate for Hippolytus to ignore a venerable goddess (σεμνὴν δαίμον'), one venerated and distinguished (σεμνην ... κἀπίσημος) among mortals.[11] Though Hippolytus accepts the principles of social comity on which his servant tries to build up this argument—that we should avoid haughtiness and embrace affability—he dismisses the particular worry about Aphrodite. Comprehensive religious fealty, he says, is a matter not of obligation but of tastes, and tastes differ: he, who considers himself "pure" (ἁγνός), does not care for those "worshipped at night."[12] (Hippolytus is a kind of observant Pentheus of the *Bacchae*, one who takes religious matters under his own consideration.) Euripides is here drawing a stark contrast between the servant's acknowledgment of norms—the "rule set down by mortals" (βροτοῖσιν ὃς καθέστηκεν νόμος) and "rules concerning the gods" (θεῶν νόμοισι)—and Hippolytus' freedom of conscience.[13] That conflict is stressed by the servant's relative maturity and conscientiousness and his formulation of Hippolytus' heterodoxy as, in effect, youthful thoughtlessness verging on hubris: Hippolytus needs to "apply his mind" (νοῦν ἔχων); he "has intense gut feelings and is speaking to no purpose" (σπλάγχνον ἔντονον φέρων | μάταια βάζει).[14] He reads Hippolytus' shirking of Aphrodite's charms as willful but naïve self-assertion founded on a self-appointed religious expertise.

The servant's intervention is a response to Hippolytus' opening reverie, a bucolic praise of Artemis. Hippolytus describes the hunting grounds where he assembled a flowery garland for her. This meadow, tended or sheltered by *aidôs*, as he says, permits only those with *sôphrosunê* "in all things always/alike" (εἰς τὰ πάντ' ἀεί) to pluck its produce; those who are bad may not.[15] Hippolytus

---

[11] Eur. *Hipp.* 107; 99, 103.
[12] Eur. *Hipp.* 102, 106; on purity and its connections to *sôphrosunê* in the play, see Segal (1970).
[13] Eur. *Hipp.* 91, 98.
[14] Eur. *Hipp.* 105; 118. A callow and problematic youth, principled but immature: e.g., Cairns (1993, 317–21). For the theme of hubris throughout the play: Fisher (1992, 412–18). Festugière (1954, 13) disagrees with the servant's (and many others') assessment: "There is nothing morbid in his case. He is perfectly normal. He simply does not yet think about love." That is because Festugière finds appealing Hippolytus' striving for communion with Artemis, for a personal religious engagement. Festugière's argument would have more attraction were the debated virtue-term *eusebeia* rather than the secular and broad-reaching *sôphrosunê*. Davies (2000) provides a more qualified version of this "pro-Hippolytus" perspective. Carson (2006, 166) finds a problem with this view: Hippolytus is simply mistaken about his beloved Artemis, who stands for more than virginity: "Gods are big. Gods can enlarge us. Artemis' view of what's good for Hippolytus is much bigger than his own; her view of sexuality sees virtue in virginity and marriage both. Flesh and change make sense to her as part of the workings of necessity, beyond human control."
[15] Eur. *Hipp.* 78–81: Αἰδὼς δὲ ποταμίαισι κηπεύει δρόσοις, | ὅσοις διδακτὸν μηδὲν ἀλλ' ἐν τῆι φύσει | τὸ σωφρονεῖν εἴληχεν ἐς τὰ πάντ' ἀεί, | τούτοις δρέπεσθαι, τοῖς κακοῖσι δ' οὐ θέμις. There are textual difficulties here—Kovacs (1995 ad loc.) proposes ὁμῶς in place of ἀεί—but on any

finishes this praise with the wish that, in his wholesale and unique dedication to Artemis, he may never change, even as he grows old.[16] Hippolytus has thus ascribed *sôphrosunê* to himself; treated its opposite as *kakia*, "badness"; and nearly equated *sôphrosunê* with *aidôs*, the latter usually thought the youthful comportment of the innocent. In describing the hunting ground as having been untouched by human interference and the flower-pickers as untouched by learning, he offers up a vision of virtue as a primal naturalness, a disposition prior to sociality or deliberate self-cultivation. Hippolytus seems to equate erotic attraction with artifice and decadence, a departure from the state of nature. He believes that the good life, one governed by *aidôs* and *sôphrosunê*, always avoids intense (marital or erotic) attachment. He seems to be pursuing an ideal of an original independent self-sufficiency, an autonomy from the claims of others, an uncomplicated mastery by oneself.[17] We see that he does not forsake pleasure altogether, or even companionship: his parting command to his servant is for him to prepare a meal: "a pleasure is, after a hunt, a full table."[18] But he desires, so it seems, always to be in command of himself; and both a god and a human have warned against this desire. The ideal of unimpeded agency is put into question.

Phaedra's Problem

Euripides juxtaposes to the archetypally free young man his exact opposite: the obstructed, self-defeating adult woman. We now see Phaedra in all her terrible excruciations: she is ill; she wants to die; she will not say what is wrong. The Chorus, baffled, diagnoses her with a feminine imbalance—"women's nature is an uneasy harmony, and with it is wont to dwell the painful unhappy helplessness of birth pangs and their folly (ἀφροσύνη)"—and, perhaps ironically, says that it has called on Artemis for succor.[19] Phaedra's nurse, for her part, bemoans Phaedra's mercuriality, always desiring what she now lacks and always requesting

---

reconstruction, Hippolytus seems to be taking a hard line, contrasting those who are totally *sôphrôn* with those who are *kakos*. (Barrett 1964, 172, who makes this observation, captures the breadth of Hippolytean *sôphrosunê* by translating it as "virtue" and defending that translation.) Note that Hippolytus allows a range of ways of being *sôphrôn*.

[16] Eur. *Hipp.* 87.
[17] Hippolytus' vision of self-sufficient agency is a profound theme of this play; see, e.g., Segal (1965, 220: "[Hippolytus'] life is a pure expression of the masculine desire to re-form his world, to make himself as free as possible of the physical and animal exigencies of his existence, to which women must yield.... His freedom is ultimately the spiritual freedom men have always sought"); Goldhill (1986, 118–21).
[18] Eur. *Hipp.* 109–10. See also Winnington-Ingram (1958, 173).
[19] Eur. *Hipp.* 131–69.

a change to her situation. She would bear her illness more easily, says the nurse, were she to do it with more calm (μετά ... ἡσυχίας).[20]

As Phaedra's delirium climaxes, she wails about going to the hunting grounds to be with Artemis.[21] This is craziness, the nurse says repeatedly.[22] When Phaedra comes to, she agrees: she lost her "good judgment" (γνώμης ἀγαθῆς) as she descended into a divinity-caused madness.[23] Nevertheless, she acknowledges her shame (αἰδούμεθα, αἰσχύνην) at what has happened, and recognizes a distinctive bind.[24] Knowing what's really going on (ὀρθοῦσθαι γνώμην) is painful, but losing that painful knowledge in a crazed state is bad; it would be best not to know anything at all (μὴ γιγνώσκοντ'), which death would allow.[25] Sanity requires acknowledging how things actually stand with oneself, owning up to oneself, and this is the normative state. But Phaedra does not feel up to maintaining that sanity, with the continued self-disclosure and consequent horror of herself that it requires. To a disgusting closeness she prefers silent self-annihilation.

The nurse moots a plausible alternative, a compromise between a suffocating self-proximity and a liberating self-destruction: a kind of psychical distance.[26] She observes that one should distinguish oneself from one's social affection (φιλία)—one should not identify with it too wholeheartedly and too irrevocably. It should be held in measure (μετρίας), "nothing too much" (μηδὲν ἄγαν). This does not mean avoiding or extirpating strong feelings—sometimes one must "draw them tight" (ξυντεῖναι) to oneself—but rather being able to modulate the degree of one's identification with them. The nurse thus advises a new attitude toward oneself: do not conflate oneself with one's passions; instead, choose when and whether to act on them. Do not flee the social world and its overlaid web of sentiments; see oneself as apart from and superior to those sentiments. Here we have a plausible and sincere view of one's self-relating agency that offers, if indirectly (the nurse has been speaking of herself rather than of Phaedra, whose problem she does not yet know), something of a solution to Phaedra's bind. Phaedra should not take

---

[20] Eur. *Hipp*. 205. The connection between *sôphrosunê* and *hêsuchia* is common; see Chapter 5.
[21] Eur. *Hipp*. 215–22, 228–31.
[22] Eur. *Hipp*. 214, 223, 232, 238.
[23] Eur. *Hipp*. 240.
[24] These terms for shame are at 244, 246.
[25] Eur. *Hipp*. 244–49.
[26] Eur. *Hipp*. 250–66. The nurse in *Hippolytus* has long had a bad reputation for her "sophistic" and even amoral, or immoral, position: see, e.g., Linforth (1914, 7: "endowed with a far duller sense of right and wrong"); Knox (1952, 10, 18–21); Norwood (1954, 74, 76, 81–83, 87: "narrow in mind," "comfortably corrupt," "this masterpiece of triviality completes her descent," "unseemly foolishness"); Segal (1965, 178–82; somewhat more generous in 1970, at 281, but skeptical at 282 and 291); Goldhill (1986, 128, 131, 136). This view might be encouraged by the failure of her love-potion scheme, as though this shows her utter corruptness. It is also accorded to her reasoning that Phaedra should try to keep on living rather than simply adhere to an impossible ideal, as though Phaedra's is the only properly "moral" stance. But as I try to show in these next paragraphs, her position is no less reasonable, and no less an ethical analysis of *sôphrosunê*, than Phaedra's (or Hippolytus'), and so Euripides is showing an ethical debate rather than lambasting one side as anti-ethical.

her affection so unbearably to heart, with its removal requiring the extinction of herself. Rather than seeing herself *as* her affections, she should treat them as adventitious, even foreign, and thus up to her whether to act on them, acknowledge them as meaningful, or do neither. She should use her rationality not to accept the full brunt of her passions but instead to perceive each passion *as* a passion, an externality internalized, something that need not on its own obligate a response. The nurse sees a self aside from its desires.

Phaedra does not respond to her attendant's speech—it takes a mention of Hippolytus to get her going and to reveal to the nurse that she can still think straight (φρονεῖς εὖ).[27] But this impression is short-lived: Phaedra comes soon to reveal her love for her stepson.[28] It is at this point that *sôphrosunê* is first mentioned in their exchange, though we have surmised its relevance so far. Aghast, and speaking of her mistress, the nurse spits out, "The *sôphrones*, albeit not willingly, love evils anyway."[29] The earlier time we saw *sôphrosunê* in the play, Hippolytus cited it as the character of the person who could frolic alone on the hunting grounds, uncorrupted by social intimacies. Here the use is even more general: the character of those who could live without intentionally desiring what is bad. So it involves (intentionally) comporting oneself with ethical norms. In the nurse's judgment, *sôphrosunê* characterizes Phaedra. But appreciating authoritative norms is consistent with feeling pulls in another direction. This love for Hippolytus has interposed itself in Phaedra's life. Phaedra has taken it seriously enough, as the nurse sees, to reveal it to be motivationally relevant to her. *Sôphrôn* as the nurse may know Phaedra to be, as guided as she may be by legitimate norms, the nurse realizes, nevertheless, that Phaedra is showing herself too weak to overcome that love.

The Nurse's Challenge

We now come to the central debate between Phaedra and her nurse. In a powerful speech, Phaedra justifies her self-annihilation as the only justified response to her passion for Hippolytus. The Chorus sees that she means that *sôphrosunê* demands this response; it praises the virtue and its appearance— "what a fine thing is *sôphrosunê* (τὸ σῶφρον) everywhere and how splendid is the repute it gains among mortals."[30] The nurse, by contrast, says that *sôphrosunê* demands something else: not a severe and uncompromising rigor but rather an

---

[27] Eur. *Hipp.* 313.
[28] Eur. *Hipp.* 347.
[29] Eur. *Hipp.* 358–59. The nurse is thinking about Phaedra alone; the plural generalizes the ethical point: Barrett (1964 ad 49).
[30] Eur. *Hipp.* 431–32: τὸ σῶφρον ὡς ἀπανταχοῦ καλὸν | καὶ δόξαν ἐσθλὴν ἐν βροτοῖς καρπίζεται.

acknowledgment of human imperfection and the impossibility of predicting the future. Whereas Phaedra idolizes *sôphrosunê* as a sensitivity to exceptionless social norms, here about sexual propriety, to be followed at the cost of death, the nurse sees it as a skill of prudent self-government, giving due weight to what we can and cannot do, what we can and cannot know.

Phaedra begins her speech with a general observation concerning a mismatch between human competence and human action: many people, despite thinking well (εὖ φρονεῖν) and having good judgment (γνώμη), bring themselves to fare or do badly (πράσσειν κάκιον).[31] The observation is so general that we do not know whether she includes herself in or excludes herself from this group, and thus whether she means to explain her own faring badly or how she differs from the others who *do* fare badly. (The ambiguity may be intentional, as a matter of dramatic irony: she may misunderstand her relative position.) In either case, Phaedra seems to be describing the risk that thoughtfulness is not enough for living well, a risk she has striven to avoid.

A problem with mortals, Phaedra says in her development of the observation, is that what we know and recognize to be noble (ἃ χρηστ' ἐπιστάμεσθα καὶ γιγνώσκειν) we do not labor hard to bring about (ἐκπονοῦμεν). Sometimes this is from idleness (ἀργίας), but sometimes it is from failing to give priority (προθέντες) to the pleasures that come from what's admirable (τοῦ καλοῦ).[32] These are two ways of being inadequately active: not having the energy to act on what one takes to be a decisive reason for action and not directing one's authorizing gaze toward the more admirable if not necessarily more immediately appealing reason for action. The latter looks more pertinent to *sôphrosunê*.

Phaedra's general account is clear so far, and she will soon explain why she decided on suicide, but she interposes a reflection on pleasure. This reflection has a famous interpretative crux that concerns *aidôs*, and by extension *sôphrosunê*:

εἰσὶ δ' ἡδοναὶ πολλαὶ βίου,
μακραί τε λέσχαι καὶ σχολή, τερπνὸν κακόν,
αἰδώς τε· δισσαὶ δ' εἰσίν, ἡ μὲν οὐ κακή,
ἡ δ' ἄχθος οἴκων· εἰ δ' ὁ καιρὸς ἦν σαφής,
οὐκ ἂν δύ' ἤστην ταὔτ' ἔχοντε γράμματα. (Eur. *Hipp.* 383–87)

and there are many pleasures in life,
long conversations and leisure—a bad enjoyment—
and *aidôs*: and there are two, one not bad,

---

[31] Eur. *Hipp.* 377–78. See Gill (2005, 159–71) for *akrasia* in Euripides and interpretative issues concerning the type of *akrasia* at issue.
[32] Eur. *Hipp.* 379–80.

and the other a burden on houses. But if the situation were clear,
there would not be two [things] having the same letters.

Phaedra has been explaining how lives go badly: people either fail to do what they realize is right, or they pursue the wrong pleasure. She takes up the second option: there are, after all, many different pleasures. She gives two examples, evidently one contrary to the *kalon* (what's admirable), the other associated with it.[33] The first, negative example is long and leisurely talks; this is suggested to her by her nurse's loquacity, as becomes clear when, after the nurse's next speech, she calls her speech "too admirable" (καλοὶ λίαν) and "enjoyable" (τερπνά).[34] Too much talk—whether of rapport-building, deliberation, or whatever—interferes with action. The second, positive example is *aidôs*; this has probably been suggested by Phaedra's own experience of it.[35] It has been long debated what kind of pleasure might pertain to *aidôs*, but if virtuous action is pleasurable for the virtuous—Hippolytus sure seems to enjoy his purity—and *aidôs* is something like a virtue, then we have our solution.[36] The profound and more sustainable pleasure of virtuous activity is the theme of Prodicus' *Choice of Heracles* as well as of Democritus, as we will see in the next chapter. At any rate, Phaedra says that there are two kinds of pleasure, one that is not bad (such as *aidôs*) and the other that is (such as chitchat).[37] This is a problem for human decision: we do not always distinguish between the two kinds of pleasure, and thinking they are both "not bad," we may happen to prefer a bad one to a good one. Thus people end up ruining themselves because, while they could understand what it would be best to do, they think the pleasures consequent to, say, temporizing are better (because easier or more immediate) than those consequent to embodying *aidôs* and thus acting correctly, and so prefer to temporize than to act.

---

[33] Kovacs (1980, 298–300) conjectures a long lacuna, with missing instances of pleasures; this conjecture is unnecessary (as Kovacs in fact appreciates).

[34] Eur. *Hipp.* 487–88, cf. 503–6. Phaedra's very speech, in its theoretical elaboration, may suggest that she too enjoys long discussions. Aristotle criticizes excessive talk, though he says that we call this "babbling" rather than "undisciplined" (τοὺς γὰρ φιλομύθους καὶ διηγητικοὺς καὶ περὶ τῶν τυχόντων κατατρίβοντας τὰς ἡμέρας ἀδολέσχας, ἀκολάστους δ' οὐ λέγομεν, *EN* 3.10 1117b33–1118a1).

[35] Eur. *Hipp.* 239–49.

[36] In Plato's *Philebus*, the *sôphrôn* person explicitly gets pleasure from *to sôphronein* (12d1–4); see Moore (2015c, 189–93); cf. Cairns (1993, 328–31) for the *Hippolytus* case. Contrast Williams (1993, 227), who calls the good *aidôs* simply "a social pleasure—a comfort or reassurance." Barrett (1964, 229–31) thinks that Phaedra does not call either form of *aidôs* pleasurable (the Greek having an anacoluthon, Phaedra forgetting her construction), only that one is the virtue that inhibits self-assertion, the other the vice of indecision.

[37] This interpretation is controversial; textually it is unclear whether *dissai* refers to *aidôs* or *hedonê*. For two *aidôs*, see, among a much wider debate, Dodds (1925); Barrett (1964, 229–31); Segal (1970, 283–92); Goldhill (1986, 135); Craik (1993); Williams (1993, 225–30). For two *hedonai*, see, e.g., Kovacs (1980); Cairns (1993, 322–36). Generally: Fitton (1967, 40–42).

With this theoretical prelude articulated, Phaedra goes on to describe her own efforts to be good. This is the work of keeping her love for Hippolytus both inactive and private; its publicity could be as bad as its consummation—or worse? First, she strove to be silent.[38] This would address the privacy issue; maybe she also thought the passion would go away, or at least become bearable. But silence didn't work: either she was still too public in her travails—and she did eventually speak her love to her nurse—or the passion did not die down. So, second, she strove "to bear well the thoughtlessness, prevailing over it by *sôphrosunê*" (τὴν ἄνοιαν εὖ φέρειν | τῷ σωφρονεῖν νικῶσα).[39] This step gets little discussion, but since it is the last step before suicide, it must reflect a psychologically important moment.[40] She describes her problem as an *anoia*, "thoughtlessness, mindlessness, lack of reason," rather than as her having a desire whose power has compelled certain undesired actions. The issue, then, as she sees it, is her inability to employ her capacity to decide what to do. She has tried to recover that capacity by means of *sôphrosunê*.[41] Phaedra thus presents *sôphrosunê* not as passion-quashing but as *anoia*-reversal. Naturally, regaining the capacity for judgment may require one's lessening the felt urgency of a passion (as we saw Aristotle describe it in Chapter 2), but she places the emphasis on the capacity that the passion is inhibiting. After all, without that capacity, a minimized passion is irrelevant. *Sôphrosunê* turns out to be the capacity to decide what to do, to aim for *to kalon*, to be *aidôs*—to venerate what is worthy of veneration.[42]

Sôphrosunê, Phaedra says, did not in the end prevail against her passion (Κύπριν κρατῆσαι), so she deemed it best to kill herself.[43] Remarkably, she takes herself to have decided this well, on the basis of strong of reasons—she says that "nobody would controvert" her (οὐδεὶς ἀντερεῖ)—and so she cannot be said to have succumbed to mindlessness! This would suggest that she retains

---

[38] Eur. *Hipp.* 394–97.
[39] Eur. *Hipp.* 398–99.
[40] It also gets little discussion in the scholarship, as Barrett (1964 ad 398–99) exemplifies: he says almost nothing except that Phaedra went from hoping the passion would die down (while being concealed) to wanting "actively to fight against it."
[41] *Sôphrosunê* and *anoia* are familiar close opposites: Eur. fr. 545 (*Oedipus*) (πᾶσα γὰρ δούλη πέφυκεν ἀνδρὸς ἡ σώφρων γυνή· | ἡ δὲ μὴ σώφρων ἀνοίᾳ τὸν ξυνόνθ' ὑπερφρονεῖ; "For every *sôphrôn* wife is naturally slave of her husband; the non-*sôphrôn* one despises her partner from *anoia*"); and Thg. 453–54 (εἰ γνώμης ἔλαχες μέρος ὥσπερ ἀνοίης | καὶ σώφρων οὕτως ὥσπερ ἄφρων ἐγένου; "if you had a portion of *gnômê* as of *anoia*, | and were so *sôphrôn* as you were *aphrôn*").
[42] Compare Norwood (1954, 84–85), in wholly different vocabulary: "*Sophrosyne* is no more 'temperance,' the refusal of self-indulgence.... [It is] chastity sword in hand, the cherishing of instincts, emotions, and thoughts that not only restrain but fortify: a vibrant loyalty to husband and children, but also, and even more, to one's own personality as utterly intimate and precious, whose annulment is damnation." Norwood seek to capture the way *sôphrosunê* amounts to the realization of one's deepest commitments: "The sense of abstract Right, as a conception of the individual spirit and a guide of individual conduct... dominates Phaedra." Admittedly, Winnington-Ingram (1958, 177) does make Phaedra's plight—her use of *to sôphronein* against "certain antecedents and circumstances," which was almost sure to fail—look quite pathetic.
[43] Eur. *Hipp.* 401–2.

some *sôphrosunê*, even if she fears a flare-up of her passion, and deems such a flare-up, whatever its form, to be absolutely unacceptable.[44] Her *aidôs* retains its efficacy, at least now, in a cool moment, away from Hippolytus.

Near the end of her speech Phaedra focalizes *sôphrosunê* again. She says that she detests those women who are *sôphrôn* in the way they speak but secretly harbor a daring that, to the contrary, is not admirable.[45] She means to avoid being one of them, who can speak of noble norms and sound actions but fail to live accordingly. Phaedra's speech has thus concerned accomplishing what one knows to be best, putting in the work and keeping the value of *to kalon* foremost in mind. True *sôphrosunê*, not merely the superficial form expressed in language, is the acknowledgment of the priority of the good. Some passions can prevent you from keeping *to kalon* foremost in mind. In those cases, your *sôphrosunê* may guide you to the best thing in the circumstances: suicide.

The nurse responds with the thesis that Phaedra, far from exercising the ultimate in *sôphrosunê*, has exercised its opposite, hubris. In her scrupulosity, the nurse says, and echoing Aphrodite's charge against Hippolytus, Phaedra has tried to be better than the gods; in general, she has ignored how humans really are. At this speech's conclusion, the Chorus hesitates to contradict what the nurse has said, even as they maintain their fealty to Phaedra. (Later they overcome their hesitation and come down hard on *erôs*.)[46]

The argument countering Phaedra's view of *sôphrosunê* starts as the nurse's "revised thoughts" (αἱ δεύτεραί πως φροντίδες), which are "wiser" than her earlier thoughts, ones she now deems impoverished (φαῦλος) because too precipitous (cf. ἐξαίφνης).[47] The nurse appears to be modeling *sôphrôn* thinking, at least as she sees it, in its flexible error-correcting pursuit of what is right, rather than an inflexible adherence to what has seemed right. In any event, the nurse says, what has happened to you is hardly as unthinkably extraordinary as you make it out to be. A goddess has afflicted you with *erôs*, as she has done to untold many other people; it would be absurd if they all responded to it with suicide. Not only is it impossible to withstand the goddess; even to try to do so expresses conceitedness (φρονοῦνθ' . . . μέγα) and superiority (περισσόν), which simply goads her on, yielding exactly the opposite of her intended outcome.[48] One should instead give in to Aphrodite's demands, so that the goddess will "come tranquilly" (ἡσυχῇ μετέρχεται) rather than violently to you.[49] The nurse's position is clear: people cannot always follow perfectly the norms of sexual propriety since the nature

---

[44] Eur. *Hipp*. 404–25.
[45] Eur. *Hipp*. 413–14: τὰς σώφρονας μὲν ἐν λόγοις, | λάθραι δὲ τόλμας οὐ καλὰς κεκτημένας.
[46] Eur. *Hipp*. 525–64.
[47] Eur. *Hipp*. 434–36.
[48] Eur. *Hipp*. 443; 445–46.
[49] Eur. *Hipp*. 444.

of *erôs* and its sources prevent it; but they can follow the norms of conscientious humility—the recognition of the limits on human control over their own passions. This is not an abdication of mentality, judgment, or agency, but a re-acknowledgment of the constraints in which those capacities are to work.

The rest of the nurse's speech gives further considerations in favor of her thesis. *Erôs* descends from a god, and thus is divine and to be revered.[50] The gods themselves feel illicit love and do not for that reason exile themselves; they concede the victories of chance.[51] These are the norms (νόμοι) too for humans: even those who think well (εὖ φρονῶν) ignore others' erotic dalliances; they have to, and are not so censorious as Phaedra fears her neighbors are. Those who give in to such passions, sure, are not altogether admirable (τὰ μὴ καλά), but as long as they keep their actions covered up, they are okay in the eyes of the wise (ἐν σοφοῖσι).[52] This is a philosophy of tolerance and moderation: "Mortals should not work too hard at their lives"; just ensure that the good outweighs the bad.[53] It is hubris (ὑβρίζουσ'... ὕβρις), the precise opposite of *sôphrosunê*, to try to do otherwise.[54] The nurse ends her speech acknowledging that, nevertheless, there are ways to try to subdue (καταστρέφου) the illness, including by means of charms.[55]

Once Phaedra decries this speech, as perniciously appealing but deploying reasoning that "destroys cities and homes,"[56] the nurse reiterates her main theme, this time more cuttingly. Had Phaedra actually been *sôphrôn*, had she not had "her bedroom pleasure," none of this would be happening; but the situation now demands this sort of response. The use of *sôphrosunê* here looks equivocal, in the way that reprises a fundamental ambiguity about the trait: it means either not having extreme desires in the first place or being able to deal with them well once one has them. But there is no reason to think that *sôphrosunê* must be only either proactive or reactive. The nurse seems to be implying that while Phaedra failed to be *sôphrôn* proactively (though through no fault of her own), she should still be *sôphrôn* with respect to her difficult situation: thus, blindly dismissing the nurse's advice is not a way to be *sôphrôn*.

The debate in this major exchange between Phaedra and her nurse has not concerned whether to be *sôphrôn* or not, or whether *sôphrosunê* is always good or not. The debate is not, in other words, of the sort we will see, in Chapter 8, between Callicles and Socrates in the *Gorgias*. It is instead over what *sôphrosunê* demands, given that one should be *sôphrôn* and that *sôphrosunê* is

---

[50] Eur. *Hipp.* 447–50.
[51] Eur. *Hipp.* 451–58.
[52] This resonates with "Worse Argument" in Aristophanes' *Clouds* from several years later; see Chapter 1.
[53] Eur. *Hipp.* 467: οὐδ' ἐκπονεῖν τοι χρὴ βίον λίαν βροτούς; 471.
[54] Eur. *Hipp.* 475.
[55] Eur. *Hipp.* 477–81.
[56] Eur. *Hipp.* 486–87.

always good. Phaedra believes it demands the elimination of illicit passions. The nurse believes it demands their de-authorization. Put more sharply than our characters put it, Phaedra treats *sôphrosunê* as a state of noninterference by shameful desires, whereas the nurse treats it as a disposition to acknowledge the ineradicability of certain desires and to deal with them in the least damaging way available. For one it is a tool of self-simplification; for the other, a tool of self-negotiation.[57]

Talk of *sôphrosunê* continues after this debate, and in a less marked way it confirms the remarks above. To save Phaedra, the nurse enacts a stratagem: to proposition Hippolytus. Her plan does not work, and Hippolytus' hatred of women flares up.[58] He concludes his speech of reaction: "Let someone teach them [sc. women] to *sôphronein* or allow me to trample over them forever."[59] Phaedra is furious, and the nurse is sorry. The latter apologizes: "I lacked *sôphrosunê*" (οὐκ ἐσωφρόνουν ἐγώ).[60] The nurse is saying that she hoped too much from her plan; she was too conceited about her insight into human affairs.[61] She failed in just what she had advised Phaedra not to do: not to think you can outwit the gods and their plans for us. Hippolytus must mean not only "let someone teach women to be sexually chaste," as he is often assumed to be saying, but also "to think what troubles they could get themselves into."

This lesson is confirmed in Phaedra's final speech before hanging herself, which she presents as her final act of self-determined will.[62] With the poison-pen letter she means to write, her nemesis Hippolytus is about to—as she puts it in her final words in the play—"learn *sôphrosunê*" (σωφρονεῖν μαθήσεται).[63] He will learn not to exult over others' misfortunes, which is to assume a superiority and an invulnerability to risk that he is not justified in assuming.[64]

---

[57] Some readers are little impressed by Phaedra. Fitton (1967, 41): "Phaedra is afraid of what people will say. That is the sum total of her morality.... Phaedra's trouble is respectability.... Phaedra is a weak good woman with no morality: under a crisis she has no definite response coming from herself." Williams (1993, 95–97): Phaedra is self-obsessed, an obsession which takes the form of conventional shame concerning her own reputation, which takes account of others' views of her, at least virtually.

[58] Eur. *Hipp.* 616–66.

[59] Eur. *Hipp.* 667–68.

[60] Eur. *Hipp.* 704.

[61] Phaedra's response to the nurse, that she should "care about [her] own things; I will arrange my own just fine" (σαυτῆς πέρι φρόντιζ'· ἐγὼ γὰρ τἀμὰ θήσομαι καλῶς, 708–9), resonates with Critias' definition of *sôphrosunê*, as we will see it in the next chapter. The relationship the two also recalls Penelope's with her maid in *Odyssey*: she accuses her maid of overstepping her bounds in trying to give authoritative advice to her mistress (Chapter 2).

[62] Eur. *Hipp.* 723.

[63] Eur. *Hipp.* 731. Remarkably, Barrett (1964 ad 728–81) doubts that this is a thematic usage of *sôphrosunê*—"I doubt whether an audience would have taken the point" that Hippolytus is so confident in his own *sôphrosunê* and of Phaedra's lack of it—on the grounds that nearly all the talk of Hippolytus' *sôphrosunê* comes later in the play. What we have just seen places doubt on that.

[64] Eur. *Hipp.* 729–30. Mueller (2011, 169–72) thinks it is to get him to keep the secret, to be silent.

Hippolytus' Self-Defense

As Theseus returns home, learns of his wife's suicide, and reads her false accusation of Hippolytus, the conversation returns, yet again, to *sôphrosunê*. After cursing his son, he accuses him of senselessness and brazenness.[65] He then addresses Hippolytus' self-imputed moral excellence. "Do you indeed accompany the gods as a man extraordinary? Are you indeed *sôphrôn* and have no taint of evils?"[66] He continues by comparing Hippolytus to a self-satisfied Orphic vegetarian mystic who intones "sententious words."[67] Theseus presents Hippolytus' self-regard as *sôphrôn* as utter hypocrisy. This purported *sôphrosunê* amounts to his following an alien, divine set of principles and being or striving to be independent of normal human desires.

Hippolytus responds to Theseus' accusation, saying that he will start where his father started, with the point about *sôphrosunê*.[68] "There is no man—though you may deny it—more *sôphrôn* than me."[69] Hippolytus immediately lists three grounds for this extraordinary boast.[70] First, he knows how to revere (σέβειν) the gods; second, he makes friends who try to do no wrong (ἀδικεῖν), who have enough *aidôs* not to call for evil deeds or do disgraceful things themselves; and third, the one evil in particular of which he has no taint is sex. So for Hippolytus, *sôphrosunê* has at least three aspects: religiosity, social morality, and sexual restraint. "But you are not persuaded by my *sôphrosunê*," Hippolytus says, recalling his father's skepticism.[71] Hippolytus sees that he cannot appeal to his virtuous character, the most important aspects of which he has just adumbrated, in exculpation; so he advances to possible motives, and shows them to be implausible. He suggests that Phaedra is not so beautiful as to corrupt him. And he explains that he would not want to marry into the kingship: he would prefer athletic victory and spending time with his friends over that leadership slog.[72]

---

[65] Cursing: 887–90. Accusing: 920: φρονεῖν διδάσκειν οἷσιν οὐκ ἔνεστι νοῦς; 936–37: φεῦ τῆς βροτείας—ποῖ προβήσεται;—φρενός. | τί τέρμα τόλμης καὶ θράσους γενήσεται; cf. 969 and also 935.
[66] Eur. *Hipp.* 948–50.
[67] Eur. *Hipp.* 952–57. Hippolytus as mystic (and quest for purity a reaction to his bastardy): Fitton (1967, 42).
[68] Eur. *Hipp.* 991–92.
[69] Eur. *Hipp.* 994–95.
[70] Eur. *Hipp.* 996–1006.
[71] I assume this is the sense given by καὶ δὴ τὸ σῶφρον τοὐμὸν οὐ πείθει σ' (1007). This responds to Theseus' comment at 949–50: σὺ σώφρων καὶ κακῶν ἀκήρατος; | οὐκ ἂν πιθοίμην τοῖσι σοῖς κόμποις ἐγώ.
[72] I agree with Barrett (1964, 353–54) that lines 1012–15 are of doubtful authenticity, though for the reason that the argument they provide is pointless (admittedly, Diggle does not bracket them). As 1010–11 and 1016–18 run, Hippolytus asks whether he would hope to take up Theseus' position by marrying Phaedra; no, he says, since I would like to be first only in athletics, not in the city. Verses 1012–15 add a series of confusing considerations: "I was foolish then—really, completely thoughtless. But is absolute power sweet even to *sôphron* people? Least so, since monarchy has ruined the minds of mortals for whoever love it" (μάταιος ἄρ' ἦν, οὐδαμοῦ μὲν οὖν φρενῶν. ἀλλ' ὡς τυραννεῖν ἡδὺ τοῖσι σώφροσιν; ἥκιστά γ', ἐπεί τοι τὰς φρένας διέφθορεν θνητῶν ὅσοισιν ἁνδάνει μοναρχία). (Barrett

There is something dubious about Hippolytus' self-exultation as *sôphrôn*, which expresses none of the humility attributed to the virtue by Phaedra's nurse or even by Phaedra herself. To be sure, his argument sounds reasonable enough. But his statements about *sôphrosunê* get focalized once again, with a double paradox in his speech's closing couplet:

ἐσωφρόνησε δ' οὐκ ἔχουσα σωφρονεῖν,
ἡμεῖς δ' ἔχοντες οὐ καλῶς ἐχρώμεθα. (Eur. *Hipp*. 1035-36)

She was exercising *sôphrosunê* despite not being able to exercise *sôphrosunê*, while we, being able [sc. to exercise it], did not put it to good use.

In his clever capping of Phaedra's plight, Hippolytus plays on the by now familiar two characterizations of *sôphrosunê*: she was not able to ignore feeling a damagingly strong passion, namely her lust for Hippolytus, but she was able to avoid satisfying it. So she lacked *sôphrosunê* from the perspective of the content of her present desires (some were too strong to ignore), but she possessed it from the perspective of her reasoning about those desires (she recognized that some were too strong and that she would therefore have to take drastic measures for them not to impel her action). To make sense of Hippolytus' claim, we must see that these are not two senses but rather two focal points on a virtue that reflects a complex human situation: our having a capacity to treat only certain desires as motivationally relevant.[73] Nor is it that Phaedra mostly lacked *sôphrosunê* but pulled it together once and so had *sôphrosunê* for a moment.[74] We have already seen that *sôphrosunê* is equivocal between having bad desires that one ignores and not having them at all. So did she or didn't she have *sôphrosunê*? Euripides

---

replaces the manuscripts' εἰ μή with ἐπεί τοι.) Whichever lines we accept, Hippolytus casts doubts on the idea that *sôphrôn* men like himself would find kingship attractive. (Barrett ad 1013 thinks that "Th. cannot, in suggesting a motive, *admit* that virtue in Hipp.," and so Barrett assumes that this use of the term "cannot refer to the virtue of *sôphrosunê* on which Hipp. prides himself." There may well be some paradox in Hippolytus' having just said that Theseus denies his being *sôphrôn* and then using his being *sôphrôn* as part of an argument, but Hippolytus' self-confidence would probably allow him to do so.)

[73] This contradiction has been an important crux. It has so consternated scholars that A. E. Housman (1888, 242-45), for example, conjectured a noun, σωφρόνη, to alleviate it, since according to him we would otherwise have to read "she was virtuous though unable to be so," which he believed to be impossible. Taking the semantic rather than lexical route to distinguish meanings looks like this: "Though she lacked self-control, she acted with good sense" (Shaw 2007 ad loc.); paradoxically similar: "Phaedra behaved with self-control although she had not the power to be chaste" (North 1966, 81).

[74] E.g., Norwood (1954, 89-90): "The aorist sense of ἐσωφρόνησεν is to be taken as ingressive," translating: "Though chaste she could not live, yet chaste she died." Similarly, Barrett (1964 ad 1034-35); Halleran (1995, 238).

has shown an indeterminacy in this question, and Hippolytus himself seems confused.

Hippolytus is not confused, however, about his own case. He ascribes *sôphrosunê* to himself and expresses no doubt about it at all; he admits only that it did not repay his efforts to develop or maintain it. That self-regard gains clearest expression near the end of his conflict with his father. He wishes he could look at himself (ἐμαυτὸν προσβλέπειν) and bewail his misfortunes; his father responds with a direct condemnation of Hippolytus' egotism: "You are much more practiced at revering yourself than in being just and acting piously toward your parents"—that is, in effect by Hippolytus' own analysis, in being *sôphrôn*.[75] And once again, as though unwilling to release himself from the vindicating self-appraisal, Hippolytus' final claim, before leaving his home, addressed to his friends, is that they will never know a man more *sôphrôn* than he.[76] To psychologize for a moment, the ideal of *sôphrosunê* seems to be providing the foundation of Hippolytus' self-identity; with any qualification, it seems he fears a loss of himself—and unlike Phaedra, he does not feel that any such loss is justified.

That final claim is repeated as Hippolytus is brought in, mortally wounded, from the sea. "Here I am, the reverent one (ὁ σεμνός), god-venerating; he I am, the one excelling all others in *sôphrosunê*. . . . In vain have been my efforts of piety toward men."[77] He continues in his identification with that virtue, incredulous that it could not secure his well-being.[78] When his beloved Artemis enters the conversation with him, she says that Aphrodite hated his *sôphrosunê*.[79] This sounds rhetorical: Aphrodite must have hated the partial way Hippolytus exercised *sôphrosunê*. Nevertheless, the gods appear to disagree about the proper expression of *sôphrosunê*. Artemis' affirmation of Hippolytus seems to be an affirmation of his strident sexual innocence and construction of that as the whole of this particular virtue rather than of the broader-minded rationality suggested as a meaning of *sôphrosunê* over the previous fourteen hundred lines. Aphrodite's rejection of Hippolytus amounts to her judgment that his gloss of *sôphrosunê* as piety leads him into inconsistency, since he, impiously, does not revere her. Thus the play ends in an unanswered question: How does sexual restraint or even

---

[75] Eur. *Hipp.* 1078–79; 1080–81.
[76] Eur. *Hipp.* 1100.
[77] Eur. *Hipp.* 1364–69.
[78] Hippolytus' unrelenting confidence about his rectitude to the very end has confirmed to many readers some adverse judgment against him. See, e.g., Dodds (1925, 103–4): "As Phaedra does violence to αἰδώς in the name of αἰδώς, so does Hippolytus to σωφροσύνη in the name of σωφροσύνη: each is the victim of his own and the other's submerged desires masquerading as morality"; Barnett (1964, 403, ad 1364–67): "Still in his last agony the same unshaken certainty of his own perfection: his blindness to the defects of his narrow puritanism stays with him to the end, and lets him see in his fate nothing but blind irrational injustice."
[79] Eur. *Hipp.* 1402: σωφρονοῦντι δ' ἤχθετο (and thus not *sôphrosunê* itself, as an abstract principle, but Hippolytus' instantiation of it, so to speak).

vehement asexuality contribute to the great ideal of *sôphrosunê*, especially in contrast to or in relation with epistemic flexibility and humility?

The *Hippolytus* as a Play about *Sôphrosunê*

I have said that the *Hippolytus* is the earliest full-scale reflection on *sôphrosunê* from classical Greece. To be sure, it is not an easy reflection to use: no remark reflecting an authoritative position, it sets problematically partial understanding against problematically partial understanding, and no character speaks more theoretically than befits her or his local and immediate purposes. Yet its length, its polyphony, and the precision with which Euripides has filled out and tuned his characters' views of *sôphrosunê* for maximum dramatic conflict make up for its indeterminacy.

Among many subsidiary issues about *sôphrosunê*, two stand out; they turn out to be closely related. One concerns the relationship between a salient quality of *sôphrosunê*, namely sexual chastity; the virtue in its broader personal construal, as autonomy, namely freedom from unauthorized incentives to action; and the virtue in its broadest social construal, as moral excellence, here recognition of the dignity of others. The other subsidiary issue concerns the absoluteness of this ideal of autonomy, involving either total extirpation of unauthorized desires; depreciation of their motivational power while allowing them to stay; or acting with moderation on whatever persistent desires one has, accepting them as having some pertinence even if one does not wholeheartedly identify with them.

The character of Hippolytus brings out the first concern: he sometimes sees his sexual abstinence as somehow coextensive with *sôphrosunê* writ large, and the question comes up, for his servant as much as for the audience, whether he in fact embodies *sôphrosunê* writ large, and whether his idealization of his *sôphrosunê* blinds him to his failure to embody it. But the problem is not only that he might mistake an aspect of *sôphrosunê* for the virtue exercised across a mature life; he might see *sôphrosunê* as demanding an emptying out of *erôs*, which is the passionate attachment to other people and indeed the impulse for sociality as such, rather than a rational integration of erotic attachment into a mature life.

The character of Phaedra brings out the second—and, we now see, related—concern: she cannot see *sôphrosunê* as anything but vanquishing her illicit desire, either through hard work on herself or eventual self-extinction. Perhaps her inability to see *sôphrosunê* otherwise reflects her social condition as a woman held to a high standard of marital fidelity and a mother of children who will suffer whatever disgrace gets attached to her. Whatever the facts, her nurse sees her reading of the ideal of *sôphrosunê* as unnecessary and, indeed, inadequately rational, failing to account for the naturalness—the unavoidability and the acceptability—of certain passions. Those passions may eventually disappear or they may be managed, either by moderate satisfaction or by erecting situational and not merely psychic obstacles to their satisfaction. In other words, love, even the illicit sort, is not to be extirpated, as foreign to one's self, but safely incorporated as part of one's unavoidable complexity.

On the reading of the play given above, Hippolytus wants it both ways: for *sôphrosunê* to be praiseworthy as a virtue for a whole life and also the simple, and ultimately less praiseworthy, matter of asexuality; in so wanting it both ways, he shows a failure of *sôphrosunê* as self-knowledge and acknowledgment of the most authoritative of norms. Phaedra, for her part, wants the praiseworthiness of *sôphrosunê* to come from its difficulty as a total self-overcoming, amounting to a total self-annihilation, rather than from the difficulty of living on in compromise, in acknowledging desires whose position with respect to her "self" will always be ambiguous. The destruction of both figures seems Euripides' verdict of misunderstanding. And yet that may not be the lesson, in case we are to see Aphrodite's jealousy or Artemis' partisanship as causally central and not metaphorical. But even there, only the details about *sôphrosunê* change, not the overall evaluation. The issue remains a concern for the meaning of autonomy and self-constitution: what does it mean to judge for oneself what reasons for action to have? The desire called *erôs* brings this question into sharpest relief: it is the severest and most ornery desire, but also the one most tightly set into a vision of the life that is one's own. In short, Euripides provides a messy picture of *sôphrosunê*, but a messiness that is altogether salutary, for it treats the strain to live up to its as yet unarticulated ideal as a central problem in human life.

Bacchae

We will discuss *Bacchae* rather more briefly than *Hippolytus*. It dramatizes a simpler, though no less profound problem about *sôphrosunê*: Is it the ideal of the insightful, calm, and reserved person, or is it the ideal of the reverential? These might usually seem to go together, such that no problem arises; but as he did in *Hippolytus*, Euripides prizes them apart. This play asks: What if the reverence is not for Aphrodite or Artemis but for Dionysius, whose rites enjoin frenzy and ecstasy, the standing outside the very self that *sôphrosunê* has been thought to constitute? By play's end, Euripides seems to advise following the gods, whatever they may enjoin. What this really means, and how self-contradiction in a polytheistic order may be avoided, are questions raised though not answered. *Sôphrosunê* is treated, in the end, as commitment to authoritative norms, but which and whose are the most authoritative, and what that commitment entails, are questions left open.

The play begins with a series of statements about the irreverence of Pentheus, king of Thebes. In a parallel to the prologue of the *Hippolytus*, the god Dionysus notes Pentheus' failure to give him prayers or libations and Pentheus' desire to surpass the gods altogether.[80] Then the seer Tiresias, implicitly contrasting Cadmus and himself with Pentheus, praises their own "good sense" (εὖ φρονοῦμεν) for "not despising" (οὐ καταφρονῶ) the gods; they do not think they can see through and rationally undercut (οὐδὲν σοφιζόμεσθα) age-old religious traditions.[81] Pentheus, in his first scene, proves these charges: the ecstatic rites dedicated to Dionysus are, in his view, fabricated, opportunities for women to drink heavily and sneak trysts with men; indeed, they are really dedicated to Aphrodite instead![82] And the foreigner inciting such riotous behavior is himself hubristic (ὕβρεις ὑβρίζειν), "introducing a new divinity to mankind."[83]

Tiresius goes on to defend the Dionysiac in a speech that the Chorus afterward praises, saying, "You are *sôphrôn* in honoring a great god" (329). Tiresius' speech deals with *sôphrosunê* in several ways; two are most important here. Tiresius justifies madness (μανία), the putative opposite of *sôphrosunê*, as in fact enabling future prediction (μαντική).[84] And he says that the Dionysiac rites do not corrupt *sôphrôn* women:

οὐχ ὁ Διόνυσος σωφρονεῖν ἀναγκάσει	314
γυναῖκας ἐς τὴν Κύπριν, ἀλλ' ἐν τῇ φύσει	315
[τὸ σωφρονεῖν ἔνεστιν εἰς τὰ πάντ' ἀεί]	316
τοῦτο· σκοπεῖν χρή· καὶ γὰρ ἐν βακχεύμασιν	317
οὖσ' ἥ γε σώφρων οὐ διαφθαρήσεται. (*Bacch*. 314–18)	318

Dionysius will not force women to *sôphronein*
with respect to Cypris, but in their nature—
[*sôphronein* is in it always and in every way]
—is this. One must consider: for even in Bacchic frenzy
the *sôphrôn* woman will not be corrupted.

Tiresius' reasoning for this paradoxical conclusion—that Bacchic frenzy, despite involving abdication from self-control, does not corrupt those with *sôphrosunê*—has long been a textual crux. Each of the first four lines has seemed problematic, as indeed have both of the uses of the verb *sôphronein*. These confusions affect to what extent we can learn about *sôphrosunê* from this passage.

---

[80] Eur. *Bacch*. 45–46: θεομαχεῖ.
[81] Eur. *Bacch*. 196–203 (Diggle brackets 199–203; Kovacs does not); cf. 266–68, 330–36, 895.
[82] Eur. *Bacch*. 218–25.
[83] Eur. *Bacch*. 237, 256. On the theme of hubris throughout the play, see Fisher (1992, 443–52).
[84] Eur. *Bacch*. 298–301; cf. Pl. *Phdr*. 240a–b, specifically discussing *sôphrosunê*, *mania*, and *mantikê*.

The initial line, 314, has been subject to three editorial emendments, each of which depends on attitudes about *sôphrosunê*. When this passage is quoted by Stobaeus (remarkably, as the very first excerpt in the chapter of his collection of Greek wisdom on *sôphrosunê*), we find not σωφρονεῖν but its negation, μὴ σωφρονεῖν. This is also the reading of a corrector of the P manuscript of Euripides' play.[85] The thought seems to be that, given this is praise of Dionysus, it would be ridiculous for Tiresias to praise Dionysus for failing (οὐχ) to make women *sôphronein*, which is something good. A dropped negation would have it that we should not blame Dionysus for making women fail to *sôphronein*: it is not *his* fault that they lose their self-restraint. Samuel Musgrave in the late eighteenth century agrees that a negation was accidentally dropped, but also that σω- was added (perhaps to preserve the meter): he reads μὴ φρονεῖν—Dionysus does not make women *fail to reason*. David Kovacs in the recent Loeb edition avoids the strained double negative by proposing παραφρονεῖν—Dionysus does not make women *crazy*.[86] In these cases, the τοῦτο of 317 refers to women's failure of reason or craziness or thoughtlessness; Tiresias is saying that women are crazy or thoughtless by nature, not because of Dionysus, and so the god is not to blame. Given the statement at the end of the passage, this must mean that whichever women are in fact crazy are so from nature, or that those who are *sôphrôn* had to get there on their own. But it is unclear how that last statement provides any explanation for the previous observation about Dionysus' noninvolvement, which is a problem, since the "one must consider" (σκοπεῖν χρή) and "for even" (καὶ γὰρ) indicate that it must serve as some kind of explanation.

Fortunately we can make sense of the uncorrected manuscript reading.[87] The sentiment expressed at 314–15 could be taken as either concessive or corrective. The concessive reading: Granted, Dionysus does not make women *sôphronein* in sexual matters, but reverencing him through manic dance does not make those who are already *sôphrôn* lose it.[88] Sexual continence is not Dionysus' ambit, but neither is sexual incontinence. Assuming (as most editors do) that line 316 is an interpolation, the unparalleled locution "but in their nature is this" (ἀλλ' ἐν τῇ φύσει τοῦτο) presumably means that those women who are *sôphrôn* are so naturally.[89] Given that their *sôphrosunê* is natural, not contingent on a whimsical god's will, some ritual frenzy will hardly drive it out. The corrective reading: It

---

[85] Stob. 3.5.1, 4.23.8; Eur. *Bacch*. MS P².

[86] Kovacs (2002) does not print his suggestion, only †σωφρονεῖν†, but he translates the line as "Dionysus will not compel women to <u>act foolishly</u> where sex is concerned." Further discussion at Kovacs (2003, 122).

[87] Diggle (the source of the text above) is unmoved by other editors' interventions here.

[88] Dodds (1960 ad 314–18): "It is not Dionysius' part to force chastity on women: you must look for that (the moral factor) in human character; for even in the ecstatic rite the pure will not lose her purity"; Barrett (1964, 175) similarly.

[89] For the idea of natural virtue, compare Eur. *Hipp*. 967: Theseus asks whether Hippolytus claims that foolishness (τὸ μῶρον) is not in men but is "inborn in women" (γυναιξὶ δ᾽ ἐμπέφυκεν).

is not Dionysus who makes women *sôphronein*; that is already in their nature, if they are in fact *sôphrôn*. And thus, as before, their chastity will not depend on the god.

The second appearance of σωρονεῖν in its line of context (316) is more readily rejected. It is missing from Stobaeus' quotation of the passage, and the line already appeared, in similar form, in *Hippolytus*.[90] The line makes sufficient sense in the mouth of Hippolytus, who wishes to make emphatic the breadth and stability of his *sôphrosunê*. It makes little sense coming from Tiresius, who has no reason to proclaim the extent and duration of women's *sôphrosunê*, and the line leaves the τοῦτο of the next line hanging. Presumably some scribe, who knew the earlier play, interpolated it here.[91]

So this five-line passage raises two questions that will later be formulated by the Socratics, especially Xenophon, Antisthenes, and Plato: about the behavioral effects on virtues—can they be lost by letting oneself go?—and about their origin in divine dispensation or in nature. On the present reading of the text, a paean of sorts to Dionysus, Tiresius says that at least one virtue in particular cannot be lost in at least one way in particular, and that *sôphrosunê* comes by nature. (Hippolytus had made a related point in his opening speech: he praised the *sôphrosunê* that owes nothing to teaching [διδακτὸν μηδέν] but that comes by nature, *Hipp.* 79.)

This speech does not convince Pentheus; he still thinks the visitor is messing up marriages.[92] The Chorus, accordingly, returns to its charges: a hubristic Pentheus fails in piety and exemplifies lawless foolishness (ἀνόμου... ἀφροσύνας). What he should have instead is "the quiet life" (ὁ τὰς ἡσυχίας βίοτος) and thoughtfulness (τὸ φρονεῖν); Dionysus brings peace, wisdom, and moderation.[93] Eventually Pentheus and Dionysus meet, and squabble. Dionysus accuses Pentheus of impiety; Pentheus replies that Dionysus disdains (καταφρονεῖ) both himself and Thebes, and orders him seized.[94] Dionysus rejects the order: "I, being *sôphrôn*, say to you, who is not *sôphrôn*, that I must not be [seized]" (αὐδῶ με μὴ δεῖν σωφρονῶν οὐ σώφροσιν).[95] Pentheus retorts that he has more authority (κυριώτερος); Dionysus in turn denies that he has any self-knowledge at all: "You do not know how you are living, what you are doing, or who you are" (οὐκ οἶσθ' ὅ τι ζῇς, οὐδ' ὃ δρᾷς, οὐδ' ὅστις εἶ).[96] We see here what we saw already in *Medea* and *Hippolytus*, a disagreement over the proper recipient of the praise as *sôphrôn*.

---

[90] Eur. *Hipp.* 80; see above, n15.
[91] Dodds (1960 ad 314–18) advises, to preserve the line, to emend to εἰ τῇ φύσει τὸ σωφρονεῖν ἔνεστιν εἰς τὰ πάντ' ἀεί, τοῦτο σκοπεῖν χρή; Seaford (1996 ad 316) makes a similar suggestion.
[92] Eur. *Bacch.* 353–53; cf. 487.
[93] Eur. *Bacch.* 387–89, 420–29.
[94] Eur. *Bacch.* 476, 490, 502, 503.
[95] Eur. *Bacch.* 504.
[96] Eur. *Bacch.* 506.

Here the debate shows the centrality of this virtue-term to the issue of authority. *Sôphrosunê* is the competence to make authoritative decisions, and this authority amounts to self-understanding. Being *sôphrôn* means appreciating one's habits, actions, and character, and in particular the grounds or justification for each of them.

The play continues relentlessly to Pentheus' doom and makes his failure of *sôphrosunê*, and the success of others' *sôphrosunê*, a recurrent theme. Dionysus does not worry about Pentheus' anger because "a wise man practices a *sôphrôn* good-temperedness (εὐοργησία)," and Pentheus' huffiness (πνέων ... μέγα) is actually easy to bear (ῥᾳδίως ... οἴσω), as perhaps most mortal complaints should be.[97] The messenger returns with a report that the Bacchic women in the forest were lying around in a *sôphrôn* way and were amazingly well-ordered (θαῦμ' ... εὐκοσμίας), in particular without wine or sexual escapades.[98] Dionysus reiterates this to an enchanted Pentheus: "you'll see how unexpectedly (παρὰ λόγον) *sôphrôn*" they are.[99] Of course this does not presage an awakening of Pentheus' moral perception: his lesson will be final. The Chorus anticipates the Bacchic women's destruction of Pentheus in a most disquieting stanza. It chants: "justice shall be manifest" (ἴτω δίκα φανερός) for the "ungodly, unjust, unlawful" (ἄθεον ἄνομον ἄδικον) Pentheus, who with unjust judgment (ἀδίκῳ γνήμᾳ) and lawless anger (παρανόμῳ τ' ὀργᾷ) thought he could accomplish forcibly what cannot be so mastered. The following six lines are confounded; I include only three of them, though they can hardly be translated in current form:

†γνώμαν σώφρονα θάνατος ἀπροφάσιστος
εἰς τὰ θεῶν ἔφυ
βροτείῳ τ' ἔχειν ἄλυπος βίος. (Eur. *Bacch.* 1002–4)

a *sôphrôn* judgment [acc.] ... death [nom.] ... is unhesitating
toward the things of the gods,
and to carry on mortally is a griefless life.

These lines must be reconstructed, and there is no consensus how to do so. The later part of the passage is clear enough: accept the authority of the gods; do not second-guess them. A *sôphrôn* judgment would have done this. Pentheus lacked it. He is about to die (992–96). But this does not explain the first line. E. R. Dodds emended to γνωμᾶν σωφρόνισμα θάνατος, "death is a corrector of his purposes,"

---

[97] Eur. *Bacch.* 640–41; cf. 647. Seaford (1996 ad 641, 647) wonders whether Dionysius' calm self-control has "a mystic significance," reflecting the contented happiness of the initiated gazing upon the uninitiated (ad 621–22).
[98] Eur. *Bacch.* 686–88, 693. Cf. Gold (1977).
[99] Eur. *Bacch.* 940.

and in this he is followed by major editors.[100] The problem is that death does not make Pentheus more *sôphrôn*, much less his judgments. And the Chorus goes on to emphasize the importance of reverencing and honoring the gods and rejecting customs that go beyond justice (τὰ ... ἔξω νόμιμα δίκας ἐκβαλόντα).[101] So while Euripides' meaning remains uncertain, he apparently intends to treat *sôphrosunê* as a fundamental virtue for human-divine relations, which is to say for human nature.

Such an interpretation matches two of the play's valedictory comments.[102] The messenger concludes his speech on the disaster that befell Pentheus:

τὸ σωφρονεῖν δὲ καὶ σέβειν τὰ τῶν θεῶν
κάλλιστον· οἶμαι δ' αὐτὸ καὶ σοφώτατον
θνητοῖσιν εἶναι κτῆμα τοῖσι χρωμένοις. (Eur. *Bacch.* 1150-52)

Sôphrosunê and reverence toward the divine is
finest; and I think this is the wisest
possession a mortal can use.

Later, Dionysus tells a grieving Cadmus that if he had worked to *sôphronein*, when he was not willing to do so, he would be happy now (1341-43).

Thus the play identifies *sôphrosunê* with recognition of and obedience to the divine, and puts this at the heart of human flourishing. It finds this acknowledgment of the gods more fundamental to human excellence than either a tranquil bodily composure or a mental acuity that sees through myth. Such was the debate here: how wild and traditional can *sôphrosunê* be while still being a virtue? Very much, Euripides' Dionysus says, as long as the normative element remains.

Tragic *Sôphrosunê*

Euripides dramatizes the debates about *sôphrosunê* like no other writer, seeming to recognize the common currency in Heraclitus' vaunt, that *sôphrosunê* is the

---

[100] Dodds (1960 ad 1002-4); Seaford (1996 ad 1002); Kovacs (2002 ad 1002; 2003, 134). Murray had already proposed re-accenting γνώμαν (s. acc.) to γνωμᾶν (pl. gen.). Dodds' reasoning is rejected by Campbell (1956, 61-63), who prefers a major rewrite: γνώμᾳ σωφρονεῖ θνατὸς <ὃς> ἀπροφάσι-|στος ἐς τὰ <τῶν> θεῶν ἔφυ, βροτείῳ γένει τ' ἀλύπος βιοῖ. "Wise in his sobriety is the mortal who is by nature unquestioning in face of the decrees of the gods and who lives in a manner uninjurious to humankind." Giudice Rizzo (2007), which contains a full review of the scholarship, proposes repunctuating to make γνώμαν σώφρονα the end of the previous thought: τὰν ἀνίκατον ὡς κρατήσων βίᾳ γνώμαν σώφρονα, "si avvia per vincere con la forza l'invincibile mente saggia" (p. 184): you, Pentheus, in your angry and atheistic craze, "set out to overcome with force the invincible wise mind."
[101] Eur. *Bacch.* 1009-10.
[102] Dodds (1960 ad 1150-52) and Seaford (1996 ad 1150-53) assure us that these are no mere platitudes.

greatest virtue. That the virtue can be so heated an object of discord reveals not just its existential profundity but also, and more specifically, the simultaneous approbation of and doubts about the ideals of (religious) purity, (psychological) self-mastery, and (intellectual) clarity. Hippolytus stood for an austere set of desires; Phaedra for a hidden inner life; Pentheus for seeing past convention and mystification. Each fought to avoid submission to heteronomous inclinations; each sought to be the agent of his or her own life.

The issues that have arisen in these two play—plus *Medea*—recur in the texts discussed in the remainder of the book. What is the natural state of our desires, if one can speak of a "natural" state, and how are they best to be dealt with? How, if at all, can talking and reasoning through problems deal with ornery desires? What image of self-restraint, self-control, or self-construction best captures the challenges and ideals of *sôphrosunê*? In the next two chapters, we address Euripides' exact contemporaries—Critias, Antiphon, Thucydides, Democritus, and Socrates—and among their writings and influences we will see again the power and richness of the fifth-century debates about *sôphrosunê*.

5
The Late Fifth Century

Four More Authors

We have seen, in Chapters 1 and 4, the force and dynamism of the debates about *sôphrosunê* in the late fifth century. Writers of the period queried how its presence might be determined, what psychological condition it assumes, what effort or circumstance brings it about, to what extent it actually conduces to current visions of personal flourishing, and how its self-ascription might be blinkered in one way or another. Disagreement pervaded this culture-wide discussion, but it was a disagreement predicated on some foundational agreement. *Sôphrosunê* was a hugely important capacity, the capacity to deliberate and act well, with eyes open to the normative considerations proffered by world, cosmos, and one's conscience. This meant not being distracted by one's insistent desires to do otherwise than that to which one was committed. Herodotus queried the breadth of considerations relevant to deciding whether someone could still act well (or was instead in the tunnel vision of craziness); Euripides dramatized contrasting views about the role of problematic desires in a successful life; Aristophanes gave expression to the cynical rejection of sophronistic pieties.

These are not the only representatives of that fifth-century debate, however, and this chapter will give close consideration to the four most important others: Critias, Antiphon, Thucydides, and Democritus. To be sure, this does not exhaust the relevant authors from the period. Sophocles, whose complete and fragmentary plays often deploy *sôphrosunê* language at key moments, makes *sôphrosunê* thematic especially in *Ajax*, though not so much as an object of debate; his usage will be noted in Chapter 11 (on Aristotle).[1] If Protagoras discussed *sôphrosunê* we would know it only through the evidence of Plato's dialogue about him, to be explored in Chapter 8. A fragment of a speech by Thrasymachus will be mentioned below in the section on Thucydides, and Prodicus' *Choice of Heracles* will be cited in Chapter 13. Some important authors have no instance of *sôphrosunê* in their extant work, notably Gorgias, Hippias, and the anonymous authors of the pseudo-Xenophontic *Constitution of the Athenians* or the

---

[1] *Sôphrosunê* in *Ajax*: see esp. Goldhill (1986, 145–46, 156, 159, 190–96); see also North (1966, 58–61).

Anonymus Iamblichi.² Yet while these authors' texts prove that not every ethical issue came in for a *sôphrosunê*-focused analysis, they reveal a capacious interest in the constellation of issues around the virtue.

In any event, the four authors of the present chapter have remarkable things to say about *sôphrosunê*, philosophically interesting on their own and contributing substantially to our understanding of the topography of the term's debate; scholarship has not generally given these aspects of their thought much attention. Plato ascribes to Critias a definition of *sôphrosunê*, and the dialogue in which he does so, *Charmides*, seems to suggest the definition is historical. It is a fascinating and appealing definition, one that (on Plato's reconstruction) registers an improvement on earlier attempts at fathoming the virtue. Antiphon acknowledges the importance of the virtue and observes its relationship both to action and to desire. He takes and argues for a position in a field of possible positions about *sôphrosunê*: that it means not acting badly, or having the right desires, or not being overwhelmed by the wrong desires. He opts for a desire-suppression model, but in doing so acknowledges, as our earlier evidence shows he must, that this is not the only possible model; indeed, while plausible, it is not obviously the best model. Antiphon also takes and argues for a position in another field of possible positions: that *sôphrosunê* does or does not involve reason and good intentions, and so in what way, if any, it can be described as self-mastery. Thucydides makes the presence and significance of a civic-level *sôphrosunê* a core issue in at least two crucial speech exchanges in his book on the Peloponnesian War, and in doing so shows a usage of the term not readily seen elsewhere: as a virtue of a city in geopolitical context, and not just of its population in ethnographic terms. And Democritus, to whom a half-dozen statements about *sôphrosunê* are attributed by the time of Stobaeus, had an ethical theory that, while not in the remaining fragments explicitly about *sôphrosunê*, seems to have taken *sôphrosunê* as a central goal. Each author describes a self-constitution through the discrimination between motivational sources.

Critias of Athens

Critias, a cousin of Plato's mother and erstwhile associate of Socrates, has long been best remembered as a spokesman for the murderous and democracy-subverting "Thirty" oligarchs, at the close of the Peloponnesian War (404–403 BCE), who ruled Athens for eight months;³ philosophers remember him best as

---

² The *Anonymus Iamblichi* will be discussed in Chapter 8 for its use of the term "most self-controlled" (ἐγκρατέστατος, 98,17). It is often assumed, though not proved, that this text is from the late fifth or early fourth century.
³ The key sources are Xen. *Mem.* 1.2.31 and *Hell.* 2.3.15–2.4.10, 2.4.19–21; Diod. *Sic.* 14.4.5–5.3, 33.2–3; Philostr. *VS* 1.16.

an (unwitting) besmircher of Socrates' reputation.[4] He is little remembered—as even Aristotle noted—for his life preceding the political terror, which was most of it: no political activities are definitely recorded for him until around 410 BCE, when he was in his mid-fifties.[5] In his young and middle adulthood, he seems to have lived a vigorously creative intellectual life, writing prose and poetry across a range of genres: sympotic elegy, cutting-edge drama, political histories, rhetorical pattern-books, and belletristic reflections.[6] From an elite and cultured Athenian family that traced its lineage back toward Solon, he had the resources to listen, talk, think, and write in ways that distinguished him in Greek culture. Later authors esteemed his works highly, frequently quoting, discussing, or imitating them.[7] His importance was such that Plato included him in four dialogues (*Protagoras, Charmides, Timaeus,* and the eponymous *Critias*).[8] Plato presents him as a notable thinker about *sôphrosunê*, perhaps as *the* thinker of the virtue from the later fifth century with whom to reckon. This is not generally acknowledged, since his role in the violent Thirty has often seemed to undercut whatever pretensions he may have had to understanding or embodying *sôphrosunê*; but this does not follow.[9] Indeed, he should probably be thought the next major proponent and exegete of the virtue after Heraclitus (other than Socrates; see Chapter 6), though with a marked political turn.[10] The confluence of his interests in sympotic drinking-norms, contrasts in the constitutional success of Sparta, Thessaly, and Athens, self-regulating moral

---

[4] See, for the tensions between Socrates and Critias, Pl. *Chrm.* 176c8–d5 (a possible allusion); Xen. *Mem.* 1.2.12–39; [Pl.] *Ep.* 7.324e; Aesch. 1.173; (and as an example of later formulations) Ael. Aristid. 2.335, 3.434. For reflection on the relationship, see, e.g., Grote (1852, 8.232–80, which also covers the life of Critias in a still effective way) and, intriguingly though speculatively, Danzig (2014).

[5] Arist. *Rhet.* 3.16 1416b26–29. Critias is almost always thought to have entered the historical record as one of those accused, probably speciously, for involvement in the mutilation of the Herms in 415, based on the reference to a "Critias" in Andocides' *On the Mysteries* 47; but there is no independent evidence for the identity (see Humphreys 2018, 443). Nor is there any good evidence for Critias' involvement in the 400 of 411 (*pace* [Dem.] 58.67). The earliest reliable reference to Critias is in connection with Phrynichus' corpse (Lyc. 1.113) after 411.

[6] For complete coverage of the life and works of Critias, and relevant scholarship, see Moore and Raymond (2019).

[7] A16–20 DK; see Breitenbach (2003) and Gotteland (2018).

[8] An imitator of Plato's also includes Critias in the *Eryxias* (see Donato 2018, 175–81, for discussion). Controversy continues over the identity of the "Critias" in *Timaeus* and *Critias*; an important skeptic is Nails (2002, 106–11); the most recent novel argument in favor is in Aloni and Ianucci (2016), adding to strong arguments in Rosenmeyer (1949) and Davies (1971, 322–35).

[9] The usual assumption is that his government acted in ways antithetical to *sôphrosunê*, and its actions must have flowed from a deep character flaw (a lack of *sôphrosunê*) in himself (a view encouraged by Xen. *Mem.* 1.2.24, on Critias' experiences in exile in "lawless" Thessaly). A more complex assumption is that Critias sought to create a city governed by *sôphrosunê*, and his flawed understanding of the virtue led to the flawed regime; for this kind of assumption, see Tuozzo (2011, 53–70). In either case, we lack the evidence to track the relationships between Critias' reflections on morality, his intentions with respect to the government of the Thirty, and the explanations of the Thirty's months of extralegal execution and eventual civil war. A helpful study is Pownall (2012).

[10] Such a view is adumbrated in Gottesman (2020).

behavior, and gnomic maxims may explain his attention to the virtue.[11] At any rate, our best evidence for this thought comes from Plato's *Charmides*, from which with some labor and care we might extricate it; corroborating evidence comes from Athenaeus' quotation of one of Critias' elegies and Critias' other symposium-related work, including his *Spartan Constitution*.

Plato sets the *Charmides* in 429, at the beginning of the Peloponnesian War.[12] He peoples it with historical personages in actual situations, so though he writes some decades after its purported events, we might assume a basic historical verisimilitude. The dialogue presents Critias as having a memorable position about *sôphrosunê* that he advances within a larger debate about the virtue. Indeed, Plato's analysis of that position, Critias' definition of *sôphrosunê* as "doing one's own things," cited eight pages into the dialogue, occupies, in one form or another, the remaining sixteen pages of conversation.[13] Critias in the dialogue also makes other statements about *sôphrosunê*, for example, that the Delphic maxim "Know yourself" essentially means "Be *sôphrôn*" (Σωφρονεῖ); that *sôphrosunê* can just as much be glossed as "having a knowledge of knowledge"; and that a city, to be completely well run, needs only to be organized by *sôphrosunê* or led by *sôphrôn* leaders.[14] Presumably these three further statements reflect Critias' actual views, but their juxtaposition and examination belong more properly to Plato's fourth-century work and overall argument about *sôphrosunê* seen with Socratic eyes, and so their treatment will wait until Chapter 9.[15] Critias' express or initial definition of *sôphrosunê* is the focus here.

In the dialogue, talk of *sôphrosunê* gets going once Socrates asks Charmides, Critias' younger cousin, over whom he is legal guardian, whether he really has "an adequate share" (ἱκανῶς . . . μετέχειν) of the virtue in him; the question arises because Critias has said that everyone believes Charmides' possession of it surpasses all others.[16] Charmides does not give an answer; to loosen him up, Socrates proposes that Charmides say what he takes *sôphrosunê* to be, on the grounds that his possession of it would reveal itself to him, both its presence and what it is like.[17] In other words, Charmides is to define the virtue and then defend

---

[11] Drinking norms: Ath. 10.432d–433b (= B6; see below), 11.463e–f (= B33), 11.483b–c (= B34). Constitutions: B31–37. Self-regulating moral behavior: the "Sisyphus" fragment. Gnomic maxims: Σ Eur. *Hipp.* 264 (attributing the μηδὲν ἄγαν to Chilon of Sparta); Philostr. *VP* 1.16 (γνώμας δὲ πλείστας ἑρμηνεύων; see Condello 2014).

[12] Date: Planeaux (1999); Nails (2002, 311–12); Lampert (2010, 237–40).

[13] I take it that all the reformulations are simply that, and not rejections of Critias' original thesis; similarly, Press (2018, 23); Moore and Raymond (2019, xxxiv, 77).

[14] Delphic maxim: 164d3–165a7; having a knowledge of knowledge: 166c1–174e7; well-run city: 171d2–172a3, 173a7–d5.

[15] For other scholarly discussion, within a broad scholarship on the *Charmides* from the past half-century, see notably Irwin (1995, 35–44); Schmid (1998); Tuozzo (2011); Tsouna (2022).

[16] Pl. *Chrm.* 158c3–4 (note the similarity to Heraclitus B116; see Chapter 2, p. 59) and 157d1–4 (this exchange implies a social interest in exemplary manifestations of a virtue).

[17] Pl. *Chrm.* 158e6–159a4. There are reasons to doubt Socrates' seriousness about this method; see Moore (2015c, 73–75); Moore and Raymond (2019, 54–56).

his definition; if he cannot defend it, then he will not have proffered evidence that the virtue really does reveal itself to him.

Charmides fails adequately to defend his first two definitions of *sôphrosunê*—"some state of tranquility" (ἡσυχιότης τις) and "a sense of shame" (αἰδώς)—and then presents a definition that he says he learned from someone (as we find out, Critias): "doing one's own things" (τὸ τὰ ἑαυτοῦ πράττειν).[18] The contrast between the first two proffered definitions and the third tells us about the status of those respective definitions. The first two must have seemed intuitively plausible, even obviously true, to Charmides. This is not to say, of course, that they were "his" ideas, as though he invented them. The association of tranquility and shame with *sôphrosunê* was commonplace. Just as in Phocylides and *Clouds* we saw that *sôphrosunê* involves "walking in the roads well-orderedly" (βαδίζειν ἐν ταῖσιν ὁδοῖς εὐτάκτως, 964), so too in the *Charmides* it is "doing everything in an orderly way, and with tranquility—walking in the streets" (τὸ κοσμίως πάντα πράττειν καὶ ἡσυχῇ, ἔν τε ταῖς ὁδοῖς βαδίζειν, 159b2); and as in Homer, *Hippolytus*, and *Clouds*, one is not to scandalize *aidôs*; so too in the *Charmides*, *aidôs* is the very thing itself.[19] The point is that the commonplace associations would be available to a fifth-century Charmides, as an educated speaker of Greek; his definitions required no real conceptual insight on his part.[20] At the same time, he does not recall them as explicit teachings, as definitional explanations of the virtue, as at all imposed upon him by lexical legislators. As he reflects on the norms he would have thought himself to (be seen to) have exemplified or strived for, he probably thinks first of his composure and his self-restrained respect for his elders. Interpreting *sôphrosunê* as tranquility or the sense of shame would have seemed right and natural for Charmides, since he understands what it means to be tranquil and what it means to exercise a sense of shame; he believes himself to embody both; and those interpretations, if true, would vindicate the claims about his superlative possession of *sôphrosunê*. He advances his first two definitions as ones that he has independent, as it were subjective, grounds to accept.

The third definition differs. From the start, Charmides identifies his having heard it from someone else, apparently *as* a definition, and as an unfamiliar and unintuitive one. Its plausibility he does not feel; it does not self-certify. It is part not of the common language of *sôphrosunê* but of the theoretical response to *sôphrosunê* as an object of study. Charmides says to Socrates, "Tell me what you think about the following regarding *sôphrosunê*. I've just remembered something

---

[18] Tranquility: 159b3–160d3 (cf. Kosman 1983); shame: 160e3–161b2 (cf. Raymond 2018); introduction of "doing one's own thing": 161b3–7.

[19] For the connection to tranquility, see also Epicharmus fr. 101 PCG; Soph. fr. 64; Xen. *Lac. Pol.* 3.4; with shame: Soph. *Aj.* 1075.

[20] At 159a6–7 he is asked whether he "knows how to speak Greek" (ἑλληνίζειν ἐπίστασαι), with the implication that, if so, he can articulate his experiences by drawing on familiar formulations.

I heard someone say—that *sôphrosunê* is 'doing one's own things.' See if you think the person who said this was right."[21] Charmides recalls an assertion about *sôphrosunê*, one he seems not to have found altogether compelling, perhaps because, as the ensuing conversation suggests, he did not altogether comprehend it. This points to a background debate about the meaning of *sôphrosunê*, with the person from whom Charmides heard this definition contributing a novel proposal with questionable success. The definition abstracts more from lived experience than Charmides' first two definitions, presumably so that it might pertain to more departments of life: "tranquility" mainly describes those bodily or mental changes that occur predictably and with low amplitudes, such that others can readily ignore them; a "sense of shame" mainly describes the restriction of one's actions to those considered socially acceptable. But what the third definition gains in explanatory range—and further, in other dimensions of definitional success, such as accuracy, irrefutability, or cleverness—it buys at the cost of recognizability or ready applicability to difficult cases. Whereas we feel immediately what counts as tranquil walking, and feel, too, that it manifests an ideal of *sôphrôn* public comportment, we do not so immediately feel what counts as "doing one's own things" or, even if we did, feel it as an ideal of *sôphrosunê*. Thus the bulk of the trust we might have in the plausibility of this kind of definition comes from its source (and the reasoning or insight underwriting the source's confident assertion); and thus we must assume the source to be an actual or putative lexicographical or ethical expert. Charmides asks whether "the person who said this was right," not whether the position is right or sustainable, even though the answers to these questions should entail one another.

Socrates reacts immediately to Charmides' focalizing of the author of the view: "You rogue ... you heard this from Critias here—or from some other wise man (του τῶν σοφῶν)."[22] Socrates must be guessing, having been gone for three years, but it is an educated guess, evidently recognizing Critias' fingerprint: either Critias' talk of "doing one's own things" from earlier years, or his interest in *sôphrosunê*, or his propensity to present clever definitions in competitive contexts, or all three. Socrates' "or from some other wise man" at once admits his uncertainty and positions Critias as a "wise man," someone situated to give high-grade moral advice, often conceived of as doing so in competitive contexts.[23] What follows in the dialogue is a dramatically marked exchange. Critias flatly denies Charmides' getting the definition from him, though technically, we might

---

[21] Pl. *Chrm.* 161b4–7. Translations of the *Charmides* from Moore and Raymond (2019), here modified.

[22] Pl. *Chrm.* 161b8–c1.

[23] The recent relevant background literature is Griffith (1990); Martin (1993); Tell (2007); Kurke (2011, 95–115).

note, he does not deny authorship of it.[24] Some pages later, however, he comes to accept authorship, though without explaining his earlier denial.[25] This happens when Charmides bungles the definition's defense, taking his time in doing so, and then disavows blame for his having done so. He says that just as he has no idea what the definition means, perhaps its author has no idea either. Critias can take the abuse no longer, excoriates Charmides for impugning an author's understanding on the basis of his hearer's understanding, and then says, to Socrates, that he in fact accepts ownership of the definition and is willing to defend it. Whatever reason he had for wanting Charmides to defend his definition by himself, he now wants to show its plausibility.

The many antics in this dialogue connected to owning and disowning the definition draw attention to its being Critias'—the historical Critias'. The timeline of the *Charmides* has it that Critias publicized the idea in the years of Socrates' absence, 432–429. This sounds about right: it makes sense given the evidence from Aristophanes' *Clouds*, of concerted debate about *sôphrosunê* from the 420s, and more precisely matches the debate about *sôphrosunê* we will study in Thucydides' account of the beginning of the Peloponnesian War (at the end of this chapter) and in Euripides' *Hippolytus*, set in 428 (in the previous chapter). Given the centrality of the definition to the entire dialogue, the importance of Critias otherwise to Plato's writings, and the availability of Critias' writings, it would make little sense at this point to hoist a fictitious definition onto his relative. There just is no positive reason to doubt the historicity of the definition.[26] But that only leads us to be able to ask: What did Critias mean by defining *sôphrosunê* as "doing one's own things"?

This definition has a number of appealing qualities, though whether they outweigh its vagueness or riddling quality is yet to be seen. I have already mentioned its abstractness, and thus applicability to any department of life. I add now that it presents the virtue in terms of (a qualification of) action. Neither "tranquility" nor "a sense of shame," the earlier definitions, need represent any action at all; both may seem merely inhibitory of action. Such, at any rate, contributes to their failure as definitions of a virtue, since sometimes, it would seem, one must *do* something. "Doing one's own things" emphasizes action, albeit a subset of possible actions.

---

[24] "It appears he heard it from someone else... he certainly didn't get it from me" (ἔοικεν... ἄλλου· οὐ γὰρ δὴ ἐμοῦ γε). Critias' response could be literally true if, though the definition is his, Charmides heard it through an intermediary, someone who reports a conversation from which he was absent, a not implausible situation given Charmides' apparent innocence of the explanation. Yet Socrates later says that his "suspicion had been entirely right: Charmides had heard this last response about *sôphrosunê* from Critias" (162c4–6). This may well be consistent, if Socrates allows for indirect hearing and rejects Critias' technicality. Otherwise, Critias simply lies. There are good and less savory reasons for his doing so, none specifically relevant here.

[25] Pl. *Chrm.* 162c1–e6.

[26] Diels-Kranz (1952) accept it as 88 B41a. Some scholars have assumed that Critias' definition is Socrates' definition warmed over (notably Lampert 2010, 178–92); but there is no evidence for that.

It does not define the virtue circularly,[27] but also does not define it so blatantly descriptively—again, among the failures of "tranquility" and "a sense of shame," which could count as either good or bad. It defines the virtue based on something interpretative and in effect normative: "one's own things." And this points to another aspect of the definition: it involves a conception of selfhood. Acting in a *sôphrôn* way is none other than acting in a unified way—with the unity proper to oneself.

But why *this* definition? The background consideration seems to be the polarity "quietness, quiescence" (ἀπραγμοσύνη) vs. "(over-)involvedness" (πολυπραγμοσύνη).[28] Those unimpressed by democratic litigiousness and imperial expansion and compromise accused their advocates, litotically, of *polupragmosunê*, "doing too much."[29] Disvalued as "meddlesomeness" or "getting into others' business," the term identifies a norm, namely of action, and the direction of its breakage, namely toward excess. Criticism went in the other direction, too. Those unimpressed by aristocratic hauteur and conservative disengagement accused their advocates, hyperbolically, of *apragmosunê*, "doing nothing."[30] Disvalued as "dropping out from the common good," it identifies a breakage of the norm in the other direction, namely toward deficiency. Of course, those accused of *polupragmosunê* believed themselves to be admirably responsive to the need for change and worldly engagement, seeking honor and the goods which it rewards; and those accused of *apragmosunê* believed themselves to be abstaining from only some actions, namely bad or improper ones, or from political change motivated by a thirst for progress.[31] In any event, a form of the debate about political engagement, on either the personal or the civic level, took the euphemistic form of *prattein polla* or *oliga* ("doing much" or "little"): how active to be.

From this debate came Critias' middle way, premised on a discovery: the problem was not with too much or too little action, which could hardly be objectively measured or freed from context, but with action that was not one's own. Hence *idiopragmosunê* or *idiopragia*, the compound words that later clinched Critias' definition, *to ta heautou prattein*, "doing one's own things."[32] Critias

---

[27] This sort of problem is thematized in *Meno* 78d3–79c9.

[28] On this polarity, see Thuc. 2.60–64; also Ehrenberg (1947); Adkins (1976); Lateiner (1982).

[29] The related *philopragmosunê* (φιλοπραγμοσύνη) is nearly contemporaneous, in Pl. *Rep.* 8.549e; Arist. *Top.* 111a10; adj. in Lyc. 3; Is. 4.30; abs. n. in Cratin. fr. 27d.

[30] See esp. Carter (1986, 38–51).

[31] The "Better Argument" in Aristophanes' *Clouds* says that the (implied) *sôphrôn* life will include a competition with a *sôphrôn* age-mate in a grove filled with *apragmosunê* (1005–6); compare Eur. *Hipp.* 74–86 (discussed in the previous chapter). See Dover (1968 ad 1007) for the ancient interpretation of *apragmosunê* as the name of a flower (a name presumably on the model of our "forget-me-not," "impatiens," or "love-in-idleness" [*Midsummer Night's Dream* 2.1.174]). An early fifth-century red-figure vase fragment (Ath. Nat. Mus., Acropolis coll. F42) seems to contain the line σοφροσσυνεν ενι κλα[δοις σ]μιλα[κος "*Sôphrosunê* covered in the branches of the *smilax* (oak/yew/bindweed)."

[32] *Idiopragia* appears first in Pl. *Laws* 875b7, linked with *pleonexia*. Cp. *autopragia*, discussed in Chapter 11. The common translation of Critias' definition as "minding one's own business" is probably too critical and reactive.

surely did not invent the locution "Do your own thing!" nor discovered the snide wisdom behind "Leave others alone!" or "Mind your own business!," but may well have nominalized it as a definition for a virtue, specifically *sôphrosunê*.[33] (It need not be for *sôphrosunê* alone, as Plato's *Republic* shows; see Chapter 9.)

This brilliant definition of *sôphrosunê*, emphasizing as it does action and selfhood, might, for all that, seem vapid. Is it any clearer what counts as doing "one's own thing" in any particular domain of life than what counts as doing "too much"? It seems that what counts as one's own is what one ought to do, given the order of norms in which one finds oneself, or, in other words, doing what is good specifically for you. Such is how Socrates responds immediately to Critias' definition: You are saying that *sôphrosunê* is doing what one ought, doing what is good?[34] (This is in effect what Socrates says in the *Gorgias* [see Chapter 8], so the idea is not crazy.) Still, Critias must be onto something in emphasizing the indexical aspect: the "ought" and the "good" are with reference to "oneself." And indeed, Critias goes on again to modify his definition to emphasize the knowledge of oneself involved; *sôphrosunê*, as he puts it, practically *is* knowing oneself.[35] That must be because the specialness in being *sôphrôn* lies not only in deciding to do what happens to be one's own, but also in knowing what actually is one's own: there, in the selection or identification, is the particular achievement lauded by the term *sôphrosunê*.[36] Evidence for this comes from two directions: the shoal on which Charmides' definitional attempts capsized was knowing what "one's own" means, and the entire second half of the dialogue takes up the meaning of "knowing oneself" (by contrast with knowing other things), without ever explicitly rejecting the "doing one's own things" (aspect of the) definition.

"Doing one's own things" does, then, sound like a mature gloss on the earlier uses of *sôphrosunê* we saw in Chapter 2. In Homer, the *sôphrosunê* of Apollo and Telemachus labels decisions made in accord with—we now say—one's stable concerns, commitments, and social and self-constituted identity (where stability is a matter of discovery or interpretation). Of course, a continuity between the Homeric and Critian accounts of the virtue requires "one's own" to refer to what's stable rather than to what's fleeting, even if the fleeting sometimes has a more urgent inner presence. So the continuity of Critias' definition with earlier implicit definitions requires that the idea of one's "self" should pick out a subset of one's mental contents, and specifically a subset of one's experiences and judgments— namely, from the temporal perspective, the stabler ones. It does not require, of course, that in Homeric Greek there be a notion of "selfhood" that so refers.[37] It means, instead, that the Homeric idea of *sôphrosunê* implied that its characters,

---

[33] Cf. Hom. *Il.* 6.490; Soph. *El.* 678; Thuc. 1.68.1; Xen. *Lac. Pol.* 7.2.
[34] Pl. *Chrm.* 163e1, 164b3.
[35] Pl. *Chrm.* 164d5–165b5.
[36] This kind of argument in found in [Pl.] *Alc.* 133c18–d2; see Chapter 6.
[37] On this issue, see Gill (2008); Jeremiah (2012); *OCD*[4] s.v. "the self in Greek literature."

or readers, could conceive of an (at least approximate) internal distinction between some desires and others, those which should not motivate and those which should, those which flicker in and out depending on dynamic situations and those whose grip seems relatively independent of such dynamism. This division occasioned the division between what is properly oneself and what is only incidentally or imperfectly oneself.

In archaic poetry, as we have read it, *sôphrosunê* meant acting on something we would now deem principle by contrast with impulse. This is an idea that does not require reference to "oneself." Yet we see there a forerunner of the idea of a self, a glimmer of which we see in Critias' formulation, as something that, paradoxically enough, finds its reality less in the contingent rise and fall of one desire after the next, which seem maximally "inside," than in one's recognition of and adherence to regular patterns of valuation. The thought arises, still anachronistically formulated, that one is a self only when one has principles. From "my *norms*" we can infer "*my* norms."

This is Critias' abstract definition of *sôphrosunê*, given in probably political debate concerning the term, as reported and assessed in Plato's *Charmides*. We return to the debate about *polupragmosunê* when we discuss Thucydides. Critias also has a nondefinitional usage of *sôphrosunê* found in the fragments of his poetry. The Roman-era collector of classical poetry Athenaeus quotes from Critias' "Elegies" on the topic of Spartan symposia. It seems likely to come from Critias' *Spartan Constitution*, which presumably cites those institutional or dispositional arrangements in Sparta that, in the author's judgment, account for its excellence. Critias has been saying that compulsory drinking, of the sort found in Athens and of which he disapproves, is the result of (too frequent) toasts and the relentless passing around of a shared vessel of wine.[38] He describes the negative effects and then lauds the non-Athenian alternative, which seeks moderation:[39]

> εἶτ' ἀπὸ τοιούτων πόσεων γλώσσας τε λύουσιν
> εἰς αἰσχροὺς μύθους σῶμά τ' ἀμαυρότερον
> τεύχουσιν· πρὸς δ' ὄμμ' ἀχλὺς ἀμβλωπὸς ἐφίζει,
> λῆστις δ' ἐκτήκει μνημοσύνην πραπίδων.
> νοῦς δὲ παρέσφαλται· δμῶες δ' ἀκόλαστον ἔχουσιν
> ἦθος· ἐπεισπίπτει δ' οἰκοτριβὴς δαπάνη.
> οἱ Λακεδαιμονίων δὲ κόροι πίνουσι τοσοῦτον

---

[38] The connection between drinking and happiness is a major subject of early Greek debate, as we have already seen in Theognis and Xenophanes; for closer contemporaries to Critias, see Panyassis frr. 19–22; Ion fr. 744, fr. eleg. 26–27; Antiphon B76; Eur. *Cycl.* 503–43; Antisth. 197 SSR.

[39] Text from Gerber (1999) with one modification, translated by Christopher C. Raymond and the author.

ὥστε φρέν' εἰς ἱλαρὰν ἐλπίδα⁴⁰ πάντ' ἀπάγειν
εἴς τε φιλοφροσύνην γλῶσσαν μέτριόν τε γέλωτα.
τοιαύτη δὲ πόσις σώματί τ' ὠφέλιμος
γνώμῃ τε κτήσει τε· καλῶς δ' εἰς ἔργ' Ἀφροδίτης
  πρός θ' ὕπνον ἥρμοσται, τὸν καμάτων λιμένα,
πρὸς τὴν τερπνοτάτην τε θεῶν θνητοῖς Ὑγίειαν,
  καὶ τὴν Εὐσεβίης γείτονα Σωφροσύνην.

ἑξῆς τε πάλιν φησίν·

αἱ γὰρ ὑπὲρ τὸ μέτρον κυλίκων προπόσεις παραχρῆμα
  τέρψασαι λυποῦσ' εἰς τὸν ἅπαντα χρόνον·
ἡ Λακεδαιμονίων δὲ δίαιθ' ὁμαλῶς διάκειται,
  ἔσθειν καὶ πίνειν σύμμετρα πρὸς τὸ φρονεῖν
καὶ τὸ πονεῖν εἶναι δυνάτους· οὐκ ἔστ' ἀπότακτος
  ἡμέρα οἰνῶσαι σῶμ' ἀμέτροισι πότοις. (Critias B6, 8–27)

Then, from this sort of drinking their tongues slip
  into disgraceful language and they make their bodies
dim: a dark mist settles on their eyes,
  and oblivion melts memory from their hearts.
The mind falters: slaves become undisciplined in
  character; wealth-draining extravagance bursts in.
But Spartan sons drink only as much
  as will restore their thoughts to
cheerful hope, their tongues to sociability and measured laughter.
  This sort of drinking is beneficial for body,
judgment, and property; it is well suited to Aphrodite's works
  and to sleep, safe harbor from toils;
and to Health, the most pleasing of gods to mortals;
  and to *Sôphrosunê*, neighbor of Reverence.

And thereafter Critias says, again:

For toasting with cups beyond measure, though it brings
  immediate pleasure, causes everlasting pain.
But Spartan habits rest on level ground:
  eating and drinking moderately so they are able to think well
and work hard. There's no special day set aside
  for soaking the body with immoderate drinking.

---

[40] Emperius: ἀσπίδα codd.

Sôphrosunê is the capping and final term in Critias' praise of Spartan drinking, found in a sort of priamel of its benefits: from somatic, psychic, and practical benefits, to sexual and dormitive success, and culminating in health and that which is as valuable as piety. It is even apotheosized into a mythic genealogy. It represents the avoidance of the seven listed sins of overdrinking: (1) a shameful over-speaking, (2) weakness of body, (3) imprecision of vision, (4) forgetfulness, (5) a faltering (παρασφάλλω) mind, (6) undisciplined dependents, and (7) an uncontrolled household. None is absolutely distinctive of drinking, and so Critias, like Theognis, brings up *sôphrosunê* as relevant to drinking culture but not restricted to or defined by it. Health and piety have much broader domains than nonintoxication. And Critias says specifically that moderate drinking is simply "well-matched" or "harmonized" with moderate living.

From Critias' list of drinking's sins we may infer the list of traits of the *sôphrôn* person, who is evidently capable of doing all and only his own things: quiet; strong or hearty of body; clear-eyed; clear-minded; thoughtful; and with those under one's command disciplined and obedient. We have seen many of these traits already cited, for instance in Aristophanes; the image is of one who sets up no obstacles to action, least of all narrow-mindedness or an inability to reason (to exercise a stable mind). Our study of Xenophon, in Chapter 7, will further justify us in saying that *sôphrosunê* means acknowledging and having the capacity to adhere to authoritative norms: this seems the best explanation of its being "the neighbor of Piety" or, as Xenophanes puts it in a similar poem, "giving good consideration to the gods always."[41]

Antiphon's Theory

Later writers linked Critias with Antiphon (ca. 480–411) as powerful intellectuals who eventually led coups against the Athenian democracy.[42] Thucydides calls Antiphon superior to all other Athenians in virtue (ἀρετή) and in the power of his thought and expression, disinclined to public participation given his reputation as "terribly clever," but deemed the most capable advisor for others' legal or political needs.[43] This is plausibly the same Antiphon as the "Antiphon the sophist" Xenophon depicts in conversation with Socrates about the charging of tuition for instruction; the author of the famed "Tetralogies" (irresolvable moot capital cases) and numerous forensic addresses, including three extant speeches on murder cases; and the author of various other works of intellectual literature, including on cosmology and dream interpretation.[44] He is best known now for

---

[41] Xenoph. B1.24.

[42] Joint mentions of Antiphon and Critias are in, e.g., Galen *In Hippocratis librum De officina commentarii iii*, p. 656 (Kühn, vol. 18.2); Hermog. *Peri Ideôn* B401,25 (Rabe); Poll. 2.58 (and less meaningfully in Dion. Hal. *Thuc.* 51 and *Isae.* 20; [Plut.] *Vita Antiphonis* 1.1 832d–e).

[43] Thuc. 8.68.1–2.

[44] Xen. *Mem.* 1.6. For the debate about one Antiphon or two, see Gagarin (1997) and Pendrick (2002, 1–26).

an ethically controversial fragment found in the Oxyrhynchus papyri evidently from his *On Truth*—there he argues that justice is following the law, but law is distinct from nature, and so acting justly goes against nature; the costs of acting justly may thus outweigh the risk of acting unjustly in secret or with impunity.[45] We do not know whether he was asserting this view or simply mooting it. In any event, he was obviously interested in the virtues.

The fifth-century CE anthologist Stobaeus cites three fragments of Antiphon's writings on *sôphrosunê*.[46] One of them is a single sentence:

ὅστις δὲ τῶν αἰσχρῶν ἢ τῶν κακῶν μήτε ἐπεθύμησε μήτε ἥψατο, οὐκ ἔστι σώφρων· οὐ γὰρ ἔσθ᾽ ὅτου κρατήσας αὐτὸς ἑαυτὸν κόσμιον παρέχεται. (Antiph. B59/D56)

Whoever has neither desired nor touched disgraceful or bad things is not *sôphrôn*: he has not rendered himself orderly by having overcome something.

Antiphon gives a conflicted-desire analysis of *sôphrosunê*: it amounts to doing the right thing despite having the desire to do otherwise, perhaps even the vivid desire caused by proximity to its satisfaction. Just as courage makes sense only as action through fear, and thus as a management of one's strong inclinations, *sôphrosunê* makes sense only as action through enticement, management of another kind of inclination. So the virtue is not expressly one of going in the correct direction but of being able to choose well between different directions.

Antiphon claims that *sôphrosunê* is the rendering (παρέχεται) of oneself orderly (κόσμιον).[47] And to have rendered oneself orderly is to have overcome something (ὅτου κρατήσας), a desire for something bad or disgraceful. So *sôphrosunê* is a kind of orderliness, a putting of one's actions into a norm-adhering line. In Homer, the verbal form related to being "orderly," *kosmein*, is used for a general's organizing his soldiers;[48] more widely, the propositional

---

[45] For treatments, see Guthrie (1971, 107–13); Cairns (1993, 360–63, with 344–51); Pendrick (2002, 315–77); Bonazzi (2020b, 84–89).

[46] The following are at Stob. 3.5.57 ("On *sôphrosunê*"), 3.20.66 ("On anger"), 4.22.66 ("That it is not good to marry"). LM 9.71 express some doubt about the authenticity of the twelve Stobaeus-Antiphon quotations, yet Pendrick (2002, 39–40), on whom their doubt relies, allows only that some scholars have thought (on quite weak grounds) to attribute some of them to Antiphon's contemporary and homonym, Antiphon of Rhamnous. I, however, suspect these are the same Antiphon; at any rate, the passages would be from the same era.

[47] The middle voice of παρέχεται is unusual; in Antiph. 5.20 and 5.24 it means "to produce, furnish [witnesses]." Pendrick (2002) translates ambiguously: first "makes himself" (205), then "show[s] oneself such and such" (409): the first emphasizes self-constitution, the second appearance. Jeremiah (2012, 98) suggests that both meanings are present: in his gloss, "making oneself such-and-such in a way that can be seen by others" (98n36); my "rendered himself" follows this interpretation. Parallel constructions are at Lys. 7.41; Isoc. 18.18; Isae. fr. 30. On παρέχω used reflexively for self-cultivation, see Isoc. 2.20, 3.34, 38, 45, 51, 60, 63.

[48] Hom. *Il.* 14.379.

phrase *kata kosmon* means "in order," of a sequence of things or moments.[49] Antiphon speaks of an orderliness of oneself achieved by oneself. But his is an orderliness achieved against strong opposition—against desires pressing for counternormative action. So, in a case of *sôphrosunê*, one makes oneself orderly by rejecting calls to action made by bad desires.

The debate this fragment contributes to concerns which person exemplifies *sôphrosunê*. Does the virtue mark the person who feels no shameful or harmful enticements at all, or by contrast the person who, feeling those enticements, can disregard them? Is it a matter of desiderative purification or rather of psychic distancing and evaluative discernment? Is the ideal person simple, or is he or she complex? To be sure, these need not be incommensurable positions: continual self-overcoming may suffocate the bad desires; better-trained desires may allow for more reliable self-control. At any rate, Antiphon highlights for *sôphrosunê* the success in inner struggle, and thus the question of choice or endurance.

The centrality of that inner struggle, and what success depends on, is developed in a much longer remark by Antiphon, this one more ostensibly paradoxical:

ὅστις δὲ ἰὼν ἐπὶ τὸν πλησίον κακῶς ποιήσων δειμαίνει, μὴ ἃ θέλει ποιῆσαι, ἁμαρτὼν τούτων, ἃ μὴ θέλει ἀπενέγκηται, σωφρονέστερος. ἐν ᾧ γὰρ δειμαίνει, μέλλει· ἐν ᾧ δὲ μέλλει, πολλάκις ὁ διὰ μέσου χρόνος ἀπέστρεψε τὸν νοῦν τῶν θελημάτων· καὶ ἐν μὲν τῷ γεγενῆσθαι οὐκ ἔνεστιν, ἐν δὲ τῷ μέλλειν ἐνδέχεται γενέσθαι.[50] ὅστις δὲ δράσειν μὲν οἴεται τοὺς πέλας κακῶς, πείσεσθαι δ' οὔ, οὐ σωφρονεῖ. ἐλπίδες δ' οὐ πανταχοῦ ἀγαθόν· πολλοὺς γὰρ τοιαῦται ἐλπίδες κατέβαλον εἰς ἀνηκέστους συμφοράς, ἃ δ' ἐδόκουν τοὺς πέλας ποιήσειν, παθόντες ταῦτα ἀνεφάνησαν αὐτοί. σωφροσύνην δὲ ἀνδρὸς οὐκ ἂν ἄλλου ὀρθότερόν τις κρίνειεν ἢ ὅστις τοῦ θυμοῦ ταῖς παραχρῆμα ἡδοναῖς ἐμφράσσει αὐτὸς ἑαυτὸν κρατεῖν τε καὶ νικᾶν ἠδυνήθη αὐτὸς ἑαυτόν. ὃς δὲ θέλει χαρίσασθαι τῷ θυμῷ παραχρῆμα, θέλει τὰ κακίω ἀντὶ τῶν ἀμεινόνων. (Antiph. B58/D55)

Whoever, coming against a neighbor to do him harm, fears lest he mess up what he wishes to do and so carry off what he does not wish, is more *sôphrôn*. For in his fear, he delays; and in his delay, the intervening time often turns his mind away from what he had wished. This [turning] is not possible for something that has already happened, but it can happen in the case of delay. But whoever thinks he will do harm to neighbors but will not suffer it himself is not *sôphrôn*. Hopes are not everywhere a good thing: for such hopes have thrown many into irreversible misfortune; and what they thought to do to their neighbors they

---

[49] LSJ s.v. I.
[50] Pendrick (following Bücheler) conjectures a μὴ preceding γενέσθαι.

evidently suffered themselves. Someone would very correctly judge nobody to have *sôphrosunê* but whoever blocks the immediate pleasures of his heart and is able both to control himself and to be victorious over himself. He who wishes to gratify his heart immediately wishes worse things in place of better ones.

The paradox that opens this fragment is that while *sôphrosunê* seems characteristic of the efficient agent, it rightly applies to the inconstantly malicious coward in the very midst of his doubting of his efficacy. This is something of a joke, since the application of *sôphrosunê* to this man seems hardly a matter of praise. Our coward wanted to do ill; fear that he would fail pushed pause; while on pause, he came no longer to want to do ill; so, in not doing ill, he overcame the desire to do so. As the previous fragment states, this is what *sôphrosunê* is. If any reason was involved, this was by happenstance and it had no force against the desire for ill; only the neutralization brought about by fear of mishap calmed the mind sufficiently for a happier desire to arise.

The reverse of the ineffective dastard who is *sôphrôn* despite himself is the self-confident villain who thinks he may act with impunity but suffers what he sought to mete out, and therefore lacks *sôphrosunê*. This man seems to have satisfied his initial desires, and therefore realized agency, but from a broader vantage he has not: he did not intend to undergo the misfortune he threw himself into. His confidence was unjustified, since it failed to account for the serious risks incurred by his endeavor. These are the risks that the coward felt so strongly.

Antiphon concludes this comparison with a direct statement about *sôphrosunê*. Rather than formulate it as overcoming bad desires, as in the previous fragment, here he formulates it as waiting a moment before acting on a new desire. Before it was an evaluative condition; now it is a temporal one. *Sôphrosunê* is not doing whatever one feels like doing; it involves a cool moment of distance from a desire, giving a better desire the chance to bloom. *Sôphrosunê* applies only when triumphing over a bad desire, of course, because nobody would celebrate with a virtue-term the triumph over a good desire; the implication is that the desire that one temporizes about *is* a bad one. Its enervation during the delay comes to the same point as in the previous fragment. Again, as before, the role of reasoning goes unmentioned as irrelevant.

The repetition of self-reflexive language in fragments B59 and B58 is striking. Here that language is even doubled, "being able both to control oneself and be victorious over oneself" (αὐτὸς ἑαυτὸν κρατεῖν τε καὶ νικᾶν ἠδυνήθη αὐτὸς ἑαυτόν). Each of the three self-reflexives focalizes an "I" that is some aspect of oneself that is superior to another aspect of oneself. They suggest that one identifies oneself more closely with the acting-on-the-good-desires than with the bad desires themselves, even if those bad desires are more immediate, more intimately connected to the heart, and even if the acting-on-the-good-desires is possibly an accident of nerves and caution. If *sôphrosunê* is the acting on those good desires, and an orderliness that allows for that action, and in an overarching way the virtue seems a matter of efficacy, of power and agency, then power and agency come from organizing oneself into a person who acts on one's good desires. If so, what I most truly am is my commitment to what is consistent and good, which is precisely for those good desires to be decisive. Thus, according to Antiphon, *sôphrosunê* is the virtue that is predicated, first, on there being different and inconsistent desires clamoring to influence my actions; second, on my being constituted more by my longer-term desires than by those "immediate pleasures of one's heart"; third, on those longer-term, or less-evanescent, desires winning out; such that, fourth, *my* actions are those that flow from *who I really am*, namely the longer- rather than shorter-term desires.

These claims get clear corroboration in other work by Antiphon. He uses the verb *sôphronizein*, "to make *sôphrôn*," twice in his *Tetralogies*. The *Tetralogies* are likely the earliest extant prose works in Greek, presented as a trio of four-part moot court cases. Both times he uses the verb, he means muting the efficacy of one's immediate inclinations to action. The First Tetralogy concerns a capital charge for street murder; the prosecutor believes he has circumstantial evidence for the defendant's guilt, given prior conflict between the defendant and the victim. Before the murder in question occurred, the accused had been wronged by the victim and was afraid of a suit the victim brought against him. This fear and anger at the injustice "blocked his *promêtheia*," which is his capacity for rational judgment, and so he committed the murder.[51] For anybody else, the prosecutor says, no matter how much they wanted to kill the victim, the danger and disgracefulness of committing such a murder "would have been sufficient to *sôphronizein* the felt intensity of their judgment" (ἀρκοῦσα ἦν σωφρονίσαι τὸ θυμούμενον τῆς γνώμης), and so they wouldn't have done it.[52] The risk to their well-being and reputation would counterbalance whatever prior considerations in favor of killing the victim they had. This is precisely the case described in fragment B58: delay causes reconsideration, the bad desire is overcome, and this is *sôphrosunê*.

The Third Tetralogy depicts the prosecution of a young guy for killing an old guy who he perceived as starting a fight with him. The prosecutor doubts the ferocity of the old guy's assault, observing that old men are less inclined than young men to get drunk and angry and thus they have less desire to harm others: their experience with wine, bodily weakness, and fear of youthful power *sôphronizein* them.[53] Old men are *sôphrôn* because they do not have such strong desires (they

---

[51] On *promêtheia* as rational judgment, not mere "hesitation" or "caution," see Moore (2015a).
[52] Antiph. 2.3.3.
[53] Antiph. 4.3.2.

do not get so drunk); they cannot act effectively on such desires (they are not so strong); and they do not want to act on such desires (they are no so robust against others' retaliation). So again, their better desires overcome their worse, thanks to the realities of aging. The defendant later rebuts this notion by saying that the prosecutor has overplayed this *sôphronizein* among old men; he thinks they do not always overcome their worse desires.[54] As with the earlier Tetralogy, and again as in B58, *sôphronizein* is credited with preventing some immediate, worse, and evidently less stable desire from being motivationally decisive. In some cases, those desires may be de-intensified, but the more important case is that they lose their authority, no matter their strength.

One more fragmentary statement by Antiphon on *sôphrosunê* includes the virtue in a list of effortful personal concerns. Though Antiphon does not here analyze the virtue, he reveals its centrality in ethical and social life. The term comes up in a warning against marriage: hard enough it is to care for oneself; to care for two would be too hard.

ἐγὼ γάρ, εἴ μοι γένοιτο σῶμα ἕτερον τοιοῦτον οἷον ἐγὼ ἐμαυτῷ, οὐκ ἂν δυναίμην ζῆν, οὕτως ἐμαυτῷ πολλὰ πράγματα παρέχων ὑπέρ τε τῆς ὑγιείας τοῦ σώματος ὑπέρ τε τοῦ καθ' ἡμέραν βίου ἐς τὴν ξυλλογὴν ὑπέρ τε δόξης καὶ σωφροσύνης καὶ εὐκλείας καὶ τοῦ εὖ ἀκούειν. (Antiph. B49/D57, 19–24)

For, if there were for me another body such as I have for myself, I would not be able to live, so much effort I furnish for myself, regarding health of my body, and getting what I need for daily life, and reputation and *sôphrosunê* and renown and good name.

Staying healthy and working a job involve a lot of work (πολλὰ πράγματα παρέχων), and on top of that personal life-support is maintenance of one's public persona: one's reputation (δόξη), *sôphrosunê*, renown (εὔκλεια), and good name (τὸ εὖ ἀκούειν). It was traditional to be concerned about the *sôphrosunê* of marital partners.[55] Here *sôphrosunê* must involve acting well in ways that could be known outside the house and that are laborious or challenging.[56] This suggests

---

[54] Antiph. 4.4.2.

[55] Hipponax (fr. 182) says that the best marriage for a *sôphrôn* man is to a woman with a "fine disposition" (τρόπον . . . χρηστόν), one who is good-natured (εὔνουν) and stable (βεβαίαν), for only this will "preserve the household" (οἰκίαν σῴζει μόνη). Semonides (fr. 7.108) treats *sôphrosunê* as the primary desideratum for a wife, and notes that one who may *seem* (δοκεῖ) most *sôphrôn* may not actually be so.

[56] This string of four nouns has received much editorial scrutiny and emendation because of its seeming redundancy and because when later in the fragment Antiphon recapitulates the burdens of caring for a spouse, he lists only four items: health, livelihood, *sôphrosunê*, and *eukleia*, cutting the last four items down to two. Wilamowitz deletes *sôphrosunê* and *eukleia* from the first list (so that when they appear in the second list they provide rhetorical variety for their putative synonyms, *doxa* and *to eu akouein* from the first list); Meineke deletes only *to eu akouein* (figuring that having three

overcoming those persistent and hard-to-extinguish desires to do unseemly or bad things that have a social component, for example acting on jealousy, anger, laziness, captiousness, acquisitiveness, or lust.

Whatever we think about this intriguing fragment, Antiphon's global take on *sôphrosunê* seems distinctive, determinate, thoughtful, and consistent. The psychology, evaluative language, reflexivity, and conception of self-constitution that Antiphon advances in his writings about the virtue all reward further reflection. And in their nuance and dialectical presentation we see him responding to ongoing debates about the nature and ascription of the virtue.

Thucydides

Thucydides writes his history of the Peloponnesian war at the end of the fifth century, perhaps even after Socrates' execution, having thus already absorbed a half-century's worth of intellectual and political agony.[57] Though he does not cite Critias (his book cuts off in 411, before Critias had significant political notoriety), he does discuss Antiphon, as we have seen, and the sophistic movement evidently influenced him, both rhetorically and analytically; he relocates the sophists' debates about goodness and virtue to the political oratory of the same time—or he finds it there, and perhaps sharpens the dialectic.[58] The debates about the nature of *sôphrosunê* he re-creates are the most striking, in part because of their centrality to his narrative across its eight books, but mostly because of the distinctiveness of his vision of the virtue. What he has to say about *sôphrosunê* is usually analyzed through his contrast between Spartan and Athenian sensibilities, and their changes through the war.[59] But we see something else

---

items in this list would not be excessive); Diels revises τοῦ εὖ ἀκούειν to ἐς τὸ εὖ ἀκούειν (with about the same reasoning). Blass fr. 131, LM 9.76–77, and Pendrick (2002, 194) do not emend. Pendrick defends the text by saying that the four terms have the rhetorical effect of accumulation; but he also claims that *sôphrosunê* means "reputation for σωφροσύνη" (387). He does not note, however, that this would be an unparalleled use of the term, and anyway he does not translate in accordance with his claim, rendering instead: "honor, prudence, glory, and reputation" (195). North (1966, 88), has a similar view, claiming without argument that the term can mean "only 'outward reputation, won by good moral conduct.'" But then she complicates this view by saying that "this connotation recalls the external type of sophrosyne depicted . . . in the *Clouds* . . . and the superficial definitions of the virtue offered in the early part of Plato's *Charmides*." Those may be understandings of the virtue that have outward appearances, but are not for that reason merely "reputations."

[57] For post-399 dating, see Pouilloux and Salviat (1983, 391–403; 1985) and Munn (2000, 5–6, 11–12, 305–6, 316–27, 433n57, 434n61). OCD^4 (Wade-Gery) considers 399–98 as the latest likely date.

[58] Thucydides says he revised the speeches he heard: Thuc. 1.22; see Hornblower (1991), 1.75 for discussion. Studied with Gorgias and Antiphon: Philostr. *VS* 1.9.3; *Suda* α. 2745. On the relationship between sophistic and para-sophistic thought, see Billings (2021). On Thucydides' thinking through ethics, Pearson (1957).

[59] E.g., North (1966, 100–115); Rademaker (2005, 201–21).

about it when we study it dialectically, as a contentious term that plays a role in arguments about political morality. It presages something of the analysis of a city-wide *sôphrosunê* in Book 4 of Plato's *Republic* (discussed in Chapter 9). But the virtue has a more complex role in this even longer piece of prose. It gets close to the idea of self-sufficiency, being content with what one has and thereby avoiding graspingness in foreign affairs and thus internationalism of any sort; but it can also mean acknowledging and acting upon whatever norms are normative, such that sometimes a city feels it must reach beyond its borders.

Two debates, both from Book 1 of the *History*, illuminate Thucydides' thinking about *sôphrosunê*. The terms of those debates recur through the bulk of the *History*.

Corcyreans vs. Corinthians at Athens (433 BCE)

The very first speech-debate in Thucydides' *History* is the programmatic rhetorical conflict between the Corcyreans and the Corinthians litigated before the Athenians at the start of the Peloponnesian War.[60] The Corcyreans are requesting an alliance with Athens to protect themselves against the ominous growth of the Corinthian navy. They know their request is awkward, since during peacetime they had avoided any such alliance, an alliance which would have benefited the Athenians monetarily and perhaps militarily; the Corcyreans seem to want a costless alliance, in force only when it will be to their own active advantage. So they try immediately to justify this apparent opportunism. "What earlier seemed to us *sôphrosunê*, of not sharing in the hazards of foreign alliances, namely the judgment of one's neighbor, has come around to seem irresolute and weak."[61] Their justification amounts to an explanation of their earlier mistake. They thought they were living up to an ideal, of *sôphrosunê*, but they now see that they were not being *sôphrôn*; they were failing to make the right commitments. What they took to be *sôphrosunê* was autonomy, an independence of decision-making—not being forced to act on the judgments of those with whom they allied. Dependence on such judgments can be dangerous. Thus the Corcyreans had earlier thought, as they now report it to the Athenians, that they had committed themselves to acting on the basis of their own judgment, being master of their destiny, and being all the safer for that. But now they think, so they say in

---

[60] Programmaticity: Morrison (1999). For an approach to the ethics in this exchange, see Pearson (1957, 231–33).

[61] Thuc. 1.32.4: καὶ περιέστηκεν ἡ δοκοῦσα ἡμῶν πρότερον σωφροσύνη, τὸ μὴ ἐν ἀλλοτρίᾳ ξυμμαχίᾳ τῇ τοῦ πέλας γνώμῃ ξυγκινδυνεύειν, νῦν ἀβουλία καὶ ἀσθένεια φαινομένη. Hornblower (1991, 77) renders *sôphrosunê* here as "wisdom"; he makes no mention of the concept's being thematic until his note on 1.37.2 (τὸ σῶφρον, "a wise moderation"): "Another pair of speakers throw the same idea back and forth." Later this author renders the noun as "prudence" (e.g., ad 1.68.1, 1.79.2).

exculpation, that they were not actually so committed; they were simply afraid to make any commitment at all. Surely allying with the Athenians would have been better, but they could not get themselves to appreciate that fully, or to have the courage to enter the world stage. So they request forgiveness for having been mistaken in their "uninvolvement" (ἀπραγμοσύνη); they did not mean anything bad (κακίας) by it.[62] In an echo of Critias' thinking about *sôphrosunê*—not getting involved in others' affairs, but still doing what one ought—the Corcyreans apologize for their isolationism, which they had wrongly dignified as self-determination. They see now that any hope they may have of self-determination requires coordination with stronger states; making their own decisions does not mean being the only party to any decision-making. In their quest for autonomy, they had fallen into a "lazy neutrality," which is not a principled position at all.[63]

Thucydides develops this argument about *sôphrosunê* in the opening lines of the Corinthians' response. They deny that the virtue-ideal explains anything. "They say, on the topic of alliance, that it was because of *sôphrosunê* that they never entered one; but they made this their practice from deviousness, not from virtue; they wanted no ally because they did not want a witness to their injustices, and they did not want the disgrace of requesting one."[64] According to the Corinthians, the Corcyreans never actually believed that they were acting as they ought; they were never simply mistaken about the demands of *sôphrosunê*, taking it to counsel isolation rather than cooperation. They were not confused at all; they were in fact driven by the goal of privacy, to advance their illicit ends with impunity, and to support their reputation for strength. What motivated them was the desire to indulge themselves and to dissemble about their vulnerabilities, neither of which motivation is virtuous.

The Corinthians go on to interpret the terms of the Fifty-Years Peace, the conditions of which are presently at issue. On the Corinthian construction, the Peace allows alliance by previous unaligned cities should three conditions be met. The first two are simple: the previous unaligned city does not ally in order to cause harm, and it has not recently deserted another alliance.[65] The third, which deploys the verb *sôphronein*, is an interpretative crux for our understanding of the term.[66] The Peace, the Corinthians say, is for "whoever will not make, for those accepting them, if they *sôphronein*, war rather than peace" (ὅστις μὴ τοῖς δεξαμένοις, εἰ σωφρονοῦσι, πόλεμον ἀντ' εἰρήνης ποιήσει). That is, the rights and responsibilities of the Peace may be afforded to cities just in

---

[62] Thuc. 1.32.5.
[63] The term is from Hornblower (1991, 77).
[64] Thuc. 1.37.2: Φασὶ δὲ ξυμμαχίαν διὰ τὸ σῶφρον οὐδενός πω δέξασθαι· τὸ δ' ἐπὶ κακουργίᾳ καὶ οὐκ ἀρετῇ ἐπετήδευσαν, ξύμμαχόν τε οὐδένα βουλόμενοι πρὸς τἀδικήματα οὐδὲ μάρτυρα ἔχειν οὔτε παρακαλοῦντες αἰσχύνεσθαι.
[65] Thuc. 1.40.2
[66] See Marchant (1905 ad loc.).

case their joining an alliance does not bring about war. The conditional "if they *sôphronein*" seems to apply to those already in an alliance, but its meaning is not immediately clear. Thomas Hobbes renders it this way: the Peace is for those who "bring not a war with them instead of peace to those (if they be wise) that receive them." To be sure, it cannot be the wisdom *of* receiving them that is a relevant qualification (if *sôphronein* means that); maybe it is the wisdom of the receivers generally. Perhaps the framers of the Peace recognized that any alliance could lead to war, were the parties to it foolish or overextended, and this fact could end up preventing all alliance whatsoever; the qualification means to disallow only those alliances that would cause war even to *sôphrôn* states.[67] But this might seem a strange condition to build into an international legal instrument. Thus it could be that Hobbes imagines the parenthesis "if they be wise" as a kind of editorial interjection spoken over the shoulder of the city deciding whether to accept a candidate new league member: should they *sôphronein*, they would themselves accept alliance only with those who would not bring war with them. There would be an alliance only if, in having done their due diligence, the receiving parties see that peace rather than war would result.[68]

The point is that, whatever our interpretation, it seems that one could *sôphronein* as well as ally; *sôphrosunê* does not mean absolute political independence. The Corcyreans had already in effect recognized or at least asserted this, in their *mea culpa*: We thought *sôphrosunê* demanded isolation, but we were wrong! *Sôphrosunê* may demand instead diffidence in alliance-making, doing so only for a select group of reasons. We will see later a debate over the proper form of geopolitical *sôphrosunê*, as either no-exceptions isolationism or a selective international participation, and if the latter, what the group of legitimating reasons includes.

The Corinthians conclude their speech against the Corcyreans with one more reference to *sôphrosunê*. It would be more *sôphrôn* for the Athenians to allay the suspicions they have raised about Megara than, by allying with the Corcyreans, to

---

[67] This may be the view of Morris (1891 ad loc.): "[T]his condition applies to the whole clause, and not to τοῖς δεξαμένοις only; and the force of it will be felt if, instead of 'who will not cause war instead of peace to his new friends' (τοῖς δεξαμένοις), we substitute its positive equivalent: 'who will permit peace to be maintained by his new friends' *if they exercise ordinary discretion*; i.e. no new allies should be received who will render ordinary discretion unavailing to prevent war, as the Corcyraeans are sure to do." Marchant (1905 ad loc.) similarly interprets *sôphronousi* as applying "to the whole sentence" and glosses confusingly, "as they—*those to whom they make the application*—know if they are prudent."

[68] This may be the rough implication of Lattimore (1998, 22): "and does not bring those who accept the alliance, if they reflect on it, war instead of peace," though it really is not easy to understand what relevance the alliance acceptors' reflection has to the matter. Smith (1919), struggling, seems to assume that the text has lost a negation: "and whose adhesion will not bring to the power that is mad enough to receive them war instead of peace." Jowett (1881 ad loc.) goes a similar way, imagining words that are not in our text: "and who will bring war instead of peace to those who receive him, or rather, if they are wise, will not receive him on such terms."

act unjustly on the basis of fear and uncertain predictions of the future.[69] It would be so because they would not incur the instantaneous wrath of the Corinthians—it would be more prudent; they would be acting more from their long-term interest than instantaneous feelings of gratification or power. *Sôphrosunê* is a matter of assaying all relevant considerations and doing what is best overall.

In this first debate, we see two perspectives on *sôphrosunê*. It can mean being motivated only by those judgments one takes as properly one's own; the *sôphrôn* city does not treat others' judgments as authoritative. We could take this self-sufficiency as an instantiation of prudence, doing what is safe, predictable, and within one's control, though the Corcyreans present it rather in self-constituting terms, as concerning whose judgment to treat as authoritative. The Corinthians recognize *sôphrosunê* so glossed as a "virtue" and thus an admirable ground or justification of action, not just a prudent one. This is the second perspective. The Corinthians realize that *sôphrosunê* is so admirable that it may be used rhetorically as cover for something else. As we see in their concluding exhortation to the Athenians, it involves acting justly—that is, not harming others to their disadvantage but one's own benefit—and reasonably. Thus isolation may be *sôphrôn*, but sometimes it might not be.

Corinthians vs. Spartans (432 BCE)

The second debate about *sôphrosunê* in Thucydides' *History*, again in a programmatic early position, again involves the Corinthians, this time with the Spartans. The opening sentence of the Corinthians' speech returns to the Corcyrean view: "Your confidence, Lacedaemonians, in your constitution and your interactions among yourselves establishes you as less trusting toward others, should we have something to say; while your *sôphrosunê* comes from this, you're also more ignorant about external affairs."[70] This is the *sôphrosunê* that the Corcyreans claimed they thought they stood for: a commitment to principles promulgated by and to oneself, and separation from any claims on oneself by external parties. The Corinthians are explaining Spartan *sôphrosunê*, evidently an admirable stability and reliability, but also citing its cost, an inflexibility and perhaps even failure on its own terms. After all, as the Corcyreans accepted, *sôphrosunê* is consistent with alliance, which involves accepting the judgment of others.

---

[69] Thuc. 1.42.2.
[70] Thuc. 1.68.1: Τὸ πιστὸν ὑμᾶς, ὦ Λακεδαιμόνιοι, τῆς καθ' ὑμᾶς αὐτοὺς πολιτείας καὶ ὁμιλίας ἀπιστοτέρους ἐς τοὺς ἄλλους ἤν τι λέγωμεν καθίστησιν· καὶ ἀπ' αὐτοῦ σωφροσύνην μὲν ἔχετε, ἀμαθίᾳ δὲ πλέονι πρὸς τὰ ἔξω πράγματα χρῆσθε.

The Corinthians go on to castigate the Spartans for their inactivity, their unwillingness to aid their allies by invading Athens. You are at peace (ἡσυχάζετε) because you defend yourselves through delay (μελλήσει).[71] By contrast with the innovative Athenians, who accomplish whatever they resolve to do, you just preserve what is already there and make no further decisions, even leaving tasks incomplete; you do not do as much as you can, you do not trust your judgments, and you fear never escaping difficulties.[72] In sum, in your delaying and refusing to respond to injustice, you actually fail to keep the peace; in ignoring the claims of your allies, you are doing them an active injustice.[73]

The Spartan king Archidamus responds, speaking directly to the Spartans.[74] His response proves the longest apology for *sôphrosunê* yet found in Greek literature:

> Καὶ ἀνανδρία μηδενὶ πολλοὺς μιᾷ πόλει μὴ ταχὺ ἐπελθεῖν δοκείτω εἶναι. . . . οὗτοι καὶ καθ' ἡσυχίαν τι αὐτῶν προΐδωμεν. καὶ τὸ βραδὺ καὶ μέλλον, ὃ μέμφονται μάλιστα ἡμῶν, μὴ αἰσχύνεσθε. σπεύδοντές τε γὰρ σχολαίτερον ἂν παύσαισθε διὰ τὸ ἀπαράσκευοι ἐγχειρεῖν, καὶ ἅμα ἐλευθέραν καὶ εὐδοξοτάτην πόλιν διὰ παντὸς νεμόμεθα. καὶ δύναται μάλιστα σωφροσύνη ἔμφρων τοῦτ' εἶναι· μόνοι γὰρ δι' αὐτὸ εὐπραγίαις τε οὐκ ἐξυβρίζομεν καὶ ξυμφοραῖς ἧσσον ἑτέρων εἴκομεν· τῶν τε ξὺν ἐπαίνῳ ἐξοτρυνόντων ἡμᾶς ἐπὶ τὰ δεινὰ παρὰ τὸ δοκοῦν ἡμῖν οὐκ ἐπαιρόμεθα ἡδονῇ, καὶ ἤν τις ἄρα ξὺν κατηγορίᾳ παροξύνῃ, οὐδὲν δὴ μᾶλλον ἀχθεσθέντες ἀνεπείσθημεν. πολεμικοί τε καὶ εὔβουλοι διὰ τὸ εὔκοσμον γιγνόμεθα, τὸ μὲν ὅτι αἰδὼς σωφροσύνης πλεῖστον μετέχει, αἰσχύνης δὲ εὐψυχία, εὔβουλοι δὲ ἀμαθέστερον τῶν νόμων τῆς ὑπεροψίας παιδευόμενοι καὶ ξὺν χαλεπότητι σωφρονέστερον ἢ ὥστε αὐτῶν ἀνηκουστεῖν, καὶ μὴ τὰ ἀχρεῖα ξυνετοὶ ἄγαν ὄντες τὰς τῶν πολεμίων παρασκευὰς λόγῳ καλῶς μεμφόμενοι ἀνομοίως ἔργῳ ἐπεξιέναι, νομίζειν δὲ τάς τε διανοίας τῶν πέλας παραπλησίους εἶναι καὶ τὰς προσπιπτούσας τύχας οὐ λόγῳ διαιρετάς   (Thuc. 1.83.1–84.3).

> Let no one consider it cowardice when a large group does not rush to attack a single city. . . . [We would need capital and have to take total responsibility, so] let us give these matters some forethought in peace. About the slowness and delay, which they blame us especially for, feel no disgrace. For in being hasty you would more slowly come to a conclusion, on account of your unprepared endeavor; and we dwell in a city that has always been free and most highly regarded. It can surely

---

[71] Thuc. 1.69.4, cf. 2.
[72] Thuc. 1.70.2–3.
[73] Thuc. 1.71.
[74] Thuc. 1.79.2: Thucydides says he was "reputed for being intelligent and *sôphrôn*," which is Thucydides' sole use of *sôphrosunê* as a personal quality anywhere in the *History*; it may be an exception that proves the rule, since Archidamus is a direct advocate of Spartan *sôphrosunê*.

be that this [for which we are blamed] is a wholehearted *sôphrosunê*. For thanks to this we alone do not get hubristic with our successes, and disaster affects us less than it does others; and when we are urged on by praise, we do not go against our resolutions and, pleasurably stirred up, head into dangers; nor, when we are provoked by accusation are we more likely to be convinced through our annoyance. Thanks to our good order we have become both fine fighters and prudent: the former, because a sense of shame is the greater part of *sôphrosunê*, and courage likewise of shame; and prudent, because we are educated in too unschooled a way for despising the laws and in too *sôphron* a way—thanks to our strictness—for disobeying them, nor being too clever in useless matters do we go about making appealing speeches impugning our enemies' preparations but execute those plans in quite another way, but we consider our neighbors' considerations to be akin to ours and eventualities not to be discernable by reason.

Archidamus argues against the charge that Sparta simply fails to act when action is called for. *Sôphrosunê* is not cowardice (ἀνανδρία), a vice with which the virtue is equated again, during the plague, by cynical Athenians.[75] Adequate action needs preparation and deliberation; hurry undermines agency. *Sôphrosunê* is the very virtue that has kept Sparta free and in high repute. Evidently, as opportunities multiply, desires remain stable, and as others encourage the Spartans to act, their tried-and-true norms of action remain stable.[76] What the Spartans deem right to do, in effect, depends not on external incentives—the perceived vulnerabilities and announced enticements of foreign states—but ground rules to which the state has committed itself. This *sôphrosunê* and orderliness in dealing with the world bring about the power to act, both affectively, as excellent fighters (πολεμικοί), and intellectually, as prudent people (εὔβουλοι).

---

[75] Thuc. 3.82.2.
[76] This statement has an important parallel in the longest fragment from Thrasymachus, a younger contemporary of Protagoras, innovator in rhetorical practice and theory, with developed reflections on politics and justice (see Pl. *Rep.* 1.336c–354a, *Clit.* 406a, 410d–e, with Guthrie 1971, 295–97; Betti 2011). It is a reflection on the Athenian Constitution evidently in the aftermath of the Sicilian expedition (B1/D16, sometimes dated to 411 BCE; see Fuks 1953, 102–6). For close discussion, see White (1995, 308–18). Thrasymachus reflects on the relationship between desires and their satisfiability: ἡμεῖς δὲ μετὰ μὲν τῶν ἀγαθῶν ἐσωφρονοῦμεν, ἐν δὲ τοῖς κακοῖς ἐμάνημεν, ἃ τοὺς ἄλλους σωφρονίζειν εἴωθεν. The usual situation, found throughout the world, is that when people of some city can get much, they end up desiring even more; when they can get little, they end up shrinking their desires to fit their straitened circumstances. Athens differs: when we could get much, he says, we kept our desires small; but when we could get only a little, we desired to have yet more than that. So the extent of one's desires may be variously determined. Sometimes it depends on judgments or hopes of satisfiability, where desires keep growing as others are fulfilled, with a consequent overgrowth of desires; sometimes it depends on social norms. Perhaps this means that desire is especially mimetic: if in others it grows, then in you it does too; if not, then not. Thrasymachus treats *sôphrosunê* as having psychic and behavioral elements: one must regulate one's desire, and one must also regulate the behaviors consequent to one's (as yet unregulated) desire. (North 1966, 115, judges Thrasymachus' thinking here "utterly conventional," but in fact there is insight involved in its use.)

Archidamus' argument for this two-part claim about *sôphrosunê*'s role in agency is unparalleled in Greek literature and bears the extraordinary logical equations celebrated in the sophistic period. The conclusion is that *sôphrosunê*, despite its attendant hesitation, is not cowardice. The first part gives the steps from good order (εὔκοσμον) to fine fighters (πολεμικοί). It does so through a series of implied and approximate equivalents. Orderliness is (implicitly) the same as *sôphrosunê*; *sôphrosunê* is largely, and therefore effectively, having a sense of shame (αἰδώς); having a sense of shame is (implicitly) the same as shame (αἰσχύνη); courage (εὐψυχία) is largely, and therefore effectively, having shame; and courage (implicitly) underwrites being fine fighters—perhaps especially under the guise of orderly military formations. Archidamas allows an imperfect overlap between *sôphrosunê* and the sense of shame (an overlap seen frequently already) but treats the overlap as sufficient for his purposes. The basic reasoning is that those who are *sôphrôn* have a sense of shame—the fear of incurring disgrace, the negative social judgment levied at those who fail to meet communal norms. Archidamas does the same with the next approximate equivalence, between shame and courage: imperfect but close enough. Evidently it is a fear of disgrace that animates courageous action—such, at any rate, was thought to explain Thebes' Sacred Band.[77] *Sôphrosunê*, then, is an acute sensitivity to the force of guiding rules, those taken as normative by everyone else. The recognition that one should follow them is more authoritative, or weightier, than the desire not to. (In Chapter 8, we will see in Plato's *Gorgias* an alternative argument for *sôphrosunê*'s subsumption of courage.)

The second part of Archidamus' argument involves the same view of *sôphrosunê*, but focused now on law-abidingness rather than on socially admired actions. Spartan soundness of judgment, Archidamus says, has three sources, all of them linked to a recognition of ignorance. Not having learned much about foreign affairs, the Spartans cannot compare their laws to those of other states and find their own wanting and unworthy of respect; by being quite *sôphrôn*, having had a "strict" upbringing, they simply cannot fail to follow their laws; and realizing that it is a fantasy to believe they could see better into their enemies' preparation or the outcome of any conflict than their enemies could see into their own or into that same outcome, they do not play the rationalizing game and reconstrue their laws. This *sôphrosunê* involves humble self-knowledge: appreciating that one cannot act from omniscience, one acts instead from principle, and in the process one avoids those self-undermining choices typical of the hubristic overreacher.

---

[77] For this passage, see also Dover (1974, 118–19); Nussbaum (1986, 508n24); Hornblower (1991, 129); Cairns (1993, 358). The Athenians in the "Melian dialogue" contest this rosy view of shame (αἰσχύνη), 5.111.2–3.

Thus Archidamus argues in favor of Spartan *sôphrosunê*, which to outsiders looks like cowardly hesitation but is, as it turns out, the only reliable way to get anything done. Spontaneity, which strikes the eye as courage, is really rashness, and it tends to be driven by an unreflective expectation for the future that is based on past successes or other people's exhortation. Large-scale actions take planning and orderly rule-following, not gut reaction. *Sôphrosunê* does not counsel against war-making itself; indeed it constitutes martial effectiveness. But it counsels in favor of war-making only in the presence of principled reasons.

Archidamus advances the least compromising argument in favor of *sôphrosunê* to be found in the *History*. The remainder of Thucydides' text, from this vantage, amounts to a sequence of responses and qualifications. Two further speeches given to the Peloponnesian League in Book 1 take issue with Archidamus' isolationist interpretation. Another Spartan, Sthenelaides, gives a brief competing address to the Spartans: if we really *sôphronein*, then we will not look on dispassionately while our allies are wronged, and we will not hesitate (μελλήσομεν) to avenge them, given that they are not hesitating to suffer ills.[78] Being *sôphrôn* does not mean caring only about local affairs. It means acting well, on the basis of considered reasons; in fact, preserving one's friends' well-being provides a reason for action. Archidamus treated delay as the time during which one marshaled one's powers, but sometimes that for which one needs those powers must be dealt with now: the world is not static, and not every decision can be as fully prepared for as one would like. Archidamus explains why *sôphrosunê* looks self-abnegating but is actually self-actualizing; Sthenelaides explains why *sôphrosunê* looks self-involved but is actually also other-concerned. For both speakers, the virtue amounts to one's following norms rather than passing fancies, but whereas Archidamus mainly has norms of practical success in mind (wait until all one's materiel has been gathered; don't fix what ain't broke), Sthenelaides recognizes other norms, including one's incurred obligations.

In a later speech, the Corinthians develop Sthenelaides' critique:

δι' ὅπερ καὶ μὴ ὀκνεῖν δεῖ αὐτοὺς τὸν πόλεμον ἀντ' εἰρήνης μεταλαμβάνειν. ἀνδρῶν γὰρ σωφρόνων μέν ἐστιν, εἰ μὴ ἀδικοῖντο, ἡσυχάζειν, ἀγαθῶν δὲ ἀδικουμένους ἐκ μὲν εἰρήνης πολεμεῖν, εὖ δὲ παρασχὸν ἐκ πολέμου πάλιν ξυμβῆναι, καὶ μήτε τῇ κατὰ πόλεμον εὐτυχίᾳ ἐπαίρεσθαι μήτε τῷ ἡσύχῳ τῆς εἰρήνης ἡδόμενον ἀδικεῖσθαι. ὅ τε γὰρ διὰ τὴν ἡδονὴν ὀκνῶν τάχιστ' ἂν ἀφαιρεθείη τῆς ῥᾳστώνης τὸ τερπνὸν δι' ὅπερ ὀκνεῖ, εἰ ἡσυχάζοι, ὅ τε ἐν πολέμῳ εὐτυχίᾳ πλεονάζων οὐκ ἐντεθύμηται θράσει ἀπίστῳ ἐπαιρόμενος.
(Thuc. 1.120.3–4)

---

[78] Thuc. 1.86.2.

And they [various states] too ought not shrink from exchanging peace for war. It is characteristic of *sôphrôn* men that, if they are not wronged, they stay quiet; yet characteristic of good men that, should they be wronged, they leave peace for war and at the right opportunity leave war to come back into agreement, and that they neither exult in their good luck in war nor suffer injustice from enjoying the quietness of peace. For he who shrinks back for the sake of pleasure will very quickly, if he stays quiet, be deprived of that same blissful state that caused him to hold back, and he who overreaches because of his good luck in war does not take to heart his exulting in an untrustworthy boldness.

The Corinthians emphasize that, to be a virtue, *sôphrosunê* must combine peacetime tranquility with wartime sensitivity to injustice and harm, though also a desire to return to peace if possible. Spartan temporizing, which at first looked like indecisive delay, then was redescribed as forces-marshaling, is now re-redescribed as a fixed preference for pleasure over toil. This quiescence is not a characteristic of good men, who seek to right wrongs, and it is not prudent, for it fails to defend the very leisure it seeks to maintain. The Corinthians thus give moral and prudential reasons in favor of *sôphrosunê*, considered as a virtue of good men. The point is not that *sôphrosunê* is sometimes a moral virtue, sometimes a prudential one. It is that good action has a number of ways of being spelled out, and *sôphrosunê* amounts to an acknowledgment of a range of reasons for action.

Versions of this debate recur through the remainder of Thucydides' book. In his speech to the Athenians about the Mytileneans, Cleon takes up Archidamus' argument and makes it even sharper: strict obedience to worse laws is better than irreverence toward better laws; *amathia* with *sôphrosunê* is better than cleverness with indiscipline (ἀκολασία).[79] Diodotus, in his response to Cleon, broadens the application of civic *sôphrosunê*: it is not just deviation-free law-abidingness; it is deliberating well in assemblies, listening well to advisors, and adopting the right criteria of choice.[80] In a debate before the Spartans, the Plataeans appeal to *sôphrosunê* as respect for past association, acknowledgment of the badness of suffering, and resistance to undue Theban pressures to ignore those moral conditions.[81] The Thebans in turn excuse their own past actions by attributing them to a government that lacked *sôphrosunê* and was thus akin to a law-ignoring tyranny.[82] And so forth.[83]

---

[79] Thuc. 3.37.3.
[80] Thuc. 3.42.5, 3.43.5, 3.44.1.
[81] Thuc. 3.58.1, 3.59.1.
[82] Thuc. 3.62.3.
[83] Thuc. 4.18.3–4 (Spartans to Athenians) and 4.28.5 (Thucydides' comment on Cleon's speech); 4.60.1, 4.61.1, 4.64.4 (Hermocrates to the Sicilians); 6.6.2 (Thucydides regarding Syracuse); 6.11.7 (Nicias to the Athenians); 6.29.2 (Alcibiades' paraphrased speech to the Athenians); 6.41.2 (anonymous general to the Syracusans); 6.78.2, 6.79.2 (Hermocrates to the Syracusans) and

In Thucydides' reflection on linguistic cynicism in Book 3, he notes that aristocrats treated *sôphrosunê* as their preferred slogan, as democrats praised *isonomia*.[84] But this does not mean that, for Thucydides or in reality, *sôphrosunê* was a purely rhetorical ideal, a meaningless term for anything the speaker wants. To be sure, there is much flexibility of application and disagreement about its proper application. Does *sôphrosunê* require isolationism or alliance and warmaking? It is hard to say. But this is a feature of all virtue-terms, justice and reverence and wisdom alike, and not a knock against *sôphrosunê*. In fact, we see remarkable commonality across the uses: it means following the more stable of one's principles, either those codified in a city's own constitution or in the moral order acknowledged by all Greeks. To the extent these two sources of principles, nation and cosmos, conflict, *sôphrosunê* means following the more stable or authoritative of them. It is a matter of probably unending ethical—and political— debate to know which it is. This is what Thucydides shows us.[85]

Democritus of Abdera

Democritus, a younger contemporary of Critias', Antiphon's, and Thucydides'— and an encyclopedic writer who shared their interests—also contributed to debates about *sôphrosunê*. Specifically, in what may have been the first ever book of ethics, he may have developed an overall ethical theory for which *sôphrosunê* was the prime virtue.[86] The content of that book, on "cheerfulness" (εὐθυμία), is known only in fragments; but those fragments, along with many fragments attributed by Stobaeus to Democritus (possibly including some of those under the name "Democrates"),[87] at least five of which expressly include

---

6.87.5 (Athenians to the Syracusans); 8.1.3, 8.24.4 (Thucydides on Athenians and Chians); 8.53.3 (Peisandros to the Athenians); 8.64.5 (Thucydides: after Athens gave *sôphrosunê* and freedom from tribute [ἄδειαν τῶν πρασσομένων] to cities, they forwent law-boundedness [εὐνομία] and advanced to total independence).

[84] Thuc. 3.82.8. For Thucydides' analysis here of the changing use of virtue terms, see Allison (1997, 163–86).

[85] Edmunds (1975, esp. 75–82) has also argued for the centrality of *sôphrosunê* to Thucydides' ethical outlook, though taking a different path.

[86] North (1966, 118–20): "sophrosyne is the key to the sensible hedonism of Democritus; this note runs all through his ethical maxims"; similarly, Bailey (1928, 200–202, more broadly 188–212); Nill (1985, 85, more broadly 75–91). Barnes (1982, 532–33) at least allows that Democritus' *gnômai* can best be said to "offer a systematic theory of prudence" and advocacy for "moderation in all things."

[87] On the reliability of ascriptions of the maxims of "Democritus" and "Democrates" to Democritus himself, and for the plausibility of reconstructing an ethical theory from them, see West (1969) and M. R. Johnson (2020); for "Democrates," see in particular *DPhA* D.68. Kahn (1985) accepts a narrow range of fragments as authentic, and doubts Democritus engaged in "theorizing," but Kahn can rely on those fragments to show continuities between Democritean and Socratic reflection. Procopé (1989) argues that even the putatively political fragments have a mostly personal-ethics foundation.

the term *sôphrosunê*, show Democritus in active dispute with the disparagers of *sôphrosunê* as depicted in Aristophanes' *Clouds*. We lack a direct definition of *sôphrosunê* of the sort found in Critias and Thucydides' Archidamus, though the exhortative quality of the statements constituting Democritus' book makes this unsurprising.[88] But unlike in Critias and Thucydides, in Democritus we have a rich framework of ethical reflection, concerned with the goal of life and the role of pleasure in it.[89] What we learn is that the best life depends on *sôphrosunê*, and this for a range of reasons.[90]

The most important of the *sôphrosunê* statements is a defense of the virtue's role in the subjectively happy life—what we might imagine to be the cheerful life:

B211/D244: σωφροσύνη τὰ τερπνὰ ἀέξει καὶ ἡδονὴν ἐπιμείζονα ποιέει (Stob. 3.5.27)

Sôphrosunê increases enjoyments and makes pleasures better.

Democritus appears to be arguing against a position of the sort advanced by the *Clouds*' Worse Argument and by Plato's Callicles. *Sôphrosunê*, according to that adverse perspective, decreases enjoyment and worsens one's pleasures. This is an inference from the belief that enjoyment and pleasure come from the unimpeded pursuit and achievement of one's desires combined with the belief that *sôphrosunê* is a matter of impeding that pursuit. Stobaeus does not quote Democritus' explanation for his opposed view, if he ever wrote out an explanation, but we can guess at the implied reasoning. *Sôphrosunê* is the virtue that makes it such that in satisfying a desire, one leaves as little residue of pain, suspicion, or agitation as one can. One can say, then, that it increases satisfaction both quantitatively and qualitatively. The argument thus responds to both simple and sophisticated hedonisms. It is not stated here how *sôphrosunê* works, but it must

---

[88] On the literary form, see M. R. Johnson (2020). Aristotle claims that Democritus moved in the direction of definition (*Metaph.* M.4 1078b20), but he has in mind only physical definitions, e.g., "the hot and the cold."

[89] Annas (2002) argues for Democritus' (proto-)eudaimonism. This follows on doubt whether we should call Democritus a hedonist, even if qualifiedly (as "enlightened," for example; SEP s.v. "Democritus" §7), especially since it is hard to determine what Democritus sees as the precise relationship between pleasure and *euthumia* (Gosling and Taylor 1982, 29–37); see McGibbon (1960: skeptical), Taylor (1967: we should, as long as we focus on the enjoyment of a life as a whole), and, earlier, Vlastos (1945–46, 596: nobody in the fifth century was worried about vaunting pleasure). Kirk, Raven, and Schofield (1983, 431–33) are distinctly unimpressed by the "theoretical" standing of Democritus' ethics, finding most of it "traditional common sense," and, despite their book being a reader in Presocratic thought, quote only fr. 3. Similarly skeptical, but more willing to entertain the details (and quoting B211), is Barnes (1982, 530–35).

[90] Wolfsdorf (2013, 13–17), argues for the importance of (a kind of) self-knowledge in Democritus' thinking: "the individual can achieve a good life by understanding his nature, his power and thus limitations, and conjointly his place within the world."

not be merely by impeding desire-satisfaction.[91] For, if it did, it would not allow an increase in enjoyment and would make pleasures only fewer, not necessarily better (except, perhaps, on average).

Other Democritean maxims about *sôphrosunê* focus not on the increase in pleasure but on the decrease in or at least control over want. "Chance sets a lavish table; *sôphrosunê* provides self-sufficiency" emphasizes the virtue's role in determining one's desires, either ignoring or pruning those that would press for extravagant consumption.[92] Similarly, "Being *sôphrôn*, one bears poverty with reasonableness": one can make one's wants better fit the circumstances, even if not altogether eradicate them (since poverty must still be endured).[93] *Sôphrosunê* is a core desideratum of the good life: "Strength and good looks are the goods of youth; *sôphrosunê* is the flower of old age"; "A father's *sôphrosunê* is the best message for his children"; "Living badly without thought or *sôphrosunê* or reverence, Democrates said, is not living badly, but is dying over a long time."[94] Stobaeus includes three more Democritean statements in his chapter on *sôphrosunê* (3.5) that do not include the term *sôphrosunê* but that, to his mind, capture distinctive issues about the virtue. The first is key for thinking of *sôphrosunê* as the power of discrimination between desires: "Not every pleasure ought one to choose, but the one dependent on what's fine (ἐπὶ τῷ καλῷ)."[95] Showing the nearness of justice and *sôphrosunê*, we have the related idea, "A just love: craving fine/beautiful things unhubristically."[96] We are not to follow Hippolytus and avoid passion altogether; we are simply to avoid going to extremes with it. Finally, there is a statement that seems to say that eating moderately gives one a better night's sleep.[97]

These might all seem free-floating maxims, of conventional flavor. But against the background of Democritus' most distinctive ethical statements, they have substance, really claiming that *sôphrosunê* has, in a way not always attended to, central importance in a full and independent life. This is the virtue, rather than courage, or theoretical insight, or piety, that people must strive to acquire—for *sôphrosunê* allows one to attain the good in life in light of an avoidable condition: diverse and accumulating desire.

---

[91] Kahn (1985, 5, 15–17) reads Democritus through a "combat" model that may be misleading to the extent it implies that psychic force must overwhelm passions.

[92] Democr. B210/D277 (= Stob. 3.5.26): τράπεζαν πολυτελέα μὲν τύχη παρατίθησιν, αὐτάρκεα δὲ σωφροσύνη.

[93] Democr. B291/D318 (= Stob. 4.44.70): πενίην ἐπιεικέως φέρειν σωφρονέοντος.

[94] Democr. B294/D317 (= Stob. 4.50.20): ἰσχὺς καὶ εὐμορφίη νεότητος ἀγαθά, γήραος δὲ σωφροσύνης ἄνθος; B208/D396 (= Stob. 3.5.24): πατρὸς σωφροσύνη μέγιστον τέκνοισι παράγγελμα; B160/D280 (= Porph. *de abst.* 4.21.6): τὸ γὰρ κακῶς ζῆν καὶ μὴ φρονίμως καὶ σωφρόνως καὶ ὁσίως Δημοκράτης ἔλεγεν οὐ κακῶς ζῆν εἶναι, ἀλλὰ πολὺν χρόνον ἀποθνήσκειν.

[95] Democr. B207/D242 (= Stob. 3.5.22):'Ηδονὴν οὐ πᾶσαν, ἀλλὰ τὴν ἐπὶ τῷ καλῷ αἱρέεσθαι χρεών.

[96] Democr. B73/D266 (= Stob. 3.5.23): Δίκαιος ἔρως, ἀνυβρίστως ἐφίεσθαι τῶν καλῶν.

[97] "A short [or 'long'?] night never comes for self-sufficiency of nourishment" (B209/D255 [= Stob. 3.5.25]: Αὐταρκείῃ τροφῆς σμικρὴ νὺξ οὐδέκοτε γίνεται—Hense emends σμικρὴ to μακρή; the problem seems to be knowing what the Greek saying is).

The longest verbatim ethical fragment of Democritus gives the relevant framework, starting with this statement: "*Euthumia* comes about for men by moderate joy (μετριότητι τέρψιος) and a balanced life (βίου συμμετρίη)." Democritus' fragment continues: excesses and deficiencies alike put the soul off balance and into discontent. One may not merely wish away these failures of moderation. One must take a deliberate and thoughtful approach: reflect (ἔχειν τὴν γνώμη) on what is possible and judge to be sufficient that which one already has (τοῖς παρεοῦσιν ἀρκέεσθαι). One must tamp down one's daydreams of the desirable and awesome—in particular, other people's supposedly great lives—and picture instead how poorly off others are compared to oneself. Otherwise the rising feelings of animosity, envy, and hostility will destroy one's life, both because of the unlawfulness their satisfaction may involve and because of the earlier-mentioned imbalance and discontent.[98]

In another fragment, generally considered the beginning of *On euthumia*, Democritus admonishes people not to get too involved in (other people's) affairs (χρὴ μὴ πολλὰ πρήσσειν—"one ought not to be *polupragmôn*") in private or public contexts, not to exceed one's own capacity and nature (δύναμιν... τὴν ἑωυτοῦ καὶ φύσιν), and not to expect continued good fortune. Again the intellectual effort is prominent: one must "be on guard... by thought" (ἔχειν φυλακήν... τῷ δοκεῖν) and prefer the appropriate rather than the abundant.[99] Elsewhere, Democritus exhorts "not setting one's pleasures on mortal things," which may be the changeable or evanescent ones.[100] For example: "All those who make pleasures come from the belly, having overlooked (ὑπερβεβληκότες) what is appropriate as far as food, drink, and sex are concerned, all their pleasures are small and short-lived, and arise only for as long as they are eating or drinking; but their pains are many.... There is nothing valuable in them but a brief delight before the need for them returns."[101]

Democritus' ethical theory starts in the view that cheerfulness is our goal, and that it is constituted somehow by pleasure. But Democritus knows that pleasure as the satisfaction of desire will not, on its own, ensure cheerfulness.[102] This is for a range of complex reasons, related to the ways we acquire and experience desire within social and physical contexts. The mimetic desire of envy, which increases the more one fantasizes about other lives (probably as imagined solutions to one's own dissatisfactions), brings great ill: one may become unpleasantly

---

[98] Democr. B191/D226 (= Stob. 3.1.210). For commentary, see Warren (2002, 44–48).
[99] Democr. B3/D228 (= Stob. 4.39.25). Evidence that it began *On euthumia* is from Sen. *Tranq.* 13.1. See Warren (2002, 53); M. R. Johnson (2020, 222). LM express doubt that this is verbatim.
[100] Democr. B189/D227.
[101] Democr. B235/D248.
[102] See, e.g., McGibbon (1960).

resentful, unpleasantly incapable of sharing in social success, unpleasantly punished for breaking the law, and unpleasantly discombobulated as one desires one inaccessible thing after another. In general, desires grow fast, and their satisfaction depends on unpredictable future conditions; unsatisfied new desires may cause more pain than can be offset by increased satisfaction of others of those new desires.[103] And the troublesome satisfaction of yet other desires may yield benefits that are so much briefer than the intervening pain of the desires themselves.

The solution to the problems of hedonism starts at "moderation of desires"—cheerfulness does not vary proportionally with desire—but goes far beyond it. One must work, through pivots of attention and analyses of one's conditions, to construct one's desires to be for those things that are readily satisfiable, stable, and compatible with others' interests. A cheerful life depends as much on acuity of judgment about the suitability of one's desires as it depends on instrumental cleverness about their satisfaction. Arius Didymus summarizes: "He [Democritus] says that [happiness] consists in distinguishing and discriminating (διορισμοῦ καὶ διακρίσεως) pleasures, and that this is the finest and most advantageous thing for humans."[104] Democritus emphasizes one's having to acknowledge the better desires in place of learning how to deal with whatever desires may haphazardly come about. The power to live cheerfully involves self-knowledge of various sorts, and an appreciation of tranquility, a self-reliance and norm-following:[105] "Do not feel more ashamed around people than around yourself, and don't bring about bad ends whether nobody or every single person will see you. Rather, feel shame most around yourself, and establish this as law for one's soul, so as not to do anything detrimental."[106] So *sôphrosunê* must be the intellectual work enjoined in *On euthumia*: a self-scrutiny that assesses the nature of one's desires and works to make only the best of them motivating.[107]

---

[103] Cf. Democr. B219/D257: "Appetite for money, unless bounded by satiety, is much harder to manage than extreme poverty; for greater appetites produce greater wants" (χρημάτων ὄρεξις, ἢν μὴ ὁρίζηται κόρῳ, πενίης ἐσχάτης πολλὸν χαλεπωτέρη· μέζονες γὰρ ὀρέξεις μέζονας ἐνδείας ποιεῦσιν); B233/D246: "If one should go beyond what's moderate, the most enjoyable things would become most unenjoyable" (εἴ τις ὑπερβάλλοι τὸ μέτριον, τὰ ἐπιτερπέστατα ἀτερπέστατα ἂν γίγνοιτο).

[104] Stob. 2.7.3i. See Annas (2002, 174–78) for discussion.

[105] B119/D274: "most things in life an intelligent sharp-sightedness straightens out." Vlastos (1945–46, 57–62) speaks of this in terms of wisdom and self-mastery.

[106] Democr. B264/D386: μηδέν τι μᾶλλον τοὺς ἀνθρώπους αἰδεῖσθαι ἑωυτοῦ μηδέ τι μᾶλλον ἐξεργάζεσθαι κακόν, εἰ μέλλει μηδεὶς εἰδήσειν ἢ οἱ πάντες ἄνθρωποι· ἀλλ' ἑωυτὸν μάλιστα αἰδεῖσθαι, καὶ τοῦτον νόμον τῇ ψυχῇ καθεστάναι, ὥστε μηδὲν ποιεῖν ἀνεπιωήδειον. See esp. Cairns (1993, 363–70).

[107] Compare Socrates at Xen. *Symp.* 2.17 who says he dances regularity, despite its risibility, to make his eating and sleeping more pleasurable (ἥδιον ἐσθίειν καὶ καθεύδειν): he acts against social disesteem and probably the discomfort of toil out of understanding of a longer-term benefit.

Sôphrosunê in the Late Fifth Century

This chapter has given us four fresh vantages on fifth-century talk about *sôphrosunê*. Critias, who lauds *sôphrosunê* in the Spartan value hierarchy, gives a political rather than a psychological analysis of the virtue. Manifesting the virtue means recognizing what roles and pursuits are suitable for oneself and acting to advance only them: this is "doing one's own things." Antiphon plays with the term's laudation of inner struggle breaking toward what's good, and in particular with the question whether one must intend, with reason, that good end. Thucydides' politicians praise *sôphrosunê* geopolitically, as resisting the subordination of one's government to another's and resisting the making of premature policy decisions. Democritus gives a psychological analysis parallel to these two larger-scale analyses: *sôphrosunê* means not satisfying one's immediate or most insistent desires, but instead discriminating cautiously between those one has. In Chapter 3 we saw the connection to self-knowledge; in Chapter 4 we saw the connections to purity, reputation, religious reverence, and sanity. This chapter has added the connection to self-government in the micro-, meso-, and macrocosm. And the definitions and debates here develop those seen already in Chapter 1, concerned with the horizon of considerations appropriate to any sort of leader.

We now turn to a sequence of chapters concerned with Socrates and his intellectual progeny. He and the oldest of them came of age in this very fifth-century intellectual milieu. We will see them re-posing questions, redramatizing conflicts, and reattempting solutions to the problems that have arisen in the past several chapters.

6
The Figure of Socrates

A Problem of Evidence

Socrates of Athens is the most celebrated talker about and embodiment of *sôphrosunê* in his fifth-century milieu. His peculiar dalliance with Alcibiades, his heartiness on military campaign and in battle, his integrity in legal crises, and his dogged pursuit of argument support the latter. Xenophon and Plato, studied in subsequent chapters, provide the best evidence for the former. This chapter shows how some other contemporaries and near-contemporaries saw or took inspiration from him in their own thinking about *sôphrosunê*: playwrights of Old Comedy, Antisthenes, another Socratic (who may be Antisthenes) whose work was excerpted in Stobaeus, and the author of the Platonic *Alcibiades* (who may be Plato).

It seems probable that, as a circulator in elite Athenian culture, Socrates supported the reflections on *sôphrosunê* we see in Critias, Euripides, Antiphon, and Aristophanes.[1] He may even have contributed to popularizing theoretical discussion of *sôphrosunê* in general. What in detail his own views were, however, it would be very hard to say.[2] I suspect that the recurring set of considerations—assumptions, commitments, counterexamples—found across Socratic literature does preserve things Socrates said, but these can hardly be disentangled from the evolving tropes of that literature itself. There is little that counts as direct evidence. The earliest collection of notes made on Socratic conversations known to us is ascribed to Simon, a shoemaker and shopkeeper in the Athenian agora; only the titles, of about thirty discussions, are known, and none is "On *Sôphrosunê*."[3] Nor do any of the titles attributed to Socrates' other close companions, such as Crito, Glaucon, Simmias, or Cebes, refer to *sôphrosunê*.[4] The comic fragments

---

[1] On Socrates' circulation, see D'Angour (2019). Socrates with Critias: Plato's four dialogues featuring Critias, with Xen. *Mem.* 1.2.12–38 and Aesch. 1.173. With Euripides: Satyrus *Vit. Eur.* fr. 38iv + 39i; DL 2.18; Anon. *Vit. Eur.* 4–4; *Suda* ε 3695 (relatedly, Ael. *VH* 2.13 and Cic. *Tusc.* 4.63). With Antiphon: Xen. *Mem.* 1.6. With Aristophanes: Pl. *Symp.*

[2] On the "Socratic problem," see esp. Redfield (2018); also Ford (2008); Dorion (2011); Moore (2015c, x–xiii).

[3] DL 2.122–23. The titles need not be contemporary, but they probably reflect the most prominent topic in each conversation. The evidence from Simon has generally been doubted (e.g., Kahn 1996, 10), but on inadequate grounds; for discussion, see Nails (2002, 261–62); *DPhA* s.v. "Simon d'Athènes le cordonnier"; Molinelli (2018); Moore (2020b, 153–54).

[4] DL 2.121, 2.124–25.

about Socrates do not treat the word as a catch-phrase or a characteristic topic of discussion.[5] In the passages of Aristotle that appear to speak of the historical Socrates, none highlights *sôphrosunê* as a special or distinctive interest; Aristotle focuses instead on claims about courage and *akrasia*.[6] And in the six quotations attributed to Socrates by Stobaeus in his chapter on *sôphrosunê* (3.5), none actually mentions *sôphrosunê* explicitly.

Nevertheless, there is a constellation of considerations about *sôphrosunê* connected to Socrates that do not come directly from Plato or Xenophon. They are not for that reason more historically valid or interpretatively perspicuous. But they are informative, further hints of an ongoing late fifth-century and early fourth-century discourse about *sôphrosunê*.

We begin with the remarks about Socrates found in Old Comedy; these authors see Socrates' putative *sôphrosunê* in his austerity with respect to the conventional desires and as connected somehow to his intellectual commitments, but they also doubt the efficacy of his lauded desire-control. They thereby doubt the rhetoric of *sôphrosunê* and the mastery over the humdrum bodily impulses that it represents, either in general or in the extreme cases represented by Socrates. We then turn to a less adverse witness, Antisthenes, Socrates' earliest great associate, who says some pointed things about *sôphrosunê* and, more substantively, identifies the qualified value of pleasure as a motivation for action. He supplies, like Democritus, an implicit *sôphrosunê*-as-a-way-of-life, this one presumably inflected by his time with Socrates. Next we consider the many references to Socratic views in Stobaeus' chapter on *sôphrosunê*. Stobaeus presents a view of Socrates as *sôphrosunê* theorist that is largely independent of the Platonic and Xenophontic traditions, and while the authenticity of the remarks, namely as direct quotations of Socrates, could be doubted, their general tenor seems consistent with views ascribable to Socrates. In fact they seem likely excerpted from a Socratic author such as Antisthenes. Finally, we study the Platonic *Alcibiades*, where Socrates explicitly, but without argument, equates *sôphrosunê* with self-knowledge. To be sure, this work may well be by Plato himself, but there are plausible reasons for supposing it not to be—the strongest evidence being its lack of dramatic and thematic complexity relative to works with similar topics, such as *Charmides* or *Symposium*.[7] Whoever the author and whatever its date of composition, in its depiction of Socrates tête-à-tête with Alcibiades, outside a definitional context, it provides a distinctive, and still somewhat pretheoretical, perspective on Socratic *sôphrosunê* as having come fully to understand, and thereby to be properly committed to, the content of one's desires. In other words,

---

[5] See *SSR* I 1 1–18.
[6] Collected in Deman (1942); for discussion, see Moore (2019b).
[7] The best recent exponents of authenticity are Denyer (2001) and Jirsa (2009).

I suspect that the *Alcibiades* preserves Socrates'—or the Socratics'—suspicion that *sôphrosunê*, self-knowledge, and self-constitution are ideas that go closely together.

Socrates in Old Comedy

In Chapter 1, we studied the *agôn* of Aristophanes' (revised) *Clouds*, which debated the value of an education putatively conducive to *sôphrosunê*. The contestants of that debate were two teachers in Socrates' Thinkery, "Better Argument" and "Worse Argument." Neither speaks in Socrates' voice, to be sure. But their central position in his intellectual-pedagogical enterprise, and their jockeying to take over the education of Pheidippides that Socrates initiated, allows that we might take both as somehow representing his views. Could we see in Socrates a surprising merger, on the one side, of a conservative virtue-lauder who exhorts his pupils to demurely Spartan behavior with, on the other, someone who looks to be, in his loquacious scrutiny of the virtue, a libertine skeptic of all traditional values? Whether this could be a coherent merger, or is meant to seem to be one, is another question; in any event, it is an appealing hypothesis. More to the point, the topic of this *agôn* suggests that Aristophanes associated Socrates and the problem of *sôphrosunê*'s value in personal maturation, what we have called "self-constitution."

We know that Aristophanes had significant interest in *sôphrosunê* elsewhere.[8] In the parabasis of the revised *Clouds*, Aristophanes mentions his earliest play, *Banqueters*, from 427 BCE, which, in his telling, contrasted a father's two sons, one whom he calls *sôphrôn*, the other "buggered" (καταπύγων).[9] Their schooling anticipates what the Thinkery offers, in particular linguistic novelties.[10] The play appears to describe their relative successes in life vis-à-vis *sôphrosunê*. Given Aristophanes' sensitivity to the problematic ethical and pedagogical terrain to which citations of *sôphrosunê* belong, we have reason to look closely at his portrait of Socrates in light of that sensitivity. In the (revised) *Clouds*, Socrates' actions are presented as largely independent of bodily desire: occupying his time are scientific investigation, reflection, and the education of others. Socrates appears as an

---

[8] For a brief discussion, see Moore and Raymond (2019, xxxii).

[9] Ar. *Nub.* 529 (= test. iv). Dover (1989, 143) gives large compass to this contrast: "almost 'the well-behaved and the badly behaved.'" The contrast requires that *sôphrosunê* indicate an active by contrast to a submissive role (in life).

[10] The *katapugôn* boy learns fancy language, including from "orators" and Alcibiades, and he speaks against cultivating noble excellence (καλοκἀγαθίαν ασκοῦντας), for which his father calls him a "Thrasymachus" and assimilates his speech to the monstrosities of the legal profession (τῶν ξυνηγόρων τερατεύεται) (fr. 205). One of the boys has previously spent his time playing the aulos and lyre and now must spend his time digging (fr. 232).

advocate of self-knowledge.[11] As dean of a school that includes among its subjects speech, he cares about competence in public presentation. His freedom from material concerns is made thematic by his poverty. In sum, Socrates seems to embody what we have so far seen about the virtue, in his priority of the long-term psychic goods of knowledge and self-understanding over the immediate pleasures of banquets, sex, or luxury. And yet, despite his heartiness, Socrates seems also to fail to embody *sôphrosunê*. Perhaps not so settled in his condition of want, he steals a cloak.[12] He cares little for the gods and less for proper familial relations—his school leads Pheidippides to entertain beating his father and mother.[13] So he is also impious and unjust.[14] This ambivalent portrait, of the *sôphrôn anêr* contaminated by his opposed traits, seems intentional. Aristophanes may even encourage his spectators' finding in Socrates an incomplete or sham *sôphrosunê*, in that Socrates' failure of reverence for the most authoritative norms—toward gods and parents—undermines, in its eventuating in a burned-down school, whatever *sôphrosunê*-related value comes from his norms of investigation and self-discovery.[15] We might find that the adverse judgment available against Hippolytus, who is extravagantly *sôphrôn* in one way but evidently not in all ways, or against Pentheus, who is intensely intellectual but also religiously heterodox, leveled also against Socrates.

The other extant references to Socrates in Aristophanes and other comic dramatists corroborate this ambivalent judgment about Socrates and *sôphrosunê*. In the *Birds*, Socrates is said to Laconize, in his lack of concern for looks and his next meal (1280–83), and again to be filthy (1554). This seems to highlight the grubbier aspects of *sôphrosunê* (Socrates' endurance, his *karteria*), and the degree to which it is a put-on, a cultural fad, whose moral depths are questionable. Ameipsias casts Socrates as without a winter cloak, shoes, or concern for a meal; for Eupolis, he is a beggar, once again without a thought for his food.[16] But Socrates has not confirmed his praiseworthiness: he steals from a symposium and is full of himself, irrepressibly talkative.[17] Thus though the demotic desires for food and public estimation appear preternaturally suppressed in him, perhaps these playwrights either suspect the impossibility of such suppression, hence the thievery, or find them sublimated into or replaced by something equally dubious: never-ending talk. In brief, they seem to doubt that desire

---

[11] Moore (2015b).
[12] Ar. *Nub.* 179 and 1498; but see Tomin (1987), Kleve (1989), and Meynerson (1993) for complications.
[13] Religious heterodoxy: Ar. *Nub.* 247–53, 365–81, 423–36; lack of filial piety: 1321–1446.
[14] These charges are combined in the final substantive line of the play: Strepsiades says that Socrates has "done injustice to the gods" (τοὺς θεοὺς. ... ἠδίκουν, 1509).
[15] That comeuppance is at Ar. *Nub.* 1466–1509.
[16] Ameip. fr. 9 K-A; Eup. fr. 386 K-A.
[17] Stealing: Eup. fr. 395 K-A; self-involved: Callias fr. 15 K-A; talkative: Ar. *Ran.* 1491–99; Ameip. fr. 9.1; Eup. fr. 386.2–3.

ever gets completely controlled, believing that it at best gets redirected, and that Socrates serves as a remarkable paradigm of that redirection. This attitude toward Socrates may simply instantiate a general comic cynicism about human nature, that it is more sclerotic than social reformers wish, or it may result from the exigencies of humor, which demand overweening and self-deluding desire coming into play somewhere, even among the most moderate and self-aware of characters. Even so, it does suggest that they could put Socrates to use as an object lesson in the value of *sôphrosunê*.

Antisthenes

The proximity of Antisthenes to Socrates is richly described in Xenophon's *Symposium*, where the relationship is one of close companionship and intellectual sympathy.[18] It involved, as Diogenes Laertius memorably relates, Antisthenes' very long daily hikes to visit Socrates, from whom he learned to be hearty (καρτερίκος) and resilient in hardship (ἀπαθής).[19] Jerome of Stridon (ca. 345–420 CE) adds that upon assuming a discipleship with Socrates, Antisthenes gave up everything he owned except for a cloak, which itself came to be rather beat up.[20] This picture of a Socratic life—as one that eradicates the usual desires for comfort, ease, and social status—matches closely the contemporary picture of that life found in Old Comedy, though here shorn of the comedians' doubtfulness.

The traits Antisthenes acquired from Socrates become themes in the testimonia to Antisthenes' own views and way of life. He advocates against the pursuit of money, of vanity, and of pleasure unmediated by judgment and effort and in favor of the pursuit of virtue.[21] He believes that virtue suffices for happiness, and virtue amounts to "the strength of Socrates,"[22] a strength which is presumably the resistance to the pressures of desire.

Remarkably, the remains of Antisthenes' writings include few references to *sôphrosunê*, despite his interest in virtue and pleasure, and his taking as a paradigm of virtue someone to whom Xenophon, for instance, ascribes *sôphrosunê*, Cyrus. In the *Ajax* and *Odysseus*, for instance, no use is made of the virtue-term, and where Antisthenes lists exemplary virtues, admittedly without intention to be exhaustive, *sôphrosunê* does not appear.[23] In his discussions of Cyrus,

---

[18] Esp. Xen. *Symp.* 8.3–6 and 4.60–64.
[19] DL 6.2 = fr. 12A.
[20] Jer. *c. Iov.* 2.14 = fr. 12C, with fr. 15.
[21] Antisth. frr. 80–83; 27, 111A; 117–29; 86–90, 94B; 98–99, 103–4.
[22] DL 6.11: αὐτάρκη δὲ τὴν ἀρετὴν πρὸς εὐδαιμονίαν, μηδενὸς προσδεομένην ὅτι μὴ Σωκρατικῆς ἰσχύος.
[23] Antisth. frr. 77–78; 41A.

Antisthenes advocates without reference to *sôphrosunê* the value of toil (fr. 85) in opposition to immediate desire-satisfaction (frr. 113, 126), the importance of acting well despite the reputation it incurs for you (fr. 86A), and sticking to norms (not being παράνομον) in matters of women and more generally (fr. 14A).

Nevertheless, the several places the term does appear prove informative about him and probably about Socrates, too. Antisthenes was perhaps best known in antiquity for his provocative and paradoxical preference for madness over pleasure, a claim found in various sources.[24] Theodoret, an important source for fourth-century BCE information,[25] claims that Antisthenes valued *sôphrosunê* above all, and felt disgust at pleasure.[26] Theodoret explains: those ignorant about pleasure come to be overwhelmed by *erôs*, their guard against which they drop in believing it to be a divine passion. Evidently, whereas madness simply impairs one's self-command, as it were from the outside, pleasure gets personal buy-in to abdicate from self-command: it makes people feel justified in going really wild for pleasure. Where the chase and satisfaction seem everything, one may feel alive, powerful, admirably risk-tolerant in pursuing pleasure through one hazard and the next. Antisthenes does not reject pleasure as such: some pleasure can "come in through the doors," or result from toil, or be approved of after the fact, or in general be consistent with virtue.[27] But pleasure pursued without a bridle leaves one deluded, even hypocritical, about one's agency; hence the "disgust" Antisthenes is said to feel about it, rather than simply disapprobation, and the consequent valuation of *sôphrosunê*. From a longer-term perspective, at least certain pleasures may undermine not just the exercise of wisdom but also its cultivation.[28] Evidence from across the Socratic literature assures us that Socrates dedicated much consideration to *erôs* and its relation to *mania* and *sôphrosunê*.[29]

Theodoret's assertion about Antisthenes' valuation of *sôphrosunê* gets a kind of corroboration from Diogenes Laertius. Antisthenes would say that those who are *sôphrôn* should not learn *grammata*, so as not to be distorted ("twisted") by others (διαστρέφοιντο τοῖς ἀλλοτρίοις).[30] *Grammata* are letters and, by

---

[24] *P.Oxy.* 3659, col. II.25–28; Euseb. *PE* 15.13.7.

[25] See Stavru (2018) on Theodoret's reliability about Aristoxenus' reports about Socrates.

[26] Antisth. fr. 123B: τὴν σωφροσύνην περὶ πλείστου ποιούμενος καὶ τὴν ἡδόνην μυσαττόμενος.

[27] Antisth. frr. 124 (the meaning of "doors" is uncertain: perhaps, with Prince (2015, 378), "the rational faculty" or "self-respect"; or *kata thuras* means "invited in a civilly normative way"); 126, 127, 125.

[28] Wolfsdorf (2013, 18–20).

[29] Plato's *Phaedrus* and *Symposium* are the best preserved of these works.

[30] Antisth. fr. 161 = DL 6.103. Prince (2015, 544) has "distracted by other people's thoughts." Marcovich (1999) proposes <τοὺς σοφοὺς> καὶ σώφρονας where Dorandi (2013) gives τοὺς σώφρονας (following Frobenius) with most editors, for the unreadable ἢ σωφρονας in the manuscripts. In favor of Dorandi, Dio Chr. *Or.* 13.17, which probably follows Antisthenes (= fr. 208, see Prince 2015 comm. ad loc.), states that learning letters does not conduce to one's leading a city σωφρονέστερον καὶ ἄμεινον ("better and with more *sôphrosunê*"); it does not say that it conduces to "wiser" leadership. Dorandi's reading is more consistent with Antisthenes' attention to character development over intellectual learning.

extension, the writings assembled from them. Antisthenes seems to mean that reading generates new, foreign, and unwieldy beliefs and desires, the attraction to which is contrary to *sôphrosunê*; alternatively, reading may interfere with the toilsome self-work necessary for inner peace. In either case, reading books corrupts or distracts quixotically from one's project of becoming *sôphrôn*; and if reading is to be given up for this end, the end must be of signal importance. In either case, but especially on the first interpretation, *sôphrosunê* is not specifically control of bodily desires, since reading books would not distinctively induce gustatory or erotic desires. It must have to do with identifying with or committing oneself to the desires or beliefs one thinks it best to have (deploying Socratic strength); by not reading (i.e., relying on intellectual discovery), one avoids papering over these commitments with novel or exciting views. Socrates never comes across as antiliteracy per se, but he does quite forcefully present book-collecting and interpretation of poetry as a distraction from self-knowledge, which he otherwise connects to *sôphrosunê* (as we will see), and thus Antisthenes' quip could formulate a logical extreme of Socrates' ethic of reading oneself.[31]

Another kind of corroboration of Theodoret's ascription comes from a quotation of Antisthenes' interpretation of Homer: it includes the remark that one would not achieve *sôphrosunê* through fighting (διὰ μαχῆς), just as one would not get to justice through robbery or to immortality through the love of mortal life.[32] This argument against Antiphon's position seen in Chapter 5 has a close resonance to Socrates' observation in Plato's *Phaedo* that a *sôphrosunê* effected merely through the canceling out of contradictory intemperances hardly counts as a virtue.[33] When opposed desires cancel out, there is no reasoned choice to forgo the satisfaction of one or both desires, only an adventitious obstacle to the satisfaction of either. Just so in Antisthenes, fighting could lead to peace through attrition, but this peace would not be the virtue of keeping to oneself, of coming to be satisfied with the territory or treasure one already has. Given the similarity of argument type but difference in content across Plato and Antisthenes, we might suspect that this view of virtue, as constitutive rather than combative, and perhaps of *sôphrosunê* in particular, had Socratic origins.

Three further passages impute *sôphrosunê* interests to Antisthenes. Scholars have long surmised that Isocrates, a young contemporary of Antisthenes', has this Socratic in mind when he notes the oddness of his pedagogical competitors' having "*aretê* and *sôphrosunê*" as their teaching goals but then not trusting

---

[31] Xen. *Mem.* 4.2.1–10; Pl. *Prot.* 347c–348a; cf. Pl. *Phdr.* 229c–e.
[32] Antisth. fr. 188A-1. Prince (2015, 626) thinks we cannot document this contrast from Antisthenes' time, so she thinks the passage may be anachronistically Stoicizing; but we do see this contrast in Euripides (fr. 282.25–27).
[33] Pl. *Phd.* 68e–69b; see Chapter 8.

that their students will pay their tuition.³⁴ If scholars have rightly identified Isocrates' target, Isocrates associates Antisthenes' education preeminently with *sôphrosunê*; treats *sôphrosunê* as, like *aretê*, something to be cultivated in philosophical association; and makes *sôphrosunê* a virtue of "doing what one ought," of honoring a contract even if one would prefer to spend money or the time necessary for getting money in some other way. Thus *sôphrosunê*, as Isocrates takes Antisthenes to use the term, would amount to a thoughtful attitude toward one's desires and obligations, and an outcome of education worth paying for. We might imagine that this is the informal Socratic program formalized and monetized, even if Socrates had no monopoly on teaching *sôphrosunê*. The conceptual proximity implied by the collocation of *aretê* and *sôphrosunê* (which we have also seen in the epigraphical evidence, p. 50) further suggests that *sôphrosunê* is a core part of overall human excellence, which in the educational space of the early fourth century would amount to competence as a political actor.

Second, in a context where Xenophon may be referring to Antisthenes—he speaks of putative philosophers who claim that virtue cannot be lost—Xenophon says that they oppose *sôphrosunê* to hubris.³⁵ The context, which is of Critias' and Alcibiades' failing to stay *sôphrôn* after abandoning Socrates' tutelage, is of political extremism and violence. Hubris thus means exceeding consensual norms of respect, and *sôphrosunê* thereby the respecting of them.

Finally, a late Cynic letter tasked with clarifying Antisthenes' teaching has Simon call Antisthenes a *sôphronistês* ("disciplinarian") and say that Antisthenes might show Aristippus that, though he thinks he imitates Socrates, he (Aristippus) is in fact among the thoughtless (ἄφρων) and lives with much "delicacy" (χλιδή).³⁶ This latter term implies either "insolence" or "luxury"; the latter is more likely in the context, since the letter closes with the injunction to "remember hunger and thirst, for these have great power for those pursuing *sôphrosunê*." One practices desire-minimization by minimizing desire-satisfaction. Hunger and thirst are not the sole concerns of *sôphrosunê*, of course; they seem only salient or powerful obstacles to the development of *sôphrosunê* more generally.

A conjectural reconstruction of Antisthenes' view of *sôphrosunê* would take reconstructing his entire moral psychology, which the poverty of the evidence prevents from ever being more than a sketch of likelihoods.³⁷ Still, we might read those literary remains as informative about a Socratic orientation to *sôphrosunê*.

---

³⁴ Isoc. *C. soph.* 6 = fr. 170. For Isocrates' referring to Antisthenes, see, recently, Prince (2015, 558); Murphy (2013, 329–37).

³⁵ Xen. *Mem.* 1.2.19 = fr. 103C, with Prince (2015, 341). Cf. fr. 134 = DL 6.12, ἀναφαίρετον ὅπλον ἡ ἀρετή, "virtue is an unalienable weapon."

³⁶ *Soc. Ep.* 12 = fr. 207B.

³⁷ The major studies are Decleva Caizzi (1966); Patzer (1970); Rankin (1986); Brancacci (2015); Prince (2015); Meijer (2017).

The principal idea is an independence of decision-making and self-direction: independence from the grips of pleasure, from the (written) positions of others, from the effects of reputation. This independence is not meant to be a naive isolation from others; one must still cultivate oneself through training, study, and emulating a model. The ideal of *sôphrosunê*, which Antisthenes must, like some other Socratics, have adopted, evidently stands for this cultivation of independence, presumably a virtuous autonomy allowing one to live rightly.

Socrates in Stobaeus' "On *Sôphrosunê*"

Let us turn now to Stobaeus' *Anthology*, a fifth-century CE collection of extracts from earlier literature and philosophy, notable especially for its hundreds of unique fifth-century BCE passages; among them we find many statements attributed to Socrates.[38] Its third book (of four) concerns ethics; it proceeds by paired chapters of opposites, each constituted by dozens of fragments illustrative of the theme and organized both generically and by some scheme known only to Stobaeus himself. Chapters 5 and 6 are "On *sôphrosunê*" and "On *akolasia* ['indiscipline']." Chapter 5 has sixty-one entries: the first five come from classical playwrights, the next fifty-five from prose writers from Heraclitus to those near Stobaeus' day, and the closing one from Euripides. Entries 30–35 are attributed directly to Socrates; the two preceding entries, 28–29, quote from a letter purportedly from Xenophon reporting a Socratic statement and view; and entries 11, 13, 54–56, and 58 are citations of Socrates' statements in Platonic dialogues.[39] Thus more than 20 percent of the chapter's individual entries involve Socrates, and eight passages in a row—the longest span of a single authority in this chapter—purport to give Socrates' actual views.[40] Many of the Platonic passages will be discussed in Chapters 8–9. Those not sourced in Plato will be discussed here. It is worth noting that heretofore no scholar has taken these passages seriously as verbatim statements of Socrates' views, given both Socrates' agraphia and the dynamics of *gnômai*, whose generation seems free of the names to which they are later ascribed.[41] And yet nothing prevents their being statements of Socrates' attributed to him or members of his circle in Socratic literature, even from the first generation—the vast majority of which has been lost—and extracted without reference to author. In fact, I would not be surprised if they

---

[38] See Prince (2019).
[39] *Rep.* 3.389d; *Grg.* 507c–508a; *Phlb.* 63–64; *Chrm.* 173a–d; *Grg.* 499c–500b; *Phd.* 68c. There are also two quotations from Plato's *Symposium* from non-Socratic passages.
[40] This priority given to Socrates is not exceptional relative to the rest of the *Anthology*; see the chart in Prince (2019, 505–15) for the concentration of Socrates passages in Stobaeus' chapters.
[41] For this dynamic, see esp. Pietruschka (2019, 531–37).

came especially from Antisthenes' works, which likely included such statements and had considerable appeal.[42] At any rate, the number of such *sôphrosunê*-related remarks attributed to Socrates, and their general agreement, speaks to the likelihood that there were early Socratic texts on this subject.

Xenophon's letter to Lamprocles, Socrates' son, includes a quotation of a Socratic maxim, "Measure wealth" (πλοῦτον μετρεῖν).[43] Xenophon goes on to give Socrates' explanation of it: an immeasurable amount of property (ὑπέρμετρον κτῆσιν) is not wealth, but only that amount which is appropriate for our use (προσήκει χρῆσθαι); making a mistake about this is an incurable illness of the soul (ἀνίατον ... ψυχῆς ... τὸ ἀρρώστημα).[44] Pertinent, then, to Socratic *sôphrosunê*—at least as Stobaeus perceives it—is the healthy capacity of a person to "measure" the amount of money he needs. Wealth has significance as a resource for action; one should size it to one's intended accomplishments, for otherwise one acts inefficiently, expending needless energy accumulating resources never to be deployed. Indeed, that this is called an "incurable" illness implies that, without a way to measure the amount of money to pursue, a counterproductive accumulation will never cease. So, according to Stobaeus, Socrates understands *sôphrosunê* to be a judgment connected to the self-knowledge of both what one needs and what one ought to pursue. Stobaeus had just quoted from Xenophon's letter: "Nothing bad comes about in a man who sets *sôphrosunê* and *enkrateia* as foundation-stone (θεμέλια) of *sophia*." Xenophon must be generalizing here after having given other examples of Socrates' sayings. The statement echoes authentic Xenophontic attributions to Socrates of *enkrateia* as the foundation of virtue and *sôphrosunê* as the first step in education.[45] One must have sufficient self-knowledge and understanding not to pursue too much, and sufficient strength of will to disobey insistent desires for accumulation, and with those one can start to understand how to live.

Now we turn to the six sayings attributed directly to Socrates. Notably, none includes the term *sôphrosunê*. Interestingly, it is only a later chapter that contains a saying that does: "Socrates said that *sôphrosunê* is small needs (τὴν πενίαν ... μικράν)."[46] The emphasis there is not on combat with zealous desires but maintenance of desires that do not occasion combat. The six sayings in the "On *sôphrosunê*" chapter share this sensibility, each expressing wariness of pleasure or praise of self-sufficiency. *Sôphrosunê*, as Stobaeus understands its Socratic form, is the condition of being able to satisfy one's desires, the kind of

---

[42] See Prince (2019, 487), who expands this possibility to include Cynic literature.

[43] This is the only occurrence of the maxim in extant Greek literature. Perhaps this tells in favor of its actually being a Socratic invention. Other Xenophontic letters are addressed to Aeschines the Socratic, Crito, Soteira, Aglaitades, and Agesilaus. They are generally taken as inauthentic.

[44] *Anon. Iambl.* fr. 4.1 makes a similar fifth/fourth-century statement about the badness of the pursuit of wealth.

[45] See Chapter 7.

[46] Stob. 4.32.18.

freedom of intention and action allowed by their not growing out of bounds. I print these six sayings and discuss them in turn.

30: Δεῖ ὥσπερ Σειρῆνας τὰς ἡδονὰς παρελθεῖν τὸν σπεύδοντα τὴν ἀρετὴν ἰδεῖν ὥσπερ πατρίδα.

30: The one striving to behold virtue must elude pleasures, just as [the one striving to behold his] homeland [must elude] the Sirens.

31: Σωκράτης πρὸς τὸν πυθόμενον τίς πλουσιώτατος εἶπεν 'ὁ ἐλαχίστοις ἀρκούμενος.' αὐτάρκεια γὰρ φύσεώς ἐστι πλοῦτος.

31: Socrates said, to someone inquiring who the wealthiest person was, "the one satisfied with the least." For wealth is the self-sufficiency of [one's] nature.

32: Σωκράτης ἐρωτηθεὶς τίνων δεῖ μάλιστα ἀπέχεσθαι, 'τῶν αἰσχρῶν καὶ ἀδίκων ἡδονῶν' ἔφη.

32: Socrates, having been asked what must be most avoided, said "disgraceful and unjust pleasures."

33: Σωκράτης ἔλεγεν θεοῦ μὲν εἶναι τὸ μηδενὸς δεῖσθαι, τὸ δ' ὡς ἐλαχίστων ἐγγυτάτω θεοῦ.

33: Socrates said that whereas needing nothing belongs to god, needing as little as possible is nearest to god.

34: Ἡ αὐτάρκεια καθάπερ ὁδὸς βραχεῖα καὶ ἐπιτερπὴς χάριν μὲν ἔχει μεγάλην πόνον δὲ μικρόν.

34: Self-sufficiency is just like the short and sweet road, which has much charm with little toil.

35: Σωκράτης ἔλεγε δεῖν τὰς ἡδονὰς μὴ παρ' ἄλλων ἀλλὰ παρ' ἑαυτῶν θηρᾶσθαι, προδιατίθεσθαι δὲ τὸ σῶμα ὃν χρὴ τρόπον.

35: Socrates said that people must hunt out pleasures from themselves and not from others, and [thus] predispose the body as is necessary.

The first of these sayings, 30, on the Sirens, convinces with a beautiful image. Sirens and pleasures alike beckon you—the pilot of the ship, or the pilot of yourself—and, if you choose to respond, they alike pull you away from your goal. They cannot themselves reach you (the Sirens are not Scylla; pleasures are not cases of madness), though they present themselves as extremely desirable, as entirely worth commitment. But by hypothesis you already have a commitment, to your homecoming or your maturation, and presumably *sôphrosunê* is the maintenance of that commitment, by "eluding" or slipping past those incentives. It may take preparation to do it rather than sheer inner force in the moment.[47] Odysseus' sailors, their ears stuffed, are made ignorant of the Sirens' calls; Odysseus himself, his body tied to the mast, is made incapable of acting on those calls. Just so, you could prevent yourself from learning whatever it is that would generate those desires, as Antisthenes recommended one not learn to read, or you could prevent yourself from acting on those desires, as taking a reliable chaperone to a party might serve. The point is that extinction of desire is not what matters, and is sometimes impossible or undesirable (as it was for Odysseus); what matters is that the desire not become a decisive or competent reason for your action.

The statement about *autarchia* in 31 repeats the sentiment found in the Xenophontic letter, concerning the accumulation of just so much wealth as can finance one's projects. The language is again quantitative, not qualitative: what matters for well-being is the size of one's desire for wealth, specifically its size relative to one's other desires. The prosperity of wealth is its capacity for satisfaction; that capacity grows as the satisfaction is made easier. The gnomic "*autarchia* of one's *phusis*" seems provocatively to name *sôphrosunê* in the civic-constitutional form we saw in Thucydides: it is an agent's competence at managing her inner preferences such that she is in a ready position to satisfy them; she does not need to gather much more from beyond herself to do so. (*Phusis* in the personal context, at the time of Socrates, could refer to one's primary sensibility or core distinguishing interests.)[48] *Sôphrosunê*—or, anyway, the state of the best-off person—is here a matter of efficient deployment of power: being able to accomplish what one would, without the scramble first for extensive resource-accumulation.

Statement 32 replaces prudential with ethical language. Satisfying desires that break norms, either by exceeding one's proper domain (injustice) or otherwise acting improperly (disgrace), is wrong. The risk here addressed is not the cultivation of desires beyond what one can satisfy, a quantitative problem; it is the cultivation of desires beyond what one *should* satisfy, a qualitative problem. So 30 and 31 dealt with inefficiency; 32 deals with immorality. These provide two perspectives on *sôphrosunê*, the first agential and the second ethical. Their integration is a matter of considerable difficulty, one that Plato addresses head-on, as we will see in the next chapter. The important point is that Stobaeus wants to

---

[47] Elster (1984).
[48] See, e.g., Ar. *Nub.* 276, 486, 503, 877, 960, 1187, with discussion at Moore (2015b, 540–1).

show that *sôphrosunê* amounts to regulating oneself with both interests in mind. Norms are both hypothetical and categorical.

Statement 33 is familiar from a remark Socrates makes to Antiphon in Xenophon's *Memorabilia*.[49] It provides a new reason for esteeming minimal desires, by contrast to the earlier efficiency/prudence argument. There (e.g., in 30 and 31), one could more readily satisfy smaller desires, for one was already sufficiently powerful to do so; thus one would more readily attain happiness. Overweening desires resulted in one's being either dissatisfied or overworked. Here, by contrast, Socrates gives an argument from a recognized ideal. God is excellent; god has no (unsatisfied) desires; thus excellence is approached by having as few desires as possible. It might be thought that god is perfectly capable, a wholly actualized agent, and thus the argument is really the same, but Socrates does not here draw out that consideration. The implication is simply that god's *autarchia* is maximal; being like god is good; so *autarchia* is good.

Statement 34 has other versions in the Antisthenic tradition, as a sort of contrast to Prodicus' long and hard road to virtuous self-cultivation,[50] and thus it has a plausible Socratic provenance.[51] There is little to work on if all one does is minimize one's desires. Then they can be readily satisfied! This is the avenue not taken by Plato's Socrates against Callicles, who, as we will see in the next chapter, vaunts maximal desire-satisfaction. (This argument is excerpted elsewhere in Stobaeus' chapter on *sôphrosunê*.) This Socrates would say that it is simply too much work marshaling all the resources necessary for satisfying those desires. The ease of not doing so outweighs whatever benefit that high-velocity desire-satisfaction provides. This argument is more like the agential than the morality position about the value of *sôphrosunê*. It differs from a pure capacity position, however, in conceding a person's capacity to satisfy whatever desires he might have—Callicles hypothesizes a clever, powerful person—and thus undermining the claim that *sôphrosunê* is necessary for streamlined agency. The position is instead that this Calliclean approach is simply not worth it; it is too inefficient and onerous.

Finally, the precise meaning of 35—which says that people should find pleasure with themselves rather than with others, and predispose the body as appropriate—is something of a mystery. Susan Prince suggests an erotic context and an exhortation to masturbation, comparing it to a reference to Diogenes of Sinope.[52] But the point is probably more general, and is the one now familiar

---

[49] They are very close: Xen. *Mem*. 1.6.10: ἐγὼ δ' ἐνόμιζον τὸ μὲν μηδενὸς δεῖσθαι θεῖον εἶναι, τὸ δ' ὡς ἐλαχίστων ἐγγυτάτω τοῦ θείου, καὶ τὸ μὲν θεῖον κράτιστον, τὸ δ' ἐγγυτάτω τοῦ θείου ἐγγυτάτω τοῦ κρατίστου. Stob. 3.4.33: Σωκράτης ἔλεγεν θεοῦ μὲν εἶναι τὸ μηδενὸς δεῖσθαι, τὸ δ' ὡς ἐλαχίστων ἐγγυτάτω θεοῦ.

[50] Antisth. fr. 136.

[51] For some difficulties squaring this with Cynic doctrine, see Prince (2019, 487–88).

[52] DL 6.46; Prince (2019, 487).

from Thucydides: it is easier to satisfy one's desires when they are local and do not depend on the cooperation or availability of others. This is a matter of self-sufficiency, predictability, and reliability of action.[53] The "predisposition" or arrangement of the body presumably refers to the training of oneself so as not to have extravagant desires.

I mentioned that these sayings that Stobaeus takes to be about *sôphrosunê* plausibly go back to Socrates or early Socratic literature. At the very least, they show that later writers took Socrates as an archetypal proponent or apologist of the virtue. More substantively, they show Socrates in a characteristically dialogical guise, defending the virtue in a range of ways, both "ethical" and "nonethical," and among the nonethical ways, by appeal to various considerations. This variety is consistent with the natural supposition that Socrates did not have a robust theory of *sôphrosunê*, only a tenacious engagement in discussions about the virtue. But not every perspective on *sôphrosunê* appears here: in particular, we do not see arguments presenting *sôphrosunê* as the result of inner combat or restricted to appetitive desires. From this silence we might cautiously suppose that (this anonymous source or set of sources for) Socrates saw *sôphrosunê* as generally about domesticating one's desires, adjusting them to fit one's resources and position. These sayings do not emphasize selection between desires, though their management may require such selection, and desires not acted upon may eventually wither away. What they do show is Socrates' treatment of *sôphrosunê* as at the heart of living well.

The Platonic *Alcibiades*

Our chapter's final witness to a *sôphrosunê*-concerned Socrates and his vision of *sôphrosunê*'s significance is the longer of the two *Alcibiades* dialogues found in the Platonic corpus. This dialogue served for centuries as an introduction to Plato's dialogues and, relatedly, to the character of Socrates. A vigorous debate in the past two centuries has queried the likelihood it was actually written by Plato. The dialogue seems to lack the complexity, richness, and depth, both dramatically and dialectically, found in similar-length dialogues by Plato. The question of authorship does not resolve directly to the question of historical validity about Socrates, since it could be deeply influenced by Plato and other Socratic writings, and the author might have had no personal knowledge of Socrates. Its being by Plato could mean that it was written at the beginning of his career, but not much follows from that. The dialogue is important here because its Socratic discussion of *sôphrosunê*, which analyzes it as a kind of self-knowledge, has

---

[53] Cp. *Anon. Iambl.* 4.6.

an appealing simplicity, something explicable but not yet so problematized or theorized as we find it in the *Phaedo, Gorgias, Republic,* and *Charmides*. Yet the *Alcibiades* shares an animating idea with those four dialogues, that *sôphrosunê* is the virtue of the successful civic actor, the political agent; it is the capacity that Alcibiades seeks. It is an agency that depends on recognizing with precision one's most characteristic desires. I suspect that the idea goes back to Socrates.

At what appears to be the very climax of the dialogue, where Socrates is persuading Alcibiades that, to achieve the power he desires, he must come to know himself, the two interlocutors agree that knowing oneself amounts to *sôphrosunê*.[54] The lines immediately preceding this agreement are the most famous of the dialogue: Socrates has drawn an analogy, for understanding self-knowledge, of an eye that sees itself best by seeing its reflection in the most precise mirror, namely the surface of the eye of another person. They infer from this analogy that a soul knows itself best in the most divine and rational portion of another soul.[55] What is strange, however, is that scholarship on the dialogue has given almost no attention to this agreement identifying *sôphrosunê* and self-knowledge, especially not its meaning or argumentative impact. Olympiodorus, from whom the most thorough ancient commentary comes, makes only a brief esoteric comment.[56] The introduction to the leading English translation of the dialogue does not mention it.[57] The most recent commentary on the dialogue notes only a rhetorically interesting feature of it.[58] The best historical study of the dialogue offers only somewhat incidental comments about it.[59] And yet the equation, and the way it is made, amounts to a major statement about *sôphrosunê* from the Socratic perspective.

Just before the key identification of the virtue, Alcibiades has accepted what about himself he must most know—the aspect of his soul where there is knowing and thinking—and which actions contribute to a soul's having virtue and wisdom. His having accepted this hardly suffices for his then coming to know himself, of course; Socrates does not say how Alcibiades is to know that aspect of his soul. Instead, Socrates proceeds without pause to his next question.[60] In fact

---

[54] *Alc.* 133c18.
[55] *Alc.* 133a4–c16.
[56] Olymp. *in Alc.* lec. 28. This, the final lecture, is introduced with the lemma "But we agree that knowing oneself," but the long précis of this section of the *Alcibiades* does not mention *sôphrosunê*. Olympiodorus does eventually comment on this line itself: "For it was also pointed out earlier that *sôphrosunê* is appropriate to reversion, because it rides upon *epithumia*, around the part [of the soul] most remote [from reason]. Hence, since our nature is unable to be still, and cannot go further, it returns to its betters. Because of this, they say 'good habits are unstable at their peak'" (tr. Griffin).
[57] Hutchinson (1997, 557) does write that "the virtues of soul that he needs to acquire are the intellectual skills that give it the authority to rule, over its body and over other people as well."
[58] Denyer (2001, 238, cf. 222). The summary of the relevant section, at p. 237, does not even mention *sôphrosunê*.
[59] Renaud and Tarrant (2018, 59, 74, 76).
[60] I note that most treatments of the dialogue obscure this continuity by breaking the sections up at this point: see, for example, Olympiodorus and Denyer (2001, 229, 237).

he asks the question twice, once at c6 and again, in a section usually judged a later interpolation, at c15–16:

[1] ΣΩ. οὕτω καὶ ἑαυτὸν ἂν γνοίη μάλιστα (c6) *and* οὕτως ἂν μάλιστα ὁρῷμεν καὶ γιγνώσκοιμεν ἡμᾶς αὐτούς (c15–16)
ΑΛ. Φαίνεται (c7) *and* Ναί (c17)
ΣΩ. Τὸ δὲ γιγνώσκειν αὑτὸν ὡμολογοῦμεν σωφροσύνην εἶναι;
ΑΛ. Πάνυ γε. (*Alc.* 133 c18–19)

SOCRATES: And in this way one will most know himself *and* And in this way we will most see and know ourselves.
ALCIBIADES: Apparently *and* Yes.
SOCRATES: And we agreed that knowing oneself is *sôphrosunê*.
ALCIBIADES: Definitely.

Socrates here refers back to 131b5 (text [5] below), where they had already drawn the equivalence, though there they gave no reasons to accept the equivalence; indeed, it was posited only in the protasis of a conditional. Yet at no point earlier in the conversation did Socrates explicitly exhort Alcibiades to become *sôphrôn*; Alcibiades cannot have been waiting for Socrates to explain how to do so. Alcibiades wants to become a competent leader. So the equivalence cannot really be tendentious. What follows is Socrates' next question, expecting a negative answer:

[2] Ἆρ' οὖν μὴ γιγνώσκοντες ἡμᾶς αὐτοὺς μηδὲ σώφρονες ὄντες δυναίμεθ' ἂν εἰδέναι τὰ ἡμέτερα αὐτῶν κακά τε καὶ ἀγαθά; (*Alc.* 133c21–23)

So if we neither knew ourselves nor were *sôphrôn*, would we be able to know, of our things, the ones that are bad and the ones that are good?

The claim is that achieving self-knowledge and *sôphrosunê* is necessary—and presumably sufficient—for knowing both what things are one's own (implied here) and how good they are (made explicit here). This sets Socrates up to conclude his long protreptic argument about leadership. One must know one's own things—and by extension, others' things—in this way to qualify as any sort of ruler and as happy, which are Alcibiades' real ambitions.[61] Thus Alcibiades has a compelling reason to seek self-knowledge and spend time with Socrates. At this level of abstraction, Socrates' move is straightforward enough.

But how relevant is *sôphrosunê* to the argument? Its equivalence with knowing oneself is ascertained, as though it is to replace occurrences of knowing oneself,

---

[61] *Alc.* 105a–c.

but then, in the protasis of [2], there is no such replacement. Socrates speaks of being *sôphrôn* as well as, not instead of, knowing oneself. Socrates' point becomes clearer as we survey the few but wide-ranging uses of *sôphrosunê* and its adjectival and verbal cognates in the dialogue. The earliest use arises in the description of one of the four tutors of a Persian prince:

[3] ὁ δὲ σωφρονέστατος μηδ' ὑπὸ μιᾶς ἄρχεσθαι τῶν ἡδονῶν, ἵνα ἐλεύθερος εἶναι ἐθίζηται καὶ ὄντως βασιλεύς, ἄρχων πρῶτον τῶν ἐν αὑτῷ ἀλλὰ μὴ δουλεύων. (*Alc.* 122a4–7)

The [tutor reputed as] most *sôphrôn* [teaches him] not to be ruled by any one of the pleasures, so that he may be accustomed to be a free man and truly a king, ruling first over the things in himself and not being a slave.

This passage suggests that *sôphrosunê* amounts to being ruled by no pleasure and to being free as befits a king, and ruling over what is within oneself. It does not say so determinately, however, since Socrates says here only what the particular tutor will teach. There is a distinction between the virtue and tailored lessons in the cases of the other tutors. The "wisest" tutor teaches Zoroastrian magic and kingship (τὰ βασιλικά), but presumably *sophia* has a broader scope and more abstract definition than piety and statesmanship. The same goes for justice: the "justest" tutor teaches "truth-telling" (ἀληθεύειν). So rule over rather than by pleasures, with its consequent freedom of action and rule, may be a part of *sôphrosunê* but need not be the whole or even dominant or authoritative part of it. Nevertheless, pleasures or desires, and their relative authority in decision-making, must have some pertinence to *sôphrosunê*.

The next appearance of *sôphrosunê* in the *Alcibiades* conversation arises less than half a page later, when Socrates provides another humbling model for Alcibiades: the Spartans. Remarkably, paragons both of luxury and of austerity manifest *sôphrosunê*:

[4] εἰ δ' αὖ ἐθελήσεις εἰς σωφροσύνην τε καὶ κοσμιότητα ἀποβλέψαι καὶ εὐχέρειαν καὶ εὐκολίαν καὶ μεγαλοφροσύνην καὶ εὐταξίαν καὶ ἀνδρείαν καὶ καρτερίαν καὶ φιλοπονίαν καὶ φιλονικίαν καὶ φιλοτιμίας τὰς Λακεδαιμονίων, παῖδ' ἂν ἡγήσαιο σαυτὸν πᾶσι τοῖς τοιούτοις. (*Alc.* 122c4–d1)

And again, if you wish to look to the *sôphrosunê* and orderliness of the Spartans, their confidence and composure, self-esteem and organization, courage and hardiness, persistence and competitiveness and ambition, you would judge yourself a child in all these respects.

150 THE VIRTUE OF AGENCY

Given its position in the list, *sôphrosunê* appears to be the most characteristic virtue of the Spartans.[62] Whether it is a matter of asceticism or management of bodily desires is not so obvious. As we saw in our study of Thucydides, for example, in the Spartan context *sôphrosunê* means insulating oneself from foreign influence, relying mainly on one's inner direction, and in general being loyal to one's long-standing commitments.[63] Granted, these uses apply to the city of Sparta as a corporate actor, in the context of foreign affairs, but they are not presented as metaphorical or derivative of psychological uses. *Sôphrosunê*'s proximity to *kosmiotês* ("orderliness") here, a similar pairing of the two terms in Plato's *Gorgias* (508a), and the collocation with a range of other traits all in the sphere of self-directedness, suggest it means acting in a patterned, predictable, and not impetuous way: having a principled or at least habitually unified way of acting.

We will see later the coherence of the Persian and Spartan cases, the dialogue's two "background" uses of *sôphrosunê*, which are not explicitly connected to our focal argument, [1] and [2]. The next use of *sôphrosunê* in the dialogue, nine pages later on, is the first so connected. Socrates is arguing about the nature of the "oneself" one knows in knowing oneself: it is the soul, by contrast to the body or what pertains to the body. Tradesmen, for instance, know only the latter. Socrates draws an inference:

[5] Εἰ ἄρα σωφροσύνη ἐστὶ τὸ ἑαυτὸν γιγνώσκειν, οὐδεὶς τούτων σώφρων κατὰ τὴν τέχνην. (*Alc.* 131b4–5)

So if *sôphrosunê* is knowing oneself, not one of them [i.e., tradesmen] is *sôphrôn* on account of his skill.

This is the place where the equivalence between *sôphrosunê* and knowing oneself first arises, the target of the back-reference in [1]. With Alcibiades' immediate agreement to this conditional, Socrates goes on to infer that this explains why gentlemen do not go into these trades: they would lack virtue were they to do so. Then Socrates allows that the same lack of virtue pertains to those treating bodies and those seeking money—the latter, he notes, "do not do their own things" (οὐ τὰ αὑτοῦ ἄρα ἔτι πράττει, 131c3). Why Socrates brings up the equivalence and why Alcibiades accepts it is a question to be addressed in light of the following four considerations.

First, Socrates provides no reasons to accept the equivalence, and Alcibiades accepts it without any. This suggests that the equivalence is familiar and entirely plausible. Critias allows it in the *Charmides*, and before him, though less directly,

---

[62] What this means ends up being complicated: see Humble (1999); Herrmann (2018b).
[63] Thuc. 1.32.4.5, 1.68.1.3, 1.84.2–3.

Heraclitus in his fragments, as we have already seen. Second, neither of the earlier discussions of *sôphrosunê* in the dialogue anticipates the equivalence with knowing oneself. In [3], the language is of "ruling"; in [4], none of the Spartan skills is put in cognitive terms. Yet, it would be hasty or even wrong to assume that *sôphrosunê* must have a distinct meaning here—a mistake made by Ficino (in 1484), translating the first two as *temperantia*, the last ones as *prudentia*. Integration or overlap may well be possible. Neither earlier passage provides a definition or complete gloss. Further, there may be ways that "knowing oneself" could be understood in terms of "being authoritative over one's motivations" or in terms of the stable dispositions of character typified by ideal Spartans. Third, Socrates' immediate dialectical reason here for mentioning the equivalence is to explain the disreputable ethical status of tradesmen. Saying that they do not know their souls presumably does not impugn them enough; indeed, it could sound irrelevant, even commendable. But saying they lack *sôphrosunê*, and that money-makers do not do their own things, must sound quite bad to Alcibiades—even if they amount to the same thing. The traditionally ethical terms have more charge, even if one were to appreciate that the properties they denote are epistemic attitudes.

Fourth, just before passage [5], knowing oneself was equated with knowing one's soul, in contrast to knowing one's body. The meaning here is uncertain: there is no overwhelming evidence that this means "know what a soul *is*," namely, what its metaphysics are. But some clues come from the place in the dialogue where Socrates discusses the maxim *gnôthi sauton*. Not long before this passage, the Delphic injunction was said to exhort knowing something about the "itself" itself (αὐτὸ ταὐτό).[64] Socrates says that while he and Alcibiades intended to investigate this "itself" itself, they only got to knowing about "oneself," as an individual, something to whom we can attribute belongings or contingent properties. Knowing what "itself" means might imply knowing something about unity or distinctiveness or identity—and thus knowing a criterion of distinction. We thus see another parallel to the *Charmides*: Charmides fails to defend the definition "doing one's own things" because he has not thought enough about what it is to be "one's own," lacking any usable criterion for identity (161d1–162b1). Then, in the *Alcibiades*, the other, earlier reference to *gnôthi sauton* came at 124b, in the peroration to Socrates' Royal Fable, whence came texts [3] and [4]. Knowing oneself there involves knowing and not merely thinking you know the objects of your desires, which means knowing what they actually are. This seems to mean discovering or knowing what in fact one values. The third notion of knowing oneself comes up later, in the eye-seeing-itself passage (133c). There knowing oneself is doing whatever it is that goes best with another person's exercising his knowledge and reflection in concert—presumably what Socrates

---

[64] *Alc.* 129b1. On this reading, see Denyer (2001 ad loc).

has been doing with Alcibiades. Namely: testing, modifying, and realizing one's commitments, what one takes to be true and good.[65]

The equivalence between *sôphrosunê* and knowing oneself is treated as uncontroversial and helpful for the exhortation of Alcibiades, yet it is challenging and unclear enough to animate the conversation in the *Charmides*. And while it is not obvious how the equation would work out, trying to figure it out leads to reconsidering both sides of the equation: discerning and determining the norms on the basis of which action that could be called yours could be done.

Socrates mentions *sôphrosunê* four more times at the end of the dialogue:

[6] Οὐκ ἄρα οἷόν τε, ἐὰν μή τις σώφρων καὶ ἀγαθὸς ᾖ, εὐδαίμονα εἶναι. (*Alc.* 134a13–14)

So one cannot be happy if one is not *sôphrôn* and good.

[7] Οὐκ ἄρα οὐδ' ὁ πλουτήσας ἀθλιότητος ἀπαλλάττεται, ἀλλ' ὁ σωφρονήσας. (*Alc.* 134b4–5)

So it's not by being rich that one avoids suffering but by being *sôphrôn*.

In these two passages Socrates takes a strong line: *sôphrosunê* is something like the key desideratum in seeking the flourishing life. In [6], *sôphrosunê* seems to have about as much generality as goodness. In [7], we see the charge against a rosy view of wealth as automatically useful for living well, a charge akin to what we saw in Stobaeus' collection of Socratica, with the imputation that wealth in fact is not a relevant consideration.[66]

[8] Οὐκ ἄρα ἐξουσίαν σοι οὐδ' ἀρχὴν παρασκευαστέον σαυτῷ ποιεῖν ὅτι ἂν βούλῃ, οὐδὲ τῇ πόλει, ἀλλὰ δικαιοσύνην καὶ σωφροσύνην. (*Alc.* 134c9–11)

So you ought to prepare for yourself neither power nor authority to do what you'd like for yourself, or the city, but justice and *sôphrosunê*.

[9] Δικαίως μὲν γὰρ πράττοντες καὶ σωφρόνως σύ τε καὶ ἡ πόλις θεοφιλῶς πράξετε. (*Alc.* 134d1–2)

For when you and the state act justly and *sôphronôs*, you will be acting as the gods love.

---

[65] On these three passages about self-knowledge in the *Alcibiades*, see Moore (2015c, 101–35).
[66] See again *Anon. Iambl.* fr. 4.

Socrates generalizes again, bringing back *dikaiosunê* from earlier in the conversation. This pair is traditionally something of an exhaustive conjunct in Socratic literature, as *Protagoras* and *Rival Lovers* (138a10) suggest.

The survey of uses of *sôphrosunê* in the *Alcibiades* completed, we can revisit the double inference from [1] knowing oneself to being *sôphrôn* and then [2] from both of those to knowing the goodness of one's things—one's belongings and actions—and (thus) of others' things.

Regarding the first inference, there is the superficial observation that the equivalence is treated as familiar—from Heraclitus, and Critias, and Critias' assumption that Socrates would assent to it. But even if it is familiar, is it also cogent? Would really knowing one's desires—as knowing oneself is glossed at 124b—be the same as mastering them, as *sôphrosunê* is glossed in [3]? It might after all seem so, since upon knowing their full extent or configuration, one could try to structure one's life to satisfy them. If one did not know them fully, however, one might be continually blinkered by one's failures to satisfy them all the way; they would be popping up at inconvenient moments. Would knowing oneself qua self, something "itself"—knowing oneself as portrayed at 129b—be the same as maintaining an inner integrity, a unity, an essential core—as *sôphrosunê* is glossed in [4]? Would knowing what amounts to wisdom and virtue—knowing oneself as portrayed at 133c—be the same as being good, which is whatever constitutes being god-beloved when that is combined with justice? The *Alcibiades* appears to provide the resources for accepting this theoretically rich equation of *sôphrosunê* and knowing oneself.

The dialogue prompts another hypothesis: If having a virtue means knowing what's good in some context, then *sôphrosunê* accounts for knowing whether one's things are good or not. Knowing something "more properly" includes knowing the things that belong to it (130e7), and so knowing yourself accounts for knowing your belongings. So together they get us to the goodness and badness of one's belongings. There is something paradoxical here: we need both *sôphrosunê* and knowing oneself, as it were distinctly; and yet, they were just said to be the same thing. Yet the equivalence was cited in [1] probably just to get *sôphrosunê* into the argument. *Sôphrosunê* then may have sufficed to derive the claim about knowing the value of one's things—the term is ethically charged in a way self-knowledge is not. But if the things one knows in self-knowledge are, in the end, ethically salient things, like one's commitments, then even self-knowledge is ethically charged. *Sôphrosunê* may not have the really apparent self-examining aspect that knowing oneself does—the first *Charmides* definition of it as "tranquility" shows this; it is not obviously reflexive at all—but if tranquility, etc. requires acting on only certain authorized motivations, then it does ultimately require a sufficient quantity of self-examination. Thus knowing oneself and *sôphrosunê* are the same thing, but with different historical associations; together they clinch the protreptic argument against Alcibiades.

The arguments I have just made are tentative, though I believe the dialogue has sufficient depth to warrant this type of exploration. What matters for this chapter is that the dialogue's Socrates gives the virtue a profound role in political power. And it is properly political power, rather than simply tyrannical power, that embraces or unites the agential and ethical aspects of *sôphrosunê*. For Alcibiades to do what he wants to do rather than to be tripped up by misapprehensions of his own goals, for example by setting his sights in the wrong direction and willingly undergoing the wrong preparation, he needs self-knowledge, and this is *sôphrosunê*. This is the agential aspect. But he also needs to know what is due to him and what to others; so he needs a self-knowledge realized as the sense of justice, and this is also *sôphrosunê*. This is the ethical aspect. Thus Socrates' charge to Alcibiades, through the pen of the *Alcibiades* author, is to become *sôphrôn*, for only then will he be the decision-maker or even change-maker he most truly wants to be.

A Socratic *Sôphrosunê*

The circumstantial evidence is extensive that Socrates distinguished himself among his fellow intellectuals for embodying an ideal of *sôphrosunê* and for talking about and even exhorting others to an ideal of *sôphrosunê*. Depending on the historical reliability of the theses and explanations Xenophon attributes to Socrates, we may even have direct evidence for Socrates' views of *sôphrosunê*; something similar could be said of Plato's depictions. At least these two authors provide further circumstantial evidence for the association of the virtue and the man. (What they do say about *sôphrosunê*, in particular through Socrates, will come out in Chapters 7–10.)

What is the meaning of the evidence marshaled in this chapter? The comic dramatists, for genuine or literary reasons, doubted that Socrates' remarkable self-mastery could be for real: in quelling some desires, he diverted psychic force elsewhere: either it never went away, as the cases of stealing show, or it transmuted, as the cases of excessive talk show. Aristophanes, who places Socrates in a play effectively about *sôphrosunê*, offsets his otherworldly rationality, which is a commitment to seemingly higher norms, against his self-glorifying religious radicalism, which is a failure of commitment to the highest norms. In his appearances in Old Comedy, Socrates serves as a problem case for *sôphrosunê*—just as Hippolytus and Phaedra did, as we saw in Chapter 4. He appears to embody certain aspects of it, such as giving little attention to food, warmth, or popular esteem, but in the process forgetting other aspects, such as justice or piety. These judgments are not assuredly sound, given the comedic imperative and rhetorical conservatism. But they do show that Socrates incited reflection on *sôphrosunê*, and perhaps more important from this book's perspective, through Socrates' counterexample, these judgments show how people thought of *sôphrosunê*, even if implicitly. *Sôphrosunê* does more than control one's bodily desires; it also involves recognition of human and divine laws.

The life of Antisthenes, insofar as it reflects a Socratic, even if more literary mode of being, looks consistent with the laudable side of Socrates' comic persona. Here we probably find an explicit advocacy of *sôphrosunê*, both as a way of life and as a subject or goal of teaching. The testimonia about Antisthenes emphasize a Cynic self-sufficiency, a wariness about pleasure but not a monkish austerity toward it, and a life oriented by virtue and unconcerned with mere creature comforts. Besides Socrates, Antisthenes admired Heracles, Odysseus, and Cyrus. So for him *sôphrosunê* amounts not to the suppression of desire or pleasure but to practical excellence, the capacity to get done what really matters to oneself. This has a prudential and an ethical side, an indefatigability and undistractability as much as an orientation toward what is right.

Stobaeus, conceivably following in an Antisthenic tradition, sees Socrates as the standard-bearer of *sôphrosunê*; his judgment is not the result of mechanical sorting of gnomic statements to chapters, because none of the statements attributed to Socrates in his chapter on *sôphrosunê* includes the word.[67] In those statements we see an appraising attitude toward pleasure: neither a rejection nor a celebration of it, but an awareness that getting pleasure is not reason by itself to satisfy a desire. They exhort doing what one can to avoid enlarging one's desires; this probably involves taking up psychic distance to them, recognizing that they are instruments of action, not authoritative directions about what to do.

The *Alcibiades* has no more certain historical value than these other sources of evidence for Socrates-vis-à-vis-*sôphrosunê*, but it does have much greater argumentative detail. The key lesson is the association of *sôphrosunê* with self-knowledge. This association is meaningful, since it serves in two key dialectical maneuvers and, lacking any explicit substantiation, is treated as an unsurprising thing for Socrates to say. Given the linkage between the two associated concepts and the proper recognition of one's desires, and its avoiding a rhetorically implausible argument against desire suppression—such a maneuver is unlikely to gain Alcibiades' assent—*sôphrosunê* comes to seem a capacity for unimpeded

---

[67] This is not altogether precisely put, since Stobaeus could be mechanically relying on an earlier collection of gnomic statements about *sôphrosunê*; nevertheless, *somebody* used their judgment, and Stobaeus presumably did as well, given that he seems unlikely to have copied chapters wholesale from earlier anthologists.

action, unimpeded, that is, by ignorance and self-ignorance. Given the other evidence just surveyed about Socratic *sôphrosunê*, this picture of the virtue as involving knowing what one is about, what principles most drive oneself, and how recognizing the dignities of others contributes to reaching one's goals, seems once again Socratic.

7
Xenophon on *Sôphrosunê* and *Enkrateia*

Xenophon among the Other Fourth-Century Theorists of *Sôphrosunê*

We have just seen that we can count neither Antisthenes nor the Academic *Alcibiades* author as wholesale theorists of *sôphrosunê*, even though both wrote about the virtue. The evidence for the first is simply too exiguous, and the second, while making the concept argumentatively crucial, does not make it thematic. The situation improves as we turn to Plato and Aristotle. Plato treats specifically of *sôphrosunê* throughout his oeuvre, albeit aporetically or programmatically; Aristotle, though giving it less space, assesses it with his characteristic intensity and directness. Not only do these authors say much more about *sôphrosunê* than others; they differ in their interpretations of it in theoretically fundamental ways. As Plato surveys the capacities a person needs to go well through life, he seeks to explain the centrality of *sôphrosunê* to Greek discussions of human maturity—and, in so doing, he ends up presenting *sôphrosunê* as something of a metavirtue, either as virtue in general or as a prerequisite for other virtues. Aristotle, by contrast, though still acknowledging maturation's dependence on *sôphrosunê*, fits the virtue to a much narrower domain of a person's experience of the world.

Xenophon serves our narrative as a bridging figure, in two ways: between the less theoretical and the more theoretical Socratics; and between the Platonic-maximal and Aristotelian-minimal interpretations of the virtue. He is a diagnostician of well-reputed polities, such as Sparta, Persia, and Athens, concerned with the capacity of their institutions to promote *sôphrosunê* among the other virtues necessary for a stable and flourishing state. Even more fundamentally, he is a moralist, writing of figures such as Socrates, Cyrus, and Agesilaus as models and proponents of the virtue. In this respect he is an apologist, too, in particular of Socrates' way of life, an explicator of the role that *sôphrosunê* played in Socrates' provocative teaching and example. Xenophon is not the familiar sort of moral philosopher, in that he does not seek principally to distinguish terms and justify assumptions. But, a member of contemporary intellectual trends, wanting to explain and encourage, he does do moral philosophy. He is a substantial participant in fourth-century debates about *sôphrosunê*. The worst that could be said about Xenophon's status as a theorist of *sôphrosunê* is that he never wrote a passage that answers the question "What precisely is *sôphrosunê*?" But he gets close often, identifying cases or failures of *sôphrosunê*, defending the value of the virtue, and relating it to similar virtues and traits.

In fact, Xenophon's relative lack of philosophical pretension makes him valuable as an informant about the nature of *sôphrosunê*: he speaks of it as he thinks his audience will appreciate it, with a proximity to colloquial usage.[1] To be sure, he is hardly innocent of philosophy. As a student of Sparta he will have been influenced by both Critias and those others around Socrates who analyzed the city, with its putative *sôphrosunê* a salient feature. And as a student of Socrates and the other Socratics, he will have absorbed Socrates' discussions about the virtue itself.[2] But he is not led, as with Aristotle, to what we will see as a reductive systematization or, as with Plato, to exploratory brainstorming or imaginative reconstruction. The generic variety of his work implies that he intends to have readers who are not prepared for surprising or counterintuitive views about *sôphrosunê*, who do not see the concept as puzzling or radically problematic, but who see the virtue instead as a stable and recognizable part of the moral landscape, even if of indefinite scope and uncertain moral priority.

Xenophon mostly follows the way people around him, especially intellectuals, talk about *sôphrosunê*, but he does so with attention to statements about the virtue itself, especially those that come from debates about the virtue's application or implication. Thus we can attribute a view or interpretation of *sôphrosunê* to him. He gives us an at times imprecise or indeterminate view, to be sure, but it is nevertheless a substantive set of distinctive and interlocking positions. It is the first quasi-systematic account of *sôphrosunê* we have seen, and so it is valuable for theoretical and intellectual-historical reasons. And despite the influence of Socrates and other intellectuals, we can suppose that in some respects it represents and elaborates a basically consensus view of the Greeks of the early fourth century.

Two related aspects of Xenophon's analysis stand out and repay investigation. First, Xenophon makes especially clear that *sôphrosunê* amounts to acknowledging authoritative norms. This means recognizing that certain norms should guide one's actions, which in turn means acting, as far as possible, in accordance with those norms. These norms may be divine, civic, or prudential, and thus are neither inherently other-directed or self-directed, though Xenophon's meliorism tends to bring them together. So *sôphrosunê*, to put it in the present-day argot, is responsiveness to reasons; it is not specifically a matter of enlightened self-interest or moral selflessness. Second, Xenophon introduces *enkrateia*, "inner power," as a partner to *sôphrosunê* in discussions of human maturity.

---

[1] For Xenophon's audience, see Christ (2020).
[2] For Socrates' influence on Xenophon, see Luccioni (1953); Anderson (1974, 20–45); Higgins (1977, 13–43); Johnson (2021, 1–13).

He once lauds *enkrateia* as the "foundation" or "footing" (κρηπίς) of virtue and often presents as the key desideratum of education and self-cultivation; and yet he treats it as somehow significantly different from *sôphrosunê*.[3] He does not always insist on this difference, to the point of allowing some characters to speak as though they were interchangeable; some readers have come to believe that he equates the two.[4] But the difference between the two is real, philosophically purposeful and interesting, and highly informative about Xenophon's interpretation of *sôphrosunê*. As we will see, *enkrateia* describes the capacity to withstand desire's urgent call, either by hardening oneself to that call or by weakening the call itself. This allows Xenophon to present *sôphrosunê* as the commitment to authoritative norms; *enkrateia* does the work of controlling desires sufficiently to allow that commitment, and *sôphrosunê* guides which desires *enkrateia* will control. Other virtue-terms present other partially overlapping aspects of sound decision-making: wisdom, the identification of those norms; endurance, the temporal stability of one's *enkrateia*; self-sufficiency, the reduction of desires for things other than necessities. But his attention to the special work described as *enkrateia* is Xenophon's signal contribution to the clarification of *sôphrosunê*'s special work.

Looking forward, we will see Plato agreeing with Xenophon about the meaning of *sôphrosunê*, but doing so largely without reference to *enkrateia*; where Plato does mention *enkrateia*, he is in effect acknowledging the popular connection between the two states. For Plato, the control of desire and the commitment to authoritative desire that control allows belong to the same competence, *sôphrosunê*. Aristotle, by contrast, resumes from Xenophon a distinction between *sôphrosunê* and *enkrateia*, but not the same one. They agree that *enkrateia* is tasked with overcoming or neutralizing the force of desires, that it is not itself good-oriented, and that it is therefore not properly a virtue. They disagree markedly about the scope of *sôphrosunê*: whereas Xenophon attributes to it norm-following in general, Aristotle sees it as having moderate desires specifically for food, drink, and sex and the insight to decide precisely how or when to act on those desires. As it happens, these are three of the desires for which Xenophon thinks *enkrateia* is most necessary (along with those for sleep and relaxation). So while Aristotle basically accepts Xenophon's account of *enkrateia*, what Xenophon concedes to *sôphrosunê* Aristotle redirects to something new: *phronêsis*, action-guiding insight.

What we see in this and the next few chapters, then, is a range of responses to a single problem, one that earlier debate has begun to reveal: How are we to

---

[3] Xen. *Mem.* 1.5.4 for κρηπίς.
[4] Louis-André Dorion defends the equation view throughout his commentary on the *Memorabilia* (Bandini and Dorion, 2003–11); see his Dorion (2003) specifically on *enkrateia*. But see Johnson (2021, 173–76) for a critique of the equation.

conceive the control of desires in respect to the ideal of *sôphrosunê*? This is a problem because desire-control is neither the exclusive nor sometimes even the primary capacity lauded by appellations of *sôphrosunê*. As we have seen in previous chapters, the term has instead lauded those who take a considered perspective on their actions, who acknowledge what ought to be acknowledged. The relevance of desire-control is of course evident here—but its precise connection is not. These fourth-century theoretical reflections on *sôphrosunê* work to clarify that connection.

Sôphrosunê beyond the Socratica

Most of Xenophon's analytic remarks about *sôphrosunê* appear in the Socratic writings, the *Memorabilia* in particular.[5] But they make the most sense against his broader patterns of usage of the term. The most invariant of his formulae is one seen elsewhere in historiography, the monitory "If you *sôphronein*, then you . . ."; that is, if you look before you leap, this is what you will or will not do.[6] This suggests that the verb, at least, is concerned with a basic norm of well-deliberated action: not treating the inclination that happens to absorb the most of one's attention as the best available reason to act. We find the same sense of having done one's due diligence in the other parts of speech. Members of the cavalry would make more *sôphrôn* horse-buying decisions if they knew that any violent steeds they acquired might be dismissed from service; a *sôphrôn* military tactic is to go where the enemy is weak, even at the cost of long travel; a *sôphrôn* leader trusts thoughtful advisors; *sôphrôn* parties do not fight each other over slight differences.[7]

These are so far prudential concerns: should you fail in *sôphrosunê*, you will fail to achieve your intended results, whether it be success as a cavalry man, defeat of one's enemy, political leadership, or civic preservation. This is of course not altogether distinctive of *sôphrosunê*; failures in other virtues also block great achievement.[8] But Xenophon sometimes speaks of the value of *sôphrosunê* more broadly. He can treat it simply as being good and doing what is right.[9] This moral formulation becomes ritualized in the context of young men, who in Sparta show

---

[5] See Róspide López and Martín García (1995, 206–7) for the Socratica; Crusius, Koch, and Güthling (1969, 112–13) for the *Memorabilia* (with glosses); Sauppe (1869, 127) for the minor forms.

[6] Xen. *Hell.* 2.3.34, 7.1.24; *Anab.* 5.8.24, 6.2.11, 7.3.17, 7.6.41; *Cyr.* 3.2.13, 4.2.24, 8.3.32.

[7] Xen. *Hipparch.* 1.14.3, 4.14.1; *Hell.* 6.2.39, 6.3.5. Cf. *Cyr.* 1.6.26, 5.3.43 (reasons for marching in silence), 5.4.44 (safest vs. fastest retreat); 8.5.13 (an official's knowing where his subjects live).

[8] Xen. *Hell.* 7.3.6.

[9] Xen. *Hiero* 9.8.2; *Cyn.* 12.7–9, 13.15.5 (the reasonable scholarly doubts about Xenophon's authorship of ch. 13 not undermining the point but lessening the evidence of Xenophon's use of this formulation).

their *sôphrosunê* by walking with their hands under their cloaks, in silence, with eyes down—they bother nobody and prevent themselves from even the chance of provocation.[10] They combine obedience and self-restraint, valuable as states of noninterference and nondistraction, with the future value of the cultivated capacity for rule-following, valuable as a prerequisite of self-rule.

Indeed, Xenophon's more substantive remarks about *sôphrosunê* connect it to rule-following. Sometimes the point is simply that a *sôphrôn* person willingly obeys another.[11] In some cases, however, obedience becomes a greater capacity, the autonomy necessary for sound leadership. In the *Anabasis*, young Persians are said to learn *sôphrosunê* above all at the king's court, which is where young men learn to "rule and be ruled." Cyrus, among them, was reputed most respectful (αἰδημονέστατος) and obedient (πείθεσθαι), and he exhibited the qualities befitting a good leader.[12] In his *Agesilaus*, Xenophon reports the view that the Greeks would be happy (εὐδαίμων) if they should fixedly follow the laws (ἐν τοῖς νόμοις ἠρεμοῦντες διαμένοιεν), but that they would be strong (ἰσχυρός) in addition if they should *sôphronein*.[13] *Sôphrosunê* is not merely law-abidingness; it seems related to practical competence and resilience. Several paragraphs earlier, Xenophon had said that Agesilaus worked without cease, never avoided danger, and lacked any stinginess concerning money or effort; and that, in addition to doing good works, he also modeled obedience to the law and complaisance even toward those who acted wrongly. All these character traits conduce to efficacy, both individual and corporate. Thus *sôphrosunê* would amount to committing oneself not just to the city's laws, promoting civic stability and comity, but also to those higher norms that promote civic power.

Among these remarks about *sôphrosunê*, Xenophon includes one debate about the virtue's nature and acquisition, one that gives historical resonance to a theoretical passage in the *Memorabilia*.[14] In *Cyropedia*, Tigranes, son of the Armenian king, asks Cyrus to stop his postconquest punishment of his father. It is true, Tigranes says, that his father did wrong, but in being vanquished militarily by the Persians, he has already become *sôphrôn*. And *sôphrosunê* is a preeminent value: without it, none of the other virtues are useful (οὐδ᾽ ἄλλης ἀρετῆς οὐδὲν ὄφελος): neither strength, nor courage, nor wealth, nor political position; and with it, friends are useful, servants good. Cyrus is perhaps not wholly convinced

---

[10] Xen. *Lac. Pol.* 3.4.5. This passage echoes the Better Argument's position about *sôphrosunê* in *Clouds* and, before that, Phocylides' remark; we will see it again in *Charmides*. For discussion, see Moore (2023). The *sôphrosunê* of these young men is compared favorably to that of young women; for the theme, see *Ages.* 6.7.4. See also Humble (2021, ch. 3).
[11] E.g., Xen. *Cyr.* 3.2.4, 8.6.10; *Anab.* 7.7.30 (related to but not identified with fear).
[12] Xen. *Anab* 1.9.3.
[13] Xen. *Ages.* 7.3.
[14] Xen. *Cyr* 3.1.16–22. For context, see Danzig (2017, 305–11).

that he should yet relent; he expresses surprise that Tigranes' father could really have become *sôphrôn* so quickly. He had assumed that *sôphrosunê* was something learned (a μάθημα), a transition from being thoughtless (ἄφρονος) to being thoughtful (φρόνιμος): evidently an intellectual state of understanding, the competence to do certain kinds of reasoning. But if so, Cyrus seems to imply, it would be like a language or skilled art, something the acquisition of which would take more than a day. Tigranes must by contrast be assuming, he says, that it is a "state of the soul" (πάθημα ... τῆς ψυχῆς); this must be something which, perhaps like an emotion or mood, could strike one instantaneously. These opposing views about *sôphrosunê* reflect a debate between active and passive perspectives on the virtue—the capacity to figure out how to do things correctly versus the inertia of not acting incorrectly. One is the perspective of agency, the other the perspective of imperturbability.

Tigranes seeks a rapprochement between the two perspectives. He explains how his father, like anybody else, could become willing to submit (πείθεσθαι ἐθέλει) to the superior party. He describes it as a process of self-knowledge: Cyrus' actions made his father *sôphrôn* (σωφρονίζειν) when they helped him realize the inefficacy of his ambitions. He had been aiming for liberty, but his thoughtlessness led him to become enslaved; he had been aiming for accomplishment, and accomplished none of it; and it was Cyrus who outwitted him at every step. Cyrus had a stronger army and was plainly more competent in every respect. Tigranes' father came to realize that his failure was no accident, nothing that might be overcome with better luck or provisioning next time. Cyrus was simply better. *Sôphrosunê* does not mean simple obedience, but a willing obedience, the recognition of righteous authority in the agent you follow. By contrast with blind or thoughtless obedience, *sôphrosunê* involves self-understanding. Tigranes gives a dignified construction to his father's discovery: he does not cower; he respects.

We have seen *sôphrosunê* as a kind of autonomy-rich obedience, a following of rules the legislation of which one approves. What is notable is that none of the above discussions of *sôphrosunê* emphasize or even reference control over one's bodily desires. Surely many instances of action that call for praise of *sôphrosunê* or rebuke of its absence could be described as cases where desires were or were not controlled. But for Xenophon here *sôphrosunê* labels good, norm-following decision-making, whether that is in line with the rational norms of fact-finding and reasoning or the external norms of a city or community. Xenophon does care about desire management and minimization, and he allows *sôphrosunê*'s relevance to it, but his practice is to describe that under another head: *enkrateia*. He is not excessively scrupulous about his labeling, however, and desire-control is central to *sôphrosunê*, howsoever labeled, and so the places where Xenophon treats *sôphrosunê* and *enkrateia* simultaneously reward study.

A confusing but especially important case concerns Agesilaus. He is something of a model of virtue for Xenophon.[15] He exercised *sôphronein* during good times (εὐπραξίαι), while being courageous and reliable (εὐθαρσής) during bad ones.[16] He was reverent toward god rather than impious; just rather than unjust; *sôphrôn* rather than hubristic; and self-controlled (ἐγκρατής) rather than incontinent (ἀκρατής).[17] Here we have a canon of virtues. Whether mutually exclusive or not, each is salient in its own way. *Sôphrosunê* is opposed to hubris rather than *akrasia*: so it pertains immediately to the respect of rules, be they divine, civic, or social, rather than to the defeat of desires.[18] Ungoverned desires could surely contribute to hubris, but they need not; one could also imagine an utterly self-controlled hubris. More important, the social and moral judgments between the two negative states, and thus the two positive states, differ. This may be clear enough here, but elsewhere Xenophon puts less space between the two states. A series of early chapters speak directly to Agesilaus' individual virtues: piety (3), justice (4), courage (6), wisdom (6.4–7), additional virtues later.[19] Chapter 5 does not specifically address *sôphrosunê* or *enkrateia* but rather begins by speaking to Agesilaus' immunity to such pleasures as defeat many other people—namely those for alcohol, food, sleep, and sex—and goes on to praise his excellence in endurance and hardiness.[20] Xenophon then speaks specifically of an *enkrateia* concerning sex (ἀφροδισίων ἐγκρατείας), which involves mastery (κρατεῖν) over one's desires; but he glosses this as an instance of *sôphrosunê* (τὸ σωφρόνημα), and generalizes to say that Agesilaus lived in the open to keep his *sôphrosunê* on display.[21] In this exhortative context, and given his clarity later, Xenophon's indifference to distinctions here seems excusable if also evidence of the terrain shared by the two states.

A similar collocation occurs in *Cyropedia*. There Xenophon reprises the Persian education that we earlier saw in *Anabasis* and summarizes the consequent virtues of Cyrus. The basic program in Persia, Xenophon says early in his tale, is to ensure that its youth never desire (ἐφίεσθαι) to do anything base or shameful, a condition the attainment of which involves considerable structure and observation. Xenophon goes on to discuss four curricular topics: justice, *sôphrosunê*, obedience, and *enkrateia*.[22] The youth learn and practice justice by undergoing formal trials for the kinds of crime they might commit against

---

[15] See generally Anderson (1974, 162–69); Higgins (1977, 76–82); Powell and Richer (2020, esp. the chapters by Powell, Richer, Humble, and Pontier); Humble (2021, 221–37, with qualifications).
[16] Xen. *Ages.* 11.10; cf. 5.7 (always *sôphrôn* in public).
[17] Xen. *Ages.* 10.2.
[18] Fisher (1992); Danzig (2017, 304: "Being respectful of one's superiors").
[19] Xen. *Ages.* 7: φιλόπολις (patriotism); 8.1–2: τὸ εὔχαρι (graciousness); 8.3–4: μεγαλογνωμοσύνη (elevation); 8.5: πρόνοια (foresight); etc.
[20] Xen. *Ages.* 5.1–2 (ὅσαι... ἡδοναὶ πολλῶν κρατοῦσιν ἀνθρώπων); 5.2–3, endurance.
[21] Xen. *Ages.* 5.4–7.
[22] Xen. *Cyr.* 1.2.3–9.

others. Notable among them are trials for ingratitude toward the gods, parents, country, and friends, a state they could be held to exhibit in the form of shamelessness (ἀναισχυντία). About *sôphrosunê* he gives no content except to say that the youth must see adults being *sôphrôn* and their service as night watchmen contributes to their *sôphrosunê*, though evidently only because they remain in the public eye.[23] Obedience is manifest toward officers; *enkrateia* is about food and drink.[24] Xenophon separates *sôphrosunê* from inner control of desires and external submission to authority, though we may think its expression generally amounts to both. That it is best learned from adults going about their day in a *sôphrôn* way, and enforced by being on the public stage, suggests that Xenophon here conceives of it like *aidôs*, a self-restraint in light of social norms. Adults succeeding at being *sôphrôn* would exhibit the possibility of self-monitoring and self-management, the idea being that they could act badly but choose not to. Having to live in public shows that there may be few internal checks on counternormative action; only other people's disapprobation would serve the regulatory function. Xenophon makes none of this explicit, indeed seeming to assume the transparency of the term *sôphrosunê*, and he suggests that the behavioral territory of *sôphrosunê*, so to speak, overlaps with that of obedience and *enkrateia*. But the conceptual distinctiveness of *sôphrosunê* he retains.

At the end of *Cyropedia*, Xenophon presents Cyrus as a model of virtue. What he says about Cyrus tracks approximately what he said about the Persian curriculum, of which Cyrus was a beneficiary. Cyrus displays a substantial acknowledgment of the gods, and thus avoids the shameless ingratitude toward them that the Persians reproach under the heading of justice.[25] Further results of the first Persian curricular unit are Cyrus' justice and a sense of shame.[26] Cyrus then shows he values obedience (πείθεσθαι), albeit by honoring above all those who show it toward him; this reflects the third step in the Persian education.[27] The final two qualities Cyrus exhibits Xenophon presents separately, *sôphrosunê* and *enkrateia*, each receiving slightly more content than before.[28] Cyrus' *sôphrosunê* is the opposite of hubris. It may even be distinct from *aidôs*: those who embody *sôphrosunê* avoid shameful things (τὰ αἰσχρά) even when outside the public eye, which is all one can ask from the sense of shame.[29] *Aidôs* inhibits counternormative action from fear of observation (or internalized guilt),

---

[23] Xen. *Cyr.* 1.3.7 and 9.
[24] Xen. *Cyr.* 1.3.8: πείθεσθαι τοῖς ἄρχουσι; ἐγκράτειαν γαστρὸς καὶ ποτοῦ.
[25] Xen. *Cyr.* 8.1.23–25.
[26] Xen. *Cyr.* 8.1.26–28.
[27] Xen. *Cyr.* 8.1.29.
[28] Xen. *Cyr.* 8.1.30–32.
[29] Xen. *Cyr.* 8.1.31. This line is doubted as an interpolation by Nitsche (1879, 61) as lacking a point here and consequently bracketed by Hug (1883), but retained by Gemoll and Peters (1968) and Delebecque (1978).

whereas *sôphrosunê* amounts to a positive commitment to normative action. *Enkrateia*, for its part, gets a fuller definition: it involves never being distracted in the pursuit of the good by the pursuit of pleasures and being willing to toil (and thus exhibit endurance) in anticipation of fine pleasures.[30] This version of the distinction thus suggests that *enkrateia* pertains particularly to desire-control and delayed gratification, whereas *sôphrosunê* pertains particularly to acting in accordance with norms: not breaking them, as a hubristic person would, and acting in accordance with them even more reliably than *aidôs* would cause them to, which is sensitive mainly to social pressure.

The linguistic background of *enkrateia* may explain its paradoxical status as both definitely distinct from *sôphrosunê* and occasionally overlapping with it. Xenophon's use of the term has a mostly fourth-century provenance—a new connotation and a certain indeterminacy. The earliest uses of the adjective *enkratês*, found in fifth-century tragedy, simply meant "hard and powerful" in contrast to brittle and unreliable: internally strong rather than stronger by comparison with or over another.[31] Its most common use describes something's having political or military command over subsidiary parts of that thing, as a league has power over its member cities.[32] But it can mean being in charge of other things, such as one's own resources, especially if they can be seen as internal to one's domain: in Plato's *Cratylus*, for instance, Socrates observes that his interlocutor "does not have command over an inheritance" (οὐκ ἐγκρατὴς εἶ τῶν πατρῴων), and is thus poor.[33] The *Anonymus Iamblichi*, a text supposed to be from the fifth or early fourth century, may mark the earliest application of the term to one's desires, which are being treated as something internal:

καὶ μὴν ἐγκρατέστατόν γε δεῖ εἶναι πάντα ἄνδρα διαφερόντως· τοιοῦτος δ' ἂν μάλιστα, εἴ τις τῶν χρημάτων κρείσσων εἴη, πρὸς ἃ πάντες διαφθείρονται, καὶ τῆς ψυχῆς ἀφειδὴς ἐπὶ τοῖς δικαίοις ἐσπουδακὼς καὶ τὴν ἀρετὴν μεταδιώκων· πρὸς ταῦτα γὰρ δύο οἱ πλεῖστοι ἀκρατεῖς εἰσι. (*Anon. Iambl.* fr. 4.1 = Iambl. *Protr.* XX 98,17–23)

---

[30] Delebecque (1978, 95n1) is so impressed by this passage to say that it is as though Cyrus has been following the teachings of Socrates; Sansalvador (1987, 434n343), similarly, finds a *Republic*-style ideal city here.

[31] [A.] *PB* 55: "with *enkratês* strength strike with your hammer" (ἐγκρατεῖ σθένει ῥαιστῆρι θεῖνε); Soph. *Ant.* 474: "overly hard attitudes (σκληρ' ἄγαν φρονήματα) fall; the stiffest iron (τὸν ἐγκρατέστατον σίδηρον) snaps in a fire"; Soph. *Ph.* 75: "so that, if he sees me, he being *enkratês* of [his] bow, I am dead, and you" (ὥστ' εἴ με τόξων ἐγκρατὴς αἰσθήσεται, | ὄλωλα καὶ σὲ προσδιαφθερῶ ξυνών).

[32] One example will suffice: Hdt. 8.49: "in which of the lands over which they are in charge would it be advisable to have a sea-battle?" (ὅκου δοκέοι ἐπιτηδεότατον εἶναι ναυμαχίην ποιέεσθαι τῶν αὐτοὶ χωρέων ἐγκρατέες εἰσί). Similarly, Soph. *OT* 941; Hdt. 9.106.2; Thuc. 1.118.2.5, 5.35.5.4; Isoc. 6.45 (ca. 366 BCE), 5.21, 90, 100 (346 BCE).

[33] Pl. *Crat.* 391b.

And every man ought preeminently to be superlatively *enkratestatos*. And this is how someone would especially be, should he be superior to money, in the face of which everyone is corrupted and, not trying to spare his soul, should he have been serious about just things and pursued virtue—for it is in the face of these two that most people are *akrateis*.

The anonymous author has been explaining how a person might become as virtuous as possible. In the immediately preceding passage, he gives the first part of an answer: he should benefit others by supporting the laws and justice, and not, as might be imagined, through money distributions, which have significant drawbacks.[34] The present passage gives the second part of an answer: he should not let his desires for money and for preserving his life dictate his actions, as they do for many people. Indeed, in many cases these are the same desire, the desire to have the resources to buy oneself out of the various deadly adversities one might run into. Being *enkratestatos* means not letting one's desire for money or life win out over one's desire to do the right thing. Being *akratês* means being too weak to prefer the latter to the former desires. Our author explicitly uses the language of "desire" (ποθοῦσιν, ὀρέγεται) in later sentences of this passage.[35]

In the fourth century, *enkrateia* could especially concern the desire for money, as evidenced in an Isocratean letter from around 340.[36] But we come increasingly to see what we find in Xenophon: an application to all those desires that could derail one from what one more genuinely wants to achieve, in particular living virtuously. Isocrates' *Nicocles*, written sometime in the second quarter of the fourth century, includes a prototypical example:

> καὶ δεινὰ ποιεῖν ὅσοι τοὺς μὲν ἄλλους κοσμίως ζῆν ἀναγκάζουσιν, αὐτοὶ δ' αὑτοὺς μὴ σωφρονεστέρους τῶν ἀρχομένων παρέχουσιν. Πρὸς δὲ τούτοις τῶν μὲν ἄλλων πράξεων ἑώρων ἐγκρατεῖς τοὺς πολλοὺς γιγνομένους, τῶν δ' ἐπιθυμιῶν τῶν περὶ τοὺς παῖδας καὶ τὰς γυναῖκας καὶ τοὺς βελτίστους ἡττωμένους· ἐβουλήθην οὖν ἐν τούτοις ἐμαυτὸν ἐπιδεῖξαι καρτερεῖν δυνάμενον, ἐν οἷς ἔμελλον οὐ μόνον τῶν ἄλλων διοίσειν, ἀλλὰ καὶ τῶν ἐπ' ἀρετῇ μέγα φρονούντων. (Isoc. 3.38–39)

And they act terribly who force others to live in an orderly way but do not render themselves more *sôphrôn* than their subjects. Add to this, I saw that

---

[34] Anon. Iambl. fr. 3.
[35] Anon. Iambl. fr. 4.2, 4.4.
[36] Isoc. *ep.* 4.4: "Nobody is superior to him [Diodotus] in the capacity for speech and advice-giving; he is most just and *sôphrôn* and *enkratês* about money" (καὶ εἰπεῖν καὶ βουλεύσασθαι μηδενὸς ἧττον αὐτὸν δύνασθαι καὶ δικαιότατον καὶ σωφρονέστατον εἶναι καὶ χρημάτων ἐγκρατέστατον). Isoc. *ep.* 9.13 gives a related grouping, though without the qualification (ἐγκρατέστατος καὶ δικαιότατος καὶ πολιτικώτατος).

many are *enkrateis* otherwise but are overwhelmed by their desires for boys and women; I wished, thus, to show myself capable of enduring in these things, in which I intended, not only to be superior over others but even over those with high views of their virtue.

Having distinguished being *enkratês* from being *sôphrôn*—where *sôphrosunê* means living in terms of some ordering principles—Isocrates provides a specific case of *enkrateia*, which in general means enduring the potent calls of desire, namely not being overwhelmed by sexual desire. The speaker identifies with some part of himself that is superior to subordinate aspects of himself just as it (and he) is superior to other people; this is apparently the seat of virtue.

In the course of a century, the term *enkratês/enkrateia* became personalized and psychologized. The original meaning, a kind of intransitive "strength" or "integrity" by contrast to the transitive "strength over," came to apply to hierarchical composite items, like a political association, with a hegemon who has strength over its various dominions, and thus to human beings, who come similarly to be thought of as hegemons over their various dominions, namely their desires. We see that psychological use by the date of the *Anonymus Iamblichi*. The negative terms, *akratês/akrasia*, seem to have undergone a similar transition, though we know it mostly in personal contexts. Their earliest references indicate weakness and incapacity, either in general or over a specific body part, like one's tongue.[37] By the date of the *Anonymus Iamblichi*, however, we see *akrasia* as giving undue authority to self-undermining desires (as fr. 4.1, quoted above, shows). There are some other notable early philosophical usages that get at desire control. There is a statement attributed to Democritus:

ὑγιείην εὐχῇσι παρὰ θεῶν αἰτέονται ἄνθρωποι, τὴν δὲ ταύτης δύναμιν ἐν ἑαυτοῖς ἔχοντες οὐκ ἴσασιν· ἀκρασίῃ δὲ τἀναντία πρήσσοντες αὐτοὶ προδόται τῆς ὑγείης τῇσιν ἐπιθυμίῃσιν γίνονται. Democr. (B234/D240 = Stob. 3.18.30)

Humans beg the gods—by their prayers—for health, not knowing that they have in themselves the power for this: doing the opposite, in their *akrasia*, they become betrayers—by their desires—of their health.

Human *akrasia* is the inability to withstand health-destroying desires; people should realize that they have, in principle, the capacity to withstand them. In the opening of the *Dissoi Logoi*, another anonymous text probably from the same period, the author argues that things are sometimes good, sometimes bad:

---

[37] General bodily weakness or incapacity: Hipponax fr. 115,12 (West); Soph. *OC* 1236. No power over tongue: [A.] *PB* 884; Ar. *Ran.* 838. Much Hippocratic evidence corroborates this.

σκέψομαι δὲ ἐκ τῶ ἀνθρωπίνω βίω, ὧι ἐπιμελὲς βρώσιός τε καὶ πόσιος καὶ ἀφροδισίων· ταῦτα γὰρ ἀσθενοῦντι μὲν κακόν, ὑγιαίνοντι δὲ καὶ δεομένῳ ἀγαθόν. καὶ ἀκρασία τοίνυν τούτων τοῖς μὲν ἀκρατέσι κακόν, τοῖς δὲ πωλεῦντι ταῦτα καὶ μισθαρνέοντι ἀγαθόν. (*Diss. Log.* 1.2–3)

I will look into this in the case of human life, in its concern for food and drink and sex: for to the weak these are bad, but to the healthy who need them they are good. Well, so *akrasia* in these is bad for the *akrateis*, but for those who sell and profit from them they are good.

This author focuses on desire for three particular types of thing, items that can be sold (so they produce good) and of which people sometimes consume too much (so they produce bad).

Still, most of the recorded uses of *akratês/akrasia* come from the Hippocratic corpus, since *akrasia* as general or local incapacity tends to be a medical matter. It is in the fourth-century philosophical corpora that we see everyone using it as Xenophon does, not as overall or bodily weakness but as inability not to act on powerful and detrimental desires. An interesting study would work out how "desires" came to be construed as inward property, as instruments of subagential entities, but we cannot do that now. The point of this history is to show that *sôphrosunê* and *enkrateia* have very different linguistic and contextual origins; they may have come close at some point, but then diverged again in Xenophon and Aristotle.

Let us return to Xenophon. Even when he is not analyzing *sôphrosunê*, Xenophon in the non-Socratic works reveals his understanding of the virtue. Generally, exercising the virtue means giving due consideration to the range of reasons for or against some action, in contrast to acting simply on one's immediate inclination (e.g., taking the easy route). From this "intellectual" perspective, *sôphrosunê* means deliberating in terms of the norms of rationality. But this does not just mean "prudence," acting in the way that best suits one's interests. For there are other norms—divine, civic, or familial—and *sôphrosunê* means the capacity to follow them, too. *Sôphrosunê*, seen this way, differs from justice in being not specifically directed toward social duties; it differs from *enkrateia* in being not specifically described as control over bodily desires. It is among the essential traits of a successful life.

Socratic *Sôphrosunê*

In his Socratic works Xenophon gives much direct attention to *sôphrosunê*. It is in the *Memorabilia* particularly that we get nearly explicit arguments for *sôphrosunê* as commitment to authoritative norms. We also get the sharpest distinction between *sôphrosunê* and the desire-control of *enkrateia*, though as in the non-Socratic works, here they sometimes overlap and the relevance of bodily drives to *sôphrosunê* becomes informatively ambiguous. Neither *Apology* nor *Symposium* treats *sôphrosunê* so much as a subject of inquiry, but the concept has a central role in both, so we will start there. (We discuss the *Oeconomicus* in Chapter 13.)

Among the notorious differences between Xenophon's *Apology of Socrates* and Plato's is the content of the Apolline oracle about Socrates. According to Plato, it was a "no" answer to the question "Is anybody wiser than Socrates?" According to Xenophon, Apollo told Chaerephon that nobody was more free, just, or *sôphrôn* than Socrates.[38] Whatever explains the difference between the anecdotes, in Xenophon's account *sôphrosunê* is among the three highest traits, if one must spell out the way someone is good (or wise). Xenophon gives a bit of familiar content to *sôphrosunê* later in the *Apology*. Socrates, defending himself against Meletus' charge that he has corrupted the youth, says that nobody under his care has turned bad in any of the following five ways: going from piety to impiety; from *sôphrosunê* to hubris; from economy (εὐδίαιτος) to extravagance (πολυδάπανος); from moderate drinking to drunkenness; or from some state to being overcome (ἡττημένον) by another base pleasure.[39] The rhetorical order seems to start from the worst offense and trail off onto smaller problems. *Sôphrosunê* is akin to piety but distinguished from it; it precedes a personal regimen that is well-regulated; that in turn precedes the specific risks of alcohol; and then Socrates generalizes from the case of drinking. It seems unlikely that all five conversions are implied to be ways in which a person may be bested by a base desire, even if they could be so glossed.

In the following passage Socrates defends Apollo's statement that nobody is more free, just, or *sôphrôn* than he, and in the process he may seem to give evidence for a desire-control *sôphrosunê*:

τίνα δὲ ἀνθρώπων ἐλευθεριώτερον, ὃς παρ' οὐδενὸς οὔτε δῶρα οὔτε μισθὸν δέχομαι; δικαιότερον δὲ τίνα ἂν εἰκότως νομίσαιτε τοῦ πρὸς τὰ παρόντα συνηρμοσμένου, ὡς τῶν ἀλλοτρίων μηδενὸς προσδεῖσθαι; σοφὸν δὲ πῶς οὐκ ἄν τις εἰκότως ἄνδρα φήσειεν εἶναι ὃς ἐξ ὅτουπερ ξυνιέναι τὰ λεγόμενα ἠρξάμην οὐπώποτε διέλειπον καὶ ζητῶν καὶ μανθάνων ὅ τι ἐδυνάμην ἀγαθόν;
(Xen. *Ap.* 16)

---

[38] Xen. *Ap.* 14. Xenophon has Socrates say that Chaerephon "asked about me" (ἐπερωτῶντος... περὶ ἐμοῦ) and Apollo "responded" (ἀνεῖλεν). This is too loose to determine what language Chaerephon's question actually used.

[39] Xen. *Ap.* 19.

Do you know anyone less enslaved to his bodily desires than me? Any freer person, since I accept neither gifts nor payment from anyone? Would you reasonably consider anyone more just than one who, so in step with the things he has, needs nothing from others? And how would someone not reasonably proclaim me a wise man, who from the time I began to understand language have never left off searching for and learning what good I could?

Socrates is vindicating the claim about his superlative *sôphrosunê* by appealing to his not being enslaved to bodily desires. But he is not thereby identifying *sôphrosunê* with desire-control. First, he speaks of enslavement, and thus of the question of the practical authority of his desires, not merely their strength or unwieldiness. Second, similarly, he may be speaking only of a characteristic but nonexhaustive quality of *sôphrosunê*: freedom is surely broader than having no financial obligations, and justice is broader than needing nothing from others. Action independent of bodily desire is probably the most commonplace realization of *sôphrosunê*, even if this is its negative and incomplete formulation. What it leaves out, perhaps, is how Socrates does treat his desires.

In *Symposium* we see the perspective-relativity of *sôphrosunê* when it appears in the two parties to an asymmetrical erotic relationship. Beautiful Autolycus, the object of the host Callias' affections, is twice called *sôphrôn*: he embodies it along with *aidôs*, as befits a young man, and he embodies it along with strength, endurance, and courage, neither luxuriating in opulence nor languishing in weakness.[40] He is neither immaturely self-assertive nor enervated by the pursuit of needless goals; his activity and competence come of a sort of restraint, his recognition of both social and practical or evaluative norms. Callias, for his part, is *sôphrôn* in not getting erotically overheated.[41] He is disciplined in his desires and the actions that could conduce to desire aggravation. So we see that the salient content of *sôphrosunê* depends on the role or situation: in one case, norm sensitivity matters more, in another, desire management.

Xenophon's *Apology* and *Symposium* feature *sôphrosunê* in ways that *Memorabilia* explores more deliberatively. Xenophon has cause there to philosophize about *sôphrosunê* because he says that it was a particular topic of Socrates' discussions. It was one of the "human matters" with which he occupied himself exclusively, rather than the religious innovation for which he was charged. In a programmatic statement, Xenophon lists seven pairs of topics of Socrates' discussions: what's pious and impious; the noble and disgraceful (καλόν . . . αἰσχρόν, or "beautiful and ugly"); the just and unjust; *sôphrosunê*

---

[40] Xen. *Symp.* 1.8 (ἁβρότητι χλιδαινομένου οὐδὲ μαλακίᾳ θρυπτομένου) and 8.8.
[41] Xen. *Symp.* 1.10 and 4.26.

and *mania*; courage and cowardice; state and statesman; and government and governor.⁴² Xenophon concludes that these are some of the matters Socrates believed knowledge of which makes one an excellent person (καλοὺς κἀγαθούς), while ignorance of them is slavish (ἀνδραποδώδεις). This is a remarkable list: as the curriculum for the efficacious citizen, it includes the cardinal virtues found in Plato (minus wisdom), fineness itself, and two types of political or leadership knowledge. *Sôphrosunê*, in the exact middle, is in estimable company. As for the missing wisdom, Xenophon later says that Socrates did not separate it from *sôphrosunê*.⁴³

Here in 1.1 Xenophon lists the topics; he reports what Socrates said about them later, in various places across the *Memorabilia* (see Table 7.1). The sequence of discussions at *Memorabilia* 4.6 corresponds best to that programmatic list. It begins: Socrates made his companions better at discussion (διαλεκτικωτέρους), as we may see through examples of the way he discussed various subjects. Six of the seven topics mentioned at 1.1.16 arise, in similar order: first piety, beauty, and justice; then courage, the state, and government. The list lacks only *sôphrosunê*.

In place of a discussion of *sôphrosunê* in 4.6, we have discussions of wisdom and the good—which were themselves missing from the programmatic

Table 7.1 Discussions of Fundamental Concepts in *Memorabilia*

Topic (Book/Chapter)	1.1._	1.2–2.1	3.9._	4.3–5	4.6._
Piety, impiety	16	1.3.1–4		4.3	2–5
Beautiful, ugly	16				9
Just, unjust	16		5	4.4	5–6
Sôphrosunê, madness	16	1.2	4, 6, 7	4.3	
Courage, cowardice	16		1–3		10–11
State, statesman	16				14
Government, governor	16		10–13		12
Wisdom			4–5		7
Good			5		8
Enkrateia		1.3, 1.5, 2.1		4.5	

---

⁴² Xen. *Mem.* 1.1.16.
⁴³ In the *Dissoi Logoi* (whose chapters follow a scheme remarkably like this one), *sôphrosunê* and *sophia*, along with their opposites, are treated in a single section, 5.1: ταὐτὰ τοὶ μαινόμενοι καὶ τοὶ σωφρονοῦντες καὶ τοὶ σοφοὶ καὶ τοὶ ἀμαθεῖς.

list—but they are not presented here as standing in for *sôphrosunê*. It could be that Xenophon feels he has discussed the virtue enough already. There are discussions of *sôphrosunê* on at least three extended occasions elsewhere in the *Memorabilia*, and references to the virtue elsewhere. None is a direct definition, but together they give a coherent and robust picture of *sôphrosunê*.

Xenophon has two reasons for discussing *sôphrosunê*. The first is Socrates' having occupied himself with such conversations rather than others, from the belief that knowing about *sôphrosunê* contributes to one's overall excellence. The second is Socrates' having been accused of not having exercised or taught *sôphrosunê*, and thus of having corrupted his fellow Athenians. Both reasons assume the fundamental normative importance of the virtue.

Given the dominant apologetic function of *Memorabilia*, Xenophon's initial discussions of *sôphrosunê* respond to the accusations of corruption. Xenophon closes his book's first chapter, on Socrates' conventional piety—where he introduces Socrates' human-level conversation topics—with this exasperation: "I marvel that the Athenians were ever persuaded that Socrates was not *sôphrôn* toward the gods (περὶ τοὺς θεοὺς μὴ σωφρονεῖν), despite his having never said or done anything impious toward them." He was truly "most pious" (εὐσεβέστατος).[44] In identifying *sôphrosunê* and *eusebeia* here, as he does again in *Memorabilia* 4.3, Xenophon shows that *sôphrosunê* means acknowledging the authority of the gods; Socrates has been accused of not acknowledging them. Then, near the beginning of the second chapter, which responds to the corruption-of-youth charge, Xenophon observes that Socrates was in effect accused of teaching political capacity before he taught *sôphrosunê*.[45] And yet, as Xenophon responds at length, that was not true.

To be sure, the overall strategy Xenophon adopts to defend Socrates would repay close attention.[46] What matters to our study of *sôphrosunê* is something other than this strategy; it is the way Xenophon continues to put the virtue in complex relationship with *enkrateia*. This is because he also draws Socrates as the preeminent man of *enkrateia*, one who, as he does with *sôphrosunê*, manifests it and benefits his companions most by facilitating their own manifesting of it. His discussions of *enkrateia* in *Memorabilia* 1.2 through 2.1 and beyond present the scope of *enkrateia* in overlapping but various ways, with indeterminate relationships with "endurance" and "self-sufficiency." It is worth reviewing Xenophon's (nonsystematic) statements here.

Xenophon's initial discussion, at 1.2–2, asserts that Socrates is the "most *enkratês*" about "sex and stomach" (ἀφροδισίων καὶ γαστρός); "most enduring"

---

[44] Xen. *Mem.* 1.1.20; further, see Johnson (2021, 63–70).
[45] Xen. *Mem.* 1.2.17. This could be Xenophon's term rather than the accuser's, who is cited elsewhere in these chapters.
[46] Pangle (2018, 23–39); Johnson (2021, 71–102).

about cold and heat and every toil; and he brought his needs (δεῖσθαι) through education to a moderate level (πρὸς τὸ μετρίων). The consequence is that Socrates did not make others irreligious, lawless, gluttonous (λίχνους), sexually uncontrolled (ἀφροδισίων ἀκρατεῖς), or weak and irresolute in their commitment to work (πρὸς τὸ πονεῖν μαλακούς). Xenophon seems thus to distinguish *enkrateia* from endurance, where the former deals with food and lust (though in the list of consequences, *akrasia* pertains explicitly only to lust). In the next chapter (1.3.7-9), Xenophon speaks to Odysseus' being *enkratês* about food, and discusses *aphrodisia* (though twice saying that sexual desire is controlled by *sôphrosunê*, 1.3.8, 9). He concludes chapter 3 by claiming to have covered Socrates' views about eating, drinking, and sex (though he has not actually discussed drinking). In chapter 5 he says that *enkrateia* is the possession of a gentleman, and gives several examples. A general would do poorly if he were defeated by his stomach, wine, sex, labor, and sleep. A person would do poorly if he prefers food, wine, and women to his friend. Socrates displays *enkrateia* by "mastering his bodily pleasures (τοῦ σώματος ἡδονῶν ἐκράτει) but also those that come from money."[47] This is the section where Xenophon says Socrates treats *enkrateia* as the foundation or footing (κρηπίς) of virtue. In chapter 6, the discussion with Antiphon, Xenophon says that Socrates' constant training kept him from being enslaved by his belly, sleep, or anything lascivious (λαγνεία).[48]

In Book 1, then, Xenophon is especially concerned with Socrates' command of his own bodily desires and Socrates' advice that others command their own. This command is generally called *enkrateia*, and five desires are exemplary: those for food, drink, sex, sleep, and relaxation. The first three get relatively more attention but are not treated as definitionally distinct.

Book 2 begins with the *Memorabilia's* most capacious gloss on *enkrateia* yet. Xenophon writes that "Socrates exhorted his companions to exercise *enkrateia* in their desire for food and drink and sex and sleep and cold and heat and labor."[49] Too capacious, scholars have thought. The earliest modern editorial tradition brackets "in their desire" (πρὸς ἐπιθυμίαν), evidently on the thought that the last three are not matters of desire but of endurance; the most recent critical edition brackets "cold and heat and toil" instead, on the same reasoning.[50] Yet in the subsequent discussion with Aristippus, a man Xenophon judges as rather *akratês*, Socrates argues that the capacity for leadership takes control of hunger, thirst, sleep, sex, the aversion to work, and oversensitive avoidance of cold and

---

[47] Xen. *Mem.* 1.5.6.
[48] Xen. *Mem.* 1.6.8.
[49] Xen. *Mem.* 2.1.1: ἀσκεῖν ἐγκράτειαν πρὸς ἐπιθυμίαν βρωτοῦ καὶ ποτοῦ καὶ λαγνείας καὶ ὕπνου καὶ ῥίγους καὶ θάλπους καὶ πόνου.
[50] Bessarion (1521), followed recently by Marchant and Todd (1923 ad loc.); Brandini and Dorion (2003-10, 2.113-16).

heat. In Prodicus' *Choice of Heracles*, which Socrates reprises for Aristippus, Vice encourages Heracles to enjoy food, drink, sights, sounds, love, and guilt-free sleep.[51] The manuscript text appears fine, then; Xenophon appears to be saying that *enkrateia* is strength about desires, basically bodily drives, and Socrates draws attention to those desires that would most familiarly enervate a leader. Later chapters support this view. When Socrates returns to the topic of friendship, he says that a good friend must "rule over his stomach and love of drinking and lust and sleep and laziness"; in sum, he must be "*enkratês* over the desires of the body."[52] Late in Book 4, Socrates says that *akrasia* inhibits the endurance (καρτερεῖν) of hunger, thirst, sexual desire, and sleep deprivation (4.5.9).

For Xenophon, then, there is a fluidity between *enkrateia* and *karteria* as well as *autarchia*: even if each term emphasizes some domain of human struggle, they do not do so in mutually exclusively ways. Further, there is a changing canon of salient desires, always including those for food and sex, sometimes including that for drink, and occasionally for leisure and mild temperatures. The relevant prototype changes, from martial man to aristocratic man to urban man. So we should not expect precision or determinacy in the content of *enkrateia* and its boundaries.

Having seen Xenophon's view of *enkrateia* in the Socratic works, we can turn to his major discussions of *sôphrosunê*, studying especially the way in which control of bodily desires comes into play there. *Sôphrosunê* first becomes a focus of discussion in Xenophon's defense of Socrates against the corruption-of-youth charge. The accuser asks: Hasn't Socrates caused his associates to despise the constitution and to be violent?[53] No, says Xenophon: Socrates and his associates have practiced being thoughtful (φρόνησιν ἀσκοῦντας).[54] Well, maybe in general, but, the accuser rejoins, what about Critias and Alcibiades, who were his associates and obviously despised the constitution and were violent? Even Xenophon concedes that Critias was utterly rapacious, violent, and murderous, and Alcibiades was utterly out of control, hubristic, and violent.[55] This is a more difficult charge, and one that leads Xenophon into a several-part response comprising the bulk of Book 1, chapter 2.

Xenophon begins by explaining why Critias and Alcibiades became Socrates' associates. They saw him "living most self-sufficiently (αὐταρκέστατα ζῶντα) and with the least amount of inputs, having extraordinary inner control over all his pleasures (ἡδονῶν . . . πασῶν ἐγκρατέστατον), and in conversations able

---

[51] Xen. *Mem.* 2.1.24.
[52] Xen. *Mem.* 2.6.1: ἄρχει γαστρός τε καὶ φιλοποσίας καὶ λαγνείας καὶ ὕπνου καὶ ἀργίας; 2.6.5: ἐγκρατής . . . τῶν διὰ τοῦ σώματος ἡδονῶν.
[53] Xen. *Mem.* 1.2.9.
[54] Xen. *Mem.* 1.2.10.
[55] Critias: κλεπτίστατός [A] or πλεονεκτίστατός [BΦ] τε καὶ βιαιότατος καὶ φονικώτατος; Alcibiades: ἀκρατέστατός τε καὶ ὑβριστότατος . . . βιαιότατος.

to make whatever use he wished of his interlocutor." Only the third of these capacities really appealed to them. They were supremely ambitious, wanting to do everything by themselves (πάντα δ' ἑαυτῶν πράττεσθαι) and to keep all the fame for themselves. Thus they wanted to learn from him only what they took to be his complete competence in speech and action (ἱκανωτάτω λέγειν τε καὶ πράττειν): for they wanted to do politics (ἐπραττέτην τὰ πολιτικά).⁵⁶

So Critias and Alcibiades wanted Socrates' power—the skill in speech that allowed him to be perfectly persuasive—but not the psychic condition correlated with or causative of that power. It is unclear here how precisely Xenophon thinks Socrates' three extraordinary capacities go together, though one assumes that the third depends on the first two—this would give a satisfying indictment of Critias and Alcibiades, wanting the ends without the means.⁵⁷ Presumably the cultivation of speech-prowess depends on not needing to spend time harvesting resources for and combating the distractions of an unruly desire set.

Xenophon next anticipates an objection: Why did Socrates let Critias and Alcibiades learn how to do politics (τὰ πολιτικά) before or without teaching them *sôphrosunê*? Oh, but he didn't: he modeled and taught *sôphrosunê* to them first. He showed that he was *kalokathagos*; and he "talked excellently about virtue and the other human matters," presumably the topics listed at 1.1.16. And proof that this is what he taught is that they learned it: they were *sôphrôn* as long as they were with him, and genuinely so, not just from fear but from the belief that this was the best way to act.⁵⁸ By talking about *sôphrosunê* and the other virtues, evidently a person could become *sôphrôn*. Despite Xenophon's not saying how, we can probably infer the process from the examples of such discussions later in the *Memorabilia*. In Book 4, chapter 3, Socrates gives a naturalistic reason for being *sôphrôn* toward the gods; in Book 3, chapter 9, he links *sôphrosunê* to other already valued goods, such as safety from insanity. Thus discussion of *sôphrosunê* may include reasons to adopt it, ways to embody it, and the scope of its influence.

In the third step of the defense here, Xenophon addresses another objection: virtue is never lost, so if Critias and Alcibiades lack *sôphrosunê* (in being *hubristai*), then they must never have had it. What follows Xenophon presents as his own retort; it involves a complex sequence of reasoning.⁵⁹ The objector assumes, as Cyrus had, that *sôphrosunê* is something learned (μάθησις), and that someone who has learned some knowledge does not later become ignorant of it. Xenophon has a trio of responses, playing on *sôphrosunê* as an acquired competence, as something learned, and as only one possible source of one's motivations.

---

⁵⁶ Xen. *Mem.* 1.2.12–16.
⁵⁷ This view seems partially vindicated by the connection drawn between *enkrateia* and conversation-success in Xen. *Mem.* 4.6; see qualifications in Johnson (2021, 86–95).
⁵⁸ Xen. *Mem.* 1.2.17–18.
⁵⁹ Pangle (2018, 26) emphasizes the first-person language here.

First, only those who exercise their bodies have the power to do bodily things; just so, only those who exercise their soul have the power to do psychic things, namely, "doing what one ought and abstaining from what one ought." So even if someone is already *sôphrôn*, Xenophon continues, he should keep the company only of the virtuous; otherwise he will be undone. *Sôphrosunê* is like bodily fitness: an extinguishable capacity for action. It is also the capacity to act in accordance with "oughts," that is, norms.[60] Second, even things you've learned and not merely practiced can be lost, as the case of the forgetting of poetry clearly shows. When words of advice (τῶν νουθετικῶν λόγων) are forgotten, so too what the soul experienced that caused it to desire *sôphrosunê*.[61] The reasons to be *sôphrôn* vanish if they are not rehearsed repeatedly. Third, we see people lose *sôphrosunê* all the time—those who take to drink or to love lose the power to care about what they ought and to avoid what they ought.[62] Contranormative desires never go away; they continually exhort the soul, "Don't *sôphronein*, but hurry up and gratify us and the body."[63] With these three examples, Xenophon implies that becoming *sôphrôn* is more complex than having some truth imprinted ineluctably on one's mind: one may lose the strength or tone to act well; one may forget why or how to do it; and one may forget, in any particular instance, that one should do it. *Sôphrosunê* is then a disposition, a standing attempt, what I have called a commitment to act in some way, and commitments are psychic states that must be made robust, that must be borne in mind, and that must not be obscured by more visceral captivations of one's attention.

And so it was with Critias and Alcibiades. While they were young, during the period when they would otherwise have been most thoughtless and out of control (ἀγνωμονεστάτω καὶ ἀκρατεστάτω), Socrates kept them *sôphrôn*; and yet once they left his care and companionship, they confronted and crumbled under many bad influences, even as Socrates maintained his own *sôphrosunê*.[64]

Xenophon's insistence on the term *sôphrosunê* is in part dialectical: he is giving a response to the objection that Socrates did not teach Critias and Alcibiades *sôphrosunê*. But it is also substantive. Critias and Alcibiades caused Athens problems not specifically due to failures of *enkrateia* as traditionally conceived, as though they were gluttons, alcoholics, laze-abouts, or enervated weaklings.[65] Quite the opposite: they were highly ambitious and had the energy and political

---

[60] Xen. *Mem.* 1.2.19–20.
[61] Xen. *Mem.* 1.2.21.
[62] Xen. *Mem.* 1.2.22.
[63] Xen. *Mem.* 1.2.23: μὴ σωφρονεῖν, ἀλλὰ τὴν ταχίστην ἑαυταῖς τε καὶ τῷ σώματι χαρίζεσθαι.
[64] Xen. *Mem.* 1.2.24–28; 1.2.29–47 recounts other stories from Critias' and Alcibiades' times with and without Socrates.
[65] Compare Pangle (2013, 19). Xenophon does identify their weakness for sex *Mem.* 1.2.24, 29. This could be a telling weakness, but it is not treated as explanatory or fundamental; Xenophon does not psychologize them as having sought power *for* the sex.

focus to match. Their violence and hubris expressed their desire to have power over others and exercise their will, without concern for the norms of a unified society. One suspects that, had they really so lacked *enkrateia* (rather than *sôphrosunê*), Socrates could hardly be held responsible for not fixing them and that, further, they would not have gotten as far as they did. *Enkrateia* is the foundation for any reliable action at all; a Socratic lesson, to be sure. But Critias and Alcibiades are charged, repeatedly, for doing something other than what they ought to do. Their failure of *sôphrosunê* is a failure to act correctly. *Sôphrôn* action, which is enabled by *enkrateia*, is more than self-controlled action.

That *sôphrosunê* and *enkrateia* capture different ethico-psychological aspects of practical life comes into sharper focus later in the *Memorabilia*. The clearest case is in Book 4, where Xenophon describes a typical Socratic curriculum, what Socrates teaches ambitious young people.[66] He uses Euthydemus as a running example throughout this book, as a young man who decides to associate with Socrates to reach his aspirations (ἀξιόλογος γενέσθαι).[67] Xenophon seems to want to show what Critias and Alcibiades would have gotten from spending time with Socrates. He presents Socrates' students as seeking to become excellent in speech, action, and problem-solving (τὸ ... λεκτικοὺς καὶ πρακτικοὺς καὶ μηχανικοὺς γίγνεσθαι), basically what Critias and Alcibiades wanted.[68] As Xenophon wrote about that case, he writes again here, that Socrates does not start by satisfying his students' ultimate desires. He believes that they need first (πρότερον) to acquire *sôphrosunê*. For, without it, their acquired capacities for action could be used indifferently for injustice and other bad things. For Xenophon the prime issue is not the capacity for action but the right direction of that action.

Xenophon goes on, in Book 4, chapter 3, to explain how Socrates taught *sôphrosunê*; in chapter 4, justice; in chapter 5, *enkrateia*, which supports the capacity for action at all (being *praktikôteros*); in chapter 6, competence in speech (being *dialektikôteros*); and in chapter 7, self-sufficiency and knowledge of the various fields. Structurally, then, Xenophon separates *sôphrosunê* from *enkrateia*, treating *enkrateia* as necessary for accomplishing anything, *sôphrosunê* for accomplishing the proper things. And of course Socrates must teach *sôphrosunê* and justice first, even if they are in a way more ethically advanced, so that his students do not become *enkratês* but ungoverned.

The content of chapter 3 leaves no question about the separation of *sôphrosunê* and *enkrateia*. This is despite Xenophon's not having Socrates define *sôphrosunê* itself. Prompted, it would seem, by the charge seen in Book 1 that Socrates failed to *sôphronein* with respect to the gods—whose promulgated norms are surely

---

[66] See Moore (2018b).
[67] Xen. *Mem.* 4.2.40.
[68] Xen. *Mem.* 4.3.1.

the most authoritative of all—Xenophon says that Socrates started (πρῶτον) by "trying to make his associates *sôphrôn* with respect to the gods."[69] The problem for Euthydemus, as Socrates sees it, is that he has not yet considered how carefully the gods have outfitted humans with what they need. So Socrates goes through their benefactions: light, night, stars, moon, seasons, water, fire, sun, livestock, other useful and beautiful things, sense perception, reason, language, and prophecy.[70] He goes on to note that such benefits evidence not just the gods' benevolence but also their existence.[71] Thus, Euthydemus should revere (σέβεσθαι καὶ τιμᾶν) the gods.[72] Euthydemus agrees that he should, but, he wonders, how could he ever express his full gratitude? Socrates responds, "By the law of the city" (νόμῳ πόλεως)—namely, by observing the customary holy rites.[73] He summarizes:

πῶς οὖν ἄν τις κάλλιον καὶ εὐσεβέστερον τιμῴη θεοὺς ἤ, ὡς αὐτοὶ κελεύουσιν, οὕτω ποιῶν; ἀλλὰ χρὴ τῆς μὲν δυνάμεως μηδὲν ὑφίεσθαι· ὅταν γάρ τις τοῦτο ποιῇ, φανερὸς δήπου ἐστὶ τότε οὐ τιμῶν θεούς. χρὴ οὖν μηδὲν ἐλλείποντα κατὰ δύναμιν τιμᾶν τοὺς θεοὺς θαρρεῖν τε καὶ ἐλπίζειν τὰ μέγιστα ἀγαθά. οὐ γὰρ παρ' ἄλλων γ' ἄν τις μείζω ἐλπίζων σωφρονοίη ἢ παρὰ τῶν τὰ μέγιστα ὠφελεῖν δυναμένων, οὐδ' ἂν ἄλλως μᾶλλον ἢ εἰ τούτοις ἀρέσκοι· ἀρέσκοι δὲ πῶς ἂν μᾶλλον ἢ εἰ ὡς μάλιστα πείθοιτο αὐτοῖς; (Xen. *Mem.* 4.3.16–17)

So how could someone more excellently and reverently honor the gods than by doing whatever they command? But you ought not do less than you're capable of. For when someone does that, clearly there you're not honoring the gods. So you ought, when doing all you can to honor the gods, to expect with confidence the greatest of goods. For there are no others from whom someone being *sôphrôn* should expect more than from those capable of providing the greatest help; nor could he be more *sôphrôn* than by pleasing them. And how better can he please them than by being as obedient as possible to them?

---

[69] Xen. *Mem.* 4.2.2; earlier charge at 1.1.20. Xenophon says that people recorded various of Socrates' discussions regarding *sôphrosunê peri theous* and that his story in *Memorabilia* 4.3 presents just one of them; Xenophon is saying that the historical Socrates really did take up this topic, whether or not his current formulation is historically accurate. (It is not obvious that Plato himself recorded any such versions: the *Euthyphro* does speak of piety but not in terms of *sôphrosunê*.) For further reflection on Xenophon's reasons for starting with *sôphrosunê peri theous*, see Bandini and Dorion (2003–11, 2.2.118–19); see also Lorch (2009); T. L. Pangle (2018, 182–89); Sebell (2021, 90–103, who reads this section as principally concerning piety, not *sôphrosunê*). L. S. Pangle (2013, 20) claims that Euthydemus here learns only a "simulacra of moderation, or a fairly conventional piety and justice ... not the moderation of Socrates," but this is not argued for.
[70] Xen. *Mem.* 4.2.3–12.
[71] Xen. *Mem.* 4.2.13–14.
[72] Xen. *Mem.* 4.2.13, 14, 17.
[73] Xen. *Mem.* 4.2.16.

"*Sôphrosunê* with respect to the gods" thus means acknowledging that the laws concerning the god's propitiation are authoritative for us. We respect and thus obey those laws not because doing so benefits other people, or because it benefits us, but because it is the right thing to do: the gods deserve it. And they deserve it because of their relationship with us.

It is strange that Xenophon does not discuss *sôphrosunê* generally; though the charge against Socrates may have been a religious radicalism called *peri tous theous mê sôphronein*, the salient problem with Critias and Alcibiades was surely not their disregard of religious ritual;[74] nor does disregard of sacrifices seem to explain the injustice and evil-doing Xenophon warns about for those who never learn *sôphrosunê*.[75] Xenophon is rather killing two birds with a single stone, Socrates' teaching of *sôphrosunê* and of reverence. The norm-acknowledging virtues were closely linked, anyway, given the preeminence of divine norms. The next chapter of *Memorabilia* 4 concerns justice, and the argument there is that justice is following the law, whether written or unwritten, civic or household, human or divine, contractual or moral.[76] Since Xenophon has treated reverence as *sôphrosunê* regarding the gods, we have good reason to think that justice is equivalent to *sôphrosunê* regarding humans, despite his not saying so. If this were so, it would explain the considerable overlap between or proximity of the terms: *sôphrosunê* comes to seem, most abstractly, following authoritative rules; justice comes to seem rule-following specifically in the human sphere.

Whatever the relation, the analysis of *sôphrosunê* here in 4.3 makes no reference to desire-control; the contrast with the chapter following the one on justice, which concerns *enkrateia*, puts into bright relief the absence of such reference. There, in 4.5, Xenophon presents Socrates as deeming *enkrateia* necessary for anyone intending to do what he chooses, and good for anyone intending to do what is proper. The argument turns on the value of freedom. A person is not free who is impeded from doing the best things (μὴ δύναται πράττειν τὰ βέλτιστα) by his being ruled by bodily pleasures (ἄρχεται ὑπὸ τῶν διὰ τοῦ σώματος ἡδονῶν); indeed, freedom just *is* doing what a person considers best.[77] Those ruled by bodily desires—the "impotent" or "uncontrolled" (οἱ ἀκρατεῖς)—are said to be enslaved to them, and are said to be forced to do dishonorable evils.[78] These akratics believe they will get the most pleasure, but they are wrong; only *enkrateia*, and thus the freedom to choose, allows them to do what will actually provision them with pleasure. Xenophon shows this for both the bodily and

---

[74] Alcibiades was charged in the Affair of 415, and someone named Critias was momentarily implicated in it before being exonerated (it was plausibly not this one), but Xenophon seems not even to allude to these cases.
[75] Notwithstanding Pownall (2016).
[76] See further Xen. *Mem.* 4.4.19–25 on unwritten universal divine laws.
[77] Xen. *Mem.* 4.5.3.
[78] Xen. *Mem.* 4.5.4–5.

nonbodily desires. The pleasure that comes from eating, drinking, sex, rest, and sleep is greatest when one has waited as long as possible, so that the deprivations become as intense as possible. And yet *akrasia* means not being able to endure (καρτερεῖν) the slightest deprivation: the moment you feel a tinge of hunger, you eat; and this yields very little pleasure. *Enkrateia* as endurance is the capacity to wait strategically to act on those bodily desires. Then, *enkrateia* allows one to focus on the cultivation of nonbodily pleasures too, for example learning good things, working on oneself and household management, and becoming useful to friends and city. Euthydemus, warming to this argument, observes that, when one is bested (ἥττονι) by bodily pleasures, one can give no attention to virtue at all (πάμπαν οὐδεμιᾶς ἀρετῆς).[79] Socrates extends this point: "Only those with *enkrateia* can investigate the most significant things and, sorting them out by kind, in word and deed, choose the good and reject the bad."[80]

So *enkrateia* means resisting bodily desire to the advantage of bodily and nonbodily pleasures. In particular, it provides one of the ingredients for doing what is right. Another ingredient is the exercise of *sôphrosunê*. *Akrasia* hinders the exercise of wisdom (σοφία) because it prevents a person from learning about (καταμανθάνειν) and attending to (προσέχειν) what is useful, directing one instead to what is pleasurable; the result is that a person often confuses good and bad and so chooses the latter.[81] Just so, *akrasia* hinders the exercise of *sôphrosunê*, which is "caring for what is appropriate" (ἐπιμελεῖσθαι ὧν προσήκει).[82] It obstructs both wisdom and *sôphrosunê*, where wisdom seems to be the investigative capacity of coming to know what is good, and *sôphrosunê* seems to be the commitment to act on that basis. *Enkrateia* is the "foundation" of virtue because it gives the psychic space, by being a mechanism of desire-control, to act for reasons other than the visceral urgency of some appetitive prompting. *Enkrateia* and *sôphrosunê* work together, with wisdom, but they are not for all that conceptually identical. Xenophon's account of human maturation has, so to speak, internal and external requirements: you must both quell the inner turmoil as well as identify the external guidelines for action. Without a say in desire's impact on thought and action, the latter is impossible; without the capacity to follow guidelines, there is no reason to suppress one desire rather than another.

The overlap between wisdom and *sôphrosunê* seen here at *Memorabilia* 4.5.6 becomes thematic in an earlier chapter. Book 3, chapter 9 reports Socrates'

---

[79] Xen. *Mem.* 4.5.10–11.
[80] Xen. *Mem.* 4.5.11: ἀλλὰ τοῖς ἐγκρατέσι μόνοις ἔξεστι σκοπεῖν τὰ κράτιστα τῶν πραγμάτων, καὶ λόγῳ καὶ ἔργῳ διαλέγοντας κατὰ γένη τὰ μὲν ἀγαθὰ προαιρεῖσθαι, τῶν δὲ κακῶν ἀπέχεσθαι. Johnson (2021, 163–78) discusses this passage at length.
[81] Xen. *Mem.* 4.5.6.
[82] Xen. *Mem.* 4.5.7: Τοῦ δὲ ἀντὶ τῶν ὠφελούντων τὰ βλάπτοντα προαιρεῖσθαι ποιοῦντος καὶ τούτων μὲν ἐπιμελεῖσθαι, ἐκείνων δὲ ἀμελεῖν πείθοντος καὶ τοῖς σωφρονοῦσι τὰ ἐναντία ποιεῖν ἀναγκάζοντες οἴει τι ἀνθρώπῳ κάκιον εἶναι;

evidently idiosyncratic or at least distinctive views about several fundamental ethical concepts, all connected to the unity of virtue: the teachability of courage (1–3); the identifiability of justice and the other virtues with *sophia* (5–6); *mania*, the opposite of wisdom, as a failure of self-knowledge (6–7); and so on.[83] In section 4, Xenophon discusses Socrates' understanding of wisdom and *sôphrosunê*, in particular whether one could have one without the other:[84]

> σοφίαν δὲ καὶ σωφροσύνην οὐ διώριζεν, ἀλλὰ τῷ τὰ μὲν καλά τε καὶ ἀγαθὰ γιγνώσκοντα χρῆσθαι αὐτοῖς καὶ τῷ τὰ αἰσχρὰ εἰδότα εὐλαβεῖσθαι σοφόν τε καὶ σώφρονα ἔκρινε. προσερωτώμενος δὲ εἰ τοὺς ἐπισταμένους μὲν ἃ δεῖ πράττειν, ποιοῦντας δὲ τἀναντία σοφούς τε καὶ ἐγκρατεῖς εἶναι νομίζοι, Οὐδέν γε μᾶλλον, ἔφη, ἢ ἀσόφους τε καὶ ἀκρατεῖς· πάντας γὰρ οἶμαι προαιρουμένους ἐκ τῶν ἐνδεχομένων, ἃ οἴονται συμφορώτατα αὑτοῖς εἶναι, ταῦτα πράττειν· νομίζω οὖν τοὺς μὴ ὀρθῶς πράττοντας οὔτε σοφοὺς οὔτε σώφρονας εἶναι.[85] (Xen. *Mem.* 3.9.4)

He did not distinguish between wisdom and *sôphrosunê*, but deemed the person who recognizes what things are fine and good and so does them, and who knows what things are disgraceful and so guards against them, as the

---

[83] For the problem of the unity of virtue in the Socratic context, see Kahn (1976).

[84] This identification is displayed in Plato's *Protagoras* (332c–333b), but that argument goes by way of their shared opposite; Xenophon disaggregates these issues across sections 6 and 7. Aristotle also brings up the equation as a debater's argument (*Top.* 108a2). For helpful discussion of this issue, especially in light of *Mem.* 3.9.5, see Morrison (2010, esp. 233–34). Kahn (1996, 394–95) simply states that 3.9.4 is "a free, slightly confused variation on" the *Protagoras* passage. For further discussion of this passage, see Seel (2006, 35–38); Pangle (2013, 17, somewhat confused); Weiss (2018, 300–304); Johnson (2021, 161–63).

[85] Text from Bandini and Dorion (2003–11), except replacing their ἀκρατεῖς εἶναι νομίζοι with ἐγκρατεῖς εἶναι νομίζοι. ἐγκρατεῖς is found in the Venetus Marcianus 368, though corrected to ἀκρατεῖς in accordance with the other medieval manuscripts. Marchant (1923) in his Loeb edition follows Sauppe in accepting ἐγκρατεῖς (see Delatte 1933, 115n3; but note that Marchant in the Loeb gives the wrong translation of ἐγκρατεῖς as "vicious"). Marchant (1901) had earlier, in his Oxford Classical Text edition, preferred ἀκρατεῖς, as do recent scholars, including Bandini and Dorion (2003–11, 2.1.91); Jones and Sharma (2018, 80); Johnson (2021, 161). I believe ἐγκρατεῖς is the superior reading, however, since it has the questioner aiming to show the absurdity of Socrates' nondistinction of wisdom and *sôphrosunê*. "So, Socrates, you hold wisdom and *sôphrosunê* to be the same; yet on the reasonable assumption that *sôphrosunê* is the same as *enkrateia*, how can you explain someone who knows what is right, and so is wise, but does not do it—are you really going to say that he is *enkratês*? Who knows whether they are also *sôphrôn*, but surely you cannot think that they are also *enkratês*, self-controlled!" The reading ἀκρατεῖς would seem to require a sort of negative question: "But don't you in fact think that such-and-such a person is wise but actually *akrateis*?" There are three additional reasons in favor of reading ἐγκρατεῖς. The pair "*sophos* and *enkratês*" is a better setup for Socrates' total reversal in his answer, "*asophos* and *akratês*!" Socrates' final rejection, νομίζω οὖν τοὺς μὴ ὀρθῶς πράττοντας οὔτε σοφοὺς οὔτε σώφρονας εἶναι, seems to require it. And some manuscripts that contain the ἀκρατεῖς reading in the challenge have Socrates' response as οὐδέν γε μᾶλλον, ἔφη, ἢ ἀσόφους τε καὶ ἀμαθεῖς, "Not so much that as unwise and ignorant," which seems redundant and inapt, and the clumsy result of trying to avoid an awkward duplication of ἀκρατεῖς across two sentences.

wise and *sôphrôn* one. And being further asked whether he thought that those who know what they ought to do but do the opposite are wise and *enkratês*, he responded, "Not so much that as unwise and *akratês*: for I think that everyone, choosing from among the available options what they consider most beneficial for themselves, does those things. Thus I think that those acting incorrectly are neither wise nor *sôphron*."

Socrates does not argue for the identity of wisdom and *sôphrosunê*; he allows for their conceptual or semantic distinctiveness. He observes rather their factual or ideal coincidence. Xenophon does not make Socrates' reasoning perfectly clear, but there is a natural way to read the initial paraphrase of Socrates' thinking, given the parallel syntactic structure. Wisdom is the recognition of what's fine and good and the knowledge of what's disgraceful; *sôphrosunê* would then be the acting on the basis of what is fine and good and not acting in accordance with what is bad. *Sôphrosunê* would be the capacity to follow the judgments of value, here made by wisdom, and to treat some of them as authoritatively action-guiding, not merely theoretically interesting. Socrates' second statement, the one in direct quotation, provides us the same view. Wisdom judges which among the available options is best; that option chosen, *sôphrosunê* is a person's treating the best option as the decisive reason to act.

Socrates' second statement is an answer to a question obviously prompted by his first statement. If wisdom and *sôphrosunê* coincide in a person, how are we to understand someone who apparently knows what is right but seems not to act in accordance with it? How could we possibly hold that this person is both wise and *enkratês*, which traits go together (on the interrogator's assumption that *sôphrosunê* is functionally equivalent to *enkrateia* here), even though the person who does not act in accordance with wisdom seems precisely opposite, *akratês*, incontinent and weak-willed? Socrates agrees that this person could not be both, but rather than claim that he is wise and *akratês*, Socrates denies the assumption that he is even wise. Socrates does so by articulating a moral psychology: what everyone does is whatever he happens to think is best for himself. The interrogator imagines that someone who does something evidently irrational, to the extent that he is *akratês*, knew what to do but was prevented from doing it by being overwhelmed by some unauthorized desire. Socrates claims by contrast that the person simply failed to know what was best for himself; he did what he intended, but his intention was based in ignorance, the absence of wisdom. That person has picked the wrong desire to be the one to act from. *Akrasia* means not being able to discern the real value of things.

So the questioner's sorry person is not wise; but why, according to Socrates, is he also not *sôphrôn*? After all, might it not have taken considerable strength of will for him to have executed his chosen albeit stupid goal, to have defended himself against his desires to act otherwise? Two answers suggest themselves. First, the *sôphrosunê* of the putatively *sôphrôn* idiot would not be helpful for him; his tenacity in acting on his erroneous judgment would not be admirable; and yet virtues are admirable, laudable states of character, and so that tenacity should rather be called "drivenness" or "stubbornness," something evaluatively neutral or even pejorative. Thus the unwise man cannot be *sôphrôn*—that is, in a good state—by sticking to his self-undermining judgments, since doing so is bad.

A second answer is more psychological than analytic: the proposed person, who fails to do what he knows he ought to, acts in a manner that does not reflect what we would expect to see from the exercise of *sôphrosunê*. For example: his friend has suffered a great loss, and he knows that he should call on his friend to offer support. But he does not do so. Presumably his fear of misspeaking, distaste for awkwardness, and worry that it will take too long outweigh for him the benefit, evident even to him, of simply reaching out. If he does not call on his friend, according to Socrates he has miscalculated what the right thing to do is; so he is not wise. Yet we do not think that he is exhibiting *sôphrosunê* in acting on his judgment that he should not call on his friend, because it surely does not *feel* or *look* like he is: he does not seem to be bearing down and sticking to that judgment, staying away, despite the Siren song, the massive and insidious appeal, of calling on his friend. In other words, he does not seem to be exercising any skillful filtering of desires but instead simply to be going whither the strongest desires lead. Indeed, the very fact that he judged staying away as the best choice seems a result of his judgment of value depending exactly on the strength of the impulse rather than on some better criteria.

Thus Socrates' view about *sôphrosunê* makes sense: it is an acknowledgment of what actually provides authoritative guidance in life, and this acknowledgment involves treating certain desires as decisive despite there possibly being other, viscerally more urgent desires.

Xenophontic *Sôphrosunê*

Xenophon recognizes two elements in one's maturation and attainment of agency: the exercise of *enkrateia* and that of *sôphrosunê*. For actions to be one's own rather than those of the noisiest of one's desires—in other words, to act freely, to act on the basis of one's authority as master of oneself—one must exercise *enkrateia*. That is resisting or enduring the call of desires. It is the capacity to find reasons to act elsewhere than in the prominence of a strongly felt desire. This capacity is neither specifically other- or self-oriented, but it is self-constituting: it allows one to be responsive to a range of reasons, and thus to have plans to attain, for example, whatever is best for one's city or oneself.

Sôphrosunê, by contrast, is that responsiveness to reasons, laws, or otherwise judgments of action-guiding value. This is rational agency. It is acting in accordance with and from divine, social, and prudential norms, recognizing their authority, whatever their justification. Such is to be called acting piously, justly, and sensibly. Like *enkrateia*, *sôphrosunê* is not specially other- or self-oriented, but is again self-constituting: it is sticking to the best reasons to act. We might then see *enkrateia* and *sôphrosunê* as negative and positive formulations of agency: *enkrateia* amounts to not acting on the basis of the strongest desire; *sôphrosunê* amounts to acting on the basis of the best reason. They are, conceptually, different capacities, but the emphasis on one rather than the other will depend on context.

This is a judicious and attractive division between moral-psychological terms. We will see that Plato does not avail himself of the division, though he recognizes its existence in *Gorgias*, *Republic*, and *Laws*. Consistent with the prevailing usages in the Greek language, *sôphrosunê* does for Plato the work of both terms. Their connectedness in Xenophon makes this unsurprising, even unremarkable. The worry might be that Plato leaves *sôphrosunê* to do too much. But in the first place, this is not his problem; the language already saddled the term with this grand scope; if this virtue-term is capacious and superior to other states, so be it. And in the second, Plato's not having decided to remove the desire control from the norm commitment makes the virtue that much more interesting, since it requires that we consider how self-cultivation takes both inside-focused and outside-looking attention. It makes the effort of *sôphrosunê* like the effort of coming to know oneself, what one is committed to and how one stands with respect to those commitments—with which it is repeatedly identified.[86]

We will then see Aristotle's alternative inventory of moral-psychological terms. Like Xenophon he distinguishes *enkrateia* and *sôphrosunê*. His account of *enkrateia* is akin to Xenophon's: it is concerned with withstanding the press of desire. But his account of *sôphrosunê* is not: while it involves reason, formulated as *phronêsis*, it concerns principally the having so moderated the desires for food, alcohol, and sex as not to require *enkrateia*—the counterforce of endurance—to act for reasons other than their satisfaction. *Sôphrosunê* remains important in agency: it means freedom from the constant distraction of certain bodily desires. It remains aloof from the other- vs. self-interested distinctions, given that the benefit of nongluttony, nondrunkenness, and nonlustfulness redound both to oneself and others. It even remains important for rational agency, since it gives a person space to think about the best way to live, from both the action-by-action and the overall perspective. Nevertheless, *sôphrosunê* is no longer rational agency itself, as it was in both Xenophon and Plato.

---

[86] Moore (2015c); for Xenophon, see ch. 10.

8
Plato 1—*Sôphrosunê* and the Capacity for Action

Plato as Theorist of *Sôphrosunê*

It is Plato more than any other classical Greek thinker who sees *sôphrosunê* as the virtue of agency, the capacity to act, the legitimate responsibility for doing what one does. He establishes the virtue's centrality to the human ideal of maturity, independence, and activity by having characters across the dialogues praise, critique, and otherwise contemplate it; he also has them advance sophisticated arguments about its nature. We have seen a similarly extensive interest in the virtue in Euripides and Xenophon. But the theoretical analysis has no fifth- or early fourth-century correlate. Plato is unique for his continuous, even if aporetic, incomplete, and puzzling explanations of the virtue's foundational role in self-constitution and civic affairs, and for the creative linkages he draws between it and various ethical, psychological, epistemological, and political positions.

By contrast with Plato, Xenophon endeavored to distinguish *sôphrosunê* from *enkrateia*, such that the first would concern acknowledgment of authoritative norms and the second would concern the prevention of unauthorized desires from directing one's action. The first was to be a matter of judgment and end-setting, the second of internal-milieu management. While Xenophon did not always keep the distinction between them crisp, he usually did in his major statements about human aspiration to virtue. Plato, for his part, makes much less effort to apportion norm-acknowledgment and desire-suppression between the two capacities. As befits the language available to him as he started his writing career, the virtue called *sôphrosunê* does both tasks: it allows one to be reason-guided and it keeps the various strong pleasures from knocking one off these guide rails. Plato's brilliance comes out especially in the ways his characters describe and analyze the virtue given its double burden. They strive to combine the epistemic aspect, which involves doing whatever one learns the right thing to be, and the affective aspect, which involves not being so distracted as to be unable either to learn or to apply what one has learned. Combining these is difficult; people tend to think of *sôphrosunê* as one thing or another, either as a kind of knowledge that is hard to delimit or as a practice of self-limitation that is hard to valorize. Dialogues from across Plato's career show versions of the problem or candidate solutions. None gives a direct and determinate theory of *sôphrosunê*. But together they articulate better than the work of any other author the importance of, the trickiness concerning, and the points of contention about this virtue.

The dialogues written later in Plato's career deal with the challenges of defining *sôphrosunê* in a way less commonly found in those from earlier in his career. These later dialogues sometimes observe that the term *sôphrosunê* is used in two ways: sometimes it emphasizes desire-suppression only; at other times it highlights the involvement of reason, intelligence, and even wisdom. The desire-suppression type, crucial as it is for human maturation, will not bring it wholly about; for that one needs the rational type. This observation about two uses of *sôphrosunê* in the later dialogues helps us see that even in the earlier dialogues Plato recognized this ambiguity, though his characters dealt with it in their own ways.

An illustration of the late-dialogue phenomenon, which neatly clarifies the *sôphrosunê*-assessing challenges faced throughout Plato's writings, is found in the *Phaedo*. Socrates has come to say that philosophy is the practice of dying, because it, somewhat like death, involves the separation of soul from body. A result is that philosophers, unlike nonphilosophers, face their mortality with courage. As it turns out, courage is a distinctive trait of philosophers. But courage is not their only distinctive trait.

> οὐκοῦν καὶ ἡ σωφροσύνη, ἣν καὶ οἱ πολλοὶ ὀνομάζουσι σωφροσύνην, τὸ περὶ τὰς ἐπιθυμίας μὴ ἐπτοῆσθαι ἀλλ' ὀλιγώρως ἔχειν καὶ κοσμίως, ἆρ' οὐ τούτοις μόνοις προσήκει, τοῖς μάλιστα τοῦ σώματος ὀλιγωροῦσίν τε καὶ ἐν φιλοσοφίᾳ ζῶσιν; (Pl. *Phd.* 68c8–12)

> And then *sôphrosunê*, too—what even many people call *sôphrosunê*, not being undone by desire but thinking little of it and being orderly—is this not appropriate to those alone who most distinctively think little of their bodies and who live philosophically?

As Socrates presents it here, *sôphrosunê* is generally understood in two guises: as a capacity regarding desires and as an overall disposition. The capacity involves not allowing desires on their own to be motivationally decisive: the person with *sôphrosunê* is not overwhelmed or stunned (μὴ ἐπτοῆσθαι) into acting on a desire. She can instead assess the relative value of a desire from above, as it were; she does not give it outsized significance (ὀλιγώρως ἔχειν), and instead recognizes it as just one of potentially many inclinations. The disposition is one of orderliness, a unity of parts, the following of a pattern or set of guidelines rather than jerking from one adventitious impulse to another. Socrates makes no claim against the common understanding of *sôphrosunê* here; his point concerns only who most characteristically has the virtue. This means he needs to explain the absurdity (ἄτοπος) of most people's condition with respect to courage and *sôphrosunê*.[1]

Socrates begins with the case of courage: for most people, their stolidity before death comes from the fear of greater evils. It does not come, Socrates implies, from a special capacity that deals with the power or consequences of one's desires or overall disposition. He spells this out in the case of *sôphrosunê*:

τί δὲ οἱ κόσμιοι αὐτῶν; οὐ ταὐτὸν τοῦτο πεπόνθασιν· ἀκολασίᾳ τινὶ σώφρονές εἰσιν; καίτοι φαμέν γε ἀδύνατον εἶναι, ἀλλ' ὅμως αὐτοῖς συμβαίνει τούτῳ ὅμοιον τὸ πάθος τὸ περὶ ταύτην τὴν εὐήθη σωφροσύνην· φοβούμενοι γὰρ ἑτέρων ἡδονῶν στερηθῆναι καὶ ἐπιθυμοῦντες ἐκείνων, ἄλλων ἀπέχονται ὑπ' ἄλλων κρατούμενοι. καίτοι καλοῦσί γε ἀκολασίαν τὸ ὑπὸ τῶν ἡδονῶν ἄρχεσθαι, ἀλλ' ὅμως συμβαίνει αὐτοῖς κρατουμένοις ὑφ' ἡδονῶν κρατεῖν ἄλλων ἡδονῶν. τοῦτο δ' ὅμοιόν ἐστιν ᾧ νυνδὴ ἐλέγετο, τῷ τρόπον τινὰ δι' ἀκολασίαν αὐτοὺς σεσωφρονίσθαι. (Pl. *Phd.* 68e2–69a4)

What about the orderly people [who are not philosophers]? Aren't they in the same situation—they are *sôphrôn* through a kind of indiscipline? To be sure, we claim this to be impossible; all the same, their situation with this simple *sôphrosunê* turns out to be like this. Out of fear that they will be deprived of some pleasures that they desire, they abstain from one set [of pleasures] by being controlled by another set [of pleasures]. To be sure, they call indiscipline being ruled by pleasures; all the same, it turns out that they control some pleasures by being controlled by other pleasures. This is like what I just now said, that they have been made *sôphrôn* by some kind of indiscipline.

Nonphilosophers have *sôphrosunê* too when they do not act on certain desires and remain orderly. But the explanation for their attainment of *sôphrosunê* differs from that of the philosophers. The nonphilosophers do not deploy a capacity to withstand the impressions of desires and they do not think little of their desires. They instead have some desires that are so strong as to cancel the effect of competing desires. The orderliness is imposed not intentionally from above, so to speak, but unintentionally from within; it is a fiction of unity caused by the inevitable success of a single desire. These nonphilosophers do not have superior attitudes toward their desires; they just have desires of unequal strengths.

---

[1] On the structural differences between the arguments about courage and *sôphrosunê*, see Gallop (1975, 98–102).

Socrates qualifies this *sôphrosunê* that results from desire competition: it is "simple" (εὐήθη), a consequence of a fortunate character rather than of thoughtfulness. And the person in this state has been "sophronized" (σεσωφρονίσθαι), made to be *sôphrôn*, rather than realized the virtue on his own. This qualified *sôphrosunê* is to be contrasted with the "true" (ἀληθής) virtue. He gives the contrast in a monetary analogy:

Ὦ μακάριε Σιμμία, μὴ γὰρ οὐχ αὕτη ᾖ ἡ ὀρθὴ πρὸς ἀρετὴν ἀλλαγή, ἡδονὰς πρὸς ἡδονὰς καὶ λύπας πρὸς λύπας καὶ φόβον πρὸς φόβον καταλλάττεσθαι, [καὶ] μείζω πρὸς ἐλάττω ὥσπερ νομίσματα, ἀλλ' ᾖ ἐκεῖνο μόνον τὸ νόμισμα ὀρθόν, ἀντὶ οὗ δεῖ πάντα ταῦτα καταλλάττεσθαι, φρόνησις, [καὶ τούτου μὲν πάντα] καὶ μετὰ τούτου [ὠνούμενά τε καὶ πιπρασκόμενα] τῷ ὄντι ᾖ καὶ ἀνδρεία καὶ σωφροσύνη καὶ δικαιοσύνη καὶ συλλήβδην ἀληθὴς ἀρετή, μετὰ φρονήσεως καὶ προσγιγνομένων καὶ ἀπογιγνομένων καὶ ἡδονῶν καὶ φόβων καὶ τῶν ἄλλων πάντων τῶν τοιούτων· χωριζόμενα δὲ φρονήσεως [καὶ] ἀλλαττόμενα ἀντὶ ἀλλήλων μὴ σκιαγραφία τις ᾖ ἡ τοιαύτη ἀρετὴ καὶ τῷ ὄντι ἀνδραποδώδης τε καὶ οὐδὲν ὑγιὲς οὐδ' ἀληθὲς ἔχῃ, τὸ δ' ἀληθὲς τῷ ὄντι ᾖ κάθαρσίς τις τῶν τοιούτων πάντων καὶ ἡ σωφροσύνη καὶ ἡ δικαιοσύνη καὶ ἀνδρεία, καὶ αὐτὴ ἡ φρόνησις μὴ καθαρμός τις ᾖ. (Pl. *Phd.* 69a6–c3)

My blessed Simmias, for this is not the correct way to buy virtue, exchanging pleasure for pleasure and pain for pain and fear for fear, and more for less, as it is with money, but this alone is the correct currency for which all those things should be exchanged—wisdom—and through which and with which all of them are in truth to be bought and sold; courage and *sôphrosunê* and justice and, to summarize, true virtue are so only with wisdom, where pleasures and fears and all other such things are added or subtracted. But separated from wisdom, such virtue that is an exchange of these for one another is a kind of illusion and is really slavery and nothing healthy or true; but truth is really a kind of purifying of all such things, and *sôphrosunê* and justice and courage, and wisdom itself, are some kind of purification.

True *sôphrosunê*, Socrates says here, is "with wisdom" (μετὰ φρονήσεως). While the meaning of the currency analogy is uncertain, clearly this wisdom accounts for the virtue's being a kind of mastery rather than the kind of slavery experienced by the *sôphrôn* nonphilosophers in thrall to their strongest desires.[2] And the philosopher's *sôphrosunê* is a "purification" (καθαρμός, cf. κάθαρσίς) of her pleasures and other feelings, not their elimination but their modification,

---

[2] On the currency analogy, see Archer-Hind (1883, 181–86); Gallop (1975, 102–3); Irwin (1977, 322n2; 1995, 195–95); Weiss (1987); Bobonich (2002, 23–31).

presumably such that they are still felt but without compulsion.³ *Sôphrosunê* always means not acting on certain pleasure-seeking desires. Yet without wisdom, this resistance to certain desires—especially those for bodily pleasure, for money, and for social standing, as the previous discussion specified—comes only from the efficacy of other desires; with wisdom, by contrast, this resistance comes from something else, namely being in charge of (κρατεῖν, ἀρχεῖν) the desires on which one acts.⁴

This passage from the *Phaedo* presents two ways of thinking about *sôphrosunê* corresponding to two ways to appear orderly and resistant to certain desires; it distinguishes them in terms of their relationship to agency. The nonphilosopher's *sôphrosunê* is a condition of slavery (to one's desires); the philosopher's *sôphrosunê* is a condition of mastery (of one's desires). Using language from Christine Korsgaard, the first amounts to conflict, the second to self-constitution.⁵ Both forms are familiar from analyses we have seen before, the first most strikingly in Antiphon's writings (Chapter 5). Plato here sharpens the contrast and introduces "wisdom" as the key differential.

But the *Phaedo* leaves open more questions than it answers. What is this wisdom of? Why is it to be considered "with" (μετά) the other virtues rather than in place of them? How does *sôphrosunê* with wisdom prevent one from keeping the desires in their place without simply extirpating them? How does it make a person "orderly"? And does one even need the language of wisdom to make the relevant claim? This book's triad of chapters on Plato studies the six dialogues that attend most closely to these questions, the promises and problems of *sôphrosunê*. The present chapter, focusing on the *Protagoras* and *Gorgias*, investigates *sôphrosunê*'s seeming overlap with the other virtues, wisdom not excluded. The *Protagoras* involves the most direct argument for the unity or reciprocity of virtue. The *Gorgias*, like the *Phaedo*, contrasts two accounts of *sôphrosunê*, one a desire-suppression model and the other a unity-preserving model, the former which seems to suppress agency, the latter which represents agency, in part by subsuming all the other virtues to it. The next chapter, focusing on *Republic* and *Charmides*, traces out two new arguments for *sôphrosunê*'s status as the virtue of agency, one in an affective key, the other in an epistemic key. In the *Republic*, *sôphrosunê* is distinguished from wisdom; Socrates posits *sôphrosunê*'s capacity to acknowledge authoritative reasons for action. In the *Charmides*, Socrates tests Critias' construal of *sôphrosunê* as a form of self-knowledge; this is a promising idea, but Critias' defense founders on a misprision about the kind of knowledge

---

³ On the talk of purification, see Marechal (2021) for sympathetic discussion and bibliography, notably Woolf (2004: aligned), Ebrey (2017: opposed). For general considerations, see Bobonich (2002, 16–42, esp. 16–18, 19).

⁴ At 68c1–2, Socrates referred to people who were φιλοσώματος, φιλοχρήματος, and φιλότιμος.

⁵ Korsgaard (1999 and 2009) with reference to the *Republic*.

relevant here. The third Plato chapter, focusing on the *Statesman* and *Laws*, studies two dialogues where *sôphrosunê*'s relationship with wisdom becomes a focus of analysis. Seen in light of the *Phaedo*, these two dialogues show Plato's concern with this specific problem, the difficulty of distinguishing *sôphrosunê* as doing what one ought from *sôphrosunê* as knowing what one ought to do. To be sure, issues cross freely between dialogues and chapters, and I have not ordered all the dialogues chronologically; but this grouping of dialogues brings out key elements of Plato's thinking about *sôphrosunê*.

Here we turn first to the *Protagoras*. Three important issues arise. Protagoras slips without remark between shame (αἰδώς) and *sôphrosunê* as core virtues in the development of human civilization. Socrates tries to convince Protagoras that *sôphrosunê* is equivalent to wisdom, because the opposite of both is foolishness (ἀφροσύνη). And Protagoras and Socrates disagree about the identification of *sôphrosunê* with "doing/faring well" (εὖ πράττειν)—does this mean hypothetically, such that whatever end one has, one sticks to it, or categorically, such that one's end also happens to be good? The dialogue furnishes no theory of *sôphrosunê*, instead poignantly articulating the issues a theory would need to address.

We then turn to the *Gorgias*. Though the dialogue's first half depicts a conversation about justice, early in Socrates' great exchange with Callicles the topic shifts to *sôphrosunê*. Callicles sees *sôphrosunê* as the inhibition of one's will, the forgoing of desire-satisfaction; since he also sees the condition of human agency as courage plus intelligence—figuring out how to do what one wants and then taking the risks to achieve it—he sees *sôphrosunê* as a perversion of agency. To get Callicles to see *sôphrosunê* otherwise, Socrates lays out the virtue in a new way, now arguing from the equivalence of *sôphrosunê* and orderliness (the second half of the *Phaedo* conception of *sôphrosunê*). From orderliness Socrates draws an equivalence with doing what one ought, and then with the possession of all the virtues, and then with flourishing. Again furnishing no final theory of *sôphrosunê*, this dialogue at least builds up a plausible view of the virtue, one with the rhetorical benefit over the less theorized but commonsense desire-suppression model.

The *Protagoras* and the Unity of Virtue

Plato's *Protagoras* depicts Socrates' discussion with Protagoras, a celebrated thinker who professes to teach his students virtue sufficient for their flourishing at home and in society. The two men talk about virtue's teachability, the unity of its various instances, and the way a virtue could contribute to a happy life. The topic of *sôphrosunê* arises in the first part of their conversation, becomes thematic in the second part, and recedes into the background in the third. Plato has not written this dialogue to explore *sôphrosunê*. But in its survey of the span of virtue and the structure of its arguments, it reveals, like no other dialogue, *sôphrosunê*'s fundamental role in explaining successful human action. Not only do we see civic life enabled by *sôphrosunê*; we see how its absence makes one foolish and its presence allows tasks to get done.

The topic of *sôphrosunê* arises in the mythological half of Protagoras' "Great Speech."[6] Here he gives a mythological account of the origin of human civilization that focalizes the origins of human skill and virtue. Protagoras says that cities must avoid civil strife to maintain their unity and stability against the destruction wrought by wild animals; this civic comity requires virtue. This virtue he gives as a pair, first calling them "right" (δίκη) and "respect" (αἰδώς, a sense of shame), later, referring to the same ones, "justice" (δικαιοσύνη) and *sôphrosunê*.[7] These are to be sufficient for keeping cities together, but in his short speech Protagoras does not explain why he selects these two virtues in particular. The implication seems to be that, unlike courage, thoughtfulness, religiosity, generosity, or friendliness, these favor social integration. Or together they may have served, in late fifth-century parlance, as a polar expression for "virtue in general." In any event, Protagoras does not distinguish between the two virtues. Some readers have thought that right/justice pertains especially to socially relevant actions in light of others' interests, and respect/*sôphrosunê* to socially relevant actions in light of one's desires; but the speech does not countenance this distinction, if it even has any analytic purchase.[8] Nor does Protagoras explain, much less note, his shift from respect (αἰδώς) to *sôphrosunê*.[9] Aristotle says that thinkers earlier than he tended to conflate the two, and we have already seen and will continue to see evidence of such conflation.[10] Perhaps Protagoras implies that "respect" is the older concept or is one that involves a more naive ethics or moral psychology; or perhaps he merely wishes to have linguistic variety. We cannot say, and the matter arises again only in other dialogues.[11]

---

[6] In favor of this speech reflecting what the historical Protagoras actually or would actually have said: Guthrie (1971, 64, 266); Nill (1985, 4–22); Beresford (2013); Manuwald (2013). The "Great Speech" is often attributed to "On the Original State [of Man]," Περὶ τῆς ἐν ἀρχῇ καταστάσεως, DL 9.55 (see Guthrie 1971, 63n3). Protagoras' political-theoretic sensibility is supported by Aristoxenus' charge that Plato's *Republic* basically recapitulated Protagoras' *Antilogikos*: DL 3.37. North (1966, 87–88; 1979, 79, 89–88) discusses this speech as inaugurating the treatment of *sôphrosunê* as a political virtue.

[7] First pair: 322c2, 4, 7, d5; second pair: 323a1–2, b4–6.

[8] For example: *SEP* s.v. "Protagoras," §5.1: "*aidos* corresponding to the component that enables each to govern himself in his conduct toward other human beings and *dike* to the norms which regulate the social intercourse among human beings." Cf. Šegvić (2004).

[9] Nor the parallel shift from δίκη to δικαιοσύνη, which needs explanation, according to Havelock (1969, 50).

[10] Arist. *EE* 3.7 1234a21–23.

[11] Nill (1985, 43–46, with 14) argues that the *sôphrosunê* mentioned in the Great Speech was obviously ethical and other-regarding, and so when Socrates suggests that the opposite of *sôphrosunê*

Nevertheless, our questions become in a sense Socrates': his only reaction to Protagoras' speech is his claim to want to know how Protagoras understands the relationship between the major virtues. That is because Protagoras spoke indiscriminately about the various virtues.[12]

ἔλεγες γὰρ ὅτι ὁ Ζεὺς τὴν δικαιοσύνην καὶ τὴν αἰδῶ πέμψειε τοῖς ἀνθρώποις, καὶ αὖ πολλαχοῦ ἐν τοῖς λόγοις ἐλέγετο ὑπὸ σοῦ ἡ δικαιοσύνη καὶ σωφροσύνη καὶ ὁσιότης καὶ πάντα ταῦτα ὡς ἕν τι εἴη συλλήβδην, ἀρετή· ταῦτ' οὖν αὐτὰ δίελθέ μοι ἀκριβῶς τῷ λόγῳ, πότερον ἕν μέν τί ἐστιν ἡ ἀρετή, μόρια δὲ αὐτῆς ἐστιν ἡ δικαιοσύνη καὶ σωφροσύνη καὶ ὁσιότης, ἢ ταῦτ' ἐστὶν ἃ νυνδὴ ἐγὼ ἔλεγον πάντα ὀνόματα τοῦ αὐτοῦ ἑνὸς ὄντος. (Pl. *Prot.* 329c2–d1)

You were saying that Zeus sent justice and respect to humans and, throughout the speech it was said by you that justice and *sôphrosunê* and piety and all these were, in a word, sort of one—virtue. Now talk through these same things for me, making precise whether what virtue is is one, where justice and *sôphrosunê* and piety are parts of it, or rather whether the things that I just mentioned are all names of one single thing.

Protagoras answers that he thinks the various virtues are parts of virtue; a person can have some but not others; each is different from the other; and *sophia* is the best part.[13] Socrates' question has come from a pedagogical concern: if the virtues differ, presumably Protagoras will have to teach a range of things; but, if they do not differ, he will have to show how a single object of instruction can have such outsized benefit for his students' lives. Further, if Protagoras has the competence to teach about virtue at all, he should know precisely what being virtuous means. Protagoras' answer leaves Socrates unsatisfied.

It is in the testing of Protagoras' answer that Socrates twice gets into the details of *sôphrosunê*. His overall strategy is to equate overlapping pairs of the five canonical virtues such that they all turn out to be the same: justice and piety,

---

is foolishness, and thus that *sôphrosunê* is also a prudential and self-regarding virtue, he is testing Protagoras' attitude toward "other-regarding behavior['s being] compatible with self-interest." But it is not obvious that Protagoras implies this about the virtue in the Great Speech. Denyer (2008 ad 322c1–2) thinks, by contrast, that "such vagaries present a crack where Socrates can insert the wedge of his question about the unity of virtues." Helpful discussion, connected to *aidôs*, is in Cairns (1993, 355–60).

[12] Protagoras at 323a7: δικαιοσύνης τε καὶ τῆς ἄλλης πολιτικῆς ἀρετῆς; at 324a1–2: ἡ ἀδικία καὶ ἡ ἀσέβεια καὶ συλλήβδην πᾶν τὸ ἐναντίον τῆς πολιτικῆς ἀρετῆς; at 325a1: δικαιοσύνη καὶ σωφροσύνη καὶ τὸ ὅσιον.
[13] Pl. *Prot.* 329d4–330b6. See O'Brien (2003) for the types of virtue relations discussed here, and Irwin (1995, 79–81) for the "reciprocity" vs. the "unity" theses, two ways for virtues to be the same.

sôphrosunê and wisdom, *sôphrosunê* and justice, wisdom and courage.[14] It is the middle two pairs that concern us.

The equation of *sôphrosunê* and wisdom works by reference to shared opposites (by contrast to the argument via the denial of *akrasia* in Xenophon's *Memorabilia* 3.9.4, studied in the previous chapter). Protagoras agrees that foolishness (ἀφροσύνη) is the absolute opposite of wisdom (σοφία). Then he agrees that those who act correctly and beneficially (πράττωσιν . . . ὀρθῶς τε καὶ ὠφελίμως) exercise *sôphrosunê*. And yet those who do not act correctly act foolishly and do not exercise *sôphrosunê*. So *sôphrosunê* is the opposite of foolishness. He agrees that each thing with an opposite has only a single opposite. Since foolishness has at its opposite both wisdom and *sôphrosunê*, they must be the same thing.[15] Protagoras accepts the conclusion reluctantly (μάλ' ἀκόντως: "not really voluntarily").

Of particular interest here is the definition of *sôphrosunê* as "acting well and beneficially." It is a capacity for sound action that, notably, can be described without reference to desire-suppression or orderliness. The action is sound because it achieves its aim (hence "correctly"), and the aim is a good one (hence "beneficially"). The implied contrast is with actions that are too hasty to be brought off or that end up satisfying a poor intention. Notable, too, is that neither "correctly" nor "beneficially" is given specification. The action may be subjectively or objectively correct—accomplishing what the actor wanted, or what the action in general is supposed to do—and it may be beneficial to oneself or others. *Sôphrosunê*, while potentially a moral, other-regarding notion, is here only a capacity for (excellent) action.

Protagoras does not explain his reluctance to admit Socrates' overall conclusion. It may be from competitive spirit, not wanting to clinch his own argumentative defeat. But it could also come from his notion of *sôphrosunê*. As we have seen, in his mythological speech he equates *sôphrosunê* with respect (αἰδώς); this might lead him to judge the opposite of *sôphrosunê* to be hubris or shamelessness, not foolishness. If so, a person could act foolishly not just from ignorance but also from disregard of communal norms. In that case, *sôphrosunê* would be distinct from wisdom and knowledge, since knowing how to act would be insufficient for being *sôphrôn*; the *sôphrôn* person would also have to respect social norms. Nevertheless, Protagoras does accept Socrates' conclusion, and realizes he must, since he accepted the premises. He accepts the usages of the term *sôphrosunê* that Socrates offers to him. Accordingly, Protagoras' conflicted admission here probably reflects something formal about the contemporary notion of *sôphrosunê*. It means the capacity to act in accordance with certain norms,

[14] Justice and piety: 330b8–331b7; wisdom and courage: 349e1–361a1.
[15] Pl. *Prot.* 332a4–333b3.

but these norms may include practical norms as well as social norms. Socrates' argument emphasizes the first, practical norms; acting in accordance with them amounts to having expertise and knowledge. It de-emphasizes the second, social norms, which could apparently be ignored even by someone who knows what they are and knows how to follow them. The disagreement, then, reveals something crucial about *sôphrosunê*, as the capacity to be norm-governed, where the content of those norms is not itself part of the definition of the virtue.

The next argument that Socrates advances in his unification of the virtue seeks to equate *sôphrosunê* with justice. Socrates asks: Could someone exercise *sôphrosunê* in doing wrong—doing an injustice? Protagoras says that people would generally think so, though he would feel ashamed to agree with them.[16] Prompted for his own view, he concedes that some people do exercise *sôphrosunê* when acting unjustly (τινές . . . σωφρονεῖν ἀδικοῦντες). His reasoning has been foreshadowed by the previous argument: exercising *sôphrosunê* is "thinking well" (εὖ φρονεῖν) or, what is the same, "deliberating well" (εὖ βουλεύεσθαι). In doing an injustice with *sôphrosunê*, one does it with a clear mind and effectively rather than thoughtlessly and foolishly. Socrates rejoins: Yet acting effectively is "acting well" (εὖ πράττουσιν), and this "well" implies that the actions yield "good things" (ἀγαθά); and "good things" are whatever are beneficial to people (ὠφέλιμα τοῖς ἀνθρώποις). But injustice necessarily does not benefit people. And so one could not do injustice well. And so one could not do injustice while exercising *sôphrosunê*.

The disagreement turns on the meaning of "acting well" (εὖ πράττειν), just as the previous argument turned on the meaning of "acting correctly and beneficially." Acting well may involve having the means fit the end, which itself may require successful thought and deliberation. Acting well involves satisfying norms of practical rationality. This is what Protagoras meant. But acting well may also involve having good and admirable ends. Acting well may involve satisfying other norms, whether social or otherwise. This is what Socrates meant, and also what Protagoras realized people would expect it to mean, such that it would be shameful to claim that one could act unjustly but with *sôphrosunê*.[17] Protagoras does not accept Socrates' refutation. He presses Socrates on the specific

---

[16] At *Rep.* 6.491b9–10, Socrates observes that *sôphrosunê* can take someone away from philosophy if he does not have a good upbringing, suggesting that the term can refer simply to efficacy of action. Denyer (2008 ad *Prot.* 333c2–3) expresses doubt that there are "many, or even any, who said [this] outright," but then he recognizes that Protagoras may have in mind those "advocates of *Realpolitik* [who] sometimes use *sôphrosunê* and its cognates to mean a hard-headed and clear-sighted idea of where one's interests lie, and [means] to claim that *sôphrosunê* requires one to forget about considerations of justice." He gives as a qualified example Thucydides' Diodotus (3.44); but even he, Denyer says, is counselling only that one overlook injustice, not that one ought to commit it.

[17] In the *Meno* (73a8–9), Meno agrees with Socrates that "successfully managing" (εὖ διοικεῖν) anything, whether city, household, or any other enterprise, takes doing it *sôphronôs* and justly (σωφρόνως καὶ δικαίως).

beneficiaries of the goods (ἀγαθά) in which acting well eventuates. A contradiction arises only if doing well benefits the same people that doing injustice harms. But maybe benefits need not be universal: an injustice may harm one's enemy but benefit oneself. Maybe not; the world could be such that an actor is benefited only when others are also benefited. But this would be a feature of the world, not of *sôphrosunê*; *sôphrosunê* could be, in itself, neutral about the beneficiaries of the actions it enables.

After these two arguments about *sôphrosunê* in the *Protagoras*, we have a view of the virtue and an open question. The view is that *sôphrosunê* is acting well, correctly, and beneficially, actions that are supported by thinking and deliberating well. So *sôphrosunê* means acting sensibly, in awareness of the relevant considerations and stably committed to some end, by contrast with acting spontaneously or whimsically in response to some passing desire. Put this way, it probably means appreciating how this action fits into one's overall goals, such that the action advances the overall purposes of the actor. Telemachus could almost be said to have acted successfully were he to have announced to the suitors the return of his father in a way proper to announcements—loudly, clearly, aptly, etc.—but it would not in general count as a successful action unless it advanced what he *really* wanted, namely to help his father retake control of his household. So acting well probably means not just adopting the proper means for whatever end there may be, but also ensuring that the end is *one's* (ongoing) end. The open question concerns the beneficiaries of this successful action. The end is beneficial, but beneficial for whom? As we have seen in previous chapters, there is no consensus, or rather no belief that there is a determinate answer to this question. And this is as one might expect since, after all, we act for a range of reasons, including for a range of beneficiaries.

Sôphrosunê and justice amount to the same thing when "acting well" does not mean acting for one's benefit to the detriment of others. Whether it does not mean this is uncertain. This explains the uncertainty of the relationship between those two virtues in Protagoras' Great Speech, and the inconclusiveness of the argument about their coincidence after that speech. The remainder of the dialogue does not solve the issue directly. The long technical argument in the dialogue's second half deals with the equivalence of courage and knowledge, concluding that even (or at least) for the hedonist, living well takes wisdom. But this does not address whether courage or wisdom takes others' interests into consideration.

So the *Protagoras* is indeterminate on this issue, whether *sôphrosunê* is self-, other-, or neither-regarding; and this is so for two reasons, internal and external. Protagoras' lessons in virtue, as excellence in running a household and participating in a state, seem not to take a stand on the issue; and Socrates is not immediately concerned to undermine *that* aspect of his profession. This is the internal reason. The external reason is that the indeterminacy also prompts reflection on the nature of virtue—especially as we try to reconstruct Socrates' arguments for virtue-coincidence—and thus the dialogue prompts us to do some important philosophical work. If we are sympathetic to Socrates' perspective, we will probably be inclined to find that *sôphrosunê* involves acting in ways that do not harm others.

It may perhaps seem remarkable that "desire-satisfaction" did not come up in the *Protagoras* analyses of *sôphrosunê*. The virtue determines the status of an action *qua* action, not explicitly the suppression of desires. This contrast, between action-excellence and desire-suppression, becomes thematic in *Gorgias*. The question of *sôphrosunê*'s beneficiaries comes up again at a key argumentative point in that dialogue, as does its coincidence with other virtues, in particular with justice. The core dialectic in *Gorgias* concerning *sôphrosunê* is its crucial role as the virtue of agency: what it takes to be fully a doer in one's own life.

Debating the Value of *Sôphrosunê* in the *Gorgias*

The first half of the *Gorgias* concerns justice explicitly: Socrates reveals Gorgias' inconsistency about his teaching of justice to his students, and he reverses Polus' preference for doing injustice over suffering injustice, persuading him that wrongdoers ought to look forward to their punishment.[18] In fact, in the dialogue's first forty-four pages, no character uses the word *sôphrosunê*. The interlocutors' attention to justice is explained by their focus on rhetoric's power in the civic sphere, the democratic power to persuade assemblies about the just thing to do and the tyrannical power to exercise personal rule and thereby arrogate what is others' to oneself. When Callicles first joins the conversation, skeptical about Socrates' argumentative success—he accuses Socrates of repeated equivocation—the topic remains justice.[19] And so it remains when Callicles offers his putatively radical sociopolitical theory, claiming that the conventional praise of justice is an ideology of the weak and comes from those who are unable to protect themselves otherwise from the overreach of the strong, and that justice actually denotes the success in that overreach by the strong.[20]

It is only once Socrates presses Callicles on the identity of the "stronger" or "superior" that *sôphrosunê* arises; once it does, and the conversation comes to concern the best way of life more than the correct sociopolitical theory, *sôphrosunê* becomes the focal idea of the conversation.[21] Set at the very

---

[18] Pl. *Grg.* 449a1–481b5.
[19] From Pl. *Grg.* 481b6. At 477c3–5, injustice is seen as an icon of a bad soul, and so here justice is either the prime virtue or the most relevant virtue.
[20] Pl. *Grg.* 483b4–484c34.
[21] This has not generally been recognized; the introduction to neither Dodds (1959) nor Irwin (1979 1–12, esp. 8, 12) makes reference to *sôphrosunê*.

argumentative heart of the *Gorgias* is a debate about the value of that virtue. The debate does not occasion the fine-grained discussions of the virtue's structure that we will find in the *Republic* and *Charmides* and does not equate it with wisdom or justice as we saw in the *Protagoras*, but it brings urgency to such careful discussions and refines some of their findings. Callicles disagrees with Socrates about *sôphrosunê*'s contribution to agency: he believes that it impedes doing what one intends, and is thus contra-agential; Socrates judges it essential for doing what one intends, and is thus pro-agential. Their disagreement turns on their attitude toward a person's desires. Callicles treats all desires as, so to speak, equally one's own and equally deserving of satisfaction; Socrates treats only those desires directed toward what's good as worthy of one's affirmation, commitment, and identification with, and thus deserving of satisfaction. This difference about desires amounts to a difference about agency. For Callicles, robust agency comes through satisfying one's desires, and the more desire-satisfaction there is, the more agency there is. This is because for Callicles we are our desires; to be actualized as ourselves is for our desires to be realized. For Socrates, robust agency comes through satisfying only good desires, and the better those desires, the more agency there is. This is because for Socrates what's good is what we ultimately desire; to be actualized as ourselves is for our desires for the good to be realized. Thus Callicles, taking *sôphrosunê* as the limitation of desire, judges it harmful to agency; Socrates, taking it in the same way, judges it conducive to agency.

Callicles' natural right theory is that the "stronger," or the "superior," or the "better," or the "more excellent"—he keeps changing this formulation—deserve to rule and to have more.[22] This variability of descriptor annoys Socrates, however, and so he prompts Callicles to choose one. Callicles accedes to the view that the "more thoughtful" (φρονιμώτεροι) are those who deserve to rule.[23] This specification solves several problems at once: how could a single person be "stronger" (ἰσχυρότεροι) than a mass of people; how could the "superior" (κρείττους) be deemed so except by their actually ruling; how could the term "better" (βελτίοι) be anything but completely vague? But Socrates finds new problems with "more thoughtful": more thoughtful about what? Callicles eventually specifies; he means

οἳ ἂν εἰς τὰ τῆς πόλεως πράγματα φρόνιμοι ὦσιν, ὅντινα ἂν τρόπον εὖ οἰκοῖτο, καὶ μὴ μόνον φρόνιμοι, ἀλλὰ καὶ ἀνδρεῖοι, ἱκανοὶ ὄντες ἃ ἂν νοήσωσιν ἐπιτελεῖν, καὶ μὴ ἀποκάμνωσι διὰ μαλακίαν τῆς ψυχῆς. (Pl. *Grg.* 491b2–6)

---

[22] On Callicles' view, see Barney (2017, §§4–5).
[23] Pl. *Grg.* 489e8.

the ones who are thoughtful about civic matters, specifically how to manage them well, and who are not only thoughtful but also courageous, sufficiently able to bring to completion what they have in mind to do, and not to stop short from feebleness of soul.

Here we have a description of civic agency: understanding how to accomplish satisfactorily such tasks as exist in the city, and having the fortitude and stamina to accomplish them completely.[24] Such cognitively and affectively competent people—like those in the *Protagoras* who think and act well—are the ones Callicles believes should rule the city, and justice is their having more than the ruled.[25]

This is where Socrates turns the conversation from politics to psychology, and does so around the pivot of *sôphrosunê*. The language of ruling and being ruled gives him an idea. Are you saying, Socrates asks, that the rulers are to have more than themselves? Is each ruler not also to rule himself (ἕνα ἕκαστον . . . αὐτὸν ἑαυτοῦ ἄρχοντα), and thus be ruled by himself; or is each only to rule over others, and not be ruled by himself? Callicles wants Socrates to say more about this "ruling oneself"; presumably Callicles does not see a relevant parallel between ruling over others and one's self-directed activities. Socrates responds:

οὐδὲν ποικίλον ἀλλ' ὥσπερ οἱ πολλοί, σώφρονα ὄντα καὶ ἐγκρατῆ αὐτὸν ἑαυτοῦ, τῶν ἡδονῶν καὶ ἐπιθυμιῶν ἄρχοντα τῶν ἐν ἑαυτῷ. (Pl. *Grg*. 491d10-e1)

[I don't mean] anything fancy—just what lots of people would say: being *sôphrôn* and *enkratês* with respect to oneself, ruling the pleasures and desires that are in oneself.

Socrates says that self-rule is familiar enough: it is whatever *sôphrosunê* and self-control (being *enkratês*) are.[26] The relationship that a leader has with his citizens—answering their petitions only when he finds it appropriate to do so—is the relationship that one has with one's desires. The conclusion Socrates draws against Callicles' account of justice is that the deserts of ruling cannot in any

---

[24] Similarly, Irwin (1995, 103–6, 125–26).
[25] Pl. *Grg.* 491d2-3: πλέον ἔχειν τούτους τῶν ἄλλων, τοὺς ἄρχοντας τῶν ἀρχομένων.
[26] Dorion (2007, 2012, 2018) is impressed at this use of *enkratês* in the psychological sense, given its absence in dialogues (presumed) earlier than it, especially *Charmides* and *Protagoras*, and takes it as evidence that only now does Plato believe in a partitioned soul, whereas earlier the idea of "self-mastery" struck him as ludicrous, despite other Socratics using the term (including perhaps Socrates himself). But it is equally possible, as we saw in the previous chapter, that the term did not enter into common parlance with this psychological use until this time. (Dorion does not attempt to show that such use predates the *Gorgias*.) Furthermore, even here *enkrateia* is presented as something that other people are talking about, not an idea that Plato or Socrates is committed to as especially informative of their technical psychology.

simple way be getting more than the ruled, if one also rules over oneself, and it is absurd to get more than oneself.[27] Socrates says that he is appealing to a familiar view of *sôphrosunê* and *enkrateia*, though he is not affirming it. He thus brings out its desire-management aspect. This explains why he does not distinguish *sôphrosunê* and *enkrateia* here: they both help describe "self-rule." *Sôphrosunê* may especially pick out someone's qualifications to rule, for instance his meeting certain epistemic or psychological conditions, and *enkrateia* someone's strength to rule, for instance, his ability to ignore or quell strong desires; but those differences are not pertinent here.

Callicles does not respond to this amusing charge against his theory, for instance by showing a disanalogy between the two kinds of rule or accepting a way in which a person could be more than his desires. He instead explodes about *sôphrosunê*: "By *sôphrôn* people you mean foolish (ἠλιθίους) people!"[28] It is clear where his concern is to be found. And with this Callicles goes on to give his antisophronic moral psychology. Callicles' basic argument is, first, that "one's desires being ruled" is equivalent to "one's being ruled," and this is equivalent to "being a slave." Second, slaves are not happy. Third, no ruler in seeking his happiness would seek also to be ruled. Thus, no ruler would seek to be *sôphrôn*. The first premise might seem strange, equating one's desires being ruled with being ruled oneself, given that it is oneself who is doing the ruling of them; one's desires are hardly being directed by some outside master. That this premise does not strike Callicles as strange, however, reveals his vision of human nature, and helps us sharpen the contrasting Platonic vision that so esteems *sôphrosunê*. We can articulate Callicles' vision in two ways. One way is to say that, for Callicles, one—one's *self*—just is one's desires. So any rule or suppression of one's desires is a suppression of one's self—of oneself. Agency is realized with the satisfaction of those desires, just as slavery means foregoing one's own desire-satisfaction for the satisfaction of someone else's desires. The other way is to say that Callicles does not envision a self as something that treats its desires as options for action among which it is to choose. For him, agency does not involve selection or deployment. In either case, according to Callicles, it is the desires, not that which might judge those desires, that is sovereign. From this perspective, his vision of the self is profoundly unhierarchical, even democratic.

Actually, Callicles does not see the self as wholly unhierarchical, constituted solely by desires. There is something beyond the desires. We see this when he gives his advice for living correctly: you should leave desires alone and let them grow large without disciplining them (δεῖ τὸν ὀρθῶς βιωσόμενον τὰς μὲν ἐπιθυμίας τὰς ἑαυτοῦ ἐᾶν ὡς μεγίστας εἶναι καὶ μὴ κολάζειν).[29] Callicles allows

---

[27] Cf. Pl. *Chrm.* 168c–d.
[28] Pl. *Grg.* 491e2.
[29] Pl. *Grg.* 491e8–9.

that one might not leave them alone and instead try to shrink and discipline them. He recognizes a capacity to manage one's desires, and even a capacity to decide whether to manage them. Further, he says, one should be capable of "servicing" (ὑπηρετεῖν) one's desires through one's courage and reason, to ensure that each is satisfied (ἀποπιμπλάναι).[30] So, of course, the desires are not self-sufficient; they have helpers. The desires are the normative core of the person: what they want is what I am. The other human faculties service or minister to them, as staff members minister to a board of trustees. The less interference and the more competence embodied in those faculties (= the staff members), the greater the efficacy or potency of the desires (= the trustees). What matters is that the ends are set by the desires, by the trustees, not by the servants enabling the means. The contrast with the Platonic Socrates' perspective is that for Socrates the manager of the desires, not any desire in particular, is the authority.

The rest of Callicles' rejoinder is amplification and reiteration. Those full of "incapacity" (ἀδυνυμία), unable to bring about fulfillment of their pleasures (οὐ δυνάμενοι ἐκπορίζεσθαι ταῖς ἡδοναῖς πλήρωσιν) due to their lack of courage (ἀνανδρία), praise *sôphrosunê* in post hoc rationalization.[31] Running into obstacles, they adulate self-obstruction. Calling the grapes sour, they say that unsatisfiable desires should not be satisfied, and in not being able to act as they wish they say that they are more truly actors. Limitation they treat as discrimination.

Callicles' speech causes Socrates to reset the program for the conversation's remainder: Socrates aims to compare "this pair of lives, the *sôphrôn* and the undisciplined (ἀκόλαστος) one." He hopes to bring Callicles to accept that the former, which is more orderly (κόσμιος) and satisfied with what it has, is more choiceworthy than the latter, which is always unfulfilled.[32] Whereas Callicles thought that he became greater the more numerous his desires, actually he is setting himself up for failure: he will never be able to act as robustly as he intends. Socrates formulates his rejoinder to Callicles—to many readers his most theoretically sophisticated opponent, hedonism's strongest exponent, and the logical extreme of Gorgianic democracy—as praise of *sôphrosunê*'s centrality to the good life. The position against which Socrates argues, which I have called "democratic," has it that each desire, as long as it has not yet been completely satisfied, has equal claim to satisfaction. Socrates' own position, by contrast, is the "orderly" life, and thereby the *sôphrôn* one. Callicles' "undisciplined" life is not an orderly one.[33]

---

[30] Pl. *Grg.* 492a1–2.
[31] Pl. *Grg.* 492a5–c8.
[32] Pl. *Grg.* 493d9–10; 493c8–d3.
[33] Socrates accuses Callicles of "not being in agreement" (οὐ... ὁμολογήσει) with himself, "being in discord" (διαφωνήσει) in his entire life, and "being out of tune" (ἀναρμοστεῖν); he goes on to say that he would rather have many other people not agree with and contradict him than, "considering just me, being out of concordance and speaking in opposition to myself" (ἕνα ὄντα ἐμὲ ἐμαυτῷ

In the first stage of his argument, Socrates seeks to undermine Callicles' equal respect for each desire. But he does not do so by saying that desires may demand contradictory, self-undermining, or inefficient actions, though he does note that this may occur—a disorganized life may lead to many changes of directions.[34] He argues instead that certain desires have bad ends that Callicles would not deign to pursue. Callicles' theory had been end-neutral: it cares only about the efficacy of the means to the desire satisfaction, and the number of desires, since total pleasure is the sum of those satisfactions. Socrates convinces Callicles that he cannot remain end-neutral. No matter how satisfiable and satisfying, it would not be good for certain desires to be satisfied; one could not identify with them. Socrates gives the example of the desire to scratch an itch: pleasurable as doing so might be, it is hard to see how success here could be judged good, seen to contribute to happiness and one's sense of worth as a powerful doer, or identified with as a meaningful part of one's life.[35] An even more damaging example for the democratic view is the desire for passive sexual experience: evidently pleasurable and something catamites desire, it is a desire that Callicles actively rejects as bad. Callicles accepts that only certain pleasures are good, and so only certain desires are affirmable.

Socrates' effort to show that desires are to be satisfied for the sake of the good, not for their own sake, was not, however, enough to demonstrate the superiority of the *sôphrôn* over the undisciplined life. He proceeds to the second stage of his argument. This stage has a feature unique in the Platonic corpus: Socrates goes through it twice, once with Callicles, and then, once Callicles refuses to answer further questions, a second time, now modified to avoid whatever caused Callicles to balk before.[36] This makes the reasoning here especially emphatic. The outcome of both spans of argument is that the successful life requires an orderliness of soul that is properly called *sôphrosunê*. The first time he goes through this argument (the "first pass," 500a6–505c2), Socrates concludes that desires must be restrained and disciplined, and thus that being disciplined is better for the soul than being undisciplined. In the redo (the "second pass," 506c6–508a8), Socrates takes a different tack: he argues that *sôphrosunê* includes all other virtues, and thus its presence in someone means that he is perfectly good and capable of action, and it is in this way that he lives happily. Here Socrates comes to praise

ἀσύμφωνον εἶναι καὶ ἐναντία λέγειν) (482b8–c3). For discussion, see, e.g., Woolf (2000); Kamtekar (2004).

[34] Pl. *Grg.* 493a5: ἀναπείθεσθαι καὶ μεταπίπειν ἄνω κάτω.
[35] Pl. *Grg.* 497c8–e2.
[36] For earlier discussions of this argument, see Adkins (1960, 273–74); Friedländer (1964, 2.268–69); Jaeger (1965, 2.145–56); Irwin (1979, 214–21; 1995, 109–10); Curzer (1991); Benardete (1991, 61, 72–75, 85–90); Kahn (1996, 142–45); Newell (2000, 30–33); Manuwald (2003); Stauffer (2006, 127–38); Gastaldi (2021).

sôphrosunê largely without invoking the restraint of desire, which is what caused Callicles to balk. His quietness about desire-restraint has a strategic purpose: to skirt Callicles' prejudices. But it also has a substantive point: as we saw already in the *Protagoras*, *sôphrosunê* is not essentially a restraint of desire; it is a disposition to act well, to be a competent and responsible agent.

The first-pass argument is connected to the antihedonistic argument that preceded: Callicles agrees that picking out (ἐκλέξασθαι) what is good from among the possible pleasant ends of action takes being skilled or expert (τεχνικός). Yet experts work not at random (οὐκ εἰκῇ) but instead, seeking to give some form (εἶδός τι) to whatever it is they are working on, put its respective parts into order (εἰς τάξιν ... τίθησιν). They seek to make those parts appropriate to and harmonized with (πρέπον ... ἁρμόττειν) one another, to the point that the whole is regular and orderly (τεταγμένον ... κεκοσμημένον). Even doctors, for example, arrange and order the body (κοσμοῦσι ... συντάττουσιν).[37] Thus an expert is so called not for effectiveness in satisfying his desires but for his capacity to create orderliness. Because the person living well, who chooses only the good pleasures to seek, is an expert, he will also somehow be creating orderliness.

The perspective next shifts from the expert to the object of his work. To the extent the expert puts things in order, the result of his effort is good (χρηστός) when it shares in regularity and order (τάξεως ... κόσμου). The soul is no less an object of skillful work than the body or any manufacture.[38] Asked what this psychic orderliness is called, Callicles demurs, but he accepts Socrates' suggestion: it is a regularity and order (τάξεσι ... κοσμήσεσιν), which in the soul is called lawfulness and law (νόμιμον ... νόμος), whence people become lawful and orderly (νόμιμοι ... κόσμιοι). Such people, they agree, embody justice and *sôphrosunê*.[39]

This argument has gone from the agreement that we seek only good pleasures to the agreement that doing so well requires *sôphrosunê* because it requires skillfulness. (It does not simply require courage and intelligence, notably.) There has as yet been no direct reference to the suppression of desire. Desire comes up, however, in the practical application of this finding that follows. The good orator, Socrates says, having Callicles in mind, must work to instill *sôphrosunê* in those in his audience. If they have it, he may allow them to satisfy their desires, but those who do not have it are to have their desires restrained (εἴργειν ... τῶν ἐπιθυμιῶν) and corrected (κολάζεσθαι), just as a doctor disallows the ill from doing whatever they wish.[40] Callicles goes with Socrates this far. He balks, however, when Socrates draws the conclusion and makes it pointedly about him: correction is better for the soul than indiscipline, contrary to Callicles' earlier thought (ὥσπερ

---

[37] Pl. *Grg.* 503e3–504a5.
[38] Pl. *Grg.* 504a8–b5.
[39] Pl. *Grg.* 504d1–4.
[40] Pl. *Grg.* 505b1–7.

σὺ νῦν δὴ ᾤου, 505b10). Probably Callicles had been imagining himself as one of the healthy, whose desires were not to be corrected; he was not anticipating Socrates to treat indiscipline, for Callicles a freedom from external interference, as a state of unhealthiness. To be fair, Socrates may be moving too fast, even if Callicles also fails to draw the right inferences. Socrates has gotten Callicles' agreement that the good person is *sôphrôn*, and that the psychically unhealthy person needs correction. But Callicles needs to see more clearly that the *sôphrôn* person is also happy, due in particular to his capacity to act well, and that the undisciplined person will be unhappy, due in particular to his failure to act well. Otherwise he is stuck seeing only that it is good to be well-ordered and that disorder needs to be ordered, but not that indiscipline is a failure of order. After all, *akolasia* simply means "not disciplined," and from Callicles' hopeful perspective, the man of intelligence and courage gets everything done that he needs to, thanks especially to his never having been disciplined.

We turn now to the second pass of Socrates' argument about *sôphrosunê*. This pass comes in three parts, arguing that the *sôphrôn* soul is good and that the *sôphrôn* person is happy, concluding with some further considerations about *sôphrosunê*. The first part, a ten-step argument, is familiar, though it makes key premises more explicit:

First part: a *sôphrôn* soul is good (506c6–507a2)

1. The pleasant is not the same as the good; the first is done for the sake of the other. (c6–8)
2. We are good thanks to the presence of the good. (d1)
3. We are good when some virtue is present in us. (d2–4)
4. The finest way for virtue to be present is through arrangement (τάξει) and correctness (ὀρθότητι) and skill (τέχνῃ). (d5–8)
5. By arrangement (τάξει) the virtue of each thing is something having been arranged (τεταγμένον) and ordered (κεκοσμημένον). (e1)
6. Something is good when some order (κόσμος τις), the proper (οἰκεῖος) one for it, is present in it. (e2–3)
7. A soul having its own order (κόσμον) is better than a disordered (ἀκοσμήτου) one. (e4–5)
8. The soul having order (κόσμον) is orderly (κοσμία). (e6)
9. An orderly (κοσμία) soul is *sôphrôn*. (507a1)
10. A *sôphrôn* soul is good (ἀγαθή). (a1–2)

As in the earlier pass, Socrates delays the arrival of *sôphrosunê* until near the end of the sequence, through its identification with the orderly soul. And as he did in the earlier argument, here too he takes this identification as a commonplace.

Callicles, who is asked for his view immediately after, again does not balk; Socrates has scrupled to avoid saying anything controversial.[41] Nevertheless, the equivalence with *sôphrosunê* is doing considerable work. Whether it really is a commonplace we will exam in a minute.

Before studying this sequence of reasoning, we should notice what the argument is not. Socrates does not reason that (i) having virtue is good, (ii) *sôphrosunê* is a virtue, so (iii) having *sôphrosunê* is good. This is because Callicles would presumably query as question-begging the assumption that *sôphrosunê* always counts as a virtue. He has already claimed that *sôphrosunê* is just a proud name for desire-inhibition, a screen necessary only for those too incompetent to satisfy the desires they have.[42] Yet Socrates does cite (i) in step 3, that having a virtue is good. So he will have to defend (i), and then link *sôphrosunê* to virtue through some intermediate term that does not present it as desire-suppression. Thus his emphasis on "arrangement" (τάξις), an emphasis that takes the form of a flurry of synonyms, cognates, and rephrasings.

Step 4 implements this strategy. Socrates states that the best way to come to have virtue is through arrangement (τάξις), correctness (ὀρθότης), and skill (τέχνη), not by random. In the first pass, Socrates said that experts approach their tasks with a form in mind, seeking to impose order; virtue came into the argument later. Here Socrates introduces virtue earlier and impersonalizes the account, speaking not of experts but of "the best way" of doing something, skillfully or technically being an aspect of that best way.[43] He gets what he needs in step 5, rendered more fully by E. R. Dodds as "So it is due to a principle of design (τάξις) that excellence is in each case something which has design and harmonious order."[44] Socrates is inferring that some excellent state is organized because it has been introduced in an organized way. An excellence is successfully introduced when done carefully; a careless way would not actually or fully introduce it at all. The excellence of a ship, for instance, is navigability; this is to be introduced through skill, which involves the orderly calculation of dimensions and deployment of materials; its excellence can hardly be expected to come together by chance. We might then translate step 4 as "Something's excellence is most effectively brought about by orderly, scrupulous, and technically informed means." The fact that some excellence comes about through an orderly process means that excellence itself involves being ordered: the navigability of a ship involves its

---

[41] Dodds (1959, 331) believes that when Socrates abandons discussion with Callicles, he does so in part to make claims to which he cannot anticipate agreement; but this does not make sense of Socrates' particular arguments.

[42] Pl. *Grg.* 491c8–492c10.

[43] Dodds (1959 ad 506d6): "Plato does not deny that excellence *can* arise spontaneously, but thinks there is a better, because more reliable, way of producing it."

[44] Dodds (1959 ad loc.).

being balanced and streamlined, and this balance and streamlining are products of orderly construction.

Because excellence is a cause of goodness, and excellence is a state of being ordered (κεκοσμημένος), Socrates simplifies and says that something's being orderly (κόσμιος) in its proper way makes it good. This has been argued by appeal to our ideas about production: systematic efforts yield excellences, and thus those excellences must be themselves systematic. To finish his argument, Socrates now needs only to link being orderly to *sôphrosunê*. For this he can rely on familiar ways of speaking. Of course we saw the equation of *sôphrosunê* and orderliness in the *Phaedo*. In the *Charmides*, Charmides' first definition of *sôphrosunê* is "doing everything in an orderly (κοσμίως) way and with tranquility."[45] In the *Clouds*, Better Argument speaks of *sôphrosunê* for young men as walking in order (εὔτακτος); in *Spartan Constitution*, Xenophon refers to the very practice as an exercise in *sôphrosunê*.[46] We already saw this in Phocylides,[47] and it appears in Thucydides and much early fourth-century writing.[48]

The idea throughout this literature is that being *sôphrôn* is being cool, calm, and collected; it represents a maturation from out of the frenetic and spontaneous wildness of babies and children. It is a freedom from tics, spasms, and the other nonrational explosions of organic energy. Nothing Callicles says or does suggests he would not admire the orderly life in this respect, the one that has given up the prerogatives of youth, that takes seriously adult political activity, that reflects the superiority of intention over bodily randomness.

Socrates has thus argued for the goodness of *sôphrosunê* by attending to its involvement in the valorization of the calm and collected life. True enough, in the *Charmides* the dispositional partner of being orderly, "some state of tranquility" (ἡσυχιότης τις), did not survive Charmides' defense. Charmides could not show what made being tranquil good, and he could not circumscribe tranquility sharply enough to defend it against potential counterexamples, such as appropriately quick but not tranquil music or calculation.[49] But this ambiguous relationship between calmness and orderliness does not mean that *sôphrosunê* is not orderliness. Indeed, Socrates has already explained the good-making properties of orderliness—(functional) excellence seems to depend on order. While Callicles could make various attacks on Socrates' premises, the basic structure of this argument is plausible. Socrates has argued for the goodness of *sôphrosunê* by appeal to its representation as an inner orderliness, and a more

---

[45] Pl. *Chrm.* 159b3; see Chapter 5.
[46] For the *Clouds*, see Chapter 1; for *Spartan Constitution*, see Chapter 7.
[47] Fr. 11 W; see again Chapter 1.
[48] Thuc. 1.84.3; Ar. *Pl.* 563–64; Lys. 3.4, 14.12, 19.16, 21.19.
[49] In Plato's *Statesman*, the Eleatic Visitor notes problems with *sôphrosunê* as quietness: see Chapter 10.

general consideration that orderliness is the foundation of excellence in most any sort of being.

We should note at this point that there has been no claim that the orderly soul is particularly good for me or for you; its goodness is not relativized. This is because, on this model, goodness depends not on the satisfaction of anybody's desires or the advancement of anybody's interests but on the execution of function. We do not specify a ship's navigability as being specifically good for the ship or the pilot or the passengers; it is good for the sailing.

From the goodness of *sôphrosunê* Socrates now argues for the happiness of the person who possesses it. He needs this argument because he cannot merely assume that good people are happy. Indeed, just as Callicles doubted that the virtues are good, even had he accepted that the virtues are good, he would have doubted that possessing such good things would conduce to one's happy flourishing. For Callicles, flourishing depends instead on one's activity, one's power, one's ability to satisfy one's desires. Socrates' argument addresses this concern.

Part 2: The *sôphrôn* man is happy (507a4–c7)

11. The *sôphrôn* man does what he ought (τὰ προσήκοντα πράττοι) toward gods and men. (a7–9)
12. The former is doing what is just; the latter is doing what is reverent. (b1–3)
13. Doing what is just and reverent is being just and reverent. (b3–4)
14. The *sôphrôn* man is courageous and endures against desires to do what he ought not. (b5–9)
15. The *sôphrôn* man, having the three other virtues, is a perfectly good man. (c1–3)
16. This good man does well and finely (εὖ τε καὶ καλῶς πράττειν) whatever he does. (c3)
17. This doing-well man is blessed (μακάριον) and happy (εὐδαίμονα). (c4)

This argument relies on a key assumption and several key inferences: *sôphrosunê* is doing what one ought; thus it involves all the canonical virtues; the four canonical virtues constitute perfect goodness; perfect goodness means competent action; competent action amounts to flourishing. The end of the argument is likely the most convincing to Callicles. While Callicles did not originally present his view of flourishing in terms of competent action, claiming instead that it was the satisfaction of maximal desires, his view involves it. After all, Callicles does not advocate the proliferation of desires for their own sake; a good life involves many desires only if they are to be satisfied, which means acting effectively in their satisfaction. His critique of Socrates is that his philosophizing preempts action; he spends too much time in idle chatter, which undermines one's action-guiding beliefs and action-motivating desires.

Step 11, the first assumption of this second part of the argument, might appear rather less convincing. It does not follow from the previous claim about *sôphrosunê*, which was that it is having an orderly soul. It instead picks up on another commonplace about the virtue. The clearest formulation of this commonplace elsewhere in Plato's dialogues may be found in Socrates' exchange with Critias. Both agree that "the one who does what he ought exercises *sôphrosunê*."[50] They treat exercising *sôphrosunê* as acting appropriately, as required by duty or obligation or norms. This is the action-formulation correlate of the earlier comportment formulation, the excellence of the orderly soul. A well-ordered ship, for example, does what it ought: it sails whither the pilot directs it; it changes speed depending on the sails and rowing; it stays afloat even in harsh weather.

It is a commonplace that *sôphrosunê* applies to actions done toward gods and men. As we saw in the previous chapter, when Xenophon describes Socrates' lessons about *sôphrosunê*, he gives as a long example his education of Euthydemus into *sôphrosunê* regarding the gods.[51] When he describes Critias' and Alcibiades' failure to remember Socrates' lessons in *sôphrosunê*, by contrast, he gives as examples failures to treat other humans appropriately.[52] Justice and piety are subcategories of *sôphrosunê*: both emphasize one or another domain of appropriate action. Given overlap between *sôphrosunê* and justice in much sixth- and fifth-century literature, and between *sôphrosunê* and piety in the same literature, this view should be seen as plausible. The connection to courage, too, for example in the character of Socrates as portrayed in the beginning of the *Charmides*, is not unique, even if this is more controversial, as we will see in Chapter 10. *Sôphrosunê* involves, in addition to doing what one ought, not avoiding doing what one ought, no matter how strong the feelings in opposition are; that is, as much as it involves a positive action, it also involves "endurance" (ὑπομένοντα καρτερεῖν) against negative impulses. So whereas justice and piety emphasize one or another object of action, courage emphasizes the inner management of fear and pain.

So now we have four of the canonical virtues. (It is not clear why wisdom is absent, but Socrates really needed only the link from courage, to which Callicles is already committed, to *sôphrosunê*, to which he was not yet.) The claim at step 15 is that together the four virtues constitute the perfect man, a claim also found in *Republic* 4 (with wisdom in place of piety).[53] Socrates infers from goodness to the doing of things "well and finely." A good instance of something does well

---

[50] Pl. *Chrm.* 164b4: ὁ τὰ δέοντα πράττων ... σωφρονεῖ; cf. *Rep.* 1.336d1: τὸ δέον.
[51] Xen. *Mem.* 4.3; cf. Thg. 1135–42.
[52] Xen. *Mem.* 1.2.14.
[53] Pl. *Rep.* 4.427e3–7; see Chapter 9.

whatever it does. Socrates might instead have tried to infer directly from "doing what's appropriate" to "doing well and finely what one does," skipping the analysis of the unity of the virtues and the redescribing of the person with all the canonical virtues as the perfectly good person, but his seeming digression has two dialectical benefits. First, it makes *sôphrosunê* seem especially capacious, governing all of the valuable actions in life. Second, to *sôphrosunê* it subordinates courage, a virtue Callicles has already treated as central in his vision of the flourishing life.

We have already supposed that the final inference would be appealing to Callicles; so we may now reflect on the argument overall. Without this argument, Callicles would have assumed that *sôphrosunê* was a curtailment of action, a self-limitation across many departments of life. But with the argument, he should think that *sôphrosunê* is not a curtailment of action: it is what makes any purposive action excellent. Of course, it really is both: *sôphrosunê* disallows much behavior, namely all that is inappropriate; what it makes go well and finely is a subset of all putatively possible actions. But the focus is on the capacity to act well whenever one acts. This is Callicles' concern: that he *can* act. Actions count as *actions*, rather than random behaviors, when they are motivated by reasons and not merely caused by physical impacts; so a behavior is an action when backed by the reason that one *ought* to do it. This is readily seen in the language of excellence. A ship is sailing when, as an excellent ship, balanced and streamlined, it goes where it ought to go, namely, where the pilot, using the tiller and rudder, directs it. Otherwise, it is merely drifting. Its going other than where it ought to go is not really sailing (the relevant action), even if it is a kind of movement.[54]

Sôphrosunê is the capacity to act on reasons, to follow norms, that pertain to one's effects on gods and other people. Following such norms is what makes one's actions count as intentional, as expressions of one's power and individuality, as coming from *oneself*. It makes one an agent. *Sôphrôn* people flourish because they are not mere passive sufferers of the world's and their bodies' purposes. They flourish because they are precisely those who can do what *they* want, and what they want is what *they* have reason to want.

At this point Socrates has effectively completed his positive argument. He continues, however, with some further considerations.

Part 3: Consequences about *sôphrosunê* (507c9–508a4)

18. Individuals (people or cities) must get disciplined (κολάζεσθαι) if they are still undisciplined. (d3–6)

---

[54] A similar conclusion is drawn in Irwin (1995, 116–17).

19. The standard (σκοπός) of personal or civic action is to have justice and *sôphrosunê* be present. (d6–e1)
20. Trying to satiate undisciplined desires (ἐπιθυμίαι) amounts to living as a pirate. (e1–3)
21. Being a pirate prevents partnership and friendship with gods or men. (e3–4)
22. The universe is called a *kosmos* because heaven and earth, gods and men, are said to be held together by community, friendship, orderliness, *sôphrosunê*, and justice. (e5–508a4)

Sôphrosunê is to be engendered through "getting disciplined" (κολάζεσθαι) if one is undisciplined. The argument that pertains to individuals also pertains to cities, and perforce to civic leaders—one of which Callicles aspires to be. Once the city has been brought into consideration, Socrates pairs *sôphrosunê* with justice, which allows him to link the present discussion with the remainder of the *Gorgias* conversation and to emphasize the social component, law and law-guidedness. He delays until here (step 20) his first reference to desire (ἐπιθυμία); he says that the disorder of desires is utterly bad, and that trying to fulfill such desires is piratical. Being piratical is particularly bad because it prevents joint action—a badness due, presumably, to its impeding corporate agency. Finally, the joint action preserved only by *sôphrosunê* can be seen on even a cosmic scale, as what constitutes the world as we know it.

Socrates has gotten most of the way through his celebration of *sôphrosunê* without discussing desire. He speaks of psychic orderliness in part 1 and of norm-following in part 2. Only at the midpoint of part 3 does he bring up desires (ἐπιθυμίαι), though still not equating *sôphrosunê* with their mitigation. Having disciplined desires is an important part of living with *sôphrosunê* and flourishing. Because the range of desires one has does not seem itself to impinge on one's acting as one ought, having undisciplined desires must amount to having desires that are so forceful that they motivate contranormative action. After all, well-disciplined desires would be those that motivate suitably and do not interfere with acting on the best of them. Socrates' more interesting proscription is against "trying to sate them [sc. one's desires]" (ταύτας ἐπιχειροῦντα πληροῦν). It sounds strange to forbid desire-satisfaction itself, until we realize that what he means is that we should not treat desire-satisfaction as an end in itself, as Callicles explicitly has. We should instead try to do what we ought to do. This will often include eating and drinking and sleeping, but the reason for doing these things is that we ought to do them—on certain occasions, in certain ways—rather than because they are desires that are open to satisfaction. The existence of a desire is not itself a reason for action. The two conditions, undisciplined desires and desires satisfied for their own sake, are presumably linked: the discipline of desires assumes that only some should be satisfied, in some ways; from this vantage, the satisfaction of *any* desire in *any* way is not to be countenanced.

"Piracy" so described—aimed at desire-satisfaction itself—prevents common action (κοινωνία) and friendship (φιλία). Sometimes you might desire an end that requires cooperation, but sometimes you might desire complete independence. Though Socrates does not draw out the conclusion, we can assume that the satisfaction of remarkably many of our desires requires concerted action— partnership or friendship—and so we run into another way in which the lack of *sôphrosunê* impedes action.

Socrates' concluding remarks show that the considerations of *sôphrosunê* scale to all levels of analysis—cliques, cities, even that of the cosmos (and we will see the same in the final fragment of Iamblichus' letter on *sôphrosunê*, in Chapter 13).[55] They replicate in microcosm the conversation's conclusion in an eschatological myth. But by contrast to the richness of that final myth, these last considerations are not developed. I think Socrates believes he has already made his argument at the crucial level—that of personal agency and flourishing—and wants at this point only to adumbrate some cases reflecting the total importance of virtue.

So, *sôphrosunê* is a virtue or excellence of the orderly soul; it involves a person's doing what he ought, with the result that everything he does is done well and finely. The consequent flourishing depends on this fine action. While it is *one's* action at issue, flourishing does not depend on those actions earning goods for oneself (rather than for others). Callicles' view had been that skill allowed one to satisfy one's desires, and the good would be one's own. This is not inconsistent, of course, with desiring to benefit others; but on Callicles' view, the reason to satisfy that desire is not the good of another (which is in a sense accidental); it is that one has that desire, and it is good for oneself to satisfy it.

Socratic *Sôphrosunê*

This passage, the pseudo-exchange with Callicles, prompts an important question about Socrates' rhetorical strategy: Why does Socrates treat *sôphrosunê* as the solvent for the impasse between Callicles and himself—rather than, for example, justice or wisdom? It may simply be because Callicles and he already brought up *sôphrosunê*; but I also think that *sôphrosunê* has come to be the most contentious and interesting virtues in personal and civic debate. What is more important for us is that the passage also prompts substantive questions. For example: How precisely is the soul (made to be) orderly? If well-ordered things

---

[55] On this cosmic level of analysis, see Irwin (1979, 224–26); Rosella Schluderer (2016).

always have parts, what parts does Socrates have in mind? If disciplining a soul contributes to its becoming orderly, and virtues must come about "by arrangement," how are we to imagine this process? And if *sôphrosunê* at the same time is "doing what one ought," how, if at all, does an orderly soul conduce to one's following such norms of action? Or might one think of it the other way, that by following norms one is able to unify oneself into having an orderly soul?

The dialectical situation of Socrates' pseudo-exchange with Callicles makes it such that he neither does nor needs to answer these questions. He wants to give the shape of the argument rather than analyze and justify it with full rigor. What matters is the twin ideals of self-coordination and norms-obedience, ideals that arose also in the context of the *Protagoras*. But it is not the case that this sketchy argument has only an ad hoc, rhetorical, or occasional pertinence for Plato's Socrates. For while the questions just raised go without an answer in the *Gorgias*, they do not go unaddressed elsewhere by Plato. In fact, Plato gives two sets of (partial) answers, in two dialogues. Those answers, though distinct in appearance, share their fundamental visions of *sôphrosunê*. This means that some of the details—specifically, the answers to the immediately preceding questions—do not matter so much, since they are replaceable by others. What matters is that these accounts explain the signal importance of the virtue attributed to it in this exchange. *Sôphrosunê* really is, on these accounts, what brings about a person's selfhood, their self-constitution as a rational agent, that which allows them to act at all. And this is the source of human flourishing.

9
Plato 2—Two Formulations of Agency

The *Republic* and *Charmides*

The *Protagoras* deployed *sôphrosunê* in two ways: as a key but untheorized ingredient in Protagoras' story of the rise of political community, and twice as a virtue to be identified with another virtue in Socrates' argument about the unity of the virtues. In the first way, Protagoras treated *sôphrosunê* as necessary for concerted human action, argumentatively equivalent to respect (αἰδώς), and somehow paired with justice. In the second way, Socrates observed wisdom and *sôphrosunê*'s shared opposite, "foolishness," a kind of incompetence in action, and doubted whether someone could meaningfully be said to act unjustly with *sôphrosunê*, that is, to do bad things with calm effectiveness. The dialogue thereby indicates the virtue's centrality in thinking about personal and political action, though it gives no account of the virtue's having this quality, and leaves open the degree to which it is a "moral," other-regarding quality.

The *Gorgias* goes further in accounting for *sôphrosunê* as a virtue of agency, in part because Socrates faces a Callicles who impugns *sôphrosunê* as stupidly action-negating. Callicles sees it as the suppression of those desires whose satisfaction gives purpose and glory to life. *Sôphrosunê* impedes the work of his two virtues of agency, namely courage and intelligence. Socrates builds up a response that depends on the view that anything's or anybody's efficacy depends on its well-orderedness and that *sôphrosunê* is essentially good order. He then argues that the other canonical virtues instantiate *sôphrosunê*. Thus *sôphrosunê* is the virtue of agency in general, and other virtues' agency-entailing qualities redound to *sôphrosunê*. Though these two arguments have several steps, they are also compressed, and Socrates does not explain or justify many of their assumptions. Thus in both *Protagoras* and *Gorgias*, we see hints or outlines of a Socratic-Platonic perspective on *sôphrosunê* as agency, but little realization of this vision. For more, we turn to two further dialogues.

The *Republic* and the *Charmides* provide, in striking ways, complementary treatments of *sôphrosunê*. From the perspective of their arguments' contents, they are remarkably non-overlapping. None of the candidate definitions in the *Charmides*—tranquility, respect or the sense of shame (αἰδώς), doing one's own things, doing good things, and knowing oneself—appears as a gloss on

The Virtue of Agency. Christopher Moore, Oxford University Press. © Christopher Moore 2023.
DOI: 10.1093/oso/9780197663509.003.0009

sôphrosunê in the *Republic*, not even to be rejected.[1] And none of the *Charmides'* interlocutors presents *sôphrosunê* as the proper relationship between types of desires, as might seem intuitive and which approach drives the analysis found in the *Republic*. Plato cannot therefore be said to have written the longer dialogue to overturn or resolve his putatively earlier confusion about the virtue expressed in the shorter dialogue, at least not in any explicit way; the two dialogues seem rather to speak from and to different (if interestingly related) concerns about the virtue.

From a more programmatic perspective, however, the *Republic* and *Charmides* overlap a lot. Most significant, the definition of *sôphrosunê* attributed to Critias in the *Charmides*, "doing one's own things," which is never exactly refuted or rejected in that dialogue, is offered up as the working definition of justice in *Republic* 4.433a–b, again never refuted or rejected; and those two virtues are notoriously similar in the longer dialogue. Similarly, though the *Republic* conversation ostensibly aims at insight into justice, Socrates talks at length with Plato's brothers about *sôphrosunê* several times. And just as the *Charmides* confronts paradoxes of reflexivity arising in certain accounts of *sôphrosunê*, so too the *Republic* confronts related paradoxes of reflexivity in its analysis of the virtue. The two dialogues may even share important elements of political-generic background: the *Republic*'s analysis of the Spartan constitution, and the many elements of such a constitution in the design of Kallipolis, may well respond to Critias' constitutional theorizing, which seems an implicit subject of the *Charmides*.[2]

This complementarity suggests that Plato's most important reflections on *sôphrosunê* are revealed jointly in these two dialogues.[3] What we see here, in short, is that the *Charmides* focuses on Critias' important position on *sôphrosunê* and develops the epistemic formulation of the virtue; the *Republic* focuses on the larger psychic context of *sôphrosunê* and develops its affective formulation. We will see that the epistemic formulation, where *sôphrosunê* relates to self-knowledge, is equivalent to the affective formulation, where *sôphrosunê* relates to psychic harmony, even though they differ in vocabulary and emphasis. Both ground a shared conception of personal agency as one's coordination with objective norms and thereby the constitution of oneself as a "self."

I argued earlier that the extant reflections on *sôphrosunê* from fifth-century Athens—by the sophists, Thucydides, and Euripides especially—reveal active debates about the virtue; this debate is continued in these two dialogues. This is obvious about the *Charmides*, as its presentation of Critias makes clear. But it is

---

[1] Cf. Rademaker (2005, 241).
[2] See Menn (2005).
[3] See also Rabinowitz (2015). For differences, however, see Santas (1973, 110); Lobo (2006); Tsouna (2018, 18).

also the case of the *Republic*. Plato does more there than give diligent attention to each of the four canonical virtues; Socrates' discussion of *sôphrosunê* flows from actual background notions and confusions about it. Because it is the more robust and celebrated dialogue about virtue—though not necessarily the more conclusive one—we start with the *Republic*.

The Affective Account of the *Republic*

Socrates initiates two major discussions of *sôphrosunê* in the *Republic*—one when discussing the education of the young guardians (in Book 3) and one when looking for the nature of justice writ large and small (in Book 4).[4] He presents the latter as a more considered view, though hardly as definitive or exhaustive; the earlier one he presents as sufficient only for their immediate purposes.[5] For that reason, let us begin with the Book 4 account; we will later turn to the more ad hoc account, which proves consistent with the considered view.

Having imagined a city as a more visible proxy for the soul, Socrates says that they need to look in it for justice.[6] Having constructed it as wholly good, he infers that it is wise, courageous, *sôphrôn*, and just—and he assumes that this allotment of virtues is exhaustive, such that if we find what corresponds to the first three virtues, we will know that what remains corresponds to justice.[7] Plato presents this inference, assumption, and method of finding the remainder as unexceptionable; Socrates does not justify them, and his interlocutors do not query them.[8] Not everyone in Plato's world would accept that list of virtues, of course: Meno's list of virtues puts in place of "justice" the virtue "generosity" (μεγαλοπρέπεια) and trails off in an ellipsis: "and a whole lot of others" (ἄλλαι πάμπολλαι).[9] What vindicates Socrates' position about the completeness of the four virtues is unclear, but it does show the analytic work done by canons, exemplary virtues coming to stand in for a complete array of them.[10] In any event,

---

[4] For *sôphrosunê* across the *Republic*, see North (1966, 169–76); Rademaker (2005, 317–21, 341–49); Tsouna (2018, 18–24). Many other studies of the dialogue do not include discussion of it; for instance, Vlastos (1969: "Psychic Harmony").

[5] Bobonich (2002, 43–45), by contrast, believes that the Book 3 account is "non-philosophical," the Book 4 one "philosophical."

[6] Pl. *Rep.* 4.427c6–d7.

[7] Pl. *Rep.* 4.427e6–428a1.

[8] For similar lists of virtues, see *Meno* 78d3–e3; *La.* 199d4–e8; *Symp.* 196b5–197b9 (provided by Agathon, on which see Hug (1876), 104–5 and Robin (1930), lxvii–lxix, considering a Gorgianic precedent, and Ausland (2013), 8), as well as our passages at *Prot.* 329c3–6, 329e2–330a1 and *Grg.* 507a–b.

[9] Pl. *Meno* 74a4–6 and again 88a6–b1 (in the later list, *sôphrosunê* comes first; in the earlier, it comes second). In the *Republic*, *megaloprepeia* means having a capacious perspective, *Rep.* 6.486a8–10; and Aristotle treats it as the virtue of well-capitalized generosity, *EN* 2.7 1107b17 and 4.2 1122a18–1123a18.

[10] For explanations of or reflections on their presumed exhaustiveness, see Adam (1902 ad 427e); Cornford (1912, 248–53: they are indexed to the ages of man); Hackforth (1913, 266: it is a

Socrates deals easily with the first two virtues. Wisdom is not just any knowledge but the knowledge distinctive of civic leaders, which judges of the whole city and its internal as well as external relations.[11] Courage is the "preservation" (σωτηρία) of acquired beliefs against the onslaught of fears and other passions, and is the distinctive virtue of the auxiliaries.[12]

Only two virtues remain, and Socrates floats the idea that he and his interlocutors might skip the inquiry into *sôphrosunê*.[13] He does not say why he makes this suggestion. Perhaps he wants to measure Glaucon's interest in the virtue; might Glaucon find it politically or personally less important or interesting than justice? Alternatively, perhaps Socrates wants to see whether Glaucon thinks *sôphrosunê*'s identity with or difference from justice is so obvious that they can skip ahead to the search for the latter, without risk of confusing it with *sôphrosunê*.[14] In any event, by asking whether they could investigate justice without fussing first with *sôphrosunê*, Socrates puts in question the virtue's philosophical import and distinctiveness, evidently reflecting mixed contemporary attitudes toward it.[15]

Glaucon rejects Socrates' shortcut. He does not see how they could skip the inquiry into *sôphrosunê*, and he wants to hear Socrates' account of it. Thus Glaucon must not think that the nature of this virtue is obvious—or (though he does not hint at this) at least thinks that Socrates will show it to be less obvious than he had assumed, which is probably what happened for the first two virtues.

The Book 4 Account

Socrates starts from the broad comparative perspective, identifying the virtues mainly with respect to one another (ὥς γε ἐντεῦθεν ἰδεῖν, "at least from this

---

popular view); Larson (1951, 396); North (1966, 172); Cross and Woosley (1966, 103); Sparshott (1970); Guthrie (1975, 535); White (1979, 114–15); Annas (1981, 110–11); Pappas (2003, 74–75); Ausland (2013, 11). On the concept of cardinal virtues as exhaustive generally, see Auerman (1876); Hammond (1892); Kunsemüller (1935); Carr (1988); Oderberg (1999). There is the problem about "piety," which comes and goes in Plato's lists of virtues as well as in the cardinal virtues through antiquity; see Dihle (1968) and Dalcourt (1963, 57).

[11] Pl. *Rep.* 4.428b1–429a3.
[12] Pl. *Rep.* 4.429a8–430b9. This *sôtêria* account of courage mirrors the etymology of *sôphrosunê* found in the *Cratylus* (see Chapter 2); it is provocatively paradoxical, because this preservation happens by throwing oneself into battle. For the significance of *sôtêria* in Plato, see Menn (2013).
[13] Pl. *Rep.* 4.430d3–4.
[14] Ferrari (2003, 38–39) claims that Socrates himself wants to skip over *sôphrosunê*, on the grounds that this virtue alone "requires the city to contain better and worse elements," and Socrates is regretful, even if realistic, about needing to introduce such hierarchy. Yet Socrates' first gloss on *sôphrosunê*, as "harmony," does not imply hierarchy, and his earlier explanations of wisdom and courage, which located each in specific parts of the soul, implied that higher parts were looking out for lower parts.
[15] In the *Laws*, the Athenian twice speaks of silence about the nature of *sôphrosunê*; see Chapter 10.

vantage").[16] Compared to wisdom and courage, *sôphrosunê* is "more like" (προσέοικεν μᾶλλον) some kind of "agreement and harmony" (συμφωνίᾳ τινὶ καὶ ἁρμονίᾳ).[17] Wisdom of the relevant sort had just been located only in the leaders, and courage of the relevant sort only in the warriors. Socrates presents *sôphrosunê* differently, as a coordination of various psychic parts rather than as a property of a single psychic part.[18] Notably, it is not a property exclusively of the third psychic part, "appetite"; conceivably his interlocutors would have anticipated such an answer. The appetite, so to speak, has fundamental importance to any animal, motivating the pursuit of all things needful. But human virtue represents the refinement of one's actions beyond the impulse of the strongest of one's present desires, and, presumably, that refinement would have to come from outside the basal layer itself (which contains only those impulses). Wisdom and courage provide two sources of refinement; *sôphrosunê* provides a third, one that more saliently involves the cooperation of the various psychic elements.[19]

Another difference between *sôphrosunê* and the two previous virtues comes in the way the three are discussed. The psychic locations of wisdom and courage were taken as obvious, and the basic form of their activity was thought to be pretty straightforward. What remained to be decided about wisdom was the content of the knowledge that constituted it; the question about courage was the meaning of Socrates' putting it in terms of "preservation." Unlike in those previous cases, however, *sôphrosunê* is presented at first only by comparison to two

---

[16] Pl. *Rep.* 4.430e1. Adam (1902 ad 430e) glosses instead "on a first view," citing *Pol.* 289d, *Rep.* 4.432b, 10.595b (similarly Griffith in Ferrari and Griffith 2000: "my first impression is that . . ."); Quandt (2020, n2143) gives "from my own vantage," explaining, "Socrates confesses it is his own idea," and compares to 2.368c7, 4.427e6, 4.428a11. How this difficult phrase is interpreted determines the epistemic confidence Socrates is expressing toward his formulation.

[17] Pl. *Rep.* 4.430e1-2.

[18] Very many have ignored this point, attributing the virtue (mostly?) to the appetitive class; for two instances, see Cornford (1912, 249); Adkins (1960, 285-93). See also North (1979, 106).

[19] It seems that even wisdom and courage could be described "harmonically," to the extent that, if a person's actions are going to be informed by them, their lower-level desires need to be sufficiently weak so as not always to trump higher-level intentions. Demos (1957a, 400) is sensitive to this: "[S]ophrosyne is *more* like concord . . . than the other two virtues. The sense of a common loyalty is of the *essence* of sophrosyne while it is only a consequential attribute of wisdom and courage." But Demos is also representative in thinking that the reason *sôphrosunê* is not a virtue of the lowest part is that the lowest part is irrational (ἀλόγιστος) (cf. Lorenz 2006, 44-48, though Bobonich 2017 doubts the relevance of the claim that the lowest part is irrational). Yet the putative irrationality of the lowest part would seem to prevent it from agreeing with the rule of the higher part (as the analysis of *sôphrosunê* here would seem to require). More important, it is not clear why we should expect the virtue to be "of" the lowest part, unless we are seduced by the desire for parallelism and a simple psychology of "one part—one virtue," which otherwise has no linguistic or phenomenological evidence in its favor. Interestingly, Pappas (2003, 76-77) does not wonder about the failure of the parallel because he sees the definition of *sôphrosunê* as (helpfully?) suggested by the earlier definitions: "[T]he simpler virtues have brought Socrates to look for virtues in the city's class structure, [so] he can define self-mastery as the harmonious domination of one class over the rest." For the view that *sôphrosunê* cannot really be separated from courage, see Irwin (1995, 224-29).

even more general concepts—"agreement" and "harmony." Since these are merely metaphors, Socrates shows that he has no uncontroversial first-approximation definition ready to hand, or at least does not want to reveal one, perhaps for pedagogical reasons.[20] Anyway, Glaucon does not quite see the point; evidently this is not a standard gloss on the virtue.[21]

So Socrates tries again, in a syntactically odd statement:

κόσμος πού τις, ἦν δ' ἐγώ, ἡ σωφροσύνη ἐστὶν καὶ ἡδονῶν τινων καὶ ἐπιθυμιῶν ἐγκράτεια, ὥς φασι, κρείττω δὴ αὑτοῦ λέγοντες οὐκ οἶδ' ὅντινα τρόπον. (Pl. *Rep.* 4.430e4–6)

Evidently *sôphrosunê* is some kind of order, and an *enkrateia* of [certain] pleasures and desires, as they say, speaking of "mastering oneself"—I know not in what way.[22]

Socrates here gives three commonplace formulations of *sôphrosunê*.[23] We have seen each before: "order" in *Phaedo* and *Gorgias*, "*enkrateia* of pleasures" in *Gorgias*, and "mastering oneself" in Antiphon.[24] Each presents *sôphrosunê* as a kind of concord between or integration of multiple parts: an orderly arrangement, control over various subagents, and mastery of some subordinate aspect of oneself. But Socrates is not simply listing three separate glosses; they are mutually explanatory.[25] *Enkrateia* of pleasures and desires, as a kind of order, is presented as self-mastery. Mastering oneself must mean unifying one's disparate and willful aspects into a self, as a hegemon's mastering its empire means unifying its far-flung and questionably loyal clients into a state or league. Yet this raises a paradox. If you master someone else, you bring an independent person under your control; but to master yourself would seem to require that the "yourself" being

---

[20] See Lynch (2017, 22) on the vague likeness, and generally on the "harmony" definition. Aristotle emphasizes the metaphoricity here: *Top.* 123a34–36, 139b33.

[21] Perhaps this should not be surprising, if Socrates' definition of justice is itself nonstandard (Annas 1981, 121).

[22] Contrast the Grube/Reeve translation found in Cooper (1997, 1062): "Moderation is surely a kind of order, the mastery of certain kinds of pleasures and desires. People indicate as much when they use the phrase 'self-control' and other similar phrases." Closer to my translation is Shorey (1930 ad loc.): "Soberness is a kind of beautiful order and a continence of certain pleasures and appetites, as they say, using the phrase 'master of himself' I know not how; and there are other similar expressions." For the syntax, see Quandt (2020, n2144).

[23] He says there are more such (ἄττα τοιαῦτα) synonyms or paraphrastic expansions of the virtue-term, suggesting a much talked about virtue (*Rep.* 4.430e6–7).

[24] Plato uses the noun *enkrateia* only one other time in his corpus, in *Republic* 3.390b3 (ἐγκάτειαν ἑαυτοῦ . . . νέῳ), in the dialogue's other discussion of *sôphrosunê*. The adjective in the psychological use appears only slightly more frequently, notably *Grg.* 491d10–e1; *Phdr.* 256b1; *Symp.* 188a7; *Laws* 1.645e8, 8.839b3, 8.840c5.

[25] Hackforth (1913, 269–70) disagrees; he believes that *harmonia* is incompatible with self-mastery, since he thinks the one feels effortless whereas the other demands much effort.

mastered is in a way both independent and constitutive of yourself. Fortunately, a desire is the sort of thing that at once has a certain independence, a sort of alien psychic or bodily thing, and a constitutive role in one's personality, a manifestation of one's actual commitments. Treating a desire as coming from a "lower part" of one's soul figures its quasi-agency, as being on the periphery of one's self. Of course, Socrates does not say all of this here; so far he avers only that "they say similar such things just as a clue to" the nature of *sôphrosunê*.[26]

Whether or not "self-mastery" is the newest of the three formulations, Plato depicts sensitivity to reflexives as a hallmark of Socratic discussion.[27] Here Socrates wonders how a thing that masters could be the very thing that is mastered, when there is just one self (ὁ αὐτός) in question.[28] He answers that this phrase "seems to want to say" that in the same person (ἐν αὐτῷ τῷ ἀνθρώπῳ), considered in psychic terms (περὶ τὴν ψυχήν), there is something that is better and something that is worse.[29] It is to cases of the naturally (φύσει) superior aspect being *enkratês* over the inferior aspect that the phrase "mastering oneself" applies, approvingly. "Self-mastery" is a loose, derelativized way of saying "mastery of one aspect of oneself over another aspect of oneself."

In giving this gloss, Socrates is saying that the phrase "mastering oneself" arises in the practice of ethical approbation. In these cases, people conceive of praiseworthy actions as those that issue from the desires that are more closely accommodated to a person's long-term, deeper, or truer interests, despite the evident strength of their other desires. Despite their strength, those other desires are less expressive of the person being praised, not because they are less vivid but because they have not been unified with the overall package—or judged to be worth unifying.

Socrates treats of the opposite case in the same way. "When by some bad upbringing and association the better part, which is smaller, is overpowered by the worse, which is larger," the person undergoing this is rebuked (ἐν ὀνείδει ψέγειν) and called "self-overcome" (ἥττω ἑαυτοῦ); he is "undisciplined" (ἀκόλαστον).[30] This adds two details to the picture. The better part of the self is "smaller" than the worse part. This will have a notable political parallel: the leadership class is smaller than the worker class. But it must also have phenomenological plausibility in the psychic case. Maybe the realm of our quasi-alien desires feels vast, dominating our attention, memory, and texture of life. It could be that this realm maps to our bodies, our appearance, our belongings, and our social position,

---

[26] Pl. *Rep.* 4.430e6–7.
[27] Socrates presses on it in Critias' definition of *sôphrosunê*, "doing one's own things," as we saw in Chapter 5. For other later fifth-century uses, see Jeremiah (2012, 94–110, 142–49).
[28] Pl. *Rep.* 4.430e9–431a1.
[29] Pl. *Rep.* 4.431a3–b2.
[30] Pl. *Rep.* 4.431a7–b2.

which together are larger than the realm of the part that could possibly master them, the brain or heart. In any event, Socrates suggests that *sôphrosunê* or its absence does not feel like two equal parts of oneself clashing and then neutralizing each other; it feels like the more expansive part submitting to the narrower. The second detail is that that submission depends on a person's proper upbringing and association. The smaller part's natural superiority is not its invariant superiority; to gain its advantage it must undergo the right kind of education. Socrates may have in mind the education described in Book 3, which primes the virtues, or any education that improves a person's ability to seek and identify what is good.[31]

Next we get specification of the two parts in a way that blends the psychic and political. The larger part comprises the many and various desires, pleasures, and pains found among the women, slaves, children, and other non-citizen members of the city. The smaller part comprises the desires found in the few who are naturally and educationally best. These desires are "simple and measured, led by reasoning accompanied by thoughtfulness and correct belief (μετὰ νοῦ τε καὶ δόξης ὀρθῆς λογισμῷ ἄγονται)."[32] The *sôphrôn* city is the one in which the desires of the lesser masses "are mastered" (κρατούμενοι) by the "desires and intelligence" (ἐπιθυμία καὶ φρόνησις) of the few. This pair looks to be a hendiadys for "reason-directed desires."

No desire limits itself, but all desires can be limited. In the self-mastering city, the desires of the mastering part have been limited by reason, and they in turn limit those of the mastered part. Socrates does not say how that limitation occurs. A common picture of *enkrateia* as an inner force may suggest it does so through compulsion, if of a clever sort. Somehow the reasonable desires outfox the unreasonable ones. Or, at the political level, those with the reasonable desires outfox those with the unreasonable ones. If so, the mechanism is unspecified. In fact, compulsion seems to provide the wrong model. Socrates, after all, describes *sôphrosunê* as a "friendship and agreement (συμφωνία) between [the parts], when the ruler and ruled share the belief (ὁμοδοξῶσι) that the calculating part must rule and they abstain from civil strife against it."[33] The appetite, typically considered irrational, is here able to follow reason; it is at once unruly and deferential.[34] This is not implausible. People with unreasonable desires can on some

---

[31] See Pl. *Rep.* 3.410a7-9: Οἱ δὲ δὴ νέοι, ἦν δ' ἐγώ, δῆλον ὅτι εὐλαβήσονταί σοι δικαστικῆς εἰς χρείαν ἰέναι, τῇ ἁπλῇ ἐκείνῃ μουσικῇ χρώμενοι ἣν δὴ ἔφαμεν σωφροσύνην ἐντίκτειν. Burnyeat (1997) provides general considerations in favor of this thesis.
[32] Pl. *Rep.* 4.431c5-6.
[33] Pl. *Rep.* 4.442c9-d2.
[34] Annas (1981, 116-17) puts the paradox this way; she does not resolve it, but prefers the "compulsion" side; Irwin (1995, 227-21) prefers the obedience side. Bobonich (2013) gives an attractive formulation of the paradox and, by contrast, finds it a "puzzle": the *Republic* seems not to offer a mechanism for the lower desires' responsivity to the "best overall" judgments of the upper ones (see also Bobonich 2002, 219-20, 242-45, 254).

issues treat people with reasonable desires as worth following. This can happen when they see that their interests are better served by doing so. Perhaps, then, one's appetites might be thought capable of "seeing" that their interests, such as food consumption, would be well-served by subordinating themselves to one's reason, which after all can care about a person's getting something to eat. Further, as Socrates describes it, the ruling part involves reasonable desires, desires that have been made reasonable through a proper upbringing. He thereby directly allows for desires that are variably responsive to reasons. To be sure, this does not altogether sort out the relationship between reason and desire, but it helps us appreciate that our very humanity may depend on the tractability of desire to reason.[35]

Just as the inferior masses are "mastered by" the elite, and thereby recognize their authority in setting the norms for action, the elite recognize their own authority and so provide guidance for everyone else. They must take an interest in the total project, whether it be the city or the soul, expending effort and orienting themselves such as to influence others, and appreciating that they and only they can succeed.[36] As Socrates says later, "it is fitting for the rational [part of the soul] to rule, being wise and taking due consideration (προμήθεια) for the whole soul, and the spirited [part of the soul] to attend to it and be its ally."[37]

Thus *sôphrosunê*, Socrates says, is an agreement between two parts of the city or the person concerning internal rulership. This concludes Socrates' Book 4 analysis of *sôphrosunê*. We can now highlight some key points. First, Socrates describes the desires that *sôphrosunê* deals with only negatively as those that are not "simple and measured, led by reasoning accompanied by thoughtfulness and correct belief." Second, these unruly desires are at least indirectly responsive to reason, through their management by a well-brought-up set of reasonable desires. A *sôphrôn* soul or city is one where, whatever desires there are, only those motivate action that are consistent with reason; in Socrates' metaphor here, the potentially unruly desires follow the lead of the ones that understand what to do. What we may conclude is that *sôphrosunê* is not the strength to tamp down certain desires but rather the capacity to make decisive for action only those desires that are informed by understanding. This capacity unifies the *sôphrôn* person or city as a "self" because what had been a mass of various impulses, each with its own provenance and direction, becomes the desiderative or human resources to propel a corporate body structured as norm-guided.[38]

---

[35] Thus evidently Socrates' question whether he is like the Typhon in Pl. *Phdr.* 230a1; cf. Moore (2015c, 147–50).
[36] On "whole soul," cf. *Rep.* 4.441e4.
[37] Pl. *Rep.* 4.441e3–5. On this use of προμήθεια, see Moore (2021, 87–107).
[38] That Socrates and Plato accept this ethical-normative conception of selfhood is the argument of Moore (2015c).

Relation to Justice (δικαιοσύνη)

Many readers of the *Republic* have had difficulty distinguishing *sôphrosunê* from justice in Book 4; understanding this difficulty will itself tell us something about *sôphrosunê*.[39] After finishing his analysis of *sôphrosunê*, Socrates turns to the analysis of justice. This will take some work; Glaucon admits he cannot see where it will fit into their scheme. Socrates says that they have been talking about it the whole time. They built their city on the foundation of a single idea, labor specialization: people should do the one kind of work that naturally best suits them.[40] To this reminder Socrates adds:

> καὶ μὴν ὅτι γε τὸ τὰ αὑτοῦ πράττειν καὶ μὴ πολυπραγμονεῖν δικαιοσύνη ἐστί, καὶ τοῦτο ἄλλων τε πολλῶν ἀκηκόαμεν καὶ αὐτοὶ πολλάκις εἰρήκαμεν. (Pl. *Rep.* 4.433a8–b1)

> And then, to be sure, we've even heard that "doing one's own things" and "not meddling" is justice from many others and have often said it ourselves.

From this Socrates infers:

> τοῦτο τοίνυν, ἦν δ' ἐγώ, ὦ φίλε, κινδυνεύει τρόπον τινὰ γιγνόμενον ἡ δικαιοσύνη εἶναι, τὸ τὰ αὑτοῦ πράττειν. (Pl. *Rep.* 4.433b3–4)

> So my friend, I said, justice seems to be this, realized in a certain way: doing one's own things.

Justice conceived as each doing his own thing, Socrates continues, is the "power" allowing the other three virtues to come about and preserving them once they have done so.[41] In particular, people skilled in one profession are not to try to serve in another profession; should nonwarriors act as warriors, for instance, the city might fail in courage.

The argument for the definition of justice at 4.433a1–b4 is worth scrutinizing:

1. Labor specialization is central to the good city. (a1–6)
2. People say that justice is doing one's own things and not interfering with others. (a8–b1)

---

[39] Demos (1957a, 402), in a paper about the difference, admits to having no idea how to distinguish them. Hirzel (1874) is the first major study of this question.
[40] Pl. *Rep.* 4.433a1–6.
[41] Pl. *Rep.* 4.433b8: ὃ πᾶσιν ἐκείνοις τὴν δύναμιν παρέσχεν ὥστε ἐγγενέσθαι, καὶ ἐγγενομένοις γε σωτηρίαν παρέχειν, ἕωσπερ ἂν ἐνῇ.

3. Labor specialization is doing one's own things and not interfering with others. (assumed)
4. Justice is doing one's own thing and not interfering with others. (b3–4)

In this reconstruction, Socrates reports what he claims is a common belief and justifies that belief by appeal to the labor-specialization principle, which had already been argued for in Book 2.[42]

This argument for the definition of justice gives several reasons for pause. There is the suppression of premise 3. Socrates needs that premise to ward off a plausible alternative view of "doing one's own things," namely one where everybody does *all* "their own things": each person grows his own barley, makes his own shoes, sails his own ships. Only if "doing one's own things" means doing only those things one is naturally best at doing does labor specialization express justice. There is also the baselessness of premise 2. We have no other evidence of people's having said this about justice.[43] To be sure, we lack many potential sources of evidence. But this empirical claim is so important to the central claim of the *Republic* that its being unsupported is troubling. Where we *do* see the phrase "doing one's own things" in Plato, it is twice associated with *sôphrosunê* (in the *Charmides* and *Timaeus* 72a4–6), as it is in Thucydides and implicitly in Xenophon.[44] Indeed, Plato's Critias advances "doing one's own things" as a definition of *sôphrosunê* so provocative that the entire *Charmides* is dedicated to it and its transformations, and no character there suggests that it properly applies to justice.

The infrastructure of the *Republic*'s argument about justice cannot detain us, but two potential resolutions relevant to *sôphrosunê* suggest themselves. Perhaps *sôphrosunê* and justice were so conceptually proximate that if "doing

---

[42] It is worth noting that in the Book 2 "city of pigs," whose sole structural point was its total division of labor, labor specialization was not said to be justice; but Socrates was constructing a city with the aim of finding that virtue, and since the city of pigs seems not to exemplify wisdom (nobody is setting ends), courage (nobody is fighting wars), or *sôphrosunê* (nobody is a leader or follower, and nobody has an opportunity for immoderation), it seems that the only virtue it could exemplify is justice. North (1966, 170) claims that "Justice and sophrosyne of a kind undoubtedly exist in the city," but she does not explain. At n39, she adds, again without argument, "Presumably *sophia* and *andreia* do not exist there, since the classes to which they belong do not yet exist; as individual virtues, however, they may be present in the souls of citizens."

[43] Scholarship has generally defended Socrates' statement by saying things like "the statement need not refer to any passage in the dialogue" (Cornford 1941, 127n1), which is true enough, or as Cornford also says, "If 'justice' here is taken in the wide sense of 'the right way to behave,' 'right conduct,' this has, of course, been stated several times in the *Republic*"—though then it is hard to see justice as at all differentiated from the other virtues. Similarly Adam (1902 ad loc.) and Shorey (1930 ad loc.). Vlastos (1969, 509) says that Socrates "seizes on the catch phrase ... as a convenient stand-in for this maxim," namely, "Keep to that line of social conduct by which, given your natural endowments and skills, you can contribute maximally to the happiness and excellence of your polis." Annas (1981, 120), by contrast, simply judges this an unpersuasive argument, to be improved upon in the sequel.

[44] Thuc. 1.68.1 and Xen. *Lac. Pol.* 7.2; see Moore and Raymond (2019, xxxiii) for more discussion.

one's own things" glossed the former it also glossed the latter.⁴⁵ But unless we accept Socratic unification of the virtues, we do not have evidence for that proximity, and the surrounding pages of the *Republic*, which argue against virtue-unification, provide evidence to the contrary. Further, if "doing one's own things" were so available as a definition of justice, we might expect it to arise as a candidate definition in Book I.

A different kind of resolution to the puzzle, "Isn't it odd to say that people were always glossing justice as 'doing one's own things'?," was proposed by James Adam in 1902, in what happens to be the most recent full commentary on the *Republic*.⁴⁶ (Despite that, his proposal has virtually never been acknowledged.)⁴⁷ Adam wonders whether the manuscripts at 433a8–b1 simply contain the wrong word, misprinting *dikaiosunê* for *sôphrosunê*.

> Perhaps δικαιοσύνη after πολυπραγμονεῖν is an error for σωφροσύνη, and Plato is here deliberately *correcting* the popular view. If so, καὶ μὴν—γε means "and yet," i.e. in spite of what we now say that Justice is εἰς ἓν κατὰ φύσιν, "we and others have also said that Temperance is τὰ αὑτοῦ πράττειν." Adimantus assents. "Well," continues Socrates, "it is apparently (not Temperance, but) Justice which is τὰ αὑτοῦ πράττειν." This view gives a much better sense to καί in καὶ τοῦτο, and ἡ δικαιοσύνη receives the proper emphasis.⁴⁸

Adam suggests the following reading: we have accepted the importance of labor specialization to the just city; it is a commonplace that *sôphrosunê* is doing one's own things, including not getting into others' business; yet we would do better to say that it is in fact *dikaiosunê* that is doing one's own things, as we see when we appreciate that not getting into others' business is a virtue grounding labor specialization, and this labor specialization seems essential to the just city. Adam's argument is definitely attractive. Even if Critias' definition of *sôphrosunê* as "doing one's own things" was proprietary and novel as of 429 BCE, given its plausibility and appeal (as discussed in Chapter 5) it may have caught on among those in his orbit, Socrates and Glaucon in particular.⁴⁹ An early copyist could have written the wrong word, attracted by the surrounding claims about *dikaiosunê* and the

---

⁴⁵ North (1966, 173n49) claims that "the definition of justice *borrows* from the traditional concept of sophrosyne" (my italics) and that "it shows that [Plato] is *widening* the hitherto narrow and legalistic scope of *dikaiosunê* by endowing it with some of the attributes of sophrosyne" (again my italics).
⁴⁶ Adam (1902). The closest equivalent is Quandt (2020), an online textual commentary.
⁴⁷ The sole exception I know is Vorwerk (2001, 38n29), who denies it on the grounds that it has no manuscript authority (as Adam acknowledges) and that the two virtues are "almost equated" (which is not to the point).
⁴⁸ Adam (1902, ad εἰρήκαμεν γάρ, 433b). Christopher C. Raymond focused my attention on Adam's proposal.
⁴⁹ Howland (2018) argues for the proximity between the social worlds of the *Charmides* and *Republic* and for a (close) friendship between Critias and Glaucon.

feeling that discussion of *sôphrosunê* had already finished. Unfortunately, we cannot settle the matter here.[50]

We may now return to the putative contrast drawn between justice and the other three virtues and the relevance of that contrast for our understanding of *sôphrosunê*. Justice was said to be the "power" allowing the three other virtues to come about and preserving them once they came about; this power was the principle of each doing his own things. It was said that without this fourth virtue the city would not flourish. But it is hard to see what justice really adds or, put the other way, why it would need the other virtues. For instance, a warrior would manifest *sôphrosunê* in his acknowledgment that the rulers alone should rule; if he knew (through some rudimentary self-knowledge) that he is not himself a ruler, he would not rule. He would manifest justice in effectively the same way, in not doing anything that is proper for rulers to do, knowing that he is not himself a ruler, and for that reason not ruling.

What, then, prevents justice from being either pointless or a virtue sufficient for goodness?[51] Well, perhaps this: justice tells you to do your own thing; *sôphrosunê* tells you that sometimes you need to take guidance from or give guidance to others. So justice allows a community of independent and mutually respectful citizens; *sôphrosunê* allows those independent and mutually respectful citizens nevertheless to work together as a community.[52] The intensity of human desire demands justice: people want more than is compatible with everyone's having what they want. The incoherence of human desire demands *sôphrosunê*: people want a more divergent set of things than is compatible with everyone's having what they want. But is this too fine-grained a distinction? Maybe it is not that an unjust person desires too much but that he desires what is not his, a problem not of intensity but of object. Maybe it is not that a person

---

[50] Slings (2003) does not cite this proposal in his apparatus but does cite an alternative emendation, evidently sensitive to the odd form of argument. This emendation is by Richards (1893, 253), who notes what looks to be a redundancy: "what in the later sentence is said to be ἡ δικαιοσύνη is already said to be δικαιοσύνη in the earlier." Richards thinks Plato means "whereas doing your own work has often been described as just (*i.e.* one just thing among many), we may now take it to be absolutely coextensive and identical with justice." So he proposes δίκαιον ἐστί in place of the first δικαιοσύνη ἐστί, a less drastic emendation than Adam's, though equally speculative.

[51] Annas (1981, 119) seems to make justice sufficient for goodness when she describes the difference between the two virtues. She makes *sôphrosunê* responsible for recognizing one's relative superiority or inferiority and *dikaiosunê* for recognizing "the full scope of one's position in a particular class in a state which requires cooperation from all classes . . . [where] one has to . . . know what one's natural talents are and the ways these should be developed for the common good": justice seems thus to subsume *sôphrosunê*.

[52] Demos (1957a, 401), tries out a version of this harmonization vs. differentiation view but rejects it on the grounds that Socrates says that justice also involves cooperation and that injustice is the absence of "shared understanding" (ὁμόνοια, 1.351d4d), and that this view does not explain the fundamentality of justice. Kosman (2007, 132) is more sanguine about this view.

lacking in *sôphrosunê* desires a jumble of things but desires something too much. In any event, the *Republic* simply does not elaborate the difference between these two virtues.⁵³

The ambiguity between justice and *sôphrosunê* teaches us important facts about Plato's conception of *sôphrosunê*. *Sôphrosunê* shares justice's scope and purpose: both pertain to all desires, and both aim to integrate and unify those desires; desire integration and unification allows the virtuous person to live an effective and intelligent life.⁵⁴ And, despite Socrates' remarks, it does not seem that one is more rudimentary than the other. Neither seems more concerned with baser or simpler desires, or more private or internally directed than another, or less infused with reason. And so, if the *Republic* vaunts justice as the way to the life of successful action, as thus the virtue of agency, it would seem to do so for *sôphrosunê* as well.

The Book 3 Account

Sôphrosunê's status as a virtue of agency may seem clear enough from the Book 4 discussion, but it may seem less clear from the equally involved discussion of the virtue in Book 3. The focus here is on obedience to authority and mastery of desires. As it turns out, however, this complex account is compatible with the one we have just studied.

Book 3 begins with Socrates' explaining how young people in the hypothetical city are to be educated into courage: through redacting the parts of poetry that encourage the fear of death.⁵⁵ Then, after a few reflections on laughter and lying, Socrates asks whether the young also need *sôphrosunê*.⁵⁶ Of course they do, says Adeimantus. Socrates goes on:

---

⁵³ Weiss (2012, 169–89) argues at length that there is no serious distinction between *sôphrosunê* and justice, and this is intentional, and for rhetorical purposes: Glaucon already accepts the intrinsic value of *sôphrosunê*, and so Socrates simply imports that definition to justice, whose intrinsic value would otherwise be impossible to show, since its value depends exclusively on benefit to others (and then indirectly on those benefited). One weakness of Weiss' reductive argument is its inadequate exploration of *possible* distinctions between the two virtues. Larson (1951, 395–98) advances a mitigated and less ad hominem version of this thesis, arguing that Plato in the *Republic* redefines justice in the direction of *sôphrosunê* because he thinks it should be seen as broader than its largely "legal" background would allow. Rowe (1979) thinks that while Plato desires *sôphrosunê* and justice to be different, he fails to distinguish them, thanks his dubious analysis of justice. Kahn (1976, 29) believes that between the two virtues there is biconditionality but no intentional equivalence.

⁵⁴ Cf. Kosman (2007, 116–32). Lorch (2012) makes the interesting claim that *sôphrosunê* is the virtue that recognizes how difficult becoming just actually is.

⁵⁵ Pl. *Rep.* 3.386a6–388d7.

⁵⁶ Pl. *Rep.* 3.388e1–389a7 (laughter); 389b2–d5 (lying).

σωφροσύνης δὲ ὡς πλήθει οὐ τὰ τοιάδε μέγιστα, ἀρχόντων μὲν ὑπηκόους εἶναι, αὐτοὺς δὲ ἄρχοντας τῶν περὶ πότους καὶ ἀφροδίσια καὶ περὶ ἐδωδὰς ἡδονῶν;
(Pl. *Rep.* 3.389d9–e2)

Isn't *sôphrosunê*, as most people think of it, principally these sorts of things: being obedient to rulers, and being rulers themselves over the desires for drinks and sex and food?

Adeimantus again agrees, and Socrates considers the poetry that would and would not encourage *sôphrosunê*. Starting with the first part of the gloss, about obedience to rulers, they express their approval of the commander Diomedes' charge to "sit quietly and be persuaded by my words" and the report of the Achaeans' "marching silently, fearing their commanders"; they express their disapproval, by contrast, of Achilles' insult of his superior, Agamemnon.[57] Socrates then turns to the next part of the gloss, about ruling desires: he disapproves of lines praising feasts, lamenting starvation, and representing the distraction and villainy into which sexual lust leads even the gods.[58]

At this point Socrates has picked out the kind of Homeric material that education in *sôphrosunê* must exclude when treated in the rough-and-ready terms adumbrated above. Socrates gives equal attention to both directions of ruling (ἄρχειν): allowing yourself to be ruled as befits your subordinate status, and ruling the desires that should be subordinate to yourself. Thus the picture of *sôphrosunê* matches what we see in Book 4: acknowledging sources of authority, both others and oneself. What differs is the attention to three specific bodily desires. As we will see in Chapter 11, Aristotle takes moderation of those three to define the scope of *sôphrosunê*. There remains a profound difference in Socrates' and Aristotle's analysis of *sôphrosunê*, since Aristotle's theory of *sôphrosunê* does not mention obedience to authorities, which Socrates' view puts in first place. Nevertheless, eating, drinking, and having sex are treated as important to this Book 3 conception of *sôphrosunê*. Socrates says that desires for these three activities are examples (τοιάδε) of the ones *sôphrosunê* must deal with that most people (ὡς πλήθει) think are the principal ones (as I translated above), literally the "biggest" (τὰ μέγιστα). "Biggest" could mean most essential for understanding the nature of the virtue, but it could also mean the most viscerally strong, the most psychically prominent in the experience of *sôphrosunê*'s

---

[57] Pl. *Rep.* 3.389e4–390a3. This last is a complicated case: Agamemnon has been drunk (οἰνοβαρές).
[58] Summary: 3.390a4–6; stories: 3.390a8–c8. For the rich background context of the passages quoted here, see Lake (2018, 92–100). Remarkably, Cornford (1941, 79), in his close analysis of the dialogue, simply skips over these paragraphs.

managing desires, or, what seems most likely to me, the most salient, the cases that come most readily to mind.[59]

Whichever way Socrates meant "biggest," the view of *sôphrosunê* presented here represents the view of "many people," a group that perhaps has not thought carefully about the scope of the virtue.[60] For the sake of Socrates' curricular adjustments, evidently it suffices to specify what people take *sôphrosunê* in the main to include.[61] The triad of eating, drinking, and sex does recur throughout the dialogue, often in the context of drinking parties and as the typical desires of tyrants and those who have failed to exercise reason and virtue. In some of those cases, Socrates compares those people to cattle or mentions their violent attempts at desire-satisfaction.[62] But since some tyrants are abstemious and have delusions of more than gastronomic grandeur, Socrates must simply be giving illustrations of the ways people notoriously, evidently, and uncontroversially go wrong. He never says that *sôphrosunê* is solely the control of these consummatory and copulative desires.

In fact, Socrates continues his analysis of *sôphrosunê*-cultivating poetry by saying that it should concern the excellence of those who can "endure anything."[63] This suggests that the virtue is a strength against any desire or deprivation.[64] He gives some examples. Odysseus exhorts himself not to retaliate against the suitors; he is to endure the urge for vengeance. Achilles is to ignore his thirst for money.[65] Achilles is also to forgo acting angrily against divine norms—he is not to disobey or disrespect gods, desecrate corpses, or mistreat war prisoners.[66] Indeed, since his father, Peleus, was most *sôphrôn*, Achilles in turn should never be described as agitated (ταραχῆς πλεώς) by avarice or contemptuous of (ὑπερηφανία) gods and men.[67]

After this sequence of examples, Socrates discusses further heroic and divine character traits that are inconsistent with an education in *sôphrosunê*. These

---

[59] A little later, lust is said to be the "biggest and sharpest" (μείζω ... ὀξυτέραν) of the pleasures (3.403a4), and therefore especially inconsistent with *sôphrosunê* (3.402e2–3).

[60] Some earlier translators thought that ὡς πλήθει meant "in general," but this would force a harsher inconsistency with the Book 4 discussion of the virtue. North (1966, 170) treats "as usually understood" or "for the majority" as also meaning "interpreted on a popular level."

[61] Adam (1902 ad loc.): "Plato is warning us not to regard his account of σωφροσύνη here as scientifically accurate and complete. It is the most obvious and conspicuous aspects of self-control which poets should chiefly impress upon the multitude, and to these Plato confines his attention."

[62] E.g., *Rep.* 3.398e, 9.571c, 9.573a, 9.586a.

[63] Pl. *Rep.* 3.390d1: καρτερίαι πρὸς ἅπαντα.

[64] Nettleship (1901, 96–98) sees *sôphrosunê* in the *Republic* as "control of excessive feeling in general"; he also sees Plato divide this into three categories: obedience to authorities; control of appetites; and control of wantonness, insolence, and pride.

[65] Pl. *Rep.* 3.390d7–391a1: δωροδόκους ("bribe-taking") and φιλοχρημάτους ("avaricious"). The same point is made at *Rep.* 8.555c8. There is no analysis here of money as simply an instrument of bodily-desire satisfaction.

[66] Pl. *Rep.* 3.391b1–6.

[67] Pl. *Rep.* 3.391c1–6.

negative examples again show that *sôphrosunê* means adhering to noble norms without capitulating to distractions, such as the hope for vengeance, wealth, or self-assertion. It means giving priority to one's standing obligations to one's work, community, and gods over one's roiling desires for pleasure, ease, or esteem.

The picture of *sôphrosunê* from Book 3 ends up matching the picture of it from Book 4. Here in Book 3 *sôphrosunê* is glossed as acting only on those desires that accord with authoritative principles. Socrates' two-aspect gloss on *sôphrosunê* presents this in two directions, outwardly and inwardly. Outwardly, a person decides on which desire he should act by attending to the guidelines of his superior, whether that be a human leader, the legion of the gods, or the community in which he is a member. Inwardly, a person directs his attention to his desires in general, ensuring that none causes a distraction from following such guidelines. In Book 4, Socrates analyzed *sôphrosunê* as a unification, a self-ification, of the desires. Those potentially distracting desires for oral intake and physical contact, for wealth and glory, and for vengeance and domination are to be satisfied only when doing so is compatible with one's reason-guided desires, where reason discovers those authoritative principles. Because of the city-soul analogy there, Socrates says that the lower desires, on the periphery of the self, should conform themselves to higher ones, at the heart of the self. This language, which gives agency to the desires themselves, is not found in the Book 3 picture. Nevertheless, both accounts appreciate that *sôphrosunê* means bringing a person's complex set of desires or goals into coherence *and* having that coherence be laudable: *which* coherence it is is set by authoritative norms. This is *sôphrosunê* as the normative constitution of oneself.[68] An education in *sôphrosunê*, then, is not merely an overcoming of one's animal nature, or the preservation of time for reflection free of piercing impulses, but the creation of a coordinated and norm-governed system of motivating desires: the constitution of agency.

The Epistemic Account of the *Charmides*

Critias' formulation of *sôphrosunê* as "doing one's own things" in the first half of the *Charmides*, as discussed earlier, never proved self-evidently true. But Critias also never rejects this definition focused on the virtue's practical and self-regarding dimensions, and Socrates never suggests that it has to go. Critias instead transforms it twice. In the first transformation, Critias introduces an

---

[68] Socrates' range of other remarks about the virtue throughout the *Republic* conforms with this picture of *sôphrosunê* as rational agency. The true opposites of *sôphrosunê* are indiscipline, hubris, and craziness (3.403a2, 3.403a6, 9.573b4); the cynical equivalent is cowardice (ἀνανδρία) (560d3). These are all morally condemnatory descriptions of the ineffective or overly prideful person, one who exaggerates his independence and authority.

explicitly normative dimension, defining *sôphrosunê* as "doing good things."[69] This is a remarkable idea, since it identifies *sôphrosunê* with virtuous activity simpliciter. Critias comes to abandon this formulation, however, when Socrates observes that one may do good things unknowingly; Critias decides that the *sôphrôn* person must also know that he is doing good things.[70] Critias does not explain this epistemic criterion, but he must think that doing good unknowingly is equivalent to doing good accidentally, and thus not being wholly responsible for the good's coming about. Critias presumably has in mind an epistemic picture of agency: agents bring about what they intend to bring about. Critias' original "doing one's own things" may have had this epistemic component implicitly—doing one's own thing presumes that you know what is your own—and Critias now makes it explicit.

Rather than modify his definition to "doing well knowingly," which would at once express the practical, normative, and epistemic dimensions of *sôphrosunê*, Critias zeroes in on the epistemic component. He reprises the self-regarding component from his original formulation: *sôphrosunê* is "knowing oneself."[71] This surprising reformulation has two features immediately and decisively in its favor. Because it is also the Delphic injunction, it already carries the deep ethical significance that Critias presumably wants to ascribe to *sôphrosunê*.[72] And then, because of its generality, it treats *sôphrosunê*'s deep ethical significance as coming from its being the virtue of intentional action, of knowing what one is doing and thus being its proper source; in short, of being an agent. Indirectly, this newest formulation has a third feature in its favor: Socrates' own manifestation of *sôphrosunê*, as identified and displayed throughout the dialogues, not least in the *Charmides* itself, gets linked explicitly with his (pursuit of) self-knowledge. A fourth feature in favor of Critias' "knowing oneself" definition is metatextual: it comes at the very midpoint of the dialogue, and nearly all the second half of the dialogue deals with it. Finally, an extratextual fifth feature in its favor is the Heraclitean precedence for it.[73] I infer, therefore, that Plato takes it very seriously, and does so because it seems on the right track.

The inference that "knowing oneself" really does get at *sôphrosunê* comes under stress, however, from two directions. First, Socrates' analysis of the definition in the dialogue's second half, following up on Critias' assumptions, seems deliberately obtuse. On that analysis, "knowing oneself" as imagined by Critias is shown not to be possible, much less beneficial, and thus not definitional of

---

[69] Pl. *Chrm.* 163e1–11.
[70] Pl. *Chrm.* 164a1–c6.
[71] Pl. *Chrm.* 164d4.
[72] On the significance of this passage, see North (1979, 61–65); Tuozzo (2000; 2011, 184–88); Morgan (2009); Moore (2015c, 60–71); Tsouna (2022, 159–69).
[73] Cf. Courcelle (1974, 18).

sôphrosunê. The perversity of this result does not lead either interlocutor to source their difficulties to Critias' image of self-knowledge.[74] Second, as indicated earlier in this chapter, the *Republic*'s official definition of *sôphrosunê* does not say anything about "knowing oneself"; far from defining it this way, the dialogue does not even mention self-knowledge.[75] On a developmentalist view of Plato, one might assume that the aptness of "knowing oneself" depended on Socrates' so-called intellectualism, a perspective abandoned or modified by the time of the *Republic* for one that appreciates the power of nonintellectual desire. On a less theory-laden view, the "knowing oneself" view could seem too ad hominem, plausible only in light of Critias' idiosyncratic vision of *sôphrosunê*, or, even if it does have broad enough validity, not the most perspicuous or powerful view, perhaps because of its vagueness and indeterminacy.[76] These stresses do not, however, disqualify the hypothesis, as I will show.

I begin with Critias' inability to sustain the "knowing oneself" definition. Critias asserts that self-knowledge is really knowledge of knowledge. This is his crucial assertion, because Socrates eventually reveals Critias' inability to defend the identification of *sôphrosunê* with his distinctive conception of the knowledge of knowledge. Socrates has not impugned the promise of self-knowledge itself, nor even of a knowledge of knowledge conceived in some other way. Why Critias dilates on the knowledge of knowledge reveals his understanding of *sôphrosunê* and self-knowledge. He takes *sôphrosunê* to have profound ethical value. And self-knowledge, too, uniquely so. For it to have a unique value, self-knowledge must differ from every other kind of knowledge. Critias decides that self-knowledge differs radically in the kind of thing it is knowledge *of*. Whereas every other kind of knowledge is about something other than itself, for example facts, phenomena, operations, or whatever else is to be learned, self-knowledge is knowledge of itself. Since what it is is knowledge, self-knowledge is knowledge of knowledge.

This "knowledge of knowledge" formulation makes good sense of some cases of self-knowledge. Consider the just-preceding exchange. Critias said that the *sôphrôn* person knows what he is doing when he is doing well, for example the doctor when healing successfully. Doing well in these cases depends on knowing what he is doing, for example knowing the medical art. Thus the *sôphrôn* person knows that he knows what he is doing. He has knowledge that he has knowledge. He can distinguish his expertise from mere lucky guesses or feelings of certitude. He can thus choose to act only in the ways he knows how to act. He can be fully

---

[74] For this first kind of problem, see Moore (2015c, 85–91).
[75] For self-knowledge in the *Republic*'s later books, see McCabe (2015); Ambury (2019).
[76] See Annas (1985); Moore (2015c, 239–46). Santas (1973, 109) believes that in the *Charmides* Plato simply does not know what *sôphrosunê* is. Garver (2018), by contrast, thinks that Critias' *sôphrosunê* is simply and dubiously an oligarchic virtue.

responsible for his actions; his actions may be caused by him, not by chance or some external force.[77] And he can identify what others know, and thereby delegate tasks to those who know how to do them. Thus the *sôphrôn* person is an agent in his own life and, if he is its leader, in the life of his city. One suspects that it is the civic leadership aspect, the expert coordination of the city's constituent parts, that especially attracts Critias' attention.[78]

Spelled out this way, Critias' knowledge-of-knowledge proposal has striking parallels with Socrates' harmony proposal in *Republic* Book 4. There Socrates spoke of the rational part giving authoritative direction to the desiderative part: at the political level, the government directs the populace; at the psychic level, reason directs the appetites. The populace and appetitive parts are not to be extinguished; they are simply to be guided to act, as they are able, in appropriate ways. They start out ill-coordinated and impetuous; they need supervision. Just so, in the *Charmides*, the knowledge-knowing leaders tell which workers to do what; they facilitate a division of expertise among the populace. Since people in general lack sufficient self-knowledge, they need supervision. In both dialogues, an informed leadership and capable mass are to be unified by rational principles—both dialogues end up emphasizing the understanding of what's good. And once unified, a person or a city may do what it truly intends to do; its actions are no longer the result of accident or peripheral feeling.

Yet Critias cannot sustain his new definition of *sôphrosunê*. Socrates presses it on two points: whether it is possible and, if so, whether it would yield any benefits. Critias cannot show that either would be the case. This may mostly impugn Critias' argumentative capacities, but it also puts up challenges to any account of agency.

Socrates begins by pressing on the possibility that knowledge could ever be wholly reflexive, taking only itself as its object (knowledge's form, so to speak), and not the usual objects of knowledge (knowledge's content, so to speak). He gets there by scrutinizing an assumption that Critias makes, that the knowledge of knowledge must do more than identify which epistemic states count as knowledge—it must also identify which knowledge something is a case of. Critias assumes that *sôphrosunê* can distinguish knowledge from mere opinion and also medicine, say, from navigation. Yet Critias expects too much from a wholly (or "formally") reflexive knowledge. Socrates shows this through analogy to other reflexive intentional states. In the case of vision, for instance, we have

---

[77] Cf. Arist. *Metaph*. E.2 1026b37–1027a5: "A housebuilder brings about health only by happenstance, for doing so is not in his nature but that of the doctor (though the housebuilder might also be a doctor).... Thus we say that it is happenstance, and though it is as if he brings it about, properly speaking he does not" (καὶ τὸ ὑγιάζειν δὲ τὸν οἰκοδόμον συμβεβηκός, ὅτι οὐ πέφυκε τοῦτο ποιεῖν οἰκοδόμος ἀλλὰ ἰατρός, ἀλλὰ συνέβη ἰατρὸν εἶναι τὸν οἰκοδόμον.... διὸ συνέβη, φαμέν, καὶ ἔστιν ὡς ποιεῖ, ἁπλῶς δ' οὔ).

[78] Pl. *Chrm*. 171d1–172a5; 173a7–d5.

reflexive seeing—we see sight—only when an instance of seeing manifests itself in the usual content of sight, namely color. We see ourselves seeing, for example, by looking in a mirror and focusing on the color pattern around the eyes and upper face typical of a person's looking at something. Just so, it would seem we could have reflexive knowledge only if what we know manifests itself in the usual content of knowledge, namely something concrete and learnable.[79] A student knows that she has understood a lesson—knows a case of knowledge—when that knowledge manifests itself in a perfect quiz score. Critias has not shown how an intentional state could grasp itself in its form—as a case of that intentional state—without also grasping its content (you cannot see a window that is too clear), and yet he repeatedly asserts that his brand of reflexive knowledge takes no content as its object.

Socrates brings up a bigger problem for reflexive knowledge. To the extent knowledge is a relational property (X knows Y), its possibility depends on the possibility of other reflexive relational properties. Yet the relational property "being double" cannot be reflexive, since something cannot be double itself (for it would also have to be half of itself). Other relational properties, like "moving something" or "burning something," are doubtfully reflexive. So knowledge is doubtfully reflexive.[80] Critias does not give an example of knowledge successfully applying to itself. So he gets stuck: he cannot show that knowledge of knowledge is possible, either in isolation from first-order objects of knowledge or in general.

The major obstacle to Critias' definition of *sôphrosunê* is his desire for epistemic purity. He wants knowledge of knowledge to be an expertise solely about knowledge. He wants this to make it unique. And he wants it to be the perfect leadership virtue. Cities are complex entities, needing lots of problem-solving expertise. Should a civic leader need to know these fields herself, she would be taking on a severe epistemic load. Some leadership theorists accept this load as the price to be paid; they counsel prospective leaders to learn military, financial, agricultural, and every other important kind of knowledge.[81] But others offer shortcuts around this burdensome polymathy to a single architectonic expertise. Gorgias and Polus advise that a leader learn rhetoric; with that expertise, she can mobilize generals, accountants, farmers, and others, without having to know what they know.[82] Critias shares the "learn-one-thing" vision. Instead of persuasive speech, however, Critias counsels "what knowledge is." As he sees it, if you apply that knowledge-identifying knowledge, you end up knowing where all the individual cases of knowledge are. With this knowledge, you can now delegate

---

[79] Pl. *Chrm.* 167c4–168a8.
[80] Pl. *Chrm.* 168b2–169a7.
[81] Xenophon accepts this, not least in his tale of Socrates' advice to Plato's brother Glaucon (*Mem.* 3.6).
[82] Pl. *Grg.* 452d–e, 456a–b.

tasks perfectly, without having to micromanage. But if, as Socrates suggests, reflexive knowledge is doubtful—the capacity to know a case of knowledge—then delegation is impossible. And even were reflexive knowledge possible, it would not help with effective delegation unless it included what the cases of knowledge were *of*; and by Critias' hypothesis, it does not include that. Agricultural tasks might then be delegated to doctors. And this is not effective leadership. The shortcut ends up in brambles.

Critias fails to defend his knowledge-of-knowledge idea, but its attractions make it worth trying to salvage. Salvaging it means no longer seeing *sôphrosunê* as a shortcut. *Sôphrosunê* cannot delegate by itself. The *sôphrôn* leader needs to know who has what knowledge. To do this perfectly, she would need to know the various fields of civically relevant knowledge herself. Assigning medical tasks to a doctor takes her ability to distinguish someone with medical knowledge from someone who lacks it and from someone who has a different knowledge, such as rhetoric. This ability is medical knowledge itself. But if the leader already has this medical knowledge, then he does not need to delegate. Of course, she might have only a few true beliefs about medicine, enough to figure out who probably is a doctor even if not enough to weed out the most sophisticated imposters. In this case, she would have more cause to delegate but less confidence in its success. The more you need to delegate, the less effective it is to do so. The more effective it is, the less you need it. So *sôphrosunê* is not a shortcut. How, then, is it at all beneficial?

Socrates has an idea. Critias has been assuming a situation where various people already have various fields of expertise, and the task is to assign tasks correctly among them. Socrates assumes a different situation, one where people still need to acquire knowledge. Socrates notes that learning would improve if "knowledge were kept in view" (προσκαθορῶντι τὴν ἐπιστήμην). If you knew what knowledge is, and so what counted as knowledge, you could test to see whether your (or somebody else's) beliefs failed to meet the strictures of knowledge.[83] And if they did in fact fail, and thus you came to acknowledge a lack of expertise, knowing what knowledge is could suggest better ways to keep trying to acquire that expertise. *Sôphrosunê* so understood could never confirm that something is knowledge in a certain field, but it could deny that something is knowledge (in general and thus also in a certain field), and thereby prescribe caution in acting on its basis. This has profound leadership relevance, allowing one to debunk misplaced confidence, as Socrates does with Critias in the *Charmides* and reports doing with many other statesmen, poets, and orators in the *Apology*. It also allows one to test one's own presumptions of expertise. Socrates highlights this in the *Charmides*, and acknowledgments of his investigative and epistemic

---

[83] Pl. *Chrm.* 171d1–172c3; see Moore and Raymond (2019, 97–98, 110–12).

inadequacies provide a basso continuo to the conversations across the dialogues. Besides testing, the knowledge of knowledge could recommend ways to improve the epistemic reliability of one's beliefs.

Rendered Socratically, *sôphrosunê* as the knowledge of knowledge is the capacity to forbear from acting on epistemically shaky grounds and from delegating to those with epistemic deficiencies. This could seem to Callicles a dissipation of agency, sensitive only to the hesitation, diffidence, deferral, inaction. But to Socrates it is a condition of agency, since it ensures that one's decisions derive from actual expertise.[84] Similarly, it may seem a weakness that the Socratic examiner can help reveal inadequacies in a person's views but cannot ensure that this person won't try to act anyway. Yet what she does do is help her interlocutor to adopt the same self-scrutiny and commitment to action-guiding knowledge that she has. She helps her interlocutor learn the knowledge of knowledge, helping her become *sôphrôn*.

Reading Critias' "knowledge of knowledge" from a Socratic perspective has a further consequence. *Sôphrosunê* cannot be the burden of a single leader or corps of leaders; it must be shared throughout society.[85] Anyone who believes himself an expert or wants to rely on an expert needs this auxiliary expertise-assessment and -acquisition expertise. A doctor realizes that she can practice medicine but that only a certain professional contact, who is a business attorney, can structure a fair insurance scheme. The self-knowledge and complementary skill at assessing others' knowledge that here together constitute *sôphrosunê* amount to mutual agreement concerning the execution of various social functions. This may involve acknowledging some people as expert legislators or administrators and others as expert executors of subsidiary functions.

This consequence legitimizes Plato's attention to Critias' definition of *sôphrosunê*, especially as reformulated on the prompting of Socrates. It implies an attractive view of the virtue as relevant to political arrangements. It also returns us to the *Republic* conception. A civic-scale *sôphrosunê* involves everyone's acknowledging everyone else's respective authority and responsibility. Each party to the civic constitution does their own things; central to this is disavowing omniscience and giving due respect to those who know, both leaders and those with a more local expertise. But not only does the *Charmides* give an epistemic parallel to the *Republic* model of *sôphrosunê*; it may also supplement it. We did not notice self-knowledge as an ingredient in the *Republic*'s picture of *sôphrosunê*, but we might now say that the capacity for a psychic part in a *sôphrôn*

---

[84] Clark (2018) takes a similar view, claiming that *sôphrosunê* amounts to knowledge of the value of one's specific intentional states—in other words, the ability to evaluate their aptness. And Kosman (2020, 75, 85) argues that "*sôphrosunê* produces . . . a robust but appropriate self" as a virtue of self-consciousness.

[85] A point approached by Adams (2020).

soul to recognize its relative authoritativeness just *is* that part's self-knowledge. For instance, the lower part of the soul can appreciate that it needs to rely on the higher part only when it can appreciate the incompleteness or inaccuracy of its vision of the good, and also, since it can distinguish between the concept of an actual good and that of an apparent good, that the higher part has a sharper vision of the good.

Platonic Agency

We have now seen two complementary formulations of *sôphrosunê* as the virtue of agency. Seen epistemically, *sôphrosunê* is the capacity to act on knowledge and not adventitious views. Seen epithumatically, *sôphrosunê* is the capacity to act on rational desires and not haphazard or even habitual impulses.

The *Charmides*, a short dialogue, ends aporetically; the analysis floated here did not undergo rigorous Socratic testing. The *Republic*, despite being much longer, was no less conversational, tentative, and incomplete.[86] So despite the theoretical attitude Socrates has taken toward *sôphrosunê* in these two dialogues, we cannot attribute to him or Plato a robust, capacious, or systematic theory of *sôphrosunê*, at least not with total confidence.

Compared to the other Socratics and to Aristotle, Plato does not distinguish *sôphrosunê* and *enkrateia* and, as we have already seen, he often leaves the connection between *sôphrosunê* and wisdom nebulous. Obviously for Plato these virtues or capacities belong in close connection, and it is worth talking about them together. This is what we see Plato do especially in the *Laws*. In the *Statesman* he brings up the ambiguous relation between *sôphrosunê* and courage, too—associated dramatically in the *Charmides*, and bound by *sôtêria* language in the *Republic*. So to those two dialogues we next turn.

---

[86] Cf. Peterson (2012, 90–165).

10
Plato 3—*Sôphrosunê* with Wisdom in Two Late Dialogues

Two Late Dialogues

The centrality of *sôphrosunê* to the *Charmides* and the *Republic* makes unexceptionable the idea that *sôphrosunê* plays a major role in Plato's political theorizing. In the shorter dialogue, this came out in two ways. Charmides, among the best prospects for the next generation of leaders, is praised as superlatively *sôphrôn*; Socrates wonders whether he really is, and whether his cousin and guardian, Critias, knows enough about the virtue to guide his development in it. His and Critias' political leadership, at least the last months of it (in 403 BCE), are known from history, in their participation in classical Athens' greatest civic turmoil. This is Plato's inquiry into *sôphrosunê* from the prosopographical perspective. From the analytic perspective, Socrates discusses the benefits of *sôphrosunê* in terms of civic success, as a virtue that conduces to a city's flourishing, and does so through a sort of epistemic supervision: determining who knows what, and ensuring that actions flow from those who know how to do them. Naturally these two perspectives intersect: the importance of Charmides' and Critias' being *sôphrôn* depends on their providing that epistemic supervision. Yet without a successful definition of *sôphrosunê*, or a vision of a political constitution that would institutionalize this epistemic supervision, the *Charmides* does not provide a program for sophronizing a city.

The *Republic* comes to a similar point, if with less evident historical irony.[1] Book 3 describes the literary-poetic curriculum of the guardians who are to acquire *sôphrosunê*. Book 4 describes the fundamental organization of the city that is to be *sôphrôn*. Though both reveal Plato's insight into *sôphrosunê*, they too hardly amount to a constitutional proposal. For one, a leader's education in *sôphrosunê* requires more than well-selected cultural performances. For another, the *sôphrôn* city requires that all classes, not just the leaders, share in the virtue, but Socrates and his friends do not set out the ethical education of the

---

[1] Our knowledge of the *Republic*'s historical irony is limited by the little we know about Glaucon and Adeimantus, though some authors believe Glaucon, with Critias, came to a bad end (e.g., Howland 2018). For what irony is to be found in Book 1, see Gifford (2001).

other classes. (There is the added problem that Socrates' analysis of *sôphrosunê* undergoes no scrutiny.)[2]

From neither dialogue did we expect elaborated policy proposals. Two dialogues from later in Plato's life might seem to fill in this absence. The *Statesman* and the *Laws* turn their concern from the nature of *sôphrosunê*—neither defines the virtue—to its promotion within the populace: from analysis they turn to practice; from the abstract and puzzling they turn to the concrete and stable. These dialogues are worth studying as further evidence for the seriousness with which Plato takes *sôphrosunê*, a seriousness predicated on the virtue's crucial status in a person's maturation as a rational decision-maker.

These two dialogues do more, however, than identify *sôphrosunê*'s core role in constitutional design. They complicate its analysis in the way we have already seen adumbrated in Plato's *Phaedo*, in Chapter 8; in Xenophon's *Memorabilia* 3.9, in Chapter 7; and implicitly throughout Plato's and Xenophon's works. The question: How, if at all, is wisdom part of *sôphrosunê*? It is identical? Or is it always or usually coextensive? Or is it a necessary constituent? Or are there two kinds of *sôphrosunê*, one an unreasoning disposition, the other the same disposition but now guided by wisdom? The *Statesman* treats *sôphrosunê* in the first instance as a normatively neutral inclination to tranquility and reserve—in effect Charmides' first definition in the *Charmides*. This *sôphrosunê* becomes valuable with the addition of thoughtfulness, in the form of true belief about the times to be tranquil and reserved and the times not to be. The *Laws*, a much longer dialogue, takes several perspectives: in one, that *sôphrosunê* is a condition for the goodness of any other virtue; in another, that it is a set of desires that often but not always conduce to good and moderate action; in a third, near the dialogue's programmatic beginning, a textual crux on exactly this question obfuscates Plato's view. Neither dialogue provides a satisfactory resolution to the question, but they allow the question to be asked with new clarity. And Aristotle, probably in the same decades, will address it directly, distinguishing between two kinds of *sôphrosunê*, a natural and an "authoritative" version, the latter amounting to the addition of wisdom or thoughtfulness, *phronêsis*, to the former. Aristotle's solution is not altogether clear, but its motivations may now be.

The *Statesman*

The *Statesman* presents *sôphrosunê* as centrally important to civic life and culminates in an analogy between weaving and leadership.[3] The king must

---

[2] See Peterson (2011, 90–165) on the lack of examination of views set out in the *Republic*.
[3] Pl. *Pol*. 306a1. For the significance of this ending: Rosen (1995, 182–90); Lane (1998, 171–82); Rowe (2000, 251–53).

integrate, as warp and woof, two types of citizens, those with distinctive and even antithetical dispositions. The dispositions are those associated with courage and *sôphrosunê*.

The dialogue's concluding section begins with an abstract point: the Eleatic Visitor says that it is hard to understand the relationship between a "part of virtue" and "virtue" itself. People tend to consider the parts of virtue to be sympathetic (φίλος) to one another, and perhaps those in philosophical circles would argue against the view that the parts are "different in kind." Nevertheless, the Visitor observes, while courage and *sôphrosunê* are both parts of virtue, they are so different as to be opposed.[4] In a city full of people manifesting the various virtues, those people might not be sympathetic to one another. The job of a statesman is to unify them.

The Visitor achieves this view of virtue's disunity by attending to the behavioral aspects of *sôphrosunê* that Socrates elsewhere de-emphasizes. People use the term *sôphrosunê*, he says, when they praise things that happen "gently" (ἠρεμαίας); they call tranquil and *sôphronika* admirable actions, whether mental or practical, when they are slow and soft (βραδέα καὶ μαλακά), sounds that are smooth and deep (λεῖα καὶ βαρέα), rhythm and music that are suitably slow (ἐν καιρῷ βραδυτῆτι), and in general, all that they call orderly (τὸ τῆς κοσμιότητος).[5] This description of *sôphrôn* actions, as walking and talking and doing everything else calmly and peaceably and in an orderly way, is familiar from Phocylides, Aristophanes' *Clouds*, and Xenophon's *Spartan Constitution*. It is notably an extension of Charmides' first definition of *sôphrosunê* in the *Charmides*. Courage, by contrast, people associate with "quickness, intensity, and sharpness, of mind, body, and voice,"[6] which are the opposites of slowness and softness that Socrates brought up when evaluating Charmides' first definition.

But the lesson of the *Charmides* is not lost on the Visitor; he does not think that people judge every case of gentleness a case of *sôphrosunê*. Gentle actions are praised as *sôphrôn* only when they are done at the right time (τοῦ καιροῦ), just as intense actions count as courageous only when they are done at the right time.[7] The linguistic evidence shows this, he says: when slowness would be inappropriate, a slow person or action is called "cowardly and sluggish" (δειλὰ καὶ βλακικά); when sharpness and intensity are not called for, a person with those qualities is called "hubristic and manic" (ὑβριστικὰ καὶ μανικά). So *sôphrosunê* is

---

[4] Pl. *Pol.* 306b9–11.
[5] Pl. *Pol.* 307a8–b2. The present instance is the only use of σωφρονικός in Plato; it also appears in Xenophon once (*Mem.* 1.3.9) and several times in Aristotle, once where the "natural virtues" are discussed (e.g., *Rh.* 1390a14; *EN* 6.13 1144b5).
[6] Pl. *Pol.* 306e4–5.
[7] Pl. *Pol.* 307b9, cf. b6: ἄκαιρα.

not properly a gentle disposition; it is having that disposition and acting on it at the right time. And courage likewise.[8]

The Visitor eventually identifies the condition that allows one to act on those gentle dispositions at the right time and thus be *sôphrôn*: true and stable beliefs (ἀληθῆ δόξαν μετὰ βεβαιώσεως) about what is fine, just, and good.[9] These beliefs (τῶν δοξῶν) transform a person with an orderly nature (τὸ τῆς κοσμίας φύσεως) from someone at risk of being merely simple-minded (εὐηθείας) into someone genuinely *sôphrôn* and thoughtful (ὄντως σῶφρον καὶ φρόνιμον) about civic affairs.[10] Accordingly, *sôphrosunê* is the natural disposition to gentleness governed by stable true beliefs about the norms that govern human life; and being *sôphrôn* is tantamount to being *phronimos*, thoughtful or wise. It is notable that the Visitor does not expressly stipulate that a person needs knowledge of what's good; he treats as sufficient beliefs that are correct and unchanging. Insofar as virtue is concerned, Socrates in the *Meno* despaired of distinguishing knowledge and stable true belief (97a–98c). It is also notable that the Visitor does not say that *sôphrosunê* is the disposition to gentleness supplemented by *phronêsis* but rather that the disposition plus stable true beliefs amount to *sôphrosunê* and *phronêsis* alike. He does not quite identify *sôphrosunê* and *phronêsis*, for conceivably *phronêsis* could name those stable true beliefs. But he may think that being *phronimos* is being "thoughtful in action," and that a gentle disposition allows for such thoughtfulness. The result would be that *sôphrosunê* and *phronêsis* are two aspects of the same capacity, the former emphasizing the gentleness, the latter emphasizing the timeliness.

The Eleatic Visitor has, at any rate, distinguished two uses of the term *sôphrosunê*: what is a syndrome of dispositions rather than a virtue; and what is a virtue, a state that involves stable true beliefs about action-guiding norms. It is the task of the statesman to induce these stable true beliefs into his citizenry. But the statesman has more than this epistemic task; he also has to deal with those dispositions. The Visitor claims that people have two opposed character types, a *sôphrosunê* type and a courage type, and that cities polarize this opposition. Patterns of romantic attraction and heredity mean that those of the *sôphrosunê* type tend to marry and concentrate those traits in their offspring; the same goes for the other type. This surely inhibits community integration. But this increased gentleness and intensity affect individual levels of agency. People who are especially orderly, for instance, readily accept the tranquil life and keep to themselves.

---

[8] On the complicated relationship between virtues and natural dispositions here, see Kamtekar (2021, 218–29); for dissatisfaction with the course of the argument, see Irwin (1995, 339–41).

[9] Pl. *Pol.* 309c5. Cp. *Rep.* 4.430b3–4, on courage as "the power and preservation of correct belief (δόξης ὀρθῆς)" about what is fearful, etc., and similarly *La.* 192c8, where courage is suggested to be endurance (not a virtue) plus wisdom (μετὴ φρονήσεως καρτερία).

[10] Pl. *Pol.* 309e5–8. Lane (1998, 179) argues that this passage brings back the familiar four-member canon of virtues.

Their retirement seems to protect their identity and independence; by seeking to do only their own thing, they *can* do their own thing, which is a good way to conceive of their agency. Those who are especially intense, similarly, live with self-assertion and do not submit to others' wills; they too do as they wish. And yet too much of these dispositions subvert that agency. The excessively gentle end up at the mercy of attackers, becoming vulnerable to enslavement.[11] The Visitor says that those who have too strong a sense of shame (αἰδοῦς ... λίαν πλήρης ψυχή)—he means those whose *sôphrosunê*-related traits dominate—become rather torpid (νωθεστέρα) and end up quite maimed (ἀναπηροῦσθαι).[12] Those who are too headstrong come to the same end: they fight too much, which increases the risk of loss and destroyed lands, and of becoming enslaved to their enemies.[13] The purely tranquil person underplays her power, and the purely intense person overplays her power; both lose control of their own lives. Continued agency requires that those dispositions be diluted and diffused. Within an individual there must be both inclinations, to gentleness and to intensity, to be acted upon at various times; within a city there must be specialists in both ways of acting.[14] The Visitor calls this eugenics and social organization "weaving." One disposition is moderated by looping it around another; harshly yellow and obscurely black yarns blend into an attractive dusky orange. The dispositions themselves, natural as they are, are not restrained, only reduced in potency.

The statesman combines weaving and teaching, the dispositional and the epistemic, to bring about properly actualized citizens. His people, having stable true beliefs about what to do, can rely now on their gentleness, now on their intensity. Their virtues have been unified: while they are distinctive in their natural substratum, they are governed by the same understanding and coincide in a successful person. From the Visitor's perspective, *sôphrosunê* is not the unique virtue of agency (even if he gives the majority of his attention to it); it is one of two, courage being the other one. As we saw in Chapter 8, courage is Callicles' agency-related virtue of choice, and Callicles is the best antitheorist of *sôphrosunê* we have seen; in the *Gorgias*, *sôphrosunê* was Socrates' preference. The Visitor thus provides a kind of rapprochement between Callicles' and Socrates' views. Intense boldness is no more valuable, by itself, than a self-denying reticence; they must be mixed, with this mixture governed by an intelligence (as Callicles realizes) that amounts to an understanding of fundamental norms (as Socrates advances). Of course, Socrates in the *Gorgias* already provided an integration, treating courage as an expression of *sôphrosunê*. And in the *Statesman*, the Visitor allows

---

[11] Pl. *Pol.* 307e1–308a2.
[12] Pl. *Pol.* 310d10–e3.
[13] Pl. *Pol.* 308a4–9.
[14] Pl. *Pol.* 311a6–9: *sôphrôn* rulers are cautious, just, and capable care-takers, but they lack a certain keenness (δριμύτητος), a sharp and practical vigor (ἰταμότητος ὀξείας καὶ πρακτικῆς).

that "true *sôphrosunê*" amounts to true thoughtfulness, being able to act gently when the occasion calls for it (and not when it does not).

The *Statesman* focuses in a distinctive way on virtue and agency, equally attentive to the range of relevant dispositions and the epistemic capacities needed to govern them. Other Platonic dialogues did not give such an expressly balanced view, at least not one in this vocabulary, but retrospectively we can see their having come to the same point. The *Protagoras*, for example, did not draw out these separable components, though Protagoras, who identified *aidôs* with *sôphrosunê*, seems to have treated of the virtue as self-restraint, and Socrates, who identified *sôphrosunê* with wisdom, seems to have treated of the virtue as understanding what to do. The *Republic*, with its joint language of desire-mastery and authority-obedience, combined in its own terms the dispositional and the epistemically norm-governed, even as it gave a distinctive role to wisdom. The *Gorgias*, as we have seen, dramatizes a pivot from talking about *sôphrosunê* as de-intensification to talking about it as the excellence at accomplishing what one ought to accomplish. And the *Charmides* got closest, explicitly entertaining gentleness and *aidôs* as definitions of *sôphrosunê*, but eventually finding that it is reliably beneficial only if it involves knowledge of what's good.

Throughout his literary career, Plato circles around the problem of *sôphrosunê*, animating a range of conversations, each with its own starting point, about the way the virtue underwrites human maturity and rational agency. We now turn to Plato's final—evidently incomplete but provocatively so—statements about *sôphrosunê*.

The *Laws*

Plato's *Laws* begins from an outlook related to the one in the *Statesman*: some constitutions promote courage but not *sôphrosunê*; city founders should cultivate both virtues in their citizenry, but especially *sôphrosunê*. Unlike the *Statesman*, however, the speakers in the *Laws* gloss these two virtues not in terms of characteristic modes of behavior but the valence of the psychological impulse they manage. Courage overcomes, endures, and controls pains; *sôphrosunê* manages pleasures. And whereas in the *Statesman* the Eleatic Visitor emphasizes balancing or integrating these virtue-associated dispositions and conveying stable true beliefs about the fine, just, and good, in the *Laws* the Athenian Visitor emphasizes the education of people's desires from the earliest age. In the *Statesman* case, sound beliefs allow for the exercise of one's dispositions at the right moment. This allows continued independence, the avoidance of submission to another's will. In the *Laws* case, the problem is less a matter of autonomy than of morality: a successful action may not benefit others. One can desire something whose attainment is incompatible with others' interests, and such desires do not make for a flourishing city. People must align their own interests with others', through the instruments of cultural education.

Just as the *Laws*' analysis of *sôphrosunê* differs from that of the *Statesman*, it differs from that of the *Charmides* and *Republic* as well. It develops none of the candidate definitions in the shorter dialogue. While the *Republic* Book 3 investigation of *sôphrosunê* includes control over some pleasure-directed desires, which constitutes the focus of the *Laws*' analysis, it also adds obedience to authorities, not a focal-point of the *Laws*. The *Republic* Book 4 investigation is even further away, formulating the virtue as agreement within the soul about the most authoritative kinds of reason for action, a discussion of psychic divisions of power that does not recur in the *Laws*. And the *Laws* does not take the same approach as the *Protagoras* or *Gorgias* do: except implicitly in one case, there is no equivalence drawn with wisdom or justice, and it is not presented as psychic orderliness. But as with the *Statesman*, which we saw differing in vocabulary and emphasis from the earlier dialogues but preserving a moral-theoretical sensibility, so too the *Laws* should be seen as asking its own questions about the virtue, and coming to answers similar in content, if distinct in formulation.

We will see that the *Laws*' presentation of *sôphrosunê* as control over pleasures, a counterpart of courage's control over pains, serves as the clearest bridge between Plato's and Aristotle's *Nicomachean Ethics* accounts of the virtue. This is not surprising, given that Plato wrote it in the years of Aristotle's active ethical reflection, and Aristotle studied the dialogue closely. There are divergences, notably that Plato's Athenian does not so expressly restrict *sôphrosunê*'s scope to "natural" "bodily" pleasures, as Aristotle does; he is willing to treat it as a more broadly foundational virtue. Yet he also wants to consider more precisely the relationship between *sôphrosunê* and wisdom, as the Eleatic Visitor did, and as Aristotle will. Indeed, given the indeterminacy of the Athenian Visitor's position on this view, we might expect Aristotle to do him better. To some extent Aristotle does provide a more precise account; but, as we will see in the next chapter, it leaves many questions open. In any event, the *Laws* is extraordinarily long; we will here focus on three issues that address this relationship between virtue and reason.[15] Most interesting is a textual crux about the precise point. Then I look at two formulations of the idea of self-control. I finish by studying the famous image of the marionette puppet from Book 1.

---

[15] On the major themes, see Laks (2000).

"... with or without *nou*"

The *Laws* begins with an implicit question: what should a constitution aim for? The Athenian Visitor allows that the Spartan and Cretan constitutions aim at virtue, but he criticizes this aim for its partiality, given that it aims only at courage, a part of virtue. This observation occasions a speech on the so-called human and divine goods toward which every legislator should aim. The Athenian gives ranked lists of the four types of each kind of good. He starts with the so-called lesser goods, which in turn depend on the greater.

> ἔστι δὲ τὰ μὲν ἐλάττονα ὧν ἡγεῖται μὲν ὑγίεια, κάλλος δὲ δεύτερον, τὸ δὲ τρίτον ἰσχὺς εἴς τε δρόμον καὶ εἰς τὰς ἄλλας πάσας κινήσεις τῷ σώματι, τέταρτον δὲ δὴ πλοῦτος οὐ τυφλὸς ἀλλ' ὀξὺ βλέπων, ἄνπερ ἅμ' ἕπηται φρονήσει· (Pl. *Laws* 1.631c2–5)

The leader of the lesser [goods] is health; beauty is second; the third is strength in running and all the other physical activities; and in fourth place is a wealth that is not blind but is sharp-sighted—that is, taking its lead from *phronêsis*.

Then he gives the greater goods:

> ὃ δὴ πρῶτον αὖ τῶν θείων ἡγεμονοῦν ἐστιν ἀγαθῶν, ἡ φρόνησις, δεύτερον δὲ μετὰ νοῦ[ν] σώφρων ψυχῆς ἕξις, ἐκ δὲ τούτων μετ' ἀνδρείας κραθέντων τρίτον ἂν εἴη δικαιοσύνη, τέταρτον δὲ ἀνδρεία. (Pl. *Laws* 1.631c5–d1)

Now, the one that is first and leader of the divine goods is *phronêsis*; second *meta nou[n]* is a *sôphrôn* state of the soul; from these, mixed with courage, would be the third, justice; and fourth is courage.

The lesser tier of goods, ranked from best to worst, is health, beauty, strength, and wealth if properly directed. The Athenian does not explain this ranking; he probably takes it as the basically consensus view about the ingredients to an overall happy life, and wealth unqualified probably seems to him not a good at all.[16]

---

[16] The same four lesser goods appear at *Meno* 87e, though with the order of beauty and strength reversed. At *Laws* 2.661a6–b4, the Athenian ranks these goods now omitting an explicit reference to strength: they are said to be health, beauty, wealth, then "a great many other things," including excellent perception, and the tyrant's ability to do whatever he desires, and then immortality (λέγεται γὰρ ὡς ἄριστον μὲν ὑγιαίνειν, δεύτερον δὲ κάλλος, τρίτον δὲ πλοῦτος, μυρία δὲ ἄλλα ἀγαθὰ λέγεται· καὶ γὰρ ὀξὺ ὁρᾶν καὶ ἀκούειν καὶ πάντα ὅσα ἔχεται τῶν αἰσθήσεων εὐαισθήτως ἔχειν, ἔτι δὲ καὶ τὸ ποιεῖν τυραννοῦντα ὅτι ἂν ἐπιθυμῇ, καὶ τὸ δὴ τέλος ἁπάσης μακαριότητος εἶναι τὸ πάντα ταῦτα κεκτημένον ἀθάνατον εἶναι γενόμενον ὅτι τάχιστα). This list mirrors one found in a drinking song that Socrates quotes in the *Gorgias*: ὑγιαίνειν μὲν ἄριστόν ἐστιν, τὸ δὲ δεύτερον καλὸν γενέσθαι, τρίτον δέ, ὥς φησιν ὁ ποιητὴς τοῦ σκολιοῦ, τὸ πλουτεῖν ἀδόλως (451e3–5; this scolion is 890 *PMG*,

The ranking of the greater tier of goods—*phronêsis*, something instantiating *sôphrosunê*, justice, and courage—also goes without explanation, as do the qualifications and explanations. This time, however, it is harder to see that this gradient reflects communal agreement about the virtues, since, after all, the Spartans and Cretans seem to have vaunted courage above all.

Relevant to us is the precise state of the second entry, about *sôphrosunê*. There is a textual crux concerning the prepositional phrase. Our Plato manuscripts all record μετὰ νοῦν σώφρων, with νοῦν spelled with a terminal nu. That reading also appears in a late-antique witness to that passage, Stobaeus (c. fifth-century CE).[17] But two other late-antique witnesses to the passage, the manuscripts of Eusebius (fl. ca. 300 CE) and Theodoret (fifth century), record μετὰ νοῦ σώφρων, that is, νοῦ spelled without the terminal consonant, as does an early Arabic translation.[18] As it turns out, most recent editors follow these latter witnesses, against the Plato manuscripts.[19] The difference is significant: νοῦν (*noun*) is the accusative, νοῦ (*nou*) the genitive, and the meaning of the preposition μετά (*meta*) differs depending on the case it takes. In the reading from the Plato manuscripts (hereinafter the "MS reading"), with the accusative, *meta* means "after," furnishing "and second, following mind [*nous* = *phronêsis*] (sc. which is first), is a *sôphrôn* state of the soul."[20] In the "Eusebian reading," with the genitive, *meta* means "with," furnishing "and second, a mind-accompanied *sôphrôn* state of the soul."[21] The relevance for the ranking of divine goods is clear. On the MS reading, a *sôphrôn* state of the soul is simply second-best, behind *phronêsis* but ahead of justice and courage. On the Eusebian reading, by contrast, a *sôphrôn* state of the

and includes "being young with friends" [ἡβᾶν μετὰ τῶν φίλων] in fourth place). The Athenian gives this Book 2 list while arguing that certain so-called goods are not actually good without virtue, either justice (2.661b7, d2), or justice and piety (b6), or justice and all the other virtues (ἀρετῆς ἁπάσης, c4). For lists of human goods, see Kurke (2011, 347–51).

[17] Stob. 2.7.4a,25 (though Wachsmuth [in Wachsmuth and Hense 1884–1992] emends the text to μετὰ νοῦ to bring it into line with Eusebius and Theodoret). Such is the reading printed in Stallbaum (1859; this happens to be the basis of the long in-print Jowett translation of the *Laws*). Bobonich (2002, 124), who provides the most careful analysis of the related philosophical issues, also follows the direct tradition, but does not discuss his reasons. So too Pangle (1980, 10 with 515n27) who otherwise follows des Places' text (which prints μετὰ νοῦ).

[18] Eusebius *Praep. evang.* 12.16.4,2, μετὰ νοῦ, ed. Mras (1956); Theodoret *de cur.* 6.34,10, μετὰ νοῦ (νοῦν V), ed. Raeder (1904). A manuscript in the Bodleian library's oriental collection, Marsh 539, contains the Arabic *ma'a l-'aql*, "(along) with the intellect" (Moseley 2018, 173), obviously translating μετὰ νοῦ.

[19] E.g., Baiter, von Orelli, and Winckelmann (1839); Schanz (1879); Burnet (1907); des Places (1951). Laks (2022, 206n3) follows these editors and Schöpsdau (1994, 184) on the grounds that the manuscript reading is, while possible, "less interesting."

[20] The equivalence of *nous* and *phronêsis* is indicated several lines later, at 631d5.

[21] Or as in Saunders (1970) (found also in Cooper 1997): "the habitual self-control that uses reason"; Bury (1926): "rational temperance of soul"; Schofield and Griffith (2016): "a rational state of soul characterized by self-control"; Rowe (1979, 344), "a ἕξις of soul which is temperate in a reasoned way."

soul is second-best only when *nous* is added to it; the implication might be that, like wealth, it could readily be imagined in its unqualified state, and in that case, it would be either less good or not a divine good at all.

This crux brilliantly captures a problem that has been coming into view across the decades of *sôphrosunê* debate we have studied. Resolving it would clarify the relation that Plato's Athenian sees between *sôphrosunê* and reason. Seen from another angle, it would clarify the default kind of *sôphrosunê* at play here: either the dispositional sort of the *Statesman*, to which something epistemic must be added to achieve full virtuehood, or the ideal sort already treated as normative in the other dialogues, one in which a dispositional and an epistemic component need not be distinguished, perhaps because they are already so mutually infused. *Sôphrosunê* and reason would be relatively distant if a *sôphrôn* state of the soul was one that had the power to control some of its desires, but not know which of them, or when, or how much, or if its actions were sometimes inappropriately slow, gentle, and smooth. This is the possibility contemplated in the *Statesman*, where a useful city leader would make sure that dispositionally *sôphrôn* people would *also* have stable true beliefs about the good. This possibility would also presage Aristotle's view of *sôphrosunê* as a desire-moderation somehow perfected, made authoritative by, and ultimately directed by *phronêsis*. But *sôphrosunê* and reason would by contrast be relatively near if a *sôphrôn* state of the soul just meant following authoritative norms, or having self-knowledge, or being able to do what's good. Socrates has adopted this position through the works of Plato and Xenophon studied in the previous three chapters. The contrast may be put in high language: is *sôphrosunê* a virtue of agency, or only the raw material for such a virtue? Is it more like reason itself or is it more like self-mastery and endurance? The difference between a *sôphrosunê* that needs a rational supplement and one where it is already built in may seem unimpressive. But the debates of the fifth and early fourth centuries show that it matters. People want to know whether *sôphrosunê* is basically a form of desire-control that, depending on its degree of rational supplement, can go more or less well, or the capacity for norm-governance, such that an unreasoning *sôphrosunê* hardly makes any sense.

Patterns of Greek usage seem to tell in favor of the MS reading, "[second] after 'mind' (acc.)." Across Greek literature, the locution δεύτερον δὲ μετὰ ("and second after . . .") has about twenty instances, and in all but two cases, both close in time to Eusebius and Theodoret, the *meta* is followed by an accusative.[22] Thus, for centuries, Greek literature has parallels only for the MS reading of "after 'mind'." But we can understand how this mistake could have been introduced by the time of the Eusebian reading. In Plato, the genitive form μετὰ νοῦ by

---

[22] Lesbonax *Politicus* 3,5 (δεύτερον δὲ μετὰ τοῦ βαρβάρου γενόμενοι καὶ σύμμαχοι κείνῳ καταστάντες); Σ Eur. *Or.* 1651 (δεύτερον δὲ μετὰ τρεῖς γενεὰς Κέφαλος).

itself (that is, not following by a construction like "and second") is rather more common than the accusative form μετὰ νοῦν. This means that a scribe would be more likely to change from the MS to the Eusebian reading—either accidentally or intentionally—rather than vice versa; put in other terms, for a Plato copyist, μετὰ νοῦν would be the lectio difficilior. Earlier dialogues by Plato also tell in favor of the MS reading, since they generally treat "mind" or "thoughtfulness" and *sôphrosunê* as parallel virtues.[23] *Republic* Book 4, for instance, treats wisdom, *sôphrosunê*, and courage as each their own thing; the *Protagoras* identifies wisdom and *sôphrosunê* rather than subordinating the latter to the former. Yet textual patterns may not seem decisive, and Plato may have changed his mind about the way to present the virtues. We need thus to look at evidence from the *Laws* itself. In the end, as is the case with most cruxes, there will be no definitive solution, but appraising the evidence from the perspective of the crux draws out the mid-fourth century sensitivity to our question: how does *sôphrosunê* relate to wisdom?

The most important recent commentator on the early books of the *Laws*, Susan Suavé Meyer, addresses this issue, and favors the Eusebian reading, as do most though not all recent scholars.[24] She does not discuss the linguistic evidence or the relationship with the *Republic*, both of which pose problems for her position. She instead relies on two interpretative arguments, one internal to the *Laws* and one external. First, were the Athenian not to stipulate the addition of reason to a *sôphrôn* state of the soul, it would be strange to see, as Meyer puts it, "the moderate disposition... not... accompanied (or informed) by intelligence" yet higher ranked than the third-place divine good, namely justice, "of which intelligence is identified as a component" (given that it is composed of the two items above it and one below it).[25] She doubts that a state without reason could be ranked above a state with reason. Second, there are "instances of moderation that are foolish or otherwise lacking in wisdom" in other dialogues, and so too here.[26]

---

[23] An exception is found in *Meno* 88b1–8: courage without knowledge or wisdom or *nous* is rashness, and harmful; so too *sôphrosunê* and *eumathia* (μετὰ μὲν νοῦ καὶ μανθανόμενα καὶ καταρτυόμενα ὠφέλιμα, ἄνευ δὲ νοῦ βλαβερά).

[24] See n19 above.

[25] Meyer (2015, 112): "On the MS reading it would be 'a moderate disposition of the soul' that is 'second... after intelligence (*meta noun*)'; so described, the moderate disposition need not be accompanied (or informed) by intelligence, unlike the third-place divine good (justice), of which intelligence is identified as a component."

[26] England (1921, 1.213) takes the same view (which is worth quoting): after citing 710a and 696d (discussed below), he writes, "The stress laid, all through this passage, and elsewhere in the *Laws*, on the importance of the *conjunction* of the virtues is in favor of Eusebius' reading. (We might almost say Plato holds that one virtue by itself, or at all events the natural tendency to it, needs to be *corrected* by another... In different passages in the *Laws* we are told that two things are necessary to perfection of character: (1) the natural disposition to a particular virtue must be trained in action...; (2) one virtue cannot stand alone; it must be helped by others. Above (630a ff.) the Athenian speaks of πιστότης as involving συμπᾶσα ἀρετή, and we might call this τελέα δικαιοσύνη—'perfect righteousness.' In the present passage he uses δικαιοσύνη in the narrower sense. All this shows that our present discussion

The first argument has limited power. While justice is said to be a mixture of reason, *sôphrosunê*, and courage, still it is ranked lower than reason alone, lower than *sôphrosunê* either alone or combined with reason, though higher than courage alone.[27] This means that the Athenian ranks reason diluted with other virtues lower than reason undiluted. Those virtues by themselves are of lower though not of negligible value. Consider a reconstruction of Meyer's reading:

1. Reason
2. [Reason +] *sôphrosunê*
3. Reason + *sôphrosunê* + courage = justice
4. Courage

This means that courage, being worse than both reason and *sôphrosunê*, dilutes the potency of the whole mixture. This means, in turn, that there is a way *sôphrosunê* alone could be worse than reason by itself but better than a state comprising a mixture of it with reason and courage: namely, if courage was more worse than *sôphrosunê* than reason was better than *sôphrosunê*. We might even expect it to be so, given the nearness of *sôphrosunê* and reason (e.g., *sophia*) elsewhere in Plato, which would make reason only marginally better than *sôphrosunê*.

The second argument, that because Plato countenances a *sôphrosunê* "without reason" (ἄνευ νοῦ) elsewhere the Athenian would have to indicate, for the sake of clarity, a "*meta nou*" *sôphrosunê* here, is more complicated. Meyer first points to two places outside *Laws*, *Euthydemus* 281c and *Statesman* 306a–b, for evidence about that attitude toward *sôphrosunê*.[28] We have already seen the passage from *Statesman*: it is where the Visitor observes that courage and *sôphrosunê* are distinct parts of virtue, and that each part by itself, when ignorant of the right occasion to act, tends to destruction. But we saw that in this dialogue the Visitor seems really to be talking about the behavioral dispositions that express the virtues; he (and so Plato, too) is not committed to the view that *sôphrosunê* simply *is* these behavior dispositions. Nevertheless, the Visitor does have to specify that *sôphrosunê* is reliably good only when accompanied by true beliefs about the fine and good and just. Thus he admits that people can conflate the dispositional adjuncts of *sôphrosunê* with *sôphrosunê* itself. It is conceivable that the Athenian recognizes this conflation, hence his qualification, which serves to

---

is *practical*, not speculative. The author wants us to have in mind the perfect character, and the way to produce it, rather than a classification of the virtues, or a scientifically exact nomenclature for a treatise on Moral Philosophy.)"

[27] See Irwin (1995, 347–49) on the relationship here between *sôphrosunê* and courage.
[28] The prepositional phrase *meta nou*, "with mind," occurs in several Platonic dialogues: *Pol.* 297b1, 8; *Rep.* 4.431c5; *Tim.* 29b6, 46e4, 47d3; *Laws* 12.948d3.

disambiguate. But why does the Athenian place the dispositional *sôphrosunê* (albeit upgraded with reason) among the divine goods and, perhaps more poignantly, why doesn't he specify that courage has a place on this ranking only when reason accompanies it, too?

In the *Euthydemus* passage, Socrates is arguing with Clinias that happiness depends on the possession of goods and their knowledgeable use. So necessary for happiness is *phrônesis* and *sophia*, Socrates says, that without them, the less use of one's possessions the better.[29] Thus without intelligence it would be better to be poor, weak, out of favor, lazy, slow, and of diminished eyesight and hearing—for then one would do less, and thus make fewer mistakes, and thus live less miserably. In the middle of this list of inhibitory states, Socrates asks: "Would one do less if one were courageous and *sôphrôn* or if one were a coward?"[30] The expected answer is "coward." The point is a familiar Socratic one: if from ignorance you risk pursuing the wrong goal, you would be better off not being able to pursue any goal at all. Meyer infers from Socrates' question that he is contemplating an ignorant person, someone lacking reason, who nevertheless has (an *aneu nou*) *sôphrosunê* that would allow him to pursue his misguided goals. For the sake of his protreptic demonstration, Socrates may in fact be contemplating this, but he seems not to commit himself expressly to the possibility. He wants only to show that, without knowledge, inaction is better than action; accordingly, he gives a list of action-benefiters, of which *sôphrosunê* and courage are signal examples. This is the notable thing, Socrates' considering *sôphrosunê* to be as action-enabling as courage rather than (as Callicles would have it) its action-inhibiting opposite. He is not making a statement about the connection between *sôphrosunê* and reason.

These two non-*Laws* parallels for a reason-deprived *sôphrosunê* are provocative but not decisive for the present reading. Relevant evidence from the *Laws* is not much more decisive.[31] In the dialogue, what *sôphrosunê* adds to a person's capacity to lead points in two directions. The Athenian observes that legitimacy for ruling does not come from wealth, speed, beauty, or strength.[32] In fact, he says, legitimacy comes from nothing other than virtue. But then he revises himself, claiming that it comes from nothing other than *sôphrosunê*, even if a person has the other virtues.[33] For instance, we would avoid those who despite being very

---

[29] Pl. *Euthd.* 281b4–c3.
[30] Pl. *Euthd.* 281c6–7: Πότερον δὲ ἀνδρεῖος ὢν καὶ σώφρων ἐλάττω ἂν πράττοι ἢ δειλός;
[31] Meyer (2015, 113).
[32] Pl. *Laws* 3.696b3: πλούτῳ διαφέρων, ἐπεὶ οὐδ' ὅτι ταχὺς ἢ καλὸς ἢ ἰσχυρός: as we have seen, this is comparable to the list at 1.631c2–5, which adds only "health" and condenses strength and speed to "strength in running." In the ancient period, evidently nobody thought that "health" would qualify someone for rule, presumably on the grounds that nobody exceeds everyone else (demonstrably) in health.
[33] Pl. *Laws* 3.696b4: ἄνευ τινὸς ἀρετῆς, οὐδ' ἀρετῆς ἧς ἂν σωφροσύνη ἀπῇ.

courageous were undisciplined rather than *sôphrôn*;[34] technical experts, even if they were intellectually competent in their trade, if they were not *sôphrôn*, would never be just, and we would avoid them;[35] indeed, unless he had *sôphrosunê* we would never see someone wise (σοφόν) who "keeps his pleasures and pains in tune with, and following, right reason."[36] The Athenian has separated wisdom and competence from *sôphrosunê*. Without the capacity to act on reasons rather than simply react to feelings, not even verve or knowledge would lead to good ends. So, on the one hand, we have here *sôphrosunê* evidently without wisdom. But, on the other hand, there is no implication that this wisdom-independent *sôphrosunê* needs a supplement of reason for its full instantiation.[37] *Sôphrosunê* is treated here as already capable and reliable at maintaining focus—ignoring problematic desires, acting only on those consistent with the norms to which one is committed.[38] Wisdom is evidently the capacity to identify the right action to do, whether technical or moral. *Sôphrosunê* allows for that identification to be decisive to action.

What follows, however, complicates the previous picture of *sôphrosunê*. The Athenian follows up his earlier observation, continuing to determine the conditions of an honorable public leader. "Would the situation of *sôphrosunê* being all alone without any of the rest of virtue in some soul rightly be honored or dishonored?"[39] The Athenian's interlocutor does not know how to answer; he has no words at hand about the person who is *sôphrôn* but who exhibits none of the other virtues. The Athenian says he is right not to know what to say: neither a positive or negative response would sound right (παρὰ μέλος).[40] He does not explain what he means. We can guess that he would not want to deride the value of having *sôphrosunê*, and yet having *sôphrosunê* alone, without wisdom or courage or justice, might seem hardly sufficient for an honorable life of leadership.[41] Commitment to norms by itself is not an obvious ticket to glory. The Athenian goes on to say more about his interlocutor's silence:

---

[34] Pl. *Laws* 3.696b10: μὴ σώφρονα δὲ ἀλλ' ἀκόλαστον.

[35] Pl. *Laws* 3.696c2–6.

[36] Pl. *Laws* 3.696c8–10: τὸν τὰς ἡδονὰς καὶ λύπας κεκτημένον συμφώνους τοῖς ὀρθοῖς λόγοις καὶ ἑπομένας.

[37] See Bobonich (2002, 185) on the indeterminate relationship between wisdom and *sôphrosunê*.

[38] Bobonich (2002, 185) on *sôphrosunê*: it enables "agents to use Dependent Goods in virtuous action, by (1) enabling them to form and retain rational overall judgments, and (2) to act on their rational overall judgments once formed."

[39] Pl. *Laws* 3.696d4–6: Σωφροσύνη ἄνευ πάσης τῆς ἄλλης ἀρετῆς ἐν ψυχῇ τινι μεμονωμένη τίμιον ἢ ἄτιμον γίγνοιτ' ἂν κατὰ δίκην.

[40] Pl. *Laws* 3.696d8.

[41] In his 1959 lectures on the *Laws* at the University of Chicago, Leo Strauss presents the issue as concerning moderation as the thing which *everyone* can have (as supported by the *Republic* 4 discussion of *sôphrosunê*), such that the question is whether moderation alone suffices for rule, namely, whether democracy is a viable political system; Strauss believes the answer is no (L. Pangle 2016, 167–68).

ΑΘ. Εἶεν· τὸ μὲν δὴ πρόσθημα ὧν τιμαί τε καὶ ἀτιμίαι οὐ λόγου, ἀλλά τινος μᾶλλον ἀλόγου σιγῆς, ἄξιον ἂν εἴη.

ΜΕ. Σωφροσύνην μοι φαίνῃ λέγειν.

ΑΘ. Ναί. τὸ δέ γε τῶν ἄλλων πλεῖστα ἡμᾶς ὠφελοῦν μετὰ τῆς προσθήκης μάλιστ' ἂν τιμώμενον ὀρθότατα τιμῷτο, καὶ τὸ δεύτερον δευτέρως· καὶ οὕτω ... (Pl. *Laws* 3.696d9–e6)

ATHENIAN: Well, that which *accompanies* things that are praised and censured would not [itself] be worthy of speech; it deserves rather some speechless silence.

MEGILLUS: It's *sôphrosunê* it seems you mean.

ATHENIAN: Yes. In any event, what is most correctly honored is whatever remains, if it is most beneficial and has this accompaniment, and whatever is second-most correctly honored is what is second-most beneficial; and so on ...

Sôphrosunê is the anonymous benefactor: it allows whatever is celebrated to be celebrated, but it is not itself celebrated. What Plato is after, I am not sure. I doubt that he means to distinguish between moral importance (as something *sôphrosunê* has) and public approbation (as something it lacks), since the Athenian emphasizes "worthiness of speech" and "correctly honored," rather than "accorded speech" and "popularly honored." Perhaps he means that the capacity to act, as essential as it is, wins no accolades; it is the actions themselves that do, and these are dictated by the other virtues one has. But this would be a cryptic way of putting it. Maybe Plato has some striking idea that he did not fully work out. Be that as it may, this exchange does not support thinking that *sôphrosunê* is a second-place virtue only if accompanied by *nous*.[42]

The Athenian repeats and expands this point fourteen pages later. To be successful, he says, a civic leader with sole discretion—a dictator (τύραννος)—should be "young, not forgetful, good at learning, courageous, and naturally magnificent," and if he's going to be any use at all, he should also have "what we said earlier has to go along with all the parts of virtue."[43] Filling in the virtue to which the Athenian alludes, just as Megillus did before, Clinias responds: "Megillus, it seems to me that the Visitor means *sôphrosunê*, as 'what has to go along with it.'" At this point the Visitor clarifies:

---

[42] England (1921, 398–99) struggles with this passage, too: "But though σωφροσύνη is to get no more praise from the public than Cordelia gave herself [England had cited *King Lear* just above], this does not mean that it is worthless.... As a personal virtue, it seems to involve a good deal of what we call *self-respect*. Notwithstanding the colourlessness which the words ἀλόγου σιγῆς seem to imply, we shall be wrong if we attach a merely negative significance to the word."

[43] Pl. *Laws* 4.709e7–8: ὃ δὲ καὶ ἐν τοῖς πρόσθεν ἐλέγομεν δεῖν ἕπεσθαι σύμπασιν τοῖς τῆς ἀρετῆς μέρεσι.

ΑΘ. Τὴν δημώδη γε, ὦ Κλεινία, καὶ οὐχ ἥν τις σεμνύνων ἂν λέγοι, φρόνησιν προσαναγκάζων εἶναι τὸ σωφρονεῖν, ἀλλ' ὅπερ εὐθὺς παισὶν καὶ θηρίοις, τοῖς μὲν ἀκρατῶς ἔχειν πρὸς τὰς ἡδονάς, σύμφυτον ἐπανθεῖ, τοῖς δὲ ἐγκρατῶς· ὃ καὶ μονούμενον ἔφαμεν τῶν πολλῶν ἀγαθῶν λεγομένων οὐκ ἄξιον εἶναι λόγου. (Pl. *Laws* 4.710a5–b2)

ATHENIAN: Yes, at least its conventional form, Clinias, though not what someone would speak of in an exalted way, as when he forces *sôphronein* to be *phronêsis*—it's what flowers naturally, unprompted, in children and animals, sometimes not controlling one's pleasures, sometimes controlling them. And we claimed that if this were wholly apart from the other goods we were discussing, it would not be worth talking about.

The Athenian contrasts a conventional or popular use of *sôphrosunê* from its exalted use. This allows him to make a substantial modification of his previous claim. We hold back praise of an isolated *sôphrosunê* only if we have the popular use in mind. This is the natural though weak or even irregular capacity to control desires, which at best prevents passion's wholesale hijacking of one's deliberation. There are several reasons not to praise it: it is innate; it is imperfect; and it does not seem normatively guided. Maybe it is also preparatory but not sufficient for honorable actions, as we supposed earlier. The Athenian allows that *sôphrosunê* in an exalted sense, however, could be praised on its own. Its identification with *phronêsis* might suggest that it is now sufficient for honorable action: *sôphrosunê* just is the capacity to act well. The norms of noble action are, in effect, built in or assumed. This could be what its identification with *phronêsis* means. Though the Athenian does not say who would "force *sôphronein* to be *phronêsis*," we have seen much evidence over the past four chapters that this is a Socratic idea, and that Socrates' idea is largely consistent with earlier thinking about *sôphrosunê*. Socrates and others have taken *sôphrosunê* as a great good virtue, one that suffices for commendable public action.[44]

The Athenian's popular *sôphrosunê* looks like other cases of *sôphrosunê* studied earlier in this chapter and in Chapter 8. It is closest to the *Statesman*'s pre-virtuous dispositions of gentleness. It is less close to the *Phaedo*'s cross-canceling desires. In those two cases, full or true *sôphrosunê* was realized through the addition of

---

[44] In the famous "likeness to god" passage in the "Digression" of the *Theaetetus* (176b), Socrates says that this likeness comes about in "justice and piety with *phronêsis*" (ὁμοίωσις δὲ δίκαιον καὶ ὅσιον μετὰ φρονήσεως γενέσθαι). *Sôphrosunê* is not included. One might think this is because the gods do not need it (Plotinus *Enn.* 1.2.1,10–12); but they do not obviously need the others either (1.2.1,17–21). Perhaps the reason is that *phronêsis* stands in for *sôphrosunê*, too. One also wonders about the "with" (μετά) here: does Socrates mean that justice and piety have the right quality only when accompanied by *phronêsis*, or is *phronêsis* simply a third and equal virtue?

reasoning. In the present case, however, the Athenian does not explain how one goes from the innate popular version to an exalted phronetic version, if he even believes that there *is* such an exalted version to attain. Indeed, he does not even say that the exalted version is the popular version plus *phronêsis*, but rather that it is equivalent to *phronêsis*. While this account is a cousin of those found in the other dialogues, it does not allude to or assume them. It does not tell us how to resolve the *meta nou[n]* question.

The Athenian has spoken of a *sôphrosunê* that is not equivalent to *phronêsis*, that may in fact lack it, at least as much as children and animals lack *phronêsis*. He goes on to recapitulate: this *sôphrosunê* allows a state "efficiently and effectively" to flourish maximally.[45] And of course the state can do so only when its dictator has all the competences of leadership, being "young, *sôphrôn*, good at learning, not forgetful, courageous, and magnificent."[46] But now we must wonder: what happened to the reason or wisdom that we supposed had to accompany *sôphrosunê*? Is it built in or not?

In what follows, Plato again leaves it uncertain. The Athenian returns to the character-traits of the rare but successful dictator in a culminating paragraph of this discussion: he loves *sôphrôn* and just things and, like Nestor, has a superlative power of speech surpassed only by his superlative *sôphrosunê*.[47] His city will flourish, so the Athenian summarizes, when "the greatest power in a man meets with *phronein* and *sôphronein*."[48] Nestor's good judgment and the perfect prince's intelligence are here associated with *sôphrosunê*—not directly identified, since the Athenian speaks of Nestor's *sôphrosunê* as even more remarkable than his persuasive capacities, which may well depend on his intelligence, but not opposed. No matter how vague the relationship assumed between *sôphrosunê* and *phronêsis* is, clearly *sôphrosunê* is not simply perfected by *phronêsis*.

Against this ambivalent background, we may return to the target passage, and re-ask our question. When the Athenian puts a *sôphrôn* state of the soul second to wisdom, does he need to stipulate that he has in mind the kind of *sôphrosunê* that is accompanied by reason and not the popular name for a set of behavioral traits? Does he really need to disambiguate them here? I would think not, since a distinction between types of *sôphrosunê* is not made until Book 4, despite much talk of *sôphrosunê* before then. Of course, the Athenian may already be thinking about such a distinction, but it does not seem relevant here and, anyway, the Book 1 discussion of *sôphrosunê* seems not to square with the

[45] Pl. *Laws* 4.710b5–7: εἰ μέλλει πόλις ὡς δυνατόν ἐστι τάχιστα καὶ ἄριστα σχήσειν πολιτείαν ἣν λαβοῦσα εὐδαιμονέστατα διάξει.

[46] Pl. *Laws* 4.710c5–6: νέος, σώφρων, εὐμαθής, μνήμων, ἀνδρεῖος, μεγαλοπρεπής.

[47] Pl. *Laws* 4.711e1–3: τὴν Νέστορος ἐάν ποτέ τις ἐπανενέγκῃ φύσιν, ὃν τῇ τοῦ λέγειν ῥώμῃ φασὶ πάντων διενεγκόντα ἀνθρώπων πλέον ἔτι τῷ σωφρονεῖν διαφέρειν; cf. e6–7.

[48] Pl. *Laws* 4.711a1–2: ὡς ὅταν εἰς ταὐτὸν τῷ φρονεῖν τε καὶ σωφρονεῖν ἡ μεγίστη δύναμις ἐν ἀνθρώπῳ συμπέσῃ.

discussions in Books 3–4, suggesting that they were written with different issues in mind. In the later books, *sôphrosunê* undergirds and accompanies the other virtues, making them possible and thus valuable. In the early book, by contrast, which in fact focalizes *sôphrosunê* as a virtue the city should strive to inculcate in its population, the Athenian does not present *sôphrosunê* specifically as a helpmeet. *Phronêsis* is ranked highest without reference to any accompaniment by *sôphrosunê*; justice is not said to be "accompanied" by *sôphrosunê* but rather partially constituted by it; courage is, like *phronêsis*, given without any reference to *sôphrosunê*-accompaniment.

To be sure, the way the Athenian lists and ranks the four "human goods," the non-virtues health, beauty, strength, and wealth, might give some support for the Eusebian reading. The fourth good, wealth, earns its place only in a qualified mode, when it is "not blind but is sharp-sighted—that is, taking its lead from *phronêsis* (ἄνπερ ἅμ' ἕπηται φρονήσει)." This could be a parallel for a *sôphrôn* state of the soul accompanied by *nous*. It would not be a robust parallel, however, because wealth is accompanied by something from another list, not something immediately above it in its own list. And there are other charges against the Eusebian reading. There is the problem mentioned earlier, that it would be strange for *sôphrosunê* to be posited as "with *nous*" but not courage, which presumably needs it just as much. Justice is presented as a mixture of courage with "those" (ἐκ τουτῶν), which seems to refer to the two levels preceding it; but it would be redundant to include *nous* at the second level when *phronêsis* just appeared at the first, as though justice were "*phronêsis* + *sôphrosunê* + *nous* + courage."[49] Finally, the Athenian can be heard to be giving strong list-signposting: "First is x; second, following x*, is y; from those [x and y], mixed with z, is, third, w; and fourth is w" (where x* is a gloss on x).

The disagreements among ancient readers and contemporary commentators about our target passage point at a complex element in Plato's attitude toward *sôphrosunê*. He unifies its norm-following aspect and the desire-control aspect. Xenophon, by contrast, separates them into *sôphrosunê* and *enkrateia*, respectively. And as we will see in the next chapter, in Aristotle's account *sôphrosunê* refers to the desire-control aspect, the management of the natural bodily desires sufficiently so as not to give work to *enkrateia*, whose task it is to hold out against excessive desires. Now, as we will see, Aristotle believes that *sôphrosunê* involves *phronêsis*; it is the addition of *phronêsis* that ensures *sôphrosunê* is a virtue and not merely a natural tendency. So, the Eusebian "*meta nou*" anticipates the Aristotelian analysis, as the *Statesman* and a passage or two in the *Laws* do as

---

[49] Aristotle shows awareness of difficulties here in *Top.* 150a4–13. It is notable that at the end of the *Laws*, where the Athenian queries the relationship between the four canonical virtues, he makes no reference to the compositionality of individual virtues (12.963a–965e), and yet he does treat *nous* as the leading (ἡγεμόνα) virtue, the one toward which the other three should look (βλέπειν) (963a8–9).

well. But Plato's *Laws* as a whole does not reflect the Aristotelian analysis; it keeps alive the dominant view of *sôphrosunê* as *the* virtue to be reckoned with, central to the possibility of agency as such.

Sôphrosunê as self-management

We have just discussed one indeterminacy in the *Laws*' view of *sôphrosunê*, which we have seen throughout these chapters to be a central ingredient in Plato's thinking about rational agency. A related indeterminacy appears elsewhere in the early pages of the dialogue. It is the formulation of the self-directed condition sometimes indicated by *sôphrosunê*. Early in the conversation, Clinias describes Crete's success as dependent on its standing capacity to win any fight at any point, adopting the realpolitik perspective that every city is in constant undeclared war with every other city. He continues by saying that each Cretan person has a war against himself going on inside himself; evidence is that personal success is called being victorious in that war of oneself with oneself.[50] He equates this internal victory with "overcoming oneself" (ὁ μὲν κρείττων αὑτοῦ).[51] He comes to agree, with the Athenian, that this is more important than overcoming others. Overcoming oneself means, as Clinias says, not being overcome by pleasures.[52] The Athenian reformulates this as "not lacking the cultivation to endure pleasures and not being forced into doing anything disgraceful."[53] (These pleasures are later seen to include those of sex, drink, and partying.)[54] By later in the first book of the *Laws*, however, the Athenian refers to "ruling oneself" (ἄρχειν αὑτῶν) as the mark of goodness.[55] And this is done through "calculation" (λογισμός), which measures pleasures and pains.[56] One may wonder about the shift in language, from defeating and triumphing over oneself, to ruling and calculating about oneself.[57] The earlier is conflict talk, where one set of forces vanquishes another set, namely the counter-aretaic desires. The latter is

---

[50] Pl. *Laws* 1.626e2–5: Κἀνταῦθα, ὦ ξένε, τὸ νικᾶν αὐτὸν αὑτὸν πασῶν νικῶν πρώτη τε καὶ ἀρίστη, τὸ δὲ ἡττᾶσθαι αὐτὸν ὑφ' ἑαυτοῦ πάντων αἴσχιστόν τε ἅμα καὶ κάκιστον. ταῦτα γὰρ ὡς πολέμου ἐν ἑκάστοις ἡμῶν ὄντος πρὸς ἡμᾶς αὐτοὺς σημαίνει.

[51] Pl. *Laws* 1.626e6; cf. 627b7–8.

[52] Pl. *Laws* 1.633e3–6: καὶ πάντες που μᾶλλον λέγομεν τὸν ὑπὸ τῶν ἡδονῶν κρατούμενον τοῦτον τὸν ἐπονειδίστως ἥττονα ἑαυτοῦ πρότερον ἢ τὸν ὑπὸ τῶν λυπῶν.

[53] Pl. *Laws* 1.635c6–8: ἀμελέτητοι γιγνόμενοι ἐν ταῖς ἡδοναῖς καρτερεῖν καὶ μηδὲν τῶν αἰσχρῶν ἀναγκάζεσθαι ποιεῖν.

[54] Pl. *Laws* 1.636b5, 637a2–6.

[55] Pl. *Laws* 1.644b7.

[56] Pl. *Laws* 1.644c9–d3: Πρὸς δὲ τούτοιν ἀμφοῖν αὖ δόξας μελλόντων, οἷν κοινὸν μὲν ὄνομα ἐλπίς, ἴδιον δέ, φόβος μὲν ἡ πρὸ λύπης ἐλπίς, θάρρος δὲ ἡ πρὸ τοῦ ἐναντίου· ἐπὶ δὲ πᾶσι τούτοις λογισμὸς ὅτι ποτ' αὐτῶν ἄμεινον ἢ χεῖρον, ὃς γενόμενος δόγμα πόλεως κοινὸν νόμος ἐπωνόμασται.

[57] Meyer (2015, 168–71; 2018) takes the shift as meaningful; Dorion (2007, 135) and Wilburn (2012, 26n3) do not; see Bobonich (2002, 289) generally.

constitution talk, where something has authority over the rest, exercised through its reasoned assessment of the situation. The earlier we might call "enkratic," the latter "sophronic"; such, anyway, is Aristotle's eventual distinction between self-domination and self-management. These competing portrayals of self-control, already discussed in the *Phaedo*, have perhaps been reflected through the *Laws*' ambiguous accounts of *sôphrosunê* already discussed above. Clinias had already allowed that there are three ways in which an unjust member of one's city gets dealt with: kill him; he agrees to be ruled; laws are established such that everyone is friends.[58] The last is most constitutional.

The Athenian's discussion of "calculation" introduces a famous image, the marionette puppet as model of the person qua agent.[59] Though calculation is not referred to as *sôphrosunê*, the role it shares with the virtue in (putatively) ruling a person suggests identifying them. But there is an interpretative crux in this image: the operation of "calculation" in the internal economy of decision is unclear. The basic picture starts with the "emotions" (τὰ πάθη)—what we passively experience, including pleasure and pain, and their expectations fear and confidence—analogized to the puppet's strings. These cords tug on us (σπῶσίν τε ἡμᾶς). When opposing emotions pull against one another, they bring about opposing actions (ἀλλήλαις ἀνθέλκουσιν ἐναντίαι οὖσαι ἐπ' ἐναντίας πράξεις) in us, across the dividing line between virtue and vice (οὗ δὴ διωρισμένη ἀρετὴ καὶ κακία κεῖται).[60] Emotion causes inner conflict, erratic self-undermining, and no constant commitment to the good. But we are not at the total mercy of emotion. The puppet has another string, the cord of calculation. "This story has it that we must always comply with (συνεπόμενον) one of the things that pulls at us (μιᾷ ... τῶν ἕλξεων) and never abandon it, but that we are to pull against the other strings."[61] Whereas the other cords are iron-stiff, the cord of calculation is made of gold and is thus soft and pliable (μαλακή). Because of its gentleness (πρᾶος), we must "always cooperate" (ἀεὶ συλλαμβάνειν) with it, so that it may win out over the other kinds of cord (νικᾷ τὰ ἄλλα γένη).[62] And when it does, we may speak properly of "self-overcoming" (τὸ κρείττω ἑαυτοῦ).[63]

On this model, self-mastery—being an agent in one's life—is not a matter simply of the proper desire winning out over the improper one. All one's desires are in conflict and are outside one's control, and it is adventitious whether they result in virtuous action. It is something else that brings about agency, one's actions' being one's own. This is presented as the golden cord of calculation. The

---

[58] Pl. *Laws* 1.627c–e.
[59] For the image, see esp. Bobonich (2002, 260–67).
[60] Pl. *Laws* 1.644e1–4.
[61] Pl. *Laws* 1.644e4–6: μιᾷ γάρ φησιν ὁ λόγος δεῖν τῶν ἕλξεων συνεπόμενον ἀεὶ καὶ μηδαμῇ ἀπολειπόμενον ἐκείνης, ἀνθέλκειν τοῖς ἄλλοις νεύροις ἕκαστον.
[62] Pl. *Laws* 645a2–b1.
[63] Pl. *Laws* 645b2.

cord has a kind of external power, so it may seem ultimately no different from the force of emotion. But there is a difference: it is a power that does not succeed of its own accord. One must actively follow the golden cord, neither abandoning it nor failing to cooperate with it. The Athenian calls it "fine" and "holy," something to be revered and taken as authoritative. This image reflects the experience of calculation or reflection: the decision it generates is third-personal, as it were, not an expression of one's immediate will, and so we may feel passive with respect to it, especially in its appeal as normative on us; at the same time, we must have a first-personal commitment to it, taking up its dictates as our will, by contrast with our grudging or whimsical attitude toward our other desires.[64] Where is *sôphrosunê* in all this? We might imagine that *phronêsis* may be identified with the calculation itself, and *sôphrosunê* with the capacity to follow that calculation. Given that figuring out what to do and being able to do it are flip sides of the same desiderative coin, we can explain how *sôphrosunê* is sometimes identified with *phronêsis*; but given that calculation and adherence to norms are conceptually distinct, we can also easily explain how the two virtues come apart.

Two Visions of *Sôphrosunê*

Xenophon said that Socrates did not distinguish *sôphrosunê* and wisdom, but Xenophon's argument in support of this view indicated mainly that Socrates found them to coincide. In Plato, the position is rather more complicated. In *Protagoras*, they share an opposite; in *Gorgias*, they are not compared; in *Republic*, they are explicitly differentiated; and in *Charmides sôphrosunê* cannot be a first-order knowledge, but it could be a second-order knowledge or the knowledge of what's good and bad—what wisdom probably is. In none of these dialogues, however, did Socrates worry about distinguishing them. There was a sense either that the virtues are all unified somehow, or, as in *Republic*, that they simply pertain to different competences in life. In *Statesman* and *Laws*, by contrast, there *is* a worry: does *sôphrosunê* contain or involve *phronêsis* or not? There is a vision of a natural disposition akin to *sôphrosunê* that, when hydrated, so to speak, becomes the ideal form of *sôphrosunê*. There is a recognition that *sôphrosunê* is spoken of in two ways. This is a disaggregating of the desire-control aspect of *sôphrosunê* from its norm-recognizing aspect. We saw this disaggregation already in Xenophon, with the peeling off of *enkrateia*, and we will see it again, in a different form, in Aristotle. Plato differs from these contemporaries in referring to both by the same term, evidently following linguistic convention.

---

[64] Similarly, Wilburn (2012, 32–38).

11
Aristotle and the Later Fourth Century

Innovation and Departure

The decades following Plato's *Laws* evidence a period of intense discussion of *sôphrosunê*. Among Plato's immediate Academic associates alone, four wrote texts about *sôphrosunê*. Three of these texts have vanished, known only by their common title, *On Sôphrosunê*, though anonymous Academic documents from the period may retain echoes of them. But one remains, as a piece of a comprehensive system of ethics, and it witnesses a brilliant and direct confrontation of the problems and disagreements about *sôphrosunê* raised over the previous century and discovered in the previous chapters. This analysis of *sôphrosunê* distinguishes the virtue sharply from the sense of shame and respect (αἰδώς), from self-control (ἐγκράτεια), from a pre-virtue state of "natural *sôphrosunê*," and from the wisdom that is practical judgment at its highest development (φρόνησις). It describes the feeling of *sôphrosunê*, as the absence of temptation by improper desires, and provides a novel scope of its application, as a subset of the bodily desires. The three authors who wrote lost works about *sôphrosunê* are Heraclides, Speusippus, and Xenocrates. The fourth, whose work survives, is Aristotle.

Aristotle creates a distinctive, definite, and cogent account of *sôphrosunê*—surely the most determinate and provocative of his era. It resolves a range of *aporiai* and develops trends we have already seen: a bigger role for *enkrateia*, a tighter commitment to the special role of wisdom, emphasis on the bodily desires. And it fits snugly within Aristotle's theory of virtues, his moral psychology, and, most amazing, his biological psychology. But Aristotle buys his account's resolution, precision, and fit at a cost. He circumscribes the content of *sôphrosunê* more tightly than the evidence allows. He has, in fact, re-created the virtue for the purpose of theoretical integration, not for fidelity to moral discourse and ethical sensibility. It is not an altogether outlandish account, especially given the way it highlights the desires for food, drink, and sex; and the Greek language might be more transparent and efficient should the term *sôphrosunê* be revamped on Aristotelian principles. Yet Aristotle has not simply refined or rejiggered the best views of this virtue advanced by his predecessors and contemporaries; he has not "saved the appearances." Rather than continuing the conversation, he has started afresh.

Plato and Aristotle thus adopt opposing strategies for discussing *sôphrosunê*. Plato stays committed to the term's ubiquity and normative centrality in evaluative expression despite its attendant undertheorization and the consequent puzzles that arise. Aristotle rejects the term's diffuseness, seeking to carve moral discourse at its heretofore unrecognized joints. At the chapter's end, we will see some attempted rapprochements between the two accounts of *sôphrosunê*.

We begin with Aristotle's positive account of *sôphrosunê*, which appears in several Aristotelian works, and then discuss four differences Aristotle draws between *sôphrosunê* and neighboring moral-psychological states. Aristotle's account is generally applauded for its accuracy and power, receiving any criticism only at the boundaries. I show that, at least as a matter of accuracy, this applause is misplaced, as the usage by Aristotle's closest contemporary, Isocrates, shows, as does Aristotle's own usage elsewhere in his oeuvre. I then hypothesize explanations for his departure from linguistic commonplaces. Last, we turn to some views of the later fourth century from Aristotle's Peripatetic and Academic associates. Doing so shows again Aristotle's idiosyncrasy, since few people adopted or even mooted his complete system, even as they remained fascinated by, and disagreed over, the nature of *sôphrosunê*.

The Official View

Aristotle gives a focused account of *sôphrosunê* in each of the three ethical works attributed to him, each time following courage in the discussion of the particular virtues.[1] The shortest, at about half a Bekker page, comes in the *Magna Moralia* (ch. 1.21); the one in *Eudemian Ethics* is twice as long (ch. 3.2); and the one in *Nicomachean Ethics* twice as long again (ch. 3.10–12). The accounts agree, the longer ones simply adding examples, considerations, and restrictions on the application of the virtue-term.

According to the *Magna Moralia*, *sôphrosunê* concerns pleasures and pains, but not about all things. A charge of indiscipline (ἀκόλαστος), a failure of *sôphrosunê*, is not made against the excessive enjoyment of pictures or sculptures, sounds or smells; only pleasures of touch and taste can trigger that charge. This may be a complaint against Prodicus' statement that Vice encourages Heracles to enjoy not just food, drink, and sex, but also sights and sounds.[2] In any event, here *sôphrosunê* is not a matter of being totally unmoved by such pleasures; it is

---

[1] This is followed by gentleness in *MM* (1.22) and *EE* (3.3), as in Theophrastus, but liberality in *NE* 4.1 (where gentleness is deferred until 4.5). For the authenticity of *Magna Moralia*, see Cooper (1973) and, more recently, Nielsen (2018); there are also useful considerations at Barnes and Kenny (2014, 6).

[2] Xen. *Mem.* 2.1.24.

rather the state of not being so drawn by excessive delight in them (εἰς ὑπερβολὴν αὐτῶν ἀπολαύων) that one treats every other consideration for action as merely incidental, as of secondary importance (πάρεργα). The pleasures of touch and taste may provide good reasons for action if they are consistent what's noble (τοῦ καλοῦ ἕνεκεν), but not if they conflict with it. And what is noble is judged so by reason (λόγον, ᾧ δοκιμάζοντα τὸ καλὸν αἱροῦνται).[3] *Sôphrosunê* means acting on certain bodily desires when reason affirms doing so.

This *Magna Moralia* account gives no arguments, only positions, but these are well-defined. The domain of the virtue includes pleasures and pains about touch and taste, though pains only derivatively. The virtuous person desires those pleasures but not so much that he cannot see that he might need to pursue other things instead. Of striking interest already is the radical reduction of the domain of *sôphrosunê* relative to the domain explored in this book's earlier chapters, from the archaic period through Aristotle's contemporaries in Xenophon and Plato. For Telemachus as much as for Critias and Alcibiades, *sôphrosunê* might be exercised not only in withstanding an inclination to gluttony but also in the inclination to speak or act politically. Of interest too is the contribution to the debate we first saw in Antiphon's *On Concord*, which addressed whether *sôphrosunê* requires its bearer to have overcome untoward desires. In the *Magna Moralia*, the *sôphrôn* person does not want to do bad things. He has plenty of desires, but each is acceptable.

The *Eudemian Ethics* account begins with a lengthy reflection on two meanings of *sôphrosunê*'s principal opposite, "indiscipline." It can name the state of either not yet having been disciplined or cured (as in the case of children) or of being difficult or altogether impossible to cure through discipline.[4] This proemic sensitivity to the various ways people use a term induces one to expect the same linguistic sensitivity once Aristotle turns to *sôphrosunê* itself. The pleasures it governs come from taste and touch, "but, in truth," he now specifies, really only "touch."[5] Before eliminating taste from the ambit of *sôphrosunê*, Aristotle eliminates sights, sounds, and smells. "For nobody is said to be (λέγεται)" and "nobody would be deemed (δόξειεν)" undisciplined who simply wished (βούλοιτο) to take in some beautiful thing to look at or music to hear—that is, excessively.[6] He gives a rationale for this putative linguistic observation: taste and touch are the only senses through which beasts have pleasure or pain, and *sôphrosunê* concerns the desires shared with the animals. Aristotle believes that the sense of smell is merely a source of information for animals, not of intrinsic delight. He also believes that animals do not desire tastes for themselves. They do

---

[3] Arist. *MM* 1.21 1191b5–20.
[4] Arist. *EE* 3.2 1230b8: οἱ δυσίατοι καὶ οἱ ἀνίατοι πάμπαν διὰ κολάσεως.
[5] Arist. *EE* 3.2 1230b25–26.
[6] Arist. *EE* 3.2 1230b26–36.

not care to savor their food; they want only to feel it going down their throat and ending up in their belly.[7] The same may be said of gourmands, who "do not pray to have a long tongue but a crane's throat."

By appealing to animal ethology, Aristotle believes he can explain the main species of human indiscipline: drunkenness (οἰνοφλυγία), gluttony (γαστριμαργία), being oversexed (λαγνεία), and gourmandizing (ὀψοφαγία). He repeats that excess with respect to the other senses is simply not called (λέγεται) indiscipline and is censured "without rebuke" (ἄνευ ὀνείδους); such instances "are [instead] called not being self-controlled" (μὴ λέγονται ἐγκρατεῖς); people who "lack self-control" (οἱ ἀκρατεῖς) are neither *sôphrôn* nor *akolastos* but somewhere in between.[8] Of course, everyone naturally (φύσει) enjoys and desires the pleasures of touch, and many do so without being called undisciplined; rebuke is earned only when a person enjoys them too much or feels too much pain in their absence.[9]

While basically consistent with the *Magna Moralia* account, the *Eudemian* account gives arguments for the positions. Aristotle explains his restriction of the domain of *sôphrosunê* by appeal to the way people speak—what they would or would not chastise as indiscipline, its absence. He presents this as a kind of ordinary-language analysis, a fidelity to the patterns of actual Greek usage. But he then gives two kinds of biological explanation for that linguistic usage. First, all cases of indiscipline, which have to do with only two classes of desire, can in fact be shown to have to do with only one class of desire, that related to the sense of touch. Perhaps the simplicity of this explanation is to speak in its favor. Second, it so happens that desire for the pleasures of touch is the only kind of desire shared between beasts and humans. This connection gives another reason to accept the virtue's distinctly narrow domain: it is the virtue that concerns the desires experienced by all animals, which explains why people call failures of *sôphrosunê* bestial. Finally, Aristotle explains that while people may in fact be criticized for their excessive pursuit of pleasures unrelated to the sense of touch, this poses no problem for his view, since these people are still called uncontrolled (ἀκρατής), a different but actual charge.

The still longer discussion of *sôphrosunê* in the *Nicomachean Ethics* begins with a series of valuable specifications. *Sôphrosunê* and courage, the virtue it follows in Aristotle's discussion, "seem to be the virtues of the irrational (ἀλόγων) parts of the soul," and *sôphrosunê*, which unlike courage is mainly concerned with pleasure, has a restricted connection to pain.[10] Aristotle evidently sees *sôphrosunê* and courage as the pair of virtues concerned about our

---

[7] Sisko (2003, 139).
[8] Arist. *EE* 3.2 1230b36–1231a26.
[9] Arist. *EE* 3.2 1231a29–32.
[10] Arist. *NE* 3.10 1117b23–27; explained at 3.11 1118b29–1119a6. On the point about pain, see Konkoly (1998).

basic organismic fears and desires. He goes on to distinguish psychic from bodily pleasures and explains why *sôphrosunê* concerns only the latter. As he appealed to the ordinary use of ethical language in the *Eudemian Ethics*, here too he says that psychic pleasures of ambition fulfilled (φιλοτιμία) or curiosity sated (φιλομάθεια) are not relevant to Greek speakers' judgments of *sôphrosunê*; the same goes for the enjoyment felt by those who sit around swapping stories all day; it even goes (on the reverse side) for those who feel terrible when they lose their livelihood or their friends.[11] Thus *sôphrosunê* concerns only bodily pleasures, and indeed only those from a subset of the five senses. Aristotle makes more precise his view about smell (people may indeed be called *akolastos* if they delight too much in food smells, in anticipation of eating) and about taste. Taste is for "judging between flavors" (ἡ κρίσις τῶν χυμῶν) and matters to those who assess wine and chefs who are preparing a fine meal; but it is not the flavors that most people most of the time enjoy, and especially not those who eat in an undisciplined way. They enjoy the consummation itself, the feel of the food moving through, just as the pleasures of drinking and sex also come through touch.[12] But not all touch is relevant—the "most free" (ἐλευθεριώταται) kinds of touch, such as massages and warm baths at the gymnasium, belong in a different category. Touch of only certain parts of the body (περί τινα μέρη) pertains to *sôphrosunê*, as these are the sources of pleasure shared universally with animals.[13] Derision attaches to excess satisfaction here because these desires belong to us not as humans but as animals (οὐχ ᾗ ἄνθρωποί ἐσμεν ὑπάρχει, ἀλλ' ᾗ ζῷα).[14] Aristotle raises and addresses a number of additional problems in the ensuing paragraphs, especially connected to the place of pain in the account and the nearness of the mean to the extremes, but they do not affect this core of his most developed account of *sôphrosunê*.[15]

Aristotle believes that each virtue involves the moderation of a certain distinctive set of feelings. A person with a virtue has certain feelings—fear, desire for food, the inclination to help a friend—but only to the limited extent that motivates but does not inhibit noble action. *Sôphrosunê* involves the moderation of a special set of bodily desires, the natural or necessary ones, the satisfaction of which often poses no difficulty but does pose the risk of being too strong, preventing or complicating one's performance of noble action.[16] Eating

---

[11] Arist. *NE* 3.10 1117b29–1118a2. Sisko (2003, 135n4) notes that Aristotle presents himself as using an endoxic method.
[12] Arist. *NE* 3.10 1118a2–b5.
[13] Arist. *NE* 3.10 1118b5–8.
[14] Arist. *NE* 3.10 1118b3–4.
[15] Arist. *NE* 3.11–12 1118b8–1119b19.
[16] For context, see Broadie (1991, 266–71). Gottlieb (2009, 55, 59, 64) argues for *sôphrosunê* as a training rather than correction of desires.

is essential to our survival, and is usually unproblematic, and may even be distinctly valuable, but the desire to do so may become so inflamed as to cause us to act badly, whether unhealthily, repulsively, unjustly, or harshly.[17] So too drinking and having sex (with our survival considered at the species level). Thus, for Aristotle, the desires related to the most fundamental capacities of soul, nutrition and reproduction, constitute a natural group.[18] This natural group explains another aspect of the ethical centrality of *sôphrosunê*: it seems to have an ontogenetic priority. It concerns the desires budding humans must deal with first. Babies act much like beasts, driven by a manic quest for nourishment and intimacy; even as we grow up, as we labor and tire, those basal desires become especially vivid. The desires of touch may be the most visceral and insistent, their control the greatest accomplishment as we mature into our rational nature. Without *sôphrosunê*, those desires may end up being treated as ends in themselves, and it is the special competence of the virtue to see them as merely instrumental to more mature ends. Sarah Broadie puts the point most bracingly:

> By rejecting our sheer animality, Aristotelian moderation [*sôphrosunê*] affirms our humanity instead. It is distinctively human to think in terms of means to ends at all, and to desire the kinds of things—long-term health and security, participation in society—that moderate practices do so much to promote. The person who is genuinely moderate practices moderation [*sôphrosunê*] not for the sake of those results, not perhaps sheerly for its own sake, but to assert and reinforce the human nature, unique among mortal living beings, by which we value rational ends and approach them in a rational way.[19]

More generally, the sheer fit of Aristotle's *sôphrosunê* account into his psychological and biological theory—a theory that seems to avoid both the implausibilities of a Socratic intellectualist account and the metaphoricity of a Platonic political account—speaks strongly in its favor.[20]

---

[17] Nussbaum (1986, 309) finds Aristotle's moderateness refreshing by contrast with what she ascribes to Plato in his *Phaedo* and *Phaedrus* (cf. 151–53, 202–33). Kosman (2020, 80) puts it differently: it is a signal accomplishment to be at peace with respect to those strong desires, as it is admirable, in the case of courage, to be at peace with our fears.

[18] One might find it appropriate to distinguish the appetitive from the spirited desires (Bobonich 2013, 31) and judge *sôphrosunê* to concern itself only with the first. Tsouna (2018), who believes that Aristotle's view is close to common sense (19, 25, 37), finds it to be a plausible development of the *Republic* view and a response to Socrates' supposed refutation of Critias' intellectualist, universalist, reflexive, and contentless view of *sôphrosunê* discussed in the *Charmides*. On the psychological/biological grounding of Aristotle's theory here, see Sisko (2003). We should note, however, that Aristotle asserts that there is no virtue of the nutritive-reproductive part of the soul: *NE* 6.12 1144a9–11.

[19] Broadie and Rowe (2002, 27).

[20] Hutchinson (1986) speaks well to the impressiveness of Aristotle's theory of virtue in general.

Distinctions among Moral-Psychological States

In the *Eudemian Ethics*, Aristotle discusses the relationship between the sense of shame (αἰδώς) and *sôphrosunê*, which some people have regarded as highly similar—as Protagoras' Great Speech and the second definition in Plato's *Charmides* also reveal.[21] In that treatise, Aristotle analyzes shame as a middle state between two levels of emotional reactivity rather than as a virtue itself, since virtue but not shame involves action.[22] The shameless man gives no thought to the opinion of others (μηδεμιᾶς φροντίζων δόξης); the bashful man gives thought to everyone's; the man with a sense of shame gives thought only to that of the evidently reasonable (φαινομένων ἐπιεικῶν).[23] The bashful man feels pain when contemplating going against what he interprets as others' expectations; the shameless man feels no such pain. These feelings, Aristotle says, are natural, and so they contribute to the "natural virtues," what the virtues are before they have been infused with wisdom (μετὰ φρονήσεως). Just as envy or malice contributes to (natural) injustice, righteous indignation to (natural) justice, and truthfulness to (natural) wisdom, the sense of shame contributes to (natural) *sôphrosunê*.[24] And, Aristotle says, "for this very reason some people have even defined *sôphrosunê* as of this sort,"[25] namely an emotional mean state rather than a virtue.

Aristotle says no more here, and he says nothing on the topic in the *Nicomachean Ethics*, but his point clearly concerns the proximity of *sôphrosunê* and the sense of shame. Shame is a response to certain social expectations, ideally the authoritative ones. One's *sôphrosunê*-related desires may be moderated by the extinguishing pain caused by a well-adjusted sense of shame. Of course, Aristotle believes that only certain desires fall within *sôphrosunê*'s ambit; he must be thinking of the disdain expressed at a person's festival overindulgence or blinding lust. Yet the general point is that shame, which is a sensitivity to others' evaluations of propriety, conditions one's desires such that one no longer wants to do what shame inhibits. To the extent that shame sensitivity is felt toward the opinions of those who know the right way to behave, the desire-moderation will be ethically laudatory, not just ataraxic. Those who have placed *sôphrosunê* within the genus of emotional middle states (that is, unlike Aristotle) must believe that the *sôphrôn* person feels a moderate pleasure when anticipating (or upon receiving) certain things; the undisciplined person feels excessive pain when deprived of those things. The difference between the sense of shame

---

[21] Pl. *Prot.* 322c2, 4, 7, d5 with 323a1–2, b4–6; *Chrm.* 160e3–5.
[22] Arist. *EE* 3.7 1233b17–19, 1234a24–27.
[23] Arist. *EE* 3.7 1233b27–29.
[24] Arist. *EE* 3.7 1234a30–32.
[25] Arist. *EE* 3.7 1234a32–33: διὸ καὶ ὁρίζονται ἐν τῷ γένει τούτῳ τὴν σωφροσύνην.

and the experience of *sôphrosunê* is presumably that the first causes emotional reactions to social judgments, the second other to the satisfaction of one's desires.

This is an appealing distinction, and it shares much with the longer account of shame in the *Nicomachean Ethics*.[26] Aristotle's difference with his unnamed opponents concerns their treatment of *sôphrosunê* as an emotional middle state rather than as a virtue. In our present passage, *sôphrosunê* as a virtue involves choice (προαίρεσις), and by contrast with "natural virtues" (φυσικαὶ ... ἀρεταί), virtue properly involves wisdom.[27] This novel two-tier account of virtue gains clarity in the *Nicomachean Ethics*. Everyone agrees, Aristotle says, that our character traits come somehow or to some extent naturally (ἕκαστα τῶν ἠθῶν ὑπάρχειν φύσει πως): "Straight from birth, we can be just and *sôphronikos* and courageous and the rest."[28] So too animals. But this natural virtue differs from "authoritative (κυρία) virtue" in lacking reason (νοῦς).[29] Virtue in its ideal form thus has two aspects, a desiderative one that is natural, in-born, or at least developable from natural experiences (such as shame), and a rational one that is developed as a specifically human capacity. It is failing to identify these two aspects, Aristotle says, that led Socrates to his paradoxical virtue-unification: rightly judging that virtue involves reason but neglecting object-specific desire-moderation, he thought that all virtues were the same epistemic capacity, namely, *phronêsis*.[30] Socrates did not see that each virtue combines *phronêsis* with the moderation of its own kinds of desire. How Aristotle's authoritative virtue differs from his natural virtue is debatable.[31] In the present passage, he says only that without reason, the natural states are evidently harmful (βλαβεραί). In explanation he gives an elliptical and partly joking analogy. He imagines a vigorous creature without eyesight who, in motion but blind, trips up just as vigorously.[32] Evidently the creature can act for the most part but cannot avoid unexpected obstacles. And evidently the naturally virtuous person does the right thing for the most part but not when there are unexpected obstacles. The analogy suggests that authoritative virtue does not contribute accuracy to one's virtuous inclination but rather

---

[26] Arist. *EN* 4.9 1128b10–34; for details, see Raymond (2017).

[27] Arist. *EE* 3.7 1234a27–30.

[28] Arist. *EN* 6.13 1144b5–7: καὶ γὰρ δίκαιοι καὶ σωφρονικοὶ καὶ ἀνδρεῖοι καὶ τἆλλα ἔχομεν εὐθὺς ἐκ γενετῆς. It is not clear why Aristotle uses ἔχομεν here; Rackham (1926, 368n4) queries the verb, suggesting the emendment ἔσομεν; Beresford (2020, 154) translates "we're [predisposed to]."

[29] Arist. *EN* 6.13 1144b7–17.

[30] Arist. *EN* 6.13 1144b17–30.

[31] Russell (2014, 209) judges them to be far apart, with "natural virtue" effectively a childish possession; similarly Pakaluk (1992, 176–78). White (1992, esp. 154–56) and Curzer (2012, 293–307) bring them much closer, finding them to differ mainly in motivation; authoritative virtue acts from understanding; see also Viano (2007). Leunissen (2017, xv–xxvi) presents the background for the natural constituents of natural virtue. For more general issues connected to Aristotle's theory of virtue, see Lorenz (2009) and Moss (2011).

[32] Arist. *EN* 6.13 1144b10–12: σώματι ἰσχυρῷ ἄνευ ὄψεως κινουμένῳ συμβαίνει σφάλλεσθαι ἰσχυρῶς διὰ τὸ μὴ ἔχειν ὄψιν.

robustness in the face of unusual or extreme events. Reason or wisdom allows one to accommodate unforeseen enticements, unfamiliar desires, or blockages to one's usual mechanisms of self-possession.

This interpretation of authoritative virtue is not satisfying in all respects. It is strange to think that babies and animals have sufficient "natural virtue" to choose correctly whenever the situation is predictable. It is just as strange to think that, despite the centrality of wisdom and reasoning to Aristotle's account of virtue, it serves merely as a backstop against wild pitches. Without entering further into the debated interpretation, we can make several observations. First, Aristotle follows Plato, whose characters sometimes posit two levels of virtue, notably in the *Phaedo* and the *Laws*. Aristotle diagnoses what he sees as incoherent talk about *sôphrosunê* as a symptom of equivocation. *Sôphrosunê* is both intelligent and found in nonhuman mammals? It is both the result of intense training and a common proclivity? Well, yes, but that is because there are two distinct competences going under the same name. Second, what the person with authoritative virtue can really do better than the one with natural virtue is hard to say, but this problem was already identified in Plato's *Meno*, where the interlocutors wavered trying to explain the superiority of virtue as knowledge to virtue as true belief.[33] Both are equally accurate, but knowledge is less budgeable; decisions made on its basis remain good even in heavy weather. Third, Aristotle's key intuition here, that there is a kind of natural virtue, seems plausible enough. Some children do act in a *sôphrôn* way, placidly and affected little by strong desire. It is in the tough choices, where doing the right thing is obscure or unpleasant, that we admire a person for being fully and authoritatively virtuous.

Besides distinguishing *sôphrosunê* from the sense of shame and natural *sôphrosunê*, Aristotle differentiates it from *enkrateia*, "self-control" or "inner strength." The contrast here differs from that found in Xenophon, but the understanding of *enkrateia* itself is similar. For both authors, as well as for Plato, *enkrateia* is the capacity to avoid satisfying counterrational desires. In Aristotle's system, *enkrateia* is at issue only when a person has desires that urge him to act badly. Since people are virtuous only after having moderated their desires, which means never being urged to act badly, the *enkratês* person cannot be virtuous.[34] (Aristotle here, at 1151b35–1152a5, is taking issue with Antiphon's view of *sôphrosunê*.) Thus the *enkratês* person cannot be *sôphrôn*, what Aristotle acknowledges to be a controversial point.[35] For Xenophon,

---

[33] Pl. *Meno* 97a3–99a5; cf. Arist. *NE* 6.12 1143b30–32.

[34] A sympathetic discussion is in Trianosky (1988); see Callard (2017) for an alternative view. Haug (2022a, 2022b, with bibliography) deals with contemporary virtue-ethics reflection on this issue, especially taking issue with the strict discrimination between *enkrateia* and *sôphrosunê*.

[35] The debate discussed: *NE* 7.1 1145b14–17; the main point reiterated: 7.2 1146a10–11. At 7.9 1151b32–1152a6, Aristotle admits that people speak of the *enkratês* person as the *sôphrôn* person, by resemblance.

enkrateia and *sôphrosunê* were consistent, since they were different capacities (desire-control vs. commitment to authoritative norms), and in fact worked together; for Plato, *enkrateia* was, as it were, a major part of *sôphrosunê*; but for Aristotle, they are inconsistent levels of attainment, as walking and sprinting are. And further, while *enkrateia* and *sôphrosunê* exclude one another, Aristotle believes that, properly speaking, they have the same scope. *Enkrateia* "simply so put" (ἁπλῶς) concerns the "necessary" "bodily" desires of touch that *sôphrosunê* concerns.[36] It is only via a "resemblance" that the term *enkrateia* also concerns other excessive desires, including those for revenge, status, or money.[37] Thus Aristotle's *enkrateia* matches closely Xenophon's, though what Xenophon adds to Aristotle's list, for example the withstanding of fatigue and discomfort, Aristotle applies to "endurance" (καρτερία).[38] As with his argument about *sôphrosunê*, one may wonder whether Aristotle presents *enkrateia* too narrowly. He recognizes that when people think of the pleasures they struggle most against, they think of bodily pleasures.[39] But then he gives theoretical priority to those pleasures. He may have cogent reasons for doing so, but at least this misrepresents Greek linguistic patterns.[40] And it complicates the more important point of *Nicomachean Ethics* Book 7, that there are states called *enkrateia* and *akrasia* that parallel all the virtues and vices and not only *sôphrosunê* and *akolasia*.

Thus Aristotle distinguishes *sôphrosunê* from the sense of shame, from self-control, from a natural state of *sôphrosunê*, and from practical wisdom. Each of these distinctions could be controversial, even as none is implausible or incoherent. For instance, one might think that *sôphrosunê* is hardly to be distinguished from practical wisdom, or that *enkrateia* does not mean that one feels dubious desires more than in the state of *sôphrosunê*, or that the "natural"–"authoritative" spectrum involves not a qualitative but only a quantitative shift, or that *sôphrosunê* is just a transcendental sense of shame—and yet Aristotle's positions would be worthy adversaries for the person who thinks those things. What is notable is that none depends on the leading principle of Aristotle's *sôphrosunê* analysis: that it concerns the pleasures of touch. This principle has

---

[36] Aristotle's clear formulation of the question shows that the issue had been debated earlier: "Do *akrasia* and *enkrateia* concern all [the pleasures] or not?" (εἰ περὶ πάντ᾿ ἐστὶν ἀκρασία καὶ ἐγκράτεια ἢ οὔ; 7.3 1146b18–19); and his answer is unequivocal: "The *akratic* person simply so put is not so concerning all [the pleasures] but only those that define the *akolastos*" (οὔτε γὰρ περὶ ἅπαντ᾿ ἐστὶν ὁ ἁπλῶς ἀκρατής, ἀλλὰ περὶ ἅπερ ὁ ἀκόλαστος, b19–20). On the necessary (ἀναγκαῖα) pleasures as definitional of *akrasia*: 7.4 1146b24–28, 1148a5–11; 7.5 1149a19–24, 7.6 1149b25–26.

[37] Resemblance (ὁμοιότης): 7.4 1146b34–35; 1148b4–14; 7.5 1149a1–4.

[38] Acknowledgment that some treat *enkrateia* and *karteria* as the same: 7.3 1146b12; distinguished at 7.7 1150a34–b1: *karteria* involves τὸ ἀντέχειν ("holding out"), *enkrateia* involves κρατεῖν ("mastery"); and the latter is better.

[39] Arist. *EN* 7.13 1153b33–1154a1.

[40] On such reasons, see Broadie (1991, 266–71).

often been accepted as uncontroversial, but it is the least convincing aspect of the entire theory.

Sympathetic Reception and the Contrary Evidence

Ancient and modern commentators largely accept the basic soundness of Aristotle's general view of *sôphrosunê*, even as some do recognize that in Aristotle's hands it governs a much narrower range of human life than it does in the hands of other writers.[41] Aspasius and Aquinas simply summarize and explicate the view, with none of their frequent defense or critique. In the (only) two published articles specifically about Aristotle's view of *sôphrosunê*, the framework is taken for granted, with attention given only to details of the argument.[42] John Burnet wrote, "Plato always tries to extend the scope of these virtues as widely as he can, while Aristotle's chief endeavour is to narrow them down to their most literal meaning. . . . Aristotle is looking for facts by which to test his theory of goodness, and it was important for that purpose to have facts as unmistakeable as possible."[43] A recent commentary on *Nicomachean Ethics* 2–4 claims that Aristotle is "in broad conformity with standard Greek usage."[44] Another recent commentary states that "*sôphrosunê* originally connoted self-restraint in general, like the English 'moderation,' but later came to be restricted to restraint in the pleasures of the flesh. Aristotle uses the term in this narrower sense."[45] In none of these works are any charges made against Aristotle's linguistic analysis; what criticisms there are concern mainly his limiting the relevant pleasures to certain feelings on certain body parts. Some of those who do observe that Aristotle's usage is starkly narrow even defend his doing so. Terence Irwin, for instance, thinks that Aristotle, besides affirming the difference between necessary desires and the socially or idiosyncratically sourced desires, "rejects the view that there is some common explanation of over-indulgence in desires as a whole, and hence he refuses to treat over-indulgence as a single vice." Because "different forms

---

[41] Some commentators on Aristotle's theory of virtue do not even mention *sôphrosunê*, e.g., Tessitore (1996); Kraut (2006). Broadie (1991, 205) mentions it only to formulate the standard view: "Without temperance one cannot be wise . . . for too much concern with pleasure and pain destroys one's focus on the good."

[42] Young (1988); Curzer (1997). Curzer is more attentive to the narrowness in his book published fifteen years later (2012, 65–68, 77).

[43] Burnet (1900, 110).

[44] Taylor (2006, 116).

[45] Broadie and Rowe (2002, 25). MacIntyre (1988, 4) claims that Aristotle "assigned [*sôphrosunê*] a narrower, more specialized and better defined place"; Gauthier and Jolif (1959, 2.1.236–38) claim that Aristotle's use reflects the term's increasingly restricted use in Greek; Bartlett and Collins (2011, 312) present Aristotelian "moderation" as broader than Aristotle allows ("the proper disposition toward the bodily desires and pleasures") and seem to fault Plato for having a "rather broad" usage.

of over-indulgence associated with different desires need separate training," it is appropriate for Aristotle to distinguish virtues by their pedagogical and etiological sources.[46] Giles Pearson, in the *Cambridge Companion to Aristotle's Nicomachean Ethics*, gives four reasons to accept Aristotle's view, one of which is that the other senses attributed to *sôphrosunê* by other authors are relevant derivatively (though Aristotle never says so, and Pearson does not argue so), and the more significant of which is that Aristotle "appeals to how Greek speakers of his time would employ the words in question (at least on reflection).... Or at least to how those who are 'properly brought up' would" (though without evidence provided).[47] This apologetic stance is not universal, but the tolerance for Aristotle's narrowing is pretty broad.[48]

Against the view that *sôphrosunê* narrowed in its application in the later fourth century we may consider Isocrates, who lived and wrote until the decade of Aristotle's death. For him the verb *sôphronein* virtually always means "to be reasonable, sensible, prudent"—not acting on impulse or crazily, being thoughtful about what one is doing, and considering long-term consequences.[49] Once, in a use familiar from Thucydides, it has a foreign-policy connotation, opposing *polupragmonein*, which is imperial meddling; but even here it means acting on longer-term or broader considerations, since in that case, Thebes was said to have overrun its success after defeating Sparta at Leuctra.[50] More relevant is Isocrates' use of the noun *sôphrosunê*. As we found in epigraphy, he can pair it with "virtue," sometimes as what philosophers teach, *sôphrosunê kai aretê*. Here it seems less a subset of virtue than somehow equivalent or representative or a salient version of it, and generally implying knowing the right thing to do, perhaps captured with the English "sense and sensibility."[51] He also pairs *sôphrosunê* with justice and treats it as among the canonical virtues of excellent people,[52] though closer

---

[46] Irwin (1984, 323). Irwin elsewhere observes that "Aristotle's restricted conception of *sôphrosunê* tends to conceal the cognitive aspect of the Greek term, which sometimes indicates good sense, prudence and the moderation resulting from them. Aristotle is aware of this (cf. 1140b11)" (428).

[47] Pearson (2014, 124). The remaining two reasons are that the other pleasures have other relevant excesses and deficiencies and that foregrounding touch is actually a good idea.

[48] Those who recognize Aristotle's narrowing include Steward (1892, 302); North (1966, 198, 200; recognizing his expansiveness elsewhere, 204–9, and finding him still to treat *sôphrosunê* as the foundation of virtue); Sparshott (1970, 60n48: "Conformity to 'ordinary language' can hardly be Aristotle's motive: 'temperance' is used in an artificially restricted sense, piety is left out as are many ordinary virtue-words)"; Burger (2008, 80–82: as symmetrical with Plato's broadening); Brown (2009, 224); Curzer (2012) (see n42 above); Bourgault (2013, 126: "Aristotle has, unlike Plato, a narrow and heavily gendered account of *sophrosyne*"); Rabinowitz (2015, 27).

[49] Not impulsively: Isoc. *Panath.* 14; being thoughtful: *Panath.* 140, 172, 199, 237; the long term: *Bus.* 40, *Plat.* 22, *Philip.* 7. More cliché uses at *Loch.* 22; *Paneg.* 165; *Antid.* 242, 304; *Ad Alex.* 5. See also the adjective used in the same way at *Nic.* 51; *Antid.* 290.

[50] Isoc. *Pace* 58. The verb's use parallels that of the verbal form of *promêthês*, *promêtheomai*, "to watch out, take care that": the basic task of rationality; see Moore (2015a, 403).

[51] Paired with ἀρετή: Isoc. *C. soph.* 6, 20; *Hel.* 31, 38; *Areop.* 37, 38.

[52] Isoc. *Ad Dem.* 15; *C. soph.* 21; *Nic.* 29, 30; *Pace* 63; *Panath.* 138; *De bigis* 28.

to hardiness (καρτερία) and hard work (ἐργασία) than to courage.[53] Sometimes Isocrates mentions a specific application of *sôphrosunê*, though never in a limiting way: in paying debts,[54] due reverence toward the gods,[55] the bodily comportment of youth,[56] and the erotic restraint of tyrants.[57] It has the geopolitical isolationist implication observed above, along with a broader notion of political order and fairness, the opposite of hubris and tyranny.[58] Sparta exemplifies it and its complement, obedience (πειθαρχία).[59] Rather like Xenophon, Isocrates distinguishes *sôphrosunê* from *enkrateia* such that *sôphrosunê* is not so much strength with respect to and control over one's desires as the appreciation of the right things to do—in the *Nicocles*, Isocrates says that it involves forgoing pleasures that provide "no honor" (μηδεμίαν τιμὴν ἔχουσιν) and aiming instead for that reputation that comes from "good character" (ἀνδραγαθία); he thereby makes judgment central.[60] Presumably as part of maturation and acculturation to a system of values, *sôphrosunê* is especially fine in youth.[61] Isocrates' fundamental view is that *sôphrosunê* opposes doing whatever one wants, and thus it must mean acting on some principles.[62] His uses of the adjective *sôphrôn* clarify this: being *sôphrôn* is contrary to indiscipline (ἀκολασία), law-breaking (παρανομία), saying whatever one wants (παρρησία), and doing whatever one wants (ἐξουσία).[63] Indeed, Isocrates even has a Socratic moment, saying that *sôphrosunê* in students involves their working on themselves rather than acting on conceits of expertise.[64] So, since Isocrates treats *sôphrosunê* as a superlative political ideal,[65] it basically means living in accordance with a constitution, a set of norms. This quick overview of Isocrates' usage of *sôphrosunê* cognates, from the 390s till the 330s, shows that the virtue generally refers to norm-following—the disposition for rational choice and deliberation at the personal level, and constitutional stability, fairness, and self-containment at the political level. Nothing

---

[53] Isoc. *Panath.* 197; *Ad Timoth.* 3. Thus *Areop.* 4, where Isocrates claims that "lack" (ἔνδεια) and "poor condition" (ταπεινότης) bring forth *sôphrosunê*, by contrast with power and wealth, which bring about "thoughtlessness" (ἄνοια) and "indiscipline" (ἀκολασία).

[54] Isoc. *C. soph.* 6, where the matter is connected less to greediness than to doing one's duty.

[55] Isoc. *Bus.* 21; cf. Xen. *Mem.* 4.3.2–18.

[56] Isoc. *Areop.* 45; cf. Pl. *Chrm.* 159b; Xen. *Lac. Pol.* 3.4, Ar. *Nub.* 962–84.

[57] Isoc. *Nic.* 36, where Isocrates makes clear that at most only a few applications of the respective virtue are being cited; see the gloss on *dikaiosunê* immediately before.

[58] Isolationism: Isoc. *Pace* 63. Order and fairness: *Hel.* 31, 38; *Pace* 119; *Ad Archid.* 4, *Ad Timoth.* 3. At *Ad Nic.* 31, speaking of the leader's role in modeling *sôphrosunê* for his city, making it orderly (κόσμιος) and less disordered (ἄτακτος), Isocrates avers that having *sôphrosunê* is compatible with become wealthier; he appears to have something of the well-run society of the Protestant work ethic in mind here.

[59] Isoc. *Panath.* 111, 115.

[60] Isoc. *Nic.* 44; cf. *Ad Antipatrum* 4.

[61] Isoc. *Evag.* 22; *Ad Dem.* 15.

[62] Isoc. *Areop.* 37.

[63] Isoc. *Panath.* 218; *Areop.* 20; cf. *Pace* 104.

[64] Isoc. *Antid.* 290; cf. *Ad Antipatrum* 2.

[65] Isoc. *In Call.* 46; *Pace* 104; *Areop.* 13, 20; *Panath.* 151.

hints, across contexts and decades, of a use primarily or even notably concerned with bodily desires, much less exclusively those of touch.

Aside from this contemporary evidence for the infelicity of Aristotle's account of *sôphrosunê*, we have internal evidence: Aristotle employs the common usage elsewhere in his corpus. One instance appears at the conclusion of his main discussion of *sôphrosunê* in the *Nicomachean Ethics*. He says that we ascribe the name indiscipline, as the opposite of *sôphrosunê*, to childish errors, to which it is "somewhat alike."[66] He does not specify which desires children live at the mercy of, but he can hardly have in mind only those of food, drink, and sex—otherwise the faults of children and adults would be identical, not "somewhat alike," and it is hard to believe that he thinks youthful impetuosity concerns only those desires.[67] So "indiscipline" for children is broader than that for adults. He might then think—though he does not say so—that the wider childish use of indiscipline (and its opposite, *sôphrosunê*) is sometimes applied to adults in, as it were, a derivative or figurative sense. Elsewhere in the *Nicomachean Ethics*, in a gnomic temper, Aristotle says that he who rightly judges himself of little worth is *sôphrôn*, by contrast with the one who rightly judges himself of great worth, who is proud.[68] This represents a decidedly Socratic *sôphrosunê* of humble self-knowledge. A bit later, Aristotle says we sometimes praise the retiring or unambitious (ἀφιλότιμος) person as moderate and *sôphrôn*; he hereby treats *sôphrosunê* as the disposition not to pursue honor, fame, or other aspects of public acclaim.[69] Then Aristotle cites the important moral injunction to be *sôphrôn* and avoid adultery or hubris.[70] This is at once a narrower construction on *sôphrosunê* than Aristotle elsewhere gives, and a more social or political one, as refraining from outrage of domestic or private proprieties. In the *Topics*, he cites as an exemplary dialectical question "How does *sôphrosunê* differ from wisdom?," a Socratic question with *Protagoras* and *Memorabilia* provenance; *sôphrosunê* must be thought enough like prudence, good sense, or knowledge of the good for the question to have any purchase at all.[71] Aristotle claims, in the same work, that treating *sôphrosunê* as harmony *simpliciter* is merely metaphorical.[72] And he expressly opposes the view found in the *Laws*, that justice amounts to *sôphrosunê* plus courage, a view that makes sense only with *sôphrosunê* referring to more than control of some of the appetites of touch.[73] From this hodgepodge of examples,

---

[66] Arist. *EN* 3.12 1119b12–18.
[67] Aristotle acknowledges the conventional view that *sôphrosunê* is a virtue for youth: *Top.* 117a31; *Rh.* 1361a3–7, 1390b4. But he says that the young are *sôphrôn* in a special way, given their immaturity: *Pol.* 1259b22–32, 1277b17–21.
[68] Arist. *EN* 4.3 1123b5.
[69] Arist. *EN* 4.4 1125b13, 7.4 1147b28; cf. Isoc. *Ad Antipatrum* 2.
[70] Arist. *EN* 5.1 1129b21.
[71] Arist. *Top.* 108a2.
[72] Arist. *Top.* 123a34–36, 139b33.
[73] Arist. *Top.* 150a4–13.

it is clear that Aristotle knows *sôphrosunê* has broader application than he allows in *Nicomachean Ethics* 3.10–12 and its equivalent in the *Eudemian Ethics*. And he has obviously read enough of Plato's dialogues, notably his *Protagoras*, *Republic*, and *Laws* (though maybe not *Charmides* or *Gorgias*) to appreciate his teacher's rich conception of the virtue.

Indeed, we know that Aristotle read Sophocles, too. In *Oedipus the King*, Creon says that he, like anyone who "knows how to *sôphronein*," does not seek to become a tyrant, since with that power and visibility one can never sleep well, always fearing assassination.[74] In *Philoctetes*, Philoctetes denies that any *sôphrôn* mortal would ever want to come to his island, so little material or social value would it provide, and Neoptolomus sarcastically accuses Odysseus of having *sôphronein* when Odysseus threatens to accuse Neoptolomus of treachery; he would actually fail to be *sôphrôn* because such an accusation would prevent the realization of their plans.[75] And in *Electra*, *sôphronein* is twice closely related to piety, being observant of divine norms (εὐσέβεια).[76] To be *sôphrôn* is thus to be able to judge what is valuable notwithstanding the active appeal of alternative options. In none of these cases are touch-related desires salient or even relevant, and the same holds for the rest of Sophocles' oeuvre.[77]

So Aristotle's official statements about usage of the term *sôphrosunê* are questionable. His theoretical position is too neat to respect linguistic niceties. But even the theoretical position itself, with its biological substrate, is questionable. Aristotle asserts that *sôphrosunê* concerns eating, drink, and sex, and that the unity of these three is found in their sharing a sensory modality, touch, in their "necessity," in that everyone experiences them and that individual or group continuity requires their exercise, and in their universality across animals. Indeed, the unity is also found throughout everyday speech, as we have seen in Xenophon's and Plato's works. But that unity may be less definite than it seems, for each of the three desires of touch has only a loose relationship to the virtue. Drinking is the most straightforward case. Although consuming liquid is necessary and shared with animals, the associated pleasure is of "quenching," a moistening of what is dry; if this counts as touch, it is as a nonstandard instance. Even so, nobody chastises others as undisciplined for drinking too much water or milk; but even if they were to do so, excessive hydration is not what *akolasia* and *sôphrosunê* pertain to. What gets chastised is alcoholic drunkenness that leads to rowdiness or dissipation.[78] And intoxication Aristotle has not

---

[74] Soph. *OT* 589.
[75] Soph. *Ph.* 304, 1259.
[76] Soph. *El.* 307, 465. At 365 it means "to think rightly."
[77] Soph. *Aj.* 132, 586, 677, 1075, 1259, 1265; *Trac.* 435; frr. 683, 936. Some fragments refer to feminine virtue—frr. 64, 682—but need not refer specifically to sexual chastity; and two fragments have inadequate context—frr. 786, 896.
[78] See Arist. *NE* 7.14 1154a18: ὄψοις καὶ <u>οἴνοις</u> καὶ ἀφροδισίοις.

shown to be a pleasure of touch.[79] Even if the buzz, lightness, and reduced inhibition could casuistically be analyzed as a pleasure of touch, it is hard to see that it is a necessary or natural one, or one shared with all animals. Just as drink seems inadequately explained by Aristotle's touch analysis, eating is similarly dubious. Maybe the glutton likes the feeling of food, but why might he not also very much like the taste?[80] Those who gorge themselves on mush or gruel seem insane or undernourished, not reprehensibly pleasure-directed. It is snacks and treats, like chips and ice cream and butterflied lamb chops, that get consumed with indiscipline, because they taste so good. Their sumptuousness may be related to their high nutritive value (salt, fat, sugar), and thus to the natural desires, but then we might expect a more fine-grained account of *sôphrosunê*—too fine-grained, it might seem. The same criticisms might even be laid, if with less conviction, against the view of sex, which, while perhaps centrally about the sense of touch located at the genitals, involves or eventuates in other organismic feelings—and in other less-sensory feelings, including those of intimacy and sympathy.[81] So even if *sôphrosunê* concerns only food, alcohol, and sex, it is hard to see that the biological-psychological analysis, as linked exclusively to certain pleasures of touch, suffices. If so, then the "natural-kinds" or "theoretical efficiency" reasons for believing Aristotle's theory dim. Then the "three desires" view would need to stand on nonbiological grounds, for example linguistic or conventional ones (such that something else would exclude too much basking in the sun or sleeping in from the realm of *sôphrosunê*). Yet, as we have just seen, there are few such grounds.

We have been more critical of Aristotle than of the previous authors studied in this book. As a philosopher, one hopes he would take this as a compliment. He has been the only one to present the reader with a view in his own voice—and thus something to assess—rather than simply a range of statements that might be reconstructed into a constellation of ideas. He has been the only writer really to innovate on commonplace usage, abandoning the protection of the defense "Well, this is how people really speak, magniloquently and vaguely!" And he has at least tried out some meaningful distinctions between moral-psychological states that probably should not be altogether conflated, since they play different roles in our descriptive, explanatory, and evaluative practices. All the same, I am disappointed that Aristotle did not provide for *sôphrosunê* the richer account he gives of courage or justice or *enkrateia*, since I think the earlier history

---

[79] Beresford (2020, 349–50). In *Problemata* 3, we learn that "fondness for drink is a desire for something moist" (ἡ δὲ φιλοποσία ἐστὶν ἐπιθυμία ὑγροῦ τινός, 872a6–7); but this does not specify a desire for wine and is in the context of a discussion of children's not being "fond of wine" (φίλοινοι). Wine is moist and hot, but its heat is meant to explain its intoxicating effects.

[80] This is the view disputed at [Arist.] *Probl.* 28.

[81] For such concerns see Taylor (2006, 197–98, 199), with reflection on kissing and proprioception.

of the analysis of the virtue shows that it deserves it. And in forgoing that richer account, I think that Aristotle did not really face up to the challenge Plato, Xenophon, and others set out, to explain the virtue's ethical centrality.

After Aristotle

The next two chapters of this book study, in their own way, post-Aristotelian reflections on and debates over *sôphrosunê*. Chapter 12 reconstructs a Pythagorean perspective on the virtue. Though the content is traceable to a philosophical community in southern Italy active in the early fourth century, it received its formulation from Aristoxenus, one of Aristotle's leading first-generation students. Chapter 13 studies representative texts from two other Pythagorean perspectives; these uncontroversially postdate Aristotle. The first of these, attributed to the woman Phintys, probably dates to the end of the Hellenistic period or the beginning of the Imperial period and belongs to a complex "Neopythagorean" philosophical tradition for which Peripatetic and Academic thinking evidently forms the background. The second is a letter by Iamblichus, from the late third century CE, whose *Exhortation to Philosophy* evidences wide familiarity with both Aristotle and Plato. None of these texts takes Aristotle's desires-of-touch analysis as decisive or as the apt insight into the scope and relevance of the virtue. They return to the diffuser and more systemic moral significance ascribed to *sôphrosunê* found in all our pre-Aristotelian authors. The demands of *sôphrosunê* remain puzzling and worth spelling out, connected to deep assumptions about moral psychology and social organization. These texts remain worth studying for their independent and committed analyses of the virtue.

Much could explain the departure of these texts from the Aristotelian insight. And this book does not provide a comprehensive study of post-Classical debates about *sôphrosunê*, which developed in fascinating ways, eventually as the Latin and Christian virtue of *temperantia* (with offshoots as *modestia* and *moderatio*).[82] But even without canvassing the broadest philosophical scene we can be confident that the divergences from Aristotle we see in Chapters 12–13 are not idiosyncratic rebellions against the dominant perspective. The remainder of this chapter discusses the statements about *sôphrosunê* to be found by those closest in sympathy with Aristotle, his associates, successors, and epitomizers. None accepts or defends the signal aspects of Aristotle's approach to *sôphrosunê*. This could simply be a regression to the mean. But it also indicates the distance Aristotle moved from common sense, even within intellectually learned spheres.

---

[82] North (1966, 261–379).

The Aristotelian *Problemata*

The text that most directly develops Aristotelian thought is the collection called the *Problemata Physica*.[83] Chapters 27–30 deal with the canonical virtues and their opposites: courage, *sôphrosunê*, justice, and wisdom. Chapter 28, which deals with *sôphrosunê* and its opposite, *akolasia*, also discusses *enkrateia* and *akrasia*.[84] It collects seven distinct questions, combining a catechism about Aristotelian doctrine (Q2/7, Q3) with some physiological puzzles (Q1, Q4–6, Q8). Question 1 wonders why attempts at replacing one's *akolasia* with *sôphrosunê*, specifically by abandoning excessive drink or eating, causes illness; the answer involves appeal to changes of nature and details of excretion. Question 2 wonders why we speak of *akrasia*, as well as of *akolasia*, with respect only to taste and touch; it is because those are the senses we share with animals, which makes them least honored and most reproached. Question 3 explains *akrasia*'s connection to desire but not anger: desires generally contradict reason, but anger follows it. Question 4 observes that, just as we admire justice in the poor, for they abstain from what they need—evidently they struggle to give others their due, having so little for themselves—so too we admire *sôphrosunê* in the young and wealthy who also abstain from what they need, namely, enjoyment to fill their copious leisure. Questions 5 and 6 explain the greater difficulty of tolerating thirst than hunger. Question 7 repeats Question 2 with the supplement of some Aristotelian examples. Question 8 explains the lack of restraint of laughter among friends.

The author of *Problemata* 28 largely but incompletely adheres to Aristotelian doctrine. He accepts Aristotle's narrow scope of *sôphrosunê* to certain bodily desires, though not quite so narrow as does Aristotle, who sometimes obviates taste, and he explicitly rejects the pertinence of social emotions like anger despite people talking about *akrasia* in that respect. (The desires for honor and power might also be in this vein.)[85] But he disregards Aristotle's crucial distinction between *sôphrosunê* and *enkrateia*: he omits *enkrateia*'s not being a virtue, and he ignores Aristotle's contrast between having moderated one's desires and having mastered them. This may be evidence that he finds the contrast too phenomenologically subtle: when someone chooses not to have a second piece of cake, it may be hard to distinguish having overcome the desire for it and not having the desire at all. Be that as it may, the author also seems less persuaded that ordinary language supports Aristotle's analysis. He notes that limiting *sôphrosunê* to only a few sources of desire wants

---

[83] For a brief introduction to the mix of sources for this Peripatetic assemblage, see Bodnár (2015).
[84] For a close study of this chapter, attentive to the author's largely "physiological" interests, see Centrone (2015, with 327–31 on *enkrateia*).
[85] Aristotle does speak of the scope of *sôphrosunê* and *enkrateia* as of touch and taste (ἀφῆς καὶ γεύσεως) at *EN* 7.7 1150a9.

explanation, as does the exclusion of anger; he includes the restraint of laughter in this study. It also seems doubtful that the author contemplates wealthy but *sôphrôn* youth holding back from food, drink, and sex alone; it is probable that for him *sôphrosunê* pertains to an expansive range of desires, just as justice means giving others their due in a broad range of distributive relations. Finally, the author says in Question 7 that those who lack *sôphrosunê* in specifically sex, eating, and drinking are called *akratês*. This qualification on *sôphrosunê* seems to suggest that he imagines *sôphrosunê* to have broader application.

It is hard to draw robust conclusions about the Peripatetic commitment to the Aristotelian picture of *sôphrosunê* from this chapter of the *Problemata*, given its brevity, its status as repetitive assemblage, and its physiological focus. (Admittedly, Aristotle's *Nicomachean Ethics* 7, on *enkrateia*, is also quite jumbled.) Yet the author recognizes some of the idiosyncratic qualities of the Aristotelian position by contrast to the ordinary-language position on the virtue. He does not treat the Aristotelian line as capturing what *sôphrosunê* really is.

Theophrastus

The student of Aristotle's besides Aristoxenus from whom we have appreciable ethical material is Theophrastus. Several Theophrastean statements suggest a basically Aristotelian view that, nevertheless, may have drifted somewhat from Aristotle's special commitments. According to the Stoic epitomizer Arius Didymus, Theophrastus maintained an Aristotelian "mean" theory, with *sôphrosunê* between the extremes of total susceptibility to desire and total lack of desire. The *sôphrôn* man has an appetite for the right things, at the right times, to the right extent, and using reason like a ruler, "making determinations in accordance with propriety" and "in accordance with nature."[86] Otherwise in accord with Aristotle, one wonders about the scope of Theophrastus' "appetite," which could be broader than Aristotle has in mind. A clearer difference between the two philosophers comes in Theophrastus' putting *sôphrosunê* rather than courage first in his list of virtues.[87] Relatedly, Diogenes Laertius tells us that Theophrastus wrote a work called "On education, or On virtue, or On *sôphrosunê*."[88] We might

---

[86] Stob. 2.7.20,88–94: Σώφρονά τε γὰρ εἶναι οὔτε τὸν καθάπαξ ἀνεπιθύμητον οὔτε τὸν ἐπιθυμητικόν· (τὸν μὲν γὰρ λίθου δίκην μηδὲ τῶν κατὰ φύσιν ὀρέγεσθαι, τὸν δὲ τῷ ὑπερβάλλειν ταῖς ἐπιθυμίαις ἀκόλαστον εἶναι)· τὸν δὲ μέσον τούτων, ὧν δεῖ καὶ ὁπότε καὶ ὁπόσον ἐπιθυμοῦντα καὶ τῷ λόγῳ κατὰ τὸ προσῆκον ὁρίζοντα καθάπερ κανόνι σώφρονα λέγεσθαί τε καὶ κατὰ φύσιν εἶναι. Compare the closing line of Aristotle's primary discussion of *sôphrosunê*, *EN* 3.12 1119b16–18: ἐπιθυμεῖ ὁ σώφρων ὧν δεῖ καὶ ὡς δεῖ καὶ ὅτε· οὕτω δὲ τάττει καὶ ὁ λόγος.

[87] Stob. 2.7.20,81–85: σωφροσύνη, πραότης, ἀνδρεία, δικαιοσύνη, ἐλευθεριότης, μεγαλοψυχία, μεγαλοπρέπεια.

[88] DL 5.50: Περὶ παιδείας ἢ περὶ ἀρετῶν ἢ περὶ σωφροσύνης, in one book.

imagine that Theophrastus saw *sôphrosunê* as the first or most important step of maturation into virtue. Such training could conceivably go beyond moderation of the desires for food, alcohol, and sex, as even Aristotle suggests.[89]

(Quasi-)Academic Sources

Three anonymous works present Aristotelian views from an Academic perspective or Academic views from the time of Aristotle's life. (He was a member of the Academy for two decades.) Naturally, they show considerable departure from the detail of Aristotle's views. So Aristotle's theory must not have been argumentatively compelling to those who would have known it. This does not wholly impugn Aristotle himself; debate and alternative positions continued throughout the Hellenistic period, yielding no consensus about the virtue.

It is worth noting the source of these Academic perspectives. As mentioned above, three of the Academy's earliest scholarchs wrote works titled *On Sôphrosunê*. The volume of Heraclides of Pontic Heraclea (an acting scholarch) is wholly lost; all that remains is Diogenes Laertius' almost unique pronouncement that it is written in the "comic" mode.[90] The only other work that Diogenes calls "comic" is Heraclides' *On Pleasure*. Its fragments are historical anecdotes about people with a wide variety of extravagant tastes.[91] One might wonder whether the *On Sôphrosunê* depicted people with a wide range of failures or trials of *sôphrosunê*, wide enough that the work could not be called merely "On Drunkenness" or "On Love." But here is an alternative way to conjecture at its contents. If Heraclides was really writing in the fashion of comic drama, perhaps his work was in sympathy with Plato's account of comedy in the *Philebus*. There Socrates presents the comic figure as one who fails to know himself.[92] He misrepresents to himself his wealth, attractiveness, and attainment of virtue; and since the implication is that this misrepresentation is voluntary, presumably the self-aggrandizement is the result of pleasure. Thus if comedies are about failures of self-knowledge, and if Heraclides' comedy is about *sôphrosunê*, we might guess that Heraclides imagines *sôphrosunê* to be self-knowledge (as the *Charmides* and other works suggest).

We know not much more about the *On Sôphrosunê* of Plato's permanent successor, Speusippus. The Byzantine scholar Michael of Ephesus reports that

---

[89] Arist. *NE* 3.12 1119a33–b15, the lines immediately preceding those quoted in n86 above. Compare the analysis in Fortenbaugh (1983, ch. 10; 2011, 152–55, 299–300, 303n156, 309), who assumes Theophrastus' Aristotelianism.

[90] Title: DL 5.86. Mode: DL 5.88 (κωμικῶς). Diogenes calls *Of Those in Hades*, *Of Piety*, and *Of Authority* "tragic"; it's no clearer what he means about them.

[91] On *On Pleasure*, see Schütrumpf (2008).

[92] Pl. *Phlb.* 48c. For discussion, see Moore (2015c, 209–14).

Speusippus follows a mean theory of virtue, such that *sôphrosunê* is neither indiscipline (ἀκολασία) nor foolishness (ἠλιθιότης).⁹³ This term for foolishness appears in the *Republic* as what people scornfully call the sense of shame (αἰδώς): it must look like a diffidence and reserve that depends on stupidity rather than sensitivity to social norms; it is presumably what those scornful of Spartan *sôphrosunê* would call it.⁹⁴ Speusippus thus shares some part of Aristotle's view—the mean theory—but not all of it. For Speusippus, *sôphrosunê* is a preservation of discipline founded in careful thought about and responsivity to what matters, not merely inbuilt lassitude or incompetence. There is no hint that Speusippus cares principally or centrally about bodily desires.

Of Xenocrates' *On Sôphrosunê*, we know nothing. Only a curious biographical fact remains: he was thought to have been chosen as scholarch over Heraclides and Menedemus for his superior *sôphrosunê*.⁹⁵ Menedemus of Eretria, it turns out, subscribed to a tight unity of virtue thesis, such that the virtues are one, in particular *sôphrosunê*, courage, and justice, which is especially non-Aristotelian.⁹⁶

We now turn to extant texts. A brief anonymous work of ethics found its way into Aristotle's corpus as a complement to the three well-known lecture-series. Called *Virtues and Vices*, it seems to be a late-Hellenistic digest of Aristotelian-Platonic views.⁹⁷ It accepts a tripartite soul and claims that *sôphrosunê* and *enkrateia* both pertain to the appetitive part.⁹⁸ It distinguishes them on Aristotelian grounds: *sôphrosunê* involves coming to have no drive to enjoy bad pleasures; *enkrateia*, by contrast, is the deployment of reason to check a not yet moderated appetite.⁹⁹ But it differs from Aristotle by speaking generically of "bad" pleasures rather than of those founded in touch. This may have been a looseness of speech; later we see that *sôphrosunê* is not valuing (τὸ μὴ θαυμάζειν) the enjoyment of bodily pleasures. But then the author repeats his earlier phrasing: this nonvaluing amounts to having no drive for the enjoyments of any disgraceful (αἰσχρᾶς) pleasures.¹⁰⁰ One might assume that this author simply identifies the bad and disgraceful desires with the bodily desires for food,

---

⁹³ Michael of Ephesus, *In Eth. Nic.* 538,35–539,19. Tarán (1981, 442) doubts that Michael has independent access to Speusippus' works, but the reported view's difference from Aristotle's suggests he knows something about it.
⁹⁴ Pl. *Rep.* 8.560d3.
⁹⁵ *Index Acad.* 24.
⁹⁶ Plut. *Mor.* 440e. It turns out that neither Zeno of Citium nor Ariston of Chios took up Aristotle's view of *sôphrosunê*: Plut. *Mor.* 441a.
⁹⁷ Rackham (1935, 486) accepts the dating of Susemihl and Zeller to 0 CE +/- 100 years, attributing it to a Peripatetic. Doug Hutchinson suggests an earlier date, 150 BCE +/- 100 years (personal communication).
⁹⁸ Tripartition: *VV* 1.3 1249b27.
⁹⁹ *VV* 2.4 1250a7: *sôphrosunê*: ἀνόρεκτοι γίνονται περὶ τὰς ἀπολαύσεις τῶν φαύλων ἡδονῶν; *enkrateia*: κατέχουσι τῷ λογισμῷ τὴν ἐπιθυμίαν ὁρμῶσαν ἐπὶ φαύλας ἡδονάς.
¹⁰⁰ *VV* 4.5 1250b7–9.

drink, and sex. But he goes on immediately to give a new gloss of *sôphrosunê*: this virtue amounts to the fear of being justly dishonored; is equivalent to being sorted out (τετάχθαι) in life's small and large concerns; and is accompanied by good arrangement (εὐταξία), orderliness (κοσμιότης), shame (αἰδώς), and caution (εὐλάβεια).[101] To be sure, this more Platonic or Academic list of dispositions could be the public and behavioral consequences of moderation with respect to the pleasures of touch, but they don't seem so. Alternatively, the control of pleasures of touch could be an important way to achieve these broader dispositions.

In his *Life of Plato*, Diogenes attributes a summary of Platonic doctrine to Aristotle, the *Divisions*. Aristotle did not actually write it, and it is at best indirectly about Plato, but the work could have Academic roots.[102] This pamphlet defines *sôphrosunê* as "ruling over one's desires and being enslaved by no pleasure, but living in an orderly way."[103] This has closer parallels to Platonic and Xenophontic thought than to Aristotelianism in its emphasis on desiderative autonomy and principled living.

A related work, the *Definitions*, comes probably from the late fourth-century Academy.[104] It gives seven definitions for *sôphrosunê*. Aristotle's view does not appear explicitly. Since for the most part the definitions come not from Plato's dialogues but other late fourth-century sources, perhaps Aristotle's position was deliberately passed over.

Σωφροσύνη (i) μετριότης τῆς ψυχῆς περὶ τὰς ἐν αὐτῇ κατὰ φύσιν γιγνομένας ἐπιθυμίας τε καὶ ἡδονάς· (ii) εὐαρμοστία καὶ εὐταξία ψυχῆς πρὸς τὰς κατὰ φύσιν ἡδονὰς καὶ λύπας· (iii) συμφωνία ψυχῆς πρὸς τὸ ἄρχειν καὶ ἄρχεσθαι· (iv) αὐτοπραγία κατὰ φύσιν· (v) εὐταξία ψυχῆς· (vi) λογιστικὴ ὁμιλία ψυχῆς περὶ καλῶν καὶ αἰσχρῶν· (vii) ἕξις καθ᾽ ἣν ὁ ἔχων αἱρετικός ἐστι καὶ εὐλαβητικὸς ὧν χρή. (*Def.* 411e6–412a2)

Sôphrosunê: (i) a moderation of the soul concerning the desires and pleasures that come about naturally in it;

(ii) a good harmony and arrangement of soul vis-à-vis the natural pleasures and pains;

---

[101] *VV* 4.5 1250b10–13.

[102] DL 3.80–109 (*Divisiones Aristoteleae*); attribution to Aristotle at 3.80 and 3.109. For its distance from both Plato and Aristotle, take, for instance, its heptapartite analysis of εὐδαιμονία, as εὐβουλία, εὐαισθησία and bodily health, εὐτυχία ἐν ταῖς πράξεσι, εὐδοξία, and εὐπορία (DL 3.98–99), which has no obvious parallel in either author. For the history of the manuscripts of the text, see recently Moraux (1977); Dorandi (1996, 2011); Pepe (2013); Dorandi and Marjani (2017).

[103] DL 3.91: τοῦ κρατεῖν τῶν ἐπιθυμιῶν καὶ ὑπὸ μηδεμιᾶς ἡδονῆς δουλοῦσθαι, ἀλλὰ κοσμίως ζῆν.

[104] See Hutchinson's comment in Cooper (1997, 1677–78).

(iii) a concord of soul vis-à-vis ruling and being ruled;
(iv) a natural independence of action;
(v) a good arrangement of soul;
(vi) a reasoned compact in the soul about what's admirable and disgraceful;
(vii) a disposition according to which one can choose and reject as one ought.

The first two definitions speak of "natural" desires or pleasures; this does not evidently restrict them to the bodily or bestial.[105] The third definition glosses the *Republic* 4 account, emphasizing the agreement among parts about the one which has authority. The fourth definition uses an apt term, "independence of action" (αὐτοπραγία, "acting from oneself"), not otherwise found until Chrysippus (ca. 279–206 BCE).[106] This term, *autopragia*, happens to capture the idea of *sôphrosunê* argued throughout this book to be at its core. The next definition, "good arrangement of soul," is equally abstract and general, though focused on structure rather than action. While Plato speaks of *sôphrosunê* once in relation to *taxis* (order), the phrase *eutaxia psuchês* is found in this period only in a manuscript of the *Divisions* (not reproduced by Diogenes Laertius), where "good arrangement" is divided into four types (body, soul, movement, groups of people), and good psychic arrangement is ultimately defined as "orderliness" (κοσμιότης).[107] The term *eutaxia* appears elsewhere in the *Definitions*: as item (ii) above in the *sôphrosunê* definition as well as in the definitions of justice, reasonableness (ἐπιείκεια), and orderliness.[108] Elsewhere in the Platonic oeuvre *eutaxia* appears only once, in the *Alcibiades* (a dialogue of disputed authorship), in a passage that either glosses or expands the Spartan embodiment of *sôphrosunê* and "orderliness."[109] The last two definitions from the *Definitions* are

---

[105] Indeed, Hutchinson (at Cooper 1997, 1679) translates "normally" and "normal." There is no reference to "moderation of soul" (μετριότης τῆς ψυχῆς) in Plato's dialogues, though "moderation" is an important term in *Philebus* (64e6, 65b8 and d4) and *Laws* (3.701e4, 5.736e2); it is collocated with *kosmia* and near to *sôphrosunê* at *Rep.* 7.560d5. The two nouns εὐαρμοστία and εὐταξία are not collocated until Aelius Aristides, though εὐαρμοστία has three Platonic occurrences (*Prot.* 326b5, *Rep.* 3.400d10, 7.522a5). The entry in the *Definitions* for σώφρων is "having measured desire" (μετρίας ἐπιθυμίας ἔχων, 415d8).

[106] DL 7.121, Stoic and probably Chrysippan; cf. Plut. *de Stoic. repugn.* 20 1043b, Philo *de Joseph.* 66, *Quod omnis probus liber sit* 21.3. Cp. *idiopragia* discussed in Chapter 5.

[107] Marcianus codex #40 (Mutschmann 1906, 54): ἡ μὲν οὖν ἐν τῇ ψυχῇ εὐταξία ἐγγινομένη κοσμιότης καλεῖται.

[108] These form something of a network. Justice: "an agreement of the soul with itself, and good order of the soul's parts toward and with respect to one another" (ὁμόνοια τῆς ψυχῆς πρὸς αὐτήν, καὶ εὐταξία τῶν τῆς ψυχῆς μερῶν πρὸς ἄλληλά τε καὶ περὶ ἄλληλα, 411d8–e1); reasonableness: "good order of the rational soul regarding what's fine and disgraceful" (εὐταξία ψυχῆς λογιστικῆς πρὸς τὰ καλὰ καὶ αἰσχρά, 412b9–10); and orderliness: "good order of the movement of the body" (εὐταξία περὶ κίνησιν σώματος, 412d9).

[109] The list there separates *sôphrosunê* and *eutaxia*, but it is possible the latter serves, with other virtues, in part to gloss the former—*sôphrosunê* and *kosmiotês* appear, syntactically, as the prime virtues, the remainder as specifications or minor additions: εἰ δ' αὖ ἐθελήσεις εἰς σωφροσύνην τε καὶ κοσμιότητα ἀποβλέψαι καὶ εὐχέρειαν καὶ εὐκολίαν καὶ μεγαλοφροσύνην καὶ εὐταξίαν καὶ ἀνδρείαν καὶ καρτερίαν καὶ φιλοπονίαν καὶ φιλονικίαν καὶ φιλοτιμίας τὰς Λακεδαιμονίων (*Alc.* 122c4–8).

unparalleled in Greek literature, though they altogether share the sentiments of the *Charmides*, *Gorgias*, and *Republic*. I conjecture that all these definitions have been excerpted from the lost *On Sôphrosunês* of the early Academy and therefore are good witnesses to the thinking of that period.

A Solution, but the Debate Continues

Aristotle's theory of *sôphrosunê* seeks to solve a problem in the history of debate about *sôphrosunê*. What can hold instances of the virtue together while also differentiating it from other praiseworthy states? We have already seen some solutions, for example in the Socratic dialogues, and some acceptance of indeterminacy. But Plato's *Statesman* and *Laws*, as we saw in the previous chapter, reinforce the difficulty and seriousness of the problem; there really does seem to be a considerable distance between *sôphrosunê* as a gentle disposition or tendency of self-control and *sôphrosunê* as a form of good judgment. A solution was called for. Aristotle's solution was ingenious, brilliant, and not at all implausible, given the extent of clichéd talk about the desire for food, drink, and sex. But it was also a reductive exercise, in that Aristotle did not capture the range of experiences or ideals coordinated by the virtue-term and did not seek to integrate earlier investigations into the virtue. He did not save the appearances, either of the common Greek speaker or of the theorist of the virtue. This gained him few adopters, at least not among Greek speakers. Once Greek terms were removed from their everyday linguistic use, however, in their uptake or translation by Latin-writing philosophers, reductive analyses such as Aristotle's could better take hold. And so they did, into the Christian and then modern eras.

12
Pythagorean *Sôphrosunê*

The *Pythagorean Precepts* and the Early Fourth Century

Among Aristotle's greatest students, and among the most important witnesses to an alternative perspective on *sôphrosunê*, is Aristoxenus (b. ca. 370 BCE). Born in Tarentum, in southern Italy (Magna Graecia), a colony long associated with Pythagoreans and once the largest city in Greece, Aristoxenus grew up under the rule of Archytas, the great Pythagorean philosopher and friend of Plato's. Sometime in the mid-fourth century, he joined another Pythagorean community, under the tutelage of Xenophilus, and then came to Athens and the Lyceum.[1] The extraordinary breadth of his interests was matched only by that of his colleague Theophrastus and of Aristotle himself. Like Aristotle and others in his orbit, including Heraclides of Pontic Heraclea and Dicaearchus, he maintained an active research agenda on the Pythagoreans. In fact, he seems to have written five books about the Pythagoreans: *The Life of Pythagoras*, a biographical study, attending to the man's idiosyncratic regimen; *On Pythagoras and His Associates*, on the first Pythagorean community; *On the Pythagorean Way of Life*, on the practices of that community down to the fourth century; *Life of Archytas*, a biographical study of the philosopher-ruler; and *Pythagorean Precepts* (Πυθαγορικαὶ ἀποφάσεις).[2]

The *Pythagorean Precepts* is a study of the doctrines of Xenophilus' Pythagorean community, presumably one of the communities mentioned admiringly by Socrates near the end of Plato's *Republic*.[3] This seems to have been the least antiquarian of Aristoxenus' Pythagorean works; it belongs more to descriptive ethics or intellectual anthropology. It indicates the norms the community members were said to have paid fealty to, and what theory of human nature and society warranted those norms. These precepts differ from the well-known *sumbola* or exhortations attributed to Pythagoras found in Diogenes Laertius, among other authors.[4] In particular, they are not overtly metaphorical or gnomic; they instead explain how to build a sound community.

---

[1] Gell. *NA* 6.11; DL 8.15–16.
[2] For Aristoxenus on the Pythagoreans, see Zhmud (2012); Huffman (2014, 285–95; 2019).
[3] Pl. *Rep.* 10.600a–b. Plato also mentions Pythagorean communities in Thebes and Phlius (*Phd.* 61d5–e5, 57a8).
[4] E.g., DL 9.9, 17. See Thom (2020).

Aristoxenus' work summarizes or articulates Pythagorean doctrines about life-guiding matters and provides their explanations of those doctrines. Many of those doctrines concern the acquisition of *sôphrosunê*. Aristoxenus does not himself say that Xenophilus' community consciously aimed at *sôphrosunê*, and the work's few recent commentators do not emphasize it. Nevertheless, he presents it as organized by its pursuit of *sôphrosunê*.[5] As with many virtue-oriented communities, Xenophilus' may look oppressively conservative to contemporary observers, decidedly authoritarian, concerned more with rule-following than with individuality and creativity. It probably looked the same way to Athenians of a democratic tilt. But its rules followed directly from a Pythagorean understanding of human nature. It thus captures the ambiguity about the virtue's value found in discussions of this period.

The true importance of this Pythagorean community and the *Pythagorean Precepts* to the present study is that Aristoxenus ascribes to his Pythagoreans an analysis of *sôphrosunê* independent of and different from the Socratics' (and Aristotle's) in its details; yet it shares an upshot with the analyses of Xenophon and Plato. As Aristoxenus understands it, the Pythagoreans see *sôphrosunê* as central to human maturity, the ability to do what one would hope to do. They prize the virtue more for this than for its polishing down of craggy desire. They in effect also argue against Callicles' position. Callicles envisions personal actualization in the pure expression of his inner drives, as though agency were our default condition but one which we lose when society burnishes us down into sheep. Whereas Callicles praises the natural condition, the Pythagoreans scorn it. According to them, the natural condition is bad—confused, self-contradictory, and dangerously unstable. Society, and especially the rules rehearsed by elders and the tenets ascribed to the gods, is necessary for agency, for the efficacious coordination of one's desires and beliefs. Unlike the Socratic/Platonic view, the Pythagoreans do not encourage self-inquiry or the hope that dialectical encounter might discover or recall a better system of life. Parallel to the position announced by Thucydides' Sthenelaus and Cleon, they find it sufficient that some tried-and-true rules be followed, whatever the chances that better rules could one day be found. As in the view found in Thucydides, the attainment of agency is to be understood as the attainment of *sôphrosunê*.

The evidence for this Pythagorean view is to be found in a close study of the long fragments 8, 2, and 9 of the *Pythagorean Precepts*. Before turning to them,

---

[5] Tjiattas (1989) provides a brief but apt statement of the importance of the Pythagoreans' emphasis on *sôphrosunê* to the history of philosophy, especially for the formation of the "ethical agent." Gemelli Marciano (2014) emphasizes the importance of *askêsis*, though she does not discuss *sôphrosunê*, and she concludes that the Pythagoreans aimed for a "receptive consciousness" and "renunciation of the self." Gerson (2020) avers that "the *Precepts* shows neither any special concern with happiness (*eudaimonia*) nor with virtue (*aretê*) nor with the relevance of the latter to the former."

a few words about the work itself, which has been recently reconstructed and contextualized by Carl Huffman, would help. The *Pythagorean Precepts* as a through-written text is lost, but we have about ten pages of substantive fragments, some cited explicitly in Stobaeus and others incorporated into Iamblichus' cento *On The Pythagorean Way of Life*. The most immediate benefit of Huffman's recent study of the text is his reliable expansion and delineation of such fragments as are findable in Iamblichus' text—since Iamblichus never cites sources or indicates where his borrowings start or end.[6] The relationship between Aristoxenus' book and Iamblichus' is important, too, for the claim here under consideration, that *Pythagorean Precepts* focuses on *sôphrosunê*. Iamblichus addresses five Pythagorean virtues, each at length; but, as Huffman argues, Iamblichus borrows from the *Precepts*, and does so at length, only for *sôphrosunê*. The extent of that borrowing shows how much he esteemed the *Precepts*; that level of esteem suggests that had the *Precepts* discussed other virtues, Iamblichus would have borrowed from those discussions; but he did not, so the *Precepts* did not so fully discuss other virtues.[7] To be sure, the *Precepts* does not purport to be a treatise on *sôphrosunê* or to reduce politics and home life to *sôphrosunê*; a number of its fragments do not mention the virtue, and even where *sôphrosunê* comes up, other goals are mentioned. Its ambit is a way of life and its attainment, not a single virtue and its attainment. Nevertheless, as we will see, *sôphrosunê* provides a guiding concept.

Fragment 8: The Theology of *Sôphrosunê*

Aristoxenus' report of the Pythagoreans' fundamental attitude toward human nature, or at least his presentation of it at the highest level of abstraction, is found in what editors call fragment 8, though Huffman places it first in his reconstruction of the book.[8] An argument compassing theology, psychology, and sociology eventuates in an explanation of the way *sôphronismos tis kai taxis*—a paraphrasis for *sôphrosunê*, as we discuss below—comes about. In particular, the disorder of people's desires requires the positing of a supreme divine authority that somehow offers an irresistible pattern for living. The similarity with the (probably fifth-century) "Sisyphus" fragment attributed to Critias or Euripides is plain: both claim that ethical obedience requires belief in all-seeing gods.[9]

---

[6] A convenient discussion of Iamblichus' working methods is in Hutchinson and Johnson (2005).
[7] Huffman (2019, 133).
[8] Stob. 4.24.45 ~ Iambl. *VP* 174–6; Huffman (2019, 260–64).
[9] The "Sisyphus" fragment is found and attributed to Critias in Sext. Emp. *C. math.* 9.54 (= B25 DK) and to Euripides in Aët. 1.7.2 (with shorter fragments found in Chrysippus fr. phys. 1009 von Arnim; Σ Eur. *Or.* 982). A fourth-century date is given by Sedley (2013).

But whereas Sisyphus' wise man reasons that people must believe that no unjust action will go unrecognized, Aristoxenus' report concerns the management of one's inner impulsions. In both cases, however, the positing of a major (deistic) moral system serves to advance a certain virtue, here *sôphrosunê*.

Fragment 8 begins with a naturalizing account of religion:

τὸ διανοεῖσθαι περὶ τοῦ θείου, ὡς ἔστι τε καὶ πρὸς τὸ ἀνθρώπινον γένος οὕτως ἔχει ὡς ἐπιβλέπειν καὶ μὴ ὀλιγωρεῖν αὐτοῦ, χρήσιμον εἶναι ὑπελάμβανον [οἱ Πυθαγόρειοι παρ' ἐκείνου μαθόντες]. δεῖσθαι γὰρ ἡμᾶς ἐπιστατείας τοιαύτης, ἧ κατὰ μηδὲν ἀνταίρειν ἀξιώσομεν· τοιαύτην δ' εἶναι τὴν ὑπὸ τοῦ θείου γινομένην, εἴπερ ἐστὶ τὸ θεῖον τοιοῦτον <οἷον> ἄξιον εἶναι τῆς τοῦ σύμπαντος ἀρχῆς. (Aristox. *Pyth. pr.* fr. 8,6–12 = Iambl. *VP* 174,5–12)

To conceive of the divine as existing and as being disposed to give its attention to and not despise the human race, [this the Pythagoreans learned from him] to find it useful to do. For we need a kind of supervision that we will never think it worth rebelling against; and the divine is of this kind, if the divine is such as to be worthy to rule over everything.

The Greeks disputed the extent of divine concern for humans, from occasional curiosity to complete aloofness; there was no consensus about an omniscient and all-caring god. The Pythagoreans thus needed an argument for the gods' attention to us if they were to give impact to divine norms. In compressed form, we see that argument here: the gods are worthy to rule over everything; they are thus worthy to rule over humans, and so they do; ruling requires being present and conscientiously watching that which one rules; so the gods are present and conscientiously watch over humans.

Aristoxenus turns next to the relevance of this divine panopticon:

ὑβριστικὸν γὰρ δὴ φύσει τὸ ζῷον ἔφασαν εἶναι, ὀρθῶς λέγοντες, καὶ ποικίλον κατά τε τὰς ὁρμὰς καὶ κατὰ τὰς ἐπιθυμίας καὶ κατὰ τὰ λοιπὰ τῶν παθῶν· δεῖσθαι οὖν τοιαύτης ὑπεροχῆς τε καὶ ἐπανατάσεως, ἀφ' ἧς ἐστι σωφρονισμός τις καὶ τάξις. (Aristox. *Pyth. pr.* fr. 8,12–16 = Iambl. *VP* 174,12–175,1)

For they say that an animal is hubristic by nature—they are right in saying this—as well as complex in its urges, desires, and the other kinds of passion. Thus it needs such superiority and threats from which a certain *sôphronismos* and arrangement come to be.

The Pythagoreans diagnose two problems with all animals, humans included. They are hubristic, and they have diverse and disorganized desires. A single desire could suffice for being hubristic—in doing the single thing it wants to do, an animal or person could disregard and disdain social norms. It would be treating only its present-moment desire as authoritative, ignoring other possible ends. What it needs is acknowledgment of other authoritative norms, ones that come from something superior or something which, if ignored, will hurt it. Recognizing authority, perhaps with coercive assistance, amounts to having a certain (τις) *sôphronismos*. The second problem with (human) animals is that they in fact have many and diverse (ποικίλον) felt motivations to action. These "passions" (παθῶν) push this way and that, foiling long-term or significant projects. No natural coordinator or traffic controller sets them in order. Again, they need an authority to help them integrate their inclinations. This integration may be called "arrangement" (τάξις).

In this double-aspect presentation of refined motivations, *sôphronismos tis* points to conformity of one's actions to general norms, "arrangement" to the coherence of one's various desires. The former tends toward the ethical, the latter toward the practical; the former allows action in accordance with others, the latter action in accordance with oneself. Both concern agency, though the latter does so especially.

The argument speaks universally of any animal. Nevertheless, the argument obviously applies to us, since the divine supervision of humans has been and continues to be at issue. Indeed, this treatment of humans as animals has an argumentative point. At least here, these Pythagoreans do not posit a special human capacity for practical reasoning that would distinguish them from the lower animals. People cannot simply decide to limit or organize their desires or ends. Whatever salutary orientation and structure is to be found among them depends on a person's acceptance of objective norms. Self-constitution as a being with practical unity requires an external inspiration to order. Autonomy is really heteronomy, even for thoughtful beings like us.

This picture of a self-constitution that depends on an evidently higher authority is theoretically attractive. It avoids the paradoxes in explaining how a disordered being brings about its own ordering. It may also explain this fragment's rare noun-phrase, "a certain *sôphronismos*." The noun is related to a word with fifth-century provenance (τὸ σωφρόνισμα) but is not itself known from the fourth century except in Aristoxenus.[10] In its next earliest extant use, Strabo says that, in the ancient period, poets would teach (παιδεύουσιν) students not principally for the sake of distraction (ψυχαγωγίας) but for

---

[10] Huffman (2019, 309) worries this term may be a textual corruption, but the situation of a term appearing in only some fourth-century literature and then not again for several centuries is not unusual; similarities occur with *promêtheia* and *philosophêma*, the latter a fourth-century invention that had minimal success, the former a once popular term that went out of fashion (for these, see Moore (2015a; 2020a)).

sôphronismos; Strabo immediately attributes this view to Pythagoreans in general and Aristoxenus in particular.[11] The noun nominalizes *sôphronizein*, a verb we saw in Chapter 5 for making someone *sôphrôn*. *Sôphronismos* thus represents a *sôphrosunê* incarnated through directed external help, "teaching."[12] The qualifier "a certain" (τις) presumably acknowledges that the present desire-management comes not through personal teaching but through the recognition of a population-level authority and threat. This is an inducement to *sôphronismos* somewhat akin to that which a music teacher provides. How significant its difference from *sôphrosunê* is we cannot readily say. The Pythagoreans seem to want to say only that acknowledging a rule of ethical or practical guidance is to see that it cannot be broken without negative consequences; they are not concerned here with non-instrumental grounds of its acceptance.

Nevertheless, Aristoxenus goes on to give a Pythagorean exhortation to rational self-cultivation:

ᾤοντο δὴ δεῖν ἕκαστον αὐτῷ συνειδότα τὴν τῆς φύσεως ποικιλίαν μηδέποτε λήθην ἔχειν τῆς πρὸς τὸ θεῖον ὁσιότητός τε καὶ θεραπείας, ἀλλ' ἀεὶ τίθεσθαι πρὸ τῆς διανοίας ὡς ἐπιβλέποντός τε καὶ παραφυλάττοντος τὴν ἀνθρωπίνην ἀγωγήν. (Aristox. *Pyth. pr.* fr. 8,16–20 = Iambl. *VP* 175,1–5)

> They thought that each person should be conscious of his own complex nature and never forget to maintain his holiness toward and service of the divine; he should always put before his mind its attention to and monitoring of human conduct.

These instructions to the Pythagorean community assume somewhat more intellectual agency than the earlier statements. They advise exercising a degree of self-knowledge, a consciousness (συνειδότα) of one's nature (φύσεως)—an appreciation of one's problematic appetitive situation. They must think that people fail to appreciate their complexity and the route to its rectification but that they do not need to fail to appreciate this. Aristoxenus does not record here how the Pythagoreans sought to effect a consciousness of one's unperfected human nature; it may have been through the provision of examples from the animal kingdom and the discussion of the nature of desire found in later excerpts. Nor does he say precisely what they did to encourage the proper attitude toward the

---

[11] Str. 1.2.3: διὰ τοῦτο καὶ τοὺς παῖδας αἱ τῶν Ἑλλήνων πόλεις πρώτιστα διὰ τῆς ποιητικῆς παιδεύουσιν, οὐ ψυχαγωγίας χάριν δήπουθεν ψιλῆς, ἀλλὰ σωφρονισμοῦ. ὅπου γε καὶ οἱ μουσικοὶ ψάλλειν καὶ λυρίζειν καὶ αὐλεῖν διδάσκοντες μεταποιοῦνται τῆς ἀρετῆς ταύτης. παιδευτικοὶ γὰρ εἶναί φασι καὶ ἐπανορθωτικοὶ τῶν ἠθῶν. ταῦτα δ' οὐ μόνον παρὰ τῶν Πυθαγορείων ἀκούειν ἐστὶ λεγόντων, ἀλλὰ καὶ Ἀριστόξενος οὕτως ἀποφαίνεται.

[12] LSJ s.v.: "teaching of morality or moderation"; Thayer and Strong (1997) s.v.: "an admonishing or calling to soundness of mind, to moderation and self-control."

divine. But people are to remember to orient themselves toward the divine as something deserving of one's respect and effort and to reflect on the divine as oriented toward one's own activities. This two-way intellectual effort amounts to leveraging beliefs in an external authority to pattern one's own desires. It is a holding before one's mind a special kind of paradigm: whereas a paradigm alone has no reconstructive power against the force of natural psychic motions, a paradigm treated as instructions from a superior agent, which thereby harnesses feelings of fear or obedience, can provide such reconstructive power.

This, then, is a subtle approach to the problem of self-constitution. How, if I am naturally excessive and mixed up, am I to limit and organize myself? I contain no limits or powers of self-organization, otherwise I would not be naturally excessive and mixed up. The Pythagoreans proffer this solution: With the intellectual powers you do have, treat yourself as importing those limits and organizational patterns from a place that is not naturally excessive and mixed up, namely the divine realm, and from there you may become arranged and as though *sôphrôn*.

The divine provides the most important object of reverence and respect for the acquisition of *sôphronismos*. But it is not the only such object:

> μετὰ δὲ τὸ θεῖόν τε καὶ τὸ δαιμόνιον πλεῖστον ποιεῖσθαι λόγον γονέων τε καὶ νόμου . . . μὴ πλαστῶς, ἀλλὰ πεπεισμένως. [καθόλου δὲ ᾤοντο δεῖν ὑπολαμβάνειν μηδὲν εἶναι μεῖζον κακὸν ἀναρχίας· οὐ γὰρ πεφυκέναι τὸν ἄνθρωπον διασῴζεσθαι μηδενὸς ἐπιστατοῦντος.] τὸ μένειν ἐν τοῖς πατρίοις ἔθεσί τε καὶ νομίμοις ἐδοκίμαζον . . . κἂν ᾖ μικρῷ χείρω ἑτέρων· τὸ γὰρ ῥᾳδίως ἀποπηδᾶν ἀπὸ τῶν ὑπαρχόντων νόμων καὶ οἰκείους εἶναι καινοτομίας οὐδαμῶς εἶναι σύμφορον οὐδὲ σωτήριον. (Aristox. *Pyth. pr.* fr. 8,20–29 = Iambl. *VP* 175,6–176,5)

> And after the divine and the spiritual, give most heed to parents and laws, not in a sham way but being actually convinced. [For generally speaking they thought that one must take it that nothing is worse than anarchy, for humans don't have the nature to be saved without being supervised.] They approved of abiding by the customs and laws of their fathers . . . even if they were a bit worse than others. For to turn so easily away from the standing laws and become familiar with innovation neither benefits nor saves you.

The Pythagoreans acknowledge the importance of parents and laws in the provision of norms. Those norms would be valuable, however, only if a person could be convinced to follow them, if he actually found them authoritative. A merely outward or seeming obedience would not reform one's desires, and merely public obedience would not continue past one's parents' eyes or the law's ears. The laws and one's parents must be taken as legitimate guides to action, not just irritating obstacles to desire-satisfaction. Coming to believe this may be a considerable challenge, of course. Whereas belief in the gods' authority is hindered by skepticism about their concern for humans, since gods seem aloof, belief in human authority is hindered by skepticism about the correctness of those with that authority, since humans seem fallible. The Pythagoreans recognize this: the laws of one's fathers could be "a bit worse than others." Nevertheless, you should still stick with those laws for procedural reasons, as Archidamus argued in Thucydides: abandoning the prevailing laws and getting too familiar with change is worse than obeying suboptimal laws.[13] Rather than evaluating the goodness of one's inherited laws and rejecting them where they seem inadequate, one should simply accept them as good and worthy of one's obedience. Otherwise their authority will be contingent on one's judgment of their aptness, which by hypothesis is not reliable. Accepting this authority without scrutiny conduces to one's self-restraint and practical unity.

The Pythagoreans see a role for both divine and social laws. Divine laws may be thought to be perfect, gaining their authority not just from the power of their enforcement but also from their aptness to the animal condition. Obedience is predicated on accepting the perfection and awareness of the divine. Though the Pythagoreans believe that the divine, who cares for us, is worthy of our obedience, obedience seems to come largely from recognizing that the divine is apprised of everything and demands that each of us follow its rules. But these laws may not be sufficiently situation-specific, and the threat of their enforcement may not always be sufficiently present to everyone's mind. Thus there is a role for human norms, whether civic or familial, that address local issues and carry a more vivid regime of enforcement. Yet human laws may be imperfect. Their authority and their threat risk separating. So one is to treat them as similar to the divine laws, valid in any case. And the most skeptical person can still hold that law is less disordered that he himself is, and so it is worth being guided by.

Fragment 8 in effect argues that becoming more *sôphrôn* and well-arranged is a primary goal of the Pythagorean system of religious belief; achieving that internal appetitive order requires self-knowledge and various forms of intellectual effort; and one's attitude toward civic and social norms should be directed toward its promotion. This shows us an engagement with ongoing debates about *sôphrosunê* and the self-constitution of agency. The Pythagorean engagement with these debates, however, has so far been at a high level of abstraction. For more concrete statements, we now turn to the brief fragment 2, on political rule and civic organization, and then to the very long fragment 9 (from sections 200–213 of Iamblichus' *On the Pythagorean Way of Life*), which covers a range of

---

[13] Thuc. 1.84.3 and 3.37.3; see Chapter 5.

sôphrosunê-related topics. Other relevant remarks about *sôphrosunê* found in the other fragments will be mentioned at the end.

Fragment 2: The Civic Architecture of *Sôphrosunê*

Fragment 2 takes as its theme not the moral psychology of the individual becoming *sôphrôn* but the structure of the city; it is cited by Stobaeus in his section "On constitution."[14] In this overview-like passage, Aristoxenus addresses the three issues already mentioned in brackets in fragment 8 quoted above (lines 23–25): the Pythagoreans judge anarchy (ἀναρχία), the absence of leadership, to be the greatest evil; they do so because the nature of human beings requires supervision; and without that supervision humans will not be saved. What is being saved (διασῴζεσθαι) must be the human capacity to live as sober and integrated beings; without leadership, people's unchecked desires may lead them to a point of no return.[15]

The first of the three issues found in fragment 2 is familiar from Plato's *Republic* Book 4 account of *sôphrosunê*: this virtue involves mutual acknowledgment between ruler and ruled:

τοὺς μὲν γὰρ ἄρχοντας ἔφασκον οὐ μόνον ἐπιστήμονας ἀλλὰ καὶ φιλανθρώπους δεῖν εἶναι· καὶ τοὺς ἀρχομένους οὐ μόνον πειθηνίους ἀλλὰ καὶ φιλάρχοντας. (Aristox. *Pyth. pr.* fr. 2,4–6 = Stob. 4.1.49,6–9)

They claimed that rulers should be not only knowledgeable but also committed to their fellow man, and that those ruled should be not only obedient but also in sympathy with their rulers.

Ruler and ruled need an active regard for one another, with an attentiveness to one another's interests (they are to be *philanthrôpos* and *philarchôn*); and they must be able to rule correctly and to heed that rule effectively. This elaborates the Pythagorean abhorrence of anarchy and their demand for a salvatory supervision. A knowledgeable but haughty ruler might increase the distance between himself and those under him and, losing sight of the details of his fellow citizens' lives, fail to organize the state as well as possible. He might also fail to impress upon those he rules the fact that he exercises his knowledge for their benefit, not his own enrichment or pleasure, and thereby fail to win wholehearted obedience. Similarly, a nonruling member of the Pythagorean order needs to be able

---

[14] Stob. 4.1.49.
[15] Huffman (2019, 182–85).

to follow orders, but the orders can be internalized and not merely given public obeisance only when he approves of the person promulgating them, thinking he has his interests in mind. For the "saving" to happen, those ruled need to acknowledge the rulers as legitimate supervisors. Plato's Socrates does not enter into these psychological details in the *Republic*; the Pythagoreans are taking their own reflective approach to civic-level *sôphrosunê*.

The next two issues mentioned in fragment 2 are developed at length in fragment 9. Society should determine what each generation should do—children, young adults, those of mature age—so that a person never acts below his age.[16] Its goal should be to ensure proper maturity for each person. The Pythagoreans doubted that supervision at a single life-moment would suffice for the whole of someone's life. Even nutrition should be well-arranged (τροφὴν τεταγμένως) for each age. This indicates the scope of Pythagorean supervision in the interest of arrangement (τάξις) and balance (συμμετρία).[17]

Fragment 9: A Course of Life Guided by *Sôphrosunê*

Iamblichus dedicates the thirty-first chapter of his *On the Pythagorean Way of Life*, at a length of twenty-six modern sections, to the Pythagorean teaching on *sôphrosunê* (*VP* 187–213). The last thirteen (*VP* 200–13) have been shown by Carl Huffman very likely to have been excerpted, in order, from Aristoxenus' *Pythagorean Precepts*, and this is what is called fragment 9.[18] (Some earlier sections of Iamblichus' chapter on *sôphrosunê* seem to come from Aristoxenus as well, specifically *VP* 197–98, but not necessarily from the same work; see below for the possibility they come from his *Life of Archytas*.) The extent of this reliance, as we have argued, is the primary grounds for believing that the *Pythagorean Precepts* reflects a practical philosophy for which *sôphrosunê* was an organizing goal. It also presents a broad range of philosophical issues that fall under the aegis of *sôphrosunê*—broader, indeed, than any other extant ancient analysis of *sôphrosunê*.

---

[16] Aristox. *Pyth. pr.* fr. 2,7–15 = Stob. 4.1.49,9–18: ἐπιμελητέον δὲ πάσης ἡλικίας ἡγοῦντο καὶ τοὺς μὲν παῖδας ἐν γράμμασι καὶ τοῖς ἄλλοις μαθήμασιν ἀσκεῖσθαι· τοὺς δὲ νεανίσκους τοῖς τῆς πόλεως ἔθεσί τε καὶ νόμοις γυμνάζεσθαι· τοὺς δὲ ἄνδρας ταῖς πράξεσί τε καὶ δημοσίαις λειτουργίαις προσέχειν· τοὺς δὲ πρεσβύτας ἐνθυμήσεσι καὶ κριτηρίοις καὶ συμβουλίαις δεῖν ἐναναστρέφεσθαι μετὰ πάσης ἐπιστήμης ὑπελάμβανον, ὅπως μήτε οἱ παῖδες νηπιάζοιεν μήτε οἱ νεανίσκοι παιδαριεύοιντο μήτε οἱ ἄνδρες νεανιεύοιντο μήτε οἱ γέροντες παραφρονοῖεν.

[17] Aristox. *Pyth. pr.* fr. 2,15–18 = Stob. 4.1.49,18–21: δεῖν δὲ ἔφασκον εὐθὺς ἐκ παίδων καὶ τὴν τροφὴν τεταγμένως προσφέρεσθαι, διδάσκοντες ὡς ἡ μὲν τάξις καὶ συμμετρία καλὰ καὶ σύμφορα, ἡ δὲ ἀταξία καὶ ἀσυμμετρία αἰσχρά τε καὶ ἀσύμφορα.

[18] Huffman (2019, 314–24: text and translation; 324–32: extent); Dillon and Herschbell (1991, 205n13).

In fact, that Iamblichus relies on the *Pythagorean Precepts* for only half the chapter undersells the work's importance to him; this is notable, since this chapter in Iamblichus is the longest continuous extant work on *sôphrosunê* besides the *Charmides*.[19] Seeing its structure will help give context to its *Pythagorean Precepts* excerpts. (It also reflects what Iamblichus, in the late third century CE, deems significant about *sôphrosunê*.)

The first two sections of Iamblichus' chapter on *sôphrosunê* recapitulate two brief lists of undefended precepts found in an earlier chapter on purification and a later chapter on courage.[20] As it turns out, these lists present two affirmative but partially distinct defenses of the virtue. In section 187, Pythagoras exhorts people to remove from themselves "what is out of balance" (τὰ ἀσύμμετρα); also, don't eat living things or those that cause undiscipline (ἀκολασία); don't wear finery unless you're a courtesan; exercise the mind to free it from distraction; and, as a useful exercise, have a fancy banquet served up, gaze on it, but then get rid of the food before touching any of it. Section 188, evidently not from the same source, gives a broader list of maxims pertinent to *sôphrosunê*: practice silence; study difficult subjects; resist wine, excesses in food and sleep, and the claims of fame and wealth; revere one's elders; be friendly with one's contemporaries; and help people younger than you. Iamblichus' use of these precepts at several points in his *On the Pythagorean Way of Life* shows he does not think they apply exclusively to *sôphrosunê*, but since they commence this chapter (and not the others), he must think of them as characteristic of *sôphrosunê*. Pythagoras' statement about "what is out of balance" is too metaphorical to indicate much more than that he has a vision of the self that involves different parts in potentially problematic relations of dominance. The rest of the first and the whole of the second list stake out the territory of *sôphrosunê*. The first includes diverse modes of desire control, mainly with respect to food and appearance (which in turn is possibly related to sexual availability), especially such that desire does not interfere with thought. The second is broader, with a concern for moderating the desires for sleep and social power, not just gustation; discipline in thought; and proper social recognition. So Iamblichus adumbrates two basic pictures of *sôphrosunê* here: one where mind controls desire, at least partly so that desire does not distract mind; and one where mental discipline, acknowledgment of other people's worth, and desire management play equal roles.

The next six sections of *On the Pythagorean Way of Life* recount a single story, of Dionysius of Syracuse's attack on some Pythagoreans in Tarentum and the *sôphrosunê* they exhibited thereby.[21] The main party of Pythagoreans were killed

---

[19] Stobaeus' chapter "On *sôphrosunê*" (Stob. 3.5) is longer but not continuous in the same way.
[20] Iambl. *VP* 187–88; seen also at 68–69 and 223–24.
[21] Iambl. *VP* 189–94.

when they halted their escape rather than trample on a field of beans, which was proscribed by their way of life. Another Pythagorean was willing to die to preserve the secret of that proscription. And a third, his wife, bit out her tongue to ensure her silence on the matter.[22] This tale, perhaps riveting to Iamblichus, shows the Pythagoreans' extraordinary discipline or sense of obligation to the norms of their community, and the way they disdained death and fear.

Between this story and the long excerpt from the *Pythagorean Precepts* Iamblichus fills in some miscellanea. He marks an explicit return to *sôphrosunê*: the virtue enjoins silence, and especially so since control of one's tongue is the signal case of self-control (ἐγκρατευμάτων); it prohibits living with concubines; it counters sexual lust; and it draws one away from hubris. Pythagoreans advise stability of body and of mind; elimination of negative emotions by never failing to expect the unexpected, but when they do fail, withdrawing until they succeed at calming their emotions; never acting in anger; and never letting passions cause disagreement.[23]

As we can see, the first half of Iamblichus' chapter contains no arguments or dialectical development; it is a haphazard assemblage of precepts and stories pertaining to *sôphrosunê*, only sometimes linked explicitly to the virtue-term. There is no overarching thesis that explains the inclusion of the present material. Its extent and variety, however, prove informative. *Sôphrosunê* is about not having one's desires, emotions, and other passions dictate one's actions; instead, reason and the recognition of authority should dictate one's desires. Such desires go beyond Aristotle's desires for food and drink and sex; they include, for example, the impulsion to self-expression through talking, to correction of wrongs through angry retribution, and to independence through disrespecting of others. On the constructive side, the virtue involves the ability to identify the proper reasons for action.

Against this background of moral potpourri, Iamblichus' long excerpt from Aristoxenus' *Pythagorean Precepts* appears as a philosophical treatise, dense with inferences, taxonomies, and analyses. It also happens to be heterogeneous in content, lacking an explicit statement about *sôphrosunê* or appeal to its parts as evidence for that statement. Nevertheless, Iamblichus understands the quoted extent as pertinent to *sôphrosunê*—pertinent enough, indeed, to give over half his chapter to it. Iamblichus' judgment does not seem mistaken: *sôphrosunê* is mentioned in five of the fourteen sections, distributed fairly evenly.[24] It is a major statement on the virtue.

---

[22] See Dutsch (2020, 55–58) on this part of the story.
[23] Iambl. *VP* 195–98.
[24] Iambl. *VP* 201, 202, 209, 210, 211 = fr. 9 lines 19, 22, 26, 132, 148 (bis), 152 (of 176 lines).

Fragment 9 has five main topics; they are only implicitly linked together. The passage starts with the issue of epistemic authority; then reprises the need for continuous authoritative supervision of people as they grow up; then analyzes pleasure and desire, eventuating in the diagnosis of the hubris already mentioned and a refinement of the supervision already mentioned; justifies anew the careful supervision of youth; and, taking off from a claim in the previous section, that children should not have procreative sex too early, sets out some considerations about procreation, emphasizing that it needs to be really thoughtful. The submerged argument across these topics is easily surfaced: nobody is perfectly knowledgeable, but some people know more than others, and thus we should follow them, throughout our lives, since we may always have problematic desires, and these problems are not only to our own detriment but, profoundly, to that of the next generation. (The moral argument gets power from the observation that the person harmed might be one's own offspring.) From this perspective, *sôphrosunê* has a determinate form, one that gives sense to the previous crush of precepts and develops the approach found in fragment 8. *Sôphrosunê* is the recognition that one's desires are not altogether salutary, the appreciation that one cannot simply squash them by understanding what's wrong with them or wanting them to go away, and the acknowledgment that only by following some guidance from beyond oneself that is authoritative because epistemically reliable will one be able to manage those desires. *Sôphrosunê* is vitally important at every point in one's life and for the lives of one's offspring.

The argumentative details for the five main topics illuminate the dialectical conditions in which Aristoxenus' sources formulate their positions; the details shall detain us only enough to sketch these conditions out. The fragment begins with an argument for treating a community's elders, and those who have lived well, as practical authorities.[25] The argument supports the assertion that people should be supervised by authorities, since it provides some actual authorities by whom to be supervised. Diversity in opinion means that not everyone should be trusted—but also that not everyone should be ignored, for in fact some people do form relatively more sensible opinions. One should therefore follow the instructions of those with the more sensible opinions, if one wants to be "saved."

---

[25] Aristox. *Pyth. pr.* fr. 9,1–14 = *VP* 200–1: περὶ δὲ δόξης τάδε φασὶ λέγειν αὐτούς. ἀνόητον μὲν εἶναι καὶ τὸ πάσῃ καὶ παντὸς δόξῃ προσέχειν, καὶ μάλιστα τὸ τῇ παρὰ τῶν πολλῶν γινομένῃ· τὸ γὰρ καλῶς ὑπολαμβάνειν τε καὶ δοξάζειν ὀλίγοις ὑπάρχειν. δῆλον γὰρ ὅτι περὶ τοὺς εἰδότας τοῦτο γίνεσθαι· οὗτοι δέ εἰσιν ὀλίγοι. ὥστε δῆλον ὅτι οὐκ ἂν διατείνοι εἰς τοὺς πολλοὺς ἡ τοιαύτη δύναμις. ἀνόητον δ' εἶναι καὶ πάσης ὑπολήψεώς τε καὶ δόξης καταφρονεῖν· συμβήσεται γὰρ ἀμαθῆ τε καὶ ἀνεπανόρθωτον εἶναι τὸν οὕτω διακείμενον. ἀναγκαῖον δ'εἶναι τῷ μὲν ἀνεπιστήμονι μανθάνειν ἃ τυγχάνει ἀγνοῶν τε καὶ οὐκ ἐπιστάμενος, τῷ δὲ μανθάνοντι προσέχειν τῇ τοῦ ἐπισταμένου τε καὶ διδάξαι δυναμένου ὑπολήψει τε καὶ δόξῃ, καθόλου δ' εἰπεῖν ἀναγκαῖον εἶναι τοὺς σωθησομένους τῶν νέων προσέχειν ταῖς τῶν πρεσβυτέρων τε καὶ καλῶς βεβιωκότων ὑπολήψεσί τε καὶ δόξαις.

It turns out that those with relatively sensible opinions tend to be those who have lived long and well.

The elder class are thus justified on epistemic grounds to promulgate rules and the younger classes have epistemic reasons to follow those rules. This backs up the precept cited earlier in Iamblichus' chapter, that people should respect their elders. And it suggests that *sôphrosunê*, most fundamentally, amounts to following authoritative norms rather than adventitious passions or unjustified beliefs, no matter how widely the latter are shared.

Now that the legitimacy of supervision has been established on epistemic grounds, Aristoxenus returns at length to the necessity of supervision at the start of life and ceaselessly through the ages of increasing maturity. The long passage that follows is a view of education in *sôphrosunê* influenced by the idiosyncratic Pythagorean view of human development:

ἐκκρούεσθαι γὰρ αὐτὰς ὑπ' ἀλλήλων, ἐάν τις μὴ καλῶς τε καὶ ὀρθῶς ἄγῃ τὸν ἄνθρωπον ἐκ γενετῆς. Δεῖν οὖν τῆς τοῦ παιδὸς ἀγωγῆς καλῆς τε καὶ σώφρονος γινομένης καὶ ἀνδρικῆς πολὺ εἶναι μέρος τὸ παραδιδόμενον εἰς τὴν τοῦ νεανίσκου ἡλικίαν, ὡσαύτως δὲ καὶ τῆς τοῦ νεανίσκου ἐπιμελείας τε καὶ ἀγωγῆς καλῆς τε καὶ ἀνδρικῆς καὶ σώφρονος γινομένης πολὺ εἶναι μέρος <τὸ> παραδιδόμενον εἰς τὴν τοῦ ἀνδρὸς ἡλικίαν, ἐπείπερ εἴς γε τοὺς πολλοὺς ἄτοπόν τε καὶ γελοῖον εἶναι τὸ συμβαῖνον. Παῖδας μὲν γὰρ ὄντας οἴεσθαι δεῖν εὐτακτεῖν τε καὶ σωφρονεῖν καὶ ἀπέχεσθαι πάντων τῶν φορτικῶν τε καὶ ἀσχημόνων εἶναι δοκούντων, νεανίσκους δὲ γενομένους ἀφεῖσθαι παρά γε δὴ τοῖς πολλοῖς ποιεῖν ὅ τι ἂν βούλωνται. Συρρεῖν δὲ σχεδὸν εἰς ταύτην τὴν ἡλικίαν ἀμφότερα τὰ γένη τῶν ἁμαρτημάτων· καὶ γὰρ παιδαριώδη πολλὰ καὶ ἀνδρώδη τοὺς νεανίσκους ἁμαρτάνειν. Τὸ μὲν γὰρ φεύγειν ἅπαν τὸ τῆς σπουδῆς τε καὶ τάξεως γένος, ὡς ἁπλῶς εἰπεῖν, διώκειν δὲ τὸ τῆς παιγνίας τε καὶ ἀκολασίας καὶ ὕβρεως τῆς παιδικῆς εἶδος, τῆς τοῦ παιδὸς ἡλικίας οἰκειότατον εἶναι· ἐκ ταύτης οὖν εἰς τὴν ἐχομένην ἡλικίαν ἀφικνεῖσθαι τὴν τοιαύτην διάθεσιν. Τὸ δὲ τῶν ἐπιθυμιῶν τῶν ἰσχυρῶν, ὡσαύτως δὲ καὶ τὸ τῶν φιλοτιμιῶν γένος, ὁμοίως δὲ καὶ τὰς λοιπὰς ὁρμάς τε καὶ διαθέσεις, ὅσαι τυγχάνουσιν οὖσαι τοῦ χαλεποῦ τε καὶ θορυβώδους γένους, ἐκ τῆς τοῦ ἀνδρὸς ἡλικίας εἰς τὴν τῶν νεανίσκων ἀφικνεῖσθαι. (Aristox. *Pyth. pr.* fr. 9,17–40 = *VP* 201–2)

These [ages] are impeded by one another, if someone should not bring up a person well and correctly. Thus, when the upbringing of a child is fine and *sôphrôn* and courageous, a great part of this should be brought along to the age of the young man; and similarly, when the cultivation and upbringing of a young man is fine and courageous and *sôphrôn*, a great part of this should be brought along to the age of the adult—since the situation otherwise, for many people, is odd and risible. For they think children should be well-ordered and *sôphrôn* and kept away from everything deemed vulgar and unseemly, yet upon their coming to be young men they leave them—at least many people do—to do what they like. Yet young men make both childish and adult mistakes. For, to put it simply, avoiding everything that's serious and orderly, and pursuing fun and indiscipline and a kind of callow hubris, these are most characteristic of the age of the child. And from this age such a disposition comes to the next. The strong desires, and similarly the ambitious ones, and so too the other impulses and dispositions that characterize the difficult and turbulent, these come [in the other direction] from the age of men to that of young men.

A primary goal of education is *sôphrosunê*, and this virtue must be instilled at every age. Children are inclined to do whatever amuses them, unconcerned as they are about the long-term coordination of their actions or about their obligations to others. This is as we would expect from the theory of human nature discussed in fragment 8. Adults, too, however, have their own challenges, namely violent and willful emotions and aspirations for social esteem.[26] The education and cultivation of teenagers thus should emphasize *sôphrosunê*, given the broad range of ways disorderly desires impinge on their decision-making. There can be no relenting since, as we saw in fragment 8, the Pythagoreans see no evidence of an inner faculty of desire-management and of self-maintenance, one which, once primed, could preserve one's state of *sôphrosunê*. While people even when young can be responsive to rules, those rules are neither self-legislated nor self-enforced (or at least do not feel that way), so the rules must be continually externally imposed, and modified according to a changing inner nature. Given the deterioration of one's organization—one's self-constitution, so to speak—it makes sense that *sôphrosunê* would be thematized in the Pythagorean curricular and cultural systems: they must keep their normative goals constantly before their mind.[27]

Aside from pedagogical arrangements to assist in maintaining orderly citizens, the Pythagoreans give general advice about desire: beware of pleasure. Pleasure "trips and knocks one into error more than anything else."[28] Is the problem that seeking pleasure tends to fail, what we call the hedonic paradox, or that, though it succeeds, it causes one to err in other ways, what we might call the vices of hedonism? It seems both: pleasure-directedness is said to be both unseemly (ἀσχήμων, which is unethical) and harmful (βλαβερός, which is imprudent).[29] The excited desire for pleasure proves so strong as to distract a

---

[26] Cf. *Anon. Iambl.* fr. 4.5.
[27] These points are reinforced in Aristox. *Pyth. pr.* fr. 9,42–59 = VP 203–4. Cp. Xen. *Mem.* 1.2.19–23.
[28] Aristox. *Pyth. pr.* fr. 9,62–64 = VP 204: οὐθὲν γὰρ οὕτω σφάλλειν ἡμᾶς οὐδ' ἐμβάλλειν εἰς ἁμαρτίαν ὡς τοῦτο τὸ πάθος.
[29] Aristox. *Pyth. pr.* fr. 9,65–66 = VP 204.

person from his duty and from doing what is actually valuable or useful. This is because acting well requires more than mere passing thought (κρίσεως οὐ τῆς τυχούσης)—namely, serious investigation and deliberation—and so it may be derailed.[30] This critique of pleasure is familiar from the Pythagoreans' contemporary Antisthenes, who, as we saw in Chapter 5, said that pleasure was worse than madness.[31] As it was in Antisthenes' work, what is revealed here and developed in the rest of the section is that the Pythagoreans do not take issue with desire itself. Because the Pythagoreans seek to avoid actions "aimed at pleasure" (πράττειν ἡδονῆς στοχαζομένους), they believe there must be desires and actions aimed at other goals, specifically those obligations (πρακτέον) achieved with an eye to (βλέποντας) what's excellent and seemly.[32] A person's natural multiplicity of impulses, while he has them, is what *sôphrosunê* confronts; presumably many of those impulses are for incompatible pleasures or for pleasures incompatible with long-term, social, or otherwise more important ends. The impulses themselves are not bad; what is bad is, at first, their lack of integration and then, later, their own working against their integration. (There is no talk of their "subordination" to something else internal.)

With the problem of pleasure addressed—it is pleasure and not desire per se that Pythagoreans worry about—Aristoxenus can discuss their analysis of desire, so as eventually to return to their practical precepts. Desires, as has been said before, are complex or diverse and take altogether many forms (ποικίλον . . . καὶ πολυειδέστατον), whether inborn or acquired, directing the soul toward one or another instance of filling, emptying, perception, or freedom from perception. A desire may be in error (ἡμαρτημένη) for perhaps many reasons, but three above all: unseemliness (ἀσχημοσύνη), being vulgar or unfree; imbalance (ἀσυμμετρία), being too strong or enduring; and inappropriateness (ἀκαιρία), taking the wrong object for the moment—or any moment. Again, desires are not intrinsically bad, since they need not be disordered, excessive, or undefined in every case; they are just at risk of becoming bad. This becomes clearer in Aristoxenus' application of this taxonomy to explain the taste for luxury.

Aristoxenus' example concerns nutrition and its luxurious satisfaction, though he emphasizes that this is simply an example, not the core case; clothing or shelter or anything else would support his point just as well.[33] The desire to fill oneself with food is inborn and unproblematic. What comes to be acquired is the desire for food beyond the level of filling, just as much as is the desire for tableware, table servers, and livestock for putting meat on the table. As this list shows, these acquired desires are not in themselves bad. But, the Pythagoreans

---

[30] Aristox. *Pyth. pr.* fr. 9,69 = *VP* 204.
[31] Antisth. fr. 122 (see Chapter 5).
[32] Aristox. *Pyth. pr.* fr. 9,64–68 = *VP* 204.
[33] Iambl. *VP* 205–8.

observe, these are the sorts of desires that might never be satiated, and this would be the problem. Those with great means especially risk their acquired desires proliferating and growing extreme. The very quest for variety induces its own madness and disturbance; the more general concern, however, is that these unlimited desires can waste time and effort and harm oneself and others. (In the case of food and drink, since each brings its own effect on one's condition, the effects presumably add up or even amplify or pervert one another.)

The relationship between natural and acquired desires is not made immediately clear. Fragment 8 had it that diversity and insolence of desires is natural, as we see from animals. We do not learn whether animals also acquire desires from external sources. If they do not, then one's inborn desires must themselves be hazardously diverse and prone to overextension. This is not acknowledged in fragment 9, where Aristoxenus classes the (overextended) desire for more than enough food with the acquired type. The explanation is probably that Aristoxenus does not mean to individuate desires as either inborn or acquired. We are born with a desire to eat in order to fill ourselves—a desire that would be active only until we filled ourselves up. We are born with other desires, too; none need be excessive, and while there could be inconsistencies among them—the desire to eat and the desire to sleep—turn-taking solutions for their mutual satisfaction could be readily found. Yet these inborn desires, given the environment, could take new shape almost immediately. The desire for food, for example, might metamorphose into the desire for novel foods, or for the act of consumption, or for avoiding future states of hunger. These fuller realizations of one's inborn desires would be natural, so to speak: our nature is such as to allow and even encourage these developments. Thus it would be natural for our desires to develop into forms of excessive intensity and diversity.

At any rate, these developed desires must be tractable. Educators in *sôphrosunê* deal with (ἐπιμελητέον) those desires that grow up (ἀναφυομένων) from a young age (ἐκ νεότητος), ensuring that their students direct themselves toward the right things. This gives us a more precise picture of the supervisory education discussed in fragments 8 and 2: modification and redirection of desire. This makes sense of Pythagoras' precepts cited early in Iamblichus' chapter connected to austerity and self-teasing: their goal is the reshaping of labile desire.

The last section of the *Pythagorean Precepts* cited by Iamblichus concerns reproduction. A fundamental Pythagorean commitment is the heritability of virtue; offspring acquire the virtues that their parents have at the moment of procreation. Prospective parents should thus wait until becoming fully mature. The Pythagoreans formulate this maturity as having adopted a "hardworking, *sôphrôn*, and resilient" life.[34] Once potential parents have come to live

---

[34] Aristox. *Pyth. pr.* fr. 9,132 = *VP* 209: φιλοπόνῳ τε καὶ σώφρονι καὶ καρτερικῷ.

a *sôphrôn* and healthy life, they are to couple "in accordance with nature" and "with *sôphrosunê*," which brings about a *sôphrôn* and lawful child-production.[35] The reiteration of the desiderative centrality of *sôphrosunê* is striking. The Pythagoreans believe that most people hardly think at all about their condition prior to and during procreation, and yet this carelessness is the most powerful and clearest cause of human vice and badness.[36] One must orient oneself toward *sôphrosunê*, for oneself and the subsequent well-being of humanity.

This long, multistage excerpt of the *Pythagorean Precepts* thus shows how *sôphrosunê* can became an object of practical ethical and political analysis, deployed as an ideal that clarifies both the signal human struggles and the kind of life that a social organization should seek to promote. Those struggles are principally coordination of errant, boisterous desires; the relevant kind of life is one described less in terms of happiness than in the capacity to act: to be able to work consistently and effectively without self-undermining oneself. This defense of *sôphrosunê* involves a view of animal/human nature that is incompatible with the Calliclean view of pure desire satisfaction. It uses a mostly prudential argument—concern for one's well-being—mixed with a concern for piety and public esteem. That the longevity of one's community is also a desideratum makes *sôphrosunê* moral, unless each Pythagorean saw the community as merely an extension of herself or the context in which her offspring were to grow up.

The Case of Archytas

As we mentioned, Aristoxenus also wrote a *Life of Archytas*, about the Pythagorean ruler of Tarentum who flourished in the first half of the fourth century—likely a close contemporary of Xenophilus' Pythagorean community.[37] Though we know rather less about the Archytean *Life* than we do about the *Pythagorean Precepts*, we get a sense for the centrality of *sôphrosunê* to this biography as well. While this may speak to Aristoxenus' commitment to the topic—which would set him interestingly apart from Aristotle—it surely also reflects the Pythagoreans' commitment to the virtue, as the long chapter on the subject in Iamblichus' *On the Pythagorean Way of Life* suggests. We lack sufficient detail to reveal any debate about *sôphrosunê* between Xenophilus and Archytas, but the differences in emphasis found within the two corpora of fragments, whether

---

[35] Aristox. *Pyth. pr.* fr. 9,147–49 = *VP* 210: καταλιμπάνειν δὲ τῶν κατὰ φύσιν τε καὶ μετὰ σωφροσύνης γινομένων τὰς ἐπὶ τεκνοποιίᾳ σώφρονί τε καὶ νομίμῳ γινομένας.

[36] Iambl. *VP* 212–13.

[37] On Archytas, see Huffman (2005). Schofield (2014) does not associate any ethical material with Archytas.

doctrinal or simply generic or adventitious, reveal the broad horizon in which the virtue was theorized in the fourth century.

That Archytas was characterized by *sôphrosunê* is best seen in an anecdote from Aelian, plausibly attributable to Aristoxenus' *Life*: "Archytas was *sôphrôn* in various respects; he was even so in guarding against verbal disorder" (Ἀρχύτας τά τε ἄλλα ἦν σώφρων καὶ οὖν καὶ τὰ ἄκοσμα ἐφυλάττετο τῶν ὀνομάτων).[38] Aelian appears to have drawn this conclusion from a list of ways in which Archytas was *sôphrôn*. The case of language must be distinctive, and also good evidence of the breadth of Archytas' ways of being *sôphrôn*. The *sôphrôn* person guards against disorder (τὰ ἄκοσμα) with respect to words (ὀνόματα), presumably as he does against disorder in any part of his life.

Words are disorderly not from the syntactic but from an ethical perspective; to speak them is to speak contrary to social propriety. Aelian continues, "Once, though being forced (ἐβιάζετό) to say something inappropriate (τῶν ἀπρεπῶν), he was not overcome (ἐξενικήθη), but kept silent about it, and instead wrote [it] on the wall, showing what he was being forced to speak but not having been forced (βιασθείς) to say [it]." Archytas felt pressure to speak out something inappropriate, but thanks to his *sôphrosunê* he did not capitulate to that pressure, pressure which otherwise would have "overcome" him. He still expressed whatever it was he felt pressure to say, but evidently in an appropriate manner. This is a puzzling anecdote in many respects, since we may wonder what sorts of things are inappropriate to say, whence comes the pressure to say them, why his writing them on a wall could have been done freely by contrast to his speaking them in a compulsory way, and why he chose to write them at all.[39] In any event, *sôphrosunê* here must include not being overcome by this impetus to do something inappropriate and hence disorderly, with silence as a suitable response. But it may also include a transparency about oneself, a kind of openness or honesty, which would account for the importance of Archytas' revealing what he felt compelled to say. Then again, it might not be a matter of transparency; the last part may reflect the fact that Archytas had legitimate reasons for saying something. It would be a failure of *sôphrosunê* to say that thing from compulsion, for example from overweening anger or frustration, but he could *write* it freely, or at least autonomously, given the skill and effort needed to inscribe something on a wall.

From this perspective, disorderly words would be speeches driven not by reason but by feeling, just as disorderly eating or sex or striving would be instances of those actions driven not by reason but by feeling. Just as one may be entitled at times to eat rich food, one may be entitled to speak one's mind, but

---

[38] Ael. *VH* 14.19 = A11. Attribution depends on similarity to A7, discussed below. See Huffman (2005, 337–38).

[39] For clear expression of the puzzling aspects and possible resolutions, see Huffman (2005, 338–40).

in either case only when affirmed by reason. Archytean *sôphrosunê* seems to demand that legitimacy of action depends on an actual decision.

In sections 197–98 of Iamblichus' *On the Pythagorean Way of Life*, there is a story about Archytas' way of dealing with anger.[40] This story is attributed to Spintharus, who is the father of Aristoxenus and elsewhere a named source in Aristoxenus' writings. Iamblichus introduces the story by anticipating its conclusion: the Pythagoreans would not act from anger (ὑπὸ ὀργῆς), for instance to punish slaves or correct freemen who aggrieved them, and would instead wait until they reestablished their placidity of thought (ἀνέμενεν ... τὴν τῆς διανοίας ἀποκατάστασιν) before doing anything.[41] Archytas once witnessed negligence on his farm, and he became angry and annoyed (ὀργισθείς τε καὶ ἀγανακτήσας), as it was in character for him to become. But he would not punish those responsible—evidently not wanting to act from emotion. Though the quoted bit of the anecdote does not use the term *sôphrosunê*, its moral so matches the anecdote found in Aelian, and its position in Iamblichus' chapter contributes to the thought, that we might suppose that this is one of the "other ways" in which Archytas is said to be *sôphrôn*. Interestingly, in both anecdotes Archytas reveals an irascible temper: his *sôphrosunê* does not amount to a psychic tranquility, only to a capacity to prevent that psychic turmoil from dictating his actions. *Sôphrosunê* involves a psychic distance from one's passionate desires such that they can be rendered unmotivating. Indeed, nothing in these two anecdotes suggests that *sôphrosunê* even suppresses desire; it only separates desire from decision procedures by putting a moratorium on decisions and allowing desires to dissipate in time (evidently in consistency with Antiphon's view).

The most telling analysis of *sôphrosunê* in the *Life of Archytas* is a debate about the value of pleasure.[42] Athenaeus quotes a long speech from the biography given to Polyarchus the Voluptuary (τὸν ἡδυπαθῆ), a philosophical acquaintance of Archytas' and advocate of "bodily pleasures."[43] Polyarchus is contributing to a conversation about "the desires (τῶν ἐπιθυμιῶν) and, in general, the bodily pleasures." He argues for a position akin to Callicles', about the value of pleasure and the disvalue of virtue—justice, *sôphrosunê*, and *enkrateia* in particular—though his position differs in the way it construes the value of pleasure. As we will see, in Cicero's *De Senectute* we appear to have a paraphrase of Archytas' response, which comes to focus on *temperantia*, which probably translates *sôphrosunê*.

---

[40] Aristox. *VA* fr. A7; discussion in Huffman (2005, 287–92).
[41] Similar stories are told about Archytas in Cic. *Tusc.* 4.36.78 and *De Rep.* 1.38.59; Val. Max. 4.1 ext. 1; Plut. *De lib. educ.* 10d, *De sera num. vind.* 551; Lactant. *De ira* 18.4; Jer. *Ep.* 79.9.4; Procl. *De prov.* 54. Such are also told about Plato; see Riginos (1976, anecdotes 113A–C).
[42] For discussion and authenticity of A9 and A9a, see Huffman (2002; 2005, 307–37).
[43] Ath. 12.545a.

Polyarchus says, in a conversation about the desires and bodily pleasures, that he has come to find that

<ἄτοπον> τὸ τῶν ἀρετῶν τούτων κατασκεύασμα καὶ πολὺ τῆς φύσεως ἀφεστηκὸς εἶναι. ἡ γὰρ φύσις ὅταν φθέγγηται τὴν ἑαυτῆς φωνήν, ἀκολουθεῖν κελεύει ταῖς ἡδοναῖς, καὶ τοῦτό φησιν εἶναι νοῦν ἔχοντος. τὸ δὲ ἀντιτείνειν καὶ καταδουλοῦσθαι τὰς ἐπιθυμίας οὔτ' ἔμφρονος οὔτε εὐτυχοῦς οὔτε ξυνιέντος εἶναι τίς ποτε ἐστὶν ἡ τῆς ἀνθρωπίνης φύσεως σύστασις. (Aristox. VA fr. A9,10–15 = fr. 50 Wehrli)

the construct of these virtues [which Archytas had evidently celebrated] is dubious and very far from nature. For nature, when it speaks in its own voice, commands the pursuit of pleasures and says that this is for the thoughtful person. Pulling against and enslaving the pleasures is not for the mindful person, or for the fortunate one, or for the one who understands what the nature of the human constitution is.[44]

The pursuit of pleasure is natural and appropriate for the thoughtful person, as the thoughtful person can see. Virtue interferes with pleasure's authority. The first reason for accepting this view, according to Polyarchus, is that it has the implicit support of the powerful, those freest to choose their ends. Everyone upon gaining power (ἐξουσία), he says, is brought toward (καταφέρεσθαι) the bodily pleasures and believes this to be the purpose of that power, with practically everything else being put in a supporting position (ἐν παρέργου ... χώρᾳ).[45] Kings at all times—Persian, Lydian, Median, Assyrian—have pursued pleasure; and given the challenges in keeping those pleasures fresh, they have poured untold resources into one novel pleasure after the next. Indeed, not just cultural variety but also the crash of empires may be explained as consequences of pleasure-hunting.[46] The hassle of both shows how deeply people value pleasure.

So pursuing pleasure is natural and right; virtue is unnatural and wrong. Polyarchus goes on to give a genealogy of morals, to explain the mistaken belief that virtues are apt and good:

οἱ δὲ νομοθέται ὁμαλίζειν βουληθέντες τὸ τῶν ἀνθρώπων γένος καὶ μηδένα τῶν πολιτῶν τρυφᾶν ἀνακῦψαι πεποιήκασι τὸ τῶν ἀρετῶν εἶδος. καὶ ἔγραψαν νόμους περὶ συναλλαγμάτων καὶ τῶν ἄλλων [καὶ] ὅσα ἐδόκει πρὸς τὴν

---

[44] <ἄτοπον> was conjectured by Capps and accepted by Huffman, <κενόν> by Wilamowitz; neither adjective has manuscript authority, but Polyarchus has surely used some dismissive adjective that has fallen out of the manuscripts. Hence my "dubious."
[45] Aristox. VA fr. A9,15–19.
[46] Examples: A9,19–45; geopolitics: 45–48.

πολιτικὴν κοινωνίαν ἀναγκαῖα εἶναι καὶ δὴ καὶ περὶ ἐσθῆτος καὶ τῆς λοιπῆς διαίτης, ὅπως ᾖ ὁμαλής. πολεμούντων οὖν τῶν νομοθετῶν τῷ τῆς πλεονεξίας γένει πρῶτον μὲν ὁ περὶ τὴν δικαιοσύνην ἔπαινος ηὐξήθη, καὶ πού τις καὶ ποιητὴς ἐφθέγξατο "δικαιοσύνας τὸ χρύσεον πρόσωπον" καὶ πάλιν "τὸ χρύσεον ὄμμα τὸ τᾶς Δίκας." ἀπεθεώθη δὲ καὶ αὐτὸ τὸ τῆς Δίκης ὄνομα. ὥστε παρ' ἐνίοις καὶ βωμοὺς καὶ θυσίας γίνεσθαι Δίκῃ. μετὰ ταύτην δὲ καὶ Σωφροσύνην καὶ Ἐγκράτειαν ἐπεισεκώμασαν καὶ πλεονεξίαν ἐκάλεσαν τὴν ἐν ἀπολαύσεσιν ὑπεροχήν. ὥστε τὸν πειθαρχοῦντα τοῖς νόμοις καὶ τῇ τῶν πολλῶν φήμῃ μετριάζειν περὶ τὰς σωματικὰς ἡδονάς. (Aristox. *VA* fr. A9,48–64)

Lawmakers, wanting to bring the whole of humanity to a single level, and for there to be no single citizen living in luxury, made the form of the virtues rise up. They wrote laws regarding our mutual dealings, and those necessary for political community, and in particular those promoting equality in clothes and other lifestyle matters. In the lawmakers' battle against the partisans of excess, first the praise of justice grew, with some poet uttering "the golden face of justice" and even "the golden eye of Justice." Then there was an apotheosis of the very name Justice, such that some people even came to have altars and sacrifices to Justice. Next came *Sôphrosunê* and Self-Control to the party, who called high enjoyment "excess." The result: the one who is obedient to the laws and the voice of the many moderates his bodily pleasures.

Presumably in the interest of civic stability, lawmakers sought to prevent the occasions and reasons for self-assertion, which if allowed would lead to inequality, envy, and inefficiency. A suite of laws concerned with economic, political, and sumptuary matters was just the start. The vaunting of justice made obedience to these laws normative; injecting *sôphrosunê* into common discourse derogated the bald pursuit of pleasure. The moral values, which in Polyarchus' eyes are contrary to hedonistic self-interest, are explained as not actually good but as the result of the policy choices of city managers, with buy-in from cultural and religious personnel. The normative force of these virtue-ideals, in other words, is a social construction.

We may now summarize Polyarchus' view: Virtues are social fictions; they are not natural; nature by contrast supplies a reason for pursuing pleasures; and the pursuit of pleasures is not contrary to reason, but indeed the very task of a reasonable person, who heeds nature's authentic call. Virtue amounts to resisting pleasures, preventing them, despite their pressures, from determining one's actions, and to enslaving them, depriving them of any authority even to try to determine one's actions. The mindful person, appreciating how people are arranged, recognizes that this prejudice against pleasures does not make sense. We see here yet another charge against *sôphrosunê* and its candidate centrality to human activity and agency. The pursuit of pleasure and exercise of intellect come together in those people most capable of action—those with the greatest power and resources. Polyarchus reads political constitutions as sacrificing individual agency for group comity, natural excellence for conventional mediocrity.

Archytas goes on to deny all this: unresisted and unmastered pleasures are, in fact, the source of evils, and they prevent the very exercise of reason and mindfulness applauded by Polyarchus himself. In Archytas' view, apparently in response to Polyarchus, pleasure and the rejection of *temperantia* (= *sôphrosunê*) is unreliable as a means to well-being. Cicero paraphrases Archytas' argument, which allows that while bodily pleasure is natural, it is natural as a "deadly plague" is, for "our lusts spur themselves on blindly and without restraint to possess [pleasure]."[47] This is bad for two reasons. The first reason cited by Cicero is moral: these unrestrained lusts eventuate not just in decadent banquets but in the worst of illicit and impious actions:

> hinc patriae proditiones, hinc rerum publicarum eversiones, hinc cum hostibus clandestina colloquia nasci; nullum denique scelus, nullum malum facinus esse, ad quod suscipiendum non libido voluptatis impelleret; stupra vero et adulteria et omne tale flagitium nullis excitari aliis illecebris nisi voluptatis; cumque homini sive natura sive quis deus nihil mente praestabilius dedisset, huic divino muneri ac dono nihil tam esse inimicum quam voluptatem. (Aristox. *VA* fr. A9a, 9–15 = Cic. *Sen.* 40)

> From this source are born betrayal of the fatherland, from this the overthrow of the state, from this secret conversations with the enemy. To sum up, there is no crime, no evil deed which the lust for pleasure does not drive us to undertake. Debauchery, indeed, and adultery and all such shameful behaviors are aroused by no other allurements than those of pleasure. And although nothing more excellent has been given to man than intellect ... there is nothing so opposed to this divine benefaction and gift than pleasure. (tr. Huffman)

The implication is that no honorable person could esteem a pursuit that eventuated in such a life. Nevertheless, if he did not think that the loss of honor outweighed his enjoyment of the pleasure, and he thought that pleasure was the only source of value, then he could coherently pursue unbounded pleasure. Archytas' next argument, which Cicero presents as explicitly about *temperantia*

---

[47] Aristox. *VA* fr. A9a,5–8 = Cic. *Sen.* 39: *nullam capitaliorem pestem quam voluptatem corporis hominibus dicebat a natura datam, cuius voluptatis avidae libidines temere et effrenate ad potiendum incitarentur* (tr. Huffman).

(= *sôphrosunê*), seeks to undermine that exception. The heedless pursuit of pleasure undermines one's own capacity for decision-making and thus, even on the hedonistic calculus, pleasure-maximization:

> nec enim lubidine dominante temperantiae locum esse, neque omnino in voluptatis regno virtutem posse consistere. quod quo magis intellegi posset, fingere animo iubebat tanta incitatum aliquem voluptate corporis, quanta percipi posset maxima; nemini censebat fore dubium quin tam diu, dum ita gauderet, nihil agitare mente, nihil ratione, nihil cogitatione consequi posset. (Aristox. *VA* fr. A9a, 16–21 = Cic. *Sen.* 41)

> Neither is there a place for *temperantia* where lust is master, nor is virtue able to gain any foothold under the tyranny of pleasure. In order to make this better understood he used to tell people to picture someone spurred on by the greatest bodily pleasure that can be perceived. He was of the opinion that no one would have any doubt that, so long as he was enjoying himself in this way, he would not be able to think about anything, to achieve anything by calculation, anything by deliberation. (tr. Huffman)

In the first sentence, Cicero summarizes Archytas' position: *sôphrosunê* and the other virtues have no efficacy when the pursuit of pleasure takes the extremes allowed by Polyarchus' position. This might seem a narrowly aimed argument, akin to the previous argument, meant for those who valorize the virtues and virtuous behavior. But the thought-experiment of Archytas' that Cicero goes on to cite in explanation suggests an alternative. The thrall of peak pleasure hinders actions that need to be thought through; and since Polyarchus' protreptic justification of unfettered hedonism appealed to the thoughtful man, who likes to reason things through, there is the chance of inconsistency. Of course, the impact and scope of this thought-experiment is open to question; are we to infer that, just as no thought is possible during the most intense pleasure, there is reduced thought during pleasure of any intensity at all? What matters, however, is the way the picture vindicates the claim about *sôphrosunê*. For it to do so, *sôphrosunê* would have to overlap with thinking, calculating, or deliberating. *Sôphrosunê* must be part of the capacity to reason out what to do, where apoplexies of pleasure prevent it from working. It cannot simply be the virtue of suppressing pleasure, for then Cicero's point would have to be different. Archytas must think that virtue is necessary for deliberate action, and pleasure interferes with virtue. Thus the second reason levied against Polyarchus' enlightened hedonism is that it undermines *sôphrosunê*, and *sôphrosunê* is the virtue of the life of determined action that Polyarchus himself champions.

A Real-Life Community of *Sôphrosunê*

Though Thucydides' early debates in his *History* include speakers presenting their cities as committed to a kind of civic *sôphrosunê*, it is doubtful that those cities, or even their leaders, actually thought of themselves as so committed; it is maybe even doubtful that those speakers really even pressed the theme of *sôphrosunê* to the extent that Thucydides depicts them doing. Plato's *sôphrôn* cities are strictly hypothetical, written out for some hermeneutic purpose. If Critias, as has been speculated, sought to reconstruct Athens on *sôphrôn* lines, during the oligarchy of 404/3, that virtue-directed reconstruction came fast to a halt, with Critias' defeat at Munychia. The Pythagorean community of Aristoxenus' youth—perhaps like that of Archytas, at Tarentum—differs from these. That community existed, and did so for decades, and seems, on the authority of Aristoxenus, to have taken the precepts about *sôphrosunê* as constitutional. How much these precepts actually governed the life and mentality of the community's members is impossible to establish; it is difficult even in the American case, with copious archival material, to know how much its constitutional virtues matter to concrete life. And yet the fact that *sôphrosunê* could serve as a prime desideratum of a community says much about the virtue. Working from a clear-eyed theory of human motivation and a civic goal of maturity into self-governing citizens, the constitution sought to help its people in the paradoxical transformation from beings with errant desires to agents with unified goals. It could rely neither on the people's gumption purely, which was the thing to be attained rather than started from, nor the government's control purely, which would not by itself conduce to its citizens' self-control. It had to provide at once norms for people to follow and exhortations to self-knowledge that would allow people to take themselves as identifying with those norms. The concept of *sôphronismos tis kai taxis* captures this passive-active state midway between the natural state of disorder and the virtuous state of *sôphrosunê*.

Both Aristoxenus' Pythagoreans and Archytas—like their contemporary Antisthenes and other Socratics—reject hedonism. They do not reject or abominate pleasure itself, but they doubt that it provides sound guidance for action. Yet of course pleasure presents itself, so to speak, as exactly the best guidance for action. So becoming a good decision-maker—a signal quality of being a mature person and living well—involves becoming able to find and deploy grounds other than pleasure for motivating action. This capacity is what *sôphrosunê* is. How to encourage or force this finding of alternative grounds becomes the rhetorical-psychological puzzle for the Xenophilian Pythagoreans and for Archytas. They must show the unlimited pursuit of pleasure to lead to obviously bad medium- and long-term consequences, and even to bad short-term consequences; provide a window into the untutored psyche to reveal its infantile inability to remain good-directed; and institute laws that promote non-pleasure-seeking goods and can be assimilated as affirmed personal principles.

The contrast with Socrates' proposal in Plato's *Republic* is notable. The Pythagoreans do not assert a tripartite soul, or prescribe musical culture, or nominate a leadership of philosophers. Their alternative route includes a less schematic inner realm, emphasizes community law, and accepts that the rules may not be intellectually perfect. An evaluation of the respective qualities of these proposals would be appealing. Our present purpose, however, has only been to show the fundamental similarities in the visions of *sôphrosunê* and practical rationality.

13
Sôphrosunê for Later Greek Women

Gendered Virtue

We saw little explicit "gendering" of *sôphrosunê* in the previous chapters, the assumption or argument that *sôphrosunê* was distinctly for or lacked by women, or that it had a distinctly feminine cast or embodiment. It was a unisex virtue in Homer and Euripides as well as in epitaphs, and though attributed mostly to men in lyric poetry, those poets after all had men as their audience and topic in the relevant works. Yet in the fifth and fourth centuries, some people expressed views about the distribution of virtues between men and women. Plato's *Meno* witnesses the debate. There Socrates says that the nature of virtue is gender-neutral: there is no "femininely just" or "masculinely courageous" way for some action to unfold. He allows that his interlocutor, Meno, may be right to believe that the potentially excellent actions for a man are one thing, for example being involved in civic affairs,[1] and for a woman are another, for example managing her household, securing all that's in it, and following what her husband says.[2] And yet, Socrates says, they share what makes those actions actually excellent: doing them *sôphronôs* and justly.[3] So a woman's virtue is the same as a man's, even if or when exercised as a competent management of a different realm of the social order.[4] The actions or situations may differ, even systematically, but not the way they are done or dealt with. Xenophon sharpens this point in the *Oeconomicus*. A married couple is meant to work together in the joint endeavor of a household. A young wife worries aloud to her husband, "How can I work with you? What power do I have? It's all on you. My work, says my mother, is *sôphronein*." Her husband responds, "By god, that's what my father said to me, too! But *sôphronein* is for man and woman to act so that their effects are in the best possible state and that they may grow as much as possible, admirably and justly."[5] Xenophon's

---

[1] Pl. *Meno* 71e3: ἱκανὸν εἶναι τὰ τῆς πόλεως πράττειν, καὶ πράττοντα τοὺς μὲν φίλους εὖ ποιεῖν, τοὺς δ' ἐχθροὺς κακῶς, καὶ αὐτὸν εὐλαβεῖσθαι μηδὲν τοιοῦτον παθεῖν.

[2] Pl. *Meno* 71e6–7: δεῖ αὐτὴν τὴν οἰκίαν εὖ οἰκεῖν, σῴζουσάν τε τὰ ἔνδον καὶ κατήκοον οὖσαν τοῦ ἀνδρός.

[3] Pl. *Meno* 73a9: ἆρ' οὖν οἷόν τε εὖ διοικεῖν ἢ πόλιν ἢ οἰκίαν ἢ ἄλλο ὁτιοῦν, μὴ σωφρόνως καὶ δικαίως διοικοῦντα. See further 73b, e.

[4] Pl. *Rep.* 5.455d–456a makes the same point and allows that men and women may occupy the same social sphere.

[5] Xen. *Oec.* 7.14–15. For discussion, see Glazebrook (2009, 240–43).

Ischomachus, the husband, does not doubt the division of labor, which a complex household appears to require, but he does doubt the division of virtue, which it absolutely does not.

Famously, Aristotle sides in his *Politics* with Meno and against Socrates, Plato, and Xenophon.[6] He thinks that virtue does differ by social role—that is, whether ruler or follower—for example between master and slave, father and son, husband and wife. Men rule over women, even if in a nonmonarchic way, and women keep to the household. What this means for the relative apportionment of virtue, Aristotle says, is something of a paradox. *Sôphrosunê* is a focal (though not the sole) virtue under his consideration here, given its importance for both leadership and followership. While women must have the virtues if they are to be able to obey and perform their duties, with *sôphrosunê* notable among them,[7] they cannot have those virtues in the same way as men, for if they did, nothing would justify their being ruled over by them.[8] This explanatory problem is severe in the case of slaves; Aristotle resolves it by saying that slaves have the virtues, but in a markedly different way: they lack altogether the capacity for judgment (τὸ βουλευτικόν). Women, by contrast, do not lack that capacity for judgment, but in them it is "not authoritative" (ἄκυρον).[9] What precisely makes this so is uncertain, but somehow the judgment is not sufficiently decisive for action. At the end of *Politics* Book 1 Aristotle says he will later discuss more thoroughly the virtue of women with respect to men, but in our version of the *Politics* he never does.[10] In any event, Aristotle summarizes his picture of role-defined virtues: "It is clear that there is ethical virtue for everyone above mentioned, and that the *sôphrosunê* of a woman is not the same as that of a man, nor courage and justice, as Socrates believed, but whereas there is a 'ruler's (ἀρχική) courage' there is also a 'follower's (ὑπηρετική),' and similarly for the other [virtues]."[11]

Aristotle gives two examples of a difference between male and female virtue, both times evidently though not explicitly about *sôphrosunê*. He instances what he calls Gorgias' view, from which Meno says he derives his own view, as one of the praiseworthy sort given by "those who enumerate the virtues" (οἱ ἐξαριθμοῦντες τὰς ἀρετάς).[12] As an example Aristotle gives "the poet's" view of women: "Silence

---

[6] Antisthenes, too, another Socratic, seems to have held the equivalence of men's and women's virtue: fr. 134 = DL 6.12: ἀνδρὸς καὶ γυναικὸς ἡ αὐτὴ ἀρετή. Similarly, the second head of the Stoic school, Clearchus, wrote a treatise, *Men and Women Share One and the Same Virtue* (DL 7.175).

[7] Arist. *Pol.* 1259b32: *sôphrosunê*, courage, justice.

[8] Arist. *Pol.* 1259a40–b4, b10 (women ruled over by men); 1259b30–1260a1 (same virtues, different way, focalizing *sôphrosunê* and courage); 1260a2–3 and a38 (*sôphrosunê* needed for doing what has been ordered).

[9] Arist. *Pol.* 1260a12–14. In the *Nicomachean Ethics*, virtue is authoritative by contrast with nature when it includes *phronêsis* (6.13 1144b7–17).

[10] Arist. *Pol.* 1260b9–22.

[11] Arist. *Pol.* 1260a20–24.

[12] Arist. *Pol.* 1260a27–31: καθόλου γὰρ οἱ λέγοντες ἐξαπατῶσιν ἑαυτοὺς ὅτι τὸ εὖ ἔχειν τὴν ψυχὴν ἀρετή, ἢ τὸ ὀρθοπραγεῖν, ἤ τι τῶν τοιούτων· πολὺ γὰρ ἄμεινον λέγουσιν οἱ ἐξαριθμοῦντες τὰς

brings order (κόσμον) to women."[13] As it turns out, this is quoted from Tecmessa in Sophocles' *Ajax*; she is in turn quoting Ajax—this was his clever rebuke to her admonition against his crazy sword-bearing nocturnal wanderings. She calls his statement curt (βαί) and cliché (ἀεὶ δ' ὑμνούμενα), evidently unimpressed. After all, he is the one who should be exercising more *sôphrosunê*. This literary context may not altogether undercut Aristotle's point, but it leaves it somewhat unconvincing.[14] Aristotle's second concrete reference to male-female differences in virtue comes in Book 3 of the *Politics*: a man's virtue differs by constitution, that is, by whether he is ruler or only ruled, just as a man's virtue and a woman's virtue differ for the same reason: "*Sôphrosunê* and courage are different for man and woman, for a man would be deemed cowardly if he were as courageous as a woman was courageous, and a woman [would be deemed] talkative (λάλος) if she were as orderly as a man was good."[15] Here Aristotle seems only to be saying that the mean to be hit by a virtue differs (as a gluttonous dinner for me is meager rations for Milo); but that quantitative point cannot be his principal concern. He gets back to qualitative, even functional differences when he says that the skill of household management differs for men and women in that the business of the former is to "acquire" goods for the household, of the latter to "preserve" them.[16] In general, Aristotle's view seems to be this: men's and women's social roles differ, sure, but this does not mean that they are equivalently *sôphrôn* across those roles, as a sprinter and a tennis player can be equivalently nimble. The nature of those social roles, namely their different relations toward ruling and thus authority, and the relevance of ruling and thus authority to virtue, means that men and women do not instantiate *sôphrosunê* in the same way. How they differ in doing so is unspecified, but that they differ is clear.

One may wonder how to integrate Aristotle's position here with the "official" one we saw in the earlier chapter, where his analysis of *sôphrosunê* makes no gender distinctions, and it is not obvious where gender distinctions would have a place. All people generally have the so-called natural or necessary desires, for nutrition and copulation, and so all people must moderate those desires. Either women's desires in those departments are especially intractable, such that they cannot keep themselves to what they know to be good, or they get confused

ἀρετάς, ὥσπερ Γοργίας, τῶν οὕτως ὁριζομένων. διὸ δεῖ, ὥσπερ ὁ ποιητὴς εἴρηκε περὶ γυναικός, οὕτω νομίζειν ἔχειν περὶ πάντων·

[13] From Soph. *Aj.* 293: γυναικὶ κόσμον ἡ σιγὴ φέρει.
[14] On *sôphronein* as thematic in *Ajax*, see Goldhill (1986, 146, 156, 159, 190–96).
[15] Arist. *Pol.* 1377b18–23. There is textual confusion where we read λάλος, but this term is appropriate given the tenor of the Sophocles quotation above (and Phaedra's remark about problematically long talks at Eur. *Hipp.* 384). Susemihl conjectured ἀκόλαστος, which would imply that men who are lascivious and forward may still count as orderly, but not women.
[16] Arist. *Pol.* 1377b24–25.

about what is good, and so even should they moderate or control their desires, they could not do so informedly. Probably Aristotle imagined or assumed a combination of these, such that women's reasoning is just always perverted to some degree by their passions. Their wisdom (φρόνησις) does not have the same oomph as men's.[17]

At all events, whatever the precise nature of Aristotle's view, it raises an essential point about *sôphrosunê*. On his view, whereas the human realization of a man is virtuous political action and theoretical contemplation, which requires a clear mind for the exercise of *phronêsis*, the human realization of a woman is virtuous contribution to an ongoing and stable household, which principally involves restraint with respect to nutrition and copulation (though perhaps also to gossip and so forth). The same virtue, a moderate state with respect to certain bodily desires, has distinct purposes and thus distinct evidence for its realization in the two genders. In this way one might judge *sôphrosunê* for men and women to be different, fundamentally: in one case, the virtue conduces to one's full and independent agency, a rational actor equal in status with all others; in the other case, the virtue conduces to effective and reliable instrumentality, a tool for the familial and economic success of another (as Jason expects of Medea). Formulating the contrast this way opens a question of central relevance to this book's argument: When does *sôphrosunê* represent agency, and when does it represent mere instrumental efficacy? When does it represent acting as one really desires, on the basis of norms one accepts as authoritative, and when does it represent acting on the desires that the people most powerful in society determine to be the right ones? Is there a categorical agency (autonomy) and a hypothetical agency (heteronomy), ideals perhaps, but not for the same person?

Until this final chapter of the book all the writings we have studied are by men, mainly for men, usually about men. With minor qualifications for Euripides' *Medea* and *Hippolytus* and Plato's *Republic*, they hardly provide impartial reflections on women's *sôphrosunê*. This chapter studies two works, both post-Classical, that do provide, if not wholly impartial, then at least more promising reflections on women's *sôphrosunê*. One of them, *On Women's Sôphrosunê* (Περὶ γυναικὸς σωφροσύνας), is attributed to a woman, Phintys of Sparta, and comes from the late Hellenistic or early Roman period; it specifically addresses virtue-differentiation by gender and the obligations it sets on women.[18] The other, a

---

[17] See generally North (1966, 206; 1977; 1979, 47–54, 110–11); Rademaker (2005, passim). Explanations of Aristotle's position: Mayhew (1999: women are intellectually weak); Fortenbaugh (2015a, 395–404: women are naturally impulsive); Nielsen (2015, 578: women are less capable of controlling and altering lawless desires, soft); Leunissen (2017, 171: they are weak); Lienemann (2021, esp. 151–54: they have inadequate *phronêsis*). The bibliography on this issue is growing; see the references discussed in Tu (2020, ch. 4); Connell (2021); Deslauriers (2022).

[18] Dutsch (2020, 37, 161) shares the conceit that Phintys "present[s] a compromise between Meno's ideas and Socrates.'" For discussion of Phintys, see Wider (1986, 36–37); Waithe (1987, 1.26–31);

letter, "To Arete, regarding *sôphrosunê*," is addressed to a real woman named Arete and written by Iamblichus of Chalcis, a Platonist from late antiquity; it exhorts Arete to the many excellences of *sôphrosunê*. Phintys' account takes inspiration from a wide swath of Classical authors, presumably including Xenophon, Plato, and Aristotle, and Iamblichus' takes inspiration from a Socratic Platonism. So in this last chapter, though leaving the Classical period in time, we remain with it in sentiment. Neither text is an easy study. Both exist only in excerpts by Stobaeus, in the commonplace book he assembled for his son. Authorship of Phintys' text is impossible to confirm, since it circulated in a literary culture of pseudonymous treatises, to which names of early Pythagoreans were affixed as part of the practice.[19] It might seem characteristic of Pythagoreanism, given the distinctive attention that this tradition of thought gave to women. Nevertheless, Phintys' analysis of *sôphrosunê* can seem almost suffocatingly conservative.[20] Iamblichus' letter is so abstract as to appear to have little social or political relevance at all. The reality is that neither woman-oriented text seems to treat *sôphrosunê* as wholly liberatory. But working through them allows us to confront the difficulties in understanding the kind of virtue *sôphrosunê* might have been taken to be.

This, then, is the concluding study of our book, where the idea of agency runs up against the subjective vision of freedom. We have treated of agency as being able to act on one's desires when those desires are commitments to one's ideals—the norms one understands to be decisive for oneself. But what happens when those norms amount to the will of one's husband? And what if one's actions are confined to the domestic space? Is this not a false or circumscribed agency? Or, by contrast, does this show that the scope of agency, so to speak, is always

---

Nails (1989, 294–96); Huizenga (2010, 383–92); Pomeroy (2013, 106–10); Dutsch (2020, 161–70); for references to older literature, see *DPhA* s.v. "Phintys" (vol. Va, 580–82).

[19] For this literary culture, Dutsch (2020) is essential; the earlier major statement is Thesleff (1961) (with Greek texts in Thesleff 1965), with new views expressed in Thesleff (1972); briefer treatments are in Lambropoulou (1995, 122–34); Centrone (2014, 319–20, 329–33). For attention to the works attributed to women, see Wider (1986, 26–40); Waithe (1987, vol. 1); Plant (2004, 67–86); Pomeroy (2013); Harper (2013)—though note the critique of the views in all of these by Dutsch. Whether the text of Phintys was really written by a woman has been widely debated; a characteristic doubt is expressed by Lefkowitz and Fant (1992, 163–64): that text and others were "probably not . . . even written by women, but rather consist of rhetorical exercises and treatises composed by men . . . certainly the content of what they wrote deals with topics particularly dear to the hearts of men: women's duties, women's chastity, how to behave when your husband acquires a mistress (put up with it cheerfully)" (similarly Deslauriers 2012, 343–44). Pomeroy (2013, 49–53) argues that it and they could well have been written by women. Dutsch (2020) shows that the issue is not decidable and is in the end unimportant because Phintys' text, like the others attributed to women, as well as to men, make sense only within a corpus of texts; they are not meant to be expressing individual, idiosyncratic, or natural perspectives.

[20] On the place of women in Pythagoreanism, see Rowett (2014, 122–23); Centrone (2014, 333). For conservativeness, see, e.g., Deslauriers (2012, 344–48); Dutsch (2020, 141).

conditioned by context, and to think otherwise is to imagine agency as what it is not, as in ideal of unfettered and unguided spontaneous power? And, not to put too fine a point on it, isn't this imagination of unfettered power a toxically masculine dream, wherein virtue is consistent with, and even justifies, the unimpeded impressment of one's will on the world? It might seem that *sôphrosunê* ought to be seen, by contrast, as precisely the capacity to acknowledge the cosmic, divine, social, or natural rules and train one's actions in accord with them. In this case, for *sôphrosunê* to be responsive to household norms does not seem to strip it of its status as a virtue. But what, then, distinguishes passive obedience from active rule-following? This is the question we must ask.

Phintys' *On Women's Sôphrosunê*

Among the earliest philosophical texts attributed to any woman in any culture is the one attributed to Phintys. It competes for this honor with other texts from the same milieu attributed to women, such as Perictione and Theano; it is probably from around the turn to the Common Era.[21] We know Phinty's treatise as reproduced or excerpted by Stobaeus in two consecutive parts, from her Περὶ γυναικὸς σωφροσύνας, *On Women's [or a Wife's] Sôphrosunê*.[22] In the first two-dozen lines of the seventy extant lines (totaling 713 words), Phintys makes a simple but apparently bold (and Heraclitus-adjacent) claim: *sôphrosunê* is the greatest virtue (μάλιστα ἀρετά) for a woman. She goes on to explain how this is even possible and what is great about it. We might call these initial lines the theoretical part of the treatise-excerpt. Sometimes *sôphrosunê* here seems related to self-determined action; sometimes it seems mere wifely submission. What follows those first twenty-four lines until the end of the treatise-excerpt is the practical part. Here Phintys describes what she takes to be the five key sources of *sôphrosunê*: marital fidelity, modest adornment, comportment out of doors, abstention from mystery rites, and cautious sacrificing. She thereby enjoins what may seem a claustrophobic and dependent life and justifies it with a mixed bag of reasons.

Phintys' text is hardly the only entry in the Pythagorean women philosopher corpus to discuss *sôphrosunê*—but it is the only one to thematize the virtue. Perictione's similarly complex *On Women's Harmony* begins, "It is of harmony

---

[21] Wilhelm (1915) (the fullest early study) argued for the second century CE, then Thesleff (1961, 115: with complete review of earlier attempts at dating) conjectured third century BCE, but later (1972) he revises this to first century BCE. After a full assessment of the evidence, Dutsch (2020) settles on first century BCE/CE. Given the networks of texts discussed by Dutsch and for other reasons, nothing speaks in favor of a fourth-century BCE dating (as assumed by, e.g., Waithe 1987, 26).

[22] Stob. 4.23.61.

that a woman full of wisdom (φρόνησις) and *sôphrosunê* must take thought," and it concludes with a clearer reformulation: a woman is harmonious, and so can benefit all those in her circle, "if she becomes full of wisdom and *sôphrosunê*."[23] A letter from Melissa to Cleareta, whom she praises for seeking virtue, describes what it takes to be *sôphrôn* and "free" (ἐλευθέραν).[24] Myia tells Phyllis that the wet-nurse she hires should "have it together" (τεταγμένα) and be *sôphrôn*, which includes not getting angry, being too talkative, or having a bad diet.[25] Theano's first piece of child-rearing advice to Euboule is to stop spoiling her children and instead to make them *sôphrôn*.[26] And in her advice to Eurydice about growing old, Theano counsels not pretending still to be young but to acknowledge her advancing years and "practice *sôphrosunê*, as you must."[27] Phintys' text evidently takes up a core topic of these works and, in its theoretical section, scrutinizes it.

We begin with that part of Phinty's text. (I number the sentences as periodized in Thesleff's edition of the treatise.)[28] I provide a running translation.[29]

[1] Τὸ μὲν ὅλον ἀγαθὰν δεῖ ἦμεν καὶ κοσμίαν· ἄνευ γὰρ ἀρετᾶς οὐδέποκα γένοιτό τις τοιαῦτα. [2] ἑκάστα γὰρ ἀρετὰ περὶ ἕκαστον γινομένα τὸ αὐτᾶς δεκτικὸν ἀποδίδωτι σπουδαῖον· ἁ μὲν τῶν ὀπτίλων τὼς ὀπτίλως, ἁ δὲ τᾶς ἀκοᾶς τὰν ἀκοάν, καὶ ἁ μὲν ἵππω τὸν ἵππον, ἁ δ' ἀνδρὸς τὸν ἄνδρα· οὕτω δὲ καὶ <ἁ> γυναικὸς τὰν γυναῖκα. [3a] γυναικὸς δὲ μάλιστα ἀρετὰ σωφροσύνα·

[1] On the whole, a woman ought to be good and orderly; yet, without virtue, she would never come to be that way. [2] For, the excellence of each thing depends on the virtue to which it is receptive, as it is with the virtue of the eyes for the eyes, of hearing for hearing, of a horse for a horse, and of men for men: so too of women for women. [3a] And of a woman, the greatest virtue is *sôphrosunê*—

Phintys opens her work with the argument that a woman's goodness must come from her virtue, for, on a basically functional account, the goodness of anything comes from its characteristic virtue. Thus at least women, to the unexceptionable extent that they can be good (at what they do), must be able to manifest virtue.

---

[23] 142,19 and 144,24 Thesleff. Her *sôphrosunê* allows her to tolerate all her husband's bad qualities and still arrange everything for him to be pleasant, 144,17.
[24] Städele (1980, III 160, 5, cf. 16, 18).
[25] Städele (1980, IV 164, 3).
[26] Städele (1980, V 166, 3).
[27] Zanetto 3 (Theophylact Simocatta).
[28] Thesleff (1965, 151–54).
[29] The text of Phintys has also been translated into English by Taylor (1822, 69–74) (revised and republished in Guthrie 1987, 263–64); Vickie Lynn Harper in Waithe (1986, 1.26–31); Lefkowitz in Lefkowitz and Fant (1992, 163–64, abridged); Plant (2004, 84–86); Pomeroy (2013, 105–6); Dutsch (2020, 234–37); Horky (forthcoming).

That this is a functional account is supported not just by appeal to the examples of sense organs and horses but also by the collocation of "good" and "orderly, composed" that we saw in Socrates' argument in the *Gorgias*. Virtue is presented here not as an extraordinary power, which could be denied to those deemed weak, but simply as the disposition appropriate for something's being seriously or excellently (σπουδαῖον) what it is. Perhaps it makes the source of goodness available to anyone, by contrast with the natural or accidental allotments of birth, money, fortune, or beauty.

The true thesis of this work, as the opening paragraph presents it, is that a woman's characteristic virtue is *sôphrosunê*. The examples of eyes and hearing favor thinking that something is characterized by a single virtue, as the general premise in [2] asserts. Phintys qualifies this somewhat implausible claim, as it pertains to humans, by calling *sôphrosunê* not the only virtue for women but the "greatest" one (as it turns out, from within the Platonic canon). In the next excerpt we will see her justification. But we may note that Phintys does not specify a single "greatest" virtue for men; she later offers two as their leading qualities, courage and thoughtfulness [9]. Nor does she say exactly what it takes for a virtue to be "greatest"; presumably, however, it is the most salient virtue for the most important task. She does not speak of *sôphrosunê* as a precondition for the exercise of other virtues, or as the general category into which other virtues may be found.

The first words of this paragraph, "On the whole" or "In general" (τὸ μὲν ὅλον), are equivocal. They could mean that there are exceptions to what follows. But this seems doubtful; perhaps they mean instead that a woman ought to be good and orderly "overall," throughout life and not just in several areas.[30] It is unclear how this would affect the force of what follows, however, namely that a woman's *sôphrosunê* serves a specific purpose.

[3b] διὰ γὰρ ταύτας τὸν ἴδιον ἄνδρα καὶ τιμῆν καὶ ἀγαπῆν δυνασεῖται.

[3b] because of it she will be able to honor and love her husband.

Because goodness and composure for a woman distinctly involve honor and love for her husband, and *sôphrosunê* facilitates or allows for that honor and love, the greatest virtue for a woman is *sôphrosunê*. Phintys does not say that the power or value of *sôphrosunê* is exhausted by this honor and love for one's husband, or even that a woman's goodness is exhausted by spousal fealty. And yet it can seem she is saying that; argumentatively, the connections between spousal fealty and

---

[30] Less plausibly, to my eyes, Pomeroy (2013, 105) and Taylor (1822, 69) take it as disallowing exceptions: women "must be altogether good"; "ought to be wholly good and modest." Meunier (1932 ad loc.), by contrast, gives "il sied en somme à la femme"—"Putting it briefly, it befits a woman."

sôphrosunê on the one hand, and goodness on the other, are central. Both may seem counteragential, if we understand *sôphrosunê* and goodness as subordination to another person's judgment or will. *Sôphrosunê* could be seen as an ability to demote one's own interests, preferences, and goals and prioritize someone else's, an ability, as it were, to become a tool. If the goodness and attendant virtue of a woman's life are to be perfected in giving oneself up to another, then here *sôphrosunê* does not seem a virtue of agency, at least not in a familiar way.

But Phintys does not speak here of passivity. The fact that she uses the language of virtue suggests otherwise. An eye has the virtue of seeing less as a passive condition (even if the eye seems merely to sit in the orbital socket as foreign images hit it) than as an active ability (to distinguish appearances in the world). A horse is not just ridden but runs. The virtue of a man is obviously in support of his doing what he judges he ought to do. So Phintys could have in mind a *sôphrosunê* as a positive capacity. The activities treated are "honoring" and "loving," neither of which explicitly mark obedience, submission, or subordination. Indeed, "loving" as taking another's good as your own, treating another as a proper object of care, as an object of value to you, and doing all this over the long haul, requires (to put the matter charitably) a sort of desiderative agency, a constancy of purpose and a unity of attention and action. The same could be said for "honoring," which involves taking the dignity and agency of another as salient for oneself. From a religious perspective, love and respect, or devotion and veneration, characterize the most effective adulators of the divine (and this was praised by Socrates in Xenophon's *Memorabilia*); from a social perspective, they characterize the most fully actualized friends.

All the same, here Phintys leaves vague the tenor of her exhortation. She certainly does not articulate an agency of creativity or independence. But she certainly does not argue that an excellent woman should give up any powers or privileges of decision or action.

[4] πολλοὶ μὲν ἴσως δοξάζοντι ὅτι οὐκ εὐάρμοστον γυναικὶ φιλοσοφεῖν, ὥσπερ οὐδ' ἱππεύεν οὐδὲ δαμαγορέν· ἐγὼ δὲ τὰ μέν τινα νομίζω ἀνδρὸς ἦμεν ἴδια, τὰ δὲ γυναικός, τὰ δὲ κοινὰ ἀνδρὸς καὶ γυναικός, τὰ δὲ μᾶλλον ἀνδρὸς ἢ γυναικός, τὰ δὲ μᾶλλον γυναικὸς ἢ ἀνδρός.

[4] Many people perhaps believe that it is not fitting for women to philosophize, as it is not to ride horses or speak publicly, but I believe that some things are particular to men, and some to women, and some are shared by men and women, and some are more for men than women, and some are more for women than men.

In [3] Phintys announces her thesis statement; in [4] she begins her argument. Her main idea is that activities or things (τὰ ... τινα) fall into three categories: gender-particular (ἴδια), gender-neutral (κοινά), and gender-preferential (μᾶλλον). She will fill out these categories, giving them plausibility, in what follows. The precise relevance of this idea to the three actions she says are perceived to be inappropriate to women—but implicitly appropriate to men—is unclear. We would have expected to see examples of men's and women's particular activities, and then an admission that, while some activities are definitely gender-particular, not all are, and that in fact there are two ways in which they are not gender-particular. Not having any examples here of activities particular to women suggests something else is going on. Phintys may be indicating that, while philosophizing may seem untoward in a woman—in the way that the leisured pursuit of horse-riding and the political pursuit of speech-making are—she will go on anyway to philosophize, whether to do so is appropriate or not. She has already been doing some philosophizing, when she made a threefold distinction between goodness, virtue, and *sôphrosunê*.[31] The erudite distinction in the second half of this sentence is more philosophizing.

Phintys does not directly connect the development of *sôphrosunê* with philosophizing. It might seem that her philosophizing allows for the proper articulation of the ways of being *sôphrôn*, and so philosophizing contributes to *sôphrosunê*. Admittedly, she does not speak to the value of intellectual reflection on and for *sôphrosunê* in subsequent sentences. And she does not encourage other women to philosophize. Yet she implies that she herself—and women in general—may philosophize, and this philosophizing seems important for being a good and orderly woman, whether mediated or not through the virtue of *sôphrosunê*.[32]

The present sentence is another crux for deciding Phintys' radicality and view of agency. We just saw her taking a seemingly conservative line about a woman's perfection, which for Phintys is found in honoring and loving her husband. She may be deploying her philosophy for the same conservative ends: with an erudite argument, to be sure, she justifies inequality and secondary status for women. But she has also just said that people may well consider philosophizing inappropriate for women, and yet she goes on to philosophize nevertheless. So in this she seems to be taking a progressive stance; and if in this, then perhaps in what philosophizing leads her to believe, or, more specifically, in what roles are actually suitable for women. This progressive stance is not clearly the one of modern

---

[31] Nails (1989, 294–96) is nevertheless dubious about the depth of reasoning in Phintys' treatise; there is no "defense or critique of *harmonia*, moderation, or any other of the supposed normative principles on which one could build a coherent ethical system."

[32] Lefkowitz (in Lefkowitz and Fant 1992, 163) replaces "activity" language with "social role" language ("a cavalry officer or a politician"), perhaps misleadingly. Her translation has a more obvious problem, however; she excises most of the "philosophical" sentences from Phintys' text (much of [2], [4], [7], [8], [15], [16], and [22]). This editorial intervention is an object lesson in the history of studying gender in ancient philosophy.

liberalism, where *sôphrosunê* and goodness in a person amount to their being able to formulate and pursue whatever end seems upon reflection best. But perhaps the formulation of a woman's capacity to treat the well-being of her spouse as a goal befitting herself *is* progressive. Perictione's essay takes this line: "A woman's soul must become very thoughtful with respect to virtue, so that it will be just and courageous and thoughtful and adorned with self-sufficiency and hate empty reputation." From these virtues come goods to her and her home and city; when she "controls her desires and spirit" (κρατέουσα ὧν ἐπιθυμίας καὶ θυμοῦ), holiness and harmony come about, which benefit both others and herself.[33] Becoming a more competent person, and aware of the sources of well-being for oneself and those to whom one is related, means not giving in to frivolous and harmful tastes and inclinations. This may be Phintys' point as well, though she does not emphasize the personal benefit of the virtue suited for spousal support.

Phintys continues her argument about gendered virtue:

[5] ἴδια μὲν ἀνδρὸς τὸ στραταγὲν καὶ πολιτεύεσθαι καὶ δαμαγορέν, ἴδια δὲ γυναικὸς τὸ οἰκουρὲν καὶ ἔνδον μένεν καὶ ἐκδέχεσθαι καὶ θεραπεύεν τὸν ἄνδρα.

[5] Particular to a man is generalship and statesmanship and public speaking, and particular to a woman is keeping the home and staying inside and welcoming and serving her husband.

Phintys sets out two spheres of labor: outside and inside, civic and domestic. While one may suppose them to be distinguished by active (outside, civic) and passive (inside, domestic) work, they need not be so distinguished. Just as generalship and statesmanship have their characteristic activities, so too being inside the home. Phintys stresses locational difference and audience of a person's actions: for men, the public; for women, the household. Nothing about these locations and audience per se represent distinctions in agency or its scope. If one sees human nature and human agency as realized solely in public affairs, then, to be sure, Phintys de-agentializes women. But without that presumption, she need not be doing so. Phintys could be suggesting that the field of action of men is no more real, provides no better a scope for self-assertion, than that of women, who have their own proper and adequate domain. From our present-day perspective, we may see prejudice built into the distinction between fields, since they are established and enforced by men themselves. But it is not clear whether Phintys believes the same.

---

[33] 142,19–143,2 Thesleff.

318 THE VIRTUE OF AGENCY

[6] κοινὰ δὲ φαμὶ ἀνδρείαν καὶ δικαιοσύναν καὶ φρόνασιν· καὶ γὰρ τὰς τῶ σώματος ἀρετὰς ἔχεν πρέπον καὶ ἀνδρὶ καὶ γυναικὶ καὶ τὰς ψυχᾶς ὁμοίως· [7] καὶ ὡς ὑγιαίνεν τῷ σώματι ἀμφοτέροις ὠφέλιμον, οὕτως ὑγιαίνεν τᾷ ψυχᾷ· σώματος δὲ ἦμεν ἀρετὰς ὑγείαν ἰσχὺν εὐαισθησίαν κάλλος.

[6] But I claim that what is shared is courage and justice and thoughtfulness: for as the virtues of the body are proper for both men and women, so too those of the soul— [7] for as being healthy in respect of body benefits both, so too being healthy in respect of soul: and the virtues of the body are health, strength, keen perception, and beauty.

Here Phintys starts applying her three categories of gender distribution to the virtues, and gives a new argument. Obviously men and women are both good and healthy in body by means of the same virtues of the body, so those virtues of health are proper to all; they are gender-neutral. Thus men and women will be good and healthy in soul by means of the same virtues of the soul, so those virtues of soul are proper to all.[34] This list of canonical virtues oddly enough does not include *sôphrosunê*, so Phintys has just given an exemplary list (and perhaps she did not want to appear to be begging the question).

The core of this claim is that, despite jobs being gender-differentiated, health of the body and soul is not gender-differentiated. A subsidiary claim is that robust health of soul is as central to human flourishing as robust health of body. Maybe Phintys' reason is that any activity whatsoever requires both bodily and psychic health. A further claim is that the canonical virtues represent the foundation of that universal capacity for action. So human agency depends on bodily and psychic health.

[8] τὰ δὲ μᾶλλον ἀνδρὶ καὶ ἀσκὲν καὶ ἔχεν οἰκεῖόν ἐντι, τὰ δὲ μᾶλλον γυναικί.

[8] Some are more cultivated by men and are more proper to them, and some more by women.

Though Phintys goes on to talk only about the psychic virtues, she may be making a claim about all the virtues here, since popularly people may have thought that men preferentially cultivate their strength, women their beauty. But the point is that despite the psychic virtues being shared, some are "more proper" (μᾶλλον... οἰκεῖον) to one gender or the other, and (accordingly?) more cultivated (ἀσκέν) by that gender. Phintys has hereby solved, to her satisfaction, the paradox of virtues seeming both universal and gendered: everyone has all of

---

[34] On the application of the concept *andreia* to women, and its sometimes meaning "chastity" for women during the period of authorship, see Penrose (2016, 23–65).

them, but they are both naturally ("proper to") and circumstantially ("cultivated by") differentiated along gender lines.

[9] ἀνδρότατα μὲν γὰρ καὶ φρόνασιν μᾶλλον ἀνδρὶ καὶ διὰ τὰν ἕξιν τοῦ σώματος καὶ διὰ τὰν δύναμιν τᾶς ψυχᾶς, σωφροσύναν δὲ γυναικί.

[9] For great courage and thoughtfulness are more for a man both because of the structure of his body and because of the power of his soul; *sôphrosunê* is more for women.

This is the culmination of the argument for the distinctiveness of *sôphrosunê* for women, though frankly the reasoning is hard to grasp. The male-preferential virtues are ("great") courage and thoughtfulness. The explanation is not that these are necessary for civic affairs, surprisingly enough, but rather that the organization of their bodies and their psychic capacity is suitable for them. Phintys has put this in a highly vague way; probably she means that courage is more properly male, and thus more proper for them to cultivate, because their bodies have the hardiness and strength for military or naval action, and thoughtfulness is proper for men, and accordingly developed, because they have the mental vigor and flexibility for political life. In any event, she does not explain why *sôphrosunê* is more for a woman. In the case of men, she argues to their virtues from two kinds of strength ("structure of body" and "power of soul"). It is not clear whether she thinks there are additional kinds of strength that support women's virtue. She might think instead that women have *sôphrosunê* not because of some distinctive capacity but because of some distinctive need (e.g., unwieldy desires). In fact we could have read the men's need for courage, for example, as explained by their inordinate fearfulness (due to their bodily vulnerability) and their need for thoughtfulness as explained by their inordinate proclivity, thanks to a wayward soul, to get themselves into complicated fixes. Suffice it to say, Phintys does not here say what makes *sôphrosunê* "more for" women. However, given her previous definition of a woman's excellence as love and respect for her spouse, as welcoming and serving him, and perhaps her belief that women are naturally good at or apt for such love and honor, welcome and service, *sôphrosunê* could be seen as the virtue naturally suited and worth cultivating for those attitudes and skills. Perictione's treatise suggests that women provide the glue or the lubricating fluid for the household enterprise, helping integrate diverse constituencies, tolerating ornery participants, and keeping their own desires from gunking up the works. Just so, in Phintys' treatise *sôphrosunê* could be positionally apt for women, as well perhaps as something they are good at.

"Justice" has disappeared in this statement; presumably it befits men and women equally. We do not learn what this means for its role in womanly goodness.

[10] διὸ δεῖ περὶ σωφροσύνας παιδευομέναν γνωρίζεν, ἐκ πόσων τινῶν καὶ ποίων τοῦτο τἀγαθὸν τᾷ γυναικὶ παραγίνεται. [11a] φαμὶ δὴ ἐκ πέντε τούτων· [11b] πρᾶτον μὲν ἐκ τᾶς περὶ τὰν εὐνὰν ὁσιότατός τε καὶ εὐσεβείας· [11c] δεύτερον δὲ ἐκ τῶ κόσμω τῶ περὶ τὸ σῶμα· [11d] τρίτον <δ'> ἐκ τῶν ἐξόδων τῶν ἐκ τᾶς ἰδίας οἰκίας· [11e] τέταρτον δ' ἐκ τῶ μὴ χρέεσθαι τοῖς ὀργιασμοῖς καὶ ματρῳασμοῖς· [11f] πέμπτον δ' ἐν τᾷ θυσίᾳ τᾷ πρὸς τὸ θεῖον εὐλαβέα ἦμεν καὶ μετρίαν. [12] τούτων δὲ μέγιστον αἴτιον καὶ συνεκτικώτατον τᾶς σωφροσύνας τὸ περὶ τὰν εὐνὰν ἦμεν ἀδιάφθορον καὶ ἄμικτον θυραίω ἀνδρός.

[10] Thus one training in *sôphrosunê* ought to learn from what number and type of things this good comes to women. [11a] Indeed I claim there are five of them: [11b] first, from the veneration and sanctity of the marriage bed; [11c] second, from the orderliness of the body; [11d] third, from journeys from her own house; [11e] fourth, from not participating in mystery rites and celebrations of Cybele; [11f] and fifth, in being cautious and measured in her sacrifices to the divine. [12] And of these the greatest and most integral cause of *sôphrosunê* is the incorruptibility of the marriage bed and not mixing with men from beyond one's door.

We might have expected that these five things would follow from a woman's *sôphrosunê*; instead, Phintys says that one comes to be educated in *sôphrosunê*—or, indeed, comes finally to manifest the virtue fully—by having done these five things. Doing them must allow a woman the capacity to "honor and love" her husband. Honor and love are surely not equivalent to mere sexual fidelity, modest appearance, and social and religious restraint, even if these are important ingredients, since these forbearances would be compatible with icy indifference toward one's spouse, even disdain and dislike. These forbearances put a woman in the position, psychically, to honor and love her husband. Besides avoiding distraction and the direct harms to a spouse that being caught cheating would bring, if these five forbearances do really train a woman to have *sôphrosunê*, where *sôphrosunê* is what allows honor and love, then they must conduce to a woman's ability to take her spouse as rightly authoritative for her and thus due her affective and desiderative attention.

How could this be so? Not sleeping with other men, not working to entice other men, and not being where other men could be enticed [11a-c] may help one keep vivid and central the value and relevance of one's spouse.[35] Should

---

[35] Perictione, in *On Women's Harmony*, claims that when cheating on her husband (and thus neglectfully away from home), a woman begins to lie about and impugn everyone in her household (thereby becoming enemies of all), so as to present herself to her husband as the only person with goodwill and a good work ethic: 143,3–7 Thesleff.

sleeping around (and so forth) be enticing, the practice in resisting those enticements might strengthen one's commitment to more important demands. (Compare Phaedra, who apparently gives little thought to Theseus' admirable and adherence-worthy qualities.) The cynical view of this text at this point is that Phintys really just wants to list the five most important sources of foolish behavior, especially in light of domestic comity, and rather than simply saying that they are foolish and bad for a marriage—which sounds like easy marital advice—she interposes *paideusis* and *sôphrosunê* into her analysis, which end up doing no real work besides rhetorical ennobling. Less cynically, and with attention to the protreptic arc of the treatise, Phintys focuses on the ennobling education in virtue, the virtue that deserves women's primary attention for their realization as good women, and has to link five concrete actions to this education. By what practices otherwise is one to develop a virtue? For Aristotle, *sôphrosunê* would be developed by abstaining from binge-drinking, daily feasting, and a riotous sex life. In other words, by abstaining from the very actions that are representative of lacking the virtue.

In the rest of the treatise that Stobaeus excerpts, Phintys explains the importance of these five actions. Before we turn to them, we should reflect on the preceding. Phintys' argument has been philosophical, though in its laconic approach to the issues it has not been altogether satisfying. It may present an active and, as it were, affirmative approach to *sôphrosunê*, as a capacity for norm-identification and commitment, by contrast to mere submission and alienation of one's decision-making to another, but this is an uncertain interpretation. What *sôphrosunê* is, however, we have not discovered. Is it obedience, or rather a fancy veneer on obedience? It seems it is more than that, since Phintys could just as well have spoken of "obedience" (εὐπείθεια, πειθομένη) either as the ultimate disposition to develop or as the proper attitude toward one's husband. Instead she speaks of "being orderly," "honoring," "loving," "welcoming," and "serving." We might compare this to the attitude of reverence toward the gods, where cherishing a god is an active and substantial condition, one dependent on one's self-constitution as someone who can properly acknowledge the gods. The gods do not simply promulgate rules that humans are to follow; they are worthy of esteem and orientation toward. The greatness of the gods does not mean that the reverent worshiper is for that reason unable to be an agent; indeed, the worshiper's correct recognition of the ultimate or greatest source of value—as we saw in Xenophon's *Memorabilia* 4.3—is what allows them to be the most effective agent. Agency does not mean unguided freedom or an autonomy that follows norms of one's impetuous devising. So, too, in the Pythagorean household, a woman's recognizing the value of her husband, and thereby having the proper attitude toward him as so valuable, does not make her less of an agent; indeed, it makes her more of one. That is, if her husband really is an authoritative guide! (What virtues would he need to exercise in order to be so? And might a husband's authority derive from something beyond himself, such as the moral law, to which his wife might appeal directly, without spousal mediation?) Phintys does not wonder about these issues, and that she does not is a disappointment to philosophers wanting her to follow the argument whither it ought to go. But within the Pythagorean framework, holding its assumptions stable, this may be the route to redeeming Phintys' argument for *sôphrosunê* as a virtue of agency and self-constitution, being good at what one is (for).

We may now continue with Phintys' treatise:

[13] πρᾶτον μὲν γὰρ εἰς τοῦτο παρανομοῦσα ἀδικεῖ γενεθλίους θεούς, οἴκῳ καὶ συγγενείᾳ οὐ γνασίους ἐπικούρους ἀλλὰ νόθους παρεχομένα· ἀδικεῖ δὲ τοὺς φύσει θεούς, οὕσπερ ἐπομόσασα μετὰ τῶν αὐτᾶς πατέρων τε καὶ συγγενῶν συνελεύσεσθαι ἐπὶ κοινωνίᾳ βίω καὶ τέκνων γενέσει τᾷ κατὰ νόμον· ἀδικεῖ δὲ καὶ τὰν αὐτᾶς πατρίδα, μὴ ἐμμένουσα τοῖς ἐνδιατεταγμένοις. [14] ἔπειτα ἐπὶ τούτοις ἀμβλακίσκεν, ἐφ' οἷς τὸ μέγιστον τῶν προστίμων ὥρισται θάνατος διὰ τὰν ὑπερβολὰν τοῦ ἀδικήματος, ἔκθεσμον καὶ ἀσυγγνωμονέστατον εἶμεν ἁδονᾶς ἕνεκεν ἁμαρτάνεν καὶ ὑβρίζεν· ὕβριος δὲ πάσας πέρας ὄλεθρος.

[13] For, first, being a transgressor in this respect does injustice to the gods of the family, producing for the household and relatives not genuine offspring but instead bastards; and she does injustice to the gods of generation, to whom she swore with her parents and relatives to be brought together into common life for the lawful birth of children; and she does injustice even to her country, in not abiding by its system of organization. [14] Then she has failed in the respects for which the greatest of penalties is defined, death, because of the enormity of the injustice, its being unlawful and unpardonable, for the sake of pleasure, to err and commit hubris: and the end of all hubris is ruin.

[fragment break]

Phintys endeavors to explain how marital fidelity causes *sôphrosunê*. She argues the negative case. Transgression does a triple injustice, to two sets of gods and to the commonwealth. (It probably also does a triple impiety.) So, Phintys argues the complete badness of infidelity. But in this passage she says nothing about the immediate harms to one's husband: the embarrassment of being cuckolded, his feeling undesired, nobody being around to help him, his being generally distracted. What is being emphasized is breaking for the mere sake of pleasure those high normative obligations that allow for the re-creation of the human race.[36] So *sôphrosunê* here is, as clearly as anywhere in the treatise, a commitment to the most authoritative norms. Love and honor of a husband is, from this perspective, a concrete instantiation of the commitment to those universal norms for sound procreation.

At this point, Stobaeus breaks off his excerpt, and returns in his second fragment to more argument about the same topic. We do not know why he interrupts his quotation here, or what he excludes, if anything. We might reasonably assume that he has excluded nothing, given that [14] speaks of a cheater's having "failed," and [15] speaks of there being no remedy for this death-deserving failure.

[15] Κἀκεῖνο δὲ χρὴ διαλογίζεσθαι, ὡς οὐδὲν καθάρσιον εὑρήσει τᾶς ἀμπλακίας ταύτας ἄκος, ὥστε ὡς ἱερὰ θεῶν καὶ βωμὼς ποτερχομέναν εἶμεν ἁγνὰν καὶ θεοφιλάταν· ἐπὶ γὰρ ταύτᾳ τᾷ ἀδικίᾳ μάλιστα καὶ τὸ δαιμόνιον ἀσυγγνωμόνητον γίνεται. [16] κάλλιστος δὲ κόσμος γυναικὸς ἐλευθέρας πρᾶτόν τε κῦδος τὸ διὰ τῶν αὐτᾶς τέκνων ἐπιμαρτύρασθαι τὰν σωφροσύναν τὰν ποτὶ τὸν ἄνδρα, αἴκα τὸν τύπον τᾶς ὁμοιότατος ἐπιφέρωντι τῷ κατασπείραντος αὐτὰ πατρός. [17a] καὶ περὶ μὲν εὐνᾶς οὕτως ἔχει·

[15] And she should think through this fact, that she will find no purifying remedy for this failure so that she could be someone who approaches, holy and god-beloved, the sanctuaries and altars of the gods: for with respect to this injustice, even the god is altogether unforgiving. [16] The most beautiful order and leading glory of a free woman is the witnessing by her children of her *sôphrosunê* toward her husband, if their outline bears a likeness to their father who begat them. [17a] And regarding the marriage bed this is how it is ...

Phintys has turned from an argument in favor of *sôphrosunê* to a mortal threat against breaking a marital rule: for infidelity, the results are horrible, and they are irreversible. This piling on of punishments has several effects. It suggests that women are at true risk of sleeping around, and so need severe disincentives. It puts child-rearing at the center of social and religious life, as all that really matters, at least from the perspective of women. It does not advance the view that men should not sleep around with women, or that husbands should be particularly sympathetic to their wives.[37] It does not advocate a course of education, or alternative ways to spend time, to replace the interest a woman might have in

---

[36] We saw this in Chapter 12 on the *Pythagorean Precepts*.
[37] This sentiment is expressed explicitly at Perictione *On Woman's Harmony* fr. 1, 144,11–13 Thesleff, and is the entire theme of the letter of Theano to Nicostrate.

other men with interests in other valuable things. Most intriguing, however, is its suggestion that the goal of a *sôphrôn* marital fidelity is so important that its achievement is noble. This point is suggested by [16]: if one really believes that the high point of womanhood is the production of children—and, in particular, children for one's husband—and also believes that infidelity is so easy and commonplace, then *sôphrosunê*, concern for one's husband (qua male producer of children, qua citizen), is really important.

I turn more briefly to the last three paragraphs, which develop themes familiar from the literature:[38]

[17b] περὶ δὲ τοῦ κόσμου τοῦ περὶ τὸ σῶμα δοκεῖ μοι οὕτως. [18] δεῖ λευχείμονα εἶναι καὶ ἁπλοικὰν καὶ ἀπερίσσευτον. [19] ἐσσεῖται δὲ τοῦτο, αἴκα μὴ διαφανέεσσι μηδὲ διαποικίλοις μηδὲ ἀπὸ βόμβυκος ὑφασμένοις χρᾶται τοῖς περὶ τὸ σῶμα, ἀλλὰ μετρίοις καὶ λευκοχρωμάτοις· οὕτω γὰρ τὸ μᾶλλον κοσμεῖσθαι καὶ τρυφὴν καὶ καλλωπισμὸν φεύξεται, καὶ ζᾶλον οὐκ ἐμποιήσει μοχθηρὸν ταῖς ἄλλαις. [20] χρυσὸν δὲ καὶ σμάραγδον ἁπλῶς μὴ περιτίθεσθαι· καὶ γὰρ πολυχρήματον καὶ ὑπεραφανίαν ἐμφαῖνον ποττὰς δαμοτικάς. [21] δεῖ δὲ τὰν εὐνομουμέναν πόλιν, ὅλαν αὐτὰν δι' ὅλας τεταγμέναν, συμπαθέα τε καὶ ὁμοιόνομον εἶμεν, ἀπερύκεν δὲ καὶ δαμιοεργὼς ἐκ τᾶς πόλιος τὼς ἐργαζομένως τὰ τοιαῦτα. [22] χρώματι δὲ φαιδρύνεσθαι τὰν ποτῶπα μὴ ἐπακτῷ καὶ ἀλλοτρίῳ, τῷ δ' οἰκήῳ τῶ σώματος δι' αὐτῶ τῶ ὕδατος ἀπολουοέμναν, κοσμὲν δὲ μᾶλλον αὐτὰν αἰσχύνᾳ· καὶ γὰρ τὸν συμβιῶντα καὶ αὐτὰν ἔντιμον παρέξεται.

[17b] Regarding the orderliness of the things regarding the body, the following is what I think. [18] One must dress in white, simply, plainly. [19] She will be this way if she uses as clothing for her body nothing diaphanous, bejeweled, or silken, but what's measured and pale: for in this way she will avoid being made up in luxury and embellishment, and will not cause wretched envy among other women. [20] Do not drape oneself with gold or emeralds!—for it is both extravagant and shows arrogance to the people. [21] And a well-ordered city should, being organized through and through, be in sympathy and agreement, and even bar craftsmen making such things from the city. [22] The face must be brightened by color that's not imported from elsewhere but is her own, from her own body, washed with water, and must compose herself rather with her own modesty: for she will render honor for her cohabitant and herself.

Modesty of dress combats envy from other women who, because they wish they had what you have but believe they cannot get it, disdain you for having it. It

---

[38] E.g., Perictione *On Women's Harmony* fr. 1, 143,9–144,5 Thesleff; Melissa to Claerata, Städele (1980, III 160, 4–19). Similar advice is found in Xen. *Oec.* 10.

also eliminates annoyance from those who would otherwise judge you as aloof in representing yourself as better than your neighbors. *Sôphrosunê* here involves presenting oneself naturally or authentically, not as finer than one really is.[39] As *sôphrosunê* earlier amounted to respect for the gods and other norms of sexual/reproductive fidelity, here it amounts to respect for the norms of economic equality and authentic (or fair) presentation of one's natural gifts. The impact of this *sôphrosunê* on one's husband does not come through in the first of these sentences ([17b]–[21]). In [22], however, a direct appeal to the consideration of "honoring him" is made: it would dishonor one's husband to appear immodest, and it would perhaps even incite envy and judgments of arrogance.

[23] τὰς δὲ ἐξόδους ἐκ τᾶς οἰκίας ποιεῖσθαι τὰς γυναῖκας τὰς δαμοτελέας θυηπολούσας τῷ ἀρχαγέτᾳ θεῷ τᾶς πόλιος ὑπὲρ αὑτᾶς καὶ τῶ ἀνδρὸς καὶ τῶ παντὸς οἴκω· [24] ἔπειτα μήτε ὄρφνας ἀνισταμένας μήτε ἑσπέρας ἀλλὰ πλαθυούσας ἀγορᾶς καταφανέα γινομέναν τὰν ἔξοδον ποιεῖσθαι θεωρίας ἕνεκά τινος ἢ ἀγορασμῷ οἰκήῳ μετὰ θεραπαίνας μιᾶς ἢ καττὸ πλεῖστον δύο εὐκόσμως χειραγωγουμέναν.

[23] A woman [must] make a departure from the house [only for] sacrificing at public festivals for the founding god, for the sake of herself, her husband, and her whole household. [24] And then she is to get up and go neither in the middle of the night nor in the evening but when the city center is full, she being visible, making a departure for the sake of some spectacle or shopping for the household, being guided in a nice orderly fashion by one or at most two maids.

While Phintys acknowledges the importance of traditional piety, she seems concerned mainly that a woman not appear to be or actually end up going out for an assignation (as someone like Pentheus would be prone to suspect). In the mere appearance case, this might dishonor one's husband; in the actual case, it would do an injustice to the various gods and civic laws. Because Phintys recognizes that women cannot always stay inside the home, given their religious and economic

---

[39] This finds a fifth-century parallel in Prodicus' *Choice of Heracles*. We know it from Xenophon (*Mem.* 2.1.22–31) as Socrates' report of it to Aristippus in a discussion about *enkrateia* (on its fidelity, see Sansone 2004 [pro-] and Gray 2006 [anti-], with development in Dorion 2008; Wolfsdorf 2011; Mayhew 2012; Sansone 2015). Lady Virtue advocates the life of patient and effortful self-cultivation of the traditional virtues, including broadly dispersed benefaction, with superior rewards later on rather than immediate gratification, with its inferior present-moment rewards (on the argumentative details, see Wolfsdorf 2008, 7–9; 2013, 10–13; Mayhew 2012, xviii–xxi, 206–21; Anderson 2019; Bett 2020). She is distinguished by four traits: purity (καθαρότης) of body, modesty (αἰδώς) of eye, *sôphrosunê* of comportment (σχῆμα), and whiteness of garb (cf. A. *Sept.* 645–46). The comportment of Virtue's adversary, Vice, involves holding herself up with more straightness than is natural; the contrast implies that a *sôphrôn* comportment is one that is authentic and not driven by the desire to seem other than one is.

errands, she needs here to address *sôphrosunê* for those cases, though she does not add anything substantive to the argument.

[25] τὰς δὲ θυσίας λιτὰς παριστάμεν τοῖς θεοῖς καὶ καττὰν δύναμιν, ὀργιασμῶν δὲ καὶ ματρῳασμῶν τῶν κατ' οἶκον ἀπέχεσθαι. [26] καὶ γὰρ ὁ κοινὸς νόμος ἀπερύκει τὰς πόλιος ταῦ<τα> τὰς γυναῖκας ἐπιτελέν, καὶ ἄλλως καὶ ὅτι μέθας καὶ ἐκστάσιας ψυχᾶς ἐπάγοντι ταὶ θρησκεύσιες αὗται· τὰν δ' οἰκοδέσποιναν καὶ προκαθεζομέναν οἴκω δεῖ σώφρονα καὶ ἀνέπαφον ποτὶ πάντα ἦμεν.

[25] She [must] cause sacrificial prayer for the gods according to her power, but avoid the orgiastic and in-home Great-Mother worships. [26] For even the common law of the city bars women from doing these rites—including for the reason that these very worships lead to drunkenness and ecstasies of the soul; and the mistress presiding over the house must be *sôphrôn* and untouched in all things.

The final section returns to obligations of piety, which have been an ongoing theme in Phintys' treatise. Some putatively pious actions are not lawful and not *sôphrôn*, so they should not be done. *Sôphrosunê* involves self-control, especially in contexts that could lead to orgiastic or otherwise unbecoming activity.

The treatise ends here, much as its theoretical portion ended, with doubt and indeterminacy. The most charitable reading is that the work concerns women as "wives," as female members of a Pythagorean household, whose primary though not exclusive object is support of the husband through continuation of the household, namely by birthing and bringing up legitimate children. *Sôphrosunê* names the virtue whereby those wives may fix their attention on the most important thing—the love, honor, and support of their husbands—and subsequently may commit themselves to the most vital norms, including those of divine, civic, and social propriety. This text does not answer our question, Is *sôphrosunê* here the admirable virtue of self-constitution as an agent and not merely a tool of some external or internal force? But, in not answering it, it at least does not give a negative response. Perhaps it is with great canniness that Phintys skirts the issue, appealing to the Socratic and Aristotelian perspective alike: it is the virtue of agency within her proper (and even unquestioned) social sphere. At any rate, she reveals, whether wittingly or not, how difficult the question is, or, alternatively, how easily statements made about *sôphrosunê* can be taken in opposing ways.

Iamblichus' Letter About *Sôphrosunê*

In Phintys' treatise, *sôphrosunê* conduces preferentially to a woman's goodness and composure; this goodness includes honoring and loving her husband.

Establishing the actual scope of *sôphrosunê* and the goodness to which it conduces does not detain Phintys, who seeks to dignify her domestic advice by formulating it as a guide to fundamental virtue. She gives to a local and conservative goal universality and progressiveness. Nevertheless, I argued that we need not read her treatise as wholly cynical, as supporting passivity through the language of activity, as praising as self-possession the factual dispossession of oneself in subservience to another. We saw that agency may be in there nevertheless, even if it is in some way compromised.

We get a rather different account of the virtue in the other extant text explicitly about *sôphrosunê* from the post-Classical period, Iamblichus' letter to Arete. Though like Phintys' treatise it shows up in Stobaeus' *Anthology*, only this text appears—in seven excerpts, six of them continuous—in Stobaeus' chapter on *sôphrosunê*, in which it has some pride of place. (Stobaeus starts excerpting it among the first prose authors.) This letter, a protreptic to the virtue, at no point presents it as gendered. It mentions nothing about domestic relations, except incidentally praising the virtue, in a quotation from Crates, as the savior of households and cities (σῴζει μὲν οἴκους σῴζει δὲ πόλεις), saying nothing explicitly about sex or personal appearance. Indeed, it hardly speaks of the virtue as socially relevant at all. It focuses on *sôphrosunê* as the perfection of the soul, the foundation or preservation of the other virtues, and its macrocosmic iteration as the unity of the world.

For all its overt universality and Platonic background, one might wonder whether it might covertly take a gendered approach to the virtue. Questions arise from three directions. First, this is Iamblichus' only extant letter written to a woman. Topics in his other letters include the canonical virtues—justice, courage, wisdom, and virtue (in general)—and related matters, including dialectic, ruling, concord, truth, and providence. The fact that the letter written about the virtue most closely associated with women is addressed to a woman is notable. Second, in a short excerpt from another of Iamblichus' writings, "On marriage" (Stob. 4.33.57), Iamblichus says that "they" agree that a husband will rule and a wife will be ruled, not as in a master-slave or artisan-artwork relation, where the interest of one party prevails, but as in political rule, where the interests of both prevail. Iamblichus does not say who "they" are or whether he himself agrees; however, given that "they" may well be Plato and Aristotle (who we saw, at the beginning of this chapter, to have this view),[40] and given the tone, it seems likely that he does agree. So at least with respect to the household, the wife must obey the words of another who has no claim to wisdom or economic skill beyond that of being a man, and this might seem to put special pressure on her exercise of *sôphrosunê*. Third, five of the seven excerpts from the letter to Arete speak of controlling the passions, and while little else might be expected with

---

[40] See Dillon and Polleichtner (2009, 91–93).

sôphrosunê, it might seem that Iamblichus emphasizes the overcoming of weakness more here than he does in the other letters.

These incitements to scrutinize Iamblichus' text for a crypto-gendered *sôphrosunê* do not prove there is one, of course. They show only that we should think carefully, as we did about Phintys' treatise, about the commitments and motivations of the author. To be sure, Phintys and Iamblichus have markedly different goals and sentiments in writing about *sôphrosunê*: the worldly and otherworldly; the vulgar and the authentic; the practical and the theoretical; the social and the personal. The best way to formulate the difference, however, might be as descriptive and normative. Plato's *Charmides* taught a lesson about the definition of a virtue: if one wants the definition to serve also as praise, it should account for a capacity's counting as a virtue more than it should account for the distinctiveness or idiosyncrasies of that capacity. The less said about the differentiae of a virtue, the harder it may be to give concrete advice about the way to manifest that virtue rather than some other one. But the more said about its status as a virtue, the easier it is to give advice about the way to become virtuous, which, after all, is the ultimate goal. So the observation that Iamblichus looks to be writing at a level of generality that obscures gender distinctions does not mean that he must still be doing so implicitly or secretly; he may really believe that he is getting at the underlying matter for any embodiment of *sôphrosunê*. As with Phintys' text, the evidence is in the document, so to that we now turn.[41]

> Τὰ αὐτὰ δὴ οὖν καὶ περὶ πασῶν τῶν δυνάμεων τῆς ψυχῆς ἀποφαίνομαι, τὴν συμμετρίαν αὐτῶν πρὸς ἀλλήλας καὶ εὐταξίαν θυμοῦ τε καὶ ἐπιθυμίας καὶ λόγου κατὰ τὴν προσήκουσαν ἑκάστῳ τάξιν εὐκοσμίαν· καὶ τούτων ἡ τοῦ ἄρχειν τε καὶ ἄρχεσθαι ἐν δέοντι γιγνομένη διανομὴ σωφροσύνη ἂν εἴη πολυειδής. (fr. 1 = Stob. 3.5.9)

> So I declare that quite the same thing holds for all the powers of the soul, that their symmetry with one another, and the fine arrangement of spirit and desire and reason—in terms of the fitting arrangement for each—is good order; and the norm-guided coming to be of a distribution of ruling and being ruled among them would be the multiform *sôphrosunê*.

Stobaeus does not quote the beginning of Iamblichus' letter. There Iamblichus probably remarked on the "multiform" (πολυειδής) nature of *sôphrosunê*,

---

[41] For previous discussions of the letter, mostly concerned with the prosopography of Arete, see Bidez (1919, 39); Athanassiadi (2013, 18–19); Addey (2018, 424–28); also *DPhA* s.v. "Arétè" (vol. 1, 349–50). On the letter overall, see esp. Taormina and Piccione (2010, 312–17: text and Italian translation, 442–64: commentary).

perhaps as an obstacle to defining the virtue: maybe cases look too different from one another to draw easy conclusions. He probably turned then to a single power of the soul, which would manifest "good order" (εὐκοσμία), a trait sufficiently like *sôphrosunê* to be relevant, when it was internally harmonized. *Sôphrosunê*, then, would be like good order or composure between aspects of the soul. In the language of Plato's *Republic* Book 4, it would be the proper allocation of ruling and being ruled among those soul-parts. Perhaps *sôphrosunê* appears multiform because different relations of authority could be salient.

Πᾶσα μὲν γὰρ ἀρετὴ τὸ θνητοειδὲς μὲν ἀτιμάζει, τὸ δὲ ἀθάνατον ἀσπάζεται· πολὺ δὲ διαφερόντως ἡ σωφροσύνη ταύτην ἔχει τὴν σπουδήν, ἅτε δὴ τὰς προσηλούσας τῷ σώματι τὴν ψυχὴν ἡδονὰς ἀτιμάζουσα, καὶ ἐν ἁγνοῖς βάθροις βεβῶσα, ὥς φησι Πλάτων. (fr. 2 = Stob. 3.5.45)

For while each virtue disdains the mortal element, cherishing the immortal, *sôphrosunê* has this attitude quite distinctly, in its disdain for the pleasures that "nail the soul to the body," and in "standing on holy foundations," as Plato says.

The second fragment seems to follow a break in Iamblichus' reasoning, since here Iamblichus is explaining something special about *sôphrosunê* that he has already observed, but something other than its being a proper distribution of rule. He makes this first point powerfully in his letter to Sopater, "On virtue." There he writes that reason triumphs over the body, and shares in divine and not earthly qualities; thus, all virtues work to liberate oneself from, for example, the urges of the body.[42] This does not mean that bodily desires are bad; it is that they are not to be obeyed simply because they are desires. *Sôphrosunê* has as its distinctive capacity taking even the most visceral and urgent desires as mere entreaties to one's rational attention. These may be characteristically bodily desires, but *sôphrosunê* has as its scope any desire that does not tie one's decisions to a universal norm, for instance an instantaneous impulse. These norms constitute a "holy foundation," that which is objectively right, and a bulwark against that which impedes one's acting on the basis of those ideals.

Πῶς γὰρ ἡ σωφροσύνη τελέους ἡμᾶς οὐ ποιεῖ, τὸ ἀτελὲς καὶ ἐμπαθὲς ὅλον ἀφ' ἡμῶν ἐξορίζουσα; γνοίης δ' ἂν ὡς τοῦτο οὕτως ἔχει, τὸν Βελλεροφόντην ἐννοήσας, ὃς μετὰ τῆς κοσμιότητος συναγωνιζομένης τὴν Χίμαιραν καὶ τὸ θηριῶδες καὶ ἄγριον καὶ ἀνήμερον φῦλον πᾶν ἀνεῖλεν. ὅλως γὰρ ἡ τῶν παθῶν ἄμετρος ἐπικράτεια οὐδὲ ἀνθρώπους ἐφίησιν εἶναι τοὺς ἀνθρώπους,

---

[42] Stob. 3.17.17 and 3.1.49.

πρὸς δὲ τὴν ἀλόγιστον αὐτοὺς ἕλκει φύσιν καὶ θηριώδη καὶ ἄτακτον. (fr. 3 = Stob. 3.5.46)

For how would *sôphrosunê* not make us perfect, since it excises from us the whole of what's imperfect and susceptible to passion? You might recognize the truth of this from considering the case of Bellerophon, who, with Orderliness fighting alongside, eliminated the Chimaera and that whole beastly, uncultivated, and harsh tribe. For, on the whole, the immoderate predominance by the passions does not allow humans to be humans but drags them toward an irrational nature, bestial and disordered.

After another lacuna, we learn that *sôphrosunê* removes one's "susceptibility to passion," which is the "immoderate predominance" of passions over oneself—not, of course, the having of passions at all. This predominance means not being "dragged" by passions, governed by them without having a say in the matter.[43] Being dragged amounts to irrationality, bestiality, and disorder; it means not governing oneself by reason.

Ἡ δὲ μέτροις ὡρισμένοις κατέχουσα τὰς ἡδονὰς εὐταξία σῴζει μὲν οἴκους σῴζει δὲ πόλεις κατὰ τὴν Κράτητος γνώμην· ἔτι δὲ πλησιάζει πως ἤδη πρὸς τὸ τῶν θεῶν εἶδος. τοιγὰρ οὖν Περσεὺς ἐπ' αὐτὸ τὸ ἀκρότατον ἐλαύνων τῆς σωφροσύνης ἀγαθὸν ἡγουμένης τῆς Ἀθηνᾶς ἀπέκοψε τὴν Γοργόνα, τὴν εἰς τὴν ὕλην οἶμαι καθέλκουσαν καὶ ἀπολιθοῦσαν τοὺς ἀνθρώπους ἀνοήτῳ τῶν παθημάτων πλησμονῇ. (fr. 4 = Stob. 3.5.47)

The fine arrangement that restrains the pleasures to measured bounds "saves households and saves cities," as Crates quipped; further, it somehow approaches the form of the gods. For that very reason Perseus, advancing to the very height of goodness in *sôphrosunê*, following Athena, beheaded the Gorgon—the dragging of humans into bare matter and petrifying them through thoughtless satiation of the passions.

Life without *sôphrosunê* amounts to the desires' unimpeded action, and contrary to Callicles' view that such an unimpeded life is the most vital and vibrant, Iamblichus claims that in fact the opposite is true. In their unimpeded action, the desires act mechanically, turning the person into body, "bare matter," like unto stone. Not merely is the person who lacks *sôphrosunê* bestial, as in fragment 3; he is now inert and lifeless; there is no activity at all. Occupation by the Gorgon is not just monstrous; it is abiotic. Accordingly, Iamblichus calls for "restraint

---

[43] Cf. Iambl. *Protr.* ch. 20, 95,20 Pistelli; Pl. *Phdr.* 229e.

of pleasure to measured bounds." Not to its extinction, and not to some other-worldly detachment from the call of pleasure, but to a responsible and principled self-scrutiny of one's desires. The impact is extensive, to familial and political life, not just inner animation.

Ὅτι τοίνυν κρηπὶς τῆς ἀρετῆς, ὡς ἔλεγε Σωκράτης, ἡ ἐγκράτειά ἐστι τῆς γλυκυθυμίας· κόσμος δὲ τῶν ἀγαθῶν πάντων ἡ σωφροσύνη θεωρεῖται, ὥσπερ δὴ ἀπεφήνατο Πλάτων. ἀσφάλεια δὲ τῶν καλλίστων ἕξεων ἡ αὐτή ἐστιν ἀρετή, ὥσπερ ἐγὼ λέγω. (fr. 5 = Stob. 3.5.48)

> Thus self-control of one's laxity, as Socrates tended to say, is the groundwork of virtue; *sôphrosunê* is seen as the ordering of all goods, as Plato declared. And this virtue is security for the finest conditions of being, as I say.

Iamblichus here gives three statements of *sôphrosunê*'s status as a metavirtue; he will give a more precise formulation of that status in fragment 6, where it becomes clear that unified human action, and thus agency, depends on it. Here he starts with a claim probably sourced to Xenophon's *Memorabilia* 1.5.4, that self-control (ἐγκράτεια) is the foundation (κρηπίς) of all virtue. As we have seen, Xenophon often does not equate *sôphrosunê* and *enkrateia*—the former is more closely connected to norm-guidance, the latter to desire-management—but he treats the two capacities as having similar domains. In Xenophon's passage, Socrates speaks of *enkrateia* as freedom from enslavement to pleasures, for example those of food, drink, sex, and sleep.[44] (Iamblichus' "laxity," γλυκυθυμία, which may simply mean "susceptibility to pleasantness," presumably refers to these; we have no evidence for Socrates' ever having used the term.) *Enkrateia* is the foundation of all virtue because only with it can one learn or do anything good.[45] Iamblichus would himself be unlikely to equate *sôphrosunê* wholly with *enkrateia* over bodily desires, since his fragments 1 and 6 suggest a rather broader understanding of the virtue. Yet the contextual overlap between the two capacities legitimizes the claim.

The second statement is attributed to Plato, though it is not verbatim. Two recent editors believe Iamblichus has *Republic* 4.430e in mind, where, however, Plato's Socrates says only that *sôphrosunê* is "some kind of order (κόσμος)" and an "*enkrateia* over pleasures and desires" (as we saw in Chapter 9);[46] he does not extend it to "all goods."[47] Whatever the provenance of the idea, there is an

---

[44] Xen. *Mem.* 1.5.1.
[45] Xen. *Mem.* 1.5.5.
[46] Dillon and Polleichtner (2009, 66).
[47] See Olymp. *in Pl. Gorg.* 35.1 for a similar inclusion of "goods" into Socrates' account of *sôphrosunê*.

ambiguity in the meaning of *kosmos*. It could mean "ornament," per the first part of fragment 6 below, or "order," per the second part of the same fragment. The first gloss makes *sôphrosunê* something like the bloom on a fine plum, what makes that good thing really excellent; the second gloss makes it essential wherever there are conflicting goods.

Iamblichus' own contribution perhaps maintains the ambiguity of the Plato statement. Again *sôphrosunê* has its realization as a virtue by affecting other virtues. It protects whatever is most valuable in a person, presumably their other states of virtue.[48] Whether it keeps them only in pristine condition (the "ornament" reading) or prevents them from harming each other (the "order" reading) is unclear.

Ὃ δ' ἐστὶν ὄντως ὁμολογούμενον θαρρῶν διισχυρίζομαι, ὅτι δὴ δι' ὅλων τῶν ἀρετῶν τὸ κάλλος διατείνει τῆς σωφροσύνης καὶ συναρμόζει τὰς πάσας ἀρετὰς κατὰ μίαν ἁρμονίαν συμμετρίαν τε αὐταῖς καὶ κρᾶσιν πρὸς ἀλλήλας ἐντίθησι. τοιαύτη δὴ οὖν οὖσα καὶ ἀφορμὴν παρέχει ταῖς ὅλαις ὥστε ἐγγενέσθαι, καὶ ἐγγενομέναις αὐταῖς ἀσφαλῆ παρέχει σωτηρίαν. (fr. 6 = Stob. 3.5.49)

> I declare confidently what is truly agreed upon, that it is in fact through the whole of the virtues that the beauty of *sôphrosunê* extends and harmonizes all the virtues in one harmony and sets in them a symmetry and mixture with one another. This being how it is, it provides an impetus to all to come into being, and, once they have come into being, it provides a stable preservation.

Iamblichus recapitulates his claim and argument of fragments 1 and 5, and thus takes himself to have clinched his main contention. *Sôphrosunê* is a metavirtue: it does something for each virtue severally, and it brings them all together and preserves them. The second point is more important here. The sense must be that courage and piety, for example, could demand contradictory preparations or actions unless *sôphrosunê* has integrated them. Such integration presumably involves the capacity to think broadly about the range of one's incentives to action, recognizing potential conflicts and spending time coordinating one's response to them. One might feel ready to defend one's city against quick-moving besiegers ("courageous motivations") but also obligated to request the gods' assistance ("pious motivations"); *sôphrosunê* ensures reflection on the best way to do both. This exercise of rationality is an exercise in agent-defining unification. What it is to be an agent is to have the capacity to respond to complex situations with a singular determination—and not just any determination, but one with which

---

[48] For this argument, see again Olymp. *In Gorg.* 35.1. This seems to be the power that Plato's Socrates gave to justice in *Republic* 4.

one does or would choose to identify oneself. Amazingly, this power to bring the virtues into being and maintain them is the one Plato's Socrates ascribes to justice (rather than *sôphrosunê*) in *Republic* Book 4. Iamblichus' easy replacement of the one virtue with the other casts further suspicion on Socrates' dubious discrimination between the two virtues in his conversation with Plato's brothers.

Καὶ ἡ τῶν ὡρῶν τοῦ ἐνιαυτοῦ σύστασις καὶ ἡ τῶν στοιχείων πρὸς ἄλληλα σύγκρασις συμφωνίαν ἀποσῴζει καλλίστην καὶ σώφρονα. καὶ τό γε πᾶν τοῦτο διὰ τὴν κοσμιότητα τῶν καλλίστων μέτρων κόσμος ἐπικαλεῖται. (fr. 7 = Stob. 3.5.50)

Both the arrangement of the seasons of the year and the mixture of the elements with one another preserve a most beautiful and *sôphrôn* concord. And this Whole is called Orderliness on account of the ordering of the most beautiful measures.

Iamblichus' letter to Arete culminates (if it is concluding here) with reference to *sôphrosunê* as a virtue of cosmic organization; this is also as Socrates' pseudo-argument with Callicles did. *Sôphrosunê* creates unity—wholeness and order—at the grandest scale.

Thus ends Stobaeus' excerpts from Iamblichus' letter to Arete. *Sôphrosunê* for Arete is not limited to obedience; it extends to every form of order, including that of her other virtues, and to an excellence shared by all rational beings.

Aporias about Agency—Rational Choice or Quiet Submission?

Both of these post-Classical texts that take *sôphrosunê* as their theme grant a centrality to the virtue. Phintys' *On Women's Sôphrosunê* does so as a fascinating, frustrating, and ambivalent document. It makes us wonder: Does it treat *sôphrosunê* as agency, or as submissiveness? Is it doing one under the guise of the other? Is it giving a virtue-theoretical justification for the conventional social norms, social norms codifying gender inequality and feminine alienation from large-scale decision-making? Or is it, quite to the contrary, constructing a form of agency embraceable within an otherwise alienating set of traditional social norms? These questions are not wholly decidable without a closer study of the rest of Neopythagorean literature—which, thus, is a desideratum. But, together, the preceding chapters of this book have made the questions askable, even obvious. For to the extent that agency is desirable, so too the semblance of agency seems valuable; and to the extent that *sôphrosunê* involves following norms, its practice can be indistinguishable from being compelled to follow norms. Phintys' treatise proves a brilliant site for dwelling on these morally profound cases of indistinguishability and forces the questions: What is agency in an ethically dubious situation? and What is *sôphrosunê* where the putatively authoritative norms may not really be authoritative?

Iamblichus' letter to Arete is less overtly troublesome. It gives a familiarly and synoptically Platonic, and highly laudatory, account of *sôphrosunê*. The virtue separates us from the beasts, helps us fight the ongoing fight against degradation and depravity, underwrites all the other virtues, fertilizes households and cities, approximates us to the gods, and is reflected in cosmic ordering. What indeed could make us more the human beings we aspire to be? The advocacy of this virtue, in utterly gender-neutral language, to the woman Arete, however, leads to extratextual conjecture. Are women especially in need of this advice, and is the gender-neutrality rhetorically sly, grounding an argument for feminine comportment in seemingly universal language? The attribution to women of insufficient *sôphrosunê* throughout Greek thought and literature warrants the suspicion. We must also remember that Stobaeus has only excerpted this letter, for the benefit of his son; perhaps some ad hominems to Arete, either as an individual or as a woman, were excluded as irrelevant to Stobaeus' pedagogical purpose. But while we may have suspicions, we lack evidence. Given that some theorists did believe virtue was gender-neutral—the Socratics, maybe some Pythagoreans—we may assume that Iamblichus, influenced by both groups, did as well. What is important for the present study is what was important about Phintys: the conversation about *sôphrosunê* and agency may continue.

Epilogue: Translating an Ancient Virtue for Modern Times

An Interested History of a Virtue

A range of motivations might occasion writing the history of a virtue. Two seek to address contemporary issues with the (paradoxically) new resources of the past. One is of public concern: praising an ancient virtue as a virtue for our times, a forgotten human capacity and way of acting to solve our ills. Grit, simplicity, mindfulness, forbearance, or reverence: the idea is cultural revitalization through rediscovery of a powerful normative disposition. It is like the importation of putatively Asian practices of exercise and wellness to North America, filling gaps in a health regimen with long-tested but as yet ignored treatments. The program of reintroduction could prove pointless, of course: if the ancient virtue is recognizable, recalling it to our attention might seem otiose; if it is not recognizable, its acceptance might require that we have already shifted radically the way we live, as would be the case with self-abnegation and the other ascetic virtues, or utter submission and the other authoritarian virtues. The risk of pointlessness, however, could be exaggerated. The ways to achieve what we take to be good are innumerable and begin indeterminate; they must be characterized, individuated, and made salient. Rediscovering an ancient virtue is finding the way another culture identified and carved out an approach to what's good. Since we may already accept the overall good, we may accept a less-remembered avenue to it. Hence the appeal of the examples given above: grit and determination; simplicity and letting go; mindfulness and attentiveness; forbearance and toleration; reverence and appreciating what is beyond human control. All the same, books of virtue-reclamation, usually written in the popular vein, assume something that I cannot, that they recognize the current ills and know the historical virtue to succeed as treatment. Is more *sôphrosunê* what we most need? Maybe, but really I do not know if that is our particular deficit.

Another motivation is of disciplinary concern: reframing or seeking to resolve contemporary philosophical problems. Relevant here would be virtue ethics, moral psychology, or practical rationality. The hope would be that the close connection shown to obtain between *sôphrosunê* and selfhood would clarify some obscurity in one of those fields. But which obscurity, and how? This I do not know either. Further, even if I knew, I doubt the ancient reflections on *sôphrosunê* would come with enough precision to intervene in already subtle and robust fields of inquiry. So this task I leave to those who actually confront the contemporary philosophical problems, with the hope that what I have written here may catalogue the ancient resources available, as a forest survey may catalogue the compounds available to the experimental pharmacologist.

The motivation I in fact have has only indirect relevance to contemporary thought. I have wanted to find the beliefs about human and social life, and the judgments about how best to live it, that Classical Greek talk of *sôphrosunê* reveals. Such talk showed that the Greeks found this virtue to be important but confusing or controversial, hence the debates about it. It was important and confusing because it represented, or came to represent, certain essential features of maturation as a person in society, connected to gaining responsibility for one's actions, stability in identity through time, and the capacity to maintain a needy and vulnerable body. That the Greeks saw these features as unifiable under the term *sôphrosunê* provides a worthwhile hypothesis for us, that they *are* unifiable, that we can think of these features together, as part of the same capacity. Thinking of them this way may be a little alien, hence the possibility of learning from the Greeks, but not so alien as to become a matter of only antiquarian or counterfactual reflection: we too can see *sôphrosunê* as a virtue. It, or its English-language equivalent, may not have been salient as a norm for action for us, but it could become one. Other Greek terms have had this illuminating and useful effect: *psuchê, kosmos, dialegesthai, elenchus*. But all this is not to say that this book precisely *advocates* the virtue the Greeks called *sôphrosunê*. Rather it describes it, and thereby allows us to see our ethical lives through the schema of *sôphrosunê*; it is then up to us to decide whether that helps.

Translating *Sôphrosunê*

To this point in the book I have only transliterated *sôphrosunê*, as I have sought its meaning through its use and examples of its analysis. Deploying an English translation could have ended up assuming what I have instead striven to show. But I observed in Chapter 1 that there has been a long-standing assumption against the possibility of any reasonable translation. The thought has been that, whereas the other canonical Greek virtues map closely enough to English correlates—*dikaiosunê* to justice, *andreia* to courage, *eusebeia* to piety, and *sophia* or *phronêsis* to wisdom—*sôphrosunê* does not. *Sôphrosunê* has been taken to be a distinctively Greek virtue, with a semantic range somehow coextensive with no English virtue term, either as too broad, too bimodal, or too polyvalent, or simply too idiosyncratically shaped. This position has never exactly been argued for by a full survey of the English vocabulary of virtue terms or by a unifying account of *sôphrosunê* of the sort provided in this book. But many people think it.

Nevertheless, translations of the term are necessary, both in translations of texts that include the term and when discussing arguments about the term. Sometimes in long works, for example the plays of Euripides or the dialogues of Plato, the term has received multiple English translations given the translator's impression of the focal idea in one context or another. At least in the philosophical context, this has become less common, as translators recognize some readers' desire to track the contexts in which a single Greek word appears. So they seek a single translation that makes best sense of the range of contexts in which the Greek word appears and meets other criteria as well. The English term should be about as salient or familiar as the Greek term: a rare, archaic, or technical word should not translate a familiar, common, and widely used term. For a virtue term in particular, the valence or normativity should match: the Greek and English terms should refer to something equally hard to attain and valuable to have; and if there is ambivalence in the Greek (as in δεινός, "clever" or "terrible"), there should be ambivalence in the English. Ideally there should also be shared connotations and prototypes, as *andreia* and "courage" both bring to mind martial fortitude, *sophia* and "wisdom" the considered judgment of a city elder.

Older contextual translations of *sôphrosunê* sought to capture its fundamentality and breadth, going with "virtue" or "wisdom." These must be dismissed, given their failure to distinguish *sôphrosunê* from other virtues or intellectual states; for instance, Xenophon said that Socrates did not separate *sôphrosunê* from *sophia*, and this is an interesting claim only if there are two distinct words. Nevertheless, these translations have their advantages. They capture the salience and positive inflection of *sôphrosunê*. To the extent that "virtue" still euphemizes sexual constraint, it captures the ambiguity found in Euripides' *Hippolytus*; to the extent "wisdom" contrasts with spontaneity, it captures the deliberateness found in Plato's *Charmides*. Both translations advance this book's thesis, that *sôphrosunê* contributes to, to the point of constituting, human agency. Similarly overbroad translations, like "good sense," have the same pros and cons.

Another older term, for the adjective, is "chaste." This has an appropriate etymological connection with moral purity, plainness, and lack of adornment signified by *castus, castigare*. The verb "chasten" does well as a definition of the verb *sôphronizein*, "to cause to be *sôphrôn*, to educate, to tame." And it fits the explicit or implicit Pythagorean context in which we have found *sôphrosunê* frequently arising. Unfortunately the noun "chastity" in particular, but also the adjective, have simply become too sexualized in connotation; a chaste person is generally a religiously observant monk or nun whose lifelong sexual abstinence is intentional, and chastity refers somewhat bathetically to an ideal of sexual abstinence before marriage; it has become "celibacy." Aside from that, the chaste person does not seem for that reason more capable of action, even if she is thought to be better prepared for the holy life. And with "chastise" as rather too much like *sôphronizein* or *kolazein*, it lacks the intransitive aspect found in *sôphronein*.

"Temperance" is probably the most ready-to-hand and contingently transparent translation of *sôphrosunê* in contemporary English: in philosophy translations, it points (almost) unambiguously to *sôphrosunê*. It has an impressive provenance, reliant on Cicero's earliest translations of *sôphrosunê* as *temperantia* and then transferred through the Christian tradition to Modern English, with familiar usages by the time of Shakespeare (as seen in one of this book's epigrams). Its etymology has appropriate overtones, in that "proper mixture" is akin to *kosmios*, "well-ordered," and gets at aspects of *harmonia*. Yet contemporary language uses it much less often than Greeks used *sôphrosunê*; many students hardly know the term except in its association with century-old alcohol laws. It does not sound like something vigorously to strive for, having the ring rather of a default state; it is not so difficult for most people to avoid becoming alcoholic.

Another very common translation in philosophical literature is "moderation," especially in translations of Aristotle and work influenced by modern political theory. It may be, however, the least satisfactory regular translation. To the student of Greek, it would seem to refer to a *metr-* word. As an Aristotle translation, it wrongly conflates *sôphrosunê* with all the virtues, which are defined as mean states, and underspecifies *sôphrosunê* itself, which is moderation only with respect to certain bodily desires. It is rarely aspirational, salient only in its breach, though even then too bland to connote prototypical ways of being moderate or immoderate. And as with "temperance," it lacks the prudential, goal-oriented sense so prevalent in early Greek uses of *sôphrosunê*. Gregory Nagy, in recent translations of Euripidean tragedy, has favored "balance" and "equilibrium," which I class in the "moderation" family. They perhaps intimate more of an intellectual component, of weighing out or making equal, than moderation does, but their real strength over moderation is their greater aspirationality—the idea of balance suggests a narrow base on which equipoise is hard won; equilibrium suggests something hard won from a dynamic mixture. Nevertheless, they are overly general and inadequately active.

"Sound-mindedness," even more than temperance, obviously equates with *sôphrosunê* and nothing else; indeed the word was coined as a direct English translation of the Greek word, replacing its roots with English equivalents. But it serves little more than as translationese. The *Oxford English Dictionary* does not even include it in its lexicon; nobody except English-speaking students of ancient Greek philosophy would ever know the term; it accordingly has not acquired any prototypes or overtones. Further, while an admirable state, it does not appear particularly aspirational, and only the opposite, being of unsound mind, which prevents one from making enforceable contracts, has much ethical bite. It seems like an easy virtue to acquire, so easy as to be, so to speak, ours to lose. Classical scholars have often thought the same about *sôphrosunê* itself, but this is from undervaluing the Greek virtue, not from understanding its role in discursive exchange.

"Self-control," "self-restraint," and "self-mastery" capture Antiphon's conception of *sôphrosunê* as dealing with overweening desires; the terms differ mainly in the level of (self-)management implied. But this implication of management in any case is important, reflecting an active stance toward some aspect of oneself that would otherwise be wild. Though without explicit reference to intellectual processes, "control," "restraint," and "mastery" imply some degree of judgment. All are clearly aspirational, to the degree we feel our desires or habits getting the better of us. "Self-control" in particular does not sound technical or unusual; self-restraint does not either, though it comes in at a more refined register. But there are three problems with these terms as English translations. First, "self-control," "self-restraint," and "self-mastery" more familiarly translate *enkrateia*, a term theoretically distinct from *sôphrosunê*, as we have seen, in Xenophon and Aristotle, and infrequently used by Plato. Second, like *enkrateia*, they are not appreciably normative, good-oriented; like power or control in general, they are only as valuable as that which they control, restrain, or master is harmful. Third, the "self-" prefix gets ahead of the analysis: the reflexivity of *sôphrosunê*, for example in Plato, is only an eventual hypothesis or explanation, not something evidently built into sôphrosunê. In general it makes *sôphrosunê* seem more self-directed than other virtues, such as courage or justice, even though they may depend on the same amount of inner attention or "self-work."

"Discretion," rarely used as a translation of *sôphrosunê*, actually has nearly all one would need, except that in its most common contemporary usage it refers to tact and verbal restraint, which is only a subcategory of *sôphrosunê*, and its wider connotation, "the freedom to decide what should be done in a particular situation," is rather high register. The adjectival form, "being discrete," has simply come to mean "keeping things to oneself, being non-revelatory," and this does not share connotations or prototypes with *sôphrosunê*. "Prudence" would also serve well, as it represents stepping back from one's immediate desires to decide from a wider base of considerations, but the noun now sounds old-fashioned and in Greek philosophy it has been long associated with *phronêsis*.

In my judgment, the best translation for *sôphrosunê* in the Classical period is "discipline," which my colleague Christopher C. Raymond and I resolved upon in our translation of Plato's *Charmides*.[1] The leading consideration is that "discipline" is a familiar trait that, among ambitious and conscientious people, young

---

[1] Moore and Raymond (2019, xxxvi–xxxvii).

and old alike, is both highly desirable and difficult to attain. To exercise discipline is to be able to work toward whatever one takes to be good—writing a paper, training for a marathon, enduring the trials of military service, weathering political and economic turmoil (to give only the cases of the scholar, athlete, soldier, and entrepreneur)—without being turned away by visceral or insistent desires to do something else. It is the capacity to commit oneself to a principle or norm of action. Like *sôphrosunê* it has an intellectual and a nonintellectual gloss, the former its judgment of those desires whose ends conform with one's ultimate end, the latter its displacement of the urgency of one's wayward impulses and avoidance of reproach. Like *sôphrosunê* it can seem ambiguous between autonomous judgment, which is good, and social conformity, risk aversion, and nonspontaneity, which are bad. This is seen in the adverse judgment that a student is disciplined but neither creative nor insightful, or the infantry officer who is disciplined but neither bold nor attuned to her superiors' imperfections.

Epigraphical Appendix

This appendix contains and translates all entries from the *Carmina Epigraphica Graeca* (Hansen 1983, 1989) that include secure *sôphrosunê* terms (thus excluding CEG 16, 22, 480, 540). I follow the text, lineation, and conjectured dating from CEG, noting alternative reconstructions where significant, but ignore indications of orthography change and some underpoints.

CEG 30, b2 (535–30)
γ]ὰρ σόφρον ε[*sôphrôn*

CEG 34 (ca. 530)
[Ἀ]ντιλόχο : ποτὶ σε͂μ' ἀγαθο͂ | καὶ σόφρονος ἀνδρὸς | Antilochos: by the tomb of a good and *sôphrôn* man
[δάκρυ κ]άταρ[χ]σον, ἐπεὶ καὶ | σὲ μένει θάνατος.   [shed a tear,] since death awaits you too.

CEG 36 (c. 530)
[-⏑⏑ - τόδ]ε σε͂μ' ἀγαθοῦ [καὶ σόφρο]νος ἀνδρός.   This is the monument of ——, a good and *sôphro]n* man.

CEG 41 (ca. 530–20)
σε͂μα πατὲρ Κλέ[β]|βολος ἀποφθιμέ|νοι Χσενοφάντοι | Cleobulus, father of dead Xenophantus,
θε͂κε τόδ' ἀντ' ἀρετε͂ς | ἐδὲ σαοφροσύνες.   erected this monument to honor his virtue and
                                                                 sôphrosunê.

CEG 58 (ca. 510–500)
δακρυόεν πολυπενθὲς Ἀναχσίλα ἐδ' ὀλοφ|υδνὸν   Tearful, much-mourning, lamenting, I stand as a
λάινον ἔστεκα μνε͂μα καταφθιμέ|{με}νο :   stone monument of Anaxilas, who has perished:
Ναχσίο ὃν τίεσκον Ἀθεναῖοι μετέοικον   a Naxian whom the Athenians honored
ἔχ|σοχα σοφροσύνες ἕνεκεν ἐδ' ἀρετε͂ς. :   for his extraordinary *sôphrosunê* and virtue.
το͂ι μ' ἐπὶ Τιμ|όμαχος γεραρὸν κτέρας οἷα θανόντι   Timomachus placed me over him as a funeral gift
θε͂κεν Ἀ|ρίστονος παιδὶ χαριζόμενος.   Pleasing to the dead son of Ariston.

CEG 67.1 (ca. 500)
[σό]φρον, εὔ[χσύ|ν]ετος, χσε[νικ|ό]ς, πι[νυ]τός, τὰ | *sôphrôn*, keen, hospitable, prudent, knowing what's
κάλ' [εἰδό]ς …   fine …

CEG 69 (ca. 500)
[Ἀ]λκίμαχ', εὔδοχσόν σε χ[υτὲ κ]|ατὰ γαῖ' ἐκάλυφσεν, :   Honored Alkimachus, a mound of earth conceals you,
σόφρ[ονα κ]|αὶ πινυτόν, πᾶσαν ἡέχον|τ' ἀρετέν.   *sôphrôn* and prudent, possessing every virtue.

CEG 96 (430–425, Attica)
Σωσίνος Γορτύνιος χαλκόπτης.   Sosinus of Gortyna, coppersmelter.
μνῆμα δικαιοσύνης καὶ σωφροσύνης ἀρετῆς τε | A memorial of justice and *sôphrosunê* and virtue
Σωσίνο ἔστησαν παῖδες ἀποφθιμένο.   Sosinus' children erected when he died.

CEG 102 (ca. 400)
πότνια Σωφροσύνη θύγατερ μεγαλόφρονος Αἰδῶς, | Lady *Sôphrosunê*, daughter of high-minded Respect,
πλεῖστα σὲ τιμήσας εὐπόλεμόν τε Ἀρετὴν | having greatly honored you and martial Virtue,
Κλείδημος Μελιτεὺς Κλειδημίδο ἐνθάδε κεῖται, | Cleidemus Meliteus son of Cleidemidus lies here,
ζῆλος πατρί ποτ' ὤν, μητ[ρὶ δὲ νῦν ὀ]δύ[νη].   a source of pride to his father then, a pain to his
                                                                 mother now.

CEG 136 (ca. 525–500)
Ϙοσινα ηυσεμάταν θάψα [π]|έλας ηιποδρόμοιο
  ἄνδρα ἀ|[γα]θ[ό]ν, πολοῖς μνᾶμα καὶ | [ἐσ]ομένοις,
ἐν πολέμοι [φθ]ίμενον νε|αρὰν ηέβαν ὀλέσαντα,
  σό|φρονα, ἀεθλοφόρον καὶ σ|οφὸν ηαλικίαι

I buried Cosina's son Hysematas near the hippodrome,
  a good man, a memorial to many in times to come,
dying in battle, his youth in its prime destroyed,
  sôphrôn, prize-winning, and smart among his
    age-mates.

CEG 479 (early fourth century)
σῶμα μὲν ἐντὸς γῆ κατέχει, τὴν σωφ|ροσύνην δέ,
  Χρυσάνθη, τὴν σὴν ὁ | κατέκρυψε τάφος

Though the earth holds your body, the grave,
  Chrysanthe, has not hidden your *sôphrosunê*.

CEG 486 (early fourth century?)
[ἥ]δ' ἔθανεν προλιπōσα πόσιν καὶ μη[τέρα κεδνὴν] |
  [κ]αὶ κλέος ἀθάνατον σωφροσύνης [μεγάλης]. |
Ἀριστοκράτεια Κορινθία. *vvv(v)* Θεόφ[ιλος].

She died leaving her husband, her [dear] mother,
  and the immortal glory of her [great] *sôphrosunê*.
Aristocrateia of Corinth. Theophilus.

CEG 491 (early fourth century?)
σῆς ἀρετῆς μνημεῖα, | Θεοφίλη, οὔποτε λήσει, |
  σώφρων καὶ χρηστὴ καὶ | ἐργάτις πᾶσαν ἔχουσα | ἀρετήν.

Remembrance of your virtue, Theophila, will never fade,
  sôphrôn and useful and industrious, having all virtue.

CEG 494 (early fourth century?)
. . . . . . τ]όδε σῆμ' ἀγαθῆς ἣ πᾶσι | [ποθεινὴ]
[σ]ωφροσύνης ἀρετ[ῆς | εἵνεκα καὶ] σοφίας

this [is a] sign of good which is [a desire] for all,
  [because of her] *sôphrosunê*, virtue, and wisdom.

CEG 495 (early fourth century)
[σ]ῆς δ' ἀρετῆς καὶ σωφροσύν[η]ς μνημεῖον ἅπασιν |
  [λείπ]εις οἰκτρὰ παθῶν μοίρας ὑπὸ, δαίμονος ἐχθροῦ.

You leave to all a monument of your virtue and *sôphrosunê*,
  after suffering piteous things from Fate, a hateful god.

CEG 516 (ca. 380–370)
ἐνθάδε Φυλονόη κεῖται, θυγάτηρ [υ υ – –], |
  σώφρων, εὐσύνετος, πᾶσαν ἔχο[υσ' ἀρετή]ν.

Here lies Phylonoe, daughter . . .
  sôphrôn, keen, possessing every [virtu]e.

CEG 518 (ca. 375)
πᾶσι θανεῖν εἵμαρται ὅσοι ζῶσιν, σὺ δὲ πένθος
  οἰκτρὸν ἔχειν ἔλιπες, Παυσιμάχη, προγόνοις
μητρί | τε Φαινίππηι καὶ πατρὶ Παυσανίαι,
σῆς δ' ἀρετῆς μνη|μεῖον ὁρᾶν τόδε τοῖς παριόσιν
  σωφροσύνης τε

Death is decreed by fate for all those who live;
Pausimache, you left piteous mourning to your forebears,
  both to your mother Phainippe and to your father
    Pausanias,
  and a monument of your virtue for the passers-by
    to see—and of your *sôphrosunê*.

CEG 525 (ca. 360)
Γλυκέρα Θουκλείδου
  ὃ σπάνις ἐστὶ γυναικί, ἐσθλὴν καὶ σώφρονα φῦναι |
  τὴν αὐτήν, δοκίμως τοῦδ' ἔχτυχεγ Γλυκέρα

Glykera, daughter of Thoukleides.
  Glykera had genuinely what is rare in a woman—
  that she be both good and *sôphrôn*.

CEG 531 (first half of fourth century)
ἐννέα ἐτῶν ἐβίων δεκάδας, θνείσκω δὲ γεραιός, |
  σωφροσύνην δὲ ἤσκησα, ἔλιπον δὲ εὔκλειαν ἀμεμφῆ.

Nine decades having I lived, I am dying an old man,
  I practiced *sôphrosunê* and have left a blameless renown.

CEG 539 (ca. 350)
ἐνθάδε τὴν ἀγαθὴν καὶ σώφρονα γαῖ' ἐκάλυψεν |
  Ἀρχεστράτην ἀνδρὶ ποθεινοτάτην.

Here the earth hides the good and *sôphrôn*
  Archestrate, most longed for by her husband.

CEG 542 (ca. 350)
  Πεισικράτεια ἥδ' ἐστι Εὐφρονίο θυγά|τηρ, |
ἧς ψυχὴν μὲν ἔχει τὸ χρεών γ', ἣ | [τ]οῖς δὲ τέκνοισι
  τὴν ἀρετὴν ἀσκεῖν | σωφροσύνην τε ἔλιπεν.

  Here is Peisikrateia, daughter of Euphronios,
whose soul fate holds; to her children she left
  the practice of virtue and *sôphrosunê*.

CEG 543.5–6 (ca. 350)
εὐσεβῆ ἀσκήσασα βίον | καὶ σώφρονα θνήισκω,
ἡνίκα | μοι βιότου μόρσιμον ἦλθε τέλος.

After leading a pious and *sôphrôn* life I die,
when my appointed end arrives.

CEG 548 (ca. 350)
Δημητρίο[ς] | Θεοδότης.
ψυχὴ μὲν προλιποῦσα τὸ σόν, [Δημήτριε, σῶμα] |
οἴχεται εἰς Ἔρεβος, σωφροσύν[ης δὲ ?καλὴ] |
θάλλει ἀγήρατος· τύμβωι δέ σ[ε κρύψε θανόντα] |
Ἔρξις ἴσον στέρξασ' οἷσι τέκ[νοισ(ιν) u u –].

Demetrios, son of Theodote.
The soul, after leaving your [body, Demetrius],
heads toward Erebos, but [noble?] *sôphrosunê*
thrives without aging; Erxis [hid y]ou [after death]
beneath a mound,
having loved you as she did her own children.

ἄφθονον εὐλογίας πηγήν, Δημ[ήτριε, λείπεις] |
ἀσκήσας κόσμον σωφροσύνη[ν τε ?καλὴ]· |
ὧν σε χάριν στέρξασ' Ἔρξις τεκ[νοισ(ιν) u u – –] |
μνημεῖον φιλίας τεῦξε τάφ[ον u u –].

Demetrios, [you are leaving] behind an ungrudging
spring of praise,
having practiced order and [noble?] *sôphrosunê*;
for the sake of which Erxis, who loved you as she did
her own children,
has erected a grave as a memorial of friendship.

CEG 554 (ca. 350)
ἑπτὰ βίου δεκάδας πᾶσιν φίλος οὐθένα | λυπῶν
σωφροσύνης τε ἀρετῆς τε δικαιοσύνης τε μετασχών
τῆς κοινῆς μοίρας πᾶ|σιν ἔχω τὸ μέρος.

Seven decades of life, friend to all, harming nobody;
partaking in *sôphrosunê*, virtue, and justice,
I share in the fate common to all.

CEG 560 (ca. 350)
Ἀντιφῶν Εὐφάνος.
[ἀσκ]ήσαντα ὅσα χρὴ θνητὸ φύσει ἀγ[δρ]ὸς ἐνεῖνα[ι] |
[σωφρ]οσύνην, σοφίαν, γῆς με ἔ[κάλυψ]ε τάφος.

Antiphon, son of Euphanes.
Having practiced those things which must belong by
nature to a mortal man—
sôphrosunê and wisdom—a mound of earth covered me.

CEG 568 (post-ca. 350)
εἴ σε Τύχη προὔπεμψε καὶ ἡλιακίας ἐπέβησεν, |
ἐλπίδι γ' ἦσθα μέγας τῶι τε δοκεῖμ, Μακαρεῦ, |
ἡνίοχος τέχνης τραγικῆς Ἕλλησιν ἔσεσθαι· |
σωφροσύνει δ' ἀρετῆι τε οὐκ ἀκλεῆς ἔθανες.

If Fortune had sent you forth and brought you to
your prime,
you were high in our hope and expectation, Makareus,
among the Greeks a chariot-driver of the tragic art;
you died, not unrenowned for *sôphrosunê* and
virtue.

CEG 573 (post-ca. 350)
οὐχὶ πέπλους, οὐ χρυσὸν ἐθαύμασεν ἐμ βίωι ἥδε,
ἀλλὰ πόσιν τε αὐτῆς σωφροσύ[νην τ(ε) u u –]. |
ἀντὶ δὲ σῆς ἥβης, Διονυσία, ἡλικίας τε
τόνδε τάφον κοσμεῖ σὸς πόσις Ἀντίφ[ιλος].

Neither robes nor gold did she admire in life,
but her husband and her *sôphrosunê* ...
But in place of your youthful prime, Dionysia,
this tomb your husband Antiphilus adorns.

CEG 577 (post-ca. 350)
[π]άντων ὧν θέμις ἐστὶ τυχεῖν εὐδαίμοσι θνητοῖς |
ζῶσά τε ἐκοινώνουν καὶ φθιμένη μετέχω. |
ἡλικίας δὲ πόθον νεαρᾶς μνήμην τε λιποῦσα |
σωφροσύνης ἔθανον Λογχὶς ἐπωνυμίαν.

Everything which it is right for flourishing mortals to have,
I shared in while alive and partake in having perished.
I died leaving longing for my youthful age and a memory
of my *sôphrosunê*; I was named Lonchis.

CEG 584 (post-ca. 350)

ἡλικίας βαιὸν σωφροσύν[- u u -]
ἐν δεκάσιν δισσαῖσιν ἐ[τῶν ...
οἳ τάφον ἀντὶ γάμου [...

of young age, *sôphrosun*-,
twenty years old
a grave rather than marriage

CEG 585 (post-ca. 350)

σωφροσύνην ἤσκον ἀρετήν τε, ὡς χρὴ νέον ἄνδρα, |
καὶ ζῶν ἠινούμην καὶ ἐπεὶ βιότου τέλος ἔσχον, |
ὥστε θανὼν ἔλιπον λύπας προγόνοισι φίλοις τε· |
οὐ γὰρ ἔτ' ἔστιν ἰδῖν σῶμα γονεῦσιν ἐμόν.

I practiced *sôphrosunê* and virtue, as a young
   man ought,
and I was praised both while living and having
   reached the end of life,
so that, having died, I left grief to my forebears and
   friends.
For no longer can my parents see my body

CEG 590 (ca. 350–325)

ἡλικίαμ μὲν ἐμὴν ταύτην δεῖ πάντας ἀκοῦσαι·
εἰκοστῶι καὶ πέμπτωι ἔτει λίπον ἡλίου αὐγάς. |
τοὺς δὲ τρόπους καὶ σωφροσύνην ἣν εἴχομεν ἡμεῖς
ἡμέτερος πόσις οἶδεν ἄριστ' εἰπεῖν περὶ τούτων.

This age of mine, everyone ought to hear:
After twenty-five years I left the sun's beams.
As for the habits and *sôphrosunê* that I had,
My husband knows best how to speak about them.

CEG 593.6–11 (346–338)

σῶμα μὲν ἐνθάδε σόν, Διονύσιε, γαῖα καλύπτει, |
   ψυχὴν δὲ ἀθάνατον κοινὸς ἔχει ταμίας· |
σοῖς δὲ φίλοις καὶ μητρὶ κασιγνήταις τε λέλοιπας |
   πένθος ἀείμνηστον σῆς φιλίας φθίμενος· |
δισσαὶ δ' αὖ πατρίδες σ' ἡ μὲν φύσει, ἡ δὲ νόμοισιν |
   ἔστερξαν πολλῆς εἵνεκα σωφροσύνης.

Here the earth covers your body, Dionysius,
   but a common treasurer has your immortal soul.
For your friends and mother and sisters you have
      left behind
   A grief, an enduring memory of your love, when
      you perished.
Two countries loved you—one by birth, one by laws,
   thanks to your great *sôphrosunê*.

CEG 599 (fourth century)

ἥδε χθὼν ἐκάλυψε Κλεὼ τὴν σώφρονα πάντα |
δύσμορον ἡλικίας· ὀλοφύρεται ἥ σε τεκοῦσα, |
σούς τε κασιγνήτους λυποῦσα ἔθανες, δήμου φῶς, |
σὴν αὔξουσ' ἀρετὴν καὶ σωφροσύνην ἐρατεινήν.

This soil covered Cleo, who was *sôphrôn* in everything,
but ill fated regarding her age. The one who gave birth
   to you is grieving.
Your death brought pain to your brothers, oh light of
   the people,
but enhanced your virtue and your lovely *sôphrosunê*.

CEG 604 (fourth century)

Κλεαγόρα Φιλέου Μελ[ιτέως γυνή].
εἰς φῶς παῖδ' ἀνάγουσα βίου φάος ἥν[υσεν αὐτή], |
   Κλεαγόρα, πλείστης σωφροσύνης [μέτοχος],· |
ὥστε γονεῦσιν πένθος ἀγήρατον [λίπες – –]
   ἐσθλῶν ...

Kleagora of Phileus, [wife of] Melitus.
By bringing a child to life, [she] lost the light of life,
   Kleagora, [sharing in] great *sôphrosunê*.
thus you [left] for your parents ageless grief,
   excellent [things] ...

CEG 611 (fourth century)

[σ]ῶμα μὲν ἐν κόλποισι κατὰ χθὼν ἥδε καλ[ύπτει] |
[Τι]μοκλείας, τὴν σὴν δὲ ἀρετὴν οὐθεὶς [φθ]ίσει α[ἰών]· |
[ἀθά]νατος μνήμη σωφρ[ο]σύνης ἕνε[κ]α.

While this earth below hides in its bosom the body
   of Timoclea, your virtue will n[ever] [pe]rish,
   its memory immortal, thanks to your *sôphrosunê*.

CEG 624 (fourth/third century)

πατ[ρί ⌣–⌣⌣–⌣⌣–] | ἠδὲ Φιλ[– –]
[μητρί ⌣–⌣⌣–]ν ἡλικία[ν] | προλιπών·
σω[φροσύνη]ς δὲ ἀρετῆς τε πρ[όφρ]ων | τόδε τεῦξε
   πατήρ σοι
μνημεῖον θνητοῖς | πᾶσιν ὁρᾶν φανερόν.

For my father ... and Phil ...
and for my mother having left behind ... age;
In honor of your *sôphrosunê* and virtue,
your father made this monument,
that it may be visible to all mortals.

CEG 643 (350–300)
κρύπτει μὲν χθὼν ἥδε Μένωνα Πόθωνος ὃν |Ἑλλὰς
 ἤλπισε κοσμήσειν Θεσσαλίαν στεφ[ά]|νοις·
οὗ τύμβον τίμησεν Ὀρέστης, σωφρο|σύνης δὲ
 οὕνεκα πένθος ἔχει πᾶσα πό|λις φθιμένου.

This earth hides Meno son of Pothon whom Hellas
 hoped would adorn Thessaly with crowns;
Orestes honored his tomb, and due to his *sôphrosunê*,
 the entire city grieves at losing him.

CEG 662a (ca. post-350)
σωφρ[ο]σύνην τιμῶσα | δικαιοσύνην τε σέβου[σ]α |
[Ἱ]ππὼ ἐν ἡλικίαι πνεῦμ' ἔ[λ]ιπεν βιότου.

Honoring *sôphrosunê* and reverencing justice,
 Hippo, in her prime, has left the breath of life.

CEG 686.5–6 (fourth century)
αἰαῖ, σεῖο, Ϙομάλλις, ἀποφθιμένης ἀκάχηνται |
 μάτηρ θ' ἁ μελέα κουρίδιός τε πόσις, |
πᾶσά τε συγγενέων πληθύς σ' ἀδινὸν στεναχίζει
 δρυπτόμενοι χαίτας τοῦδε πάροιθε τάφου· |
ἦ γὰρ δαίδαλά τε ἔργα χεροῖν καὶ σώφρονα κόσμον |
 ἤσκησας, μῶμος δ' οὔτις ἐπῆν ἐπί σοι.

Alas, Comallis, your wretched mother and lawful
 husband are lamenting your perishing,
And the whole crowd of kinsmen loudly laments
 for you, pulling at their hair beside this grave,
For indeed you practiced both cunning handicraft
 and *sôphrôn* orderliness; no blame overtook you.

CEG 690 (ca. 360–350)
ὅστις ἄριστος ἔπαινος ἐν ἀνθρώποισι γυναικός,
 Καλλιαρίστα Φιληράτο τοῦτον ἔχουσα ἔθανεν,
σωφροσύνας ἀρετᾶ[ς] | τε· ἀλόχωι πόσις ὄνεκα τόνδε
 Δαμοκλῆς εστᾶσεν, μνημόσυνον φιλίας·
ἀνθ' ὧν δαίμων ἐσθλὸς ἕποιτο βίωι.

Whatever may be people's best praise of women,
 You died possessing, Kalliarista daughter of Phileratus
sôphrosunê and virtue. Wherefore her husband
 erected this memorial of her love,
 in honor of which may an excellent deity attend his life.

Bibliography

Abel, D. Herbert. 1943. "Genealogies of Ethical Concepts from Hesiod to Bacchylides." *Transactions and Proceedings of the American Philological Association* 74: 92–101.
Adam, James. 1902. *The Republic of Plato.* Edited with Critical Notes, Commentary, and Appendices. 2 vols. Cambridge: Cambridge University Press.
Adams, Don. 2020. "Refutation, Democracy and Epistemocracy in Plato's *Charmides.*" *Méthexis* 32: 26–44.
Addey, Crystal. 2018. "Plato's Female Readers." In *Brill's Companion to the Reception of Plato in Antiquity*, edited by Harold Tarrant, Danielle A. Layne, Dirk Baltzly, and Francçois Renaud. Leiden: Brill, 411–32.
Ademollo, Francesco. 2011. *The Cratylus of Plato: A Commentary.* Cambridge: Cambridge University Press.
Adkins, A. W. H. 1960. *Merit and Responsibility: A Study in Greek Values.* Oxford: Clarendon Press.
Adkins, A. W. H. 1968. Review of North 1966. *Gnomon* 40: 712–13.
Adkins, A. W. H. 1972. *Moral Values and Political Behaviour in Ancient Greece: From Homer to the End of the Fifth Century.* New York: Norton.
Adkins, A. W. H. 1976. "*Polypragmosune* and 'Minding Your Own Business.'" *Classical Philology* 71: 301–28.
Adomenas, Mantas. 1999. "Heraclitus on Religion." *Phronesis* 44: 87–113.
Allison, June W. 1997. *Word and Concept in Thucydides.* Atlanta, GA: Scholars Press.
Aloni, Antonio, and Alessandro Iannucci. 2016. "Writing Solon." In *Iambus and Elegy: New Approaches*, edited by Laura Swift and Chris Carey. Oxford: Oxford University Press, 155–73.
Ambury, James M. 2019. "Between Ascent and Descent: Self-Knowledge and Plato's Allegory of the Cave." In *Knowledge and Ignorance of Self in Platonic Philosophy*, edited by James M. Ambury and Andy R. German. Cambridge: Cambridge University Press, 81–96.
Anderson, J. K. 1974. *Xenophon.* London: Bristol Classical Press.
Anderson, Merrick E. 2019. "Immorality or Immortality? An Argument for Virtue." *Rhetorica* 37: 97–119.
Annas, Julia. 1981. *An Introduction to Plato's Republic.* Oxford: Oxford University Press.
Annas, Julia. 1985. "Self-Knowledge in Early Plato." In *Platonic Investigations*, Studies in Philosophy and the History of Philosophy, edited by Dominic J. O'Meara. Washington DC: Catholic University of America Press, 121–38.
Annas, Julia. 2002. "Democritus and Eudaimonism." In *Presocratic Philosophy: Essays in Honour of Alexander Mourelatos*, edited by Victor Caston and Daniel W. Graham. Aldershot: Ashgate, 169–81.
Annas, Julia. 2017. *Virtue and Law in Plato and Beyond.* Oxford: Oxford University Press.
Archer-Hind, Richard Dacre. 1883. *The Phaedo of Plato.* London: MacMillan.

Athanassiadi, Polymnia. 2013. "The Divine Man of Late Hellenism: A Sociable and Popular Figure." In *Divine Men and Women in the History and Society of Late Hellenism*, edited by M. Dzielska and K. Twardowska. Krakow: Jagiellonian University Press, 13–27.

Auerman, Gustav. 1876. "Platons Cardinaltugenden Vor Und Nach Abfassung Des Euthyphron." Inaugural diss., University of Jena.

Aurelio Privitera, Giuseppe. 1982. *Le Istmiche*. Milan: Fondazione Lorenzo Valla.

Ausland, Hayden. 2013. "On the Decline of Political Virtue in *Republic* 8–9." In *Proceedings of the Boston Area Colloquium in Ancient Philosophy*, Vol. 29, edited by Gary M. Gurtler and William Wians. Leiden: Brill, 1–26.

Bachmann, Viktoria. 2019. "The Human Being according to Nature: Self-Enquiry with Heraclitus." *Ápeiron. Estudios de filosofía—Monográfico "Presocráticos"* 11: 131–45.

Bailey, Cyril. 1928. *The Greek Atomists and Epicurus: A Study*. Oxford: Clarendon Press.

Baima, Nicholas R. 2017. "On the Value of Drunkenness in the *Laws*." *Logical Analysis and History of Philosophy* 20: 65–81.

Baima, Nicholas R. 2018. "Playing with Intoxication: On the Cultivation of Shame and Virtue in Plato's *Laws*." *Apeiron* 51: 345–70.

Baiter, Johann Georg, Johann Kasper von Orelli, and August Wilhelm Winckelmann. 1839. *Platonis Opera Quae Feruntur Omnia Acc. Integra Varietas Lectionis Stephanianae, Bekkerianae, Stallbaumianae, Scholia et Nominum Index*. Zurich: Turici Meyer & Zeller.

Bandini, Michele, and Louis-André Dorion. 2003–11. *Xénophon: Mémorables*. Paris: Les Belles Lettres.

Barnes, Jonathan. 1982. *The Presocratic Philosophers*. Rev. ed. London: Routledge and Kegan Paul.

Barnes, Jonathan, and Anthony Kenny. 2014. *Aristotle's Ethics: Writings from the Complete Works*. Princeton, NJ: Princeton University Press.

Barney, Rachel. 2017. "Callicles and Thrasymachus." In *Stanford Encyclopedia of Philosophy*, edited by Edward N. Zalta. https://plato.stanford.edu/archives/fall2017/entries/callicles-thrasymachus/.

Barrett, William Spenser. 1964. *Euripides: Hippolytos*. Oxford: Clarendon Press.

Bartlett, Robert C., and Susan D. Collins. 2011. *Aristotle's Nicomachean Ethics*. Chicago: University of Chicago Press.

Beekes, Robert. 2010. *Etymological Dictionary of Greek*. 2 vols. Leiden: Brill.

Begley, Keith. 2020. "Heraclitus' Rebuke of Polymathy: A Core Element in the Reflectiveness of His Thought." *History of Philosophy and Logical Analysis* 23: 21–50.

Benardete, Seth. 1991. *The Rhetoric of Morality and Philosophy: Plato's Gorgias and Phaedrus*. Chicago: University of Chicago Press.

Beresford, Adam. 2013. "Fangs, Feathers, and Fairness: Protagoras on the Origins of Right and Wrong." In *Protagoras of Abdera: The Man, His Measure*, edited by Johannes M. van Ophuijsen, Marlein van Raalte, and Peter Stork. Philosophia Antiqua. Leiden: Brill, 139–62.

Beresford, Adam. 2020. *Aristotle: The Nicomachean Ethics*. London: Penguin.

Bessarion, Cardinal. 1521. *De Factis et Dictis Socratis Memoratu Dignis*. Rome: Ariottus de Trino impensis Ioannis Mazochi Bergomatis.

Betegh, Gábor. 2007. "On the Physical Aspect of Heraclitus' Psychology." *Phronesis* 52: 3–32.

Bett, Richard. 2020. "Prodicus on the Choice of Heracles, Language, and Religion." In *Early Greek Ethics*, edited by David Wolfsdorf. Oxford: Oxford University Press, 195–210.

Betti, Daniel. 2011. "The Search for the Political Thought of the Historical Thrasymachus." *Polis* 28: 33–44.

Bidez, Joseph. 1919. "Le philosophe Jamblique et son école." *Revue des Études Grecques* 32: 29–40.

Bigio, Brian Jorge. 2021. "'Saving the Mind': An Etymological Inquiry into the Cognitive-Behavioral Function of the Ancient Greek Value ΣΩΦΡΟΣΥΝΗ (SOPHROSYNE)." Ph.D. diss., Stanford University.

Billings, Joshua. 2021. *The Philosophical Stage: Drama and Dialectic in Classical Athens.* Princeton, NJ: Princeton University Press.

Bobonich, Christopher. 2002. *Plato's Utopia Recast: His Later Ethics and Politics.* Oxford: Oxford University Press.

Bobonich, Christopher. 2013. "The Puzzles of Moderation." In *Platon: Gesetze/Nomoi*, edited by Christoph Horn. Berlin: De Gruyter, 23–43.

Bobonich, Christopher. 2017. "Agency in Plato's *Republic*." In *The Oxford Handbook of Topics in Philosophy (Online)*. Oxford: Oxford University Press, 1–31. https://doi.org/10.1093/oxfordhb/9780199935314.013.7.

Bodnár, István. 2015. "The *Problemata Physica*: An Introduction." In *The Aristotelian Problemata Physica: Philosophical and Scientific Investigations*, Philosophia antiqua, edited by Robert Mayhew. Leiden: Brill, 1–9.

Bollack, Jean, and Heinz Wismann, eds. 1972. *Héraclite ou la Séparation.* Paris: Les Éditions de Minuit.

Bolling, George Melville. 1925. *The External Evidence for Interpolation in Homer.* Oxford: Clarendon Press.

Bolton, Robert. 1989. "Nature and Human Good in Heraclitus." In *Ionian Philosophers*, edited by K. J. Boudouris. Athens: International Association for Greek Philosophy and International Center for Greek Philosophy and Culture, 49–57.

Bonazzi, Mauro. 2020a. "Ethical and Political Thought in Antiphon's *Truth* and *Concord*." In *Early Greek Ethics*, edited by David Wolfsdorf. Oxford: Oxford University Press, 149–68.

Bonazzi, Mauro. 2020b. *The Sophists.* Cambridge: Cambridge University Press.

Bostock, David. 2000. *Aristotle's Ethics.* Oxford: Oxford University Press.

Boudouris, K. J. 1989. "Heraclitus and the Dialectical Conception of Politics." In *Ionian Philosophers*, edited by K. J. Boudouris. Athens: International Association for Greek Philosophy and International Center for Greek Philosophy and Culture, 58–79.

Bourgault, Sophie. 2013. "Prolegomena to a Rehabilitation of Platonic Moderation." *Dissensus* 5: 122–43.

Bowie, Ewen. 2010. "Epigram as Narration." In *Archaic and Classical Greek Epigram*, edited by Manuel Baumbach, Andrej Petrovic, and Ivana Petrovic. Cambridge: Cambridge University Press, 313–84.

Bowra, Cecil Maurice. 1935. *Pindari Carmini Cum Fragmentis.* Editio altera. Oxford: Clarendon Press.

Brancacci, Aldo. 2015. "The Socratic Profile of Antisthenes' Ethics." In *From the Socratics to the Socratic Schools: Classical Ethics, Metaphysics and Epistemology*, edited by Ugo Zilioli. London: Routledge, 43–60.

Breitenbach, Alfred. 2003. "Kritias und Herodes Attikos: Zwei Tyrannen in Philostrats Sophistenviten." *Wiener Studien* 116: 109–13.

Broadie, Sarah. 1991. *Ethics with Aristotle.* Oxford: Oxford University Press.

Broadie, Sarah. 2021. *Plato's Sun-like Good: Dialectic in the Republic.* Cambridge: Cambridge University Press.

Broadie, Sarah, and Christopher Rowe, eds. 2002. *Aristotle: Nicomachean Ethics.* Oxford: Oxford University Press.

Bromberg, Jacques A. 2018. "A Sage on the Stage: Socrates and Athenian Old Comedy." In *Socrates and the Socratic Dialogue*, edited by Alessandro Stavru and Christopher Moore. Leiden: Brill, 31–63.

Brown, Lesley. 2009. *Aristotle, The Nicomachean Ethics.* Translated by W. D. Ross. Revised, with Introduction and Notes. Oxford: Oxford University Press.

Burger, Ronna. 2008. *Aristotle's Dialogue with Socrates: On the Nicomachean Ethics.* Chicago: University of Chicago Press.

Burnet, John. 1900. *The Ethics of Aristotle.* London: Methuen.

Burnet, John. 1907. *Platonis opera.* Oxford: Clarendon Press.

Burnyeat, M. F. 1997. "Culture and Society in Plato's *Republic*." Tanner Lectures on Human Values, Harvard University.

Bury, R. G. 1926. *Plato Laws.* 2 vols. Loeb Classical Library. Cambridge, MA: Harvard University Press.

Cairns, Douglas L. 1993. *Aidōs: The Psychology and Ethics of Honour and Shame in Ancient Greek Literature.* Oxford: Clarendon Press.

Callard, Agnes. 2017. "Enkratēs Phronimos." *Archiv für Geschichte der Philosophie* 99: 31–63.

Campbell, A. Y. 1956. "Notes on Euripides' *Bacchae*." *Classical Quarterly* 6: 56–67.

Carey, Christopher. 1981. *A Commentary on Five Odes of Pindar: Pythian 2, Pythian 9, Nemean 7, Isthmian 8.* Arno Press Monographs in Classical Studies. Salem, NH: The Ayer Company.

Carr, David. 1988. "The Cardinal Virtues and Plato's Moral Psychology." *Philosophical Quarterly* 38: 186–200.

Carson, Anne. 2006. *Grief Lessons: Four Plays by Euripides.* New York: New York Review of Books.

Carter, L. B. 1986. *The Quiet Athenian.* Oxford: Clarendon Press.

Centrone, Bruno. 2014. "The Pseudo-Pythagorean Writings." In *A History of Pythagoreanism*, edited by Carl A. Huffman. Cambridge: Cambridge University Press, 315–40.

Centrone, Bruno. 2015. "On *Problemata* 28: Temperance and Intemperance, Continence and Incontinence." In *The Aristotelian Problemata Physica*, edited by Robert Mayhew. Leiden: Brill, 321–36.

Chantraine, Pierre. 1968. *Dictionnaire Étymologique de la Langue Grecque: Histoire des Mots.* Paris: Klincksieck.

Chappell, T. D. J. 1993. "The Virtues of Thrasymachus." *Phronesis* 38: 1–17.

Christ, Matthew. 2020. *Xenophon and the Athenian Democracy: The Education of an Elite Citizenry.* Cambridge: Cambridge University Press.

Clairmont, Christoph W. 1970. *Gravestone and Epigram: Greek Memorials from the Archaic and Classical Period.* Mainz on Rhine: Verlag Philipp von Zabern.

Clark, Justin. 2018. "Knowledge and Temperance in Plato's *Charmides*." *Pacific Philosophical Quarterly* 99: 763–89.

Claughton, John, and Judith Affleck. 2012. *Aristophanes: Clouds.* Cambridge Translations from Greek Drama. Cambridge: Cambridge University Press.

Claus, D. B. 1981. *Toward the Soul.* New Haven, CT: Yale University Press.

Coates, Cameron, and James Lennox. 2020. "Aristotle on the Unity of the Nutritive and Reproductive Functions." *Phronesis* 65: 414–66.

Collins, Susan D. 2018. "An Introduction to the *Regime of the Lacedaemonians*." In *Xenophon: The Shorter Writings*, edited by Gregory A. McBrayer. Agora Editions. Ithaca, NY: Cornell University Press, 126–48.

Condello, Federico. 2014. "Le γνῶμαι di Crizia: Noterella a Philostr. *VS* I 16." *Quaderni di storia* 40: 151–57.

Connell, Sophia M. 2021. *Aristotle on Women: Physiology, Psychology, and Politics*. Cambridge Elements. Cambridge: Cambridge University Press.

Cooper, John M. 1973. "The *Magna Moralia* and Aristotle's Moral Philosophy." *American Journal of Philology* 94: 327–49.

Cooper, John M., ed. (D. S. Hutchinson, associate editor). 1997. *Plato: Complete Works*. Indianapolis, IN: Hackett.

Cornford, F. M. 1912. "Psychology and Social Structure in the *Republic* of Plato." *Classical Quarterly* 6: 246–65.

Cornford, F. M. 1941. *The Republic of Plato*. Oxford: Clarendon Press.

Courcelle, Pierre Paul. 1974. *Connais-Toi Toi-Même de Socrate à Saint Bernard*. Vol. 1. Paris: Études Augustiniennes.

Craik, E. M. 1993. "ΑΙΔΩΣ in Euripides' *Hippolytos* 373–430: Review and Reinterpretation." *Journal of Hellenic Studies* 113: 45–59.

Cross, R. C., and A. D. Woosley. 1966. *Plato's Republic: A Philosophical Commentary*. London: Macmillan.

Crusius, Gottlob Christian, Georg Aenotheus Koch, and Otto Güthling. 1969. *Wörterbuch zu Xenophons Memorabilien*. 3rd ed. Hildesheim: Gerstenberg.

Crystal, I. M. 2002. *Self-Intellection and its Epistemological Origins in Ancient Greek Thought*. Aldershot: Ashgate.

Curd, Patricia. 2009. "Thought and Body in Heraclitus and Anaxagoras." In *Proceedings of the Boston Area Colloquium in Ancient Philosophy*, edited by Gary M. Gurtler and William Wians Vol. 25, 1–20.

Curzer, Howard J. 1991. "Two Varieties of Temperance in the *Gorgias*." *International Philosophical Quarterly* 31: 153–59.

Curzer, Howard J. 1997. "Aristotle's Account of the Virtue of Temperance in *Nicomachean Ethics* III.10–11." *Journal of the History of Philosophy* 35: 5–25.

Curzer, Howard J. 2012. *Aristotle and the Virtues*. Oxford: Oxford University Press.

D'Angour, Armand. 2019. *Socrates in Love: The Making of a Philosopher*. London: Bloomsbury.

Dalcourt, Gerard J. 1963. "The Primary Cardinal Virtue: Wisdom or Prudence?" *International Philosophical Quarterly* 3: 55–79.

Danzig, Gabriel. 2014. "The Use and Abuse of Critias: Conflicting Portraits in Plato and Xenophon." *Classical Quarterly* 64: 507–24.

Danzig, Gabriel. 2017. "Xenophon and the Socratic Elenchos: The Verbal Thrashing as a Tool for Instilling *Sophrosune*." *Ancient Philosophy* 37: 293–318.

Davies, J. K. 1971. *Athenian Propertied Families*. Oxford: Oxford University Press.

Davies, Malcolm. 2000. "'The Man Who Surpassed All Men in Virtue': Euripides' *Hippolytus* and the Balance of Sympathies." *Wiener Studien* 113: 53–69.

De Vries, G. J. 1943. "ΣΩΦΡΟΣΎΝΗ en Grec Classique." *Mnemosyne* 11: 81–101.

Decleva Caizzi, F. 1966. *Antisthenis Fragmenta*. Milan: Varese.
Delatte, Armand. 1933. *Le Troisième Livre des Souvenirs Socratiques de Xénophon: Étude Critique*. Paris: E. Droz.
Delebecque, Edouard. 1978. *Xénophon: Cyropédie, Livres VI–VIII*. Paris: Les Belles Lettres.
Deman, Thomas. 1942. *Le Temoignage d'Aristote sur Socrate*. Paris: Les Belles Lettres.
Demos, Raphael. 1957a. "A Note on Σωφροσύνη in Plato's *Republic*." *Philosophy and Phenomenological Research* 17: 399–403.
Demos, Raphael. 1957b. "Paradoxes in Plato's Doctrine of the Ideal State." *Classical Quarterly* 7: 164–74.
Denyer, Nicholas. 2001. *Plato: Alcibiades*. Cambridge: Cambridge University Press.
Denyer, Nicholas. 2008. *Plato: Protagoras*. Cambridge: Cambridge University Press.
Deslauriers, Marguerite. 2012. "Women, Education, and Philosophy." In *A Companion to Women in the Ancient World*, edited by Sharon L. James and Sheila Dillon. Chichester: Wiley, 343–53.
Deslauriers, Marguerite. 2022. *Aristotle on Sexual Difference: Metaphysics, Biology, Politics*. Oxford: Oxford University Press.
des Places, Édouard, ed. 1951. *Platon: Les Lois*. 4th ed. Paris: Les Belles lettres.
Diels, H. 1903. *Die Fragmente der Vorsokratiker*. Berlin: Wiedmann.
Diels, Hermann, and Walther Kranz. 1952. *Die Fragmente der Vorsokratiker*. 2 vols. 6th ed. Berlin: Weidmann.
Dihle, Albrecht. 1968. *Der Kanon Der Zwei Tugenden*. Cologne: Westdeutscher Verlag.
Dilcher, Roman. 1995. *Studies in Heraclitus*. Hildesheim: Georg Olms Verlag.
Dilcher, Roman. 2013. "How Not to Conceive Heraclitean Harmony." In *Doctrine and Doxography: Studies on Heraclitus and Pythagoras*, edited by David Sider and Dirk Obbink. Berlin: De Gruyter, 263–80.
Dillon, John, and Jackson P. Hershbell. 1991. *Iamblichus: On the Pythagorean Way of Life*. Society of Biblical Literature. Atlanta, GA: Scholars Press.
Dillon, John M., and Wolfgang Polleichtner. 2009. *Iamblichus of Chalcis: The Letters*. Society of Biblical Literature. Atlanta, GA: Scholars Press.
Dodds, E. R. 1925. "The ΑΙΔΩΣ of Phaedra and the Meaning of the *Hippolytus*." *Classical Review* 39: 102–4.
Dodds, E. R. 1959. *Plato: Gorgias*. Oxford: Oxford University Press.
Dodds, E. R. 1960. *Euripides: Bacchae*. 2nd ed. Oxford: Clarendon Press.
Donato, Marco. 2018. "[Platone] *Erissia, o Sulla Ricchezza*: Introduzione, Testo Critico, Traduzione e Commento." Ph.D. diss., Université Paris Sciences et Lettres.
Donlan, Walter. 1973. "The Tradition of Anti-Aristocratic Thought in Early Greek Poetry." *Historia* 22: 145–54.
Donlan, Walter. 1980. *The Aristocratic Ideal in Ancient Greece*. Lawrence, KS: Coronado Press.
Donovan, B. R. 2003. "The Do-It-Yourselfer in Plato's *Republic*." *American Journal of Philology* 124: 1–18.
Dorandi, Tiziano. 1996. "Ricerche Sulla Trasmissione Delle *Divisioni Aristoteliche*." In *Polyhistor: Studies in the History of Historiography of Ancient Philosophy*, edited by K. A. Algra, P. W. van der Horst, and David T. Runia. Leiden: Brill, 145–65.
Dorandi, Tiziano. 2011. "Le Leidensis BPG 67C et l'histoire du texte des *Divisiones quae vulgo dicuntur Aristoteleae*." *Mnemosyne* 64: 632–38.

Dorandi, Tiziano. 2013. *Diogenes Laertius: Lives of Eminent Philosophers*. Cambridge: Cambridge University Press.

Dorandi, Tiziano, and Issam Marjani. 2017. "La Tradizione Siriaca e Araba delle Cosiddette *Divisiones Aristoteleae* Analisi e Commento della Versione Siriaca (Ed. Brock) e delle Due Traduzioni Arabe (Ed. Kellermann-Rost)." *Studia graeco-arabica* 7: 1–55.

Dorion, Louis-André. 2003. "*Akrasia* et *enkrateia* dans les *Mémorables* de Xénophon." *Dialogue* 42: 645–72.

Dorion, Louis-André. 2007. "Plato and *Enkrateia*." In *Akrasia in Greek Philosophy*, edited by Christopher Bobonich and Pierre Destrée. Leiden: Brill, 119–38.

Dorion, Louis-André. 2008. "Herakles entre Prodicos et Xenophon." *Philosophie Antique* 8: 85–114.

Dorion, Louis-André. 2011. "The Rise and Fall of the Socratic Problem." In *The Cambridge Companion to Socrates*, edited by Donald Morrison. Cambridge: Cambridge University Press, 1–23.

Dorion, Louis-André. 2012. "*Enkrateia* and the Partition of the Soul in the *Gorgias*." In *Plato and the Divided Self*, edited by Rachel Barney, Tad Brennan, and Charles Brittain. Cambridge: Cambridge University Press, 33–52.

Dorion, Louis-André. 2018. "*Enkrateia* et Partition de l'âme chez Platon." *Revue de Philosophie Ancienne* 36: 153–213.

Dover, Kenneth J. 1968. *Aristophanes: Clouds*. Oxford: Clarendon Press.

Dover, Kenneth J. 1974. *Greek Popular Morality in the Time of Plato and Aristotle*. Berkeley: University of California Press.

Dover, Kenneth J. 1989. *Greek Homosexuality*. Rev. ed. Cambridge, MA: Harvard University Press.

During, Lisabeth. 2021. "Virginity and Terror: Reading *Hippolytus*." In *The Chastity Plot*. Chicago: University of Chicago Press, 57–86.

Dutsch, Dorota M. 2020. *Pythagorean Women Philosophers: Between Belief and Suspicion*. Oxford: Oxford University Press.

Ebrey, David. 2017. "The Asceticism of the *Phaedo*: Pleasure, Purification, and the Soul's Proper Activity." *Archiv für Geschichte der Philosophie* 99: 1–30.

Edmunds, Lowell. 1975. "Thucydides' Ethics as Reflected in the Description of Stasis (3.82–83)." *Harvard Studies in Classical Philology* 79: 73–92.

Ehrenberg, Victor. 1947. "*Polypragmosyne*: A Study in Greek Politics." *Journal of Hellenic Studies* 67: 46.

Einarson, Benedict Seneca. 1927. "The Meaning of Sophrosyne." M.A. thesis, University of Chicago.

Else, Gerald. 1969. Review of North 1966. *American Journal of Philology* 90: 360–65.

Elster, Jon. 1984. *Ulysses and the Sirens: Studies in Rationality and Irrationality*. Rev. ed. Cambridge: Cambridge University Press.

England, E. B. 1921. *Plato: The Laws*. 2 vols. Manchester: Manchester University Press.

Ewegen, S. Montgomery. 2014. *Plato's Cratylus: The Comedy of Language*. Bloomington: Indiana University Press.

Fantuzzi, Marco. 2010. "Typologies of Variation on a Theme in Archaic and Classical Metrical Inscriptions." In *Archaic and Classical Greek Epigram*, edited by Manuel Baumbach, Andrej Petrovic, and Ivana Petrovic. Cambridge: Cambridge University Press, 289–310.

Ferrari, G. R. F. 2003. *City and Soul in Plato's Republic*. Sankt Augustin: Academia Verlag.
Ferrari, G. R. F., and Tom Griffith. 2000. *Plato: The Republic*. Cambridge: Cambridge University Press.
Festugière, André-Jean. 1954. *Personal Religion among the Greeks*. Sather Classical Lectures. Berkeley: University of California Press.
Fisher, N. R. E. 1992. *Hybris: A Study in the Values of Honour and Shame in Ancient Greece*. Warminster: Aris & Phillips.
Fisher, R. K. 1984. *Aristophanes' Clouds: Purpose and Technique*. Amsterdam: Adolf M. Hakkert.
Fitton, J. W. 1967. "Barrett's *Hippolytus*—A Review." *Pegasus: University of Exeter Classical Society Magazine* 8: 17–43.
Ford, Andrew. 2008. "The Beginnings of Dialogue: Socratic Discourses and Fourth-Century Prose." In *The End of Dialogue in Antiquity*, edited by Simon Goldhill. Cambridge: Cambridge University Press, 29–44.
Forster, Michael. 2006. "Socrates' Demand for Definitions." *Oxford Studies in Ancient Philosophy* 31: 1–47.
Fortenbaugh, William W. 1983. *Arius Didymus: On Stoic and Peripatetic Ethics*. New Brunswick, NJ: Transaction.
Fortenbaugh, William W. 2011. *Theophrastus of Eresus: Commentary*. Vol. 6.1: *Sources on Ethics*. New Brunswick, NJ: Transaction.
Fortenbaugh, William W. 2014. *Theophrastus of Eresus: Commentary*. Vol. 9.2: *Sources on Discoveries and Beginnings, Proverbs et al. (Texts 727–741)*. Leiden: Brill.
Fortenbaugh, William W. 2015a. "Aristotle on Women: *Politics* i 13.1260a13." *Ancient Philosophy* 35: 395–404.
Fortenbaugh, William W. 2015b. "On *Problemata* 3: Wine-Drinking and Drunkenness." In *The Aristotelian Problemata Physica*, edited by Robert Mayhew. Leiden: Brill, 100–123.
Foucault, Michel. 1985. *The History of Sexuality*, vol. 2: *The Use of Pleasure*. Translated by Robert Hurley. New York: Vintage Books.
Fränkel, Hermann. 1975. *Early Greek Poetry and Philosophy: A History of Greek Epic, Lyric, and Prose to the Middle of the Fifth Century*. Oxford: Basil Blackwell.
Frey, Jennifer A. 2022. "Temperance: Self-Control or Self-Possession." In *Neglected Virtues*, edited by Glen Pettigrove and Christine Swanton. Routledge Studies in Ethics and Moral Theory. New York: Routledge, 200–222.
Freydberg, Bernard. 2008. *Philosophy and Comedy: Aristophanes, Logos, and Erōs*. Bloomington: Indiana University Press.
Friedländer, Paul. 1948. *Epigrammata: Greek Inscriptions in Verse from the Beginnings to the Persian Wars*. Berkeley: University of California Press.
Friedländer, Paul. 1964. *Plato 2*. Translated by Hans Meyerhoff. Princeton, NJ: Princeton University Press.
Friis Johansen, Karsten. 1991. "A Poem by Theognis (Thgn. 19–38)." *Classica et mediaevalia* 42: 5–37.
Frisk, Hjalmar. 1954. *Griechisches Etymologisches Wörterbuch*. Heidelberg: Winter.
Fronterotta, Francesco. 2013. *Eraclito: Frammenti*. Milan: BUR Classici greci e latini.
Fuks, Alexander. 1953. *The Ancestral Constitution: Four Studies in Athenian Party Politics at the End of the Fifth Century B.C.* London: Routledge & Kegan Paul.
Gagarin, Michael 1997. *Antiphon: The Speeches*. Cambridge: Cambridge University Press.

Gallop, David. 1975. *Plato: Phaedo*. Oxford: Clarendon Press.
Gallop, David. 1989. "The Riddles of Heraclitus." In *Ionian Philosophy*, edited by K. J. Boudouris. Athens: International Association for Greek Philosophy and International Center for Greek Philosophy and Culture, 123–35.
Garver, Eugene. 2018. "*Charmides* and the Virtue of Opacity: An Early Chapter in the History of the Individual." *Review of Metaphysics* 71: 469–500.
Gastaldi, Sylvia. 2021. "La Sophrosyne dal *Gorgia* alla *Repubblica*: I Piaceri e la Felicità di un'Anima Ordinata." In *Platone e Il Governo Delle Passioni: Studi per Linda Napolitano*, edited by Francesco Benoni and Alessandro Stavru. Perugia: Aguaplano, 91–105.
Gauthier, René Antoine, and Jean Yves Jolif. 1959. *Aristote: L'Éthique à Nicomaque: Introduction, Traduction et Commentaire*. Louvain: Publications Universitaires de Louvain.
Geach, Peter. 1977. *The Virtues*. Cambridge: Cambridge University Press.
Gemelli Marciano, M. Laura. 2014. "The Pythagorean Way of Life and Pythagorean Ethics." In *A History of Pythagoreanism*, edited by Carl A. Huffman. Cambridge: Cambridge University Press, 131–48.
Gemoll, Wilhelm., and J. Peters. 1968. *Xenophontis: Institutio Cyri*. Rev. ed.. Leipzig: Teubner.
Gerber, Douglas. 1999. *Greek Elegiac Poetry: From the Seventh to the Fifth Centuries B.C.* Loeb Classical Library. Cambridge, MA: Harvard University Press.
Gerson, Lloyd. 2020. Review of Huffman 2019. *Bryn Mawr Classical Review*. https://bmcr.brynmawr.edu/2020/2020.10.43/.
Gifford, Mark. 2001. "Dramatic Dialectic in *Republic* Book 1." *Oxford Studies in Ancient Philosophy* 20: 35–106.
Gill, Christopher. 1990. "The Articulation of the Self in Euripides' *Hippolytus*." In *Euripides, Women, and Sexuality*, edited by Anthon Powell. London: Routledge, 76–109.
Gill, Christopher. 1995. *Personality in Greek Epic, Tragedy, and Philosophy: The Self in Dialogue*. Oxford: Clarendon Press.
Gill, Christopher. 2005. "Tragic Fragments, Ancient Philosophers and the Fragmented Self." In *Lost Dramas of Classical Athens: Greek Tragic Fragments*, edited by Fiona McHardy, James Robson, and David Harvey. Exeter: University of Exeter Press, 151–72.
Gill, Christopher. 2008. "The Ancient Self—Where Now?" *Antiquorum Philosophia* 2: 77–99.
Giudice Rizzo, Innocenza. 2007. "Euripides, *Bacchae* 996–1104." In *Il Greco, Il Barbaro e La Ceramica Attica: Immaginario del Diverso, Processi di Scambio e Autorappresentazione degli Indigeni: Atti del Convegno Internazionale di Studi, 14–19 Maggio 2001, Catania, Caltanissetta, Gela, Camarina, Vittoria, Siracusa*, edited by Filippo Giudice and Rosalba Panvini. Rome: L'Erma di Bretschneider, 181–86.
Glazebrook, Allison. 2009. "Cosmetics and *Sôphrosunê*: Ischomachos' Wife in Xenophon's *Oikonomikos*." *Classical World* 102: 233–48.
Gold, Barbara K. 1977. "Εὐκοσμία in Euripides' *Bacchae*." *American Journal of Philology* 98: 3–15.
Goldhill, Simon. 1986. *Reading Greek Tragedy*. Cambridge: Cambridge University Press.
González González, Marta. 2019. *Funerary Epigrams of Ancient Greece: Reflections on Literature, Society and Religion*. New York: Bloomsbury Academic.
Gosling, J. C. B., and C. C. W. Taylor. 1982. *The Greeks on Pleasure*. Oxford: Clarendon Press.

Gotteland, Sophie. 2018. "Critias dans la Seconde Sophistique et les Traités des Rhéteurs." In *La Muse au Long Couteau: Critias, de La Création Littéraire au Terrorisme d'État: Actes du Colloque International de Bordeaux, Les 23 et 24 Octobre 2009*, edited by Jean Yvonneau. Bordeaux: Ausonius Éditions, 179–96.

Gottesman, Alex. 2020. "The Sōphrosynē of Critias: Aristocratic Ethics after the Thirty Tyrants." In *Early Greek Ethics*, edited by David Wolfsdorf. Oxford: Oxford University Press, 243–61.

Gottlieb, Paula. 2009. *The Virtue of Aristotle's Ethics*. Cambridge: Cambridge University Press.

Gray, Vivienne. 2006. "The Linguistic Philosophies of Prodicus in Xenophon's 'Choice of Heracles'?" *Classical Quarterly* 56: 426–35.

Gray, Vivienne. 2007. *Xenophon on Government*. Cambridge: Cambridge University Press.

Green, William Charles. 1868. *Aristophanes: The Clouds*. London: Rivingtons.

Griffith, Mark. 1990. "Contest and Contradiction in Early Greek Poetry." In *Cabinet of the Muses: Essays on Classical and Comparative Literature in Honor of Thomas G. Rosenmeyer*, edited by Mark Griffith and Donald J. Mastronarde. Atlanta, GA: Scholars Press, 185–207.

Grote, George. 1852. *A History of Greece*. Vol. 8. London: John Murray.

Guthrie, Kenneth Sylvan. 1987. *The Pythagorean Sourcebook and Library: An Anthology of Ancient Writings Which Relate to Pythagoras and Pythagorean Philosophy*, edited by David R. Fideler. Grand Rapids, MI: Phanes Press.

Guthrie, W. K. C. 1962. *A History of Greek Philosophy*. Vol. 1: *The Presocratic Tradition from Parmenides to Democritus*. Cambridge: Cambridge University Press.

Guthrie, W. K. C. 1971. *The Sophists*. Cambridge: Cambridge: University Press.

Guthrie, W. K. C. 1975. *A History of Greek Philosophy*. Vol. 4: *Plato, the Man and His Dialogues, Earlier Period*. Cambridge: Cambridge University Press.

Habash, Justin. 2019. "Heraclitus and the Riddle of Nature." *Epoché* 23: 275–86.

Habib, Khalil M. 2014. "The Meaning of Socrates' Asceticism in Aristophanes' *Clouds*." In *The Political Theory of Aristophanes: Explorations in Poetic Wisdom*, edited by Jeremy J. Mhire and Bryan-Paul Frost. Albany, NY: SUNY Press, 29–45.

Hackforth, R. 1913. "The Modification of Plan in Plato's *Republic*." *Classical Quarterly* 7: 265–72.

Halleran, Michael R. 1995. *Euripides: Hippolytus*. Warminster: Aris & Phillips.

Hamilton, Edith, and Huntington Cairns. 1961. *The Collected Dialogues of Plato, Including the Letters*. Princeton, NJ: Princeton University Press.

Hammond, William A. 1892. *On the Notion of Virtue in the Dialogues of Plato, with Particular Reference to Those of the First Period and to the Third and Fourth Books of the Republic: Inaugural Dissertation*. Boston: Ginn.

Hansen, Peter Allan. 1983. *Carmina epigraphica Graeca*: Vol. 1: *saeculorum VIII-V a. Chr. n.* Berlin: De Gruyter.

Hansen, Peter Allan. 1989. *Carmina epigraphica Graeca*. Vol. 2: *saeculi IV a. Chr. n.* Berlin: De Gruyter.

Harper, Vicki Lynn. 2013. "The Neopythagorean Women as Philosophers." In *Pythagorean Women: Their History and Writings*, edited by Sarah B. Pomeroy. Baltimore, MD: Johns Hopkins University Press, 117–38.

Harris, W. V. 2011. Review of Rademaker 2005. *Gnomon* 83: 115–19.

Haug, Matthew. 2022a. "Resolving Two Tensions in (Neo-)Aristotelian Approaches to Self-Control." *Ethical Theory and Moral Practice* 25: 1–16.

Haug, Matthew. 2022b. "Silencing, Psychological Conflict, and the Distinction between Virtue and Self-Control." *Journal of Ethics* 26: 93–114.
Havelock, E. A. 1969. "*Dikaiosune*: An Essay in Greek Intellectual History." *Phoenix* 23: 49–70.
Hazebroucq, Marie-France. 1997. *La Folie Humaine et Ses Remèdes: Platon, Charmide, ou, De la Modération*. Paris: J. Vrin.
Heidel, W. H. 1913. "On Certain Fragments of the Pre-Socratics: Critical Notes and Elucidations." *Proceedings of the American Academy of Arts and Sciences* 48: 681–734.
Henderson, Jeffrey. 2007. *Aristophanes: Fragments*. Loeb Classical Library. Cambridge, MA: Harvard University Press.
Herman, Gabriel. 2006. *Morality and Behaviour in Democratic Athens: A Social History*. Cambridge: Cambridge University Press.
Herrmann, Fritz-Gregor. 2018a. "Plato and Critias." In *La muse au long couteau: Critias, de la création littéraire au terrorisme d'État: actes du colloque international de Bordeaux, les 23 et 24 octobre 2009*, edited by Jean Yvonneau. Scripta Antiqua. Bordeaux: Ausonius éditions, 83–115.
Herrmann, Fritz-Gregor. 2018b. "Spartan Echoes in Plato's *Republic*." In *The Greek Superpower: Sparta in the Self-Definitions of Athenians*, edited by Paul Cartledge and Anton Powell. Swansea: Classical Press of Wales, 185–214.
Heubeck, Alfred, Stephanie West, and J. B. Hainsworth. 1988. *A Commentary on Homer's Odyssey*. Vol. 1. Oxford: Clarendon Press.
Higgins, W. E. 1977. *Xenophon the Athenian: The Problem of the Individual and the Society of the Polis*. Albany: State University of New York Press.
Hirzel, Rudolf. 1874. "Über den Unterschied der Δικαιοσύνη und der Σωφροσύνη in der Platonischen Republik." *Hermes* 8: 379–411.
Horky, Phillip Sidney. (Forthcoming). *Pythagorean Philosophy, 250 BCE to 200 CE: An Introduction and Collection of Sources in Translation*. Cambridge: Cambridge University Press.
Hornblower, Simon. 1991. *A Commentary on Thucydides*. Vol. 1: *Books I–III*. Oxford: Oxford University Press.
Housman, A. E. 1888. "ΣΩΦΡΟΝΗ." *Classical Review* 2: 242–45.
Howland, Jacob. 2018. *Glaucon's Fate: History, Myth, and Character in Plato's Republic*. Philadelphia, PA: Paul Dry Books.
Huffman, Carl A. 2002. "Archytas and the Sophists." In *Presocratic Philosophy: Essays in Honour of Alexander Mourelatos*, edited by Victor Caston and Daniel W. Graham. Aldershot: Ashgate, 251–70.
Huffman, Carl A. 2005. *Archytas of Tarentum: Pythagorean, Philosopher, and Mathematician King*. Cambridge: Cambridge University Press.
Huffman, Carl A. 2008. "Heraclitus' Critique of Pythagoras' Enquiry in Fragment 129." *Oxford Studies in Ancient Philosophy* 35: 19–47.
Huffman, Carl A. 2014. "The Peripatetics on the Pythagoreans." In *A History of Pythagoreanism*, edited by Carl A. Huffman. Cambridge: Cambridge University Press, 274–95.
Huffman, Carl A. 2019. *Aristoxenus of Tarentum: The Pythagorean Precepts (How to Live a Pythagorean Life): An Edition of and Commentary on the Fragments with an Introduction*. Cambridge: Cambridge University Press.
Hug, Arnoldus. 1876. *Platons Symposion*. Leipzig: Teubner.
Hug, Arnoldus. 1883. *Xenophon: Cyropaedia*. Leipzig: Teubner.

Huizenga, Annette Bourland. 2010. "*Sophrosyne* for Women in Pythagorean Texts." In *Women and Gender in Ancient Religions: Interdisciplinary Approaches*, edited by Stephen P. Ahearne-Kroll, Paul A. Holloway, and James A. Kelhoffer. Wissenschaftliche Untersuchungen zum Neuen Testament. Tübingen: Mohr Siebeck, 379–400.

Hülsz Piccone, Enrique. 2013. "Heraclitus on Logos: Language, Rationality, and the Real." In *Doctrine and Doxography: Studies on Heraclitus and Pythagoras*, edited by David Sider and Dirk Obbink. Berlin: De Gruyter, 281–301.

Humble, Noreen. 1999. "*Sôphrosunê* and the Spartans in Xenophon." In *Sparta: New Perspectives*, edited by Stephen Hodkinson and Anton Powell. London: Duckworth, 339–52.

Humble, Noreen. 2021. *Xenophon of Athens: A Socratic on Sparta*. Cambridge: Cambridge University Press.

Humphreys, S. C. 2018. *Kinship in Ancient Athens: An Anthropological Analysis*. 2 vols. Oxford: Oxford University Press.

Hunter, R. L. 2022. *Greek Epitaphic Poetry: A Selection*. Cambridge Greek and Latin Classics. Cambridge: Cambridge University Press.

Hussey, E. 1999. "Heraclitus." In *The Cambridge Companion to Early Greek Philosophy*, edited by Anthony A. Long. Cambridge: Cambridge University Press, 88–112.

Hutchinson, D. S. 1986. *The Virtues of Aristotle*. London: Routledge & Kegan Paul.

Hutchinson, D. S. 1997. "Introduction to *Alcibiades*." In *Plato: Complete Works*, edited by John Cooper. Indianapolis, IN: Hackett, 557–58.

Hutchinson, D. S., and Monte Ransome Johnson. 2005. "Authenticating Aristotle's *Protrepticus*." *Oxford Studies in Ancient Philosophy* 29: 193–294.

Ireland, S., and F. L. D. Steel. 1975. "Φρένες as an Anatomical Organ in the Works of Homer." *Glotta* 54: 183–95.

Irwin, Terence. 1977. *Plato's Moral Theory: The Early and Middle Dialogues*. Oxford: Clarendon Press.

Irwin, Terence. 1979. *Plato: Gorgias*. Oxford: Oxford University Press.

Irwin, Terence. 1984. *Aristotle: Nicomachean Ethics*. Indianapolis, IN: Hackett.

Irwin, Terence. 1995. *Plato's Ethics*. Oxford: Oxford University Press.

Jaeger, Werner. 1965. *Paideia: The Ideals of Greek Culture*. 2nd ed. Translated by Gilbert Highet. Oxford: Oxford University.

Jeremiah, Edward T. 2012. *The Emergence of Reflexivity in Greek Language and Thought: From Homer to Plato and Beyond*. Leiden: Brill.

Jirsa, Jakub. 2009. "Authenticity of the *Alcibiades* I: Some Reflections." *Listy filologické* 132: 225–44.

Johnson, David M. 2005. "Xenophon at His Most Socratic (*Memorabilia* 4.2)." *Oxford Studies in Ancient Philosophy* 29: 39–73.

Johnson, David M. 2006. Review of Rademaker 2005. *Ancient Philosophy* 26: 401–4.

Johnson, David M. 2019. "Xenophon's Socrates and the Socratic Xenophon." In *Brill's Companion to the Reception of Socrates*, edited by Christopher Moore. Leiden: Brill, 150–70.

Johnson, David M. 2020. "Self-Mastery, Piety, and Reciprocity in Xenophon's Ethics." In *Early Greek Ethics*, edited by David Wolfsdorf. Oxford: Oxford University Press, 412–31.

Johnson, David M. 2021. *Xenophon's Socratic Works*. Abingdon: Routledge.

Johnson, Monte Ransome. 2020. "The Ethical Maxims of Democritus of Abdera." In *Early Greek Ethics*, edited by David Wolfsdorf. Oxford: Oxford University Press, 211–42.

Johnstone, Mark. 2014. "On 'Logos' in Heraclitus." *Oxford Studies in Ancient Philosophy* 47: 1–29.
Johnstone, Mark. 2020. "On the Ethical Dimension of Heraclitus' Thought." In *Early Greek Ethics*, edited by David Wolfsdorf. Oxford: Oxford University Press, 37–53.
Jones, Russell E., and Ravi Sharma. 2018. "Virtue and Self-Interest in Xenophon's *Memorabilia* 3.9.4–5." *Classical Quarterly* 68: 79–90.
Jowett, Benjamin. 1881. *Thucydides Translated into English: With Introduction, Marginal Analysis, Notes, and Indices*. Vol. 1. Oxford: Clarendon Press.
Kahn, Charles H. 1976. "Plato on the Unity of the Virtues." In *Facets of Plato's Philosophy*, edited by W. H. Werkmeister. Assen: Van Gorcum, 21–39.
Kahn, Charles H. 1979. *The Art and Thought of Heraclitus: An Edition of the Fragments with Translation and Commentary*. Cambridge: Cambridge University Press.
Kahn, Charles H. 1985. "Democritus and the Origins of Moral Psychology." *American Journal of Philology* 106: 1–31.
Kahn, Charles H. 1996. *Plato and the Socratic Dialogue: The Philosophical Use of a Literary Form*. Cambridge: Cambridge University Press.
Kamtekar, Rachana. 2004. "What's the Good of Agreeing? *Homonoia* in Platonic Politics." *Oxford Studies in Ancient Philosophy* 26: 131–70.
Kamtekar, Rachana. 2021. "Weaving Together Natural Courage and Moderation: 305e8–308b9." In *Plato's Statesman: A Philosophical Discussion*, edited by Panos Dimas, Melissa Lane, and Susan Sauvé Meyer. Oxford: Oxford University Press, 217–38.
Kennell, Nigel M. 1995. *The Gymnasium of Virtue: Education and Culture in Ancient Sparta*. Chapel Hill: University of North Carolina Press.
Kirk, Gregory. 2016. "Self-Knowledge and Ignorance in Plato's *Charmides*." *Ancient Philosophy* 36: 303–20.
Kirk, Gregory S. 1962. *Heraclitus: The Cosmic Fragments*. Cambridge: Cambridge University Press.
Kirk, Gregory S., J. E. Raven, and Malcolm Schofield. 1983. *The Presocratic Philosophers: A Critical History with a Selection of Texts*. 2nd ed. Cambridge: Cambridge University Press.
Kleve, Knut. 1989. "The Stolen Mantle in the *Clouds*." *Symbolae Osloenses* 64: 74–90.
Knox, Bernard M. W. 1952. "The *Hippolytus* of Euripides." *Yale Classical Studies* 13: 3–31.
Kollmann, Albrecht. 1941. "*Sophrosyne*." *Wiener Studien* 59: 12–34.
Konkoly, Damian G. 1998. "Is Temperance Ever Properly Painful?" *The Paideia Archive: Twentieth World Congress of Philosophy* 3: 168–76.
Korsgaard, Christine M. 1999. "Self-Constitution in the Ethics of Plato and Kant." *Journal of Ethics* 3: 1–29.
Korsgaard, Christine M. 2009. *Self-Constitution: Agency, Identity, and Integrity*. Oxford: Oxford University Press.
Kosman, Aryeh. 1983. "*Sôphrosunê* as Quietness." In *Essays in Ancient Greek Philosophy*, Vol. 2, edited by John P. Anton and Anthony Preus. Albany: State University of New York Press, 203–16.
Kosman, Aryeh. 2007. "Justice and Virtue: The *Republic*'s Inquiry into Proper Difference." In *The Cambridge Companion to Plato's Republic*, edited by G. R. F. Ferrari. Cambridge: Cambridge University Press, 116–37.
Kosman, Aryeh. 2020. "Self-Knowledge and Self-Control in the *Charmides*." In *Self-Knowledge: Proceedings of the Keeling Colloquium*, edited by Fiona Leigh. Leiden: Brill, 71–86.

Kovacs, David. 1980. "Shame, Pleasure, and Honor in Phaedra's Great Speech (Euripides, *Hippolytus* 375–87)." *American Journal of Philology* 101: 287–303.

Kovacs, David. 1986. "On Medea's Great Monologue (E. *Med.* 1021–80)." *Classical Quarterly* 36: 343–52.

Kovacs, David. 1995. *Euripides: Children of Heracles: Hippolytus; Andromache; Hecuba*. Loeb Classical Library. Cambridge, MA: Harvard University Press.

Kovacs, David. 2002. *Euripides: Bacchae, Iphigenia at Aulis, Rhesus*. Loeb Classical Library. Cambridge, MA: Harvard University Press.

Kovacs, David. 2003. *Euripidea Tertia*. Leiden: Brill.

Kraut, Richard. 2006. *The Blackwell Guide to Aristotle's Nicomachean Ethics*. Malden, MA: Blackwell.

Kunsemüller, Otto Gottlieb Gustav Gerhard. 1935. "Die Herkunft Der Platonischen Kardinaltugenden." Inaugural diss., University of Erlangen.

Kurke, Leslie. 2011. *Aesopic Conversations: Popular Tradition, Cultural Dialogue, and the Invention of Greek Prose*. Princeton, NJ: Princeton University Press.

Lake, Patrick K. 2018. "Plato's Homer as a Guide for Moderation and Obedience." In *Homer and the Good Ruler in Antiquity and Beyond*, edited by Jacqueline Klooster and Baukje van den Berg. Leiden: Brill, 86–103.

Laks, André. 2000. "The *Laws*." In *The Cambridge History of Greek and Roman Political Thought*, edited by Christopher Rowe and Malcolm Schofield. Cambridge: Cambridge University Press, 258–92.

Laks, André. 2022. *Plato's Second Republic: An Essay on the Laws*. Princeton: Princeton University Press.

Laks, André, and Glenn W. Most. 2016. *Early Greek Philosophy*. 9 vols. Loeb Classical Library. Cambridge, MA: Harvard University Press.

Lambropoulou, Voula. 1995. "Some Pythagorean Female Virtues." In *Women in Antiquity: New Assessments*, edited by Richard Hawley and Barbara Levick. London: Routledge, 122–34.

Lampert, Laurence. 2010. *How Philosophy Became Socratic: A Study of Plato's Protagoras, Charmides, and Republic*. Chicago: University of Chicago Press.

Lane, Melissa S. 1998. *Method and Politics in Plato's Statesman*. Cambridge: Cambridge University Press.

Larson, Curtis W. R. 1951. "The Platonic Synonyms, *Dikaiosunê* and *Sôphrosunê*." *American Journal of Philology* 72: 395.

Lateiner, Donald. 1982. "The Man Who Does Not Meddle in Politics: A *Topos* in Lysias." *Classical World* 76: 1–12.

Lattimore, Steven. 1998. *Thucydides: The Peloponnesian War*. Indianapolis, IN: Hackett.

Lebedev, A. V. 2014. Логос Гераклита: Реконструкции Мысли и Слова (с Новым Критическим Изданием Фрагментов) [*The Logos of Heraclitus: A Reconstruction of His Thought and Word (with a New Critical Edition of the Fragments)*]. St. Petersburg: Nauka.

Lefkowitz, Mary R., and Maureen B. Fant. 1992. *Women's Life in Greece and Rome: A Source Book in Translation*. 2nd ed. Baltimore, MD: Johns Hopkins University Press.

Lesher, James H. 1981. "Perceiving and Knowing in the *Iliad* and *Odyssey*." *Phronesis* 26: 2–24.

Lesher, James H. 1983. "Heraclitus' Epistemological Vocabulary." *Hermes* 111: 155–170.

Lesher, James H. 1994. "The Emergence of Philosophical Interest in Cognition." *Oxford Studies in Ancient Philosophy* 12: 1–34.

Lesher, James H. 2016. "Verbs for Knowing in Heraclitus' Rebuke of Hesiod (DK 22B57)." *Ancient Philosophy* 36: 1–12.

Leunissen, Mariska. 2017. *From Natural Character to Moral Virtue in Aristotle.* Oxford: Oxford University Press.

Lienemann, Béatrice. 2021. "Aristotle on the Rationality of Women: Consequences for Virtue and Practical Accountability." In *State and Nature*, edited by Peter Adamson and Christof Rapp. Berlin: De Gruyter, 135–56.

Linforth, Ivan M. 1914. "Hippolytus and Humanism." *Transactions and Proceedings of the American Philological Association* 45: 5–16.

Lipka, Michael. 2002. *Xenophon's Spartan Constitution: Introduction, Text, Commentary.* Berlin: De Gruyter.

Lobo, Jenifer Anne. 2006. "Theoretical and Practical Dimensions of *Sophrosyne* in Plato's *Charmides* and *Republic*." *De Philosophia* 19: 47–58.

Long, Alex G. 2008. "Wisdom in Heraclitus." *Oxford Studies in Ancient Philosophy* 33: 1–18.

Long, Anthony A. 2001. "Ancient Philosophy's Hardest Question: What to Make of Oneself?" *Representations* 74: 19–36.

Long, Anthony A. 2009. "Heraclitus on Measure and the Explicit Emergence of Rationality." In *Body and Soul in Ancient Philosophy*, edited by Dorothea Frede and Burkhard Reis. Berlin: De Gruyter, 87–110.

Lorch, Benjamin. 2009. "Moderation and Socratic Education in Xenophon's *Memorabilia*." *Polis* 26: 185–203.

Lorch, Benjamin. 2012. "The Choice of Lives and the Virtue of Moderation." *Interpretation* 39: 235–52.

Lorenz, Hendrik. 2006. *The Brute Within: Appetitive Desire in Plato and Aristotle.* Oxford: Clarendon Press.

Lorenz, Hendrik. 2009. "Virtue of Character in Aristotle's *Nicomachean Ethics*." *Oxford Studies in Ancient Philosophy* 37: 177–212.

Lougovaya-Ast, Julia. 2004. "An Historical Study of Athenian Verse Epitaphs from the Sixth through the Fourth Centuries BC." Ph.D. diss., University of Toronto.

Luccioni, Jean. 1953. *Xénophon et Le Socratisme.* Paris: Presses Universitaires de France.

Lynch, Tosca. 2017. "The Symphony of Temperance in *Republic* 4: Musical Imagery and Practical Models." *Greek and Roman Musical Studies* 5: 18–34.

MacDowell, Douglas M. 1976. "Hybris in Athens." *Greece and Rome* 23: 14–31.

MacDowell, Douglas M. 1995. *Aristophanes and Athens: An Introduction to the Plays.* Oxford: Oxford University Press.

MacIntyre, Alasdair. 1988. "*Sōphrosunē*: How a Virtue Can Become Socially Disruptive." *Midwest Studies in Philosophy* 31: 1–11.

Mackenzie, M. M. 1988. "Heraclitus and the Art of Paradox." *Oxford Studies in Ancient Philosophy* 6: 1–37.

Manuwald, Bernd. 2003. "Tugend und Wissen in Platons *Gorgias*: Zu *Grg*. 506d–507c." *Rheinisches Museum für Philologie* 146: 291–302.

Manuwald, Bernd. 2013. "Protagoras' Myth in Plato's *Protagoras*: Fiction or Testimony?" In *Protagoras of Abdera: The Man, His Measure*, edited by J. M. Van Ophuijsen, Marlein Van Raalte, and Peter Stork. Philosophia Antiqua. Leiden: Brill, 163–78.

Marchant. E. C. 1901. *Xenophontis Opera Omnia*, Vol. 2, *Commentarii; Oeconomicus; Convivium; Apologia Socratis.* Oxford: Clarendon Press.

Marchant, E. C. 1905. *Commentary on Thucydides Book 1.* London: Macmillan.

Marchant, E. C., and O. J. Todd. 1923. *Xenophon: Memorabilia, Oeconomicus, Symposium, Apology*. Loeb Classical Library. Cambridge, MA: Harvard University Press.
Marcovich, Miroslav. 1967. *Heraclitus: Greek Text*. Merida: Los Andes University Press.
Marcovich, Miroslav. 1999. *Diogenes Laertius: Vitae philosophorum*. Leipzig: Teubner.
Marechal, Patricia. 2021. "Temperance and Epistemic Purity in Plato's Phaedo." *Archiv für Geschichte der Philosophie*. https://doi.org/10.1515/agph-2021-0047.
Martin, Richard. 1993. "The Seven Sages as Performers of Wisdom." In *The Cultures within Ancient Greek Culture: Contact, Conflict, Collaboration*, edited by Carol Dougherty and Leslie Kurke. Cambridge: Cambridge University Press, 108–28.
Mastronarde, Donald J. 2002. *Euripides: Medea*. Cambridge: Cambridge University Press.
Mayhew, Robert. 1999. "Behavior Unbecoming a Woman: Aristotle's *Poetics* 15 and Euripides' *Melanippe the Wise*." *Ancient Philosophy* 19: 89–104.
Mayhew, Robert. 2012. *Prodicus the Sophist: Text, Translation, and Commentary*. Oxford: Oxford University Press.
McCabe, Mary Margaret. 2015. "From the Cradle to the Cave: What Happened to Self-Knowledge in the *Republic*?" In *Platonic Conversations*. Oxford: Oxford University Press, 208–27.
McGibbon, Donal. 1960. "Pleasure as the 'Criterion' in Democritus." *Phronesis* 5: 75–77.
Meijer, P. A. 2017. *A New Perspective on Antisthenes: Logos, Predicate and Ethics in His Philosophy*. Amsterdam: Amsterdam University Press.
Menn, Stephen. 2005. "On Plato's ΠΟΛΙΤΕΙΑ." In *Proceedings of Boston Area Colloquium on Ancient Philosophy*, edited by John J. Cleary and Gary M. Gurtler. Vol. 21, 1–55.
Menn, Stephen. 2013. "Plato's Soteriology?" In *Philosophy and Salvation in Greek Religion*, edited by Vishwa Adluri. Berlin: De Gruyter, 191–216.
Meunier, Mario. 1932. *Femmes Pythagoriciennes. Fragments et Lettres de Théano, Périctioné, Phintys, Mélissa et Myia. Traduction Nouvelle avec Prolégomènes et Notes*. Paris: L'Artisan du Livre.
Meyer, Susan Sauvé. 2015. *Plato: Laws 1 and 2*. Oxford: Oxford University Press.
Meyer, Susan Sauvé. 2018. "Self-Mastery and Self-Rule in Plato's *Laws*." In *Virtue, Happiness, Knowledge: Themes from the Work of Gail Fine and Terence Irwin*, edited by David O. Brink, Susan Sauvé Meyer, and Christopher Shields. Oxford: Oxford University Press, 97–109.
Meynersen, O. 1993. "Der Manteldiebstahl Des Sokrates (Ar. *Nub*. 175-9)." *Mnemosyne* 46: 18–32.
Miller, P. L. 2011. *Becoming God: Pure Reason in Early Greek Philosophy*. London: Continuum.
Molinelli, Sebastion. 2019. "Simon the Athenian: Archaeological, Sociological and Philosophical Remarks on a Philosopher Shoemaker." In *Shoes, Slippers and Sandals: Feet and Footwear in Classical Antiquity*, edited by Sadie Pickup and Sally Waite. Abingdon: Routledge, 133–42.
Moore, Christopher. 2011. "Socratic Persuasion in the *Crito*." *British Journal for the History of Philosophy* 19: 1021–46.
Moore, Christopher. 2012. "Socrates and Clitophon in the Platonic *Clitophon*." *Ancient Philosophy* 32: 257–78.
Moore, Christopher. 2015a. "*Promētheia* ('Forethought') until Plato." *American Journal of Philology* 136: 381–420.
Moore, Christopher. 2015b. "Socrates and Self-Knowledge in Aristophanes' *Clouds*." *Classical Quarterly* 65: 534–51.

Moore, Christopher. 2015c. *Socrates and Self-Knowledge*. Cambridge: Cambridge University Press.

Moore, Christopher. 2018a. "Heraclitus and 'Knowing Yourself' (DK 116)." *Ancient Philosophy* 38: 1–21.

Moore, Christopher. 2018b. "Xenophon's Socratic Education in *Memorabilia* Book 4." In *Socrates and the Socratic Dialogue*, edited by Alessandro Stavru and Christopher Moore. Leiden: Brill, 500–520.

Moore, Christopher. 2019a. "Introduction: Socrates' Writing as Writings about Socrates." In *Brill's Companion to the Reception of Socrates*, edited by Christopher Moore. Brill's Companion to Classical Reception. Leiden: Brill, 1–37.

Moore, Christopher. 2019b. "Socrates in Aristotle's History of Philosophy." In *Brill's Companion to the Reception of Socrates*, edited by Christopher Moore. Brill's Companion to Classical Reception. Leiden: Brill, 173–210.

Moore, Christopher. 2020a. "Aristotle's *philosophêmata*." In *Revisiting Aristotle's Fragments: New Essays on the Fragments of Aristotle's Lost Works*, edited by Antonio Pedro Mesquita, Simon Noriega-Olmos, and Christopher Shields. Berlin: De Gruyter, 49–65.

Moore, Christopher. 2020b. *Calling Philosophers Names: On the Origin of a Discipline*. Princeton, NJ: Princeton University Press.

Moore, Christopher. 2021. "*Promêtheia* as Rational Agency in Plato." *Apeiron* 54: 89–107.

Moore, Christopher. 2023. "Xenophon and the Spartan Education in *Sôphrosunê* (*Lac. Pol.* 3)." In *Xenophon Philosopher: Argumentation and Ethics*, edited by Claudia Mársico. Baden-Baden: Nomos Verlag.

Moore, Christopher, and Christopher C. Raymond. 2019. *Plato: Charmides. Translated, with Introduction, Notes, and Analysis*. Indianapolis, IN: Hackett.

Moraux, Paul. 1977. "Témoins méconnus des *Divisiones Aristoteleae*." *L'Antiquité Classique* 46: 100–127.

Morgan, Kathryn A. 2009. "Philosophy at Delphi: Socrates, Sages, and the Circulation of Wisdom." In *Apolline Politics and Poetics*, edited by Lucia Athanassaki, Richard P. Martin, and John F. Miller. Athens: European Cultural Centre of Delphi/Hellenic Ministry of Culture, 549–68.

Morris, Charles D. 1891. *Commentary on Thucydides Book 1*. Boston: Ginn.

Morrison, Donald. 2010. "Xenophon's Socrates on *Sophia* and the Virtues." In *Socratica 2008: Studies in Ancient Socratic Literature*, edited by Livio Rossetti and Alessandro Stavru. Bari: Levante, 227–39.

Morrison, James V. 1999. "Preface to Thucydides: Rereading the Corcyrean Conflict (1.24–55)." *Classical Antiquity* 18: 94–131.

Moseley, Geoffrey. 2018. "Pl. *Leg.* 631c6–7: Textual Gleanings from an Arabic Fragment." *Mnemosyne* 71: 173–76.

Moss, Jessica. 2011. "'Virtue Makes the Goal Right': Virtue and *Phronesis* in Aristotle's Ethics." *Phronesis* 56: 204–61.

Mouraviev, Serge. 2002. *Heraclitea: Édition critique complète des témoignages sur la vie et l'oeuvre d'Héraclite d'Éphèse et des vestiges de son livre*. Vol. III.3.A: *Les vestiges. Les fragments du livre d'Héraclite; le langage de l'Obscur; introduction à la poétique des fragments*. Sankt Augustin: Academia Verlag.

Mras, Karl. 1956. *Eusebius Werke. Achter Band: Die Praeparatio Evangelica, Zweiter Teil: Die Bücher XI bis XV, Register*. Berlin: De Gruyter.

Mueller, Melissa. 2011. "Phaedra's Defixio: Scripting Sophrosune in Euripides' *Hippolytus*." *Classical Antiquity* 30: 148–77.
Munn, Mark. 2000. *The School of History: Athens in the Age of Socrates*. Berkeley: University of California Press.
Murphy, David J. 2013. "Isocrates and the Dialogue." *Classical World* 106: 311–53.
Murray, Gilbert. 1911. *The Rise of the Greek Epic*. 2nd ed. Cambridge: Cambridge University Press.
Mutschmann, Hermann. 1906. *Divisiones Quae Vulgo Dicuntur Aristoteleae*. Leipzig: Teubner.
Nadon, Christopher. 2001. *Xenophon's Prince: Republic and Empire in the Cyropaedia*. Berkeley: University of California Press.
Nagy, Gregory. 1983. "Poet and Tyrant: *Theognidea* 39–52, 1081–1082b." *Classical Antiquity* 2: 82–91.
Nails, Debra. 1989. "The Pythagorean Women Philosophers: Ethics of the Household." In *Ionian Philosophy*, edited by K. J. Boudouris. Athens: International Association for Greek Philosophy and International Center for Greek Philosophy and Culture, 291–97.
Nails, Debra. 2002. *The People of Plato: A Prosopography of Plato and Other Socratics*. Indianapolis, IN: Hackett.
Nettleship, Henry Lewis. 1901. *Lectures on the Republic of Plato*. 2nd ed. London: Macmillan.
Newell, Waller R. 2000. *Ruling Passion: The Erotics of Statecraft in Platonic Political Philosophy*. Lanham, MD: Rowman & Littlefield.
Nielsen, Karen Margrethe. 2015. "The Constitution of the Soul: Aristotle on Lack of Deliberative Authority." *Classical Quarterly* 65: 572–86.
Nielsen, Karen Margrethe. 2018. "Deliberation and Decision in the *Magna Moralia* and *Eudemian Ethics*." In *Virtue, Happiness, Knowledge*, edited by David O. Brink, Susan Sauvé Meyer, and Christopher Shields. Oxford: Oxford University Press, 197–215.
Nill, Michael. 1985. *Morality and Self-Interest in Protagoras, Antiphon, and Democritus*. Leiden: Brill.
Nitsche, Wilhelm. 1879. "Bericht über die 1875–1877 veröffentlichten auf Xenophon bezüglichen Arbeiten." *Jahresbuch über die Fortschritte der klassischen Altertumswissenschaft* 9: 14–80.
North, Helen F. 1947. "A Period of Opposition to *Sôphrosynê* in Greek Thought." *Transactions and Proceedings of the American Philological Association* 78: 1–17.
North, Helen F. 1948a. "The Concept of *Sophrosyne* in Greek Literary Criticism." *Classical Philology* 43: 1–17.
North, Helen F. 1948b. "Pindar, *Isthmian*, 8, 24–28." *American Journal of Philology* 69: 304–8.
North, Helen F. 1966. *Sôphrosunê: Self-Knowledge and Self-Restraint in Greek Literature*. Ithaca, NY: Cornell University Press.
North, Helen F. 1977. "The Mare, the Vixen, and the Bee: *Sophrosyne* as the Virtue of Women in Antiquity." *Illinois Classical Studies* 2: 35–48.
North, Helen F. 1979. *From Myth to Icon: Reflections of Greek Ethical Doctrine in Literature and Art*. Ithaca, NY: Cornell University Press.
Norwood, Gilbert. 1954. *Essays on Euripidean Drama*. Toronto: University of Toronto Press.

Nussbaum, Martha. 1986. *The Fragility of Goodness: Luck and Ethics in Greek Tragedy and Philosophy*. Cambridge: Cambridge University Press.

O'Brien, Denis. 2003. "Socrates and Protagoras on Virtue." *Oxford Studies in Ancient Philosophy* 24: 59–131.

Oderberg, David S. 1999. "On the Cardinality of the Cardinal Virtues." *International Journal of Philosophical Studies* 7: 305–22.

Ollier, François. 1933. *Le Mirage Spartiate: Étude sur l'idéalisation de Sparte dans l'antiquité Grecque de l'orgine jusqu'aux Cyniques*. Paris: E. de Boccard.

Ollier, François. 1934. *Xenophon: La République des Lacédémoniens*. Lyon: A. Rey.

Onians, Richard Broxton. 1951. *The Origins of European Thought about the Body, the Mind, the Soul, the World, Time, and Fate: New Interpretations of Greek, Roman and Kindred Evidence, Also of Some Basic Jewish and Christian Beliefs*. Cambridge: Cambridge University Press.

Osborne, Robin. 1994. "Framing the Centaur: Reading Fifth-Century Architectural Sculpture." In *Art and Text in Ancient Greek Culture*, edited by Simon Goldhill and Robin Osborne. Cambridge Studies in New Art History and Criticism. Cambridge: Cambridge University Press, 52–84.

Otto, Walter F. 1954. *The Homeric Gods: The Spiritual Significance of Greek Religion*. Translated by Moses Hadas. Boston: Beacon Press.

Padel, Ruth. 1992. *In and Out of Mind: Greek Images of the Tragic Self*. Princeton, NJ: Princeton University Press.

Page, Denys Lionel. 1938. *Euripides: Medea*. Oxford: Clarendon Press.

Pakaluk, Michael. 1992. "Commentary on White." In *Proceedings of the Boston Area Colloquium in Ancient Philosophy*, Vol. 8, edited by John Cleary. Lanham, MD: University Press of America, 169–80.

Pangle, Lorraine Smith. 2013. "Virtue and Self-Control in Xenophon's Socratic Thought." In *Natural Right and Political Philosophy: Essays in Honor of Catherine Zuckert and Michael Zuckert*, edited by Ann Ward and Lee Ward. Notre Dame, IN: University of Notre Dame Press, 15–35.

Pangle, Thomas L. 1980. *The Laws of Plato*. New York: Basic Books.

Pangle, Thomas L. 2018. *The Socratic Way of Life: Xenophon's Memorabilia*. Chicago: University of Chicago Press.

Pappas, Nickolas. 2003. *Routledge Philosophy Guidebook to Plato and the Republic*. 2nd ed. London: Routledge.

Patzer, Andreas. 1970. "Antisthenes der Sokratiker." Ph.D. diss., Ruprecht-Karl-Universität zu Heidelberg.

Pearson, Giles. 2012. *Aristotle on Desire*. Cambridge: Cambridge University Press.

Pearson, Giles. 2014. "Courage and Temperance." In *Cambridge Companion to Aristotle's Nicomachean Ethics*, edited by Ronald M. Polansky. Cambridge: Cambridge University Press, 110–34.

Pearson, Lionel. 1957. "Popular Ethics in the World of Thucydides." *Classical Philology* 52: 228–44.

Pendrick, Gerard J. 2002. *Antiphon: The Fragments*. Cambridge: Cambridge University Press.

Penrose, Walter Duvall. 2016. *Postcolonial Amazons: Female Masculinity and Courage in Ancient Greek and Sanskrit Literature*. Oxford: Oxford University Press.

Pepe, Cristina. 2013. "Divisiones Aristoteleae." In *The Genres of Rhetorical Speeches in Greek and Roman Antiquity*. International Studies in the History of Rhetoric. Leiden: Brill, 235–40.
Peterson, Sandra. 2011. *Socrates and Philosophy in the Dialogues of Plato*. Cambridge: Cambridge University Press.
Pietruschka, Ute. 2019. "Syriac Reception of Socrates." In *Brill's Companion to the Reception of Socrates*, edited by Christopher Moore. Brill's Companion to Classical Reception. Leiden: Brill, 518–44.
Planeaux, C. 1999. "Socrates, Alcibiades, and Plato's τὰ ποτειδεατικά: Does the *Charmides* Have an Historical Setting?" *Mnemosyne* 52: 72–77.
Plant, I. M. 2004. *Women Writers of Ancient Greece and Rome: An Anthology*. Norman: University of Oklahoma Press.
Pomeroy, Sarah B. 2013. *Pythagorean Women: Their History and Writings*. Baltimore, MD: Johns Hopkins University Press.
Porubjak, Matus. 2013. "Theognis and the Social Role of Measure." *Electryone* 1: 54–65.
Porubjak, Matúš. 2019. "Theognis on Breeding and Learning: Why Socrates Should Have Quoted His Verses in Plato's *Meno*." *Polis* 36: 488–510.
Pouilloux, Jean, and François Salviat. 1983. "Lichas, Lacédémonien, Archonte à Thasos, et Le Livre VIII de Thucydide." *Comptes rendus des séances de l'Académie des Inscriptions et Belles-Lettres* 127: 376–403.
Pouilloux, Jean, and François Salviat. 1985. "Thucydide après l'exil et la composition de son Histoire." *Revue de Philologie, de Littérature et d'Histoire Anciennes* 59: 13–20.
Powell, Anton, and Nicolas Richer. 2020. *Xenophon and Sparta*. Swansea: Classical Press of Wales.
Pownall, Frances. 2012. "Critias in Xenophon's *Hellenica*." *Scripta Classica Israelica* 31: 1–18.
Pownall, Frances. 2016. "Tyrants as Impious Leaders in Xenophon's *Hellenica*." *Histos Supplements* 5: 51–83.
Press, Gerald A. 2018. "The Enactment of Moderation in Plato's *Charmides*." *Acta Classica Universitatis Scientiarum Debreceniensis* 54: 5–24.
Prince, Susan. 2015. *Antisthenes of Athens: Texts, Translations, and Commentary*. Ann Arbor: University of Michigan Press.
Prince, Susan. 2019. "Socrates in Stobaeus: Assembling a Philosopher." In *Brill's Companion to the Reception of Socrates*, edited by Christopher Moore. Brill's Companion to Classical Reception. Leiden: Brill, 453–517.
Prior, William J. 2002. "Protagoras' Great Speech and Plato's Defense of Athenian Democracy." In *Presocratic Philosophy: Essays in Honour of Alexander Mourelatos*, edited by Victor Caston and Daniel W. Graham. Aldershot: Ashgate, 313–26.
Pritzl, K. 1985. "On the Way to Wisdom in Heraclitus." *Phoenix* 39: 303–16.
Procopé, J. F. 1989. "Democritus on Politics and the Care of the Soul." *Classical Quarterly* 39: 307–31.
Prodi, Enrico Emanuele. 2014. "A Bibliological Note on *P. Oxy.* 659 (Pindar, *Partheneia*)." *Analecta Papyrologica* 26: 99–105.
Quandt, Kenneth. 2020. "A Commentary on Plato's *Republic*." October 10, 2020. www.onplatosrepublic.com.
Rabinowitz, Laura. 2015. "Harmony of City and Soul: Plato and the Classical Virtue of Moderation." Ph.D. diss., University of Texas at Austin.

Race, William H. 1997. *Pindar: Nemean Odes, Isthmian Odes, Fragments*. Loeb Classical Library. Cambridge, MA: Harvard University Press.

Rackham, H. 1926. *Aristotle: The Nicomachean Ethics*. Loeb Classical Library. Cambridge, MA: Harvard University Press.

Rademaker, Adriaan. 2005. *Sophrosyne and the Rhetoric of Self-Restraint: Polysemy and Persuasive Use of an Ancient Greek Value Term*. Leiden: Brill.

Radt, Stefan. 1958. *Pindars Zweiter Und Sechster Paian: Text, Scholien Und Kommentar*. Amsterdam: Adolf M. Hakkert.

Raeder, Johann. 1904. *Theodoreti Graecarum affectionum curation*. Leipzig: Teubner.

Rankin, H. D. 1986. *Anthisthenes Sokratikos*. Amsterdam: Adolf M. Hakkert.

Raymond, Christopher C. 2017. "Shame and Virtue in Aristotle." *Oxford Studies in Ancient Philosophy* 53: 111–62.

Raymond, Christopher C. 2018. "Αἰδώς in Plato's *Charmides*." *Ancient Philosophy* 38: 23–46.

Rebenich, Stefan. 1998. *Xenophon, Die Verfassung der Spartaner*. Darmstadt: Wissenschaftliche Buchgesellschaft.

Redfield, James. 2018. "The Origins of the Socratic Dialogue: Plato, Xenophon, and the Others." In *Socrates and the Socratic Dialogue*, edited by Alessandro Stavru and Christopher Moore. Leiden: Brill, 125–38.

Renaud, François, and Harold Tarrant. 2018. *The Platonic Alcibiades I: The Dialogue and Its Ancient Reception*. Cambridge: Cambridge University Press.

Richards, Herbert. 1893. "Critical Notes on the *Republic* of Plato (Continued)." *Classical Review* 7(6): 251–54.

Richardson, Nicholas. 1993. *The Iliad: A Commentary*. Vol. 6: *Books 21–24*. Cambridge: Cambridge University Press.

Riginos, Alice Swift. 1976. *Platonica: The Anecdotes Concerning the Life and Writings of Plato*. Leiden: Brill.

Rishel, Bruce. 2020. "The Divine Charioteering Model—A Guide to Moderation." *Journal of Ancient Philosophy* 14: 203–9.

Robb, K. 1986. "Psyche and Logos in the Fragments of Heraclitus: The Origins of the Concept of Soul." *The Monist* 69: 315–61.

Robin, Léon. 1930. *Platon: Oeuvres Complètes*. Vol. 2: *Le Banquet*. Paris: Éditions Gallimard.

Robinson, T. M. 1987. *Heraclitus: Fragments*. Toronto: University of Toronto Press.

Rosella Schluderer, Laura. 2016. "Psychic Kosmos: A Reading of *Gorgias* 503d–504d and 507e–508a." *Vichiana* 53: 11–21.

Rosella Schluderer, Laura. 2017. "Speaking and Acting the Truth: The Ethics of Heraclitus." *Méthexis* 29: 1–19.

Rosen, Stanley. 1995. *Plato's Statesman: The Web of Politics*. New Haven, CT: Yale University Press.

Rosenmeyer, T. G. 1949. "The Family of Critias." *American Journal of Philology* 70: 404–10.

Róspide López, Alfredo, and Francisco Martín García. 1995. *Index Socraticorum Xenophontis Operum*. Hildesheim: Olms-Weidmann.

Rowe, Christopher. 1979. "Justice and Temperance in *Republic* IV." In *Arktouros: Hellenic Studies Presented to B. M. W. Knox*, edited by Glen W. Bowersock, Walter Burkert, and Michael C. J. Putnam. Berlin: De Gruyter, 336–44.

Rowe, Christopher. 2000. "The *Politicus* and Other Dialogues." In *The Cambridge History of Greek and Roman Political Thought*, edited by Christopher Rowe and Malcolm Schofield. Cambridge: Cambridge University Press, 233–57.

Rowett, Catherine. 2014. "The Pythagorean Society and Politics." In *A History of Pythagoreanism*, edited by Carl A. Huffman. Cambridge: Cambridge University Press, 112–30.

Rumpel, Ioannes. 1883. *Lexicon Pindaricum*. Leipzig: Teubner.

Russell, Daniel C. 2014. "*Phronesis* and the Virtues (*NE* vi 12–13)." In *The Cambridge Companion to Aristotle's Nicomachean Ethics*, edited by Ronald Polansky. Cambridge: Cambridge University Press, 203–20.

Russo, Joseph, Manuel Fernandez-Galiano, and Alfred Heubeck. 1992. *A Commentary on Homer's Odyssey*. Vol. 3. Oxford: Clarendon Press.

Rutherford, Ian. 2001. *Pindar's Paeans: A Reading of the Fragments with a Survey of the Genre*. Oxford: Oxford University Press.

Sansalvador, Ana Vegas. 1987. *Jenofonte: Ciropedia*. Madrid: Editorial Gredos.

Sansone, David. 2004. "Heracles at the Y." *Journal of Hellenic Studies* 124: 125–42.

Sansone, David. 2015. "Xenophon and Prodicus' Choice of Heracles." *Classical Quarterly* 65: 371–77.

Santas, Gerasimos. 1973. "Socrates at Work on Virtue and Knowledge in Plato's *Charmides*." In *Exegesis and Argument: Studies in Greek Philosophy Presented to Gregory Vlastos*, edited by Edward N. Lee, Alexander P. D. Mourelatos, and Richard M. Rorty. Assen: Van Gorcum, 105–32.

Saunders, Trevor J. 1970. *Plato: The Laws*. Harmondsworth: Penguin.

Sauppe, Gustav. 1869. *Lexilogus Xenophonteus*. Leipzig: Teubner.

Schanz, Martin. 1879. *Platonis Leges et Epinomis*, Vol. 1: *Sex Priores Libros Legum Complectens*. Leipzig: Tauchnitz.

Schmid, W. Thomas. 1998. *Plato's Charmides and the Socratic Ideal of Rationality*. Albany: State University of New York Press.

Schofield, Malcolm. 2013. "Cardinal Virtues: A Contested Socratic Inheritance." In *Plato and the Stoics*, edited by A. G. Long. Cambridge: Cambridge University Press, 11–28.

Schofield, Malcolm. 2014. "Archytas." In *A History of Pythagoreanism*, edited by Carl A. Huffman. Cambridge: Cambridge University Press, 69–87.

Schofield, Malcolm, and Tom Griffith. 2016. *Plato: Laws*. Cambridge: Cambridge University Press.

Schöpsdau, Klaus. 1994. *Nomoi (Gesetze). Buch I-III. Platon Werke. Übersetzung und Kommentar. Band IX. 2*. Göttingen: Vandenhoeck & Ruprecht.

Schütrumpf, Eckart. 2008. "Heraclides, *On Pleasure*." In *Heraclides of Pontus: Texts and Translations*, edited by William W. Fortenbaugh and Elizabeth E. Pender. New Brunswick, NJ: Transaction, 69–92.

Scott, Dominic. 2011. "Philosophy and Madness in the *Phaedrus*." *Oxford Studies in Ancient Philosophy* 41: 169–200.

Seaford, Richard. 1996. *Euripides, Bacchae*. Warminster: Aris & Phillips.

Sebell, Dustin. 2021. *Xenophon's Socratic Education: Reason, Religion, and the Limits of Politics*. Philadelphia: University of Pennsylvania Press.

Sedley, David. 2003. *Plato's Cratylus*. Cambridge: Cambridge University Press.

Sedley, David. 2013. "The Atheist Underground." In *Politeia in Greek and Roman Philosophy*, edited by Verity Harte and Melissa Lane. Cambridge: Cambridge University Press, 329–48.

Seel, Gerhard. 2006. "If You Know What Is Best, You Do It: Socratic Intellectualism in Xenophon and Plato." In *Remembering Socrates: Philosophical Essays*, edited by Lindsay Judson and Vassilis Karasmanis. Oxford: Clarendon Press, 20–49.

Segal, Charles. 1965. "The Tragedy of the *Hippolytus*: The Waters of Ocean and the Untouched Meadow." *Harvard Studies in Classical Philology* 70: 117–69.

Segal, Charles. 1970. "Shame and Purity in Euripides' *Hippolytus*." *Hermes* 98: 278–99.

Segal, Charles. 1979. "Solar Imagery and Tragic Heroism in Euripides' *Hippolytus*." In *Arktouros: Hellenic Studies Presented to B. M. W. Knox*, edited by Glen W. Bowersock, Walter Burkert, and Michael C. J. Putnam. Berlin: De Gruyter, 151–61.

Šegvić, Heda. 2004. "Protagoras' Political Art." *Rhizai* 2: 9–36.

Shaw, Ben. 2007. *Euripides: Hippolytus*. Cambridge Translations from Greek Drama. Cambridge: Cambridge University Press.

Shoemaker, Sydney. 1963. *Self-Knowledge and Self-Identity*. Ithaca, NY: Cornell University Press.

Shorey, Paul. 1930. *Plato: The Republic*. Vol. 1: *Books I–V*. Loeb Classical Library. London: Heinemann.

Sider, David. 2013. "Heraclitus' Ethics." In *Doctrine and Doxography: Studies on Heraclitus and Pythagoras*, edited by David Sider and Dirk Obbink. Berlin: De Gruyter, 321–34.

Sisko, John E. 2003. "Taste, Touch, and Temperance in *Nicomachean Ethics* 3.10." *Classical Quarterly* 53: 135–40.

Slater, William J. 1969. *Lexicon to Pindar*. Berlin: De Gruyter.

Slings, S. R. 2003. *Platonis Rempublicam*. Oxford Classical Texts. Oxford: Oxford University Press.

Smith, Charles Foster. 1919. *Thucydides*. London: Heinemann.

Snell, Bruno. 1946. *Die Entdeckung des Geistes: Studien zur Entstehung des europäischen Denkens bei den Griechen*. Hamburg: Claassen und Goverts.

Snell, Bruno. 1953. *The Discovery of the Mind: The Greek Origins of European Thought*. Translated by T. G. Rosenmeyer. Oxford: Basil Blackwell.

Snell, Bruno. 1977. "φρένες—φρόνησις." *Glotta* 55: 34–64.

Snell, Bruno, and Herwig Maehler. 1975. *Pindari Carmina Cum Fragmentis*. Part 2: *Fragmenta; Indices*. 4th ed. Leipzig: Teubner.

Sommerstein, Alan. 1982. *Aristophanes: Clouds*. Warminster: Aris & Phillips.

Sparshott, F. E. 1970. "Five Virtues in Plato and Aristotle." *The Monist* 54: 40–65.

Sprague, R. K. 1972. *The Older Sophists*. Columbia: University of South Carolina Press.

Städele, Alfons. 1980. *Die Briefe des Pythagoras und der Pythagoreer*. Meisenheim am Glan: Hain.

Stallbaum, Gottfried. 1859. *Plato: Opera Omnia 10,1 Continens Legum Libros Priores*. Gothae: Hennings.

Stalley, R. F. 1983. *An Introduction to Plato's Laws*. Indianapolis, IN: Hackett.

Starkie, W. J. M. 1911. *The Clouds of Aristophanes*. London: Macmillan.

Stauffer, Devin. 2006. *The Unity of Plato's Gorgias: Rhetoric, Justice, and the Philosophic Life*. Cambridge: Cambridge University Press.

Stavru, Alessandro. 2018. "Aristoxenus on Socrates." In *Socrates and the Socratic Dialogue*, edited by Alessandro Stavru and Christopher Moore. Leiden: Brill, 623–64.

Strauss, Leo. 1972. *Xenophon's Socrates*. Ithaca, NY: Cornell University Press.

Steward, John Alexander. 1892. *Notes on the Nicomachean Ethics of Aristotle*. Oxford: Clarendon Press.

Sullivan, Shirley D. 1988. *Psychological Activity in Homer: A Study of Phren*. Montreal: McGill-Queen's University Press.
Suzuki, Teruo. 1989. "ΨΥΧΗ and ΛΟΓΟΣ in Heraclitus' Philosophy." In *Ionian Philosophy*, edited by K. J. Boudouris. Athens: International Association for Greek Philosophy and International Center for Greek Philosophy and Culture, 375–83.
Taormina, Daniela Patrizia, and Rosa Maria Piccione. 2010. *Giamblico: I frammenti dalle epistole*. Naples: Bibliopolis.
Tarán, Leonardo. 1981. *Speusippus of Athens: A Critical Study with a Collection of the Related Texts and Commentary*. Philosophia Antiqua. Leiden: Brill.
Taylor, C. C. W. 1967. "Pleasure, Knowledge and Sensation in Democritus." *Phronesis* 12: 6–27.
Taylor, C. C. W. 2006. *Aristotle: Nicomachean Ethics: Books II–IV*. Oxford: Clarendon Press.
Taylor, Thomas. 1822. *Political Fragments of Archytas: Charondas, Zaleucus, and Other Ancient Pythagoreans*. Chiswick: C. Whittingham.
Tell, Håkan. 2007. "Sages at the Games: Intellectual Displays and Dissemination of Wisdom in Ancient Greece." *Classical Antiquity* 26: 249–75.
Tessitore, Aristide. 1996. *Reading Aristotle's Ethics: Virtue, Rhetoric, and Political Philosophy*. Albany: State University of New York Press.
Thayer, Joseph Henry, and James Strong, eds. 1997. *Thayer's Greek-English Lexicon of the New Testament*. Peabody, MA.: Hendrickson Publishers.
Thesleff, Holger. 1961. *An Introduction to the Pythagorean Writings of the Hellenistic Period*. Åbo: Åbo Akademi.
Thesleff, Holger. 1965. *The Pythagorean Texts of the Hellenistic Period*. Åbo: Åbo Akademi.
Thesleff, Holger. 1972. "On the Problem of the Doric Pseudo-Pythagorica: An Alternative Theory of Date and Purpose." In *Pseudepigrapha: I, Pseudopythagorica, Lettres de Platon, Littérature Pseudépigraphique Juive/Huit Exposés Suivis de Discussions*, edited by Kurt Von Fritz. Entretiens sur l'Antiquité Classique. Geneva: Fondation Hardt, 59–87.
Thibodeau, Philip. 2019. *The Chronology of the Early Greek Natural Philosophers*. North Haven, CT: Cosmographia.net.
Thom, Johan C. 2020. "The Pythagorean Acusmata." In *Early Greek Ethics*, edited by David Wolfsdorf. Oxford: Oxford University Press, 3–18.
Tjiattas, Mary. 1989. "Pythagorean Askesis and the Educative Preconditions of *Sophrosyne*." In *Ionian Philosophy*, edited by K. J. Boudouris. Athens: International Association for Greek Philosophy and International Center for Greek Philosophy and Culture, 394–402.
Tomin, Julius. 1987. "Socratic Gymnasium in the Clouds." *Symbolae Osloenses* 62: 25–32.
Tonelli, Angelo. 2005. *Eraclito: Dell'origine*. Rev. ed. Milano: Feltrinelli.
Trianosky, Gregory W. 1988. "Rightly Ordered Appetites: How to Live Morally and Live Well." *American Philosophical Quarterly* 25: 1–12.
Tsagalis, Christos C. 2008. *Inscribing Sorrow: Fourth-Century Attic Funerary Epigrams*. Berlin: De Gruyter.
Tsouna, Voula. 2018. "La conception Aristotelicienne de la *sôphrosunê* dans l'*Éthique à Nicomaque* et son arrière-fond Platonicien." *Revue de Philosophie Ancienne* 36: 5–38.
Tsouna, Voula. 2022. *Plato's Charmides: An Interpretative Commentary*. Cambridge: Cambridge University Press.
Tu, Van. 2020. "Aristotle on Practical Rationality: Deliberation, Preference-Ranking, and the Imperfect Decision-Making of Women." Ph.D. diss., University of Michigan.

Tuckey, T. G. 1951. *Plato's Charmides*. Cambridge: Cambridge University Press.
Tuozzo, Thomas M. 2000. "Greetings from Apollo: *Charmides* 164c–165b, *Epistle* III, and the Structure of the *Charmides*." In *Plato: Euthydemus, Lysis, Charmides: Proceedings of the V Symposium Platonicum (Selected Papers)*, edited by Thomas Robinson and Luc Brisson. Sankt Augustin: Academia Verlag, 296–305.
Tuozzo, Thomas M. 2011. *Plato's Charmides: Positive Elenchus in a "Socratic" Dialogue*. Cambridge: Cambridge University Press.
Van Groningen, Bernhard Abraham. 1966. *Théognis: Le Premier Livre*. Amsterdam: Noord-Hollandsche Uitgevers.
Veligianni-Terzi, C. 1997. *Wertbegriffe in den Attischen Ehrendekreten der klassichen Zeit*. Stuttgart: F. Steiner.
Vestrheim, Gjert. 2010. "Voice in Sepulchral Epigrams: Some Remarks on the Use of First and Second Person in Sepulchral Epigrams, and a Comparison with Lyric Poetry." In *Archaic and Classical Greek Epigram*, edited by Manuel Baumbach, Andrej Petrovic, and Ivana Petrovic. Cambridge: Cambridge University Press, 61–78.
Viano, Cristina. 2007. "Aristotle and the Starting Point of Moral Development: The Notion of Natural Virtue." In *Aristotle and Neoplatonism: Essays in Honour of Denis O'Brien*, edited by Suzanne Stern-Gillet and Kevin Corrigan. Leiden: Brill, 23–42.
Vitek, Tomas. 2012. "False Heraclitus: Heraclitean Dubia and Their Typology." *La Parola del Passato* 384: 161–97.
Vlastos, Gregory. 1945–46. "Ethics and Physics in Democritus." *Phronesis* 54: 578–92 and 55: 53–64.
Vlastos, Gregory. 1955. "On Heraclitus." *American Journal of Philology* 76: 337–68.
Vlastos, Gregory. 1969. "Justice and Psychic Harmony in the *Republic*." *Journal of Philosophy* 66: 505–21.
Vorwerk, M. 2001. "Plato on Virtue: Definitions of ΣΩΦΡΟΣΥΝΗ in Plato's *Charmides* and in Plotinus' *Enneads* 1.2 (19)." *American Journal of Philology* 122: 29–47.
Wachsmuth, Curt, and Otto Hense. 1884–1912. *Ioannis Stobaei Anthologium*. Berlin: Weidmann.
Waithe, Mary Ellen. 1987. *A History of Women Philosophers* Vol. 1: 600 BC–500 AD. Dordrecht: Springer.
Warren, James. 2002. *Epicurus and Democritean Ethics: An Archaeology of Ataraxia*. Cambridge: Cambridge University Press.
Weiss, Roslyn. 1987. "The Right Exchange: *Phaedo* 69a6–c3." *Ancient Philosophy* 7: 57–66.
Weiss, Roslyn. 2012. *Philosophers in the Republic: Plato's Two Paradigms*. Ithaca, NY: Cornell University Press.
Weiss, Roslyn. 2018. "Pity or Pardon: Plato, Xenophon, and Aristotle on the Appropriate Response to Intentional Wrongdoing." In *Plato and Xenophon: Comparative Studies*, edited by Gabriel Danzig, David M. Johnson, and Donald Morrison. Mnemosyne Supplements. Leiden: Brill, 277–317.
Weitlich, Ernst. 1922. "Quae fuerit vocis sōphrosyne vis ac natura apud antiquiores scriptores graecos usque ad Platonem." PhD diss., University of Göttingen.
West, Martin L. 1969. "The Sayings of Democritus." *Classical Review* 19: 142.
West, Martin L. 1971. *Iambi et Elegi Graeci*. Oxford: Oxford University Press.
West, Martin L. 1974. *Studies in Greek Elegy and Iambus*. Berlin: De Gruyter.
West, Martin L. 2017. *Homerus: Odyssea*. Berlin: De Gruyter.
White, Nicholas P. 1979. *A Companion to Plato's Republic*. Indianapolis, IN: Hackett.

White, Stephen A. 1992. "Natural Virtue and Perfect Virtue in Aristotle." In *Proceedings of the Boston Area Colloquium in Ancient Philosophy*, Vol. 8, edited by John Cleary. Lanham, MD: University Press of America, 135–68.
White, Stephen A. 1995. "Thrasymachus the Diplomat." *Classical Philology* 90: 307–27.
Whitehead, David. 1993. "Cardinal Virtues: The Language of Public Approbation in Democratic Athens." *Classica et mediaevalia* 44: 37–75.
Whitehead, David. 2009. "*Andragathia* and *Aretē*." In *Greek History and Epigraphy: Essays in Honour of P. J. Rhodes*, edited by Lynette Mitchell and Lene Rubinstein. Swansea: Classical Press of Wales, 47–58.
Wider, Kathleen. 1986. "Women Philosophers in the Ancient Greek World: Donning the Mantle." *Hypatia* 1: 21–62.
Wilamowitz-Moellendorff, Ulrich. 1913. "Erkenne Dich Selbst." In *Reden Und Vorträge*, vol. 2. Berlin: Weidmann, 171–89.
Wilburn, Joshua. 2012. "Akrasia and Self-Rule in Plato's *Laws*." *Oxford Studies in Ancient Philosophy* 43: 25–53.
Wilhelm, Friedrich. 1915. "Die Oeconomica der Neupythagoreer Bryson, Kallikratidas, Periktione, Phintys." *Rheinisches Museum für Philologie* 70: 161–223.
Williams, Bernard. 1993. *Shame and Necessity*. Berkeley: University of California Press.
Winnington-Ingram, R. P. 1958. "*Hippolytus*: A Study in Causation." In *Entretiens Sur l'Antiquité Classique*, Vol. 6: *Euripide*, edited by Olivier Reverdin. Fondation Hardt pour l'étude de l'Antiquité classique. Verona: Stamperia Valdonega, 171–91.
Wolfsdorf, David. 2003. "Socrates' Pursuit of Definitions." *Phronesis* 48: 271–312.
Wolfsdorf, David. 2008. "Hesiod, Prodicus, and the Socratics on Work and Pleasure." *Oxford Studies in Ancient Philosophy* 35: 1–17.
Wolfsdorf, David. 2011. "Prodicus on the Correctness of Names: The Case of Τέρψις, Χαρά and Εὐφροσύνη." *Journal of Hellenic Studies* 131: 131–45.
Wolfsdorf, David. 2013. *Pleasure in Ancient Greek Philosophy*. Cambridge: Cambridge University Press.
Wolfsdorf, David. 2020. "The Ethical Philosophy of the Historical Socrates." In *Early Greek Ethics*, edited by David Wolfsdorf. Oxford: Oxford University Press, 169–94.
Woolf, Raphael. 2000. "Callicles and Socrates: Psychic (Dis)Harmony in the *Gorgias*." *Oxford Studies in Ancient Philosophy* 18: 1–40.
Woolf, Raphael. 2004. "The Practice of the Philosopher." *Oxford Studies in Ancient Philosophy* 26: 97–129.
Young, Charles M. 1988. "Aristotle on Temperance." *Philosophical Review* 97: 521–42.
Zeitlin, Froma. 1985. "The Power of Aphrodite: Eros and the Boundaries of the Self in the *Hippolytus*." In *Directions in Euripidean Criticism*, edited by Peter Burian. Durham, NC: Duke University Press, 52–111, 189–208.
Zhmud, Leonid. 2012. "Aristoxenus and the Pythagoreans." In *Aristoxenus of Tarentum: Discussion*, edited by Carl A. Huffman. New Brunswick, NJ: Transaction, 223–49.

Index Locorum

For the benefit of digital users, indexed terms that span two pages (e.g., 52–53) may, on occasion, appear on only one of those pages.

Aeschylus
  Agamemnon
    176-181: 48n.59
    351: 48n.60
    1425: 48n.57
    1620: 48n.58
  Choephoroi
    140: 48n.60
    786: 48n.60
  Eumenides
    44: 48n.60
    136: 48n.60
    521: 48n.59
    1000: 48n.59
  Persians
    827-28: 48n.56
  Seven against Thebes
    186: 48n.60
    568-69: 48–49
    602-8: 49n.63
    609-12: 49
    610: 48n.60
    645: 48n.60
  Suppliant Maidens
    710: 48n.60
Ameipsias
  fr. 9: 136n.16
Anonymus Iamblichi
  fr. 3: 166n.34
  fr. 4.1: 142n.44, 165–66
  fr. 4.2: 166n.35
  fr. 4.4: 166n.35
  fr. 4.6: 146n.53
Antiphon
  2.3.3: 115n.52
  4.3.2: 115n.53
  4.4.2: 116n.54
  5.20: 112n.47
  5.24: 112n.47
  B49/D57: 116
  B58/D55: 113–16
  B59/D56: 112, 114–15

Antisthenes
  fr. 14A: 138
  fr. 27: 137n.21
  frr. 77-78: 137n.23
  frr.: 80-83, 86-90, 98-99, 103-4, 117-29, 137n.21
  fr. 86A: 138
  fr. 113: 138
  fr. 122: 296n.31
  fr. 123B: 138n.26
  fr. 124: 138n.27
  fr. 125: 138n.27
  fr. 126: 138, 138n.27
  fr. 127: 138n.27
  fr. 136: 145n.50
  fr. 161: 138n.30
  fr. 188A-1: 139n.32
Aristophanes
  Clouds
    99: 12n.33
    115-16: 12n.33
    179: 136n.12
    247-53: 136n.13
    365-81: 136n.13
    423-36: 136n.13
    529: 135n.9
    889-948: 11n.25
    935-36: 11n.26
    961-1114: 11n.25
    962: 11n.28
    963: 12n.36
    964: 12n.36
    965: 12n.36
    966-968: 12n.36
    969-72: 12n.36
    973-83: 12n.36
    986: 11n.29
    991: 12n.37
    992: 12n.37
    993-94: 12n.37
    994-95: 12n.37
    997-97: 12n.37

Aristophanes (cont.)
   998-99: 12n.37
   1002: 11n.29, 12n.38
   1003-4: 12n.38
   1005-14: 12n.38
   1006: 11n.29
   1012: 11n.29
   1020-21: 13n.39
   1026-27: 12n.30
   1040: 12n.31
   1048-49: 13n.41
   1050: 13n.40
   1067: 12n.32
   1068-69: 13n.43
   1071: 12n.32
   1072-74: 13n.44
   1078: 12n.32, 13n.45
   1321-1446: 136n.13
   1466-1509: 136n.15
 Frogs
   1491-99: 136n.17
 Plutus (Wealth)
   563-64: 205n.48
Aristotle
 Eudemian Ethics
   3.2
     1230b8: 259n.4
     1230b25-26: 259n.5
     1230b26-36: 259n.6
     1230b36-1231a26: 260n.8
     1231a29-32: 260n.9
   3.3: 258n.1
   3.7
     1233b17-19: 263n.22
     1233b27-29: 263n.23
     1234a21-23: 191n.10
     1234a24-27: 263n.22
     1234a27-30: 264n.27
     1234a30-32: 263n.24
     1234a32-33: 263n.25
   4.9
     1128b10-23: 264n.26
   6.13
     1144b-7: 264n.28
     1144b7-17: 264n.29
     1144b10-12: 264n.32
     1144b17-30: 264n.30
 Magna Moralia
   1.21
     1191b5-20: 259n.3
   1.22: 258n.1
 Metaphysics
   E.2 1026b37-1027a5: 231n.77

 Nicomachean Ethics
   2.7
     1107b17: 214n.9
   3.10
     1117b23-27: 260n.10
     1117b29-1118a2: 261n.11
     1118a2-b5: 261n.12
     1118b3-4: 261n.14
     1118b5-8: 261n.13
   3.10-12: 270–71
   3.11
     1118b29-1119a6: 260n.10
   3.11-12
     1118b8-1119b19: 261n.15
   3.12
     1119a33-b15: 276n.89
     1119b12-18: 270n.66
   4.1: 258n.1
   4.2
     1122a18-1123a18: 214n.9
   4.3
     1123b5: 270n.68
   4.4
     1125b13: 270n.69
   5.1
     11129b21: 270n.70
   6.5
     1140b5: 28n.8
     1140b9: 28n.9
     1140n11-20: 28
   6.12
     11144a9-11: 262n.18
   7.1
     1145b14-17: 265n.35
   7.4
     1147b28: 270n.69
   7.7
     1150a9: 274n.85
   7.13
     1153b33-1154a1: 266n.39
 Politics
   1259a40-b4: 308n.8
   1259b32: 308n.7
   1260a12-14: 308n.9
   1260a20-24: 308n.11
   1260a27-31: 308–9n.12
   1260b9-22: 308n.10
   1377b18-23: 309n.15
   1377b24-25: 309n.16
 Rhetoric
   1416b26-29: 102n.5
   1277b17-21: 270n.67
   1361a3-7: 270n.67

Topics
  108a2: 270n.71
  111a10: 107n.29
  117a31: 270n.67
  123a34-36: 270n.72
  139b33: 270n.72
  150a4-13: 270n.73
Aristoxenus
  Life of Archytas
    fr. A7: 300n.40
    fr. A9
      5-8: 303n.47
      9-15: 303
      10-15: 301
      15-19: 301n.45
      16-21: 304
      48-64: 301–2
  Pythagorean Precepts
    fr. 2
      7-15: 290n.16
      15-18: 290n.17
    fr. 8: 286, 287
      6-12: 284
      12-16: 284
    fr. 9
      1-14: 293n.25
      17-40: 294–95
      42-59: 295n.27
      62-64: 295n.28
      64-68: 296n.32
      65-66: 295n.29
      69: 296n.30
      132: 297n.34
      147-49: 298n.35

Callias
  fr. 15: 136n.17
Critias
  B6 8-27: 109–10

Definitions
  441e6-412a2: 278
Democritus
  B3/D228: 130n.99
  B73/266: 129n.96
  B119/D274: 131n.105
  B160/D280: 129n.94
  B189/D227: 130n.100
  B191/D226: 130n.98
  B207/D242: 129n.95
  B208/D396: 129n.94
  B210/D277: 129n.92
  B211/D244: 128

  B234/D240: 167
  B235/D248: 130n.101
  B264/D386: 131n.106
  D291/D318: 129n.93
  D294/D317: 129n.94
Diogenes Laertius
  2.121: 133n.4
  2.122-23: 133n.3
  2.124-25: 133n.4
  3.37: 191n.6
  3.80-109: 278n.102
  3.91: 278n.103
  5.50: 275n.88
  5.86: 276n.90
  6.2: 137n.19
  6.11: 137n.22
  6.12: 140n.35, 308n.6
  6.46: 145n.52
  6.103: 138n.30
  7.121: 279n.106
  8.15-16: 281n.1
  9.55: 191n.6
Dissoi Logoi
  1.2-3: 168

Eupolis
  fr. 386: 136n.16
  fr. 395: 136n.17
Euripides
  Bacchae
    45-46: 94n.80
    196-203: 94n.81
    218-25: 94n.82
    237: 94n.83
    256: 94n.83
    298-301: 94n.84
    314: 95
    314-16: 95–96
    329: 94
    353-53: 96n.92
    387-89: 96n.93
    420-29: 96n.93
    476: 96n.94
    490: 96n.94
    502: 96n.94
    503: 96n.94
    504: 96n.95
    506: 96n.95
    640-41: 97n.97
    686-88: 97n.98
    693: 97n.98
    940: 97n.99
    992-96: 97–98

Euripides (cont.)
  1002-4: 97
  1150-52: 98
  1341-43: 98
  fr. 386: 136n.16
  fr. 395: 136n.17
  fr. 396.2-3: 136n.17
  fr. 545: 85n.41
  Hippolytus
    5-6: 78n.5
    13: 78n.6
    15-19: 78n.7
    28: 78n.8
    38-50: 78n.8
    74-86: 107n.31
    78-81: 79–80n.15
    79: 96
    80: 96n.90
    87: 80n.16
    91: 79n.13
    98: 79n.13
    99: 79n.11
    102: 79n.12
    103: 79n.11
    105: 79n.14
    106: 79n.12
    107: 79n.11
    109-10: 80n.18
    118: 79n.14
    131-69: 80n.19
    205: 81n.20
    214: 81n.22
    215-22: 81n.21
    223: 81n.22
    228-31: 81n.21
    232: 81n.22
    238: 81n.22
    239-49: 84n.35
    240: 81n.23
    244: 81n.24
    244-49: 81n.25
    246: 81n.24
    250-66: 81n.26
    264: 103n.11
    313: 82n.27
    347: 82n.28
    377-78: 83n.31
    379-80: 83n.32
    383-87: 83–84
    394-97: 85n.38
    398-99: 85n.38
    401-2: 85n.43
    404-25: 86n.44
    413-14: 86n.45
    431-32: 82n.30
    434-36: 86n.47
    443: 86n.48
    444: 86n.49
    445-46: 86n.48
    447-50: 87n.50
    451-58: 87n.51
    467: 87n.53
    475: 87n.54
    477-81: 87n.55
    486-87: 87n.56
    487-88: 84n.34
    525-64: 86n.46
    558-59: 82n.29
    616-66: 88n.58
    667-68: 88n.59
    704: 88n.60
    723: 88n.62
    729-30: 88n.64
    731: 88n.63
    920: 36n.21
    921: 36n.21
    948-50: 89n.66
    952-57: 89n.67
    967: 95n.89
    991-92: 89n.68
    994-95: 89n.69
    996-1006: 89n.70
    1035-36: 90
    1078-79: 91n.75
    1080-81: 91n.75
    1100: 91n.76
    1402: 91n.79
  Medea
    309-11: 8n.12
    550-51: 9n.15
    555-58: 9n.17
    559-72: 9n.19
    627-44: 10n.20
    636: 10n.20
    869-905: 10n.22
    884-85: 10n.21
    908-13: 10n.23
    1367-69: 10n.24
  Orestes
    1651: 245n.22

Gorgias
  B8/D32: 50n.67

Heraclitus
  B1/D1: 61

B2/D2: 55n.5
B17: 61, 63n.33
B22/D39: 59–60
B40: 61
B45/D98: 63n.30
B51: 63n.32
B83: 70–71
B97/D9: 61–62n.29
B101: 62–64
B112/D114a + b: 54–57, 67–74
B116/D30: 54–74
B117: 71
B118: 71
B121: 63
B129: 61, 63, 70–71
D14: 63
D26: 63
D77: 70–71
D103: 71
D114a + b: 68
Herodotus
  1.4.2: 7n.8
  1.171: 59n.21
  3.34.3: 6n.2
  3.35.2: 6n.3
  3.35.4: 6n.4
  3.64.5: 6n.6
  3.71.3: 7n.9
  4.77: 7n.10
  7.15.1-2: 7
  8.49: 165n.32
Hesiod
  Theogony
    128: 61–62n.29
    724: 61–62n.29
Hipponax
  fr. 115: 167n.37
Homer
  Iliad
    11.831: 47n.55
    14.379: 112n.48
    17.254: 34n.19
    21.462-66: 33
  Odyssey
    1.119: 34n.19
    4.157-60: 34
    23.12-15: 35
    23.29-31: 36

Iamblichus
  Protreptic
    XX 98: 165–66

On the Pythagorean Way of Life
  174: 284
  174-6: 283n.8
  175: 286, 287
  187-88: 291n.20
  195-98: 292n.23
  201: 292n.24
  202: 292n.24
  203-4: 295n.27
  204: 296n.30, 296n.32
  205-8: 296n.33
  209: 292n.24
  210: 292n.24, 298n.35
  212-213: 298n.36
Isocrates
  3.38-39: 166–67
  13.6: 140n.34, 269n.54
Lysias
  3.4: 205n.48
  14.12: 205n.48
  19.16: 205n.48
  21.19: 205n.48

Pindar
  fr. 52a.1-4: 44–45
  fr. 52a.9-10: 44–45
  fr. 94b.61-64: 45
  Isthmian Odes
    8.24-27: 46–47
    8.26: 13n.42
  Nemean Odes
    3.74: 47n.53
    4.62ff: 13n.43
  Olympian Odes
    13.6-8: 51n.75
  Paean VI
    fr. 52f.144-45: 46n.52
  Paean IX
    fr. 52k.42-46: 46n.51
  Pythian Odes
    3.63: 47
Plato
  Alcibiades
    105a-c: 148n.61
    122a4-7: 149
    122c4-d1: 149
    124b: 151–52
    129b1: 151n.64
    131b4-5: 150
    131c3: 150
    133a4-c16: 147n.55
    133c: 151–52

378 INDEX LOCORUM

Plato (cont.)
   133c18: 147n.54
   133c18-19: 148
   133c18-d2: 108n.36
   133c21-23: 148
   134a13-14: 152
   134b4-5: 152
   134c9-11: 152
   134d1-2: 152
  Charmides
   158c3-4: 103n.16
   158e6-159a4: 103n.17
   159a6-7: 104n.20
   159b2: 104
   159b3: 205n.45
   159b3-160d3: 104n.18
   161b4-7: 105n.21
   161b8-c1: 105n.22
   161d1-162b1: 151-52
   162c1-e6: 106n.25
   162c4-6: 106n.24
   163e1: 108n.34
   163e1-11: 229n.69
   164a1-c6: 229n.70
   164b3: 108n.34
   164b4: 207n.50
   164d3-165a7: 103n.14
   164d4: 229n.71
   164d5-165b5: 108n.35
   164e7: 58n.19
   165a1-10: 58n.19
   166c1-174e7: 103n.14
   167c4-168a8: 232n.79
   168b2-169a7: 232n.80
   171d1-172a5: 231n.78
   171d1-172c3: 233n.83
   171d2-172a3: 103n.14
   173a7-d5: 103n.14, 231n.78
   173a-d: 141n.39
  Cratylus
   391b: 165n.33
   411a2-4: 27n.3
   411d4-e4: 27n.4
   411e4-412a1: 27n.5
   412a1-4: 27n.6
   412a5-b1: 27n.6
   412b2-8: 27n.6
   412c1-5: 27n.6
   412c6-413d2: 27n.6
   413e1-414a6: 27n.6
  Euthydemus
   281b4-c3: 248n.29
   281c6-7: 248n.30
  Gorgias
   449a1-481b5: 196n.18
   452d-e: 232n.82
   456a-b: 232n.82
   481b1-4: 50n.67
   481b6: 196n.19
   483b4-484c34: 196n.20
   489e8: 197n.23
   491b2-6: 197-98
   491c8-492c10: 204n.42
   491d2-3: 198n.25
   491d10-e1: 198
   491e2: 199n.28
   491e8-9: 199n.29
   492a1-2: 200n.30
   492a5-c8: 200n.31
   493a5: 201n.34
   493c8-d3: 200n.32
   493d9-10: 200n.32
   497c8-e2: 201n.35
   499c-500b: 141n.39
   503e3-504a5: 202n.37
   504a8-b5: 202n.38
   504d1-4: 202n.39
   505b1-7: 202n.40
   506c6-507a2: 203-6
   507a4-c7: 206-8
   507c9-508a4: 208-10
   508a: 150
  Laws
   1.626e2-5: 254n.50
   1.626e6: 254n.51
   1.627c-e: 255n.58
   1.631c2-5: 243
   1.631c5-d1: 243
   1.633e3-6: 254n.52
   1.635c6-8: 254n.53
   1.636b5: 254n.54
   1.637a2-6: 254n.54
   1.644b7: 254n.55
   1.644e1-4: 255n.60
   1.644e4-6: 255n.61
   1.744c9: 254n.56
   2.661a6-b4: 243-44n.16
   3.696b3: 248n.32
   3.696b4: 248n.33
   3.696b10: 249n.34
   3.696c2-6: 249n.34
   3.696c8-10: 249n.34
   3.696d4-6: 249n.39
   3.696d8: 249n.40
   3.696d9-e6: 250
   4.709e7-8: 250n.43
   4.710a5-b2: 251
   4.710b-7: 252n.45
   4.710c5-6: 252n.46
   4.711a1-2: 252n.48

INDEX LOCORUM   379

4.711e1-3: 252n.47
12.948d3: 247n.28
Meno
　71e3: 307n.1
　71e6-7: 307n.2
　73a8-9: 194n.17
　73a9: 307n.3
　74a4-6: 50–51n.72,
　　214n.9
　78d3-79c9: 107n.27
　88a6-b1: 214n.9
　97a3-99a5: 265n.33
Phaedo
　68c: 141n.39
　68c1-2: 189n.4
　68c8-12: 186
　68e2-69a4: 187
　68e-69b: 139n.33
　69a6-c3: 188
Philebus
　48c: 276n.92
　63-64: 141n.39
Protagoras
　321a-2: 191n.7
　321b4-6: 191n.7
　322c2: 191n.7, 263n.21
　323a7: 192n.12
　329c2-d1: 192
　329d4-330b6: 192n.13
　332a4-333b3: 193n.15
　347c-348a: 139n.31
Republic
　3.386a6-388d7: 225n.55
　3.388e1-389a7: 225n.56
　3.389b2-d5: 225n.56
　3.389d: 141n.39
　3.389d9-e2: 226
　3.390b3: 217n.24
　3.390d1: 227n.63
　3.390d7-391a1: 227n.65
　3.391b1-6: 227n.66
　3.391c: 13n.42
　4.427c6-d7: 214n.6
　4.427e3-7: 207n.53
　4.427e6-428a1: 214n.7
　4.428b1-429a3: 215n.11
　4.429a8-430b9: 215n.12
　4.430d3-4: 215n.13
　4.430e: 331–32
　4.430e1: 216n.16
　4.430e1-2: 216n.17
　4.430e4-6: 217
　4.430e6-7: 218n.26
　4.430e9-431a1: 218n.28
　4.431a3-b2: 218n.29

4.431a7-b2: 218n.30
4.431c5: 247n.28
4.431c5-6: 219n.32
4.433a1-6: 221n.40
4.433a1-b4: 221–22
4.433a8-b1: 221
4.433a-b: 213
4.433b3-4: 221
4.433b8: 221n.41
4.441e3-5: 220n.37
4.442c9-d2: 219n.33
5.455d-456a: 307n.4
6.491b9-10: 194n.16
8.549e: 107n.29
8.560d3: 277n.94
10.600a-b: 281n.3
Statesman
　297b1: 247n.28
　306a1: 237n.3
　306b9-11: 238n.4
　306e4-5: 238n.6
　307a8-b2: 238n.5
　307b9: 238n.7
　307e1-308a2: 240n.11
　308a4-9: 240n.13
　309c5: 239n.9
　309e5-8: 239n.10
　310d10-e3: 240n.12
　311a6-9: 240n.14
Timaeus
　29b6: 247n.28
　46e4: 247n.28
　47d3: 247n.28
Plutarch
　Moralia
　　440e: 277n.96
　　441a: 277n.96

Sophocles
　Ajax
　　132: 271n.77
　　293: 309n.13
　　586: 271n.77
　　677: 271n.77
　　1075: 271n.77
　　1259: 271n.77
　　1265: 271n.77
　Antigone
　　474: 165n.31
　Electra
　　307: 271n.76
　Oedipus at Colonus
　　1236: 167n.37
　Oedipus the King (Tyrannos)
　　589: 271n.74

Sophocles (*cont.*)
  Philoctetes
    75: 165n.31
    304: 271n.75
Stobaeus
  2.7.3i: 131n.104
  2.7.4a: 244n.17
  2.7.20: 275n.86, 275n.87
  3.1.178: 54
  3.1.210: 130n.98
  3.5.1: 95n.85
  3.5.6: 54
  3.5.9: 328
  3.5.22: 129n.95
  3.5.23: 129n.96
  3.5.24: 129n.94
  3.5.26: 129n.92
  3.5.27: 128
  3.5.45: 329
  3.5.46: 329–30
  3.5.47: 330
  3.5.48: 331
  3.5.49: 332
  3.5.50: 333
  3.5.57: 112n.46
  3.18.30: 167
  3.20.66: 112n.46
  4.1.49: 289, 289n.14, 290n.16
  4.22.66: 112n.46
  4.23.8: 95n.85
  4.23.61: 312n.22
  4.24.45: 283n.8
  4.32.18: 142n.46
  4.39.25: 130n.99
  4.44.70: 129n.93
  4.50.20: 129n.94
Strabo
  1.2.3: 286n.11

Theognis
  39-42: 38
  43-52: 39n.29
  379-80: 39n.30
  384-85: 39n.31
  387: 39n.31
  395: 39n.31
  429-38: 40
  453-54: 41n.35, 85n.41
  479-83: 41–42
  497-98: 42n.39
  657-66: 41n.36
  665-66: 41n.36
  699-702: 41n.37
  753-56: 39n.31

  1135-38: 42n.40
  1135-42: 207n.51
  1139-42: 42
  1143-50: 42–43n.41
Thucydides
  1.22: 117n.58
  1.32.4: 118n.61
  1.32.4.5: 150n.63
  1.32.5: 119n.62
  1.37.2: 118n.61, 119n.64
  1.40.2: 119n.65
  1.42.2: 121n.69
  1.68.1: 121n.70, 222n.44
  1.68.1.3: 150n.63
  1.69.4: 122n.71
  1.70.2-3: 122n.72
  1.71: 122n.73
  1.79.2: 122n.74
  1.83.1-84.3: 122–23
  1.84.2-3: 150n.63
  1.84.3: 205n.48, 288–89
  1.86.2: 125n.78
  1.120.3-4: 125–26
  3.37.3: 126n.79, 288–89
  3.42.5: 126n.80
  3.44.1: 126n.80
  3.58.1: 126n.81
  3.59.1: 126n.81
  3.62.3: 126n.82
  3.82.2: 123n.75
  3.82.8: 127n.84
  4.18.3-4: 126–27n.83
  4.28.5: 126–27n.83
  4.60.1: 126–27n.83
  4.61.1: 126–27n.83
  4.64.4: 126–27n.83
  6.6.2: 126–27n.83
  6.29.2: 126–27n.83
  6.41.2: 126–27n.83
  6.78.2: 126–27n.83
  6.79.2: 126–27n.83
  6.87.5: 126–27n.83
  8.1.3: 126–27n.83
  8.24.4: 126–27n.83
  8.53.3: 126–27n.83
  8.64.5: 126–27n.83
  43.5: 126n.80

Xenophanes
  B1/D59.24: 111n.41
  B1/D59.20: 71n.50
  B2/D61.12-14: 71n.48
Xenophon
  Agesilaus
    5.1-2: 163n.20

INDEX LOCORUM   381

5.4-7: 163n.20
7: 163n.19
7.3: 161n.13
8.1-2: 163n.19
8.3-4: 163n.19
9.5: 163n.19
10.2: 163n.17
11.10: 163n.16
Anabasis
1.9.3: 161n.12
5.8.24: 160n.6
6.2.11: 160n.6
7.3.17: 160n.6
7.6.41: 160n.6
Apology of Socrates
14: 169n.38
16: 169-70
19: 169n.39
Cynegeticus
12.7-9: 160n.9
13.15.5: 160n.9
Cyropedia
1.2.3-9: 163n.22
1.3.7: 164n.23
1.3.8: 164n.24
1.3.9: 164n.23
3.1.16-22: 161n.14
3.2.13: 160n.6
4.2.24: 160n.6
8.1.23-25: 164n.25
8.1.26-28: 164n.26
8.1.26-29: 164n.27
8.1.30-32: 164n.28
8.1.31: 164n.29
8.3.32: 160n.6
Hellenika
2.3.34: 160n.6
2.3.56: 13n.44
6.2.39: 160n.7
7.1.24: 160n.6
7.3.5: 160n.7
7.3.6: 160n.8
Hipparchus
1.14.3: 160n.7
Memorabilia
1.1.16: 171n.42, 175
1.1.20: 172n.44
1.2-2: 172-73
1.2-2.1: 172
1.2.9: 174n.53
1.2.10: 174n.55
1.2.12-16: 175n.56
1.2.14: 207n.52

1.2.17: 172n.45
1.2.17-18: 175n.58
1.2.19: 140n.35
1.2.19-20: 176n.60
1.2.21: 176n.61
1.2.22: 176n.62
1.2.23: 176n.63
1.2.24: 102n.9, 176n.65
1.2.24-28: 176n.64
1.2.28-47: 176n.64
1.5.1: 331n.44
1.5.4: 159n.3, 331
1.5.5: 331n.45
1.5.6: 173n.47
1.6: 111n.44
1.6.8: 173n.48
1.6.10: 145n.49
2.1.1: 173n.49
2.1.24: 174n.51, 258n.2
2.6.1: 174n.52
3.9.4: 181-82, 193
4.2.1-10: 139n.31
4.2.2: 178n.69
4.2.3-12: 178n.70
4.2.13: 178n.72
4.2.13-14: 178n.71
4.2.14: 178n.72
4.2.16: 178n.73
4.2.17: 178n.72
4.2.40: 177n.67
4.3: 207n.51
4.3.1: 177n.68
4.3.2-18: 269n.55
4.3.16-17: 178
4.5.3: 179n.77
4.5.4-5: 179n.77
4.5.6: 180-81, 180n.81
4.5.7: 180n.82
4.5.10-11: 180n.79
4.5.11: 180n.80
Oeconomicus
7.14-15: 307n.5
Spartan Constitution
3.4.5: 161n.10
7.2: 222n.44
Symposium
1.8: 170n.40
1.10: 170n.41
2.17: 131n.107
4.26: 170n.41
4.60-64: 137n.18
8.3-6: 137n.18
8.8: 170n.40

Index

For the benefit of digital users, indexed terms that span two pages (e.g., 52–53) may, on occasion, appear on only one of those pages.

Tables are indicated by *t* following the page number

Adam, James, 214n.10–15, 216n.16, 222n.43, 223–24, 227n.61
Adkins, A. W. H., 15n.50, 17–18, 19n.66
Aeacus, 44n.45, 46, 47n.53
Aegisthus, 48
Aelian, as source for Archytas, 299–300
Aeschylus, 29n.11, 48–50, 53, 61, 64, 69
Agamemnon, 29–32, 48, 226
Agamemnon (Aeschylus), 48
agency
  Antiphon and, 114–15
  Antisthenes and, 139–40
  aporias about, 333–34
  Aristotle and, 25, 326
  ascription of, 6–7
  Charmides and, 228–29, 231, 234
  civic agency, 198
  Clouds and, 11, 14
  corporate agency, 209
  desire-control and, 3–4, 115, 138, 189–90, 196–97
  enkrateia and, 183–84
  epistemic agency, 22, 64, 73–74
  ethical agency, 23
  Euripides and, 23
  failures of, 6, 123
  freedom and, 18, 184, 311–12
  Gorgias and, 196–98, 199, 209, 210, 212, 240–41
  Heraclitus and, 22, 64, 73–74
  Hippolytus and, 81–82, 86–87
  History and, 123–24
  Laws and, 245, 255–56
  letter to Arete and, 302–3, 331
  overview of, 1–4, 14–15, 337
  personal agency, 210, 213
  Plato and, 24, 185, 189, 235, 241, 254–55
  Protagoras and, 193–94
  Pythagorean Precepts and, 282, 285, 286–87, 288–89
  Republic and, 225–28
  self-constitution and, 3, 74, 213, 288–89, 337
  self-knowledge and, 64
  Socrates and, 145, 146–47
  Statesman and, 239–41
  women and, 25–26, 310, 311–12, 314–18, 333–34
  On Women's Sôphrosunê and, 314–18
  Xenophon and, 161–62, 183–84
Agesilaus, 157–58, 161, 163
Agesilaus (Xenophon), 161, 163
agôn, 11, 23–24, 135
aidôs, 51, 79–80, 83, 84–86, 89, 104–7, 124, 163–65, 191, 212–13, 241, 263–65
Ajax, 47, 308–9
Ajax (Antisthenes), 137–38
Ajax (Sophocles), 100–1, 308–9
akrasia, 133–34, 163, 167–68, 173–74, 179–80, 193, 265–66, 274–75
Alcibiades, 126–27n.83, 135n.10, 140, 174–77, 179, 207
See also Alcibiades (Platonic corpus)
Alcibiades (Platonic corpus), 146–54
  authorship of, 146–47
  flourishing in, 152
  justice in, 149
  leadership in, 148
  orderliness in, 149–50
  overview of, 134–35, 146–47, 155–56
  Persians in, 150
  pleasure in, 149
  relation to other dialogues of, 146–47, 151–52
  scholarship on, 147
  self-knowledge in, 146–49, 150–54
  Socrates and, 146–54
  Spartans as model in, 149–51, 279–80
  wisdom in, 147–48, 153
alcohol. *See* drinking
Amphiaraus, 48–49

Anabasis (Xenophon), 161, 163–64
Annas, Julia, 128n.89, 131n.104, 217n.21, 219n.34, 222n.43, 224n.51
Anonymus Iamblichi (in Iamblichus), 100–1, 142n.44, 146n.53, 152n.66, 165–67, 295n.26
Anthology (Stobaeus). *See* Stobaeus.
Antiphon, 111–17
　agency and, 114–15
　coup planning associated with, 111–12
　courage and, 112
　depiction of, 111–12
　enkrateia account of, 112–14, 132, 217–18, 339
　orderliness and, 112–13, 114–15
　overview of, 101, 132
　reflexive language and, 114–17
　self-constitution and, 117
Antisthenes, 137–41
　agency and, 139–40
　depiction of, 137
　erôs and, 138
　fame of, 138–39
　fighting and, 139
　Homer and, 139
　hubris and, 140
　learning to read and, 138–39, 143–44
　pleasure and, 138–39
　self-knowledge and, 138–39
　Socrates and, 137–41, 155
　traits associated with, 137
　writings of, 137–38
Apology of Socrates (Plato), 169, 233–34
Apology of Socrates (Xenophon), 168–71
Aquinas, 267–68
Archidamus, 122–25, 126, 287–88
Archytas, 25, 281, 298–306
See also Life of Archytas (Aristoxenus)
aretê. *See* virtue
Aristarchus, 34n.18
Aristophanes, 11–14, 100, 135. *See also Clouds* (Aristophanes)
Aristotle. *See also Eudemian Ethics* (Aristotle); *Magna Moralia* (Aristotle); *Nicomachean Ethics* (Aristotle); *Politics* (Aristotle); *Topics* (Aristotle)
　agency and, 25, 326
　authoritative norms and, 25
　authoritative virtue and, 264–65
　contrary evidence for interpretation of, 267–73
　courage and, 133–34, 260–61, 308–9
　departure of, 257–58

　desire-control and, 245, 253–54, 258–59, 263–64
　distinctions among moral-psychological states and, 263–67
　emotional mean and, 258, 261–65
　enkrateia and, 159, 254–55, 257, 265–67, 274–75, 277–78
　etymology of *sôphrosunê* and, 28
　indiscipline and, 258–60, 270–71, 276–77
　influence of, 273–80
　innovation of, 257–58
　justice and, 263, 268–71, 272–73, 308
　moderation and, 226–27, 245, 261–68, 275–76, 338
　natural virtue and, 258, 264–65
　official view of, 258–62, 309–10
　overview of, 257–58, 280
　hronesis and, 28, 159, 245, 253–54, 310
　Plato's influence on, 242, 258, 262, 265, 270–71
　pleasure and, 260–61
　relation between virtues and, 260–62
　role-defined virtues and, 308
　self-knowledge and, 270–71
　shame and, 263–65
　Socrates and, 133–34
　sympathetic reception of, 267–73
　wisdom and, 257, 263–71, 309–10
　women and, 308–10
Aristoxenus of Tarentum, 25, 273, 281–82. *See also Life of Archytas* (Aristoxenus); *Pythagorean Precepts* (Aristoxenus)
Arius Didymus, 131, 275–76
Aspasius, 267–68
Athenian Stranger. *See Laws* (Plato)
Athens, 123n.76, 126–27n.83, 157–58, 176–77
　Critias and, 101–3, 109, 236, 305
　Corcyreans and, 118–21, 122
authoritative norms
　Aristotle and, 25
　Clouds and, 12–13
　desire-control and, 25
　enkrateia and, 185–86
　Hippolytus and, 82, 93
　Laws and, 245
　norm-following, 45, 131, 159, 162, 209–10, 253–54, 268–70
　Protagoras and, 193–94
　Pythagorean Precepts and, 25, 284–85, 294
　Republic and, 228
　Socrates and, 135–36
　Statesman and, 239–40
　Theognis and, 43

INDEX   385

women and, 322–23, 333–34
On Women's Sôphrosunê and, 322–23, 333–34
Xenophon and, 158–59, 161–62, 164–65, 168–69, 185–86
autopragia, 107n.32, 279–80

Bacchae (Euripides), 75–76, 93–98
Bandini, Michele, 173n.50, 181n.85
Banqueters (Aristophanes), 135–36
Barrett, William, 84n.36, 88n.63, 89–90n.72
Bigio, Brian, 29n.11
Birds (Aristophanes), 136–37
Bobonich, Christopher, 189n.3, 214n.5, 216n.19, 219n.34, 244n.17, 249n.37, 255n.59, 262n.18
Bollack, Jean, 57–59, 66–67, 69–70, 71
Bourgault, Sophie, 19n.64, 268n.48
Bowra, Cecil, 44n.45
Broadie, Sarah, 18n.62, 261–62, 267n.41, 267n.45
Burnet, John, 267–68

Cairns, Douglas, 79n.14, 84n.36, 112n.45, 131n.106, 191–92n.11
Callard, Agnes, 265n.34
Callicles, 50n.67, 145, 190, 196–211, 212, 234, 240–41, 282, 300
Cambyses, 6, 8
canon of virtues, 1, 4–5, 214–15, 336–37
  in Aeschylus, 48–49
  change of, according to Adkins, 17
  in epigraphy, 49–51
  in Iamblichus, 327–28
  in Isocrates, 268–70
  in Phintys, 318
  in Pindar, 47n.53
  in Plato, 192–93, 206–8, 214–15, 239, 243–44
  in the *Problemata*, 274
  in Xenophon, 163, 170–71
cardinal virtues. *See* canon of virtues
Carey, Christopher, 47n.53
Carson, Anne, 78n.4, 79n.14
celibacy, 337–38. *See also* chastity; Hippolytus
Charmides (Plato), 228–35
  agency in, 228–29, 231, 234, 235
  doing one's own things in, 103–9, 151–52, 205, 212–13, 222–24, 228–29
  epistemic account of, 228–35
  expertise in, 233–34
  inadequate definitions in, 104–5, 106–7
  knowledge of knowledge in, 103, 230–34
  moderation and, 109
  opening of, 103–4

overview of, 212–14
relation to other dialogues of, 212–13, 231, 233–34
scholarly attention on, 18
self-knowledge in, 103, 108, 189–90, 228–35
setting of, 103, 106
shame in, 104–7, 212–13, 241, 263
tranquility in, 104–7, 153–54, 205–6, 212–13
transformation of proposed definitions in, 228–29
Chastity, 19n.64, 19n.66, 21, 22–23, 75–76, 92, 95–96, 271n.77, 311n.19, 318n.34
as translation of *sôphrosunê*, 337–38
Choice of Heracles (Prodicus), 84, 173–74, 258–59, 325n.39
Christian reception of *sôphrosunê*, 273, 280, 338
Chrysippus, 279–80, 283n.9
Cicero, 303–4, 338
city of pigs, 222n.42
Clark, Justin, 234n.84
Clement of Alexandria, 49–50
Clinias (in *Euthydemus*), 248
Clinias (in *Laws*), 250–51, 254–55
clothing
  austere or white, 12–13, 324–25
  equality of, 302
  keeping hands under, 160–61
  luxurious, 291, 296–97
  making one's own, 222
  Socrates' and Antisthenes', 135–37
Clouds (Aristophanes), 5, 11–14, 104, 106, 107n.31, 127–29, 135–36, 205, 238
Clytemnestra, 48
constitution of the self. *See* self-constitution
control of desire. *See* desire-control
Cooper, John, 258n.1
Cornford, F. M., 214–15n.10, 216n.18, 222n.43, 226n.58
courage
  Antiphon and, 112
  Aristotle and, 133–34, 260–61, 308–9
  as distinctive of philosophers, 186
  epigraphy and, 49–50
  Gorgias and, 199–200, 202–3, 240–41
  Heraclitus and, 69–70
  Laws and, 243–44, 247–49, 253, 270–71
  overview of, 1–2
  Pindar and, 44, 46
  Plato and, 186–87
  Protagoras and, 192–93, 195
  Republic and, 214–16, 225, 245–46
  shame and, 124
  Statesman and, 238–40

courage (cont.)
    in Thucydides, 124
    translation of, 336–37
    wisdom and, 192–93
    women and, 308–9
    On Women's Sôphrosunê and, 318, 319
    Xenophon and, 161–62, 163, 170–71
Cratylus (Plato), 27–28, 165, 215n.12
Critias of Athens.
    absence from Thucydides, 117–18
    and Alcibiades, 140, 174–77, 207
    his definition appearing in the *Republic*, 213, 222, 223–24
    Delphic speech of, 58n.18, 103
    on drinking in his *Spartan Constitution*, 109–11
    influence on Xenophon, 158
    life in relation to the Thirty, 101–3, 236, 305
    linked with Antiphon, 111–12
    role in four Platonic dialogues, 101–3, 133n.1
    "Sisyphus" fragment, 283–84
    See also *Charmides* (Plato)
Curzer, Howard, 264n.31, 267n.42
Cyropedia (Xenophon), 161–62, 163–65
Cyrus, 137–38, 161–62, 163–65

Darius, 48
Davies, Malcolm, 79n.14
Definitions (Platonic corpus), 278–80
Delebecque, Edouard, 165n.30
Democritus of Abdera, 127–31
    akrasia and, 167
    happiness and, 127–29, 131
    justice and, 129
    moderation and, 130, 131
    pleasure and, 130–31
    self-knowledge and, 131
    self-sufficiency and, 129
Demos, Raphael, 216n.19, 221n.39
Denyer, Nicholas, 134n.7, 147n.58, 147n.60, 151n.64, 191–92n.11, 194n.16
desire-control. See also *enkrateia*
    agency and, 3–4, 115, 138, 189–90, 196–97
    Aristotle and, 245, 253–54, 258–59, 263–64
    authoritative norms and, 25
    enkrateia and, 164–65, 168–69, 180, 198–99
    Gorgias and, 196–97, 198–202
    Heraclitus and, 65
    letter to Arete and, 329–31
    Plato and, 253–54
    Protagoras and, 193, 196
    Republic and, 219–20, 228
    Xenophon and, 159–60, 162, 163–65, 168–70, 179–80

De Vries, G. K., 15n.47, 19n.66
Diels, Hermann, 63n.30, 66n.36, 106n.26, 116–17n.56
Diogenes Laertius
    on Antisthenes, 137, 138–39
    on Heraclitus, 60n.24
    on Heraclides of Pontic Heraclea, 276
    on Plato, 278
    on Pythagoras, 281
    on Socrates, 133n.1
    on Theophrastus, 275–76
Diogenes of Sinope, 145–46
Dionysus, 94–97, 98
discipline, self-discipline, 4–5, 32, 170, 291
    as definition of *sôphrosunê*, 339–40
    See also indiscipline
discretion, 19n.66, 52, 68n.42, 76, 120n.67
    as translation of *sôphrosunê*, 339
Dissoi Logoi, 167–68, 171n.43
Divisions (*Divisiones Aristoteleae*), 278, 279–80
Dodds, E. R., 91n.78, 95n.88, 96n.91, 97–98, 98n.102, 196n.21, 204–5
doing/faring well, 190, 193, 194–95
doing one's own things, 103–9, 151–52, 205, 212–13, 222–24, 228–29
Donlan, Walter, 38n.25, 44n.42
Dorandi, Tiziano, 138n.30, 278n.102
Dorion, Louis-André, 133n.2, 159n.4, 178n.69, 181n.85, 198n.26, 254n.57, 324–25, 325n.39
Dover, Kenneth, 11n.25, 11n.27, 50n.68, 107n.31
drinking, 13, 21, 168
    in Antiphon, 115–16
    in Aristotle, 258–59, 260–62, 270–72, 274–75
    in *Bacchae*, 94
    in Critias, 101–3, 109–11
    in Democritus, 130
    in Heraclitus, 71
    in Iamblichus, 291
    importance of taste, 260–61
    in Plato, 226–27, 254–55
    "temperance" and, 338
    in Theognis, 41–42
    wine, 42, 97, 109, 260–61, 272n.79
    in Xenophon, 163–64, 169, 172–74, 175–76, 179–80
    See also symposium, food and eating
Dutsch, Dorota, 292n.22, 310–11n.18, 312n.21

early history of *sôphrosunê*
    Aeschylus and, 48–49
    epigraphy and, 49–52
    etymological considerations and, 27–32, 30t

Homer and, 33–37, 38–39
overview of, 27–32, 52–53
Pindar and, 44–47
preclassical period of, 52–53
Theognis and, 37–44
eating. *See* food and eating
Einarson, Benedict, 15n.47, 29
Eleatic Visitor. *See Statesman* (Plato)
Electra (Sophocles), 271
England, E. B., 246–47n.26, 250n.42
enkrateia. *See also* desire-control
  agency and, 183–84
  Antiphon and, 112–14, 132, 217–18, 339
  Aristotle and, 159, 254–55, 257, 265–67, 274–75, 277–78
  authoritative norms and, 185–86
  definition as "inner power" or "self-control," 158–59
  desire-control aspect of, 164–65, 168–69, 180, 198–99
  development of, 165–67
  as "foundation" (*krêpis*) of virtue, 142, 158–59, 172–73, 176–77, 180, 182–83, 331
  Gorgias and, 198–99, 217–18
  letter to Arete and, 331–32
  linguistic background of, 165–66
  Plato and, 159, 185–86, 235, 265–66, 331–32
  psychologization of, 167
  Republic and, 217–20, 331–32
  self-constitution and, 158–59
  as translation of *sôphrosunê*, 339
  wisdom and, 182
  Xenophon and, 142, 158–59, 162–67, 168–69, 172–80, 182, 185–86, 265–66, 331
epigraphy, 49–52, 341
erôs, 78–79, 86–87, 92–93, 138
Eteocles, 49
etymology of *sôphrosunê*, 27–32, 30*t*
Eudemian Ethics (Aristotle), 258, 259–60, 263, 270–71
Euripides. *See also Bacchae* (Euripides); *Hippolytus* (Euripides); *Medea* (Euripides)
  agency and, 23
  overview of, 8–11, 75–76, 98–99
  self-constitution and, 75–76
Eusebian reading, 244–46, 253–54
Eusebius of Caesarea, 244–46
Euthydemus, 177–80
Euthydemus (Plato), 247–48

faring/doing well, 190, 193, 194–95
Ferrari, G. R. F., 215n.14
Festugière, André-Jean, 79n.14

Fitton, J. W., 84n.37, 88n.57, 89n.67
flower names, 107n.31
food and eating, 13, 219–20, 299–300
  acquired desire for, 296–97
  dancing's improvement of taste of, 131n.107
  with drink and sex, the desire for, 130, 168, 172–74, 226–27, 274–75
  enkrateia concerning, 163–64, 331
  and feeling going down the throat, 259–60
  gluttons, gourmands, and connoisseurs of, 259–61, 271–72
  limiting one's desire for, 291
  and the pleasures of touch and taste, 258–62, 270–72
  and quality of sleep, 129
  Spartan moderation toward, 110
  unconcern for, 136–37, 154–55, 163
Foucault, Michel, 18
freedom, 14, 18, 92, 142–43, 149, 170, 179–80, 184, 311–12
Friedländer, Paul, 50–51n.72

Geach, Peter, 18–19n.63
Gemelli Marciano, M., 282n.5
Gerber, Douglas, 39, 41n.38
Gerson, Lloyd, 282n.5
Giudice Rizzo, 98n.100
Goldhill, Simon, 77n.3, 80n.17, 100n.1
Gorgias, 100–1, 117n.58, 196, 232–33
  views on virtue, 49–50, 50–51n.72, 308–9
Gorgias (Plato), 196–210
  agency in, 196–98, 199, 209, 210, 212, 240–41
  consequences about *sôphrosunê* in, 208–10
  courage in, 199–200, 240–41
  desire-control in, 196–97, 198–202
  enkrateia in, 198–99, 217–18
  goodness in, 203–6
  happiness in, 206–8
  justice in, 191–93, 196–99, 207–9
  natural right theory in, 196–98
  orderliness in, 150, 201–2, 205–6
  overview of, 190, 196–97, 210–11
  pleasure in, 202–3
  relation between virtues in, 198–99, 201–2, 207–8
  self-constitution and, 211
  undisciplined life argued against in, 200–2
  wisdom in, 196–97, 256
  See also Callicles.

Hamilton, Edith, 19–20
happiness, 127–29, 131, 137, 145, 199, 201, 206–8, 248, 298

harmony among psychic parts, 215–25
Helen, 6–7, 34
Heracles, 13, 20, 47, 155
Heraclides of Pontic Heraclea, 276, 281
Heraclitus
  agency and, 22, 64, 73–74
  aretê and, 69–71
  authenticity of texts attributed to, 55–56, 57
  courage and, 69–70
  desire-control and, 65
  etymology of *sôphrosunê* and, 57–58
  ginôskein and, 60–65
  greatest virtue for, *sôphrosunê* as, 65–73
  logos and, 55–56, 58–59, 62–63, 65, 71, 72, 73–74
  moderation and, 69
  overview of, 54–57, 73–74
  reflexive pronouns and, 62–64
  scholarship on, 55–58, 66–68
  self-constitution and, 57–58, 73–74
  self-knowledge and, 55–65, 72, 73–74, 276
  two *sôphrosunê* fragments and, 54–57
  wisdom and, 54–56, 58, 65–68, 70–72, 73–74
Herman, Gabriel, 19n.66
Herodotus, 5–8
Hesiod, 18, 29, 37
  in Heraclitus, 61–62n.29
Hippias, 100–1
Hippocratic corpus, 63n.30, 167n.37, 168
Hippolytus, 17–18, 22–23, 76, 96, 98–99, 154–55. *See also Hippolytus* (Euripides)
Hippolytus (Euripides), 77–93
  agency and, 81–82, 86–87
  authoritative norms and, 82, 93
  conscience and, 79
  Hippolytus' problem in, 78–80
  moderation and, 87, 92, 96–97
  nurse's challenge in, 82–88
  overview of, 75–78, 92–93
  Phaedra's problem in, 80–82
  self-constitution and, 75–76, 93
  self-defense of Hippolytus in, 89–92
  self-knowledge and, 93
  shame in, 79–80, 85–86
  two versions of, 78n.4
  wisdom in, 337
Hipponax, 116n.55, 167n.37
Histories (Herodotus), 5–8
history of *sôphrosunê*. *See* early history of *sôphrosunê*
History of the Peloponnesian War (Thucydides)
  agency in, 123–24
  Corcyreans vs Corinthians in, 118–21
  Corinthians vs Spartans in, 121–27
  orderliness and, 123–25
  overview of, 126–27
  self-knowledge in, 124
Homer, 4–5, 33–37, 38–39, 108–9, 139. *See also Iliad* (Homer); *Odyssey* (Homer)
Housman, A. E., 90n.73
hubris, 42, 79, 86, 140, 163–65, 238–39, 292, 293
Huffman, Carl, 282–84, 285n.10, 290
Hutchinson, D. S., 147n.57, 262n.20, 277n.97, 279n.105, 283n.6
Hypsipyle (Euripides), 20, 76n.1

Iamblichus. *See Anonymus Iamblichi* (in Iamblichus); letter to Arete (Iamblichus); *On The Pythagorean Way of Life* (Iamblichus)
idiopragia, 107–8
Iliad (Homer), 33–34, 42, 47
indiscipline, 126, 187, 202–3, 258–60, 270–71, 276–77
intellectualism, 229–30, 262
Irwin, Terence, 192n.13, 196n.21, 216n.19, 219n.34, 238–39, 239n.8, 267–68
Isocrates, 139–40, 167, 258, 268–70
Isthmian 8 (Pindar), 46, 48

Jerome of Stridon, 137
Jones, Russell, 181n.85
Jowett, Benjamin, 120n.68, 244n.17
justice
  Alcibiades and, 149
  Aristotle and, 263, 268–71, 272–73, 308
  definition of, 1–2
  Democritus and, 129
  etymology of, 27–28
  Gorgias and, 191–93, 196–99, 207–9
  Laws and, 243–45, 247, 249, 252–53
  overview, 1–2
  Protagoras and, 191, 192–93, 194, 195
  Republic and, 213, 214–15, 221–25
  Theognis and, 39–40, 41
  translation of, 336–37
  wisdom and, 242
  women and, 319
  On Women's Sôphrosunê and, 319
  Xenophon and, 163–65, 179–80, 207

Kahn, Charles, 58–59, 58n.19, 66, 67–68, 67n.38, 68n.42, 225n.53
Kirk, Gregory, 55n.4, 55n.7, 60n.24, 67n.39, 128n.89
knowledge of knowledge, 103, 230–34

INDEX 389

know yourself. *See* self-knowledge
Knox, Bernard, 77n.3, 78n.5, 81n.26
Kollmann, Albrecht, 15n.47, 33n.15, 38n.24, 44n.44
Korsgaard, Christine, vi, 189
Kosman, Aryeh, 104n.18, 224n.52, 225n.54, 234n.84, 262n.17
Kovacs, David, 9n.14, 10n.24, 79–80n.15, 84n.33, 84n.37, 94n.81, 95

Laks, André, 55–56, 68, 69, 242n.15, 244n.19
Larson, Curtis, 225n.53
Lattimore, Steven, 120n.68
Laws (Plato), 241–56
    agency in, 245, 255–56
    authoritative norms in, 245
    calculation in, 255
    central question of, 243–44
    courage in, 243–44, 247–49, 253, 270–71
    distinctness of, 242
    justice in, 243–45, 247, 249, 252–53
    legitimacy of rule in, 248–49, 252
    moderation and, 246
    nous in, 243–54
    overview of, 241–42
    hronesis in, 251–53
    reason in, 245–49
    relation between *sôphrosunê* and *nous* in, 244–54
    self-knowledge in, 245
    self-management in, 242, 245, 254–56
    textual crux in, 243–54
    wisdom in, 242, 248–49, 252–53
Lebedev, A. V., 56n.9, 58n.18, 60n.24, 68–69n.44
Lefkowitz, Mary, 311n.19, 313n.29, 316n.32
letter to Arete (Iamblichus)
    agency in, 302–3, 331
    desire-control in, 329–31
    enkrateia in, 331–32
    gendered virtue absent from, 327–28
    influences on, 331–32
    metavirtue in, *sôphrosunê* as, 331–33
    multiform nature of *sôphrosunê* in, 328–29
    orderliness in, 333
    overview of, 326–27
    passions in, 330–31
    wisdom in, 327–28
Leunissen, Mariska, 264n.31, 310n.17
Life of Archytas (Aristoxenus), 25, 298–304
Linforth, Ivan, 78n.9, 81n.26
logos, 55–56, 58–59, 62–63, 65, 71, 72, 73–74
Lorch, Benjamin, 178n.69, 225n.54

MacDowell, Douglas, 11n.27
MacIntyre, Alasdair, 267n.45
Magna Moralia (Aristotle), 258–60
Marchant, E. C., 181n.85
Marcovich, Miroslav, 60n.24, 66, 138n.30
Mastronarde, Donald, 9n.16, 9n.18, 10n.24
maxims, 56n.8, 101–3, 127n.86, 129, 142, 222n.43, 291
know yourself, 57–58, 62, 103
Medea (Euripides), 5, 8–11, 20, 75–76
Megillus, 250
Memorabilia (Xenophon), 145, 160, 161–62, 168–69, 170–77, 171*t*, 180–81, 321–22, 331
Menedemus of Ertria, 277
Meno (Plato), 36n.21, 107n.27, 194n.17, 239, 243–44n.16, 246n.23, 265, 307–8
    canonical list of virtues in, 214n.8
Meno's list of virtues in, 50–51n.72, 214–15, 310–11n.18
Meyer, Susan Suavé, 246–48
Michael of Ephesus, 276–77
moderation
    Aristotle and, 226–27, 245, 261–68, 275–76, 338
    Critias and, 109
    the *Definitions* and, 278
    Democritus and, 127n.86, 130, 131
    Heraclitus and, 55n.4, 69
    Hippolytus and, 87, 92, 96–97
    Phintys and, 316n.31
    Pindar and, 45
    as translation of *sôphrosunê*, 14–15, 18–19, 338
Morris, Charles, 120n.67
Most, Glenn W., 55–56, 68, 69
MS reading, 244–46
Musgrave, Samuel, 95

Nails, Debra, 102n.8, 310–11n.18
Nestor, 252
Nicocles (Isocrates), 166–67, 268–70
Nicomachean Ethics (Aristotle), 18, 28, 242, 258–59, 263–66, 270–71
Nill, Michael, 127n.86, 191–92n.11
norm-following. *See* authoritative norms
North, Helen, 15–17, 19–20, 222n.42, 223n.45
Norwood, Gilbert, 78n.10, 81n.26, 85n.42, 90n.74
Nussbaum, Martha, 124n.77, 262n.17

Odysseus, 29–32, 34–35, 36, 143–44, 155, 172–73, 227, 271

Odysseus (Antisthenes), 137–38
Odyssey (Homer), 29–32, 34–36, 52
Oeconomicus (Xenophon), 307–8
Oedipus (Euripides), 20, 76n.1, 85n.41
Oedipus the King (Sophocles), 271
On Concord. *See* Antiphon
On Euthumia. *See* Democritus
On Sôphrosunê. *See* Heraclides of Pontic Heraclea; Speusippus; Stobaeus; Xenocrates
On the Pythagorean Way of Life (Iamblichus), 282–83, 290–92, 298–99, 300
On Truth (Antiphon), 111–12
On Women's Harmony (Perictione), 312–13, 320n.35
On Women's Sôphrosunê (Phintys), 310–11, 312–26
  agency in, 314–18
  authoritative norms in, 322–23, 333–34
  courage in, 318, 319
  dating of, 312
  gendered virtue in, 312–20
  greatest virtue for women in, 312–15
  justice in, 319
  marital fidelity in, 322–24
  modesty in, 324–25
  overview of, 310–14, 326
  philosophizing of women in, 315–16
  piety in, 325–26
  relation between virtues in, 314, 318–19
  self-constitution and, 321–22, 326
  wisdom in, 312–13
orderliness (*kosmiotês*, *eutaxia*)
  Alcibiades and, 149–50
  Antiphon and, 112–13, 114–15
  Gorgias and, 150, 201–2, 205–6
  History and, 123–25
  letter to Arete and, 333
  Plato and, 186–87, 190
  Protagoras and, 193
  Republic and, 217–18

Paean I (Pindar), 44–45, 46, 47
Paean VI (Pindar), 46–47
Page, Denys Lionel, 9n.18
Pakaluk, Michael, 264n.31
Pappas, Nickolas, 216n.19
Parthenian II (Pindar), 45–46, 48
Pearson, Giles, 267–68
Peisistratus, 34
Peloponnesian War, 5, 23, 101–3, 106, 118–19
Pendrick, Gerard, 112n.47
Pentheus. *See Bacchae* (Euripides)

Perictione. *See On Women's Harmony* (Perictione)
Persians, 6–8, 148–49, 301
  in Xenophon, 157–58, 161–62, 163–65
Persians (Aeschylus), 48
Phaedo (Plato), 139, 146–47, 186–90, 205, 217–18, 237, 251–52, 254–55, 265
Phaedra. *See Hippolytus* (Euripides)
Philoctetes (Sophocles), 271
Phintys of Sparta. See *On Women's Sôphrosunê* (Phintys)
Phocylides, 43–44
hronesis, 27–29, 159, 184, 239, 243–45, 248, 251–54, 264–65, 310, 336–37
piety, 1–2, 49, 91–92, 169, 192–93, 207, 325–26, 336–37
Pindar, 4–5, 32, 44–46, 49–50, 52, 64, 69, 70, 73–74
Plato. See also *Charmides* (Plato); *Gorgias* (Plato); *Laws* (Plato); *Meno* (Plato); *Phaedo* (Plato); *Protagoras* (Plato); *Republic* (Plato); *Statesman* (Plato)
  agency and, 24–25, 185, 189, 235, 241, 254–55
  Aristotle influenced by, 242, 258, 262, 265, 270–71
  challenges of defining *sôphrosunê* for, 186
  courage and, 186–87
  desire-control and, 253–54
  in Diogenes Laertius, 278
  enkrateia and, 159, 185–86, 235, 265–66, 331–32
  etymology of *sôphrosunê* and, 27–28
  norm-following and desire-control unified by, 253–54
  orderliness and, 186–87, 190
  overview of, 185–96, 210–11, 212–14, 236–37, 256
  perspective varying across dialogues of, 186
  philosophers and, 186–88
  self-constitution and, 185
  as theorist of *sôphrosunê*, 185–90
  wisdom and, 189–90, 235, 237, 256
Politics (Aristotle), 308–9
Polyarchus, 300–4
Pomeroy, Sarah, 311n.19, 314n.30
preclassical *sôphrosunê*, 52–53
Prexaspes, 6
Prince, Susan, 138n.27, 138n.30, 139n.32, 145–46
Problemata (Aristotelian corpus), 272n.79, 274–75
Prodicus. *See Choice of Heracles* (Prodicus)

INDEX   391

Promêtheia, 51n.75, 115, 268n.50, 285n.10
Protagoras, 12n.34, 100–1, 191n.6, *See also*
  Protagoras (Plato)
Protagoras (Plato), 190–96
  agency in, 193–94
  authoritative norms in, 193–94
  courage in, 192–93, 195
  desire-control in, 193, 196, 241
  doing/faring well definition in, 190, 193,
    194–95
  Great Speech in, 191, 195, 263
  indeterminacy in, 195–96
  justice in, 191, 192–93, 194, 195
  orderliness in, 193
  overview of, 190–91
  relation between virtues in, 192–95
  respect in, 191, 193–94
  self-constitution and, 211
  shame in, 191, 263
  wisdom in, 190, 192–94, 195, 241
Pythagoras, 281
  in Aristoxenus and Iamblichus, 281, 291
  in Heraclitus, 63, 70–71
Pythagorean Precepts (Aristoxenus), 281–98
  agency in, 282, 285, 286–87, 288–89
  authoritative norms in, 25, 284–85, 294
  civic architecture in, 289–90
  course of life guided by *sôphrosunê* in,
    290–98
  divine panopticon in, 284
  education in, 294–95
  fragment 2 in, 289–90
  fragment 8 in, 283–89
  fragment 9 in, 290–98
  hubris in, 284–85
  influence of, 290–91
  overview of, 281–83, 305–6
  pleasure in, 295–97
  real-life community in, 305–6
  self-constitution in, 285–87, 288–89
  self-knowledge and, 286–87, 288–89
  theology and, 283–89

quasi-Academic sources, 276–80

Rademaker, Adriaan, 16–17, 19–20, 38n.25,
  40n.34
rational agency. *See* agency
Raymond, Christopher C., ix, 104n.18, 109n.39,
  223n.48, 264–65, 264n.26, 339–40
reflexivity
  in Antiphon, 112, 117
  in Heraclitus, 62

  in Plato, 108, 213, 218, 231
  in translations of *sôphrosunê*, 339
Republic (Plato), 214–28
  affective account in, 214–28
  agency in, 225–28
  authoritative norms in, 228
  book 3 account in, 225–28, 252–53
  book 4 account in, 215–25, 228, 231, 236–37,
    242, 245–46, 252–53, 279–80, 289, 328–29,
    332–33
  courage in, 214–16, 225, 245–46
  desire-control in, 219–20, 228
  doing one's own things definition in, 221–25
  education in, 226–28
  enkrateia in, 217–20, 331–32
  harmony among psychic parts in, 215–25
  justice in, 213, 214–15, 221–25
  orderliness in, 217–18
  overview of, 212–14
  relation between virtues in, 207–8, 214–15,
    216–17, 224
  self-constitution in, 225–28
  self-knowledge in, 229–30, 231
  wisdom in, 214–17, 245–46
Rhianus, 34n.18
Richards, Herbert, 224n.50
Rowe, Christopher, 225n.53, 244n.21
Russell, Daniel, 264n.31

Schofield, Malcolm, 19n.66, 298–99, 298n.37
self-constitution
  agency and, 3, 74, 213, 288–89, 337
  Antiphon and, 117
  enkrateia and, 158–59
  Euripides and, 75–76
  Gorgias and, 211
  Heraclitus and, 57–58, 73–74
  Hippolytus and, 75–76, 93
  overview of, 3, 14–15, 17
  Plato and, 185
  Protagoras and, 211
  Pythagorean Precepts and, 285–87, 288–89
  Republic and, 225–28
  Socrates and, 135, 145
  women and, 321–22, 326
  On Women's Sôphrosunê and, 321–22, 326
  Xenophon and, 158–59
self-control. *See* desire-control; *enkrateia*
self-knowledge
  agency and, 64
  Alcibiades and, 146–49, 150–54
  Antisthenes and, 138–39
  Aristotle and, 270–71

self-knowledge (*cont.*)
  Charmides and, 103, 189–90, 228–35
  Democritus and, 131
  Heraclitus and, 55–65, 72, 73–74, 276
  Hippolytus and, 93
  Laws and, 245
  overview of, 21
  Pythagorean Precepts and, 286–87, 288–89
  Republic and, 229–30, 231
  Socrates and, 134–36, 138–39, 142, 146–49, 150–51
  Thucydides and, 124
  Xenophon and, 180–81
Seven against Thebes (Aeschylus), 48, 325n.39
Seven Sages, 58n.19
shame (*aidôs*), 51, 79–80, 83, 84–86, 89, 104–7, 124, 163–65, 191, 212–13, 241, 263–65
Sharma, Ravi, 181n.85
Shorey, Paul, 217n.22, 222n.43
Slings, S. R., 224n.50
Snell, Bruno, 17
Socrates
  agency and, 145, 146–47
  Alcibiades and, 146–54
  Antisthenes and, 137–41, 155
  Aristotle and, 133–34
  autarchia and, 144–45
  authoritative norms and, 135–36
  Clouds depiction of, 11, 135–37
  erôs and, 138, 145
  Old Comedy depiction of, 135–37
  overview of, 133–35, 154–56
  problem of evidence for, 133–35
  self-constitution and, 135, 145
  self-knowledge and, 134–36, 138–39, 142, 146–49, 150–51
  sôphrosunê-as-a-way-of-life for, 134–35
  Stobaeus' depiction of, 141–46
Sophocles, 100–1, 137–38, 271, 308–9
sôphrosunê overview, 1–26, 335–40
  agency and, 1–4, 14–15
  definitions and glosses, 2–3, 4–5
  development of concept, 4–14
  disagreement about proper attribution, 5–14
  distinctness of present volume compared to prior research, 15–18
  early bibliography, 15n.47
  epigraphical appendix, 341
  function of concept, 2–3
  lack of scholarly attention, 18–20
  methodological approach of present volume, 15–16
  moderation, 14–15, 18–19

  motivation for present volume, 335–36
  pronunciation, 1n.1
  purpose of present volume, 14–21
  reasons for studying now, 335–37
  relation to other virtues, 1–2, 5
  self-constitution and, 3, 14–15, 17
  structure of present volume, 21–26
  translation, 18–21, 335–40
  women, 21
sound-mindedness, 68n. 42, 286n.12
  as translation of *sôphrosunê*. 338–39
Sparta and Spartans, 3, 101–3, 109–11, 117–18, 121–26, 135, 158, 160–61, 213, 243–44, 268–70
  as model, 149–51, 279–80
  See also Archidamus; Agesilaus; Sthenelaides
Speusippus, 276–77
Statesman (Plato), 237–41
  agency in, 239–41
  authoritative norms in, 239–40
  balanced view in, 241
  courage in, 238–40
  doing one's own things in, 239–40
  overview of, 237–38
  hronesis in, 239
  relation between virtues in, 238
  true and stable beliefs in, 239–41
Sthenelaides of Sparta, 125–26
Stobaeus, 327
source for Antiphon, 112
source for Aristoxenus' *Pythagorean Precepts*, 282–83, 289
source for Democritus, 127–29
source for Euripides, 95–96
source for Heraclitus, 54, 55–56, 63n.30, 65, 68
source for Iamblichus' letter to Arete, 327, 328–29, 334
source for Phocylides, 43
source for Phinty's *On Women's Sôphrosunê*, 312, 323
source for Plato, 244–45
source for Socrates, 141–46
Strabo, 285–86
Strauss, Leo, 249n.41
symposium, 41, 101–3, 109
Symposium (Plato), 134–35, 138n.29, 141n.39
Symposium (Xenophon), 137, 170–71

Tarán, Leonardo, 276–77, 277n.93
taste, sense of, 258–61, 271–72, 274–75
Tecmessa, 308–9
temperance, vi, 14–15, 18–19, 223, 244n.21
  as translation of *sôphrosunê*, 338–39

Tetralogies (Antiphon), 115–16
textual issues, 7, 9n.18, 10n.24, 46, 55–56, 94–96, 97–98, 116–17n.56, 127–28, 138n.30, 151–52, 173–74, 223–24, 244–45
Theaetetus (Plato), 251n.44
Theodoret, 138–39, 244–46
Theognis, 37–43
  authoritative norms and, 43
  drunkenness and, 41–42
  etymology of *sôphrosunê* and, 37–44, 64
  hubris and, 38–39
  justice and, 39–40, 41
Theophrastus, 258n.1, 275–76, 281
Thibodeau, Philip, 54n.1
Thrasymachus, 50–51n.72, 123n.76, 135n.10
Thucydides, 100–1, 106, 117–18. See also *History of the Peloponnesian War* (Thucydides)
Tjiattas, Mary, 282n.5
Tonelli, Angelo, 60n.24
Topics (Aristotle), 253n.49, 270–71
touch, sense of, 258–62, 265–67, 270–72, 274, 277–78
Tsouna, Voula, 103n.15, 213n.3, 214n.4, 229n.72, 262n.18
Tuckey, T. G., 15n.47, 19n.66

virtue. See also courage; justice; piety; wisdom
  authoritative virtue, 264–65
  gendered virtue, 307–12, 315–20, 327–28
  metavirtue, 331–33
  natural virtue, 258, 264–65
  overview of, 1–2, 5, 335–37
  relation between virtues, 1–2, 5, 192–95, 198–99, 201–2, 207–8, 214–15, 216–17, 224, 238, 249–50, 260–62, 314, 318–19
  role-defined virtues, 308
  as translation of *sôphrosunê*, 337
Virtues and Vices (Aristotelian corpus), 277–78
Vitek, Thomas, 55n.7, 56n.8
Vlastos, Gregory, 63n.32, 128n.89, 131n.105, 214n.4, 222n.43

Weiss, Roslyn, 225n.53
West, Martin, 34n.18, 38, 40
White, Stephen, 123n.76, 264n.31
Wilhelm, Friedrich, 312n.21
Williams, Bernard, 17–18, 84n.36, 88n.57
wine. See drinking
Winnington-Ingram, R. P., 85n.42
wisdom (*sophia* or *phronêsis*)
  akrasia and, 182
  Alcibiades and, 147–48, 153
  Aristotle and, 257, 263–71, 309–10
  courage and, 192–93
  definition of, 1–2
  enkrateia and, 182
  etymology of, 27–28
  Gorgias and, 196–97, 256
  Heraclitus and, 54–56, 58, 65–68, 70–72, 73–74
  Hippolytus and, 337
  justice and, 242
  Laws and, 242, 245–46, 248–49, 252–53
  letter to Arete and, 327–28
  overview of, 1–2
  Plato and, 189–90, 235, 237, 256
  Protagoras and, 190, 192–94, 195, 241
  Republic and, 214–17, 245–46
  translation of, 336–37
  as translation of *sôphrosunê*, 337
  women and, 309–10, 312–13
  On Women's Sôphrosunê and, 312–13
  Xenophon and, 158–59, 163, 171–72, 180–83, 256
Wismann, Heinz. See Bollack, Jean
Wolfsdorf, David, 128n.90, 138n.28, 325n.39
women
  agency and, 25–26, 310, 311–12, 314–18, 333–34
  aporias about, 333–34
  Aristotle and, 308–10
  authoritative norms and, 322–23, 333–34
  courage and, 308–9
  gendered virtue and, 307–12, 315–20, 327–28
  justice and, 319
  overview of, 21, 307–12, 333–34
  quiet submission and, 333–34
  rational choice and, 333–34
  self-constitution and, 321–22, 326
  wisdom and, 309–10, 312–13
  Xenophon and, 307–8

Xenocrates, 277
Xenophanes, 70–71, 111
Xenophilus, 281–82, 298
Xenophon. See also *Apology of Socrates* (Xenophon); *Cyropedia* (Xenophon); *Memorabilia* (Xenophon); *Symposium* (Xenophon)
  agency and, 161–62, 183–84
  authoritative norms and, 158–59, 161–62, 164–65, 168–69, 185–86
  courage and, 161–62, 163, 170–71
  desire-control and, 159–60, 162, 163–65, 168–70, 179–80

Xenophon (*cont.*)
  enkrateia and, 142, 158–59, 162–67, 168–69, 172–80, 182, 185–86, 265–66, 331
  justice and, 163–65, 179–80, 207
  non-Socratic works of, 160–68
  objections anticipated by, 175–76
  as one of several fourth-century theorists of *sôphrosunê*, 157–60
  overview of, 157–60, 183–84
  self-constitution and, 158–59
  self-knowledge and, 180–81
  Socratic works of, 168–83
  wisdom and, 158–59, 163, 171–72, 180–83, 256
  women and, 307–8

Zeitlin, Froma, 77n.3, 78n.4
Zeus, 12n.32, 39–40, 46, 48, 71, 192